The New Book of

Middle Eastern Food

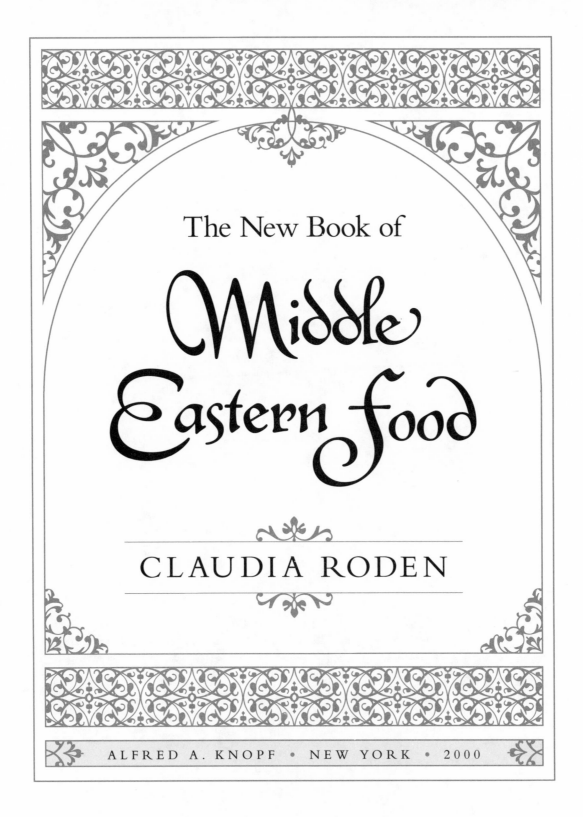

The New Book of

Middle Eastern Food

CLAUDIA RODEN

ALFRED A. KNOPF · NEW YORK · 2000

THIS IS A BORZOI BOOK
PUBLISHED BY ALFRED A. KNOPF

www.aaknopf.com

Originally published in Great Britain in 1968 by Thomas Nelson & Sons Ltd., London,
and in 1972 in slightly different form in the United States by Alfred A. Knopf, a division
of Random House, Inc. A previous revised edition was published in Great Britain by Viking,
an imprint of Penguin Books Ltd., London, in 1985.

Knopf, Borzoi Books, and the colophon are registered trademarks of Random House, Inc.

ISBN 0-375-40506-2

Manufactured in the United States of America

REVISED EDITION

To Simon, Nadia, and Anna

Contents

Photographs follow pages 84, 212, and 340.

Acknowledgments

This book has been an ongoing project, over four decades, with a second and now a third edition. So many people have contributed recipes, advice, stories, and information over the years that I cannot thank them all here, but they should know that every dish reminds me fondly of someone. I hear their voice as they described it and remember the taste and the event when they cooked it, as I remember the comments of those who ate the dish when I tried it. My parents, Cesar and Nelly Douek, are very much part of the book. My father inspired it by his enjoyment of life and appreciation of Middle Eastern food, and my mother advised and guided me enthusiastically throughout. I am also grateful for the help and affectionate support of my brothers, Ellis and Zaki.

I am especially grateful to those who contributed the very first recipes, sometimes the whole contents of their handwritten notebooks, in the very early days. Of these I would like to mention in particular Iris Galante, Lily Galante, Mrs R. Afif, my aunt Régine Douek, and my cousin Irene Harari.

Belinda Bather was a major source of the first Turkish recipes, and Mrs V. Afsharian of the first Persian ones. Josephine Salam taught me a great deal about Lebanese cooking, and Nevin Halici about Turkish regional foods. Sami Zubeida has been an invaluable help with his knowledge of the Middle East and his love of food.

I wish to record my gratitude to Maxime Rodinson, whose brilliant seminal studies in Arab culinary history and analysis of early Arab cookery manuals are the source of much of my information about the history of Arab food. I also wish to acknowledge my debt to certain Arab, Turkish, and Persian cookery books which I have consulted. A list of Middle Eastern cookery books is given in the bibliography.

I wish to thank my first editor, the late Helena Radecka, for her guidance from the early stages of my project and for her enthusiasm throughout, and my friend Jill Norman, who gave much valued advice for the second edition. I have very special thanks for Judith Jones, who has been an incredible editor for this new American edition. Her enthusiasm and very high standards, her advice, and her appreciation of good food and culinary traditions have brought out the best. It is a pleasure to work with her.

The New Book of

Middle Eastern Food

Introduction

This is an updated and very much enlarged edition of *A Book of Middle Eastern Food*—my first book, which came out in 1968. I have traveled so much, discovered so many new dishes, and accumulated so much new material that it all had to go into a new edition. The new edition is also in response to the ever-growing popularity of Middle Eastern foods in America. People have become familiar with couscous and bulgur, pita bread and fillo pastry, with eggplants, peppers, and chickpeas, and with the wide range of spices and aromatics. They are interested in new recipes and techniques which will make the dishes more accessible. The aim was to assemble the kind of dishes people want to eat and cook today—delicious, rich in flavor, exciting, healthy, and easy to prepare. The book is not only about pleasure and enjoyment, it is also a way of discovering other worlds and cultures.

My primary purpose in this edition, as in the old one, was to record and celebrate the traditional cuisines of the Middle East. But there have been great social and technological changes which have affected the way people cook and eat, both in the Western world and in the Middle East. I wanted to reflect those changes as well as our changing tastes.

Going through my first edition, I was often embarrassed at the way I expressed my enthusiasm with flowery words, and I was tempted to delete them. But then I decided to keep something of the voice I had as a young woman, in her early twenties, beginning a new life in a new world and missing the old one, enthralled by her discoveries of her own lost culture—because that is how the book came about. I am just as enthralled and committed today, but after decades in Europe I have learned verbal restraint. This is to explain that the book has been an ongoing work (there was an earlier updated U.K. edition in 1985) and that you may hear two voices and two styles of explanations.

The first edition was a labor of love on which I focused a great deal of emotion. I wrote in the introduction that it was the joint creation of numerous Middle Easterners who, like myself, were in exile; that it was the fruit of the nostalgic longing for a food that was the constant joy of life in a world so different from the Western one. The Arab sayings "He who has a certain habit will have no peace from it" and "The dancer dies and does not forget the shaking of his shoulders" applied to us.

My first recipe was for *ful medames*. I was a schoolgirl in Paris. Every Sunday I was invited with my brothers and cousins to eat *ful medames* at the home of my cousin Eric Rouleau, the French journalist, diplomat, and Middle Eastern specialist. Considered in Egypt to be a poor man's dish, in Paris the little brown beans embodied all that for which we were homesick and became invested with all the glories and warmth of Cairo. Delicious ecstasy! In their tiny one-roomed flat our hosts prepared the dish with canned *ful*. Ceremoniously, we sprinkled the beans with olive oil, squeezed a little lemon over them, seasoned them with salt and pepper, and placed a hot hard-boiled egg in their midst. Silently, we ate the beans, whole and firm at first. Then we squashed them with our forks and combined their floury texture and slightly dull, earthy taste with the acid tang of lemon, and the fruity flavor of olive oil. Finally, we crushed the egg, matching its earthiness with that of the beans, its pale warm yellow yolk with their dull brown.

But the great impulse to record recipes came when my family left Egypt for good, following the Suez Crisis in 1956 and because of Egypt's ongoing war with Israel. I was an art student in London then, with my two brothers—one a medical student, the other a schoolboy at the French Lycée. My parents arrived suddenly and were allowed to settle. My large extended family was dispersed all over the world. The sense of loss, of missing each other, the country where we had been happy, and the friends we left behind, was deep and painful. For more than ten years we continued close, intense relationships, with family and friends across countries, meeting often. We exchanged recipes as we would precious gifts. Everybody was desperately looking for them and passing them on. We had never had any cookbooks. There had been none in Egypt. Recipes had always been transferred from mother and mother-in-law to daughter and daughter-in-law, with minor exchanges between friends and family. That is why I started collecting recipes in a serious way.

Friday-night dinners at my parents' and gatherings of friends at my home became occasions to summon up the ghosts of the past. Every dish filled the house with the smells of our old homes. They conjured up memories of Egypt—of the Cairo markets and street vendors, of the *corniche* in Alexandria and the public bakehouse, of Groppi's and the Hati restaurant, and the Greek grocery down to which a constant flow of baskets would be lowered from windows above, descending with coins, and going up again with food. It is extraordinary how a smell and a taste can trigger memories.

Egypt in my time was a very mixed cosmopolitan society in the cities (it was the time of King Farouk, and I saw in the revolution). There were long-established communities of Armenians, Greeks, Italians, Syrians, and Lebanese, as well as expatriate French and British communities. Our royal family was an Ottoman Albanian dynasty, and our aristocracy was Turkish. The Jews were also mixed. My grandparents came from Syria and Turkey, and apart from the indigenous community, there were families from North Africa, Iraq, and Iran. When we ate at friends' homes we enjoyed a range of dishes from various countries. That is why I ended up covering most of the Middle East.

We were very Europeanized. We spoke French at home and Italian with our nanny. At the English School Cairo we studied English history and geography, nothing at all about Egypt or the Arab world. But past generations of my family had lived, for hundreds of years, an integrated life in the Arab and Ottoman worlds, and something of their experience filtered down to us. It was those worlds that captivated me—the part of my culture that I hardly knew, which belonged to my parents and especially my father—that I wanted to recapture. I am sometimes asked how a Jewish woman can be fascinated with Arab food and Islamic civilization, and I reply that it was also ours (with some differences) and we were part of it.

I sought out people from all over the Middle East for recipes. I hung around carpet warehouses and embassies, visa departments and the School of Oriental and African Studies in London. It must have seemed a strange thing to do in those days, but I was very lucky, and I ended up meeting some very good cooks. They explained in the minutest detail the washing and the handling of ingredients, the feel, the smell, and the color of the food, but usually omitted quantities, weights, and cooking times. I learned that to some "leave it a little" meant an hour, that "five spoonfuls" was in order to make a round figure or because five was for them a lucky number, and that a pinch could be anything from an eighth of a teaspoon to a heaped tablespoon. They were lyrical about how delicious the dishes were, and on the circumstances in which they were prepared. It gave them, I think, as much pleasure to describe the dishes as it gave me to record the recipes.

I put down every word they said. If they said, "Toast the hazelnuts in the frying pan until they are lightly browned, then rub them between your hands to detach the skins and go out in the garden and blow off the skins," that is how it went into the book. The method worked very well, but now that we can get blanched hazelnuts without skins, it sounds a little archaic. Similarly, we now have such things as pitted prunes and dried pitted sour cherries, blanched and ground almonds, and shelled pistachios, all of which make the work easier.

I gathered all kinds of dishes—humble peasant food, flamboyant Mediterranean dishes, and very elaborate, sophisticated ones. I detected a certain unity, and there were many that seemed regional variations on a theme. I tried to trace their origins and to understand the influences through the history of the area.

At the British Library in London, I was thrilled to find two medieval cookery manuals (see appendix), one translated by Professor A. J. Arberry, and the other with an analysis and extracts translated into French by Professor Maxime Rodinson. I was stunned to find similarities with the dishes that I had just gathered from family and friends. I tried many of the almost one hundred recipes and could not resist including a few in my book. Since exact measures were not given, I indicated quantities that I would choose. I have not included them in this edition because they are primarily of academic interest, and scholars have made them available today in new translations. Anyone who wishes to prepare medieval Arab banquets is best directed to the publications cited in the appendix.

I have kept in the descriptions of ceremonies, rituals, and myths, and the customs and manners relating to food, as they make the dishes more interesting by placing them in their traditional setting. I have also left in the tales, poems and riddles, proverbs and sayings, in the hope that through them a little of the wit and spirit of the people of the Middle East may be discovered.

The dishes did not retain the same power to move me over the years as they had in the beginning, but the book remained an important part of my life. It has meant a continuing involvement with the part of the world which holds my roots and for which I have a special tenderness. People always talk to me about food, and those who come from the Middle East reveal their passions and offer their own special ways of doing things. I am invited to eat and to watch people cook, and correspondents in different countries send recipes. My pockets are full of scribbled cooking instructions, my drawers full of recipes in different hands.

On the whole, I have left the original recipes as they were, with the voices and the idiosyncrasies of those who gave them. The way in which they are described best reflects the rich and varied character of very personal and much-loved cooking traditions passed down through generations in the family. I have not tried to correct spellings, pronunciations, or names, for this is an area of great complexity, with differences from one country to another. For instance, the name for bean rissoles varies from one part of Egypt to another. It is *falafel* in Alexandria and *ta'amia* in Cairo. The same dish of rice and lentils is *megadarra* in Egypt and *mudardara* in Lebanon. This is not a scholarly book, and I have not followed a system. I have generally written an Arabic name as it is most familiarly known in Egypt and as it sounded to me.

When I tell people that I am not only adding recipes but also updating and revising some of the old ones, they generally protest, asking me not to touch them, as they have worked perfectly well for them for more than thirty years. They tend to be suspicious of new versions. But things change. Cooking does not stand still: it evolves. Life is different, and different choices are made to adapt to new circumstances. The recipes in the first edition were from a time when there were no home ovens in many of the countries, let alone blenders, food processors, and freezers. People cooked on braziers and Primus stoves and outside clay ovens and sent dishes to the public oven. In a few recipes I told the reader to grind the meat three times. Who has a meat grinder now? The recipes were from a time when women did not go out to work (no woman in my family ever worked) and most had cooks and servants who cooked all day. Moreover, notions of fat-free and healthy eating had not yet taken over. As a food writer you have a responsibility. I love tradition and respect cuisines that have a past, and that is what my writing is about. But I do not wish to embalm them. Most of all, I want people to cook and to enjoy cooking and eating.

If I mention using less butter, and grilling or baking instead of frying, some of my friends are outraged, as though I am about to destroy a culture to conform to a trend of fat-free lightness. I reassure them that I have changed very little, that the new approaches do not necessarily kill the old. The important thing is to choose what is good in new ways—what makes the food more delicious and more appetizing, not less so.

In most recipes I give the alternative of butter or oil so that people can please themselves. Of course, there are changes that I do not approve of. In Morocco these days, there has been a rush to use pressure cookers to cook tagines, which were once simmered very slowly in flat clay pots with cone-shaped lids over a brazier. I am against pressure cookers, as I believe they spoil the dish—the texture of the meat is not the same, and the vegetables fall apart or they do not absorb the flavors if put in for a very short time. But a stainless-steel saucepan will do very well, even though the result is not quite the same. Dishes that need long, slow cooking are not usually labor-intensive, and you can start them off and leave them to cook while you do other things. They can also be prepared the day before.

North Africans overcook their fish, but Europeans have come to like it when it only just begins to flake. In the Middle East generally, people like their meat very cooked, never pink, but we can please ourselves. In many Middle Eastern countries, because they did not have home ovens, the custom has been to deep-fry pies. This tends to make them rather heavy, so I mostly bake them, as we did in Egypt. In America people shy away from frying eggplants because of the amount of oil they absorb. In many instances broiling or grilling is an excellent alternative.

Frozen vegetables do not have the wonderful flavors and textures of fresh ones, but some are exceptionally good. Frozen artichoke hearts and bottoms, for instance, are so good that my guests are always surprised to hear that they are frozen. Spinach too freezes well, as does the green *melokheya,* which is used for making the famous Egyptian soup of the same name. We cannot choose our wheat, wash it and dry it on the roofs of our houses, then take it to the mill to be ground while we wait. We have to deal with factory-produced bulgur and, except for very rare occasions, the precooked packaged couscous that is readily available. It is important to work out how to get the best possible results with what we have.

In traditional Middle Eastern culture, to really please your guests, you must show that you have worked very hard to prepare a meal. You have to offer an assortment of small pies, stuffed vegetables, little meatballs, and the like, which require wrapping, hollowing, filling, rolling. It is almost an insult to offer something that looks as though it took little time. You can see why people have the idea that Middle Eastern food is excessively laborious. But it does not have to be.

Many of the simpler dishes are the most appealing, and it is these that I have featured in a bigger way in the new edition. It is the special combinations of ingredients—rice and lentils with caramelized onions; bulgur with tomatoes and eggplants; artichokes and broad beans with almonds; spinach with beans or chickpeas or with yogurt—and their delicate flavoring which make them wonderful. Although often the only flavoring is olive oil and lemon juice, every country has its traditional aromatics. There is the fried garlic with cumin and coriander of Egypt, the cinnamon and allspice of Turkey, the sumac and tamarind of Syria and Lebanon, the pomegranate syrup of Iran, the preserved lemon and harissa of North Africa. The tantalizing mix of spicy hot with sweet of Morocco includes saffron, ginger, cinnamon, and cumin with hot red pepper and honey.

Many new recipes appear in every chapter. I have taken out a few of the least interesting ones. Some recipes have been replaced by a better version, and I have added many regional variations and suggestions for an alternative ingredient, a new flavoring, or an easier method of cooking. The new availability of so many products meant that I could do away with substitutes. Now there is nothing you cannot find. Many of the basic products are in the supermarkets. Some, such as sumac (the ground red berry with a lemony flavor), tamarind paste, and the sweet-and-sour pomegranate syrup or molasses made from the boiled-down juice of sour pomegranates, are easy to find in the specialty markets. You can now find sources on the Internet.

A Fashion That Goes Back
Hundreds of Years

Many things have changed since I first started recording Middle Eastern recipes forty years ago. When I told people then what I was doing, some wondered with barely veiled horror whether I was going to write about sheep's eyes and testicles. Their perception of the food was not very different from what the explorer

Charles Montagu Doughty, who traveled in Arabia around 1876, described as "lambs sitting on mountains of rice in a sea of fat." In his view the Arabs were better at making love than food.

Now top American chefs have adopted what they call eastern-Mediterranean cuisines, and couscous, tagines, pilafs, and the like appear on the menus of fashionable eclectic restaurants. Ethnic Turkish, Lebanese, Iranian, and Moroccan restaurants have opened in many cities, and street vendors sell falafel. The tumultuous events which ripped the Middle East apart in the last decades have brought cooks and restaurateurs to Europe and America. Cooking is an immigrant's trade, but newly arrived immigrants escaping from civil war or poverty usually have no catering experience. Apart from Turkey and Lebanon, where a restaurant trade began about eighty years ago, there has not been a restaurant tradition in the Middle East. This is partly because in Muslim countries women did not accompany their men eating out. Such establishments as there were, evolved from street food—just a few chairs placed beside a movable stall. The standard restaurant menu of meats grilled over embers, appetizers, and rice belongs to the street tradition. When I asked a member of one of the grand families in Morocco what restaurants she recommended, she said they had never been to a restaurant because you could not be sure of the food.

The vast and rich repertoire of home cooking with its regional and community variations remained unknown outside each locality. People of each region were interested only in their own traditional foods, and there was no way of discovering recipes from neighboring countries, or even neighboring cities, because there were no cookbooks. In Egypt in my time, no one ever had one. After we left, we wrote asking all our remaining friends to send us any cookbook they could find. The only one that arrived was an Arabic translation of a British-army cookbook left behind after the Second World War. It had recipes like "rolly polly alla castarda" and "macaroni cheese."

Today the cuisines of the Middle East have been very well documented. Most people in America are familiar with the "Arabian Delights" and the eastern- and southern-Mediterranean dishes featured in numerous books and magazines. One of the reasons for the popularity of this food is that the area has come to be recognized as "Mediterranean" (part of it is), and the healthy Mediterranean diet rich in grains, vegetables, legumes, fruits and nuts, yogurt, and olive oil has been much touted. Another reason is that Americans have come to love spices and aromatics, and these are very sensuous cuisines.

It is interesting to note that Arab foods were in fashion in other times and that many of the things that we eat today originated in the Islamic world. The popularity of Arab foods has mirrored the relationship between Europe and the followers of Islam and the relative prestige of their two cultures. It has depended on war and peace, on politics and commerce, and also on the spirit of Europe, whether people cultivated the senses or denied them, whether they were hedonist or puritan. In the full-blooded Middle Ages, when Islam was in its Golden Age, with the most advanced civilization in the world, Arab cooking had a huge impact on cooking in Europe.

At that time Christian Europe looked on the Infidels with fear and horror as pillaging and ravaging barbarians and cruel despots, but at the same time it was impressed by their wealth and power. Chroniclers of the time wrote of the magnificent courts and of the loves and excesses of the Caliphs. Travelers and merchants told of the extraordinary and exquisite foods they were served as they sat on a rug near a fountain in a fruit garden. While worrying about the odious enemy, Europe fantasized about its fabulous riches, its harems and seraglios, bazaars and minarets, about fierce warriors who chopped off heads, passionate lovers, and fantastic banquets. Europeans were captivated by the philosophical and scientific knowledge of the Islamic civilization, and soon courts and upper classes were adopting its fashions. The cooking was a stimulus and an inspiration which brought new ways of looking at food.

The Crusades created an even more avid interest, a mixture of hate for the enemy—Saracens, as they were known to the medieval West—and fascination for its exotic culture. European Crusaders remained in the Levant for generations. Antioch was occupied by the Franks and their allies between 1098 and 1268, Jerusalem between 1099 and 1187, Tripoli between 1109 and 1289, Acre between 1189 and 1291. In a paper entitled "The Saracen Connection: Arab Cuisine and the Medieval West" published in the little quarterly *Petits Propos Culinaires* (part 7, 1981), Anne Wilson described how, when they were not fighting over the holy places, the Crusaders lived on harmonious terms with the Saracens and some took Syrian, Armenian, and even Saracen wives. Those who eventually returned home were mainly well-to-do and included members of the nobility or even royal families, like Eleanor of Aquitaine and her estranged husband, Louis VII of France. The introduction of Saracen-inspired dishes in the West began in noble families.

When commerce flourished between East and West, sugar (a novelty then to Europe), rice, almonds, pine kernels, and dried fruits, such as prunes, raisins, apricots, and dates, arrived from the Levant. And with them came the aromatics which play an important part in Oriental cooking—rose and orange-blossom water, tamarind, pomegranate juice, saffron, the resin mastic, and all types of seeds, plants, and bark. The Crusaders, Orientalized by years spent in the Levant, often with a local cook in their employ, brought home the ways of handling these new ingredients. Early European cookbooks, from the thirteenth century on, show how all these foods were incorporated into Western cookery before the end of the Middle Ages.

For instance, the idea of frying cut-up pieces of meat before boiling, adopted in the thirteenth-century French *Viandier* texts, was recognized in English texts as Sarcynesse. A sweet-and-sour sauce was used early in Europe, borrowing from the Greek tradition, but the Saracens created many varied sweet-and-sour sauces for meat with sugar, date juice, or the boiled-down juice of sweet grapes partnered with verjuice (boiled-down sour-pomegranate juice) and bitter-orange juice. The

French called such fusions, which were usually spiced with cinnamon and cloves, *sarassinois* or *saraginée.* The English took the idea from the French and called the dishes "egerdouce." The coloring of food—rice tinted yellow with saffron, sweet-meats colored green with pistachios, eggs dyed vermilion—became very popular, and the use of almonds and almond milk became widespread. The "sotelties," marzipan figures offered at the end of meals, which became the fashion at all the great feasts in medieval Europe, were also an idea inspired by the Saracens.

In a conference paper for the Accademia Italiana della Cucina in 1967, Maxime Rodinson demonstrated the Oriental legacy to European cooking and traced the etymology of the names of many dishes in early Latin and European cookbooks to Persian and Arab origins. The legacy came partly through Arabic books on dietetics and medicine that had a considerable influence in Europe well into the eighteenth century. In the twelfth or thirteenth century a book of Arab dietetics was translated into Latin in Venice by a certain Jambobinus of Cremona, who called it *Liber de Ferailis et Condimentis.* This translation was one of the earliest cookbooks of medieval Europe. The original author was Ibn Jazla, a doctor in Baghdad, who died in the year 1100. Jambobinus used eighty-three of his recipes, keeping their Arab names. He indicated whether they were good for the stomach, and noted their effect on various organs and functions as well as on the tempera-ment. Many of these recipes were to reappear in other Latin cookbooks with or without dietetic information and later in Italian, French, and English translations, where their origin remains detectable by their names, as well as by the Oriental ingredients and the way the method is described.

Ibn Jazla was not the only source of Arab recipes in European cookbooks. Other recipe collections which have not been found are mentioned in various medieval works. Much later, in the early sixteenth century, Andrea Alpago, a Venetian doctor and scholar who had spent thirty years in the Orient, translated a huge treatise on medicine written by the Arab doctor and philosopher Avicenna, who was born in 980. Alpago used Arab books on dietetics to find extra informa-tion about the dishes mentioned by Avicenna and put this new material as glos-saries to each volume of the treatise.

But the most powerful influence in Europe of Arab cooking came via the Arab occupation of Spain and Sicily, and through the later occupation of the Balkans by the Ottoman Turks. The Arab and Berber armies arrived in Spain in 711 and left Andalusia in 1492. They were there for almost eight hundred years, which is plenty of time to make an impact on the food. The watermelons and artichokes that they brought from Egypt, the pomegranates from Syria, dates and hard wheat from North Africa, spinach and eggplants from Persia, and Seville oranges and cane sugar are all part of the Arab heritage. The grapes of Jerez (used to make sherry) came from Shiraz in Persia. Eight centuries of love and war left powerful legacies in the kitchen: little pies, rice dishes, vermicelli (*fideos* in Spanish), marzi-pan, almond pastries, fritters in syrup, meats with fruit, sweet-and-sour flavors, combinations of raisins and pine nuts.

Outside Granada, at the restaurant El Molino, which is also a center of gastronomic research, the old dishes, which are the origin of Spanish cooking today, are served. Many of the recipes they use are from the anonymous thirteenth-century Arabic cookery manual entitled *Kitab al Tabikh fil Maghrib wal Andalus* (*Cookbook of the Maghreb and Andalusia*). This and other Arab culinary documents have been translated and analyzed by Charles Perry, who writes for the *Los Angeles Times,* in a forthcoming book entitled *Medieval Arab Cookery,* published by Prospect Books (see appendix).

Lucie Bolens, in her book *La Cuisine andalouse, un art de vivre XIe–XIIIe siècle* (Albin Michel), gives three hundred ancient recipes translated from the Arabic, mainly from the book mentioned above. The late Rudolph Grewe translated into Spanish the fifteenth-century Catalan *Libre di Sent Sovi* and the *Libro de Ruperto de Nola.* It is fascinating to see how the cooking of Damascus, Baghdad, and Fez fused with that of rural Spain. The nostalgic tastes of the society made up of Arabs, Persians, Berbers, Christians, Jews, Greeks, Khazars, and others that was Muslim Spain, merged in a new, exuberant, convivial style of living. Some of those tastes have come to America via South America, brought by the Conquistadors.

In 827 an army of Arabs—Berbers from North Africa and Spanish Muslims (Sicilians called them all Saracens)—landed in Sicily. They brought their laws and their language, their literature, arts, and sciences. They irrigated the land and planted exotic fruits and vegetables and encouraged the rearing of sheep and goats. Stuffed vegetables, sweet-and-sour eggplant caponata, artichoke hearts with almonds, rice dishes, *cuscusu,* almond pastries, *millefoglie* (puff pastry), sorbets, and even pasta are the relics of that civilization. There is still a very thin type of pasta called by its old Arab name, *itriya.* Today, cloistered nuns in convents all over the island still make crystallized fruits, marzipan sweets with extraordinary shapes and riotous colors, pastries stuffed with almonds, and sweet couscous with nuts and dried fruit. They tell you these are Arab. Sicily is famous for her *granite* and *sorbetti* (the Sicilian dialect term *sciarbat* is the Arab word for a sorbet). According to local legend, the Arabs fetched snow from Mount Etna to make them, and the habit of mixing sugar and jasmine essence in a glass full of snow also goes back to those times. The Arab influence is still the most important in Sicily, despite the numerous other foreign occupations. And you also see it in southern Italy. In Puglia, in the "heel" of Italy, I ate *n'capriata*—mashed dried fava beans—which is like a dish we used to eat in Egypt; and *triya con i ceci*—pasta with chickpeas. During an evening of folk dancing, as guests of Prince Dentice di Frasso's Castel di San Vito dei Normanni, we were offered platters of local pastries and sweetmeats similar to those you might find in Morocco and Damascus.

The Ottoman Turks are responsible for much of the food you eat in the Balkans—in southern Hungary, Romania, Bulgaria, the former Yugoslavia, Albania, Macedonia, and Greece—which were part of the Ottoman Empire for five centuries. All that time of integrated life under Turkish rule created a shared Balkan food culture that is an amalgam of Middle Eastern and Western European traditions. The Turks are also responsible for the little cakes called "turbans" and the puff-pastry croissants of France (in the shape of the Turkish crescent), and the strudels of Vienna. What the pastry chefs and pudding makers at the Sultan's palace were up to was all the rage in Western Europe when the empire was at its peak.

Not many of the old Saracen dishes have survived from the Middle Ages in Britain, but each generation has revived a few or picked up new ones. Eliza Acton, Mrs. Beeton, Mrs. Leyel, and other cookery writers each offered a few exotic recipes to make people dream of the *Arabian Nights.* There are still traces of this early influence in the most English of foods—in Christmas pudding and mince pies, marzipan, and rice pudding—and it is a curious thought that our famous brown sauces and the mint-and-vinegar sauce for lamb perpetuate the luster of ancient Persia on our everyday tables.

Elizabeth David wrote lovingly of the foods she discovered when she lived in Cairo, Alexandria, and Greece. It is her *Book of Mediterranean Food* which slightly eased my homesickness when I moved to England, and her brilliance and integrity which inspired me to write. In an early edition she intimated that there were many more dishes in the Near East which needed to be discovered, that what she gave was the tip of the iceberg, and that was the spark that fired me.

General Features of
Middle Eastern Cuisines

The traditional cooking fats used in Middle Eastern countries in the past were *alya*—the rendered fat from a sheep's tail—and clarified butter, called *samna*. Many of the medieval recipes start with "melt tail" or "fry in tail." As a special refinement the fat was sometimes colored red or yellow. *Samna* is butter (usually made from buffalo's milk) which has been melted over boiling water and clarified by straining it through thin, dampened muslin. The impurities that cause butter to burn and darken are eliminated, as well as much of the water content. It is rich and strong with a distinctive flavor, and a little will give the same result as a much larger quantity of butter. It also keeps very well. The Indian ghee, which is sold in jars, is a type of *samna*. (See also page 46.) Today ordinary butter and oil are mostly used.

The usual oils are olive, cottonseed, peanut, corn, sunflower, and sesame. Olive oil is preferred for dishes which are to be eaten cold and for frying fish. As a general rule, people like to fry or sauté their meat and vegetables before adding water to make stews and soups in order to deepen the color and enrich the flavor. The Moroccans of Fez are an exception; their pale, delicate lamb stews are distinguished from those of the inhabitants of other Moroccan towns. Instead of frying the ingredients, they cook them from the start in water with a little oil, relying on the stocks which result, and the variety and quality of the other ingredients, to give color, texture, and body to their dishes. To them it is a crime against refinement to fry meats or vegetables destined for a stew.

The utensils and the type of heat available have to a large extent determined the style of cooking. Ovens have only recently been introduced in most homes. In the past, cooking was generally done over a type of Primus called a *fatayel* or over a brazier. It was a long, slow procedure, and pans were sometimes left to simmer overnight. This habit has remained to the present day although the necessity may have passed, and it is more usual for food to be prepared over heat than for it to be baked or roasted in an oven.

It was customary in the past, and to a lesser degree it still is even today, to send certain dishes to be cooked in the ovens of the local bakery. People would hurry about in the streets with huge trays or casseroles, sometimes balancing them on their heads. Life at the ovens bustled with activity and humor. I am told of greataunts who sealed their pans with a paste made of flour and water, ostensibly in order to cook the dish under pressure, but also to ensure that no one introduced an unwholesome, impure, or prohibited ingredient out of spite. Many people specified precisely in what position they wanted their pans placed in the enormous ovens. Others, perfectionists, sat by the ovens on wicker stools throughout the cooking time, watching their food and giving directions for the pans to be moved this way and that, in order to vary the degree of the heat. Today, dishes which would in the past have gone to the district oven (such as a roast leg of lamb surrounded by all its vegetables) are cooked in domestic ovens, but slowly, as before.

Another factor that helped to perpetuate the tradition of slow, lengthy cooking, as well as that of the more elaborate dishes, which require time and craftsmanship, is the social custom that kept women in the home until recently.

Precision and timing are not important, and no harm is done if a dish is left to simmer for an hour longer and the meat is so tender that it has fallen off the bone or the lentils have disintegrated. Nor is there any liking for red meat or underdone vegetables—unless they are eaten completely raw.

Grilling little morsels over charcoal is associated everywhere with Muslim cooking. Skewer cookery, whether it is meat, chicken, or fish kebabs (generally believed to have been developed by Turks on the field of battle), is the most popular street food in every Middle Eastern country, and it is not only street vendors who are masters of the art of using the heat of glowing embers.

Throughout the area, lamb is the favorite meat and the most available. Because of the dietary laws of the predominant religion of Islam, generally no pork is used, and no wine. Even where meat is not out of reach because of the cost, it is stretched to go far in a stew or sauce or as part of the filling in vegetables, with a half-pound serving on average four people. A wide variety of vegetables are eaten raw, or cooked in olive oil to be served cold. They are also stuffed and appear in stews or as pickles. Fruits are used in many different ways. Wheat is the staple cereal of the countryside, rice is the urban one to serve as a side dish and base to most foods. Fava beans, split peas, chickpeas, and lentils have been part of the diet since time immemorial. Much is made of them; the choice depends on what grows locally. Then there are noodles and very thin spaghetti. And a meal without bread to dip in is unthinkable; some people cannot enjoy anything without it.

Nuts have been used since ancient times in a variety of dishes and in unexpected ways. One of the regional characteristics which denote the nationality of the cook is the selective use of nuts. Where an Egyptian or a Syrian would use ground almonds or pine nuts to thicken a sauce such as *tarator* (page 93) or almond sauce (page 358), a Turk would use ground walnuts or hazelnuts. Iranians also use ground walnuts, for example in their *fesenjan* sauce (page 227) for chicken or duck, in the same way as they are used for the Circassian chicken (page 104). In Iran, pomegranate or sour-cherry sauce is added to the walnut sauce, while in Turkey it is sprinkled with the favorite garnish of red paprika melted in oil.

In most countries, it is customary to place on the table a bowl of fresh yogurt, sometimes flavored with salt, mint, and crushed garlic, to be eaten with such varied foods as *eggah,* pilafs, stuffed vegetables, salads, and kebabs. In Turkey, yogurt is used extensively as a bed for meat or vegetables, or to be poured over salads, eggs, vegetables, rice, almost anything. It is also used as a cooking medium, particularly in Lebanon, Turkey, and Iran.

Each country has developed its own special way of making a paper-thin pastry. Usually, soft dough is stretched as thin as possible; sometimes very thin pancakes are used. With melted butter brushed in between leaves, the result is a type of puff pastry.

People do not usually eat puddings or pastries at mealtime. These are reserved for visitors and festive occasions. Each country has many types of milk pudding and each has an assortment of pastries stuffed with nuts and bathed in syrup.

The flavors in savory dishes range from delicate and subtle to fierce and powerful. Persians favor dishes delicately balanced between sweet and sour, cooked with vinegar, lemon and sugar, and the juice of sour pomegranates. They share with Moroccans a predilection and a skill for combining the textures and flavors of meats and fruits. All these tastes have been adopted to some degree in the neighboring countries.

Garlic is liked, both raw and fried. Many people put a whole head in the ashes of a fire to mellow and soften to a cream. The tart taste of lemons or limes is ubiquitous in salads and many cooked dishes. A rather musty taste is obtained by Iranians and Iraqis with a dried variety, a subdued one by Moroccans with lemons preserved in salt. The faint scent of rose and orange-blossom water is evident in sweet dishes, which are sometimes made with honey instead of sugar. The Orient is so partial to the sensual pleasures of perfumes and aromatics that the widest possible variety of herbs, spices, woods, and essences are used in the kitchen.

Taste and pleasure are not the only considerations, for good healthy eating is part of the Arab philosophical doctrine of the perfect concordance of the elements of the universe with those of human nature. In the past, medical men wrote books on dietetics. Today, those who can, still strive for a balanced diet.

Understanding a Cuisine:
National and Regional Differences

Having collected an extraordinarily rich assortment of recipes from a great number of people, some of whom did not know the origins of their favorite dishes but had picked them up at some point in their wanderings—from a place they had visited, from a relative or a chance acquaintance—I tried to give them a national identity. It was impossible to class them by countries because of the overlap and similarities; there would be too much repetition. Instead, a picture emerged of one broad culinary tradition, very poor in parts, extremely varied and rich in others, and with great regional differences. There were often more differences between town and country or from one town to another than across a border, and neighboring towns in the same country sometimes had different specialties while the main towns of different countries had the same foods.

The reasons for this are to be found in the geography and history of the area. The geographical differences are extremely wide; there are large, empty deserts and lush countryside, great rivers and arid hills, green mountains, marshlands, and long coastlines. Not every country has inherited a bit of each, nor do they all have the same produce. Their cooking reflects those differences, but it also mirrors the ramified complexities of the past. The result of a shared history and the unifying influences of the Arab and Islamic and later Ottoman empires, with their inherent divisions, bitter struggles, and conflicts, has been the development of one culinary tradition that can be divided into four main branches.

The most exquisite and refined, and one of the least known abroad, is the Iranian cuisine, which is the ancient source of much of the *haute cuisine* of the Middle East. It is based on long-grain rice, which grows around the Caspian Sea. This is cooked to the highest standard of perfection and accompanied by a variety of sauces or mixed with meats, vegetables, fruits, and nuts.

In Syria, Lebanon, and Jordan the cooking is much the same, for boundaries here are only recent. It is in this patchwork of creeds and communities, where Arab revival and consciousness first took root, that what is known as Arab food is at its best. Here urban cooking is based on rice, country food on cracked wheat (bulgur). It is no accident that the area has been called the Fertile Crescent, for the soil bears the richest variety and quality of vegetables and fruits. Although some of their neighbors with a sheep-farming economy laugh at the "vegetable-eaters" of the crescent, theirs is nevertheless the most popular cuisine of the Arab world.

Turkish cuisine is the one that has influenced most countries abroad and which we have known longest and best, for the Ottoman Empire left its traces on the tables of such countries as Bulgaria, Romania, Yugoslavia, Hungary, Greece, Cyprus, Syria, Lebanon, and Egypt, and parts of Russia and North Africa. In all these countries you will find the same kebabs and rice and wheat dishes, savory pies and yogurt salads, and the nutty, syrupy pastries with paper-thin or shredded dough.

The fourth distinctive cooking style is that of North Africa, where Moroccan cuisine is especially magnificent. It is based on the couscous of the original Berber inhabitants with centuries-old echoes from Spain, Portugal, and Sicily and the more recent influence of France. Remarkably, it bears the strongest legacies from ancient Persia and Baghdad in the art of combining ingredients and mixing aromatics.

Because similar dishes turned up in several countries, I was eager to find out more about their origins. It was a thrill to discover a dish mentioned in some historical or literary work, in a poem or a proverb, and to conjure up the circumstances of its arrival in a particular place, guessing which conquering general had brought it, and why one country had adopted it while another had not.

The history of this food is that of the Middle East. Dishes carry the triumphs and glories, the defeats, the loves and sorrows of the past. We owe some to an event, or to one man: the Caliph who commissioned it, the poet who sang it, or the Imam who "fainted on receiving it."

Nothing was more valuable to me in my pursuit, or more exciting, than the discovery of writings by the French Orientalist Professor Maxime Rodinson on the history of Arab food. I am much indebted to him, and in particular to his study of early culinary manuscripts. I have dealt with these in greater detail in this new edition as I have dug deeper into them. A forthcoming book entitled *Medieval Arab Cookery,* published by Prospect Books, carries a full translation of his papers on gastronomy by Charles Perry.

A Cuisine Shaped by a Tumultuous History

A look into the past of the Middle East, a region strategically located athwart the crossroads of great cultures, shows it constantly beset by endless currents and crosscurrents, great and small wars, and all-embracing empires with factional and dynastic rivalries. All this, with the shifting allegiances, cultures, and subcultures and people spilling from one part into another, has affected the kitchen to its advantage. Here is its story.

The early origins of Middle Eastern food can be found in Bedouin dishes and the peasant dishes of each of the countries involved. In the case of Egypt, one can go back as far as pharaonic times to find the foods still eaten by the Egyptians today: roast goose, fava beans, *melokheya* soup, *bamia,* and botarga. In his *Dictionary of the Bible,* J. Hastings writes that the "Hebrews in the wilderness looked back wistfully on the cucumbers, melons, leeks, onions and garlic of Egypt; all of these were subsequently cultivated by them in Palestine." He also lists other foods mentioned in the Bible, such as varieties of beans and lentils, chickpeas, bitter herbs, olives, figs, grapes and raisins, dates, almonds, and nuts. These were prepared in a manner similar to that of the Egyptians, probably remembered by the Jews from their time in Egypt. One specialty the Hebrews adopted was fish, split open, salted, and dried in the sun. It was very useful to take on long journeys, and it is still considered a delicacy all over the Middle East.

Little is known about what the other ancient inhabitants of the region ate—the Syrians, Lydians, Phrygians, Cappadocians, Armenians, Assyrians, Babylonians, Cilicians, and Mesopotamians. But one can assume that these prosperous, civilized states had highly developed culinary traditions, undoubtedly influenced by Greek and Roman customs, which fused together at different times during their history of invasions and conquests. The inhabitants of the arid desert areas of Arabia and the Sahara produced the Spartan food still popular with Bedouins today.

The Persian Influence

The Persian Empire of c. 500 B.C. was the earliest empire to envelop the region. Macedonian Greeks followed to radiate their culture. As the Romans and Parthians fought for dominance, the states they governed assimilated their traditions—and their cooking—and while these empires were won and lost, the character and style of Middle Eastern food was born.

It is in the Persia of the Sassanid period (third to seventh century) that it blossomed. The reign of King Khosrow I inaugurated the most brilliant period of the Sassanid era, and with it the decline of Byzantine power. Alexander the Great and his successors had made part of Persia, as well as parts of India, Hellenic strongholds. The debris of Hellenic civilization remained for many centuries, mingling and fusing with the Persian and Indian civilizations. There was cross-fertilization in the kitchen as there was in philosophies, myths, and cultures. Similarities in food in these countries today, particularly between India and Persia, bear witness to these early influences.

In the reign of Khosrow II (early seventh century), Byzantium was finally defeated, and the Persian generals conquered Antioch, Damascus, Jerusalem, and Alexandria. The triumphs of this great king were matched by his growing cruelty, vanity, and greed. Enormous sums were spent on his pleasures and those of his court. Persian tales and legends describe his fantastic banquets, lavishly laid, dazzling with luxury and extravagance. In his book *L'Iran sous les Sassanides,* Arthur Christensen describes dishes popular at the time, and the court's favorite recipes. It is then that some of the dishes so familiar today made their first appearance. A "dish for the King" consisted of hot and cold meats, rice jelly, stuffed grape leaves, marinated chicken, and a sweet date puree. A "Khorassanian dish" was composed of meat grilled on the spit and meat fried in butter with a sauce. A "Greek dish" was made with eggs, honey, milk, butter, rice, and sugar—a sort of rice pudding. A "Dehkan dish" consisted of slices of salted mutton with pomegranate juice, served with eggs.

Young kid was popular; so was beef cooked with spinach and vinegar. All kinds of game and poultry were eaten; in particular, hens fed on *chènevis* (hemp seed) were hunted and "frightened" before they were killed, and then grilled on the spit. The lower part of the chicken's back was considered the tastiest. Today it is still a delicacy, sometimes called "the mother-in-law's morsel." Meat was marinated in yogurt and flavored with spices. Many different kinds of almond pastry were prepared, jams were made with quinces, dates stuffed with almonds and walnuts. All this is still done today. Our dishes were savored by Khosrow and his favorite wife, Shirin.

The decline of the Sassanids had set in by the end of Khosrow's reign, but even after this grandiose empire had crumbled, its music and its food survived. Many Arab and Turkish dishes today betray their origins by their Persian names.

Dishes Spread to the Far Corners of the Islamic Empire

The spread of Islam was the most important factor in the development of a gastronomy comparable to that of France and China. The death of the Prophet Muhammad in Arabia in the year 632 A.D. was followed by victorious wars waged by the followers of his faith. Bedouin Arabs burst out of the Arabian Peninsula, conquered one territory after another, converted it to Islam, and established an enormous Islamic Empire stretching across Asia, North Africa, Spain, and Sicily. Wherever they went with their sword, the Arabs brought their tastes and those of the countries they conquered, amalgamating and spreading the foods from one part of the empire to another.

In the early days—during the Umayyad period, when Damascus was the capital of the empire—the Arab tribes, led by the family of Muhammad, established themselves as a ruling class, separate and above their conquered subjects. The Bedouin warriors, quartered in their great army encampments, ate only once a day and kept aloof, maintaining high standards of restraint and strict, austere living. Their primitive tastes collided with the local Byzantine and Persian hedonism. They ate very simple foods which combined ingredients of agricultural and pastoral origin. Preparation was elementary—the Bedouin diet consisted of bread and dates; of mutton, with some goat and camel meat, and the milk of these animals; with the occasional game and wild berries found in the desert. The settled agricultural populations ate chicory, beets, gourds, zucchini, marrow, cucumber, leeks, onions and garlic, olives, palm hearts, fava beans, lemons, pomegranates, and grapes. A gruel called *harira* was made of dried barley meal to which water, butter, or fat was added, and flour was cooked in milk. Spices were hardly used, even though the Arabs were engaged in transporting them to Europe. They obtained too high a price on the Roman market to be used locally.

The tastes of the Prophet prevailed. His favorite dishes—*tharid,* bread crumbled in a broth of meat and vegetables, and *hays,* a mixture of dates, butter, and milk— were still popular. Muhammad had a special liking for sweetmeats and honey and he was fond of cucumbers. He also liked fatty meat. When a lamb or a kid was being cooked, he would go to the pot, take out the shoulder, and eat it. It is said that he never ate reclining, for the angel Gabriel had told him that such was the manner of kings. He used to eat with his thumb and his two forefingers; and when he had done, he would lick them, beginning with the middle one.

Over the years, Arab ranks were infiltrated and diluted by Byzantine, Persian, and the other conquered peoples. The subject classes, slowly working their way up through the evolving Islamic society to a footing of equality with the Arabs, came at last to constitute the new society themselves. The Abbasid regime was one of Persian ascendancy, with Persians flooding into Islam, transporting with them the core of their civilization. The Arabs, dazzled by the aristocratic brilliance of the Persians they had conquered, adopted their dishes with their traditions of chivalry and good living. The other subject nations—Asian, Aramaean, Egyptian, and Greek—also came to the fore later, bringing their own sometimes prestigious culinary heritage to the now cosmopolitan society.

Thus the Arabs, even though their own cooking was rudimentary, brought about the marriage of cooking styles of the ancient Mediterranean and the Near East and the opulent cooking of Persia.

In the Golden Age

In the Abbasid period, from the eighth to the thirteenth century, the Golden Age of Islam, cooking was transformed into an art which reached magnificent heights. The Islamic Empire occupied far-flung areas of the world—Egypt, and all of North Africa, nearly all of Spain, the islands of Sicily and Crete, with a few southern-Italian towns, besides the north of Arabia, Syria, Armenia, the southeast part of the Caucasus, Mesopotamia, Iraq, Persia, and Afghanistan. It was the most powerful influence in the world. Mecca was its religious center and Baghdad was the capital, the cultural and political hub. The creative culinary genius flourished especially under the reign (786–809) of Harun-al-Rashid. Culinary literature proliferated and reached the level of an art. There were two parallel trends. One, the result of the interest in food of the Abbasid upper classes, written by them or for them, was a princely activity devoted to the refinement of pleasure and to setting high standards of taste and *savoir-vivre* for the elite. Poets, astrologers, astronomers, scholars, princes, and even Caliphs took pleasure in writing about food. The other trend was the development of a branch of medicine—dietetics—and this was the work of doctors concerned with health.

Gastronomy was especially esteemed in this rich period of Arab history when the search for the most delicious combinations of food, according to increasingly subtle criteria, formed the preoccupation of a distinguished society of gourmets. The banquets at the royal courts of the Caliphs of Baghdad were proverbial for their variety and lavishness. The Caliphs commissioned people to invent dishes, to write poems about foods, and to sing their praise at gatherings which became legendary. Masudi, a writer of the time, describes in *Meadows of Gold* one such event at the court of Mustakfi, the Caliph who was blinded and deposed in 946. I quote from Professor Arberry's translation:

> One day Mustakfi said: "It is my desire that we should assemble on such and such a day, and converse together about the different varieties of food, and the poetry that has been composed on this subject." Those present agreed; and on the day prescribed Mustakfi joined the party, and bade every man produce what he had prepared. Thereupon one member of the circle spoke up: "O Commander of the Faithful, I have some verses by Ibn al-Mu'tazz in which the poet describes a tray containing bowls of *kämakh*."

Ibn al-Mu'tazz too had been a tragic prince who ruled for one day only and was put to death in 908. The poem, about a tray of hors d'oeuvres, described the different elements in an ardent and sensuous manner. Others followed with long poems to the glory of many delicacies in terms of ecstatic love.

One man recited a work by the poet, astrologer, and culinary expert Husain al-Kushâjim describing a table of delicacies, of roast kid, partridges, chickens, *tardina*, *sanbusaj, nad, buran,* and sweet lozenges. Another quoted Ibrahim of Mosul on the marvel of *sanbusaj* (little pies). Yet others glorified *harisa, madira, judhaba,* and *qata'if.* Each time, Mustakfi ordered that everything that had been mentioned in the poem should be served. They ate to the sound of music and sweet maidens' voices. Never had the narrator seen the Caliph so happy since the day of his accession. To all present—revelers, singers, and musicians—he gave money and gifts. Unfortunately, the narrator added, this Caliph was one day to be seized by Ahmad ibn Abi Shajâ' Mu'izz al-dawla the Buwayhid, who had his eyes "put out."

A ruling class had emerged whose members led a life of luxury and who devised a code of *savoir-vivre.* Manuals on how to be a connoisseur appeared. In *Meadows of Gold,* Masudi advised people to read his other work, *Ahbar Az-Zaman,* unfortunately lost, in which, he says:

One can be instructed in detail on the variety of wines, on desserts, on the manner of arranging them in baskets or on plates, either piled up in pyramids, or otherwise, a culinary summary the knowledge of which is essential and which cannot be ignored by a well-bred man. One can also read about the new fashions in the way of dishes, the art of combining aromas and spices for the seasoning; subjects of conversation, as well as the way to wash one's hands in the presence of one's host.

Development of a Court Cuisine

In 1949 Professor Maxime Rodinson published "Recherches sur les documents arabes relatifs à la cuisine" in the *Revue des Études Islamiques.* In this sociological and philological study of the history of food in the Arab world, he discusses early culinary literature, analyzes various cookery manuals (see appendix), and describes the court cuisine of the twelfth and thirteenth centuries. In what follows I have also made use of the information he gives in the entry "Ghidha" in the *Encyclopaedia of Islam.*

He describes the many changes in the new empire, which affected food habits. The spread of food products was one. Agricultural crops which had formerly been grown only in one part of the area now spread throughout it. Rice is a good example. It originated in India and was grown in Syria, Iraq, and Iran before Islam. Now it was being grown all over the Arab world and became a popular food as far away as Spain (although it did not quite take the place of wheat, which was a commodity traded on a large scale everywhere). Sugar, introduced to Iran from India shortly before the Muslim conquest, spread after this through the whole of the Mediterranean.

Large-scale transport brought food from one part of the empire to another: truffles from the desert, olive oil from Syria, dates from Iraq, coffee from Arabia. Later, a wide range of ingredients was introduced from places outside the empire. Spices, such as pepper, ginger, cinnamon, cloves, cardamom, cumin, coriander, betel, musk, mastic, and nutmeg, were brought from China, India, and Africa. In the twelfth century, dried and salted fish, honey, and hazelnuts came from Russia and the Slav countries, cheese from Sicily and Crete, wine, chestnuts, and saffron from the south of France.

Increased travel meant that cooks from parts renowned for their food were employed in distant regions. In the Middle Ages, Egyptian cuisine and cooks had a high reputation. So did the cooks of Bolu in Turkey. And there were massive migrations, with immigrants introducing their traditional dishes into their new habitat. The rulers had huge, well-equipped, and well-stocked kitchens, staffed by numerous cooks and their assistants, in which all types of dishes could be attempted.

By the tenth century there was a new prosperous elite in Baghdad which aspired to refinement. Their quest for the grand, the exotic, and the unusual led them to adopt the cuisines of foreigners whose civilizations had formerly enjoyed a certain prestige for power and glory. Hence the vogue for Iranian dishes, and later the fashion for things Turkish. The European culinary influence in the period of the Crusades can be seen in the "Franc" dishes which feature in the *Wusla* (see appendix).

Characteristics of the New Court Cuisine

The cookery manuals naturally dealt with the new styles of cooking which were constantly developing in the kitchens of the courts. These styles had not been handed down from the past and therefore needed to be recorded.

What was the style of this princely cuisine? The following features characterized it.

1. *It used expensive ingredients which only a few could afford.* Some of these were rare and came from afar, such as spices; others were newly grown on Arab soil, such as rice and sugar. Chicken and lamb were used; and so were locally grown vegetables, but not the more common ones, such as okra, beans, and figs.

Everyone knew which were the foods of the poor and which of the rich. (Proverbs, songs, and popular literature express this awareness.) Meat and rice were for the rich; lentils, beans, and honey for the poor. Although these latter foods retained their popularity, they were stigmatized in a book by al-Jahiz as the food of misers and were almost ignored in the manuscripts we have mentioned. When simple local dishes were included, they were glamorized; for example, the melted-down lamb's-tail fat was perfumed with a variety of aromatics as well as with quince and apple and dried coriander, aniseed, onion, cinnamon, and mastic, and was colored red and yellow. Bedouin dishes with dates were made grand by replacing the pits with blanched almonds. Traditional peasant dishes with wheat and lentils were enriched with meat and delicately spiced.

2. *Techniques were elaborate and sophisticated.* Methods of preserving with salt and vinegar, lemon juice and mustard were inherited from the ancient East and from classical civilizations. Fruit was crystallized in honey. Smoke-drying was said in Egypt to be a Greek process. (In the past they had dried meat by hanging thin strips in the open, or preserved it by burying it in fat.) Ancient ways were molded to the new demands of the court—a distinctive general style developed with flavors from as far as Spain and Turkistan, with regional variations.

3. *The grander dishes were Iranian.* Their origins are revealed in the Arab repertoire today by their names ending in *-ak* and *-aj.* Techniques of cooking and ele-

gant ways were adopted from conquered Iran, which had been the most prestigious civilization in the area.

4. *Koranic prohibitions were observed.* Koranic regulations and prohibitions advised by the pious specialists on religious questions were followed. No pork was used and no wine.

5. *Newly acquired tastes became fashionable.* The taste for highly spiced foods and sweet things developed; it was simply a continuation of the tastes of classical antiquity. So was the taste for sweet-and-sour which came via Iran.

6. *Visual appeal was important.* Saffron and turmeric were used for color, and much care was taken to give delight in presentation. Counterfeit dishes, such as mock brains and an omelet in a bottle, were devised as pleasant surprises.

7. *Complexity was valued.* Complexity in flavor was valued for its own sake, quite apart from the actual flavor itself. Aromatics were used in tiny quantities but in a great number and a variety of combinations. All the spices already mentioned were combined with herbs such as parsley, mint, rue, thyme, lavender, mallow, purslane, bay, and tarragon. Poppy and sesame seeds, fenugreek, rose petals, and rosebuds were used. The result was delicate and subtle and, if we go by the tastes handed down, not too strong or too hot.

Complexity in form was also esteemed. Confections which required skill, application, and time were well considered, especially if they were small and beautifully shaped. Vegetables were hollowed out and stuffed, tiny pies were filled, elegant little parcels were made with wrappings of pastries or leaves.

The Place of Dietetics and Medical Books

Dietetics was at the same time a branch of medicine and a form of culinary literature. Anecdotes of the period depict doctors sitting at the tables of Caliphs to advise them on what was good for them. (Maimonides sat for al-Malik al Afdal.)

The educated classes paid a great deal of attention to dietetic precepts, so that this science was of considerable importance. It stemmed both from the scientific medicine systematized by the ancient Greeks, whose theory of humors associated particular foods with the body's constitution and human temperament, and from the old Babylonian Persian beliefs in magic and the curative properties of plants. It incorporated local popular ideas—for instance, that dates cause ophthalmia but are good for childbirth—and penetrated deeply among the masses.

Arab books on dietetics preceded medical books, and all the early medical texts contained a long chapter enumerating, usually in alphabetical order, the positives and negatives of each food from the point of view of bodily and spiritual well-being. They also gave recipes, which were much like those circulating in the courts, and accompanied them by critical advice on what was good for the liver and the heart.

Culinary Literature Disappears, but Cooking Styles Continue

Arab culinary literature faded with the decline of the Abbasid dynasty and the brilliant civilization, which was marked by the fall of Baghdad in 1258 at the hands of the Mongols. Gastronomy continued to have its enthusiasts, but with the growth of religious puritanism they became more discreet. Those who wrote about it were no longer the aristocratic arbiters of taste but obscure people who painstakingly recorded recipes for their own use and the instruction of their servants.

Some of al-Baghdadi's recipes for stews could be word-for-word instructions for an Iranian *khoresh* or a Tunisian or Moroccan tagine of today; and we still make in my family of Syrian origin many of the dishes described in the *Wusla* (see appendix). As for the methods described in the old recipes—grinding fine, rolling into balls or oblongs, pounding in the mortar, simmering long in broth, cutting up in lozenges, bathing in syrup—they are uncannily like the ones people explained when they gave me recipes for this book. As in the past, milk puddings are thickened with ground rice and cornstarch or semolina; and the same honeyed pastries filled with chopped nuts are the usual fare of vendors in the street, to be kept preciously in boxes for festive occasions or the much-appreciated visit of an unexpected guest.

Muslim Spain

A new Arab style of cooking developed in Muslim Spain between the arrival of the Arabs with Berber foot soldiers in 711, in what became known as Al Andalus, and their departure from the Iberian Peninsula in 1492, when the Reconquista of Spain by the Christian kings was complete. The departing Moors brought the new styles with them when they settled in Morocco, Algeria, and Tunisia and initiated there a brilliant culinary renaissance.

The first emirate of Córdoba was founded by a survivor of the Syrian Umayyad dynasty. The ninth century was an era of extraordinary splendor, centered on the court of the Caliph Abd al-Rahman III. A Kurdish lute player called Abul Hassan Ali Ibn Nafi, known as Ziryab, who was from the court of Harun-al-Rashid in Baghdad and had joined the court of Córdoba as a musician, is credited with transforming the art of living in Andalusia. Apart from introducing new music, he taught people how to dress (in white in the summer, and in silk), how to wear makeup, how to cut their hair short and to dye their beards with henna. He also established rules of etiquette, table manners, and table setting and the order of serving different courses, and taught the refinements of cooking.

In the eleventh century Al Andalus had split into thirty-eight small warring

Muslim states, the kingdoms of Taifas, and by the end of the century the Castilian King Alfonso VI had retaken Toledo and begun the Reconquista (the Christian reconquest of Spain). The Almoravids, Berbers from North Africa, came in to help beat the Christians, then stayed and founded an empire. Another Berber dynasty, the Almohads, from the Atlas Mountains of Morocco, followed, making the thirteenth century a period of powerful Berber influence in Al Andalus.

Despite many wars, Muslim Spain was a tolerant, convivial civilization that loved music, song and dance, storytelling, and good food, and where the company of others was prized above all. It was an extraordinary multicultural civilization with people drawn from various parts of the Muslim world—from North Africa, Persia and Yemen, Baghdad, Egypt, and elsewhere—as well as Jews and the indigenous Mozarab Christians. It produced an exuberant type of food with dishes of various origins, which is reflected in an anonymous thirteenth-century Arabic cookery manual entitled *Kitab al Tabikh fil Maghrib wal Andalus* (*Cookbook of the Maghreb and Andalusia*), first edited and translated into Spanish by Ambrosio Huici Miranda and now translated and annotated in French and English by Lucie Bolens and Charles Perry (see appendix). Many recipes are very like those in al-Baghdadi's cookbook, calling for meats cooked with fruit, and sweet-and-sour flavors; many names of dishes end in *-ak* and *-aj,* denoting a still-powerful Persian influence. There are Syrian and Egyptian dishes, North African Berber foods, such as couscous, paper-thin pancakes, semolina sweets with dates, and many, many dishes with eggs. There is the pigeon pie now famous in Morocco, the chicken with almonds and honey, the spicy sausages (merguez), the *shakshouka*s.

The Ottoman Empire

The next empire to pick up the immense culinary fund from the derelict Caliphate, and influence the cooking of the Muslim world, was the great Turkish Ottoman Empire in the fourteenth century. Elements of Persian and Arab cuisines had come into the area when Islam was adopted in the Seljuk period (the eleventh to the end of the thirteenth century), which preceded the Ottoman.

The Turks made their first appearance in the ninth century as slave soldiers (Mamelukes) drawn from the steppelands of Central Asia for the regular armies of the Islamic empire. These Turkish slaves were formidable warriors and came to wield great power. After ruling with a number of small local dynasties, they were in control of the whole Islamic realm. A nomadic branch, the Osmanlis, or Ottomans, were to establish the most powerful Muslim and indeed world empire in history, pushing the boundaries deep into the heart of Europe. Fierce and warlike by nature, they had little sophistication about food. Their diet consisted primarily of yogurt and meat and the pasta adopted from the Chinese, whom they had fought and harassed for centuries. Shish kebabs are said to have originated on the battlefields when their invading armies had to camp outdoors in tents awaiting a new assault.

The Sultan's table, nevertheless, soon took on the luster and glamour of the Abbasid banquets. At first the Ottoman Turks adopted the Persian and Arab cuisines as their model, but they gradually developed one of their own, based on the indigenous foods of Anatolia and on those they adopted from the welter of different peoples, creeds, and ethnic groups of their empire, and especially those of their slaves who were palace cooks. (Famous Turkish dishes like Circassian chicken and Albanian liver were borrowed from their Christian subjects.) The extraordinary amalgam of dishes was the result of the unique character of the empire and its ruling class, whose members entered as the Sultan's slaves and remained slaves all their lives as part of the Ottoman Slave Household. This institution was so superior in discipline and in organizational efficiency that it allowed the empire to survive for centuries. The more able recruits were subjected to a strict course of training and turned into courtiers, husbands of princesses, even grand viziers. The profession of public slave on a high level was dangerous, all-important, and glorious—indeed, the most splendid profession in the empire—and it was open exclusively to children born of Infidels.

The royal family, the Sultan's wives, palace and government officers, the standing army—all were slaves and descendants of slaves. The Sultan himself was the son of a slave. Most were Christians or their children, and had been captured in battle or bought in markets from Barbary pirates and Krim Tartars. Some had been given as gifts by Venetian traders. They had been plucked from Caucasian highlands, from Russian forests and Eurasian steppelands, and some came from Western Europe (a few as volunteers). Wrenched from all family ties and roots, they were more ready to serve loyally. As blue eyes, rosy cheeks, and fair hair increased in the mixed population of the greatest Muslim state, so a wide variety of foods remembered from far-off lands entered the culinary pool.

The first Turkish-born cooks employed in the Palace of Topkapi were from Bolu, the mountain region where the Sultans went hunting. According to legend, they were so pleased with the young men who cooked their meats for them in the open that they brought them back to the palace.

In this extraordinary society food was all-important. The insignia of the Janissary force was the pot and spoon, which symbolized a standard of living higher than that of other troops. The titles of its officers were drawn from the camp kitchen, from "First Maker of Soup" to "First Cook" and "First Carrier of Water," and the sacred object of the regiment was the stew pot around which the Janissaries gathered, not merely to eat but to take counsel among themselves.

The courts of the glamorous and romantic Sultans, such as Mehmed the Conqueror and Suleiman the Magnificent, were notorious for their luxury and devotion to the pleasures of the table. In their kitchens, dishes from all over the world were developed and perfected. Cooks were recruited from the provinces or learned their trade early on as slave pageboys in the palace school, where they were taught to sharpen knives and swords, mix drinks, and cook the Sultan's favorite dishes for his sumptuous banquets. The most powerful grand vizier of all time, Mehmet Koprulu, started off as a young cook. Cooking was one of the most important of the arts, and everyone—poet, astrologer, physician, or prince—wrote recipes, songs, and poems about food.

The sixteenth-century Turkish poet Revani, in his *Isret Name,* deals with festive themes, and writes of the glorious banquets of the time: cultured revelers seated in a circle around crystal cups and flagons, each excelling in some art or other, debating a point of literature or philosophy, while a few musicians play the plaintive melodies of the East, a singer tells of tragic loves, and a fair young cupbearer goes her rounds. He also describes the various delicacies which figure at these banquets: sausages lying as if they were serpents keeping guard over a treasure, roast fowl dancing with delight to see the wine, grains of rice like pearls, saffron dishes like yellow-haired beauties, *börek* which might flout the sun, *chorek* shaped like the moon, jelly on which the almond fixeth her eyes, *qata'if* (vermicelli-like pastry, or *konafa,* page 436) like a silver-bodied loveling.

By the nineteenth century the decline of the Ottoman Empire was marked by corruption, inefficiency, and brutality, and society was based on sectarian allegiances. While the different countries, inspired by modern European nationalism, struggled to break free from the empire, people began to look to their own national traditions for their pleasures. Pre-Ottoman and pre-Islamic foods such as the Berber couscous and the Egyptian *ful medames* were celebrated with greater fervor, and the small sects and communities clung to their differences, making their specialties a proof of identity.

But the Turks nevertheless left their traces on the tables of the countries they conquered as an agreeable compensation for past tyrannies and spilled blood. Something of the old noble cuisine is still to be found in Istanbul (what is known as "classic" Turkish cooking is the cooking of Istanbul), while the cooking of Anatolia (the rest of Turkey), which remained largely unknown in its great regional diversity, is gaining popularity in the cities as people from the countryside invade them.

The Turkish restaurant trade is also a legacy of Ottoman times. The prestige with which professional cooks are regarded has never been equaled elsewhere in the Middle East. The strict hierarchy that reigns in restaurant kitchens—denoted by different shapes of cook's hats—was born at the palace. In the heart of Anatolia, near Lake Abant, lies the *vilayet* of Bolu, from where cooks were recruited to serve in the royal palace or the houses of the nobles. Leaving the fields to be tilled by women, all the young men went to Istanbul. At the age of twelve or thirteen, boys were sent to work in the kitchens near their fathers, uncles, or cousins, who taught them what no stranger was allowed to learn. They would go back to the village to marry, leave their wives, and return to their kitchens in Istanbul. This is how a closed society of chefs was formed, as well as guilds of specialist food producers,

> The writer Emine Foat Tugay writes about the famous Turkish chefs of Bolu in her family chronicle *Three Centuries* (1963), where she says:
>
> *Turkish cooking of the past ranked among the great cuisines of the world. Much of it has disappeared together with the excellent chefs, who had learnt their trade as apprentices in konaks and palaces, where they had to satisfy the exigent palates of their masters. They gradually worked their way up under the master chef from scullery-boy or apprentice to become third, second, and finally first assistant cook. After ten or twelve years the chef would declare his first assistant capable of working on his own account. The young cook then invited all the other chefs to a dinner which he prepared single-handed. He would choose all the most difficult dishes, and anxiously awaited their verdict, since it was they and they only who were empowered to declare him a master cook. If the dinner won the approval of the chefs, they would present him with a large silver watch on a thick silver chain, and would wrap around him, from the waist downwards, a wide striped cotton cloth which took the place of an apron, an insignia of his new status. Henceforth he was their equal.*
>
> *Every cook in Turkey is a native of the province of Bolu. They never marry anyone outside their own village, and leave their wives at home to look after their fields and to bring up the children. They take leave once a year, for two or three months, and call in a colleague of equal capacity to replace them in the interval. This custom still holds good nowadays, though otherwise the system which I have mentioned has disappeared so completely that even the now middle-aged do not remember it. The old chefs almost always brought their complete staffs with them when they were appointed and took them away with them when they left.*

such as the milk-pudding makers and pastry makers. Most cooks today still come from the region of Bolu, especially from the villages of Gerede and Mengen, where there is a catering school (you can see why the restaurant menu is standard). But the trade is no longer so jealously guarded, and many outsiders have been allowed to join, because young men are not so keen to work as hard as their fathers.

New Trends

After the collapse of the Ottoman Empire in the early part of this century, the identity of the Arabic-speaking world crystallized as an Arab world, and at the same time the influence of Europe became very important. People came to settle from all over the world. It was the Middle East of Lawrence Durrell, the Alexandria where Greek and Italian were spoken on the *corniche*, the Lebanon where most people spoke French. Italy was in Libya, the British were everywhere, the Maghreb was French. In this cosmopolitan and Europeanized climate, Western food, especially French cuisine, was considered more desirable than local foods. Restaurants and caterers offered European menus. Dishes became lighter and cooking fats more digestible, and there was a fusion of tastes of East and West. The Grand Hotel of Khartoum offered a menu reminiscent of British Rail fare, although clients could be served local food on request.

Each country began to follow its own gastronomic way and cultivate its peasant or regal past, its Arab identity or its closeness to Europe. Traditional local dishes were more openly appreciated, but many countries were too poor to make the most of their gastronomic heritage. Women went out to work when they could and impoverished bourgeoisies could no longer keep up old standards with a cuisine that required the skill of patient hands and the availability of good ingredients.

Socialism and Islamic egalitarianism created a new mood in the kitchen. Ideology elevated peasant food, and "cheap, quick, and easy" things became respectable. Presumably it was not so easy to persuade hostile servants to spend hours pounding and stuffing. The humble food, which had been stigmatized in the past as low-class and miserly, became fashionable. It had probably always been the preferred "family food"—rich in grains, beans, and vegetables, with the special touch usually bestowed on what is for the nearest and dearest—but it now also became the food for entertaining.

The oil-rich countries, generally those with a starker diet and rudimentary methods of cooking, could afford to import culinary talent from their poorer but more sophisticated neighbors. People in Egypt complained that the Saudis were taking away their family cooks. Since the Lebanese civil war, Lebanese cooks have been engaged in hotels and restaurants and their dishes have been widely adopted. And with the new mobility of businessmen, professionals, technicians, and all types of workers within the Arab world, there is a greater familiarity with the styles of cooking from one part to another. A few regional recipes have become famous; some now appear on menus of international hotels. The trouble is that, when they become standardized, something is usually lost in the flavoring (there is less garlic, for instance). Recently restaurants have become more sophisticated and enlarged their menus as tourists show their interest in local food, but too often they try to adapt to Western tastes, so that authenticity is compromised and the result is not usually good.

Social Aspects

The activities of cooking and eating reflect many subtly intricate facets of the Middle Eastern character and way of life. They are intensely social activities, while the dishes hold within them centuries of local culture, art, and tradition.

Hospitality is a stringent duty all over the Middle East. "If people are standing at the door of your house, don't shut it before them," and "Give the guest food to eat even though you yourself are starving," are only two of a large number of sayings which serve to remind people of this duty, a legacy of nomadic tribal custom when hospitality was the first requirement for survival.

Sayings of Muhammad in the Koran, folk proverbs, and religious, mystical, and superstitious beliefs set up rules of social *savoir-vivre*—sweetly tyrannical, immutable, and indisputable rules of civility and manners—to the minutest detail. They dictate the social behavior of people towards each other and sometimes submerge and entangle them in social obligations.

The ultimate aim of civility and good manners is to please: to please one's guest or to please one's host. To this end one uses the rules strictly laid down by tradition: of welcome, generosity, affability, cheerfulness, and consideration for others. People entertain warmly and joyously. To persuade a friend to stay for lunch is a triumph and a precious honor. To entertain many together is to honor them all mutually. The amount of food offered is a compliment to the guest and an indication of his importance. Failure to offer food and drink shows a dislike of visitors and brings disrepute to the host.

It is equally an honor to be a guest. Besides the customary obligations of cordiality and welcome, there is the need for the warmth of personal contact and cheerful company, the desire to congregate in groups, and the wish to please. It is common when preparing food to allow for an extra helping in case an unexpected guest should arrive. Many of the old recipes for soups and stews carry a note at the end saying that one can add water if a guest should arrive. When a meal is over, there should always be a good portion of food left, otherwise it might seem that someone has not been fully satisfied and could have eaten more.

The host should set before his guest all the food he has in the house, and apologize for its meagerness, uttering excuses such as: "This is all the grocer had," or "I was just on my way down to the confectioner's," or "For the past two weeks I have been preparing for my niece's wedding and have not had time to make anything else."

If a guest comes unexpectedly, the host must never ask why he has come, but receive him with a smiling face and a look of intense pleasure. After a ceremony of greetings, he should remark on the pleasure of seeing him and the honor of such a visit. The guest should never say right away why he has come, if there is a reason, but first inquire about the family, friends, and affairs of his host. The latter must treat his guests as though he were their servant; to quarrel with them would be a disgrace. He must never argue with them about politics or religion, but should always acquiesce. He must never ask his guests if they would like food or drink, but provide these automatically, insisting that they have them and ignoring repeated refusals.

"The first duty of a host is cheerfulness" is a maxim strictly abided by. A host must amuse and entertain, provide light gossip, jokes, and, occasionally, riddles and a little satire. He may also offer a tour of the house and an inspection of new acquisitions. A guest, in turn, must also play his role correctly. He should "guard his voice, shorten his sight, and beautify [praise] the food." That is, although he must commend everything, exclaim in admiration, and congratulate, he should not look about too much, or inspect too closely. The Koran advises him to talk nicely and politely: "Sow wheat, do not sow thorns; all the people will like you and love you." "Don't enter other people's houses, except with permission and good manners." "Beautify your tongue and you will obtain what you desire."

A guest must at first refuse the food offered to him, but eventually give in on being urgently pressed. In particular, he must never refuse dishes that have already been sampled by others of the company, as this would put them in an uncomfortable position. If he comes invited, he must bring a present, and if this happens to be a box of confectionery, the host must open it immediately and offer him some.

The Koran advises, "It is not right for a man to stay so long as to incommode his host." When a guest leaves, he must bless his host and he is under an obligation to speak well of him to others.

However, this beautifully laid-out pattern has its pitfalls. The wrong sort of admiration might be mistaken for envy, and give rise to a fear of the "evil eye," of which it is said that "half of humanity dies." Folklore provides phrases to avoid this. The words "five on your eye" are equivalent to the Western "touch wood." Blessings uttered towards various saints and the invocation of the name of God also act as a protection from evil. The person who is the object of admiration may protect himself by denouncing the reality of his good fortune and protesting that he has also been the victim of various misfortunes. However, a remark of admiration directed towards a personal possession may oblige the owner to offer it instantly and pressingly.

Cooks always cook to suit the taste of those who will eat the food. They need and expect approval. Often, dishes for the evening are lengthily discussed in the morning. Husbands express their wishes as to what they would like for dinner, and while they are eating often remark on the success of the dish. However, a few husbands of my acquaintance believe that they must criticize something in a meal or complain that the dish requires a little more of one thing or another, thereby preventing their wives from becoming complacent. Women are constantly coaxed and encouraged to surpass themselves and to perfect family favorites. Cooking ability is rated high among female accomplishments. One Arab saying goes: "A woman first holds her husband with a pretty face, then by his tummy, and lastly with the help of a *sheb-sheb* [a wooden slipper]."

Cooking is often done in company. Mothers and daughters, sisters, cousins, and friends love to talk about what they will serve their family for lunch or dinner, and they sit with or help each other to prepare delicacies which require time and skill. At all special occasions, such as family gatherings and national or religious holidays, the hostess can count on the help of many eager and generous relatives and friends, who come to help prepare the food, sometimes two or three days ahead. If they are unable to be present at the preparations, they will often send a plateful of their own particular specialty instead.

People always turn to food to mark important events. Weddings, circumcisions, religious festivals, new arrivals, in fact most occasions call for a particular dish or delicacy, or even a whole range of specialties. If these are lacking when it is customary to include them, it is a cause for offense and gossip. Criticism and disapproval are feared most by those who wish to impress and do the right or customary thing. This accounts for the fact that the fare at parties, though often extraordinarily lavish and varied, is also repetitive within each community. No table could be without stuffed grape leaves, *kahk, ma'amoul,* or *baklawa* and the usual range of delicacies. How fearful one is of the critical gaze of a guest searching for some specialty which is missing from the table!

It is said that there is a language of flowers. In the Middle East there exists a language of food. A code of etiquette for serving and presenting particular dishes expresses subtle social distinctions. Which piece, of what, and in what order gives away the status of the person who is being served. There are rules of procedure according to social and family status and age. A dignitary or the head of the family is served the best helping first. A guest who comes seldom or who comes from afar is served before one who is a regular and familiar visitor to the house. A bride-to-be is served ceremoniously at the house of her husband-to-be. But when she is married, her status drops considerably at the table (as it does everywhere else), to rise again when she is expecting a baby. Then she is often pampered and allowed to indulge in extravagant yearnings. If she gives birth to a son, her status remains high.

A person of "low extraction" who insists on sitting next to one of high birth or importance might be asked: "What brought the sardine to the red mullet?" A proverb advises men to pay respect to status, and to give to each according to his station: "Divide the meat and look at the faces." And a saying reflects this regard: "When a wealthy man comes to a feast, the host tells some poor man to get up and give his place to the newcomer."

In some parts of the Middle East where folklore is rich in beliefs about the evil eye, djinns, and omens, some foods are believed to have magical powers. Garlic is said by some to ward off the evil eye and is sometimes hung at the front door of a house to protect its inhabitants. For its disinfectant qualities it is hung on a string around children's necks during epidemics. In some parts, people do not eat brains for fear of becoming as stupid as the animal; in others, they eat them to fortify their own brains and become more intelligent. Some do not eat the hearts of birds in case they might acquire their timidity.

Certain beliefs are uncommon and localized, and few people will have even heard of them. Others are widespread in all the countries and communities. One of these is that eating yellow things will result in laughter and happiness; another, that eating honey and sweet things will sweeten life and protect one from sadness and evil. Predictably, black foods, such as very black eggplants, are considered by some to be unlucky, while green foods encourage the repetition of happy and prosperous events and symbolize a new beginning.

In the past, some foods were believed to have aphrodisiac qualities. Sheikh Umar Ibn Muhammed al Nefzawi, in his now famous sixteenth-century book, *The Perfumed Garden,* recommends various foods as cures for impotence or as powerful sexual stimulants. For the former, he recommends eating "a stimulant pastry containing honey, ginger, pyrether, syrup of vinegar, hellebore, garlic, cinnamon, nutmeg, cardamoms, sparrows' tongues, Chinese cinnamon, long pepper, and other spices"; also "nutmeg and incense mixed with honey." Among foods which "all learned men" acknowledge to have a positive effect in stimulating amorous desires are: an asparagus omelet, a fried-onion omelet, camel's milk mixed with honey, eggs boiled with myrrh, coarse cinnamon and pepper, eggs fried in butter, then immersed in honey and eaten with a little bread, and simply plain chickpeas. He assures his readers that "the efficacy of all these remedies is well known, and I have tested them." Even today, a certain belief in the aphrodisiac powers of some foods still exists. Spice shops offer all kinds of pastes and spice mixtures "to make men happy." When I asked a vendor in Egypt if he had something to make women happy, he said, "If a man is happy, the woman will be happy."

Cooking in the Middle East is deeply traditional and nonintellectual—an inherited art. It is not governed by strict rules like French cuisine, nor is it precise and sophisticated like Chinese cooking, or experimental and creative as in America today. Its virtues are loyalty and respect for custom and tradition, reflected in the unwavering attachment to the dishes of the past. Many have been cooked for centuries, from the time they were evolved, with relatively few changes. Yet all cooks feel that within the boundaries of tradition they can improvise. They can pit their artfulness and wits, their sensuous feeling for the food, its texture and aroma, to create a unique and exquisite dish with the imprint of their own individual taste.

Of the people who have given me recipes, most added remarks such as: "Personally, I like to add a little mint," implying that this was their own innovation; or "I always put double the usual amount of ground almonds," meaning that they are extravagant; or "I use dry breadcrumbs instead of soaked bread," to show their ingenuity; or, with a touch of guilt, "I use bouillon cubes instead of making a chicken stock because it is easier, but I find it very acceptable." Somebody even devised a way of stuffing zucchini without actually doing so, by curling slices around a compact ball of meat-and-rice filling and securing them tightly with a toothpick. Nevertheless, if I were to suggest to those same people a totally new taste or a totally new form or method for a dish, they would be mildly outraged or laugh incredulously at the folly of such an idea.

A capacity to absorb new cultures while still remaining true to themselves has enabled the countries of the Middle East to integrate dishes introduced by the Crusaders, those brought back by the Moors from Spain, Greek dishes, and, more recently, French, Italian, and even English dishes, and to adapt them to suit local tastes. The biggest change was brought about when the products from the New World arrived first in Spain and Portugal and gradually spread into the Middle East in the eighteenth and nineteenth centuries. Tomatoes and peppers, potatoes and sweet potatoes, string beans, pumpkins, and Jerusalem artichokes were adopted and integrated in the local cuisines and took on local flavors.

Among the dishes which evolved because of the character and style of life are the large variety of mezze, served before a meal or to accompany drinks at any time of the day. These reflect the passion that people have for leisure and the importance they attach to their peace of mind, the luxury of tranquil enjoyment which they call *keif.* It is for them a delight to sit at home on their balconies, in their courtyards, or at the café, slowly sipping drinks and savoring mezze.

The numerous stuffed *mahshi, börek, sambousek,* and pastries, all requiring artful handiwork, reflect the pride in craftsmanship and skill. The smaller they are the more esteemed, for they are more difficult and take longer. The traditional decoration of dishes, down to the humblest sauce or soup, with a dusting of red paprika or brown cumin and a sprinkling of chopped parsley is the result of a love of

Shams-Eddin Mohamet Hafiz was one of the greatest poets of Persia. He was widely respected by all Persians, and lived in his native Shiraz during the fourteenth century A.D.

On a visit to nearby Isfahan, he was the house-guest of Ali Agha Isfahani, the most prominent merchant of Isfahan. Elated by this great honor bestowed on him, Ali Agha instructed his wife that nothing but the best of food be prepared by her cooks during the Hafiz visit and only the most prominent guests be invited to the banquets arranged almost every night during this visit.

Needless to say, various dishes were prepared and they were all one better than the other. So, during the first banquet, while Hafiz really enjoyed the meal, he ended up by shaking his head and saying how much he missed the banquets and parties of Shiraz. This led Ali Agha to believe that his wife was not making enough effort to please the palate of the great poet and requested her to double the amount of food and the variety for the next evening. But again, after enjoying the meal, Hafiz shook his head and passed the same remarks about the parties of Shiraz. And this went on for several nights afterwards. While Ali Agha's household were doubling and tripling the amount of food, their eminent guest was passing the same remarks. At last Ali Agha was on the point of bursting and he took his courage into his hands and asked Hafiz as to where they were failing to please him. Hafiz replied, "You are not displeasing me. On the contrary you are almost embarrassing me by offering and wasting so much food every evening. And how can I stay at your home as long as I desire while this goes on?" That taught Ali Agha the art of preparing the adequate food for each occasion.

A STORY TOLD BY JOSEPH SHAMOON

beauty and ornamentation, the same that has produced the luscious Islamic decorative arts. The sensuous blue-and-green patterns of the ceramics are echoed in the green chopped pistachios and pale chopped blanched almonds adorning cream puddings. The crisscross patterns of the wooden balconies, behind which the women used to hide, haunt the lozenge shapes of *basbousa* and *baklawa*. The colors of confectioneries, syrups, and pickles are those of the brilliant dresses which appear at *mûlid*s (festivals).

The Traditional Table

Before proceeding to the table, guests are entertained in a different room, where they often sit on sofas at floor level. A maid comes round with a large copper basin and flask, pouring out water (sometimes lightly perfumed with rose or orange blossom) for the guests to wash their hands, and a towel is passed round.

Dining tables are low and round—large metal trays resting on a type of stool, or on short, carved, folding wooden legs, sometimes inlaid with mother-of-pearl and tortoiseshell. The trays themselves are of copper, brass, or silver, beaten and engraved, sometimes inlaid with silver or other metals. Thin threads of the metal are beaten into crevices with a little hammer, making traditional decorative patterns and writings: words of blessing, charms against the evil eye, and words in praise of Allah. Usually a number of tables are placed in the room, and the diners sit around them on cushions. Several bowls containing a variety of dishes are placed on each table for guests to enjoy the pleasure of deciding which dish to start with, and with which delicacy to follow.

Before the meal is started, the word *Bismillah* (In the name of God!) is uttered by all. In eating, a strict code of etiquette is observed. It is related that the Imam Hassan (son of Ali) listed twelve rules of etiquette to be observed. The first four are *necessary*—namely, to know that God is the Provider; to be satisfied with what he has provided; to say "In the name of God!" when beginning to eat and to say "To God be thanks!" when you finish. The next four are *customary,* and it is well to observe them, though they are not required: to wash the hands before eating; to sit with your left to the table; to eat with three fingers; and to lick the fingers after eating. The last four are rules of particular politeness: to eat out of the dish that is immediately in front of you and out of your own side of the dish; to take small pieces; to chew the food well; and not to gaze at the others at the table with you. These twelve rules form the traditional basis for the table manners of the majority of the people.

Besides these rules, there are other, subtler points of *savoir-vivre*. It is tolerated to eat with five fingers when eating food of a not-too-solid consistency, such as couscous. It is considered sociable and polite to detach choice morsels such as chicken hearts or livers, or fish roes, and to offer these to a neighbor. If one feels satiated, one should nevertheless continue to nibble at a dish from which others are still eating, since if one person stops eating everyone else may feel compelled to stop too, and the dish will be removed from the table. One must lick one's fingers at the end of a meal only. To do so before would be a sign that one has finished.

One must always talk about pleasant and joyful things and never introduce a sad or bitter note into the conversation. One must be cheerful and entertaining, and remark on the perfection of dishes, saying, "Your fingers are green!" if the hostess has prepared them or helped in their preparation; and "May your table always be generous to all!"—a phrase entertaining the hope that one will be asked to eat there again soon.

Sometimes, in parts where women have not yet become emancipated, men only are invited. Islam looks upon women with suspicion. According to Muslim tradition, the Prophet Muhammad said: "I have not left any calamity more hurtful to man than woman." In some countries, women are believed to have more power to cast the evil eye, so they are served first, before their look of longing can have a harmful effect on the food. If two people have eaten together, they are compelled to treat each other well, as the food contains a conditional curse. This is alluded to in the sayings "God and the food will repay him for it," and "Cursed, son of a cursed one, is he who eats food and deceives him who shared it with him." Host and guest in particular are tied in a relationship governed by this conditional curse. When the meal is finished, guests leave the table to go through the hand-washing ceremony again and to partake of coffee or tea.

Similar rules to these are added to Western manners in homes where Western habits of eating have been adopted. Actions and words reveal an attachment to ancient tradition. At buffet dinner parties in our house, for example, the guests stood far away from the table and had to be urged and pressed to eat. Although the mechanics of the European table, the knife and fork, and the table napkin had been adopted, the old, Middle Eastern manners and rules of *bienséance* remained.

In her beautiful book *Three Centuries,* Emine Foat Tugay describes the customary hospitality of the aristocratic Ottoman families in the early part of this century, especially during the month of Ramadan, when gates and house doors would be opened to the public:

> An Imam and a muezzin were engaged for the whole month at our house, and the latter would chant the call to evening prayer from the top of the stairs leading into the garden. Prayer-rugs facing south-east towards Mecca had been spread in the main hall for the men, and the drawing-rooms were similarly prepared for the women. As soon as a cannon boomed, announcing that the sun had set, the fast was broken with olives and bread, prior to the short evening prayer. The household, with its resident guests and any

strangers who had come in, then sat down at different tables to *iftar,* as the first meal after the fast is called. The men were all served in the *selamlik,* whether they were known to my father or not. He dined separately with his guests, but the food was the same for all. Strange women did not often come to *iftar,* nevertheless a table was always ready for the *Allah misafiri,* the guests of God. Special dishes were served at *iftar.* Black and green olives, several kinds of sliced cheese, a variety of jams, very thin slices of a sausage made of mutton, and the dried meat of mutton or turkey, the two last-named being the only foods flavored with garlic which were ever eaten in the *konaks,* had been placed, each one separately, in tiny dishes before each plate. Goblets containing sherbet always stood beside the glasses for water. The meal invariably began with soup, followed by eggs cooked either with cheese or meat, sausage, or dried meat, and usually ended after a large number of courses with the serving of *güllaj,* a sweet made from thin wafers of starch. Two hours after sunset, the muezzin again chanted his call to the last prayer of the day, the *Yatsi Namaz.* During Ramazan only, another prayer, the *Teravi Namaz,* immediately follows the *yatsi,* both together lasting over an hour. My father, with his sons and household and those of his guests who wished to participate, never missed any of these prayers. I used to pray with the other women in the drawing-room, where screens placed in front of the wide-open double doors enabled them to hear the recitations without being seen. Those who fast are permitted two meals only, the *sahur,* an hour before sunrise, and the *iftar* at sunset. During the interval nothing may pass down the throat, even smoking being prohibited, since smoke can be swallowed. The *iftars* which I have known, generous and ample as they were, would have seemed paltry in comparison with some of the gargantuan meals of former times. The following anecdote, related by Colonel Aziz Bey in my hearing, will give some idea of an *iftar* in those days.

During Sultan Mahmud II's reign, at the beginning of the nineteenth century, the Sheyh-ul-Islam, Meki Efendi, was famed for the excellence of his table. The Sultan, hearing of this, decided to put to the test the Sheyh's reputation of being both a generous host and himself a gourmet of superb excellence. Unannounced, he arrived one evening in *Ramazan,* with a retinue of forty, to partake of the *iftar* at Meki Efendi's yali. The Sheyh-ul-Islam was quietly sitting in his room beside a window which looked out on the Bosphorus, reading the Qur'an. When his servants informed him of the Sultan's arrival, he closed the holy book, kissed and lifted it to his forehead, then placed it on a high shelf. Turning to his servants he said: "Have the *iftar* served in the *selamlik,* and the *sahur* in the harem to the family." He then went down to meet his unexpected guests. The food was so abundant that, after justice had been done to each superlative dish, all were more than satisfied. After the sweetmeats had been served, cut-glass bowls containing stewed sour cherries (*vishne*) were set down to refresh jaded palates. The

Sultan, astonished that the bowls all began to drip and dissolve, wanted to know why this was happening. Meki Efendi humbly explained that the bowls were made of ice, which had been specially preserved in pits and was every day carved and adorned with intricate patterns by specialized crafts-men. The Sultan laughed and had to admit that even his own table could not boast of such luxury as this.

On a much smaller scale our own table, in readiness for any uninvited guests, was laid for sixteen every day. Without counting my father, who only lunched at home on Fridays, we were already six, my mother, three children, and two governesses. Poor Halil (then in an invalid chair for his tubercular back) ate separately. The ladies who dropped in to lunch usually brought their own children. Hala Hanim, for instance, never came without her daughter and two granddaughters. There were rarely empty seats at table. Simultaneously with ours, a second table presided over by the *bacis* was laid in another room for such guests as might be considered to be "below the salt." They were served by younger girls. At our table the three specially trained *sofracis* [servants] were reinforced by at least as many other maids. The enormous platters of food were handed round once (there were no second helpings) and then passed to an under-maid who waited outside the dining-room, to be taken to the *bacis'* table. Food was so abundant that when we had finished the dishes were still more than half-full. The staff had their meals, cooked specially for them, in the servants' hall in the basement. For each meal the cooks prepared food for twenty-five at the master's table and for forty indoor and outdoor servants; these had only five courses. They began with either soup, eggs, or a pastry stuffed with cheese, had a meat course, a vegetable dish served separately, the inevitable pilav made of rice, and lastly either a sweet or fruit.

Our "frugal" meals of six courses, which had so shocked my mother's family, always began with either fish, eggs, or *börek*, a dish comprising vari-ous kinds of pastry stuffed with cheese and herbs, or spiced minced meat. Then came meat or fowl with potatoes and salad, two vegetable courses, the first eaten cold and cooked in oil, the second in butter and served hot, pilav, each day a different kind, and either a milk pudding or pastry soaked in syrup. Fruit always finished off the meal. Coffee was served in the draw-ing-room or in summer in the entrance hall, which was delightfully cool.

Everyone publicly washed their hands before and after each meal, either in a passage beside the dining-room, which was lined with marble basins and taps, or inside, where the maids offered silver ewers and basins to the senior guests. In my mother's youth one maid had held the basin, a second poured water, and a third offered the towel. She had simplified the process; the same maid held the basin in her left hand and poured out with her right. If the guest was important enough, we children deferentially handed the towels instead of this office being performed by a servant.

Muslim Dietary Laws

The religion of Islam is the most important part of Middle Eastern culture and its dietary laws have influenced the cooking of the region. The code of religion is derived mainly from the Koran, throughout which the Prophet Muhammad mentions food many times and insists particularly on its beneficial character as a gift from God. He repeated injunctions about what kinds of food are permitted and not permitted.

So eat of what God has given you, lawful or good, and give thanks for God's favor if Him it is you serve.

Say I find not in that which is revealed to me aught forbidden for an eater to eat thereof, except that it be what dies of itself, or blood poured forth, or flesh of swine—for that surely is unclean—or what is a transgression other than (the name of) God having been invoked in it. But whoever is driven to necessity, not desiring nor exceeding the limit, then surely thy Lord is Forgiving, Merciful.

The following foods are forbidden:

1. animals dead before they are slaughtered, or those killed for reasons other than that of food
2. blood
3. pig's flesh
4. animals slaughtered as an offering to a pagan deity or in the name of the deity
5. alcoholic or fermented liquids, and all inebriating liquors, although they were favored at first; they are forbidden in cooking, too

An animal that is killed for the food of man must be slaughtered in a particular manner: the person who is about to do it must say: "In the name of God, God is most great!" and then cut its throat.

These dietary laws are observed in varying degrees of laxity throughout the Muslim world. It is very uncommon for people to eat pork. Some Muslims drink wine, and other types of alcohol such as the anise-flavored liquor arak or raki and mahia.

Flavorings, Aromatics, Condiments, and Oils

No one who has walked through a Middle Eastern spice street can never forget the intoxicating effect of mingled scents or the extraordinary displays of knotted roots, bits of bark and wood, shriveled pods, seeds, berries, translucent resins, curious-looking plants, bulbs, buds, petals, stigmas, and even beetles.

Practically every main town in the Middle East has its *attarine* or spice street in the *souk* or bazaar, where rows of very small shops—some as small as cupboards—sell spices and aromatics. Vendors lay them out artfully to tempt those passing by with their delicate shades of gold and brown and their enigmatic shapes. They sometimes roast, grate, or crush them to a powder in a mortar on demand, and sift them through a fine sieve as they did centuries ago. They fill little cones made out of tightly rolled pieces of newspaper and offer them as though they were magic potions.

The Orient is renowned for its delight in incense, perfumes, and aromatic flavorings. Since early times it was part of the spice route between the Far East, Central Africa, the Spice Islands, and Europe. The local taste for spices and for sweet dishes was inherited from ancient Egypt and the Greco-Roman world, in which spices are thought to have been used also to mask the smell of slightly "off" meat. Long before Islam, Arabia was already known as the land of spices, and Herodotus wrote that the whole country was scented with spices and exhaled a marvelously sweet odor. The country, however, was only the transit area—as were Persia and Ethiopia—for the transport trade between East and West when spices were the most highly prized merchandise because of their small volume and high prices. Their commerce, which was kept going in a small way even throughout the Muslim conquests, flourished especially during the Crusades. The middlemen—Arabs, Persians, and Saracen merchants (the last mainly Syrians and Jews)—fiercely guarded their monopoly and their sources of supply. Saracen ships brought spices from China, Tibet, Malacca, Java, and Sumatra, as well as India and Ceylon and the east coast of Africa, through the Persian Gulf and the Red Sea. Trading posts were established everywhere, and when the Arab conquests interrupted business relations with Europe, Jews became the middlemen. Goods were transferred to camels to follow the caravan routes through the Arabian desert to Palestine and Syria, or came via Cairo in boats on the Nile. Trading ships waited in the Mediterranean to carry them into Europe through the ports of Venice and Genoa. It is not surprising that the intermediaries should have succumbed to the attractions of their precious merchandise.

A certain magic still surrounds spices and aromatics, which are used not only for their taste but also for their medicinal, therapeutic, and even sometimes aphrodisiac value. For they are variously believed to increase the appetite, help digestion, or calm the nerves, to be good for the heart and circulation, to be antitoxic or sexually stimulating, and even to kill microbes. Attributes may be well founded or romantic; ginger is said to make people loving, rose water to give a rosy outlook, dill and aniseed to have digestive qualities, and garlic to be both health-giving and an antiseptic.

Almost everything that can add a touch of flavor or aroma is used in cooking. The aromatic plants most commonly used are flat-leaf parsley, cilantro (sometimes referred to as "Arab parsley"), and mint. Oregano, wild marjoram, thyme and dill, fenugreek, bay, celery and fennel leaves, chives and tarragon, purslane and rue also play their part. Herbs are so popular that they are sometimes placed in a bunch on the table for people to pick at. Cilantro is used liberally in salads as well as stews, mint marries happily with yogurt, dill is especially popular in Turkey and Iran.

All the usual spices come into use. Saffron, turmeric, cumin, coriander, cinnamon, nutmeg, allspice, cloves, ginger, cardamom, caraway, aniseed, sesame, poppy seed, fennel, dill, fenugreek and mustard seeds, sumac, peppercorns, cayenne, and paprika—all these have an important place. Each country has its favorites and its own special mixtures and combinations.

Storing and Toasting Spices

Keep your spices and dried herbs in small airtight jars, preferably in a cool, dark spot, to preserve their aroma and flavor.

Whole spices keep their flavor better and longer than ground ones, so grind them, if you can, as you need them. Toasting whole spices brings out their flavor. Toast them very briefly in a dry skillet over medium-high heat, shaking the pan and stirring until they begin to release their aroma. Remove them from the heat at once and let them cool before grinding with a pestle and mortar or in a spice mill.

Otherwise buy ground spices in small quantities, so as not to have them around for too long.

Special Flavorings and Aromatics

Barberries. Called *zereshk* in Iran, these are tart red berries used in their dried form in Persian cooking.

Bois de Panama, saponaria, erh el halawa is a pale dry wood which when boiled in water produces a thick white foam. It is used to make the cream called *naatiffe* for *karabij* (page 435) (it is also used in carpet shampoos). In America it can sometimes be found in powder form in health-food stores. It is the wood from an American tree called *Quillaja saponaria*. It can also be the root of soapwort *(Saponaria officinalis),* which has the same foaming effect.

Cardamom can be used in the pod (which can be green, white, or brown), as whole seeds, or ground.

Chilies. There are many varieties which vary in shape (most are thin and pointed), size, and degrees of pungency and flavor. They are all green to begin with and ripen through shades of yellow and orange to a bright red. They are used whole—fresh or dried—or chopped. Dried and ground, they range from the mild and sweet such as paprika, and the coarsely ground into flakes, to the fiery-hot ground chili and cayenne peppers.

Dibbis, or date syrup, is an Iraqi sweetening agent made by boiling dates until they form a pulpy mass. In the past it was poured into a basket strainer, another basket was inverted over this, and they were placed between two boards, by means of which the juice was expressed. (People stood and jumped on top.) It was then poured onto trays and allowed to evaporate in the sun; the thick syrup which resulted was stored in jars. The syrup, which looks like thick brown molasses, keeps well and is used in savory as well as sweet dishes. I have not found any of the commercial varieties particularly good. People like to mix it with tahina and eat this with bread.

Fenugreek leaves (shambabileh in Persian) are used, fresh or dried, in Iranian soups and stews. They have a pleasant bitter flavor.

Fenugreek seeds have a strange bitter taste and powerful scent. When they are soaked in water overnight they produce a bitter-tasting, viscous, jellylike substance. A relish called hilbeh (page 66) is made with it in the Yemen. A drink is made with the seeds in Egypt.

Lemons and limes are ubiquitous as flavorings in different forms. Preserved in salt, they are a North African specialty; for ways of making them see page 459. Dried limes are a specialty of Iran, Iraq, and Persian Gulf countries. One is usually enough for a stew for six. Iraqis call them *noomi basra,* Persians call them *limoo omani.* In the Arabian Gulf states, where they are much used, they are called *loomi.* They are used to flavor soups and stews and to make an infusion to drink. The usual way is to pierce with the point of a knife in a few places, or to crack them open with a hammer, or pulverize them in a food processor (in that case the pips must be removed first).

You can buy them whole or pulverized in Indian and Oriental stores. You can also make them yourself very easily. Simply leave whole small lemons or limes to dry out, preferably in the sun or, as I do, on radiators, until they are brown and very light and sound hollow when you tap them.

Mahlab is a spice obtained from the dark kernels inside the pits of small black cherries of trees that grow wild. They give a special almondy taste to breads and pastries. They are sometimes sold already ground.

Mastic is the resin exuded from small evergreen trees or bushes which famously grow on the Greek island of Chios. When tiny incisions are made in the stems in the summer, sticky oval tears of resin appear. The small (about a quarter-inch), hard translucent lumps of dried mastic must be pulverized in an electric mill or pounded and ground in a mortar with a bit of sugar before they can be used to flavor desserts. In Cairo, mastic was also used as chewing gum, mixed with a little piece of ordinary wax to soften it. It is sometimes wrongly called "gum arabic," which is a glue.

Musk, a secretion from the abdominal scent glands of the male musk deer of the Himalayas, gives a heavy scent to desserts. It is very rarely used. Seeds from the abelmusk (*abelmoschus, moschatus; ambrette* in French), which have a slight musky flavor, are a substitute flavoring.

Nigella seed (shamar in Arabic and **mavro** in Greek). These tiny black seeds with a piquant taste, also called onion seeds, are sprinkled on bread and *kahk* (page 401).

Orange-blossom water (mai qedda), produced from the blossom of the sour-orange tree, lends a delicate perfume to syrups, pastries, and puddings. As the flavor is rather powerful, and because the distilled essence can be found diluted to varying degrees of strength, it is worth adding less than the amount stated to begin with and adding more to taste.

Peppers. Many types of peppers are used. Besides the black-pepper berry and the weaker white-pepper seed freed from its powerful wrinkled black skin, there are gray peppers called cubebs and long peppers which look like a black catkin, both of which are not as strong as the black berries. All these are best bought whole and used freshly ground.

Pomegranate seeds. The juicy, shiny pink seeds of the fresh fruit are sprinkled on salads and on tahina sauce for fish. Cut the fruit in half, scoop out the seeds, and discard the bitter-tasting pith. Dried wild seeds give a sharp flavor to hummus and tahina.

Pomegranate syrup, now more usually labeled "molasses" or "concentrate," is made from the juice of sour (not sweet) pomegranates boiled down to a thick syrup. It is much used in Iranian and Syrian cooking. Some varieties are a bit too sweet for my liking. One made in Lebanon is less sweet than an Iranian variety.

Rosebuds. A powerfully aromatic variety of rose from Damascus is used to perfume strong spice mixtures. In Egypt we used to leave rosebuds about in little plates to embalm the air. I once walked into a restaurant which was a converted house in the Medina in Marrakesh to find myself treading on a soft carpet of deliciously scented rose petals.

Rose water (mai ward), the distilled essence of rose petals, is used to scent syrups, pastries, and puddings. It is weaker than orange-blossom water and can be used less sparingly. They are often used together. Because the diluted versions sold in America from various provenances vary in strength, you should adjust the quantities to taste.

Saffron. The highly prized red saffron threads—the pistils of a particular purple crocus grown in Iran, Kashmir, and Spain—are much used, especially in Persian and Moroccan cooking. There are various grades. The highest have an incomparable flavor. The threads are crushed with the back of a teaspoon and mixed with a little hot water before using. It is better to buy the threads than the powders, but in certain dishes a powder is more useful. Some commercial powdered saffron is very good and worth buying, but many are adulterated, so you must be sure of your source.

A cheap substitute sold in Egyptian and Turkish bazaars is the yellow pistils of safflowers, which give color but little flavor and a different taste.

Sahlab (also called **salep**). The bulb (or root tuber) of a type of orchid is used in powder form to thicken milk and lend a special flavor to a hot drink and an ice cream. It is quite expensive. Some that I have bought in bazaars have turned out to be low-quality adulterated with cornstarch.

Samna (clarified butter) is also used for its distinctive acid flavor. To clarify butter, heat it slowly in a pan until it is thoroughly melted and bubbling, then chill it until it is firm. Transfer carefully to another pan, leaving behind the residue at the bottom. Melt the butter again, and when it froths, strain it through a fine cloth into a jar. Make a large quantity—it keeps for months (actually, years). It gives a special acid taste to food and does not burn. Some people flavor the butter as it bubbles with aromatics such as fenugreek, caraway, or cardamom seeds. Use 1–2 table-spoons of seeds to ½ pound butter.

Sumac (or **sumak**), the dark wine-colored spice with an astringent sour flavor, is made from the coarsely ground dried berries of the sumac shrub. Iranians, Iraqis, Lebanese, and Syrians use it frequently and provide it in restaurants, particularly to sprinkle on kebabs and salads or on fish. Juice can be extracted by soaking the cracked berries—about 4 ounces in 4½ cups of water—for 20 minutes, then straining and squeezing the juice out. It is sometimes used instead of lemon juice.

Tahina paste **(tehina, tahini)** is the thick, oily pale-beige sesame meal which results from grinding sesame seeds. It is used both raw, in dips and salads, and cooked, in sauces. It keeps for a year.

Tamarind (tamarhendi) is a fat pod with large, hard shiny beans surrounded by a sour pulp. Used with sugar, it gives a delightful sweet-and-sour flavor. You can find it in Indian and Middle Eastern stores, sold semi-dried as a sticky mass of broken pods with fibers and beans, or as a moist vacuum-packed fibrous pulp. Both of these need to be soaked in water overnight; then the juice is strained and squeezed through a fine cloth. Unless you prepare a large quantity, and keep it in a jar, it is not worth the trouble of making. Many years ago you could find an Italian brand of tamarind syrup which was wonderful to use. One that is produced in Lebanon to dilute as a drink is much too sickly sweet and not suitable at all for cooking. The best alternative is tamarind concentrate—a dark, shiny paste, produce of India, which is available in plastic jars in Indian and Oriental stores. It keeps for years—no need to refrigerate. You dilute it in water or add it to the dish as it cooks.

Turmeric is often referred to as "Oriental saffron" because it imparts a bright-yellow color. The spice, the dried ground rhizome of a tropical plant, sometimes replaces saffron in Middle Eastern dishes. Where grand families use saffron, poor ones and street vendors use turmeric. But the flavor is entirely different—slightly bitter with a musky fragrance—and is also loved for itself.

Spice Mixtures

Every household has favorite spice mixtures which they blend to taste and keep in jars as ready condiments or flavorings. A few are made to be eaten with bread. The bread is broken into pieces, dipped in olive oil and then in the condiment, to pick it up. Vendors sell classic mixtures which they make up. These are often simply called "the three spices" or "the four spices." In Egypt what we called *les quatre épices* (the four spices) was a ground mixture of cloves, cinnamon, nutmeg, and pepper. "Four spices" in Tunisia may be cinnamon, pepper, rosebuds, and paprika, and in Morocco it may be cloves, nutmeg, ginger, and pepper. "Curry mixtures" of varying compositions popular in the regions neighboring India are similar to those of that country.

Baharat. In Egypt this is a mixture of ground cinnamon, allspice, and cloves which is often used with meat. In Morocco it is a mix of ground cinnamon and rosebuds.

Ras el hanout means "the grocer's head." Spice merchants in North Africa stake their reputation on a "house blend" which, according to folklore, may contain up to a hundred aromatics, though in reality it contains around twelve. The mixture generally includes cinnamon bark, nutmeg, dried rosebuds, pieces of dried ginger, cloves, cubebs (tailed peppers) and other peppers, and sometimes also the golden-green Spanish fly, renowned for its supposed aphrodisiac qualities. They are mixed and pounded together in a mortar as required.

Zaatar (or **zahtar**) is wild thyme. It is also the name of the mixture of this herb with sumac, salt, and toasted sesame seeds. The mix, which is popular in Syria, Lebanon, Israel, and Jordan, is sold in little paper cornets to dip into with bread. To make it, mix 1 part ground dried thyme, 1 part lightly toasted sesame seeds, ¼ part sumac, and salt to taste. You can buy it in jars in Middle Eastern stores.

Besar is a blend much used in the United Arab Emirates. For this, mix ½ cup cumin seeds, ½ cup fennel seeds, 1 cup cinnamon sticks, ½ cup coriander seeds, ¼ cup peppercorns, 2 tablespoons dried red chilies, ¼ cup turmeric powder. Roast all of the spices except the turmeric in a dry skillet over low heat, stirring constantly, until the spices begin to color. Then grind in a food processor and mix with the turmeric.

Relishes and Condiments

Some spice mixtures are made into a paste with oil or something moist. A covering layer of oil keeps them from spoiling.

Harissa. This very hot chili-pepper paste flavored with garlic and spices is much used in North African cooking. It can be bought ready-made in tubes and cans but it will not have the special perfume of the homemade variety. To make your own, see page 464.

Tabil is a strong-tasting Tunisian mixture of coriander and caraway seeds, garlic, and chili peppers (both sweet and fiery), ground or pounded to a paste. It is used to flavor meat-and-vegetable stews.

Zhoug. I discovered this Yemenite relish in Israel. It was so strong that a tiny drop picked up on the tip of my little finger set my throat on fire. Grind and blend the following to a paste: 1 teaspoon black pepper, 1 teaspoon caraway seed, 1 teaspoon cardamom seeds, 4 strong dried chili peppers soaked in water for an hour, 1 whole small head of garlic, a large bunch of cilantro (2 cups), and salt. Use it to flavor soups and stews, or simply to dip your bread in. It can be red or green depending on what color chili peppers you use.

Oils

On the whole, olive oil is used raw to dress salads and to sprinkle on dips. It is used for cooking vegetables to be eaten cold, and to deep-fry fish. For general all-purpose cooking, vegetable and other relatively flavorless oils—peanut oil, corn oil, and most recently the widely adopted sunflower oil—are used. Greece and Tunisia are the largest producers and the greatest users of olive oil. Nut oils such as almond, walnut, hazelnut, and pistachio were used very occasionally in the past. Sesame oil was much prized in Egypt, Syria, and Iraq. Argan oil is produced from the nut in the fruit of the argan tree, which grows exclusively in the southwest of Morocco. It is believed locally to have aphrodisiac properties.

THE LOAN OF A CAULDRON

One day the Khoja asked a neighbor for the loan of a cauldron. After he had done with it, he put a small saucepan inside and took it back to the owner. When the man saw the small saucepan, he said, "What is this?" and the Khoja answered, "Your cauldron has had a baby."

"That's good news!" said the man, and accepted it with pleasure.

Another day the Khoja wanted to borrow the cauldron again and took it home with him.

The owner waited a long time, but he noticed that the cauldron did not come back. Then he went round to the Khoja and knocked at his door. When the Khoja came and asked him what he wanted, he answered, "I want that cauldron."

"Accept my sincere condolences," said the Khoja, "the cauldron is dead!"

"What!" said his neighbor in the greatest amazement—"dead? Whoever heard of a cauldron dying?"

"Strange!—strange!" replied the Khoja. "You could believe that the cauldron had a baby, and yet you do not believe that it could die!"

BARNHAM, TRANS.,
TALES OF NASR-ED-DIN KHOJA

On Using the Book

Readers are encouraged to trust their taste and to taste often, and to allow themselves a certain freedom in preparation. This is in the spirit of a cuisine which is very personal and rich in variations, and it is what cooking is about. With some exceptions, quantities and measures need not be interpreted with too much precision. It is more important to adjust the dish as it progresses and to take more control. You cannot go wrong if you trust your taste. Anyway, measuring in cups is not as precise as weighing, since you can press ingredients down or not. And we are dealing with products of nature, and these vary.

You can have a small lemon that has more juice and is sharper than a larger one. Garlic cloves vary in size and flavor. There are many varieties, and they can be young or old and more or less strong. Tomatoes have a different taste in different countries, grown in different soils, under a different sun. Flour, even of the same variety and the same provenance, varies from one year to another in the amount of water it absorbs. Once upon a time the recommendation was to add "as much water as it takes," and there was some sense in that.

The flavor of fresh herbs is different, depending on where they were grown. Spices vary greatly too, depending on where they come from and the particular harvest. There are different grades and qualities, and if they are old they might have lost their potency, or they may never have had it. Dry herbs that have been around for some time get weaker. That is why you may have to adjust the amount of aromatics. Even rose and orange-blossom extracts, which come in bottles, can be more or less diluted according to the producer. I do not generally give precise quantities of salt in my recipes, because I believe salting is so much a matter of per-

ON THE MERITS OF TRUSTING YOUR TASTE

A Governor came to Akshehir who was rather eccentric.

"If anyone knows a good dish," said he, "I wish he would write out the recipe and we will make a Cookery Book."

He made the suggestion to one of the principal men of the town, who passed it on to the Khoja.

Next day the Khoja met this man and said, "Do you know I was thinking all night about what you told me. I have invented a rare dish—one that no one has ever heard of—quite delicious!"

When the man asked what it was, he said, "You must make a batter of garlic and honey."

The man, who was a bit of a fool, went off at once, and happening to meet the Governor, said to him, "We have a Khoja in the town, a man of much experience and quite an original character." He then proceeded to give him the Khoja's recipe.

Now, the Governor was by no means as intelligent as he was supposed to be. He answered, "How extraordinary! You don't say so!" and at once hurried home and gave orders to the cook that he was to try it for supper.

Of course it was disgusting.

The Governor was very angry and told the man who had mentioned the Khoja to him, to bring him to Government House.

"So you are the man who invented a dish of garlic and honey?" he asked.

"Your very humble servant," replied the Khoja, "unworthy though I be to have done such a thing."

"Very well," said the Governor, and gave orders that he should be made to eat some on an empty stomach next morning.

As he turned it over in his mouth he made horrible grimaces at the nasty taste, and the Governor said, "What are you making those faces for? Enjoy yourself. Take your fill of this dish you invented. Perhaps it tastes differently to the man who made it."

"Your Excellency!" said the Khoja, "this invention of mine was only a theory. I had never tasted the thing before. Now I have, and I see that theory and practice are quite different things. I don't like it, either."

BARNHAM, TRANS.,
TALES OF NASR-ED-DIN KHOJA

sonal taste and it is the one seasoning that people know how to dose and have an "eye" for even before tasting. (See "About Salt," on page 63.) It is best to start with less and add more later.

It is quite possible to substitute oil for butter in most dishes without spoiling them, and onions and garlic may be used abundantly, or omitted entirely if you don't like them.

You can be flexible in the way you plan menus. Mezze, or appetizers, can be served with drinks, as a first course, or as side dishes. You can make a casual meal out of two or three, accompanied by bread and perhaps cheese or yogurt and olives, and a large assortment can be offered at a buffet party. The traditional drinks served with appetizers are arak (or raki), the anise-flavored spirit distilled from grapes, and the Moroccan mahia made with figs or dates. Beer too goes well with appetizers. For those who do not take alcohol, fruit juices or chilled yogurt beaten with water or soda are traditional alternatives.

You can make a meal out of a soup accompanied by bread. A pie or an omelet—both of which can be quite substantial—can also serve as a one-course meal. For most of the fish dishes you may use alternative kinds of fish. Feel free to use a cheaper fish or one more easily available than the one suggested. Lamb is the traditional meat of the Middle East, but beef or veal can be used instead; and in many recipes, such as stews, meat and poultry are interchangeable. Rice, couscous, and bulgur are the staples of the area and make a good accompaniment to many dishes.

Vegetarians will find a great many ideas to make up wonderful meals. The best way to end your repast is with fresh fruit, or with dried fruit and nuts. Puddings and pastries are for special occasions.

Appetizers, Salads, and Cold Vegetables

MEZZE WA SALATAT

The custom of eating mezze—little bits of food to accompany drinks—is one of the most appealing features of the Middle Eastern way of life. It is a ritual and an institution inherited by all the Arab lands and represents an art of living. The word "mezze" derives from the Arabic *t'mazza,* meaning "to savor in little bites." Mezze are meant to be enjoyed in an unhurried way. The pleasure of savoring the food in convivial company and beautiful surroundings is accompanied by feelings of peace and serenity, and sometimes by deep meditation. You only have to witness the look of delight, approaching ecstasy, part sensual, part mystical, in men sitting in cafés to see that. And there are rules. Mezze are meant to whet the appetite, not to fill you up. There should be a variety—ideally four different items, some hot, some cold, served in small quantities. They should have seductive flavors to open the appetite, and they should be a feast for the eyes.

Most Middle Eastern meals begin with mezze, but these are not always served at the table. Sometimes there is a separate mezze table. When my father came home from work, all the family settled in the large balcony and waited for Awad the cook to bring in the drinks tray. There was arak or whisky or beer and an assortment of little bites—pieces of cheese or botarga, salted almonds, olives, pickled turnips, sticks of cucumber, radishes. At the risk of spoiling our appetite, we wolfed down the food as we watched the feluccas gliding slowly by on the Nile and listened to my father's account of his day in the Mouski. When we had guests, the array of usually elaborate delicacies that was served as mezze could be extraordinary. There were grape leaves and a variety of stuffed vegetables, fillo cheese cigars and meat triangles, little fish balls, meatballs, fried eggplant, vegetable omelets cut into squares, and all kinds of dips and salads. In the kebab houses and the cafés by the Nile, the menu had a standard list of mezze always the same and not very long. It included hummus and tahina, eggplant purees, falafel, and grape leaves.

The mezze tradition developed as a way of soaking up the drink arak, a refreshing but powerful distilled liquor made from sweet white grapes flavored with aniseed. It is called raki in Turkey and ouzo in Greece. In Iraq, dates are used to make it, while the national drink of North Africa, boukha in Tunisia and mahia in Morocco, is made from figs. The drink, affectionately called "lion's milk" because it turns cloudy when water is added, is mixed with cold water (one part arak to two of water) and served with a chunk of ice. Sometimes two glasses—one containing arak, the other iced water—are served together, to be sipped alternately.

The cooks at the Sultan's palace in Istanbul reputedly produced more than two hundred different types of mezze. Each country developed its own local specialties. In North Africa they are called "kemia." The list of foods which have come to represent mezze in the West through Lebanese and Turkish restaurants was born in the mountain resorts in the Lebanon, where arak is produced, and in the old-style meyhane—the taverns or drinking houses of Istanbul. But other types of foods are also offered as mezze in the home. I have given here a selection of those most commonly known in several different countries, but you will find many more in the chapters on savory pies, egg dishes, pickles, vegetables, meat, chicken, and fish. *Kibbeh,* for instance, and cheese cigars are famous mezze.

For a meal, following our Western way of eating only one first course, it is fine to have only one or two mezze, but for a large party when you are ready to invest more time in cooking, it is exciting for the guests to be offered a variety. A large selection of mezze makes an ideal buffet meal. Some dishes, like the Tunisian *meshweya* and the Turkish *piaz,* make a snack meal on their own, served with bread. In the recipes which follow, quantities given are usually quite large, designed for people who will be offered only one or two as a Western-style first course, so reduce the quantities if you are serving a large variety.

Salads and cold vegetable dishes are present at every type of Middle Eastern meal, both as hors d'oeuvre and as accompaniments to the rest of the meal, so serve them as a first course or together with the main dish.

Do'a or Dukkah

An Egyptian Seed, Nut, and Spice Dip

Makes 4 cups • This dearly loved Egyptian specialty is a loose mixture of nuts and spices in a dry, crushed, but not powdered form, usually eaten with bread dipped in olive oil. In Egypt it is served at breakfast or as an appetizer. It is a very personal and individual mixture which varies from one family to another. On a recent visit to Australia I was amazed to find that my mother's recipe had made it fashionable there. Wineries were inspired to produce their own adaptations of "Aussie *dukkah*" with locally grown seeds, different spices, and even ground chili pepper and now sell it in elegant packages, while restaurants put some out on little plates for people to dip in.

It will keep for months stored in a jar. To serve, pour a little olive oil on small slices of bread and sprinkle generously with the mixture. Or provide Arab bread for people to tear pieces and dip into bowls of olive oil and *do'a*.

1 cup sesame seeds

1¾ cups coriander seeds

⅔ cup blanched (skinned) hazelnuts

½ cup cumin seeds

½ teaspoon salt, or more to taste

¼ teaspoon pepper (optional)

Put each variety of seeds and nuts on a separate tray or a shallow oven dish and roast them all in a preheated 350°F oven for 10–20 minutes, until they just begin to color and give off a slight aroma. As they take different times, you must keep an eye on them so that they do not become too brown, and take each out as it is ready. Alternatively, you can toast them in a large dry frying pan, stirring constantly. Put them together in the food processor with salt and pepper and grind them until they are finely crushed but not pulverized. Be careful not to overblend, or the oil from the too finely ground seeds and nuts will form a paste: *dukkah* should be a crushed dry mixture, not a paste. Taste and add salt if desirable.

Variation

Some people use peanuts or almonds instead of hazelnuts, and some add dried mint. Some use no nuts.

A meal is often made by those who cannot afford luxuries of bread and a mixture called dukkah, *which is commonly composed of salt and pepper with za'atar or wild marjoram or mint or cumin-seed, and with one or more, or all, of the following ingredients—namely, coriander seed, cinnamon, sesame, and hummus [roasted chickpeas]. Each mouthful of bread is dipped in this mixture.*

LANE, *MANNERS AND CUSTOMS OF THE MODERN EGYPTIANS*, 1860

A Bowl of Fresh Herbs

In Persia fresh herbs are served as mezze. A bowl or platter containing a varied assortment is placed on the table at most meals for people to nibble at throughout the meal.

Wash sprigs of fresh flat-leaf parsley, mint, chives, cress, dill, cilantro, tarragon, scallions—and other fresh herbs that you like—and arrange them on a plate. Sometimes radishes are added.

❧

PERSIAN SAYING:
*"Even the worm inside
a stone eats herbs."*

❧

An ancient custom is for women to eat herbs with bread and cheese at the end of a meal. According to an old belief, this will help them to keep their husbands away from a rival. Job's tears and mandrake in particular should turn him against a "co-wife."

DONALDSON, *THE WILD RUE*

Khodrawat bel Khal
Raw and Vinegared Vegetables

A selection of raw vegetables, such as cucumbers, tomatoes, peppers, and radishes, to nibble at is a common way to start a meal.

An alternative is to turn them into instant pickles. Have carrots, turnips, cauliflower, celery stalks, and small cucumbers, all cut into thin sticks, slices, or florets. Sprinkle generously with salt and let the juices run out for an hour. Then moisten with wine vinegar and leave for a further hour before serving.

The most popular street food of Iraq is a selection called *abiadh al bedh*. Neatly arranged arrays of hard-boiled eggs, pickles, beets, tomatoes, scallions, and all types of seasonal vegetables, piled high with lavish decorations of parsley, chives, and other herbs, are pushed around the streets of Baghdad in carts. Vendors pick items on demand, slice and season them, then roll them up in a piece of bread.

Bassal bel Khal

Onions with Vinegar

Serves 6 • It is said that the Prophet Muhammad did not like the smell of onions although he liked to eat them, and he therefore asked people not to attend the mosque smelling of onion or garlic. According to numerous sayings and proverbs, onions have a low rating in Arab folklore, but they are very much appreciated and often eaten raw, quartered or sliced.

An Iranian version with added mint called *sarkeh piaz* is a relish to serve with broiled meats.

2 large mild onions

Salt

2–3 tablespoons wine vinegar

1 tablespoon crushed dried mint
(optional)

Cut the onions in half, then slice them into half-moon shapes. Sprinkle with a little salt; add the vinegar and mint. Toss the onions in this seasoning, and leave them to stand for at least 1 hour before serving. They will become soft, lose much of their pungency, and absorb the other flavors.

Serve them as an appetizer, or place them in little bowls on the table to accompany a main dish.

Variation

A Lebanese way is to sprinkle the onions simply with salt and a little sumac.

⊱✳⊰

ARAB SAYING:
"He fasted for a year, then he broke his fast on an onion" (implying that an onion is not special enough to justify fasting).

⊱✳⊰

Batarekh

*Botarga (*Boutargue *in French)*

The salted, dried, and pressed roe of the gray mullet was prized as a great delicacy since the time of the Pharaohs and is still considered so by Egyptians today. It has a deep sienna-brown color, a firm hard texture, and rich strong flavor. The taste is an acquired one which can become a passion. It is usually sold sealed in a wax coating. Remove the wax and serve it sliced very thinly on small slices of bread, either buttered or dipped in olive oil. If you like, squeeze a little lemon juice over it.

Taramosalata

Serves 8 • Gray-mullet roe was originally used in Turkey and Greece for this famous dip, but smoked cod's roe now generally replaces it. I like to use a mixture of sunflower or flavorless vegetable oil and olive oil, which allows the taste of the roe to dominate.

$\frac{1}{2}$ pound smoked cod's roe

3 slices white bread, crusts removed,
soaked in water

Juice of 1 lemon, or to taste

$\frac{1}{4}$ cup sunflower or light vegetable oil
and $\frac{1}{4}$ cup extra-virgin olive oil

Skin the smoked cod's roe and mash it in the food processor with the bread, squeezed dry, and the lemon juice.

Gradually add the oil in a thin trickle while the blades are running and blend to a creamy paste. Cover with plastic wrap and chill. If it is too liquid, do not worry—it will become thick and firm after an hour or so in the refrigerator.

Gebna Mashwi aw Makli

Broiled or Fried Cheese

Greek cheeses such as halumi, kefalotyri, and kasseri, which are hard and salty, or the popular kashkaval, are delicious cut into cubes or slices, grilled or fried, and served with a squeeze of lemon.

Cook the cheese under the broiler, until the skin begins to blister, becomes spotted with brown, and starts to melt. Alternatively, fry the cheese in hot oil or sizzling butter, rolling the pieces in flour first if you like. Serve very hot, sprinkled with lemon juice.

Fried cheese used to be served in cafés in Cairo in two-handled frying pans straight from the fire, to be eaten with bread and lemon juice.

Sidqi Effendi, in his Turkish cookery manual written in the nineteenth century, gives this recipe for grilling cheese: "Put a portion of cheese in silver paper. Wrap it up and put it over a fire. When the paper starts to glow the cheese is ready to eat and deliciously creamy. . . . This is good food which enhances sex for married men."

As soon as Goha discovered that someone had stolen the piece of salted cheese from his lunch box, he ran to the fountain.
"What are you doing here?" asked a friend. "I am waiting for the one who stole my cheese. I always come here as soon as I have eaten some."

Muhammara

Walnut and Pomegranate Paste

Serves 6–8 • There are many versions of this exquisite Turkish and Syrian relish. Serve it with bread as an appetizer, or as an accompaniment to a cooked vegetable salad, or with broiled fish or meat.

1¼ cups shelled walnuts
1½–2 tablespoons tomato paste
1 slice whole-wheat bread, crusts removed, lightly toasted
½ cup extra-virgin olive oil
2 tablespoons pomegranate syrup (also called "concentrate" or "molasses")
1 teaspoon coarsely ground red-pepper flakes or a pinch of ground chili pepper
1 teaspoon ground cumin
2 teaspoons sugar
Salt

Blend all the ingredients to a rough (not too smooth) paste in the food processor.

Cevisli Biber

Roasted Pepper and Walnut Paste

Serves 8 • This is another wonderful Turkish paste which makes a delicious canapé spread.

4 large red bell peppers

1 cup finely chopped walnuts

4 cloves garlic

Salt

Juice of ½–1 lemon

1 tablespoon extra-virgin olive oil

Pinch of chili pepper or flakes

Roast the peppers by turning them under the broiler or in the hottest oven until their skins blacken and blister, then skin them and remove the seeds (see page 84). Blend the peppers to a paste in the food processor, add the rest of the ingredients, and blend very briefly—just enough to mix them well.

Wara Einab or Dolma

Cold Stuffed Grape Leaves

Makes about 35 grape leaves • Stuffed grape leaves were served at the court of King Khosrow II in Persia in the early seventh century. There are numerous versions today of this delicacy, which is popular in every country throughout the Middle East. Meat is used in the making of hot *dolma,* and cold *dolma* are without meat. In Egypt the meatless variety is called "false" or "lying" because there is no meat, but it is the most popular. This is my mother's recipe. It is particularly aromatic. The leaves can be bought preserved in brine, but fresh ones have a better flavor. Only very young, fresh, tender ones picked in the spring will do. They freeze very well raw and wrapped in foil.

8 ounces preserved or fresh grape leaves

1¼ cups long-grain rice

2 to 3 tomatoes, peeled and chopped

1 large onion, finely chopped, or 4 tablespoons finely chopped scallions

2 tablespoons finely chopped flat-leaf parsley

2 tablespoons crushed dried mint

¼ teaspoon ground cinnamon

¼ teaspoon ground allspice

Salt and pepper

2 tomatoes, sliced (optional)

3 or 4 cloves garlic

⅔ cup extra-virgin olive oil

1 teaspoon sugar

Juice of 1 lemon, or more

If using grape leaves preserved in brine, to remove the salt put them in a bowl and pour boiling water over them. Make sure that the water penetrates well between the layers, and

(continued)

leave them to soak for 20 minutes, then change the water twice, using fresh cold water. If using fresh leaves, plunge a few at a time in boiling water for a few seconds only, until they become limp, and lift them out.

Pour boiling water over the rice and stir well, then rinse under the cold tap and drain. Mix the rice with the chopped tomatoes, onion or scallions, parsley, mint, cinnamon, allspice, and salt and pepper to taste.

Stuff the grape leaves with this mixture: Place each leaf on a plate, vein side up. Put one heaping teaspoonful of filling in the center of the leaf near the stem end. Fold the stem end up over the filling, then fold both sides towards the middle and roll up like a small cigar. Squeeze lightly in the palm of your hand. Fill the rest of the leaves in the same way. This process will become very easy after you have rolled a few.

Pack the stuffed leaves tightly in a large pan lined with tomato slices or leftover, torn, or imperfect grape leaves, occasionally slipping a whole clove of garlic in between them if you like.

Mix the olive oil with ⅔ cup water. Add the sugar and lemon juice, and pour the mixture over the stuffed leaves. Put a small plate on top of the leaves to prevent them from unwinding, cover the pan, and simmer very gently for about 1 hour, until the rolls are thoroughly cooked, adding water occasionally, a coffeecupful at a time, as the liquid in the pan becomes absorbed. Cool in the pan before turning out. Serve cold.

Variations

• Add 3 tablespoons raisins or currants and 4 tablespoons pine nuts to the filling.
• Mix ¼ teaspoon powdered saffron or turmeric with the olive oil and water before pouring over the stuffed grape leaves.

• Soak about ¼ cup dried chickpeas in water overnight. Then crush them in a mortar and add them to the filling. In this case use ¼ cup less rice. You may also use drained canned chickpeas.

Hot Stuffed Grape Leaves

Makes about 35 grape leaves

8 ounces drained preserved or fresh grape leaves
½ cup long-grain rice
8 ounces ground beef or lamb
1 tomato, peeled and chopped
1 small onion, finely chopped
3 tablespoons finely chopped flat-leaf parsley
3 tablespoons finely chopped celery leaves (optional)
1 teaspoon cinnamon
Salt and pepper
2 tablespoons tomato paste, or more (optional)
2 tomatoes, sliced (optional)
2 cloves garlic, halved or slivered
Juice of 1 lemon, or more

If using grape leaves preserved in brine, to remove the salt put them in a bowl and pour boiling water over them. Make sure that the water penetrates well between the layers, and leave them to soak for 20 minutes, then change the water twice, using fresh cold water. If using fresh leaves, plunge a few at a time in boiling water for a few seconds, only until they become limp, and lift them out.

Wash the rice in boiling water, then rinse under the cold tap and drain. In a large bowl, mix the rice with the ground meat, chopped tomato, onion, parsley, optional celery leaves, cinnamon, salt, and pepper. For a Greek flavor, add 2 tablespoons or more tomato paste.

Stuff the grape leaves with this mixture. Place each leaf on a plate, vein side up. Put one heaping teaspoon of filling in the center of the leaf near the stem end. Fold the stem end up over the filling, then fold both sides towards the middle and roll up like a small cigar. Squeeze lightly in the palm of your hand. Fill the rest of the leaves in the same way.

Line the bottom of a large saucepan with a layer of tomato slices or leftover grape leaves to prevent the stuffed leaves from sticking to the pan and burning. Pack the stuffed leaves in tight layers on top, pushing small pieces of garlic here and there between them. Sprinkle with lemon juice and add about ⅔ cup water.

Put a small plate over the rolled leaves to prevent them from coming undone, and cover with a lid. Cook the leaves over very gentle heat for about 1 hour, or until tender, adding water gradually as it becomes absorbed.

Turn out onto a serving dish and serve hot.

Variations

• A Lebanese variation adds 4 or more garlic cloves (crushed) in addition to the slivered ones and 1 tablespoon crushed dried mint with a little water about 20 minutes before the end of cooking time.

• A Greek version is served with *avgolemono* sauce. Bring 1½ cups of meat or chicken stock (you may use a bouillon cube) to the boil. Beat 3 egg yolks with the juice of 1 lemon and beat in a ladle of the stock, then pour this into the pan with the simmering stock, beating vigorously until the sauce thickens. Quickly remove from the heat, and do not let it boil, or the eggs will curdle. Pour over the stuffed leaves when you serve.

Ta'amia or Falafel

Bean Rissoles

Serves 10 • This is one of Egypt's national dishes, welcome at all times, for breakfast, lunch, or supper. The Christian Copts, who are said to be pure descendants of the ancient Egyptians, claim this dish as their own, along with *melokheya* soup (page 146). Their claim might be justified, since these dishes are extremely old. During Coptic religious festivals, and particularly during Lent, when they are not allowed to eat meat for many weeks, every Coptic family produces mountains of *ta'amia* for their own daily consumption and to be distributed to non-Coptic friends and neighbors.

Ta'amia (called "falafel" in Alexandria) are patties or rissoles made from large dried fava beans (*ful nabed*), which look white because they are sold skinless. Splendidly spiced and flavored, and deep-fried in oil, they are delicious. I have never known anyone not to like them.

The best I have eaten were in Alexandria, with my aunt and uncle. Every year they rented a flat there, the balcony of which was directly above a café which specialized in *ta'amia*. My relatives were both rather large, which was not surprising, since we always seemed to come upon them eating; and I could never visualize them eloping, gazellelike, in their youth, which was the romantic legend that was told to us.

On each visit, we would sit with them for hours on their balcony overlooking the sea. Time and again, a basket would be lowered on a rope to the café below and pulled up again with a haul of fresh *ta'amia,* sometimes nestling in the pouch of warm, newly baked Arab bread. We would devour them avidly with pieces of bread dipped in tahina salad, and then wait anxiously for the basket to be filled up again. *(continued)*

You must buy the large broad beans which are sold already skinned as "split broad beans" in Middle Eastern stores (again, they look white without their brown skins).

1 pound dried (skinless) split broad
    beans, soaked in cold water for 24
    hours

Salt and pepper

2 teaspoons ground cumin

1 teaspoon ground coriander

Good pinch of ground chili pepper or
    cayenne (optional)

1 teaspoon baking soda or baking
    powder

1 large onion, very finely chopped or
    grated

5 scallions, very finely chopped

6 cloves garlic, crushed

⅔ cup finely chopped flat-leaf parsley

⅔ cup finely chopped cilantro

Sunflower or light vegetable oil for
    deep-frying

The long soaking of the beans to soften them is all-important. After soaking, drain the beans very well and let them dry out a little on a towel. Then put them in a food processor and process until they form a paste, adding salt and pepper, cumin, coriander, chili pepper, and baking soda or baking powder (these last two release carbon-dioxide gas, which causes the paste to rise slightly and lighten). The paste must be so smooth and soft that it will hold together when you fry. Let it rest for at least ½ hour.

Add the rest of the ingredients except the oil. If you have chopped or grated the onion in the food processor, strain to get rid of the juice, or the rissoles could fall apart when you fry.

Knead the mixture well with your hands. Take small lumps and make flat, round shapes 2 inches in diameter and ¼ inch thick. Let them rest for 15 minutes.

Heat at least 2 inches of oil in a heavy pot until sizzling hot. Fry the patties in batches, without crowding them, until crisp and brown, turning them over once. Lift them out with a slotted spoon and drain on paper towels.

Serve hot, accompanied by hummus bi tahina (page 68) or baba ghanouj (page 65), a tomato-and-cucumber salad, and pita bread.

Variations

- A common version is made by dipping the *ta'amia* in sesame seeds before frying them.
- If the paste does not hold together, it usually means that the beans have not been properly mashed. You can remedy this by adding 2–3 tablespoons flour.
- A quarter-ounce dried yeast dissolved in a few tablespoons lukewarm water may be mixed into the paste, which should then be allowed to rest for an hour. The result is lighter rissoles.
- A dry falafel "ready mix" is not nearly as good as the real thing, but you can use it to make a quick appetizer. Add water as directed on the packet, and allow the paste to rest for a while. To improve the flavor, add a little finely chopped parsley, finely chopped scallions, crushed garlic, and the other flavorings called for in the master recipe to taste, then shape and fry in oil as above.
- In Syria, Lebanon, and Jordan, falafel are made with a mix of chickpeas and fava beans, and in Israel, where falafel has become the national dish, it is made with chickpeas alone. It is mostly the Israelis who have popularized falafel in the West, and their style is the one generally known abroad.

About Salt

Salt is a very important ingredient. It brings out the flavors of a dish. In recent years, after the link between high levels of salt consumption and high blood pressure was made, Americans started to use less, and as a result their palates have changed. Today they use much less salt than people do in Europe, but the taste for it still varies from one person to another. Not everyone benefits from a low-salt diet. It is necessary only for people with high blood pressure. Our bodies need salt, more or less of it depending on various factors, in particular the climate where we live. In hot countries (including parts of America), where people sweat a lot and lose salt, they need more salt and experience weakness and even fainting spells if they lack it.

Rarely do cookbooks in Europe or elsewhere in the world give quantities of salt or pepper in recipes. These are two ingredients that people are expected to gauge how much they want of.

Also, the strength and intensity of flavor of different types of salt vary according to where it originates. It depends on whether the salt has been mined from underground deposits or evaporated from seawater. Salt from the earth, extracted from underground deposits, is far less salty. Sea salt varies depending on which part of the world it comes from, how it has been collected and dried, and what minerals it contains. English sea salt, for instance, is saltier than French, which has a distinctive delicate flavor. Table salt usually has additives. Coarse-grain kosher salt does not.

I recommend finely ground sea salt. That is what I use.

It was always said that when cooking you measured with your eye, and it is true that with salt you have to trust your eye. It is usual to start with a little and to add more when you start tasting. Some salads need very little salt, whereas rice and grains need quite a bit if they are not to be terribly bland.

To Broil or Roast and Mash Whole Eggplants

Prick the eggplants in a few places with a pointed knife so that they will not burst. Turn them under the broiler until the skin is black and blistered and they feel very soft when you press them. Or place them on a sheet of foil on a baking sheet and roast in the hottest oven for about $\frac{1}{2}$ hour, or until they feel very soft when you press them, turning them at least once by one half turn. When cool enough to handle, peel the eggplants and drop the flesh into a colander. Then chop the flesh with a knife and mash it with a fork in the colander to let the juices escape.

Eggplant Caviar

Serves 4 • Roasted and mashed with olive oil and lemon juice is a common and delicious way of eating eggplants, often described as "poor man's caviar." Use firm eggplants with a shiny black skin.

2 eggplants, weighing about 1½ pounds total
4 tablespoons extra-virgin olive oil
Juice of ½ lemon, or more to taste
Salt

Broil or roast the eggplants (see page 63). Peel, letting the pieces fall into a colander with tiny holes, then chop with a pointed knife and mash to a puree with a fork or a wooden spoon, so that the juices escape through the holes of the colander.

Transfer the eggplant to a bowl and beat in the oil and lemon juice and some salt.

Variations

• For a Syrian flavor, mix in 2 tablespoons pomegranate concentrate or molasses (see page 45) instead of lemon juice, 2 crushed garlic cloves, and 3 tablespoons chopped flat-leaf parsley.

• For a spicy Moroccan version, add 1 crushed garlic clove, ½ teaspoon harissa (see page 464) or a pinch of cayenne and ½ teaspoon paprika, ½ teaspoon ground cumin, and 1 tablespoon chopped cilantro.

• For an eggplant salad, add 3 tablespoons chopped parsley, 2 chopped tomatoes, 4 chopped scallions, and ½–1 finely chopped (and seeded) chili pepper.

Borani-e Bademjan

Eggplant Puree with Yogurt

Serves 6 • This is very popular in Iran. A similar recipe, called *buran,* is to be found in al-Baghdadi's thirteenth-century cookery manual (see appendix). There, fried meatballs are added to the puree, and the dish is seasoned with ground cumin and cinnamon.

3 eggplants, weighing about 1½ pounds total
3 tablespoons extra-virgin olive oil
1¼ cups plain whole-milk yogurt
Juice of 1 lemon
2 cloves garlic, crushed
Salt
2 tablespoons chopped flat-leaf parsley (optional)

Broil or roast and peel the eggplants (see page 63).

Chop the flesh with a pointed knife in a colander to let the juices escape, then mash them with a fork or a spoon. Pour into a bowl and beat in the olive oil and the yogurt and mix vigorously until it is thoroughly blended with the eggplant puree. Mix in the garlic and salt, spoon into a serving bowl, and garnish, if you like, with chopped parsley. Serve cold.

Variations

• Instead of yogurt, add ⅔ cup fresh thick cream or sour cream and omit the oil.

• Add 3 tablespoons finely chopped fresh mint or 1 tablespoon dried.

• Garnish with ¼ teaspoon crushed saffron threads mixed with 2 tablespoons boiling water, then with 2 tablespoons of yogurt. Dribble this on top.

Baba Ghanouj or Moutabal

Eggplant and Tahina Dip

Serves 6 • This is a popular mezze in every Arab country and a regular companion to falafel. You will always find it in Lebanese and Egyptian restaurants in the West, and even in supermarkets. The smoky flavor of the eggplant and the nutty taste of tahina sharpened by lemon and garlic make a seductive combination.

> 2 pounds eggplants
> 2 or 3 cloves garlic, crushed (optional)
> Salt
> 4 tablespoons tahina (sesame paste)
> Juice of 2 lemons, or more to taste
> ½ teaspoon ground cumin (optional)
> Optional garnish: 2 tablespoons extra-virgin olive oil and 1 tablespoon finely chopped flat-leaf parsley

Broil or roast the eggplants until very soft inside (see page 63). Peel them, letting the soft flesh fall into a colander with small holes, then chop the flesh with a pointed knife and mash it with a fork in the colander, letting the bitter juices run out. Pour into a bowl and add garlic, a little salt, the tahina paste, and lemon juice, beating well and tasting to adjust the flavoring. You may use a food processor, but the texture is best when it is done by hand.

Pour the eggplant into a shallow dish and garnish, if you like, with a dribble of olive oil and a sprinkling of parsley. Serve with Arab or pita bread to dip in.

Variation

Instead of lemon juice, add 2–3 tablespoons pomegranate syrup (see page 45). Garnish, if you like, with fresh pomegranate seeds.

Tarator bi Tahina

Tahina Cream Sauce

Serves 6 • Serve as an appetizer with pita bread, or as a sauce to accompany various dishes such as fried fish, boiled vegetables, and falafel.

> ⅔ cup lemon juice or the juice of 2½ lemons, or more to taste
> ⅔ cup tahina paste
> 1–3 cloves garlic, or to taste, crushed
> Salt
> 2 tablespoons finely chopped flat-leaf parsley to garnish

Blend all the ingredients together in a food processor or blender, adding enough cold water to achieve a smooth, light cream. Taste and add more lemon juice, garlic, or salt until the flavor is fairly strong and sharp.

Serve in a shallow bowl sprinkled with chopped parsley and provide Arab or other bread to dip in it. Or use as a sauce to accompany falafel (page 61) or grilled meats and salads.

Variations

• An Egyptian way is to flavor this with ½ teaspoon ground cumin and to garnish with a sprinkling of olive oil and a dusting of cumin and chili pepper.

• For a parsley-and-tahina cream, *ba'dounes bi tahina,* stir in ½ cup finely chopped flat-leaf parsley.

• For a wonderful version rich with pine nuts, *tahina bi senobar,* fry 1–1½ cups pine nuts in a drop of oil over low heat, shaking the pan, until lightly golden, and stir them in. This is particularly good as a sauce for fried or grilled fish.

Yemeni Hilbeh

Fenugreek Relish

A curious gelatinous relish with a slightly bitter flavor is made with fenugreek seeds. It is an acquired taste that can become addictive. Eat it with bread to dip in.

The flat square yellow-brown seeds need to be crushed or ground, so it is best to buy the fenugreek in powder form. It needs to be soaked to remove some of the bitterness and to develop the gelatinous texture.

> 2 tablespoons ground fenugreek
>
> 4 cloves garlic, crushed in a garlic press
>
> 2 large tomatoes, peeled and quartered
>
> 1 tablespoon tomato paste
>
> Salt and pepper
>
> ¼ teaspoon caraway seed
>
> ½ teaspoon powdered cardamom
>
> ½ teaspoon chili pepper or more to taste

First prepare the fenugreek jelly: Pour plenty of boiling water over the ground fenugreek (2 tablespoons absorbs a large quantity of water and gives you a large amount of jelly), stir well, then let rest for at least 2 hours but preferably overnight, by which time a gelatinous mass will have settled at the bottom, leaving a clear liquid on top. Drain all the liquid off without disturbing the gelatinous substance. Now beat in about ½ cup of water, drop by drop, until the mixture is light and foamy (the beating is traditionally done with the hand and can take 10 minutes).

Blend the rest of the ingredients in the food processor, then add the drained fenugreek jelly and process to a soft, slightly frothy paste. It keeps for at least a week, covered in the refrigerator.

Variation

Mix the jelly with a few tablespoons of zhoug (page 48).

About Garlic

Garlic can be mild or strong. The heads can be large or small. They must be firm to the touch, not soft or hollow, and they should not have sprouted. To peel off the skin of a clove easily, lay it on a board with the flat of a large knife placed on top and hit the knife with one quick blow. The papery peel should lift off easily. Cut away any brown spots. If it has begun to sprout inside the clove, cut into the middle of the clove and remove the pale-green sprout, which has a bitter taste.

To crush garlic, bash it on a board under the flat blade of a large knife, then chop it or scrape it to a mush on the board. Or use a garlic press; I have used one since I was a schoolgirl in Paris, and it works very well.

Tahina bel Laban Zabadi

Tahina Cream Salad with Yogurt

Serves 4–6 • This version has a delicate flavor and is rather creamier than most. My mother discovered it in the Sudan, and has made it ever since. It can be a dip or a sauce.

- 2 or 3 cloves garlic
- Salt
- ⅔ cup tahina paste
- ⅔ cup plain whole-milk yogurt
- Juice of 2½ lemons, or more
- 2 tablespoons finely chopped flat-leaf parsley to garnish

Put all the ingredients except parsley together in a food processor or blender and blend to a smooth cream. Taste and add more salt, lemon juice, or garlic if necessary.

Pour into a shallow bowl and sprinkle on the parsley. Provide Arab or pita bread to dip in.

Serve as an appetizer, or to accompany grilled or fried meat dishes and salads.

Teradot

Tahina with Walnuts

Serves 4–6 • A specialty of Jehan, in southern Turkey, this is served as a dip with fried mussels or baked fish, or as an accompaniment to salads and boiled vegetables, such as runner beans or cauliflower.

- 1 cup walnut halves
- 2 cloves garlic
- Salt
- 3–4 tablespoons tahina paste
- Juice of 2 lemons
- 4 tablespoons chopped flat-leaf parsley

Pound the walnuts and garlic in a mortar with a little salt until the walnuts are almost, but not quite, ground to a paste. Add the tahina and lemon juice gradually, stirring well. Add a little cold water, enough to have a light creamy paste. Then mix in the chopped parsley.

You may use a blender or food processor, in which case blend the lemon juice and tahina with a little water first, to a light cream, then add the walnuts and garlic. Be careful not to overblend the walnuts, which might then lose their slightly rough texture.

Hummus Habb

Chickpea Puree

Serves 4–6 • Chickpeas are so common in the Arab world that they could be a symbol of it. The pureed version combined with tahina has become ubiquitous in the West, but this one, without tahina, called "hummus habb" or "sada," is nice too, if you dress it with plenty of lemon juice and olive oil.

1¼ cups chickpeas, soaked overnight
Salt and pepper to taste
2 teaspoons ground cumin
2 large cloves garlic, crushed, or to taste
4–5 tablespoons or more lemon juice
4 tablespoons extra-virgin olive oil
A good pinch of chili pepper (optional)
To garnish: a few sprigs of flat-leaf
    parsley and a dribble of extra-virgin
    olive oil

Drain the chickpeas and simmer in fresh cold water for 1½ hours, or until really soft, adding salt to taste towards the end.

Cool a little, extract a few chickpeas to use as garnish, and put the rest through the food processor or blender with the rest of the ingredients and enough of the cooking water to achieve a light cream. You must add the flavorings gradually and taste often. It should be distinctly sharp. Use the reserved chickpeas to garnish.

Serve in flat plates garnished with sprigs of parsley and a dribble of olive oil.

Accompany with warmed Arab or pita bread to dip in.

Hummus bi Tahina

Chickpea Puree with Tahina

Serves 4–6 • This salad puree is the most widely known and appreciated of all outside the Middle East (abroad it is known simply as hummus). It is the constant companion of shish kebab and *ta'amia* in Oriental restaurants and is also good with fish or eggplants.

1¼ cups chickpeas, soaked in cold water
    overnight
Juice of 2–2½ lemons, or to taste
2 or 3 cloves garlic, crushed
Salt
4–5 tablespoons tahina (sesame paste)

Drain and boil the soaked chickpeas in fresh water for about 1½ hours, or until they are very soft. Drain, reserving the cooking water. Blend to a puree in the food processor. Add the remaining ingredients and a little of the cooking water—enough to have a soft creamy paste. Taste and adjust the seasoning. Add more lemon juice, garlic, or salt if necessary.

Pour the cream into a flat dish and serve with Arab bread or pita.

Optional Garnishes

• Dribble 2 tablespoons extra-virgin olive oil mixed with 1 teaspoon paprika, and sprinkle on 2 tablespoons finely chopped flat-leaf parsley.
• Garnish with a good pinch of chili pepper and ½ teaspoon ground cumin, making a star design of alternating red and brown.
• Sprinkle with a few whole cooked chickpeas, put aside before blending.
• Sprinkle with ground sumac and a little chopped parsley.
• Soak and boil an extra ¼ cup of chickpeas and keep them aside to reheat just before serv-

ing. Spread the hummus in a clay dish, pour the hot drained chickpeas on top, and sprinkle with olive oil, paprika, and chopped parsley.

Variation

This is a delicious hot version. Pour the *hummus bi tahina* in a shallow baking dish. Fry 3 tablespoons pine nuts lightly in 2 tablespoons butter and pour with the melted butter over the dish. Bake for 15–20 minutes in a 400°F oven to heat through.

Ful Nabed or Bissara

Dried Fava Bean Puree

Serves 6 • For this flavorful Egyptian dip, buy the split fava beans which are sold with their brown skins removed and look creamy white.

2 onions, chopped

4 tablespoons plus 3 tablespoons extra-
  virgin olive oil

1¼ cup (skinless) white fava beans,
  soaked overnight

4 to 6 cloves garlic

Salt

Juice of 1½ lemons

1 teaspoon superfine sugar

1 teaspoon ground cumin

1 teaspoon paprika or a pinch of ground
  chili pepper (optional)

4 tablespoons finely chopped fresh dill
  or flat-leaf parsley

Fry the onions in 4 tablespoons olive oil until golden brown.

Simmer the drained beans in fresh water to cover together with the garlic for 1½ hours, or

until they are very soft, adding salt towards the end. Drain, keeping the cooking water, then turn to a puree in a food processor, adding the juice of 1 lemon and sugar and enough of the cooking water to have a soft cream.

Fold in the fried onions and serve, spread on a large plate. Sprinkle with 3 tablespoons olive oil, cumin, paprika or chili pepper, and dill or parsley. Accompany with Arab or pita bread and pass round the spices and the bottle of olive oil for people to help themselves to more.

Variations

• For a Turkish version called *fava,* add 2 large onions, cut in pieces, to the pan with the beans. When cooked, drain and puree the beans with the onions. Mix with ½ cup extra-virgin olive oil, salt, 2 teaspoons sugar, and the juice of 1 lemon. Then pour into a moistened mold and chill for 8 hours. It will become very firm. Turn out and serve sprinkled with olive oil, chopped dill, and 1 red onion cut into thin slices.

• A Tunisian version has 1½ teaspoons tomato paste and 1½ teaspoons harissa (page 464).

Fassoulia Beida

Puree of Dried White Beans

Serves 6

1¼ cups dried navy or haricot beans,
  soaked overnight
4 tablespoons extra-virgin olive oil
Juice of 1 lemon, or more
Salt and pepper
8 black olives (optional)

Drain and boil the beans in fresh water for about 1½ hours, or until very soft. Drain, keeping some of the cooking water. Save a few whole beans for garnish, and put the rest in a food processor with the olive oil and lemon juice, salt and pepper. Blend to a soft, light paste, adding a little of the cooking water to thin it if necessary.

Serve in a bowl, decorated with the whole beans and, if you like, a few black olives.

Purslane or Lamb's Lettuce and Yogurt Salad

Serves 4

1 pound purslane or lamb's-lettuce
  leaves (4 cups well packed)
1 cup plain whole-milk yogurt
1 clove garlic, crushed
2 tablespoons extra-virgin olive oil
Salt and white pepper

If using purslane, pull the leaves off the stem but do include the stem if very tender. Wash the purslane or lamb's lettuce, then wash and dry it.

Beat the yogurt with the garlic, oil, and a little salt and pepper, and mix with the leaves.

Cacik

Yogurt and Cucumber Salad

Serves 6 • This popular Turkish salad can be served as a cold summer soup. We sometimes used to drain the yogurt through a fine cloth to thicken it (see page 111), but now you can buy a thick strained Greek variety.

4–6 small cucumbers or 1 large one,
  diced or cut into half-moon slices
Salt
2½ cups plain whole-milk or thick
  strained Greek yogurt
2 cloves garlic, crushed (optional)
2 sprigs of mint, finely chopped, or 2
  tablespoons crushed dried mint, or 2
  sprigs of dill, finely chopped
White pepper

Peel and dice the cucumbers, or cut them in half lengthwise, then into half-moon slices. Unless the salad is to be served immediately, sprinkle with plenty of salt and leave for 1 hour in a colander for the juices to drain.

Beat the yogurt in the serving bowl with the garlic, mint, and pepper. Rinse the cucumber of excess salt, drain, then mix into the yogurt. Add a little salt, if necessary

Variations

• Beat 3 tablespoons extra-virgin olive oil, 1 of vinegar, and 3 tablespoons chopped dill into the yogurt.
• For a cold soup, use natural, not strained, yogurt and chop or grate the cucumber.
• A lovely alternative is to use a mixture of sour cream and yogurt in equal quantities.
• A fragrant Persian version (*mâst-o khiar*) mixes in 3–4 tablespoons raisins and ½ cup chopped walnuts. It can be garnished with a few chopped or grated radishes and dried rose petals.

Borani-e Esfenaj

Spinach and Yogurt Salad

Serves 4 • This refreshing Iranian salad has a pure and delicate flavor.

- 1 pound spinach
- 1 cup thick strained Greek-style yogurt or plain whole-milk yogurt
- 2 cloves garlic, crushed
- 3/4 teaspoon sugar
- Salt and pepper
- 2 tablespoons extra-virgin olive oil
- Juice of 1/2 lemon

Wash the spinach and remove stems only if they are thick and hard. Drain the leaves and put them in a large pan. Cover and set over low heat until the leaves crumple into a soft mass. They steam in the water that clings to them in very few minutes.

Drain, and when cool enough, squeeze out the excess water with your hands. Chop with a sharp knife and mix with the rest of the ingredients.

Variation

Another version calls for 1 large chopped onion sautéed in 1 tablespoon butter or vegetable oil.

Feta Cheese Dip

Serves 6 • You need good feta cheese for this. Serve with pita bread to dip in.

- 1/2 pound feta cheese
- Juice of 1 lemon
- 2 tablespoons vegetable oil
- 1 tablespoon olive oil

With a fork, crush the feta cheese and mash with the lemon juice and the vegetable and olive oils until smooth.

Michoteta

Feta Cheese and Cucumber Salad

Serves 6 • This strong-tasting Egyptian salad made with feta cheese is good with *ful medames* (page 328).

- 1/2 pound feta cheese
- Juice of 1 lemon
- 2 tablespoons olive oil
- 1 red Italian or large mild onion, finely chopped
- 1/2 large cucumber, peeled and diced
- White pepper

Crumble the cheese with a tablespoon of water, using a fork, and work in the lemon juice and olive oil. Mix in the onion and cucumber, and add pepper.

Shanklish

Goat Cheese Salad

Serves 4 • The salad is made in the Lebanese mountain villages with a fermented goat cheese, but you can use a strong, crumbly goat cheese.

- ½ pound goat cheese
- 1 clove garlic, crushed or mashed (optional)
- 1 mild red or white onion, finely chopped
- 2 or 3 firm ripe tomatoes, diced
- 4–5 tablespoons extra-virgin olive oil

Crush the cheese with a fork, adding garlic if using. Stir in the onion and tomatoes, and sprinkle generously with olive oil.

Salata Arabieh

Arab Salad

Serves 6 • In this most common of Arab salads, all the ingredients are cut very small. Do not prepare it too long before serving, and dress it just before serving.

- 1 small or ½ large head romaine lettuce
- 1½ red Italian or mild white onions or 9 scallions
- 2 small or 1 long cucumber
- 3 tomatoes
- 6 radishes, thinly sliced (optional)
- 3 tablespoons chopped flat-leaf parsley
- 1 tablespoon chopped fresh dill or chervil (optional)
- 2 tablespoons chopped fresh mint (optional)
- 5 tablespoons extra-virgin olive oil
- Juice of ½ lemon, or more to taste
- Salt and pepper
- 1 clove garlic, crushed (optional)

Shred the lettuce, chop the onions finely, and cut the vegetables into tiny dice, using a sharp knife. Put them in a bowl with the radishes and herbs.

Make a dressing with the oil and lemon juice, salt and pepper, and garlic if you like. Pour over the salad and mix well.

Na'na Mukhalal

A medieval recipe from al-Baghdadi for herbed vinegar:

Take fresh large-leafed mint, and strip the leaf from the stalk, wash and dry in the shade: sprinkle with aromatic herbs. If desired, add celery leaves and quarters of peeled garlic. Put into a glass bottle and cover with good vinegar, colored with a little saffron. Leave until the mint has absorbed the sourness of the vinegar so that the latter has lost its sharpness: then serve.

Leaf Salads

Rocket or arugula (*gargir*), purslane (*bakle*), and cress (*rashad*) are popular Arab salad leaves. Choose one and dress with a dribble of extra-virgin olive oil, a little salt, and a drop, if any, of vinegar or lemon juice.

About Salad Dressings

It is related that Adam was suffering with pain and complained to God; Gabriel descended from heaven with an olive tree and presented it to Adam, and told him to plant it, to pick the fruit, to extract the oil and use it whenever he had pain, assuring him that it would be a cure for all ills. . . .

DONALDSON, *THE WILD RUE*

According to folklore, it was once believed that olive oil could cure every illness except the one by which a person was destined by fate to die. People still believe in its beneficial qualities and sometimes drink it neat when they feel anemic or tired. It is used lavishly in salads and cold dishes. Prepared commercially or by peasants, it ranges from a pure, pale-golden color to green and brownish shades. Salad dressings are a mixture of olive oil and lemon juice or, less commonly, wine vinegar with salt and pepper. Boiled vegetables are always dressed with olive oil and lemon juice. Proportions are 3–4 tablespoons of olive oil to 1 of vinegar or a good deal more lemon juice—sometimes the same amount of lemon as oil.

Common embellishments are crushed garlic, scallions, chopped mild red or white onion, and chopped fresh herbs such as parsley, mint, dill, and cilantro. To give a salad a flavor of North Africa, add ¼ teaspoon harissa (page 464), or a pinch of ground chili pepper and a teaspoon of paprika, or a pinch of cumin and coriander or cinnamon. Alternatively, you can perfume the dressing with drops of orange-blossom or rose water or geranium extract, and you may use bitter-orange instead of lemon juice. Instead of adding raw crushed garlic, try boiling, broiling, or roasting the cloves in their skins until they are soft, then peel and mash them into the dressing.

Fattoush

Bread Salad

Serves 6–8 • Fattoush is a rustic country salad of Syria and Lebanon which is on the standard menu of Lebanese restaurants. The old, traditional way was to moisten and soften the toasted bread with water and a little lemon juice before imbibing it further with the dressing, which made it deliciously soggy. Nowadays it is usual to put the bread in crisp, like French croutons.

1½ Arab or pita breads

1 head romaine lettuce, cut into ribbons

3 medium-sized firm ripe tomatoes, cut into ½-inch pieces

3 small cucumbers, peeled, cut into thick slices

1 green bell pepper, seeded and cut into small slices

1½ mild red or white onions or 9 scallions, chopped

Bunch of rocket leaves, torn

Bunch of purslane leaves or lamb's lettuce, torn

Small bunch of flat-leaf parsley, chopped

A few sprigs of mint, shredded

5 tablespoons extra-virgin olive oil

Juice of 1 lemon

2 cloves garlic, crushed

Salt and pepper

1 tablespoon ground sumac

Cut open the breads and toast them under the broiler until they are crisp, turning them over once. Break them into small pieces in your hands.

Put all the vegetables in a large bowl with the onions, rocket and purslane leaves or lamb's lettuce, flat-leaf parsley, and mint.

For the dressing, mix the olive oil with the lemon juice, garlic, salt, pepper, and sumac.

Just before serving, add the toasted bread and toss well with the dressing.

Variation

For the old-style version, put the broken pieces of toast in a bowl. Moisten and soften with a little cold water or lemon juice before adding them to the salad.

Khiar bel Na'na

Cucumber Salad with Mint

Serves 4 • The fragrance of mint goes well with cucumber.

1 cucumber, peeled and sliced very thinly

Salt

3 tablespoons extra-virgin olive oil

2 tablespoons lemon juice or 1 tablespoon wine vinegar

1 teaspoon orange-blossom water, or to taste

1 tablespoon crushed dried mint leaves

Sprinkle the cucumber generously with salt and leave to drain in a colander for ½–1 hour. The salt will run away with the water, but if the cucumber is still too salty, rinse and drain before mixing with the rest of the ingredients.

Salata Horiatiki

Greek Country Salad

Serves 6 • This salad brings back for me memories of the garlands of islands floating in the deep blue sea, the plaintive sound of the bouzouki, and the sugar-cake houses.

1 head romaine lettuce, cut into ribbons

2 large firm ripe tomatoes, cut in wedges

1 cucumber, peeled, split in half through its length, and cut into thick slices

1 green bell pepper, cut in thin rings crosswise

1 large mild onion, thinly sliced, the rings separated, or 9 scallions, thinly sliced

8 ounces feta cheese, cut into small squares or broken with your fingers into coarse pieces

1 dozen or more black Kalamata olives

FOR THE DRESSING

A good bunch of flat-leaf parsley, coarsely chopped

6 tablespoons extra-virgin olive oil

Juice of 1 lemon

Salt and pepper

Put all the salad ingredients together in a large bowl. Just before serving, mix the dressing, pour over the salad, and toss.

Variations

Other possible additions to the salad are chopped dill, fennel, wild marjoram, sprigs of fresh mint, capers, and sliced pickled gherkins.

Tamatem bel Bassal

Tomato Salad with Onions

Serves 4 • Tomatoes are *banadoura* in Arabic and *tamatem* in Egypt.

1 pound firm ripe tomatoes, sliced

1 red Italian or large mild onion or 5 scallions, chopped

2 tablespoons chopped parsley or cilantro

3 tablespoons extra-virgin olive oil

1 tablespoon wine vinegar or the juice of ½ lemon

Salt and pepper

½ teaspoon ground cumin (optional)

Put the tomatoes in a bowl with the onions and parsley or cilantro. Dress with a mixture of oil and vinegar or lemon juice with salt and pepper and cumin, if using.

Radish Salad

If possible, use the very large, elongated type of radish, which can be white, violet, red, or black, and which is also called *mouli*. Slice the radishes very thinly or grate them coarsely and dress with a lemon-and-olive-oil dressing. A few drops of orange-blossom water will give it a delicate perfume. Garnish with plenty of finely chopped flat-leaf parsley.

Tabbouleh

Parsley and Bulgur Salad

Serves 6 • This is a homely version of the very green parsley-and-mint salad with buff-colored speckles of bulgur wheat you find in all Lebanese restaurants all over the world. Like many items on the standard Lebanese restaurant menu, it was born in the mountain region of Zahlé, in the Bekáa Valley of Lebanon, where the local anise-flavored grape liquor arak is produced. Renowned for its fresh air and its natural springs and the river Bardaouni, which cascades down the mountain, the region acquired a mythical reputation for gastronomy. In 1920 two cafés opened by the river. They gave away assorted nuts, seeds, olives, bits of cheese, and raw vegetables with the local arak. Gradually the entire valley became filled with open-air cafés, each larger and more luxurious than the next, each vying to attract customers who flocked from all over the Middle East with ever more varied mezze. The reputation of the local mountain-village foods they offered, of which tabbouleh was one of the jewels, spread far and wide and became a national institution. What started as a relatively substantial salad, rich with bulgur, was transformed over the years into an all-green herby affair.

When the first edition of my book came out, I received letters telling me I had too much bulgur in that recipe. One letter from Syria explained that mine was the way people made the salad many years ago, when they needed to fill their stomachs. You see, many of my relatives left Syria for Egypt a hundred years ago, and that was how they continued to make it. The following is a contemporary version.

½ cup fine- or medium-ground bulgur (cracked wheat)

Juice of 1–2 lemons, to taste

4 firm ripe tomatoes, diced

Salt and pepper

4 scallions, thinly sliced or chopped

2 cups flat-leaf parsley, finely chopped by hand

⅔ cup finely chopped mint

½ cup extra-virgin olive oil

2 Bibb lettuces or the heart of a romaine lettuce to garnish

Soak the bulgur in plenty of fresh cold water for 10 minutes. Rinse in a colander and press the excess water out. Put the bulgur in a bowl with the lemon juice and the tomatoes. Leave for 30 minutes, to absorb the lemon and tomato juices and until the grain is tender. Mix gently with the rest of the ingredients.

A traditional way of eating tabbouleh is to scoop it up with lettuce leaves.

Variation

An Egyptian version adds 1 or 2 small diced cucumbers.

Bulgur or Cracked Wheat

Bulgur or cracked wheat—wheat that has been boiled and dried, then ground—is the basis of many a salad in the Middle East. Tabbouleh has become famous, but there are others more substantial that are especially wonderful.

Kisir

Bulgur and Tomato Salad

Serves 8 • *Kisir* is a filling and luscious Turkish country salad. Chili flakes or a chili pepper give it a thrilling zing.

1½ cups bulgur (cracked wheat)

2 tablespoons tomato paste

5 tablespoons extra-virgin olive oil

Juice of 1 lemon

Salt

⅓ teaspoon chili flakes or pinch of ground chili pepper, to taste

1 fresh red or green chili pepper, very finely chopped

1 cup chopped flat-leaf parsley

⅓ cup chopped mint leaves

6 scallions, finely chopped

2 large tomatoes, finely diced

Put the bulgur in a bowl, pour plenty of boiling water on it, and leave for 20–60 minutes, until the grain is tender. Drain and squeeze the excess water out in a colander.

Add the tomato paste, oil and lemon juice, salt and chili flakes or chili pepper and mix thoroughly. You can do this in advance.

Just before serving, mix in the rest of the ingredients.

Variation

Adding 2 tablespoons of sour-pomegranate concentrate or molasses gives the grain a brown tinge and sweet-and-sour tartness.

Batrik

Bulgur Salad with Nuts

Serves 4–6 • In this nutty Turkish salad with an intense flavor, the bulgur is softened in the juice of fresh tomatoes.

¾ cup fine-ground bulgur (cracked wheat)

1 pound tomatoes, peeled, blended to a cream in the food processor

1 teaspoon tomato paste

3–4 tablespoons olive oil

Salt

A pinch or more of chili flakes or ground chili pepper

1 smallish mild onion or 5 scallions, finely chopped

½ cup walnuts or pistachios, or a mixture of the two

Mix the bulgur with the blended tomatoes and tomato paste, and leave for an hour, or until the grain has become tender. Add a little water if it hasn't.

Add the oil, salt, and chili flakes or ground chili pepper to taste.

Before serving, add the onion and walnuts or pistachios.

Salsouf

Bulgur and Chickpea Salad

Serves 6 • A rustic Lebanese salad.

1 cup bulgur (cracked wheat)

A 1-pound can good-quality chickpeas, drained

1 tablespoon dried mint

Salt

6 tablespoons extra-virgin olive oil

Soak the bulgur in plenty of cold water for ½–1 hour, then drain and squeeze the excess water out. Mix with the rest of the ingredients.

Grated Carrot Salad

Serves 4 • A Moroccan salad with an intriguing combination of flavors.

1 pound carrots, peeled and coarsely grated

½ cup black or golden raisins

5 tablespoons olive oil

1–2 tablespoons honey

Juice of 1 lemon

½ teaspoon ginger

1 teaspoon cinnamon

Salt and pepper

Mix all the ingredients together in a bowl.

Couscous Salad

Serves 6–8 • This salad, which was born in France as the North African "tabboulé," is not governed by strict rules, as is the classic Lebanese one of the same name made with bulgur. It is filling and easy to do for a large company. You can make it in advance. It does not spoil.

1¼ cups medium couscous

1¼ cups cold water

Juice of 1–1½ lemons, or to taste

6 tablespoons extra-virgin olive oil

Salt and pepper

Grated zest of 1 lemon (optional)

4 firm medium tomatoes, diced

1 cucumber, peeled and diced

8 scallions, chopped

1 large bunch of parsley, chopped

1 large bunch of cilantro, chopped

Few sprigs of mint leaves, chopped

12 black or green olives, chopped (optional)

Put the couscous in a bowl, add the water, stir well, and leave for about 20 minutes, until the water is absorbed. Fluff it up and break up any lumps with a fork.

Make a dressing of lemon and oil, salt and pepper, adding lemon zest if you like. Stir into the couscous, and mix in the rest of the ingredients. Leave for ½ hour, until the grain has absorbed the dressing, before serving.

Orange and Olive Salad

Serves 6 • The delicate nutty argan oil is particularly good in this spicy Moroccan salad. It is
made from the nut in the fruit of the argan
tree, which grows exclusively in southwestern
Morocco.

4–6 oranges

Juice of ½–1 lemon

3 tablespoons argan oil or hazelnut,
    walnut, or sesame oil

3 cloves garlic, crushed in a press or
    finely chopped

Salt

A handful of black olives

1 teaspoon ground cumin

1 teaspoon paprika

A pinch of ground chili pepper
    (optional)

Peel the oranges, removing the pith. Cut them
into slices and then into pieces. Dress with a
mixture of lemon juice, oil, garlic, and salt and
add the olives. Serve sprinkled with cumin, paprika, and chili pepper.

Lettuce and Orange Salad

Serves 4 • Another Moroccan orange salad.
Argan is the preferred oil for it in Morocco, but
you could also try hazelnut, walnut, or sesame
oil.

1 curly endive or 2 Bibb lettuces cut into
    ribbons

Juice of ½ orange

Juice of ½ lemon

½ tablespoon orange-blossom water

2 tablespoons argan, hazelnut, walnut, or
    sesame oil

Salt

2 oranges (sweet or sour), peeled and
    sliced

Dress the lettuce with a mixture of orange and
lemon juice, ½ tablespoon orange-blossom
water, 2 tablespoons oil, and a little salt. Scatter
in a wide serving dish.

Lay the oranges on top.

Other Orange Salads

Orange Salad with Orange-Blossom Water and Cinnamon

Peel 3 large oranges, taking care to remove all the bitter white pith. Slice very thinly and arrange on a plate. Sprinkle with orange-blossom water and dust lightly with ground cinnamon.

Orange and Radish Salad

In this salad, a bunch of radishes is thinly sliced, and 1 or 2 oranges are peeled, sliced, and divided into small pieces. The whole is seasoned lightly with salt and a little lemon juice.

Carrot and Orange Salad

Grate 1½ pounds of carrots, peel and cut an orange into small pieces, and dress in a mixture of the juice of 2 oranges and 1 lemon and 2 tablespoons orange-blossom or rose water. Stir in a bunch of chopped cilantro leaves. This is very refreshing to serve with a hot, spicy dish.

Turnip and Orange Salad

This salad is Tunisian.

Wash 1 pound very young, tender turnips and slice them very thinly. Macerate for an hour in a mixture of 3 tablespoons extra-virgin olive oil and the juice of 1 bitter Seville orange or 1 grapefruit, or with a mixture of orange and lemon juice (the dressing needs to be sharp), with a crushed clove of garlic, salt, and pepper. A pinch of ground chili pepper is optional.

Serve as it is with a few sprigs of parsley, or add a chopped-up orange.

Betingan bel Khal wal Tom

Eggplant Slices with Vinegar and Garlic

This is a wonderful Egyptian way of preparing eggplants. Fry, grill, or broil the slices as described on page 290. If frying, drain on paper towels. Arrange on a platter and dribble on the following dressing:

Chop 3 or 4 garlic cloves and fry them over low heat in 1 tablespoon olive oil for moments only, until they just begin to color, then mix with ½ cup white- or red-wine vinegar. Serve garnished with chopped flat-leaf parsley.

Betingan bel Rumman

Eggplant Slices with Pomegranate Syrup

This is a Syrian way. Fry, broil, or grill the slices as described on page 290. If frying, drain on paper towels. Arrange on a platter and dribble on the following sauce:

Mix 2 tablespoons pomegranate syrup (molasses or concentrate) with 1 crushed garlic clove and 4–5 tablespoons water if dressing fried slices, or with 4–5 tablespoons extra-virgin olive oil if dressing grilled or broiled slices.

Yogurtlu Patlican

Eggplant Slices with Yogurt

Serves 4–6 • This common Turkish way of serving eggplants is simple and quite delicious.

3 medium eggplants or 2 large ones,
  weighing about 2 pounds total
Salt
2 cups plain whole-milk or thick
  strained Greek-style yogurt

Fry, broil, or grill the slices as described on page 290. If frying, drain on paper towels. Arrange on a platter and serve, hot or cold, with yogurt spread thickly over each slice.

Variation

Beat into the yogurt 1 crushed garlic clove and 2 teaspoons crushed dried mint.

Domatesli Patlican Tava

Eggplant Slices with Tomato Sauce

Serves 6 • Another lovely Turkish way of preparing eggplants.

3 medium eggplants, weighing about
  2½ pounds total
Olive oil
4 cloves garlic, crushed
1½ pounds tomatoes, peeled and
  chopped
2 tablespoons red- or white-wine
  vinegar
1 tablespoon sugar
Salt
Good pinch of chili pepper
⅓ cup chopped flat-leaf parsley

Fry, grill, or broil the slices as described on page 290. If frying, drain on paper towels and arrange side by side on a platter.

For the sauce, fry the garlic in 2 tablespoons oil for a few seconds, stirring. Add the tomatoes, vinegar, sugar, salt, and chili pepper, and cook, uncovered, over low heat for about 20 minutes, or until reduced to a thick sauce. Add the parsley and let it cool.

Serve the eggplants cold, covered with the tomato sauce.

Variations

• For a Syrian flavor, add to the sauce 2–3 tablespoons pomegranate molasses or concentrate and 5 garlic cloves left whole (omit the crushed garlic).

Betingan bel Dibs Rumman

*Marinated Baby Eggplants with
Pomegranate Syrup*

Serves 4–6 • Pomegranate syrup gives this attractive Syrian specialty a sweet-and-sour flavor. Look for eggplants which are about 4 inches long.

  1 pound baby eggplants, 3–4 inches long
  Salt
  5 whole cloves garlic
  4 tablespoons extra-virgin olive oil
  2 tablespoons pomegranate syrup (also
    called concentrate or molasses)
  Juice of ½ lemon
  ¼ teaspoon ground chili pepper
  ½ teaspoon ground cumin
  3 tablespoons chopped flat-leaf parsley

Wash the little eggplants, remove caps, but leave the stems on. Cut in half lengthwise, but not right to the end, so that the halves remain attached at the stem end.

Boil in salted water with the garlic cloves for 10–15 minutes, until soft, then drain.

For the marinade, mash the boiled garlic cloves, and mix with the rest of the ingredients. Roll the drained eggplants in the marinade, opening them so that the cut sides can absorb it well.

Leave for at least 12 hours and serve cold.

Eggplants in a Spicy Honey Sauce

Serves 4 • The sauce is a splendid example of the hot, spicy, and sweet combinations which are a thrilling feature of North African cooking. Serve it cold with bread.

  2 medium-large eggplants
  Olive oil
  Salt
  3 cloves garlic, crushed
  2 inches fresh gingerroot, grated, or cut
    into pieces and the juice squeezed out
    in a garlic press
  1½ teaspoons ground cumin
  Large pinch of cayenne or ground chili
    pepper, to taste
  4–6 tablespoons honey
  Juice of 1 lemon
  ⅔ cup water

Cut the eggplants into rounds about ⅓ inch thick. Do not peel them. Dip them in olive oil, turning them over, and cook on a griddle or under the broiler, turning them over once, until they are lightly browned. They do not need to be soft, as they will cook further in the sauce.

In a wide saucepan or skillet, fry the garlic in 2 tablespoons of the oil for seconds only, stirring, then take off the heat. Add the ginger, cumin, and cayenne or ground chili pepper, honey, lemon juice, and water. Put in the eggplant slices and cook over low heat—either in batches, so that they are in one layer, or together, rearranging them so that each slice gets some time in the sauce—for about 10 minutes, or until the slices are soft and have absorbed the sauce. Add a little water if necessary.

Sweet-and-Sour Eggplant Salad

Serves 6 • Broken pieces of toasted pita bread are sometimes placed at the bottom of the serving dish to become well moistened and soggy with the dressing.

1½ pounds eggplants, cut into 1-inch cubes

Salt

½ cup extra-virgin olive oil

1 large Spanish onion, coarsely chopped

2 cloves garlic, chopped

1 pound tomatoes, peeled and chopped, or a 14-ounce can peeled tomatoes

4 tablespoons finely chopped parsley

1 tablespoon dried mint

3 tablespoons wine vinegar

1 tablespoon sugar

Pepper or a good pinch ground chili pepper to taste

Sprinkle the eggplant cubes with salt and leave in a colander for about ½ hour for the juices to drain away. Then rinse and dry.

Cover the bottom of a heavy pan with olive oil. Fry the onion in this until it is soft and golden. Add the eggplants, and stir, turning them over, for about 5 minutes. Add the garlic and stir, until it begins to color. Add the tomatoes, with their juice, the parsley, mint, vinegar, sugar, and pepper or ground chili pepper. Cook over very low heat for about 20 minutes, or until the eggplants are soft. Serve cold.

Variations

• For a Syrian flavor, instead of the vinegar add 2–3 tablespoons pomegranate molasses or concentrate and 5 or 6 cloves garlic left whole.
• Add 1 pound canned chickpeas (drained).

Zaalouk

Spicy Eggplant Salad

Serves 6 • I love this Moroccan salad. The eggplants are boiled, not fried, so it is not oily. It is best made several hours in advance so that the flavors have time to penetrate.

1½ pounds eggplants, peeled and cubed

5 cloves garlic, peeled

Salt

3 large beefsteak tomatoes (about 1½ pounds)

4 tablespoons argan oil (see page 48) or hazelnut, sesame, walnut, or mild extra-virgin olive oil

2 tablespoons wine vinegar

½ teaspoon harissa (see page 464), or a mixture of ½ teaspoon paprika and good pinch of ground chili pepper, to taste

1 teaspoon ground cumin

½ cup chopped flat-leaf parsley

Boil the eggplants with the garlic in plenty of salted water, in a pan covered with a lid, for about 30 minutes, or until they are very soft. Drain and chop the eggplants and garlic in a colander, then mash them with a fork, pressing all the water out.

Put the tomatoes in the emptied pan and cook over low heat for about 20 minutes, or until reduced to a thick sauce, stirring occasionally. Mix with the mashed eggplants and the rest of the ingredients and add salt.

Variation

Add the juice of 1 lemon (instead of the vinegar) and 1 teaspoon ground caraway or coriander.

Salatet Felfel wal Tamatem

Roast Pepper and Tomato Salad

Serves 6 • Every country in the Middle East has a roast-pepper-and-tomato combination. This is an Egyptian one.

  4 red or green fleshy bell peppers
  6 large cloves garlic, whole, in their peels
  3 large tomatoes, peeled and sliced

½ cup chopped flat-leaf parsley or
  cilantro
4 tablespoons extra-virgin olive oil
1 tablespoon wine vinegar or juice of
  ½ lemon
Salt and pepper

Roast the peppers, then peel them and remove the seeds (see box at left). At the same time, broil the garlic cloves, unpeeled, until they just begin to feel soft, turning them over once.

Cut the peppers into strips. Peel the garlic. Put peppers and garlic in a serving bowl with the tomatoes and parsley or cilantro.

Dress with a mixture of oil and vinegar or lemon, salt and pepper.

To Roast and Peel Bell Peppers

Many dishes call for roasted bell peppers (red ones are riper and have a better taste). Choose fleshy peppers. Put them on an oven tray under the broiler, about 3½ inches from the heat (or grill them on the barbecue). Turn them until their skins are black and blistered all over.

Alternatively, it is easier to roast them in the hottest oven for about ½ hour, or until they are soft and their skins begin to blister and blacken—they need to be turned once on their sides. To loosen the skins further, put the peppers in a strong plastic bag, twist it closed, and leave for 10 to 15 minutes. Another way, which has the same effect, is to put them in a pan with a tight-fitting lid.

When the peppers are cool enough to handle, peel them and remove the stems and seeds. Keep the juice that comes out, straining it to remove the seeds, as it can be used as part of a dressing.

Roast peppers can be kept for a long time in a jar, covered in oil.

Roasted Red Peppers with Preserved Lemon and Capers

Serves 4 • A North African salad.

  4 fleshy red bell peppers
  2–3 tablespoons argan (see page 48) or
    extra-virgin olive oil
  Salt
  Peel of 1 preserved lemon (see page
    459), cut into small pieces, to garnish
  2 tablespoons capers to garnish

Roast, seed, and peel the peppers as described in box at left and cut them into strips about ⅔ inch wide. Dress with argan or olive oil and very little salt, and garnish with the preserved lemon and capers.

Eggplant Slices with Tomato Sauce, and with Yogurt (page 81)

Roasted Red Peppers with Preserved Lemon and Capers (page 84)

Fava Beans with Rice and Yogurt (page 100)

Little Cheese Rolls (page 117) and Fillo Triangles with
Ground Meat, Onions, and Pine Nuts (page 118)

Pumpkin Fillo Pies (page 122)

Egg-and-Lemon Fish Soup (page 157)

Shakshouka: Eggs with Bell Peppers and Tomatoes (page 168)

Haricot Bean and Spinach Omelet (page 173)

Meshweya

Tunisian Roasted Salad

Serves 4–6 • They call it *meshweya,* which means "roasted," because the vegetables are roasted—usually over a fire. There are many versions. This one can be a meal in itself.

3 medium onions

3 green or red bell peppers

3 medium tomatoes, peeled and
  quartered

A 7-ounce can tuna in brine, drained

2 hard-boiled eggs, cut in wedges

4–5 tablespoons extra-virgin olive oil

Juice of 1 lemon

Salt and pepper

½ teaspoon caraway seeds

1 tablespoon capers (optional garnish)

8 green or black olives (optional
  garnish)

Put the onions and peppers in the hottest pre-heated oven and roast for about ½ hour, or until the skins are very browned and they feel soft, turning them over to brown their sides. Peel the onions and cut them in wedges. Peel the peppers (see page 84) and cut them into ribbons.

On a serving dish or individual plates arrange the elements of the salad—the onions, peppers, tomatoes, flaked tuna, and eggs—in a decorative way. Mix the oil and lemon juice, salt, pepper, and caraway seeds and dribble on top. Garnish with capers and olives if you like.

Ajlouke Qura'a

Mashed Zucchini Salad

Serves 4–6 • In this Tunisian salad the blandness of zucchini is lifted by the very rich flavoring.

1 pound zucchini

Juice of ½ lemon, or more

3 tablespoons extra-virgin olive oil

½–1 teaspoon harissa (see page 464)

Salt

1 or 2 cloves garlic, crushed

½ teaspoon ground coriander

½ teaspoon caraway seeds

Trim the ends of the zucchini and cut into large pieces. Boil in water for 10 to 15 minutes, until very soft.

Drain, then chop and mash in the colander to get rid of excess water. Beat the rest of the ingredients together and mix into the zucchini.

Serve cold.

Variation

Garnish with 4 ounces feta cheese, crumbled with a fork, and a few green and black olives.

Kousa bi Laban Zabadi

Fried Zucchini Slices with Yogurt

Serves 4 • For this Arab and Turkish way of serving zucchini, the vegetables may be deep-fried, grilled, or broiled.

　1 pound zucchini, cut into slices
　　lengthwise
　Olive or vegetable oil
　Salt
　1½ cups plain whole-milk or thick
　　strained Greek-style yogurt

Deep-fry the zucchini in hot oil till lightly browned, turning the slices over once, then drain on paper towels and sprinkle lightly with salt. Alternatively, brush the slices with oil and grill or broil them (see variation for broiling procedure).

　Serve hot or cold with yogurt spread over each slice.

Variations

• The yogurt may be flavored with 1 crushed garlic clove and 2 teaspoons dried crushed mint.

• To broil the zucchini, arrange the slices on a tray, brush both sides very lightly with olive oil, and sprinkle with salt. Put under the broiler, and cook, turning them over once, until browned.

• Another traditional accompaniment is a fresh tomato sauce. Use the one for eggplants on page 81.

Mashed Zucchini and Tomatoes

Serves 6 • A North African appetizer full of rich sensuous flavors.

　2 large onions, chopped
　4 tablespoons extra-virgin olive oil
　2 cloves garlic, crushed
　1 teaspoon ground cumin
　1 pound zucchini, cut into thick slices
　Salt and pepper
　2 tablespoons red- or white-wine
　　vinegar
　A good pinch of ground chili pepper
　1 pound tomatoes, peeled and chopped

Fry the onions in the oil until golden and stir in the garlic and cumin. Add the zucchini, salt, pepper, vinegar, ground chili pepper, and tomatoes. Put the lid on and cook for about 10 minutes without added water, until the zucchini slices are very soft.

　Mash with a fork or a potato masher and serve at room temperature.

Zucchini Salad with Raisins and Pine Nuts

Serves 4–6 • The combination of raisins and pine nuts was brought by the Arabs all the way to Spain and Sicily.

1 pound zucchini, thinly sliced

4 tablespoons extra-virgin olive oil

2 tablespoons pine nuts

2 tablespoons black or golden raisins, or currants

1 clove garlic, crushed and chopped

Salt and pepper

2 teaspoons dried mint (optional)

Juice of ½ lemon, or more

Sauté the zucchini quickly in the oil with the pine nuts, raisins, and garlic. Add salt and pepper and dried mint, if using, and cook, stirring, over moderate heat until the zucchini slices are just tender.

Serve hot or cold with lemon juice squeezed over the salad.

Variation

The zucchini may be left uncooked and simply macerated in a mixture of 5 tablespoons extra-virgin olive oil with the juice of ½–1 lemon and salt and pepper for at least an hour. Toast the pine nuts and add them before serving.

Kabak Muçveri

Zucchini Fritters

Serves 4 • Yogurt often accompanies these Turkish fritters.

1 pound zucchini, grated

1 large onion, coarsely chopped

Sunflower oil

3 eggs

3 tablespoons all-purpose flour

Pepper

A few sprigs of mint, chopped

A few sprigs of dill, chopped

7 ounces feta cheese, mashed with a fork

Grate the zucchini. Fry the onion in 3 tablespoons oil over medium heat, till soft and lightly colored. Add the grated zucchini and sauté, stirring, until soft.

In a bowl, beat the eggs with the flour until well blended. Add pepper and the herbs and mix well. Fold in the feta cheese and the cooked onions and zucchini.

Film the bottom of a preferably nonstick frying pan with oil and fry by the half-ladle or 2 tablespoons, turning over once, until both sides are brown. You can do a few at a time.

Drain on paper towels and serve hot or cold.

Kharshouf bi Zeit

Baby Artichoke Hearts Stewed in Oil

Serves 4 • If you want to use fresh baby artichokes, see instructions for preparing the hearts on page 282.

9 artichoke hearts, fresh or frozen
⅓ cup extra-virgin olive oil
Juice of 1 lemon, or to taste
2 cloves garlic, chopped
Salt and pepper

Put the artichoke hearts in a pan with the rest of the ingredients and barely cover with water. Simmer, uncovered, for about 20 minutes if fresh or 10 minutes if frozen, until tender. Lift out the artichokes and reduce the sauce.

Serve cold—whole if small, halved or quartered if large—in their own sauce.

Chopped Artichokes and Preserved Lemons

Serves 4–6 • This simple and delightful North African salad is easy to make with the frozen artichoke bottoms obtainable from Middle Eastern stores.

A 14-ounce packet frozen artichoke
    bottoms, defrosted
Salt
5 tablespoons extra-virgin olive oil
Pepper
1 or 2 cloves garlic, crushed (optional)
A few sprigs of dill, chopped
1 preserved lemon peel (see page 459),
    rinsed and chopped

Simmer the artichoke bottoms in salted water to cover for about 10 minutes, till just tender. Then drain and chop them coarsely with a sharp knife and mix with the rest of the ingredients.

Serve cold.

Omi Houriya

Spicy Carrot Puree

Serves 6 • Make this fiery Tunisian salad with old carrots, which taste better, and add the flavorings gradually, to taste. The color is beautiful. Serve as a dip with bread or bits of raw vegetables.

  1½ pounds carrots
  Salt
  4 tablespoons extra-virgin olive oil
  3 tablespoons wine vinegar
  2 cloves garlic, crushed
  ½–1 teaspoon harissa (see page 464) or 1 teaspoon paprika and good pinch of chili pepper
  1½ teaspoons ground cumin or caraway seeds
  ¼–½ teaspoon ground ginger

Peel the carrots and cut into large pieces. Boil them in salted water until tender, then drain and chop them with a knife or mash them with a fork.

Mix well with the rest of the ingredients and serve cold.

Variations

• Garnish with 6 green or black olives or 4 ounces crumbled feta cheese.
• Instead of cumin or caraway, add 2 tablespoons honey and 1 teaspoon cinnamon.

Ajlouk de Carottes

Mashed Carrot and Potato Salad

Serves 6 • For this Tunisian salad, use old carrots and mealy potatoes.

  4 large carrots
  3 potatoes
  4–5 tablespoons extra-virgin olive oil
  Juice of 1 lemon, or more
  Salt
  ½ teaspoon harissa (page 464) or 1 teaspoon paprika and good pinch of chili pepper
  1 teaspoon caraway seeds

Peel and boil the carrots and potatoes separately until they are soft (the carrots should be very soft). Then drain and mash with a fork or a potato masher. Put them together in a bowl, add the remaining ingredients, and mix very well.

Serve cold.

Slatit Batata Marfusa

Mashed Potato Salad with Capers

Serves 6 • Use mealy potatoes for this Tunisian salad, which is served as an appetizer and also as an accompaniment to grilled fish.

1 1/2 pounds potatoes

Salt

4–5 tablespoons extra-virgin olive oil

1 1/2 tablespoons wine vinegar

Pepper

1/2 teaspoon harissa (page 464) or a good pinch of chili pepper (optional)

1/2 cup chopped flat-leaf parsley

3 tablespoons capers, squeezed to get rid of excess vinegar

Peel and boil the potatoes in lightly salted water until soft, then drain, keeping a little of the cooking water.

Mash with the oil and vinegar and 2–4 tablespoons of the cooking water—enough to have a soft, moist texture. Add the rest of the ingredients and mix well.

Serve cold.

Slatit Batata Helwa

Sweet Potato Salad

Serves 6 • In this Moroccan salad, the curious mix of sweet and spicy is quite delicious. It is nice as it is but you may add, if you like, a handful of black olives, the chopped peel of a preserved lemon (see page 459), and a tablespoon of capers.

1 1/2 pounds sweet potatoes, peeled and cut into 1 1/2-inch cubes

1/2–3/4 teaspoon ground ginger

1 teaspoon cinnamon

1 teaspoon harissa (page 464) or a good pinch of chili pepper

Juice of 1/2–1 lemon

2 teaspoons honey

Salt

5 tablespoons extra-virgin olive oil

4 tablespoons chopped flat-leaf parsley or cilantro

Boil the sweet potatoes in just enough water to cover. Stir in the ginger, cinnamon, harissa or ground chili pepper, lemon juice, honey, and salt, and cook, uncovered, for 15 minutes, or until the potatoes are tender, turning them over once and being careful not to let them overcook and fall apart. The sauce should be reduced to a thick syrupy consistency. If it is not, lift out the potatoes with a slotted spoon into a serving dish and reduce the sauce further by boiling.

Just before the end of cooking, stir in the oil and the parsley or cilantro.

Serve cold.

Bamia

Sweet-and-Sour Okra

Serves 4 • Okra is one of the most popular vegetables in the Arab world.

1 pound small young okra

2 tablespoons extra-virgin olive oil

$1/2$–1 tablespoon sugar

Salt and pepper

Juice of 1 small lemon, or to taste

Cut off the stem ends and wash the okra. Heat the oil in a heavy skillet. Add the okra and sauté gently for about 5 minutes, turning each pod over.

Add sugar, salt and pepper, the lemon juice, and just enough water to cover the okra.

Simmer for about 15 minutes, or until the okra is tender and the liquid is reduced. Raise the heat if neccesary to reduce the liquid at the end.

Serve cold.

Mushrooms in Olive Oil

Serves 2–4 • Mushrooms are not common in the Middle East but you do find them—in Cyprus, for instance.

$1/2$ pound small button mushrooms

3 tablespoons extra-virgin olive oil

1 tablespoon water

Salt and pepper

Juice of $1/2$–1 lemon

$1/2$ teaspoon dried thyme (optional)

1 or 2 cloves garlic, crushed

4 tablespoons finely chopped flat-leaf parsley

Wash the mushrooms. Cut them in half if they are a little large.

Pour the oil and water into a frying pan. Stir in all the remaining ingredients except the mushrooms and bring to the boil. Add the mushrooms and simmer gently for about 7 minutes, or until they are tender, turning them over occasionally. Pour into a serving dish.

Taste and adjust the seasoning before serving, as its intensity changes with the drop in temperature.

Serve cold.

Mushrooms with Onions and Red Wine

Serves 6 • I was given this recipe by a lovely Cypriot. I had never come across it before. It can be made with all kinds of mushrooms. I used shiitake with a Cabernet Sauvignon and found them delicious except that the stalks remained chewy, so cut those off if you use them.

1½ large onions, sliced
4 tablespoons extra-virgin olive oil
11 ounces mushrooms, left whole, or cut in half if very large
Salt and pepper
1 cup red wine

In a saucepan, fry the onions in the oil, covered, slowly over low heat, stirring occasionally, for about 20 minutes, until soft and golden.

Add the mushrooms, salt and pepper, and the wine and cook, covered, over low heat until the mushrooms are soft—between 10 and 30 minutes, depending on the mushrooms. Take off the lid to reduce the sauce if necessary.

Loubia bi Zeit

Green Beans in Olive Oil

Serves 6

1½ pounds green beans or young runner beans
1 large onion, coarsely chopped
4–5 tablespoons olive oil
4 cloves garlic, sliced
4 tomatoes, peeled and chopped
Salt and pepper

Top and tail and wash the beans. Cut the runner beans into 2 or 3 pieces.

In a saucepan, fry the onion in oil until soft. Add garlic, and when the onions and garlic begin to color, add the tomatoes and the beans. Only just cover with water, add salt and pepper, and simmer, uncovered, until the beans are tender and the liquid is reduced.

Serve cold.

Fennel, Celery, and Cauliflower Salad

The vegetables may be served raw, but when boiled they make a very pleasant salad. The fennel gives it a faint anise flavor. Wash equal amounts of the vegetables and cut them into pieces and florets. Boil in salted water until only just soft. Dress with plenty of olive oil, lemon juice, and a little salt and pepper. The fennel has enough perfume of its own, but a little chopped fresh mint is an agreeable addition.

Turkish Tarator Sauce for Boiled Vegetables

Serves 6 • Serve this in a bowl with plain boiled or steamed vegetables such as runner beans, zucchini, or cauliflower.

2 thin slices bread, crusts removed
1 cup walnuts or hazelnuts, coarsely
   ground
⅔ cup extra-virgin olive oil
3–4 tablespoons wine vinegar
1 or 2 cloves garlic, crushed
Salt and pepper

Soak the bread in water and squeeze dry. Crumble it, and add it to the nuts in a bowl. Gradually add the olive oil, beating constantly, then stir in the vinegar and garlic, and season to taste with salt and pepper. The sauce should be very smooth and creamy.

You may use a food processor or blender. In this case add whole walnuts or hazelnuts at the end, when the rest of the ingredients have been turned to a cream, and leave the nuts slightly coarse.

Pancar Salatasi

Beet and Yogurt Salad

Serves 4 • This is a Turkish way of dressing beets.

1 pound young beets
2 tablespoons lemon juice
2 tablespoons extra-virgin olive oil
1 cup plain whole-milk yogurt
Salt
1 tablespoon finely chopped parsley to
   garnish

Cut the tops off the beets and boil them in plenty of water for 30 to 40 minutes, until tender. Peel and slice them.

Mix the lemon juice with the oil. Add yogurt and salt and beat well. Then mix with the beets.

Pour into a serving dish and garnish with chopped parsley.

Variation

An alternative dressing is olive oil and a little salt mixed with about 1 teaspoon orange-blossom water or rose water and a sprinkling of cinnamon.

Salatet Korat

Leek Salad

Serves 4 • Leeks are especially popular in Egypt.

1 pound leeks
3 tablespoons olive oil
Juice of $\frac{1}{2}$ lemon, or more
Salt and pepper
1 teaspoon dried mint
1 or 2 cloves garlic, crushed
$\frac{1}{2}$ teaspoon sugar

With a pointed knife, split the leeks lengthwise to their center and wash them carefully, fanning them out in the water to remove all traces of soil between the leaves. Discard the tough outer leaves and trim the tops and roots. Cut the leeks into 1- or 2-inch lengths and boil them in lightly salted water for 15–20 minutes or until soft, then drain and press the excess water out.

Mix the olive oil, lemon juice, salt and pepper, mint, garlic, and sugar and pour over the leeks in a serving dish. Serve cold.

Variations

• Simmer the leeks very gently with the dressing ingredients and very little water to cover, until very soft, about 20 minutes. Allow to cool in their liquid and serve cold, garnished with chopped parsley.
• Roll the boiled leeks in a sauce made by beating 2–3 tablespoons olive oil with the juice of 1 lemon, 4–5 tablespoons yogurt or sour cream, salt, and pepper. Serve cold with a sprinkling of finely chopped parsley or cilantro.

Cooked Onion Salad

In the old days people used to set onions in their skins to cook very slowly in the ashes of a fire. They acquired a sweet, mellow taste, which an hour in a low oven will also give them. Put a few in a 325°F oven for an hour or longer, until they are very soft. Let them cool, then peel and cut them into slices or pieces and dress with an oil-and-vinegar dressing. Garnish, if you like, with capers or bits of parsley, and serve cold.

Sweet-and-Sour Onions

Serves 6

1 pound little pickling onions or shallots
3–4 tablespoons extra-virgin olive oil
3 tablespoons wine vinegar
1 tablespoon sugar
2 tablespoons golden raisins
Salt and pepper
2 teaspoons dried mint (optional)

Peel the onions (one way is to plunge them for a few seconds in boiling water until the skins come off easily). Put them in a pan with the oil, and sauté, shaking the pan to brown them lightly all over. Add the rest of the ingredients and a little water, and cook, covered, over low heat for about 20 minutes, or until soft, adding more water if necessary.

Bassal bel Tamarhendi

Baby Onions with Tamarind

Serves 6 • You can find tamarind paste in Oriental stores. It gives the onions a delicious, intense sweet-and-sour taste.

- 1 pound shallots or pickling onions or simply small onions
- 3 tablespoons extra-virgin olive oil
- 1 tablespoon tamarind paste
- 1 tablespoon sugar

Poach the onions in boiling water for about 5 minutes (this makes them easier to peel) and peel them when just cool enough to handle.

In a pan just large enough to contain them in one layer, sauté the onions in the oil, shaking the pan and turning them to brown them lightly all over.

Add the tamarind and the sugar and half-cover with water. Stir well and cook, covered, over low heat for about 25 minutes, or until very soft, adding water so that it does not dry out, and lifting the lid to reduce the sauce at the end.

Serve cold.

Celeriac with Turmeric

Serves 6 • The celeriac acquires a special delicate flavor and a pale-yellow tinge.

- 2 celeriac, weighing about 2 pounds
- 3 cloves garlic, crushed
- 5 tablespoons extra-virgin olive oil
- 1/4 teaspoon turmeric
- Salt and pepper
- 2 teaspoons sugar
- Juice of 1 lemon

Peel and wash the celeriac and cut into pieces of roughly the same size (about 1 inch). Put them in a saucepan with the rest of the ingredients and enough water to cover.

Cook, uncovered for 10–15 minutes, over low heat, until the celeriac is soft and the liquid is absorbed, turning the pieces over and raising the heat, if necessary, to reduce the sauce at the end.

Serve cold.

Taratorlu Kereviz

Celeriac and Carrots with Nut Sauce

Serves 6 • In Turkey all kinds of vegetables, including cauliflower and green beans, are dressed with a nut sauce called *tarator*. Here celeriac and carrots make a good combination of flavor and color, and yogurt is a refreshing addition to the sauce.

1 large celeriac
3 large carrots
Salt

FOR THE SAUCE

1 cup hazelnuts, coarsely ground
2 cloves garlic, crushed
4 tablespoons extra-virgin olive oil
3 tablespoons wine vinegar
1 cup plain whole-milk yogurt
Salt
Pinch of ground chili pepper (optional)

Peel the celeriac and carrots and cut into matchsticks. (To peel the celeriac, you need to cut away the earth-covered exterior with a strong knife.) Boil in salted water for a few minutes until just tender and drain. Mix all the sauce ingredients and pour over the vegetables. Serve cold.

Mujadra bel Burghul

Lentils and Bulgur with Caramelized Onions

Serves 4–6 • This Lenten specialty of the Orthodox Christian communities of Syria and Lebanon can be served hot or cold. Accompany with yogurt.

About 4 cups chicken stock (page 143)
   (or you may use 2 bouillon cubes)
½ teaspoon allspice
Good pinch of chili pepper (optional)
1 tablespoon tomato paste
1 cup large brown or green lentils,
   washed
Salt and pepper
1¼ cups coarse-ground bulgur (cracked
   wheat)
8 tablespoons extra-virgin olive oil
2 large onions, halved and thickly sliced

In a large pan, bring the stock to the boil. Add the allspice, ground chili pepper (if using), and tomato paste. Stir well and add the lentils. Simmer, with the lid on, for about 15 minutes, or until the lentils are almost tender.

Add salt (taking into account the saltiness of the stock or bouillon) and pepper, and stir in the bulgur. Cook, with the lid on, over very low heat for about 10 to 15 minutes, adding a little water if it becomes too dry. Then leave for 10 minutes or longer, with the lid on, until the bulgur is plump and tender. Stir in 5 tablespoons of olive oil.

At the same time, in a large frying pan, fry the onions in the remaining oil over medium heat for about 30 minutes, stirring often, until they are very brown, putting the heat up towards the end to caramelize them. Serve the lentils and bulgur topped with the onions.

Megadarra

*Brown Lentils and Rice with
Caramelized Onions*

Serves 4–6 • *Megadarra* is immensely popular in Egypt, as it is all over the Arab world (elsewhere it is pronounced *mujadra* and sometimes called *mudardara*). It is a modern version of a medieval dish called *mujadarra,* described by al-Baghdadi (see appendix) as a dish of the poor, and still referred to as Esau's favorite. In fact, it is such a favorite that, although it is said to be for misers, it is a compliment to serve it. An aunt of mine used to present it regularly to guests with the comment "Excuse the food of the poor!"—to which the unanimous reply always was: "Keep your food of kings and give us *megadarra* every day!"

The proportions of lentils and rice vary with every family. Large quantities of dark, caramelized onions are the best part. It is served either warm or cold, as a mezze or as part of a light meal, usually accompanied by yogurt.

> **3 large onions, weighing about 1½
>   pounds total, cut in half and sliced**
> **½ cup extra-virgin olive oil**
> **1¼ cups large brown or green lentils**
> **1¼ cups long-grain rice**
> **Salt and pepper**

Fry the onions slowly in a large pan over very low heat in 3–4 tablespoons of the oil—covered to begin with, until they soften, stirring often, and then uncovered—until they turn a rich golden brown.

Rinse the lentils in cold water and drain. Cook in 4½ cups water for 20 minutes. Add half of the fried onions and the rice to the lentils. Season with salt and pepper and stir well. Put the lid on and cook over very low heat for another 20 minutes, or until the rice and lentils are tender, watching and adding water if it becomes too dry.

At the same time, put the remaining onions in the pan back on the fire, and continue to fry them, stirring often, over medium to high heat, until they are a dark brown—almost caramelized.

Serve the lentils and rice cold or warm in a wide shallow dish with the onions sprinkled on top and the remaining raw oil poured all over.

Variations

• Add 1 tablespoon tomato paste and ½ teaspoon dried red-pepper flakes or a pinch of ground chili pepper to the water with the lentils.

• Add 1 teaspoon cumin and 1 teaspoon coriander to the cooking water, or 2 teaspoons dried mint.

• In another dish of rice and lentils, called *masafi,* the lentils are turned to a puree. Red lentils, which disintegrate easily, can be used for this.

Fasulye Piyazi

Haricot Bean Salad

Serves 4 • This famous Turkish salad makes a light snack meal.

- 2 14-ounce cans of cannelini or white haricot beans
- 5 tablespoons extra-virgin olive oil
- 2 tablespoons white-wine vinegar
- Salt and pepper
- 1 mild onion, finely chopped
- 3 tablespoons chopped flat-leaf parsley
- 10 black olives
- 2 firm tomatoes, cut into wedges
- 2 hard-boiled eggs, cut into wedges

Drain the canned beans, dress with oil, vinegar, salt, and pepper, and mix with chopped onion and parsley.

Serve garnished with olives, tomatoes, and hard-boiled eggs.

Salq bi Loubia

Spinach with Black-eyed Peas

Serves 4

- 4 ounces dried black-eyed peas or a 14-ounce can, drained
- Salt
- 1 pound fresh spinach or frozen leaf spinach, defrosted
- 1 large onion, chopped
- 4 tablespoons olive oil
- Pepper

Simmer the black-eyed peas in water for about 20 minutes, or until they are tender, adding salt when they have begun to soften. They do not need soaking and fall apart quite quickly if they are overcooked.

Wash the fresh spinach, removing any thick stems, and drain. Frozen spinach must be completely thawed and have the water squeezed out.

In a large saucepan, fry the onion in the olive oil until soft and transparent. Add the spinach, put the lid on, and cook for a few minutes only, until the spinach crumples to a soft mass. If using frozen spinach, cook until tender. Add salt and pepper.

Stir the drained beans into the spinach and cook through.

Serve cold.

Salatet Adds

Lentil Salad

Serves 6

1¼ cups large green or brown lentils

Salt

6–7 tablespoons extra-virgin olive oil

Juice of 1½ lemons, or to taste

1 or 2 cloves garlic, crushed (optional)

Pepper

½–1 teaspoon ground coriander or
  cumin (optional)

3 tablespoons chopped flat-leaf parsley

Rinse and drain the lentils, and boil them in fresh water for about 20 minutes, or until tender, adding salt towards the end. Then drain.

Mix the rest of ingredients plus a little salt and pour over the lentils while still hot.

Serve cold.

Variations

• Fry 3 chopped garlic cloves in 2 tablespoons of the oil with 1 teaspoon ground cumin or coriander and stir into the lentils. Omit these from the dressing.

• Cook the lentils until they are very soft, mash to a puree, and dress as above.

Salatet Adds wal Tamatem

Lentil and Tomato Salad

Serves 6

1¼ cups large green or brown lentils

1 large onion, chopped

4 tablespoons extra-virgin olive oil or
  more

3 tomatoes, peeled and cut into pieces

Salt and pepper

2 tablespoons wine vinegar

3 tablespoons chopped flat-leaf parsley

Rinse and drain the lentils. Fry the onion in oil until lightly colored. Add the tomatoes and cook, stirring, for a minute.

Add the drained lentils, cover with water, and simmer gently for about 25 minutes, or until they are tender, adding water as required. Season with salt and pepper, add vinegar, and cook until the lentils are soft and the liquid is absorbed.

Add the parsley and, if you like, a dribble of olive oil.

Serve cold.

Salatet Hummus

Chickpea Salad

Serves 6 • This is an instant salad to make with canned chickpeas, but they must be good-quality.

A 2-pound can chickpeas

6 tablespoons extra-virgin olive oil

Juice of 1–2 lemons

Salt and pepper

1 mild onion, finely chopped

1/3 cup chopped flat-leaf parsley

Drain the chickpeas and mix with the rest of the ingredients.

Variation

Omit the onion and instead pass around a little saucer with about 8 crushed garlic cloves for people to help themselves if they want to.

ARAB SAYING:
"Rather than eat rice with eggplants, buy something to cover your hind part." (Until very recently, rice was considered an expensive dish and only for the rich. A poor man buying rice and eggplants too was therefore thought to be unnecessarily extravagant.)

Ful Ahdar bel Roz wal Laban Zabadi

Fresh Green Fava Beans with Rice and Yogurt

Serves 6 • You need young fava beans, not tough old ones. Some supermarkets sell them shelled in the season. Good-quality frozen ones are also fine to use. An Iranian grocer near where I live sells frozen skinned ones from Iran which are exceptional. The dish can be served hot or cold. The yogurt can be poured over the rice or served in a separate bowl.

1¼ cups American long-grain rice

Salt

4–5 tablespoons mild extra-virgin olive oil

Bunch of dill or mint, finely chopped

White pepper

14 ounces shelled fava beans, fresh or frozen

2 cups plain whole-milk yogurt

1 clove garlic, crushed (optional)

Pour the rice into boiling salted water. Boil hard for about 14 minutes, until it is almost but not entirely tender. Drain and put back into the pan. Stir in 3 tablespoons of the oil, the herbs, and salt and pepper to taste. Put the lid on and leave the pan on very low heat for the rice to steam for about 15 minutes, or until tender.

Boil the fava beans in salted water for a few minutes, until tender, then drain. Stir gently into the rice with the remaining oil.

Serve hot or cold with the yogurt, beaten with crushed garlic if you like and a little salt, poured over.

Patlicanli Pilavi

Pilaf with Tomatoes and Eggplants

Serves 6 • This is one of a few Turkish pilafs which are cooked in olive oil and eaten cold.

1 large onion, chopped

5 tablespoons extra-virgin olive oil

1 pound tomatoes, peeled and chopped

1 teaspoon sugar

½ teaspoon allspice

Pinch of chili flakes or ground chili
    pepper (optional)

Salt

1¼ cups long-grain rice

2 eggplants, weighing about 1 pound
    total, cut into 1-inch cubes

Olive oil or vegetable oil to fry the
    eggplants

3 tablespoons chopped dill

3 tablespoons chopped mint

In a large pan, fry the onion in 2 tablespoons of the olive oil till soft. Add the tomatoes, sugar, allspice, and chili, and cook over low heat for 10 minutes.

Add 1½ cups water, stir in some salt, and bring to the boil. Add the rice, stir, and cook, covered, over low heat for about 20 minutes, until the rice is tender and the liquid absorbed, adding a little water if it becomes too dry and begins to stick. (The tomatoes provide some of the liquid.)

In the meantime, deep-fry the eggplants in oil to cover, turning them over once, until lightly browned. Then drain on paper towels.

When the rice is done, gently fold in the dill and mint, the remaining raw oil, and the eggplants. Cover and cook a few minutes more.

Serve cold.

Tabbouleh bel Roz

Rice and Parsley Salad

Serves 6 • I like to make this Lebanese salad with basmati rice, because the grains stay very separate.

¾ cup basmati rice

Salt

Juice of 2–3 lemons

½ cup extra-virgin olive oil

Pepper

2 cups chopped flat-leaf parsley

½ cup chopped mint

10 scallions, chopped

5 firm ripe tomatoes, cut into small dice

2 hearts of romaine or Bibb lettuce to
    garnish

Pour boiling water over the rice, leave for a few minutes, then rinse and drain. Boil in salted water for about 14 minutes, then drain and pour back into the pan. Put the lid on and leave over low heat (it will steam) for 15 minutes, or until tender.

While still hot, dress with the lemon juice and olive oil and a little salt and pepper.

Just before serving, mix with the parsley, mint, and scallions. Serve topped with the tomatoes and garnished with a ring of lettuce leaves stuck around the edge of the salad.

Midye Pilavi

Mussel Pilaf

Serves 4 • In Turkey, where this dish comes from, mussels are large and fat.

About 20 large mussels or 30 small ones

2 medium onions, chopped

4–5 tablespoons extra-virgin olive oil

2 tablespoons pine nuts

½ cup long-grain rice

2 medium tomatoes, peeled and chopped

1½ teaspoons sugar

1 tablespoon raisins

Salt and pepper

1 teaspoon allspice

¼ cup chopped dill

Scrub the mussels, pull off their beards (the hairy bits that hang out of the shell), and wash them well. Discard any which are broken and those which feel very heavy or very light or which do not close when they are tapped or dipped in cold water. Put them in a pan with ¼ inch of water. Put the lid on and bring to the boil. The shells will open in 2–3 minutes. Take them off the heat and discard any which remain closed. Keep 8–10 mussels aside in their shells. Remove the others from their shells and discard the shells. Strain the liquid in the pan and keep aside.

Fry the onions in 2 tablespoons of the oil till soft and golden. Add the pine nuts, and when they begin to color, add the rice and stir for a minute or so. Add the tomatoes and the sugar and simmer 5 minutes.

Add the raisins and ¾ cup of the mussel water (add more water if necessary to make up the amount). Season with salt, pepper, and allspice and stir gently. Cook, covered, over low heat for about 15–20 minutes, until the liquid is absorbed and the rice is tender.

Stir in the remaining raw oil and the dill. Very gently fold in the shelled mussels and serve cold, arranging the mussels in their open shells on top.

GOHA'S COAT

One day Goha was invited to a wedding. He had to rush there straight from work and did not have time to get changed. The hosts took one look at him and put him at the bottom of the table. Every time a dish was passed around he was the last one to be served. All the good bits had gone and he was served very little.

The next invitation he received for a wedding, he made sure he was well dressed and borrowed the grandest coat in the neighborhood. The hosts treated him with joy and respect and he was offered the best place at the table. All the choice pieces were offered to him. One dish after another came first to him, and his plate was piled high with delicacies. Instead of eating, he started tugging at his own lapel saying, "Eat! Eat!" His neighbor looked at him in surprise and after a while bent over and whispered, "How can a coat eat?" Then Goha replied, "It's all for him, not for me!"

Slatit Hout

Fish Salad

Serves 4 • For this North African salad, use a firm white fish such as cod, haddock, or monkfish.

1 pound new potatoes
Salt
1 pound fish steaks or fillets
6 tablespoons extra-virgin olive oil
Juice of 1 lemon
Pepper
Peel of ½–1 preserved lemon (page 459), rinsed and cut into small pieces (optional)
2 tablespoons capers (optional)
3 tablespoons chopped flat-leaf parsley or cilantro

Boil the potatoes in salted water until tender. Then drain, peel, and cut into 1-inch pieces.

Poach the fish in boiling salted water for 5–8 minutes, until it just begins to flake when you cut into it with a pointed knife. Drain, let it cool, and flake it into largish pieces.

Beat the oil and lemon juice with a little salt and pepper and pour over the fish and potatoes in a serving bowl. Add the rest of the ingredients and mix gently.

Variations

• Add 2 ounces salted anchovies (chopped) and 6 green or black olives or 4 or 5 thinly sliced pickled gherkins.
• In the dressing mix 1 teaspoon ground cumin or ½ teaspoon harissa (page 464).

Koftit Ferakh

Fried Minced Chicken Balls

Serves 4–6 • Rolled into marble-sized balls, they make a nice appetizer.

2 cooked chicken quarters, preferably breasts
2 large slices white bread
Milk
1 large egg
Pinch of turmeric (optional)
Salt and pepper
Flour
Vegetable oil for deep-frying
Juice of ½ lemon (optional)

Skin and bone the chicken, and remove any sinews and hard membranes.

Remove the crusts from the bread. Soak the slices in a little milk and squeeze dry.

Put the chicken, bread, egg, and seasonings through the food processor and blend to a paste. Knead well and shape into marble-sized balls.

Roll them in flour and fry in hot oil about ½ inch deep, turning them over once, until a dark-golden color.

Serve the balls hot or cold, with a few drops of lemon juice squeezed over them if you like.

Çerkez Tavuğu

Circassian Chicken

Serves 8 • In Turkey and Egypt during the period of the Ottoman Empire, the women in the harems, the wives and concubines of the Sultans and aristocracy, were the widows and daughters captured at war. The Circassians among them were known for their beauty and their culinary skills. This classic is part of their legacy. The recipe was given by Luli Fevsi and comes from the kitchens of the old Ottoman aristocracy in Egypt. It is a cold dish which may be served as an hors d'oeuvre or as part of a buffet table.

4 chicken breast halves

4 chicken wings

1 onion stuck with 3 cloves

A few celery stalks

A sprig of tarragon or thyme

Salt and white pepper

2 thin slices dry white bread, crusts removed

2 cups walnut halves, coarsely minced or ground

1 or 2 cloves garlic, crushed (optional)

2 teaspoons paprika

2 teaspoons walnut or other oil

Put the breasts and the wings (which are to enrich the stock) in a saucepan. Cover with water (about 2½ cups), bring to the boil, and remove the scum. Add the onion and cloves, celery, and herbs and season to taste with salt and pepper. Simmer for about 15 minutes, until the breasts are tender.

Prepare the sauce. Soak the bread in a little of the stock and turn it to a paste in a blender or food processor. Mix with the walnuts in a small saucepan and add enough stock to get the consistency of porridge. Cook, stirring, a few minutes, until the sauce thickens. Add garlic, if you like, and a teaspoon of paprika, and stir well.

Skin the chicken breasts and shred into small pieces. Mix well with two-thirds of the sauce and spread on a serving dish. Cover with the rest of the sauce.

To garnish, mix the remaining paprika with the oil and dribble over the top. In Turkey, people use the oil squeezed out of walnuts, but I have not been successful with this.

Serve cold.

Hamud Shami

Lemony Chicken Jelly

Serves 6 • Although *shami* means "Syrian," this was a specialty of the Jews of Egypt. It has a strong taste of lemon and garlic. It should be made with a good, well-flavored chicken stock (see page 143). After the recipe was given to me thirty-five years ago, I never heard of it again until recently, when I was giving a lecture about Jewish food and a man complained bitterly that I had left it out of my Jewish book. So I feel obliged to leave it in here.

> 2¾ cups good chicken stock
> 1 tablespoon oil
> 2 large cloves garlic, crushed
> ¼ cup rice powder (see Note)
> Juice of 1 lemon, or a little more
> ½ teaspoon turmeric

Bring the stock to the boil. In another pan, heat the garlic in the oil until the aroma rises, then pour in a ladle of the stock.

Dissolve the rice powder in a little cold water. Beat in the garlic-flavored stock, and pour back into the pan. With the pan over gentle heat, pour the rest of the stock in gradually, stirring all the time, and bring to the boil. Add the lemon juice and turmeric and continue to cook, stirring, until the mixture becomes very thick. Pour into a serving dish.

Let it cool, and chill if you wish. The mixture will become a pale-yellow jelly. It looks beautifully translucent in a transparent bowl.

This unusual salad is delicious served with cold chicken and plain hot rice. It is often served as an appetizer, with bread or grape leaves to dip into it.

Note: Use a food processor or spice grinder to pulverize raw rice into powder.

Salatet Mokh

Brain Salad

Serves 6–8 • Brains are considered a great delicacy in the Middle East. In some parts, it is believed that they feed one's own brain and render one more intelligent. In other places, it is thought that eating brains reduces one's intelligence to that of the animal, and people who hold such beliefs cannot be persuaded to touch them. I used to have to eat them in hiding from my children, who screamed when they saw me.

> 2 sets calf's brains or 4 sets lamb's brains
> Salt
> Wine vinegar
> ½ large mild onion or 4–6 scallions, finely chopped
> Juice of ½–1 lemon, or more
> 4–6 tablespoons extra-virgin olive oil
> White pepper
> 2–3 tablespoons finely chopped flat-leaf parsley to garnish

Brains should be cooked when they are very fresh, preferably on the day they are bought. Soak them for 1 hour in cold water with salt and 1 tablespoon vinegar. Carefully remove the thin outer membranes, and wash under cold running water. Simmer gently for 10 minutes in salted water to which you have added a teaspoon of vinegar.

In the meantime, marinate the chopped onion in lemon juice. Drain the brains thoroughly and slice them. They should be firm enough to keep their shape. Arrange the slices in a single layer in a shallow serving dish.

Stir the olive oil into the onion and lemon, season to taste with salt and pepper, and sprinkle over the brains. Garnish with parsley.

Serve as an appetizer or a salad.

Kebdah Makly

Fried Liver Pieces

Serves 6 • Lamb's liver is traditionally used, but calf's liver is tastier and more tender. It is also more expensive.

- 6 slices calf's or lamb's liver
- 3 tablespoons extra-virgin olive oil plus more for frying
- 2 tablespoons wine vinegar
- Salt and pepper
- Oil
- Juice of $\frac{1}{2}$ lemon (optional)
- 2 tablespoons finely chopped flat-leaf parsley (optional garnish)
- 1 mild onion, very thinly sliced (optional garnish)

Cut the liver into 1-inch pieces, and remove any sinews or membranes. Mix the olive oil and vinegar with salt and pepper and marinate the liver for 1 hour in this mixture.

Pour the liver and its marinade into a skillet and cook over high heat for 2 or 3 minutes, turning the pieces over, until brown on the outside but still pink and juicy inside. (Liver dries very quickly and is not good overcooked.)

Serve hot or cold, sprinkled with lemon juice, and garnished with chopped parsley and onion slices if you like.

Variations

- A Moroccan way is to add a good sprinkling of paprika, and ground cumin and coriander to the frying oil.
- For a Turkish "Albanian-style" liver, cut the liver in small cubes, salt them, and dredge in flour. Deep-fry in about $\frac{1}{2}$ inch very hot sunflower or vegetable oil for 1–2 minutes until crisp and brown. Lift out with a slotted spoon and serve sprinkled with ground chili pepper or flakes, or with paprika. Accompany with sliced onions rubbed with salt and sprinkled with 2 teaspoons sumac.

A RECIPE FOR COOKING LIVER

One day the Khoja bought some liver, and as he was carrying it away a friend met him and asked how he meant to cook it.

"Oh! as usual," answered he.

"No!" said his friend, "there is a very nice way of doing it. Let me describe it to you."

He did so, but the Khoja said, "I cannot remember all these details. Write down the recipe on a piece of paper and I will cook the liver accordingly."

His friend wrote it down and handed it to him.

He was proceeding home deep in thought when a hawk pounced down, took the liver out of his hand, and flew off with it.

The Khoja, however, did not seem to mind, for he held out the recipe and called to the hawk, "What is the use of your doing that? You can't enjoy it, because I have got the recipe here."

BARNHAM, TRANS.,
TALES OF NASR-ED-DIN KHOJA

Mokh Makly

Fried Breaded Brains

Serves 6–8

2 sets calf's brains or 4 sets lamb's brains
4 teaspoons wine vinegar
Salt
Flour
2 egg yolks, beaten
White or black pepper
Fine dry breadcrumbs or matzo meal
Sunflower or vegetable oil for deep-
  frying
3 tablespoons finely chopped parsley to
  garnish
Juice of ½–1 lemon (optional)

Soak the brains for 1 hour in water acidulated with 1 tablespoon of the vinegar. Remove the thin membranes in which they are encased and wash the brains under cold running water. Drop the brains into boiling salted water acidulated with the remaining teaspoon of vinegar, and simmer for about 3 minutes. Remove, and drain thoroughly.

When cooled, cut into smallish (about 1½-inch) pieces. Gently roll the pieces first in flour, then in beaten egg yolk seasoned with a little salt and pepper, and lastly in fine bread-crumbs or matzo meal. Fry in hot oil about ¾ inch deep for a minute or two, until golden brown, turning them over once. Drain on paper towels.

Serve hot or cold, garnished with parsley and, if you like, sprinkled with lemon juice.

Brains Moroccan Style

Serves 8

2 sets calf's brains or 4 sets lamb's brains
Salt
4 teaspoons wine vinegar
3 cloves garlic, chopped
3 tablespoons oil
1 pound tomatoes, peeled and chopped,
  or a 14-ounce can tomatoes, chopped
2 tablespoons chopped flat-leaf parsley
2 tablespoons chopped cilantro
1 teaspoon paprika
Pinch of ground chili pepper, to taste
1 teaspoon ground cumin
Juice of ½ lemon
Peel of ½ preserved lemon (page 459),
  chopped up

Soak the brains for 1 hour in water acidulated with 1 tablespoon of the vinegar. Remove the thin membranes in which they are encased and wash the brains under cold running water. Drop the brains into boiling salted water acidulated with the remaining teaspoon of vinegar, and simmer for about 3 minutes. Remove, and drain thoroughly, then cut each in 2 or 4 pieces.

Fry the garlic in the oil in a large pan until it just begins to color. Add the peeled tomatoes and the rest of the ingredients (except the brains) and simmer for a few minutes. Then drop in the brains and cook gently a further 15 minutes. As good cold as it is hot.

Salatet Lissan

Tongue Salad

Serves 6

1 veal tongue

1 large onion, cut in 4

1 large carrot, cut into pieces

3 celery stalks with leaves

1 bay leaf

A few parsley stalks

Salt and pepper

FOR THE DRESSING

3–4 tablespoons extra-virgin olive oil

Juice of 1 lemon

1 or 2 cloves garlic, crushed

A few sprigs of flat-leaf parsley, finely chopped

Salt and pepper

Wash the tongue and blanch for a few minutes in boiling water. Throw out the scum with the water.

Put the tongue back in the saucepan with the rest of the ingredients except those for the dressing. Cover with fresh water and bring to the boil, then simmer until it is very tender. It will need 2–3 hours.

Drain and allow it to cool just enough to handle, then peel off the skin. If you let it get cold it will be difficult to skin. Remove the roots and return the tongue to the pot to cool in the stock.

Just before serving, cut into slices or cubes. Mix the dressing ingredients and pour over the tongue.

Variation

For a Moroccan flavor, add to the dressing ¼ teaspoon ground chili pepper, ½ teaspoon cumin, and ½ teaspoon coriander.

Yogurt

In every Middle Eastern household, the making of yogurt is a regular activity—at least it used to be. With a little experience one learns the rhythm of preparation and the exact warmth required to turn milk into yogurt. The actual preparation is extremely easy, but the right conditions are necessary for success. If these are fulfilled, the "magic" cannot fail.

Yogurt is an essential part of the Middle Eastern diet. In al-Baghdadi's medieval manual it was referred to as "Persian milk." In Iran today it is known as *mâst,* in Turkey as *yoğurt.* Syrians and Lebanese call it *laban,* Egyptians *laban zabadi,* while Armenians refer to it as *madzoon.* In parts of the Middle East, as in the Balkans, yogurt is believed by some people to have medicinal and therapeutic qualities. Longevity and a strong constitution are attributed to a daily consumption.

More recently the Western world discovered the healthful qualities of yogurt, but it is too often restricted to a minor role as a dessert, usually sweetened or synthetically flavored. Yogurt has yet to be allowed the versatility it enjoys in the Middle East, where it is, in turn, a hot or cold soup, a salad, a marinade for meat, or the basic liquid element in a meat-and-vegetable dish. The West has still to discover the vast number of dishes which are refreshed, soothed, and glorified when accompanied by yogurt, and the splendid drink called *ayran* or *abdug* (page 478), which is a mixture of yogurt and water.

The best yogurt I have ever eaten was in Turkey. It was made with water buffalo's milk and was thick and deliciously rich and creamy. A good second is the thick sheep's-milk yogurt product of Greece, which has been drained of its whey.

To Make Yogurt

If yogurt is to be adopted as an important element in cookery, it is worth learning to make it at home. All sorts of equipment have been recommended as being required: cake pans lined with padding, feather cushions, thermometers, different-sized bottles, jars, cork tops, to name but a few. Commercial firms sell sets of equipment, but you can do perfectly well without them. All that is needed is a large earthenware or glass bowl, a plate to cover it entirely or plastic wrap, and a small woolen blanket—I use two shawls.

The proportions are 1 heaping tablespoon of starter or activator (culture of the bacteria *bulgaris*) or fresh, live yogurt (I use ordinary, commercial *plain* whole-milk yogurt) to each quart of whole milk. If you increase the quantity of milk, increase that of the starter accordingly, but do not use too much of the starter, or the new batch of yogurt will be excessively sour.

Bring the milk to the boil in a large pan. When the froth rises, lower the heat and let the milk barely simmer for about 2 minutes. Turn off the heat, and allow the milk to cool to the point where you can barely dip your finger in and leave it there while you count to ten. Ten is the traditional count, but the milk must still be hot enough to sting. If you have a thermometer, the temperature should be 106–109°F. If the milk is much cooler or hotter than this, the yogurt is likely to fail.

Remove any skin that has formed on the surface of the milk. Beat the activator or plain yogurt in a large glass or earthenware bowl until it is quite liquid. Add a few tablespoons of the hot milk, one at a time, beating vigorously between all the additions. Then add the rest of the milk slowly, beating constantly, until thoroughly mixed.

Cover the bowl with a large plate or with plastic wrap. Wrap the whole bowl in a woolen blanket or shawl and leave it undisturbed in a warm place, such as an airing cupboard, for at least 8 hours or overnight. It should then be ready, thick like a creamy custard. Do not leave the bowl in the warmth too long, or the yogurt will become too sour.

As soon as the yogurt is ready, you can cool it in the refrigerator. It will keep for a week, but it is preferable to make a new batch every 4 days, using some of the previous one as an activator. This will ensure a constant supply of sweet, fresh-tasting yogurt.

For a Thicker, Creamy, Strained or Drained Yogurt

Pour the yogurt into a sieve or colander lined with damp muslin or cheesecloth and let it drain for 3–4 hours, until it is the consistency of thick heavy cream.

Labneh

Yogurt Cheese

Strained or drained yogurt becomes a creamy soft cheese which is served as a snack, for breakfast, or as a mezze, usually accompanied by olives, cucumbers, and mint. You can buy it rolled into little balls and preserved in olive oil.

To make it, mix in $3/4$–$1\frac{1}{2}$ teaspoons salt per quart of yogurt. Pour the yogurt into a sieve or colander lined with damp muslin or cheese-cloth and let it drain overnight in the refrigerator. (In the Arab world they tie the corners of the cloth together and suspend the bundle over a bowl or the sink.) The whey will drain away, leaving a soft, creamy white curd cheese.

Serving Labneh

• Eat it as it is or stir in a little extra-virgin olive oil, pepper or paprika, and, if you like, some chopped fresh mint or dill.

• In Syria they like to spread this on an opened-up piece of pita bread and roll it up to eat it. They call it *arus*—the bride.

• You can also serve *labneh* as a sweet, with honey and a dusting of cinnamon. In that case do not add salt to the yogurt.

• A lovely salad is made by mixing in a variety of raw and finely chopped vegetables such as cucumber, celery, scallions, and sweet or chili peppers.

• A very popular way of serving *labneh* is rolled into little balls. For this you must let the thickened yogurt drain for 2 days, until it is quite firm. Sprinkle the balls with olive oil and paprika. You can also keep the balls preserved in oil in a glass jar.

To "Stabilize" Yogurt for Cooking

Many Middle Eastern dishes call for yogurt as a cooking liquid or sauce which needs to be cooked—boiled or simmered—rather than just heated. Salted goat's milk yogurt, which was used in similar recipes in olden times, can be cooked without curdling, which explains why medieval recipes do not give any indication of ways of preventing yogurt from curdling. Cooking, however, causes yogurt made with cow's milk to curdle, and stabilizers such as cornstarch or egg white are required to prevent this.

1 quart plain whole-milk yogurt

1 egg white, lightly beaten, or

  1 tablespoon cornstarch mixed
  with a little cold water or milk

¾ teaspoon salt

Beat the yogurt in a large saucepan until it is liquid. Add the egg white, or the cornstarch mixed to a light paste with water or milk, and a little salt, and beat well.

Bring to the boil slowly, stirring constantly *in one direction only* with a wooden spoon, then reduce the heat to as low as possible and let the yogurt barely simmer, uncovered, for about 10 minutes, or until it has acquired a thick, rich consistency. Do not cover the pan with a lid, since a drop of steam falling back into the yogurt could ruin it.

The yogurt can now be cooked with other ingredients such as meat or vegetables with no danger of curdling.

The same process can be carried out successfully after the yogurt has been mixed with other ingredients.

Gebna Beida
White Cheese

It's the kind of cheese which you can't stop eating. It is made with rennet, which contains rennin, from the stomach of the calf. This coagulates the milk proteins, and activates the curd. Use at least 2½ quarts of milk, as the amount of cheese produced even from this quantity is really quite small.

2½ quarts milk

1 tablespoon salt, or more

4 tablespoons liquid essence of rennet

Pour the milk into a saucepan and heat gently. Add the salt and liquid rennet, and continue to heat the milk slowly until you can just bear to keep your little finger in without feeling any sting. Do not cover the pan, as condensed steam would spoil the process, and do not allow the milk to become too hot, as this will cause failure. Boiling would ruin it.

Turn off the heat and cover the pan with a cloth. The milk will separate into curds and whey. Leave undisturbed for at least 6 hours.

Pour the mixture into a colander or large sieve lined with thin damp cheesecloth or muslin, and let it drain overnight. The following day, a soft cheese will have formed. Turn it out into a small round plastic basket or mold with little holes. This will allow the cheese to dry out and to firm, and it will give it the shape and texture of the basket. Leave for a whole day before turning the beautiful, porcelain-white cheese out onto a plate.

Serve as an appetizer with olives.

Variations

• When the cheese is a few days old and quite firm, it is delicious sliced and fried with eggs.

• The same cheese, made with little or no salt, is excellent eaten with jam.

Savory Pies

In his *Kanju 'l Ishtiha* (*Treasure of the Appetite*) the fifteenth-century Persian poet of food, Abu Ishaq of Shiraz, wrote: "We came into the kitchen for this purpose, that we might show the fried meat to the pastry." The Middle East has "shown to the pastry" not only cheese, meat, and spinach—the more common fillings—but also pigeons, eggplants, pumpkin, fish, and nuts.

Savory pies are one of the most interesting features of Middle Eastern cuisines. *Sambousek, börek, bstilla,* fillo, *brik, spanakopitta, lahma bi ajeen, fatayer,* and *ataïf* are part of a vast and glorious family. Various doughs are used—flaky, puff, and fillo pastry, bread dough and pancakes, each country and community favoring a particular type. To make it more confusing, different names are given to the same pastries in different countries and communities, while sometimes the same name applies to two very different pastries. There are half-moon shapes, triangles, fingers, coils, little pots, and little parcels, as well as medium-sized pies and enormous ones. Making them requires a certain amount of skill, but it is easily acquired and worth possessing, since the results are particularly delicious and never cease to provoke general admiration. Mastering the art of making dainty little turnovers with elegant, festoon-type edges, and of folding tidy little envelopes, is part of the pleasure.

These savory pies make marvelous appetizers, particularly in their tiniest versions. They are good as a first course for buffet parties. The larger pies, such as the Moroccan *bstilla* (page 126) and the Tunisian *tagine malsouka* (page 130), make splendid main dishes.

RAGHÎF ALSINÎYYEH

An extraordinary pie or pastry is described by Abd al-Latif al-Baghdadi, the versatile Arab scholar, scientist, historian, philosopher, and traveler (not the al-Baghdadi I have quoted extensively in this book; see appendix), in an account of conditions and events in Egypt in the early part of the thirteenth century, the Kitab al-Ifadah wa'l-l'Tibar.

One of the most singular foods made in Egypt is that called raghîf alsinîyyeh. This is how it is made: they take 30 rotles (Baghdad weight) of wheat flour. They knead it with 5½ rotles of sesame oil in the same way as they make the bread called khoschinan. They divide the whole into two parts, spreading one of the two parts in a round shape of a raghîf (cake) in a copper plate made for this purpose of about 4 spans in diameter, and which has strong handles. After that they arrange on the dough three roasted lambs stuffed with chopped meats fried in sesame oil, crushed pistachios, various hot and aromatic spices like pepper, ginger, cloves, lentisk, coriander, caraway, cardamom, nuts and others. They sprinkle rose water, in which they have infused musk, over all. After that they put on the lambs and in the spaces left, a score of fowls, as many pullets, and fifty small birds, some roasted and stuffed with eggs, others stuffed with meat, others fried in the juice of sour grapes or lemon or some other similar liquor. They put above them pastry, and little boxes filled, some with the meat, some with sugar and sweet-meats. If one would add one lamb more, cut into morsels, it would not be out of place, and one could also add fried cheese.

When the whole is arranged in the form of a dome they again sprinkle rose water in which musk has been infused, or wood of aloes. They cover it again with the other part of the dough, to which they begin to give the shape of a broad cake. They are careful to join the two cakes of dough, as one makes pastry, so that no vapor escapes. After that they put the whole near the top of the oven until the pastry is solid and begins a degree of cooking. Then they lower the dish in the oven little by little, holding it by the handles, and leave it until the crust is well cooked and takes on a rose red color. When it is at this point it is taken out and wiped with a sponge, and again sprinkled with rose and musk water, and then brought out to be eaten.

This dish is fit to be put before kings and wealthy persons when they go hunting far from home or take part in pleasures in far off places; for in this one dish is found a great variety. It is easy to transport, difficult to break, pleasing to the sight, satisfying to the taste, and keeps hot a very long time.

ZAND AND VIDEAN,
THE EASTERN KEY

Fillo Pastry

Fillo (*phyllo* to the Greeks and *yufka* to the Turks) is the most common and most appealing pastry used for pies. It has replaced most other doughs that people used to make at home. The dough itself—a mixture of flour and water kneaded to a fine, firm, elastic mass—is easy enough to make, but the achievement of paper-thin sheets is extremely difficult and requires great skill. Expert pastry cooks knead the dough vigorously for a long time, until it is very elastic, and let it rest for 2 or 3 hours. Then they divide it into fist-sized balls, which are again kneaded, then rolled, pulled, and stretched as much as the dough will endure, until it becomes almost transparent. There are different ways of doing this.

I watched it being done at a small Cypriot workshop in London. The dough was pulled out by two people over large canvas sheets stretched on a large square frame which served as a table. Two electric heaters placed underneath "set" the dough immediately. At a bakery in Istanbul where a dozen men in flimsy vests worked in a permanent white haze, all covered with flour, I saw the pastry being rolled out with long thin rolling pins like broomstick handles and ending up rolled over and over on itself.

In Turkey, *yufka* is made in different degrees of thickness to suit different purposes. A thicker one is for little pies—*böreks,* cigars, coils—as a very thin pastry tears easily, and the filling has a tendency to burst out. The thinnest *yufka* is for making *baklawa.*

Fillo is now widely available frozen, and you can also find it fresh. There are different qualities, from very fine to rather thick, and packages vary in weight, and in size, thinness, and quality of sheets. A common size is 12 inches by 17 inches in a package containing about 28 sheets.

It is important to find a reliable frozen brand, as some are unsatisfactory. If packages have been frozen too long, ice crystals form and the sheets get moist and stick when defrosted.

Frozen fillo must be allowed to defrost slowly for 2–3 hours. Packages should be opened just before using and the sheets used as quickly as possible, as they become dry and brittle with the air. Cut the sheets and keep them in a pile so that the air does not dry them out. If you have to leave them for a few minutes, cover with a slightly damp cloth or plastic wrap and wrap any leftover pieces in plastic to keep them. You can put them back in the freezer.

Fillo pies with any filling except one that is too moist can be frozen and put straight from the freezer into the oven without thawing, but they will need a little more cooking time.

If the pastry is very thin, you may have to put 2 layers of fillo where one is called for.

Sigara Böregi

Little Cheese Rolls

Makes 16 • This is the most popular Turkish *börek*. The little rolls or "cigars" make ideal appetizers and canapés. It is best to use a thicker quality of fillo, which is not likely to tear during cooking. If the fillo sheets are too thin, use 2 strips together and brush with butter or oil in between. In this case you will need to double the number of sheets.

- 7 ounces feta
- 1 egg, lightly beaten
- 3–4 tablespoons finely chopped mint, parsley, or dill (optional)
- 4 sheets fillo
- 4 tablespoons melted butter or oil

For the filling, mash the feta cheese with a fork and mix with the egg and herbs.

Take out the sheets of fillo only when you are ready to use them, as they dry out. Cut the sheets into 4 rectangles each, about 12 by 4 inches, and put them in a pile on top of each other. Brush the top strip lightly with oil or melted butter. Take a heaping teaspoon of filling and place it at one of the 4-inch or shortest ends of the strip in a thin sausage shape along the edge—about 1 inch from it and 1 inch from the side edges (1). Roll up the top sheet with the filling inside like a cigarette (2). Turn the ends in when you've rolled it about a third of the way to trap the filling (3), then continue to roll (4). Repeat with the remaining fillo sheets.

Place the cigars close to each other on a greased baking sheet and brush the tops with oil or melted butter and bake at 350°F for 30 minutes, or until crisp and golden.

Serve hot.

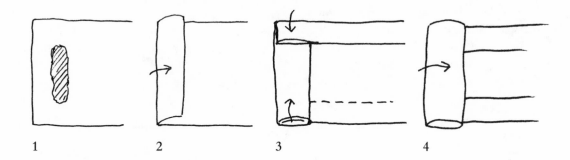

1   2   3   4

Fillo Triangles with Ground Meat, Onions, and Pine Nuts

Makes about 20 • Meat pies are traditionally little triangles. The classic Arab filling is called *tatbila*. In Turkey, where these are called *börek,* they use the thicker kind of fillo pastry for them. If your sheets are too thin and look likely to tear, use 2 strips together and brush with melted butter or oil in between.

5 sheets fillo
5 tablespoons melted butter or oil

FOR THE MEAT FILLING

1 small onion, chopped
2 tablespoons sunflower oil
8 ounces lean ground lamb or beef
Salt and pepper
¾ teaspoon cinnamon
¼ teaspoon allspice
2 tablespoons pine nuts, lightly toasted

For the filling, fry the onion in the oil till golden. Add the meat and fry lightly, crushing it with a fork and turning it over, until it changes color, adding salt, pepper, cinnamon, and allspice. Stir in the pine nuts.

Take out the sheets of fillo only when you are ready to use them, as they dry out. Cut the sheets into 4 rectangles each, about 12 by 4 inches wide, and put them in a pile on top of each other. Brush the top strip lightly with melted butter or oil. Take a heaping teaspoon of filling and place it at one of the 4-inch (or shortest) ends of the strip of fillo, 1¼ inch from the edge (1). Fold the end over the filling. Now pick up a corner and fold diagonally making a triangle (2). Continue to fold until the whole strip has been folded into a triangular packet (3), making sure that you close any holes as you fold so that the filling does not ooze out.

Place the little packets on a greased baking sheet and brush the tops with oil or melted butter. Bake at 350°F for 25 minutes, or until crisp and golden.

Variations

• Instead of oil or butter, you can brush the tops with egg yolk mixed with a drop of water before baking.
• A Moroccan filling is without pine nuts and adds ¼ teaspoon ginger, a pinch of cayenne, 3 tablespoons chopped cilantro, and 2 raw eggs to bind the meat. Deep-fry the pies in about ½ inch not-too-hot oil until golden, turning over once. Drain on paper towels, and serve hot, dusted with a little confectioners' sugar or cinnamon.

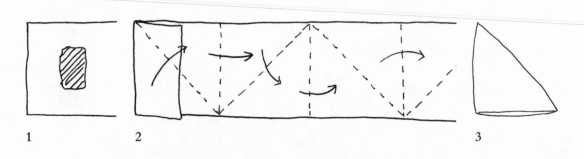

1   2   3

Fillo Triangles with Spinach-and-Cheese Filling

Spinach is a traditional filling for fillo triangles (page 118) and coils (below). Use the filling on page 131 instead of the meat filling and prepare as in the preceding recipe.

Making Fillo Coils

Cut the sheets of fillo into 2 rectangles each, about 12 inches long and 8–10 inches wide, and put them in a pile on top of each other. Brush the top strip lightly with oil or melted butter. Put a line of filling—3–4 tablespoonfuls—along one of the longer, 12-inch sides, about 1 inch from the edge and from the 2 shorter ends (1). Very carefully lift up the edge over the filling and roll up, folding in the ends when you've rolled it about halfway to trap the filling.

To be able to coil the roll without the pas-try's tearing, you have to crease it first like an accordion (2). To do this, hold the roll with both hands and very gently push from the ends towards the center. Now curve the roll very gently in the shape of a snail (3) and lift it onto a greased baking sheet. Repeat with the rest of the fillo rectangles and filling. Place all the coils close to each other on the sheet and brush the tops with oil or melted butter, or, better still, with egg yolk mixed with a drop of water. Bake at 350°F for 30–40 minutes, or until crisp and golden.

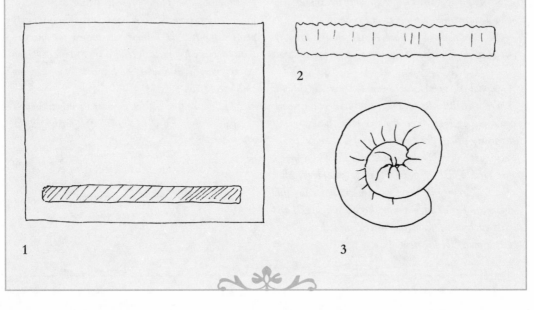

1

2

3

THE HOCA AS TAMERLANE'S TAX COLLECTOR

One day the Hoca chanced to be in Tamerlane's court when the despot's tax collector came to report on his receipts. The figures in impressive columns covered page after page of parchment, and the collector's voice droned endlessly through a recital of the sums. But, in the end, Tamerlane was not satisfied. It seems that first this account and then that one had been misrepresented. In short, the tax collector had revealed himself as a scamp and a cheat.

"So that is the way you manage your post as tax collector!" raged the testy ruler. "Well, sir, I cannot swallow such outrageous lies. But"—and his eyes glinted—"You will swallow them. Begin at once!"

"Begin what, sire?" questioned the tax collector, puzzled and frightened.

"Begin to swallow your own accounts. Quickly, now. I have other business at hand." And the lordly Tamerlane watched with increasing amusement as the wretched collector choked and gagged on the sheets of parchment. At length he had chewed and swallowed them all, and his heroic effort was rewarded on the instant by Tamerlane, who declared him no longer tax collector.

"Instead," declared Tamerlane, smiling broadly, "I appoint you, Nasreddin Hoca, to be my tax collector."

Appalled, the Hoca considered his sad plight. There was little doubt about the matter: no report could please Tamerlane. On the other hand, was it necessary to suffer such abuse for one's bookkeeping, however faulty? Suddenly the Hoca had a fine idea. This business might be managed, after all. . . . Gravely he thanked Tamerlane for his fine evidence of trust in a simple hoca's judgment, and excused himself from the ruler's presence, to prepare himself for his new office.

Every morning during the following month, Nasreddin Hoca watched with tender concern as his wife rolled fine, fresh dough to paper thinness [yufka or fillo] and baked it to form platelike pastries. Then he took the pastries to one side and on them he recorded the tax receipts of the preceding day. With painstaking care he stacked the pastries in a special cupboard where they would be protected from prying eye and tampering touch.

Finally came the day of reckoning. Taking a large wheelbarrow loaded with the precious pastries, the Hoca trundled off to Tamerlane's court, and was admitted to the ruler's presence with his curious burden.

"Ah, there you are!" exclaimed Tamerlane, slapping his hands on his knees in great satisfaction. And, "Yes, yes," he murmured as he accepted the two large leather sacks containing the taxes collected. "But where are your accounts?"

"Right here, sire," replied the Hoca, gesturing towards the load in the wheelbarrow.

Tamerlane stared in disbelief. Then, "Bring me one of those things," he demanded.

Promptly the Hoca presented him with one of the pastries, covered from end to end with finely penned figures. As Tamerlane studied the inscriptions, a smile began to spread across his face. "And what, may I ask, was your purpose in keeping your records on pastry?"

"Only, sire that either one of us might be able to swallow the reports of my labors," answered the Hoca.

WALKER, *WATERMELONS,*
WALNUTS AND THE WISDOM
OF ALLAH AND OTHER
TALES OF THE HOCA

Eggplant Fillo Pies

Makes 6 • The traditional shape for eggplant pies is a coil or snail shape, but large square packets are simple to make and don't tear as easily. And they are just as good. These pies can be served as a first course or a main dish. The Turkish eggplant filling is delicate in flavor and delicious. If you want to make them into a coil, use the method given above ("Making Fillo Coils," page 119).

2 pounds eggplants

4 eggs, lightly beaten

5 ounces mature cheddar, grated

¼ teaspoon nutmeg

Pepper

A little salt (optional)

6 sheets fillo

4 tablespoons sunflower oil or melted butter

1 egg yolk

For the filling, broil or roast the eggplants, peel them, and chop and mash the flesh (see page 63). Mix with the eggs, cheese, nutmeg, pepper, and salt (for salt, take into account the saltiness of the cheese).

Open out the sheets of fillo when you are ready to make the pies and be ready to work fast. Leave the sheets in a pile and brush the top one with melted butter or oil. Put a sixth of the filling (about 4 tablespoons) in a mound on one side of the sheet, about 3 inches from the edge, in the center (1). Let it spread over a surface of about 3 inches.

Wrap the filling up into a flat, square parcel: Fold the edge of the sheet over the filling, then very carefully lift the part of the sheet with the filling and turn over (2). Continue to turn the parcel over, folding the 2 side ends up at different turns so that the filling ends up covered with several layers of pastry on both sides (3–5).

Repeat with the remaining sheets and filling, and arrange the parcels on a sheet of foil on a baking sheet. Brush the tops with the egg yolk mixed with 1 teaspoon of water and bake in a preheated 350°F oven for 35–45 minutes, or until the pastry is crisp and brown.

Serve hot.

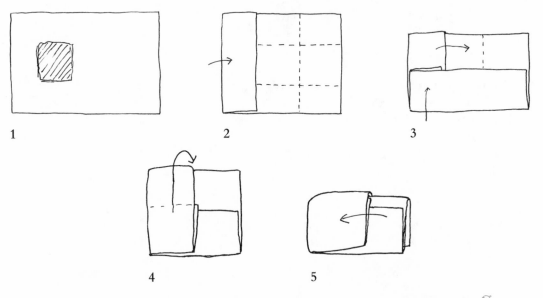

1   2   3

4   5

Pumpkin Fillo Pies

Makes 6 • These large individual pies with a Turkish filling make a wonderful first course. You need the sweet orange-fleshed pumpkin for this. It is sold in Middle Eastern and Oriental stores, almost all the year round, in large slices, with the seeds and stringy bits removed.

6 sheets fillo

4 tablespoons melted butter or
   vegetable oil

1 egg yolk

FOR THE FILLING

2 pounds orange pumpkin

2 teaspoons sugar

5 ounces feta cheese, mashed with a fork

2 eggs, lightly beaten

Peel the pumpkin and scrape off the seeds and fibrous parts. Cut the flesh into pieces and put them in a pan with about 1 cup of water. Cook with the lid on (so that they steam) for 20 minutes, or until soft. Drain and mash with a potato masher or a fork. Return to the pan and leave over high heat until all the liquid has evaporated, watching that it does not burn and stirring with a wooden spoon. The pumpkin must be quite dry. If it is wet, the pastry will become soggy.

Mix with the rest of the filling ingredients.

Open out the sheets of fillo when you are ready to make the pies and be ready to work fast. Leave the sheets in a pile and brush the top one with melted butter or oil. Put a sixth of the filling in a mound on one side of the sheet, about 3 inches from the edge, in the center. Let it spread over a surface of about 3 inches.

Wrap the filling up into a flat, square parcel. Fold the near edge of the sheet over the filling, then very carefully lift the part of the sheet with the filling and turn over. Continue to turn the parcel over, folding the 2 side ends up at different turns so that the filling ends up covered with several layers of pastry. (See drawings on page 121.)

Continue with the remaining sheets and filling, and arrange the parcels on a sheet of foil on a baking sheet. Brush the tops with the egg yolk mixed with 1 teaspoon of water and bake in a preheated 350°F oven for 35–45 minutes, or until the pastry is crisp and brown.

Serve hot.

Variation

If you want to make the pies into a traditional coil shape, use the method given above ("Making Fillo Coils," page 119).

Spinach Pies with Raisins and Pine Nuts

Serves 4 • The large individual pies make a wonderful first course.

4 sheets fillo
2 tablespoons melted butter or
    vegetable oil
1 egg yolk

FOR THE FILLING

1 pound fresh spinach
1 medium onion, chopped
2 tablespoons extra-virgin olive oil
Salt and pepper
2 tablespoons pine nuts, lightly toasted
2 tablespoons raisins

Make the filling. Wash the spinach and remove stems only if they are thick and tough, then drain. Put the leaves in a large pan with the lid on. Cook over low heat until they crumple into a soft mass (they steam in the water that clings to them). Drain and press all the water out, as it would make the pastry soggy.

Fry the onion in the 2 tablespoons of oil till golden. Add the spinach, season with salt and pepper, and cook over high heat to evaporate any remaining liquid. Stir in the pine nuts and raisins.

Open out the sheets of fillo when you are ready to make the pies and be ready to work fast. Leave the sheets in a pile and brush the top one with butter or oil. Put a fourth of the filling in a flat mound on one side of the sheet, about 3 inches from the edge, in the center.

Wrap the filling up into a square parcel. Fold the near edge of the sheet over the filling, then very carefully lift the fillo with the filling

and turn over. Continue to turn the parcel over, folding the 2 side ends up at different turns so that the filling ends up covered with several layers of pastry on both sides. (See drawings on page 121.)

Continue with the remaining sheets and filling, and arrange the parcels on a sheet of foil on a baking sheet. Brush the tops with the egg yolk mixed with 1 teaspoon of water and bake in a preheated 350°F oven for 35–45 minutes, or until the pastry is crisp and brown.

Serve hot.

Variation

Before serving, dust the tops with a little confectioners' sugar and cinnamon.

Briouat bil Kefta

Moroccan Cigars with Meat

Makes about 60 • This is elegant and tasty party fare. The pastries are called *briouat*s in Morocco, where they are made with the paper-thin pancakes called *ouarka*. Fillo makes an easy and perfect substitute. You can keep the prepared rolls uncooked in the freezer. In Morocco they are fried, but it is much easier to bake them, and the results are very good.

1 medium onion, finely chopped

4 tablespoons vegetable oil

1½ pounds lean ground beef or lamb

2 teaspoons cinnamon

½ teaspoon allspice

¼ teaspoon ginger

Salt

Pepper or good pinch of ground chili pepper

1 cup finely chopped parsley

1 cup finely chopped cilantro

5 eggs, lightly beaten

1 pound fillo sheets

¾ cup (1½ sticks) butter, melted, or ¾ cup vegetable oil

Prepare the filling. In a large skillet, sauté the onion in the 4 tablespoons oil until softened. Add the meat, spices, salt, and pepper or ground chili pepper, and cook, crushing the meat with a fork and turning it over, for about 10 minutes, until it changes color. Stir in the parsley and cilantro.

Lightly beat the eggs in a bowl and pour over the meat. Cook gently, stirring, for a moment or two only, until the eggs set to a creamy consistency. Let the filling cool. Taste and add more spices and pepper if you like.

To fill and roll the cigars: cut each sheet of fillo into three rectangles and put them together in a pile so that they do not dry out.

Brush the top one very lightly with melted butter or oil.

See drawings on page 117. Put a tablespoon of filling along one of the short edges. Roll the fillo over it. Roll up like a cigar, tucking the ends in when you've rolled it halfway so that the filling does not fall out, then continue to roll, letting the ends unfold so that they appear open. Place the rolls side by side on a greased baking sheet, brush with melted butter, and bake in a preheated 300°F oven for 35 minutes, or until golden. Serve very hot.

Variations

• You may dust the cigars with confectioners' sugar or cinnamon or with both.

• If you want to fry a few for an instant snack (they are nice fried), do so in about ½ inch not-too-hot vegetable oil, turning over once, until browned. Drain on paper towels.

Briouat bil Hout

Seafood Cigars

Use the seafood filling on page 128 and make the cigars as instructed in above recipe for *briouat bil kefta*.

Briouat bil Djaj

Chicken and Onion Cigars

Use the chicken-and-onion filling on page 129 and make the cigars as instructed in the above recipe for *briouat bil kefta*.

Ouarka, Brik, Dioul

North African Paper-Thin Pancakes

In North Africa, large ever-so-thin pancakes—called *ouarka* in Morocco, *brik* in Tunisia, and *dioul* in Algeria—are used to make large round pies and small ones in the shape of cigars, cornets, and square packets.

Making them is a highly skilled operation which requires a great deal of patience. A dough is made with hard-wheat or bread flour, a pinch of salt, and warm water, kneaded for a long time as you work in more water to obtain a soft, very moist, spongy elasticity; then the dough is left to rest for an hour covered with a

(continued)

About the Dadas in Morocco

In Morocco, cooking is a woman's thing. Men are excluded from kitchens. The great cooks—family cooks, professional cooks, those who cook for weddings and parties, the guardians of the great culinary tradition—are black women, the "dadas." Who they are is a taboo subject—the hidden face of Morocco. The women are descended from African slaves who were brought from the Sudan, which was once part of the Moroccan empire. In the seventeenth century the Sultan Moulay Ismail recruited from the states of the Sahel 150,000 slaves. The men constituted the origin of the Sherifan black guard. The women became domestics in people's homes. Some became concubines, some wives, some were freed and became midwives. In imperial Fez, it was not uncommon that men of great families chose young dadas as their fourth wives, to look after their children and cook. Their children were often recognized and took on the father's name. A form of bondage went on until not so long ago, and the women remained illiterate; that is why it is a taboo subject.

In more recent times dadas have joined cooks' cooperatives, catering for weddings and great occasions. They arrive with their helpers and their pots and pans and stay several days with the families. They shop, slaughter sheep and pigeons, prepare the *ouarka* for *bstilla,* set up the clay tagines on braziers, and prepare all the dishes while the ladies of the house and their relatives busy themselves with the sweet pastries. Some dadas have become famous itinerant specialists of one dish only or a culinary style. Some now teach at the Palais Royal Tourga, the catering school set up by King Hassan in Casablanca. The students are all young women (there were no young men when I was there) training to cook in restaurants and hotels. But the great dadas who lived all their lives in families are old now. They are disappearing. People have to learn to do without them. Some of their specialties, like the paper-thin pancakes called *ouarka,* can now be bought at the souk.

film of warm water. Lumps of dough the size of an egg are picked up with one hand and dabbed on the oiled surface of a round tray placed bottom side up over a fire. As the dough touches the tray with repeated dabs, a thin, almost transparent film of pastry is built up and gradually expanded into a round about 12 inches in diameter.

In North African markets the pancakes are sold by weight, covered in plastic wrap. In France, where they are mass-produced and sold in vacuum packs, they have become very popular with the top chefs, who use them as we use fillo. I hope they will be sold in the United States sometime in the future.

You can use Chinese spring-roll skins or a fine fillo pastry instead of *ouarka,* although the result is not quite the same. I started using fillo for Moroccan pies more than thirty years ago, but I always felt a little guilty about it until a young Moroccan cook, who had been sent to Disneyland to demonstrate Moroccan cooking at an international festival of tourism, told me about her team's experience. They had not anticipated the extent of the demand for *briouat* (pies) and ran out of pastry. A Lebanese contingent nearby lent the Moroccan cooks fillo, and they went on to make the pies with fillo. They turned out to be perfectly satisfactory.

Bstilla

Pigeon (Squab) or Chicken Pie

Serves 6–8 • Variously pronounced *bstilla, pastilla,* and *bisteeya,* it is one of the great dishes of Morocco, described as "food for the gods." Vast quantities are made in huge trays for weddings and grand occasions. The version with pigeons is the most prestigious.

Moroccans say the dish was brought back by the Moors from Andalusia after the Reconquista, but in Andalusia, at El Molino, the center of gastronomic research outside Granada, where they serve it as a historic dish, they say it was brought to Spain from Morocco. In a thirteenth-century Andalusian culinary manuscript in Arabic (see Lucie Bolens, appendix) there is a recipe for a pigeon omelet which is almost identical to the filling for *bstilla.*

The preparation of the pastry called *ouarka* requires much skill and experience (see page 125). You can buy it vacuum-packed in French supermarkets, so perhaps we will be able to find it in America soon. Store-bought sheets of fillo make an excellent alternative. There are two famous versions. The one of Fez is the most surprising, with its sweet-and-savory combination, but you must also try the sharp lemony one of Tétouan, which is given as a variation. The cooked birds are not deboned in Morocco—the bones are left in the pie—but it is much more pleasant to eat the pie without them.

FOR THE FILLING

2 squabs or 1 3½-to-4-pound chicken
3 tablespoons sunflower or vegetable oil
1½ large onions, finely chopped or
    grated
Salt and pepper

½ teaspoon ground ginger

¼ teaspoon powdered saffron (optional)

2 teaspoons ground cinnamon plus more
   to garnish

6 eggs, lightly beaten

1 cup chopped flat-leaf parsley

½ cup chopped cilantro

1½ cups blanched almonds

2–3 tablespoons sugar

½ cup (1 stick) butter, melted, or
   ½ cup vegetable oil

14 sheets fillo pastry

Confectioners' sugar to garnish

Cut the squabs or chicken into pieces. Put them in a pan with 2 tablespoons of the oil, onions, salt and pepper, ginger, saffron (optional), and 1 teaspoon cinnamon. Add just enough water to cover. Simmer with the lid on for 1½ hours, or until the flesh is so tender that it falls off the bones, adding a little water as required.

Lift out the squabs or chicken, leaving the sauce in the pan, remove skin and bone, and cut the meat into smallish pieces.

Reduce the sauce to about ⅔ cup. Pour in the eggs and stir over low heat until the mixture is creamy and nearly set. Stir in the parsley and cilantro; season with salt and pepper.

Coarsely chop the almonds and fry them briefly in 1 tablespoon of oil, stirring and shaking the pan to brown them lightly all over. Drain on paper towels and mix with the sugar and 1 teaspoon cinnamon.

Now assemble the pie. Brush a large pie or cake pan, about 13 inches in diameter and 1½–2 inches deep, with melted butter or oil.

Fit a sheet of fillo in the dish so that the ends fold well up the side and overlap the edges. If this is not possible, use overlapping sheets of fillo. Lay 6 sheets of pastry on top of each other, brushing melted butter or oil evenly between each layer.

Spread the pieces of boned pigeon or chicken neatly over the pastry and cover with the egg mixture. Lay another 4 sheets of fillo on top, brushing each one with melted butter or oil. Sprinkle the fried almonds, sugar, and cinnamon mixture evenly over the top layer, then bring the overhanging bits of sheets up and fold them over the almond mixture. Cover with the remaining sheets of fillo, brushing each layer except the top one with melted butter or oil. Tuck the top sheets down inside the pan, underneath the pie.

Bake in a preheated 400°F oven for 30 minutes, until the top is crisp and golden brown. Very carefully turn over the pie onto a baking sheet and bake a further 15 minutes, or until the other side is brown.

Serve hot, turned out upside down again onto a serving platter. Dust the top with confectioners' sugar and make a pattern of crisscrossing parallel lines with cinnamon.

Variation

For a Tétouan *bstilla,* omit the sugar and add the juice of 1 lemon or more to the sauce. Sprinkle the top of the pie with cinnamon.

Bstilla bil Hout

Individual Seafood Pies

Makes 6 • These individual Moroccan pies are made with the paper-thin pancake-type pastry called *ouarka* (page 125), but fillo can be used. They are deliciously spicy and herby, with masses of parsley and cilantro. Serve them as a first or as a main course.

1¼ pounds firm white fish, such as cod
    or haddock
Salt
5 tablespoons extra-virgin olive oil
Juice of 1 lemon
½–1 teaspoon cumin
1½ teaspoons paprika
Good pinch of ground chili pepper
2 cloves garlic, crushed
1 cup chopped flat-leaf parsley, or more
1 cup chopped cilantro, or more
8 ounces cooked, peeled large shrimp
6 sheets fillo pastry
About 4 tablespoons vegetable oil
1 egg yolk

Poach the fish in salted water very briefly, until it just begins to flake, then drain. Remove the skin and flake it into pieces.

In a bowl, mix the olive oil and lemon juice with the cumin, paprika, and ground chili pepper, the garlic, parsley, and cilantro. Put in the fish and shrimp and turn to cover all the pieces with this marinade.

Open out the sheets of fillo when you are ready to make the pies and be prepared to work fast. Leave the sheets in a pile and brush the top one with vegetable oil. Put a sixth of the filling mixture in a flat mound on one side of the sheet, about 3½ inches from the edge, in the center. Let it spread over a surface of about 3½ inches.

Wrap the filling up into a flat square parcel: Fold the nearest edge of the sheet over the filling, then very carefully lift the part of the sheet with the filling and turn over. Continue to turn the parcel over, folding the 2 side ends up at different turns so that the filling ends up covered with several layers of pastry. (See drawings on page 121.)

Continue with the remaining sheets and filling, and arrange the parcels on a sheet of foil on a baking sheet. Brush the tops with the egg yolk mixed with 1 teaspoon of water and bake in a preheated 350°F oven for 35–45 minutes, or until the pastry is crisp and brown.

Serve hot.

Trid

Chicken and Onion Pies

Serves 8 • Trid is described as the poor man's *bstilla*. It is also said that the Prophet would have liked it best. He is known to have been fond of onions, and here a huge mass is reduced to a creamy sauce. I prefer it too.

5 large onions, weighing about 3½
    pounds total
4 tablespoons sunflower oil
½–¾ teaspoon ground ginger
1½ teaspoons cinnamon plus more to
    sprinkle on top at the end
Salt
Juice of ½ lemon
4 chicken fillets—all breast halves, or
    2 breast halves and 2 legs (skinless)
1 cup finely chopped cilantro
8 sheets fillo pastry
4 tablespoons melted butter or
    vegetable oil
1 egg yolk
Confectioners' sugar to sprinkle on
    (optional)

Chop the onions—in batches in the food processor, if you like. Put them in a large saucepan with the oil, ginger, cinnamon, a little salt, lemon juice, and the chicken fillets. Put the lid on and cook on low heat for about 15 minutes.

Take out the chicken pieces and continue cooking the onions uncovered so that the liquid evaporates. Cook until the onions have been reduced to a creamy sauce and you can see the oil sizzling (it takes about 1 hour), stirring every so often.

Cut the chicken into smallish pieces and put them back in the pan with the onion sauce. Add the cilantro and mix very well. Taste and add salt and flavorings if necessary.

Open out the sheets of fillo when you are ready to use them and leave them in a pile. Brush the top one with melted butter or oil.

Take about an eighth of the chicken-and-onion mixture and put it in a flat mound on the sheet about 3 inches from one edge, in the middle. Fold the edge over the filling, and turn the parcel over with the filling, folding the side ends of the sheet up at different turns so as to end up with a flat parcel with several layers of pastry on either side. (See drawings on page 121.)

Continue with the rest of the fillo sheets and filling, and place all the parcels on foil on a baking dish or baking sheet. Brush the tops with the egg yolk mixed with 1 teaspoon of water. Bake in a preheated 350°F oven for 35 to 45 minutes, until crisp and golden.

Serve hot. Pass round the confectioners' sugar and cinnamon for people to sprinkle on if they wish.

Variation

Another Moroccan pie has a filling of cooked chicken (3 half breasts) mixed with 1 fried chopped onion, ½ pound potatoes boiled and mashed, some chopped parsley, 2 chopped hard-boiled eggs, and 2 raw eggs (as a binder). It is served hot, accompanied with lemon wedges.

Tagine Malsouka

Meat and Haricot Bean Pie

Serves 6 • This rich Tunisian pie makes an interesting main dish.

1 pound lean lamb, cut into ¾-inch
  cubes

2 tablespoons vegetable oil

Salt and pepper

¼ teaspoon powdered saffron (optional)

½ teaspoon ground cinnamon

A 15-ounce can white haricot or navy
  beans, drained

6 eggs

½ cup (1 stick) butter, melted, or ½ cup
  vegetable oil

12 sheets fillo pastry

1 egg yolk, to glaze

In a saucepan, brown the meat in 2 tablespoons oil. Cover with water, and season to taste with salt and pepper, saffron if used, and cinnamon. Bring to the boil and simmer slowly and gently, covered, for about 1½ hours, until the meat is very tender, adding a little water if necessary to keep the meat covered and letting the sauce reduce at the end. Stir in the drained beans.

Break the eggs into the pan and keep stirring over low heat until the eggs begin to set but are still creamy.

Brush a large baking dish with melted butter or oil and fit 4 sheets of fillo pastry into the dish, one on top of another, so that the edges come up over the sides of the dish, brushing melted butter or oil between the layers. Spread half of the meat stew evenly over the top, and cover with another 4 sheets of pastry, again brushing each one with melted butter. Cover with the rest of the stew and the remaining sheets of pastry, each one except the top one brushed with melted butter or oil. Brush the top one with beaten egg yolk and bake in a 350°F oven for the first 40 minutes. Then raise the heat to 425°F and bake for 10–15 minutes longer, until the pastry is crisp and a deep-golden color. The eggs in the stew should have set firmly.

Making a Large Layered Greek-Style Fillo Pie

Use a large baking pan a little smaller than the sheets of fillo. Brush it with oil or melted butter. Place half the package of fillo, or about 7 sheets, one on top of another, at the bottom of the pan, brushing each sheet with melted butter or oil and letting the sheets come up along the sides.

Spread the filling evenly on top. Then cover with the remaining sheets, brushing each, including the top one, with melted butter or oil.

With a sharp-pointed knife, cut into 2-inch squares or diamonds with parallel lines, only down to the filling, not right through.

Bake at 350°F for 30–45 minutes, or until crisp and golden. Cut along the cutting lines, this time right through to the bottom, and serve hot.

Spanakopitta

Large Spinach Pie

Serves 16–20 • The large, famous Greek pie is much quicker to make than the little triangles and cigars. It is not finger food but makes an excellent first course or main vegetarian meal.

2 pounds fresh spinach

5 ounces feta cheese

4 ounces cottage cheese

4 eggs, lightly beaten

½ cup dill, finely chopped (optional)

¼ teaspoon grated nutmeg

Salt and pepper

14 sheets fillo pastry

½ cup (1 stick) butter, melted, or about

   ½ cup olive or vegetable oil

Wash the spinach and cut off any hard stems, then drain. Put the leaves in a pan and cook with the lid on and no extra water for a few minutes only, until they crumple into a soft mass. (They steam in the water that clings to them.) Drain and press out the excess liquid, which could make the pastry soggy. Return to the pan and dry it out further, stirring, over high heat.

Mash the cheeses together with a fork. Add the eggs, spinach, dill, nutmeg, salt if necessary (take into account the saltiness of the cheese), and pepper.

Follow the instructions for "Making a Large Layered Greek-Style Fillo Pie" above (page 130).

Serve hot.

Tyropitta

Large Cheese Pie

Serves 16–20 • The filling is a traditional one for the famous Greek pie. A milder-tasting alternative (see variation) was adopted in Britain by my contemporaries from Egypt. Both make a lovely teatime savory as well as a snack meal accompanied by salad.

1 pound cottage cheese

1 pound feta cheese, mashed with a fork

4 eggs, lightly beaten

Pepper

4 tablespoons finely chopped dill,

   chervil, mint, chives, or parsley

14 sheets fillo pastry

½ cup (1 stick) butter, melted, or

   ½ cup vegetable oil

Put the cheeses with the eggs in a bowl and mix thoroughly, until well blended. Add pepper and stir in the herbs.

Follow the instructions for "Making a Large Layered Greek-Style Fillo Pie" on page 130. Serve preferably hot.

Variations

• Paint the top sheet with 1 egg yolk mixed with 1 teaspoon water (do not brush with butter), and sprinkle with sesame seeds.

• For another filling which is not traditional and does not sound very nice but is actually wonderful, put ½ pound edam, ½ pound gouda, ½ pound cheddar, all cut into pieces in the food processor with ½ pound cottage cheese and 4 eggs, and blend to a homogeneous mass.

BÖREK IN A TURKISH HOUSEHOLD

We excelled in pastry, which we called börek. Served at the beginning of a meal, as in my mother's family and at home, or at the end of a meal, as in some other houses, it was always stuffed either with cheese and herbs, or with spiced minced meat. The difference lay in the dough and the manner of its cooking. Börek was not among my own favorite dishes, and I do not remember all the varieties which were made with a dough which resembled the French mille feuille. I preferred such as were made of a paste rather like noodles, and which were boiled. Both the Tartar börek and the piruhi were made of thinly rolled-out dough. The former was cut into squares, stuffed with cream cheese and herbs and folded into triangles, boiled and eaten with yogurt; with piruhi, the little squares were left open and minced meat was sprinkled between them. Browned butter was poured over it. The best börek of this kind is the su börek, or water börek, so named because it too is boiled. Afterwards the dough is spread in layers in a round flat börek dish made of silver, with a high edge, half of it being filled with cream cheese and the other half with minced meat or chicken. Browned in the oven it is a dish for kings.

The undeniable king of all böreks is called, when rolled to look like a cigarette, sigara börek, and when rolled into a ball the size of a walnut, ceviz börek. Very few cooks nowadays are able to make it as it should be and once was produced. I once saw it in the making. The kitchen at Moda, which was in the garden half-way between the harem and the selamlik, was out of bounds. None the less my brothers and I decided to see what it was like. We passed through the dining-room for the men-servants, into the large old-fashioned kitchen with its enormous range and adjoining larder. Thence we went on into the pastry-room. Wide marble-topped tables stood beneath the windows which overlooked the garden. Mustafa, his back to us, stood at one of the tables in front of an open window. He was rolling out an enormous sheet of dough. Suddenly he caught hold of two of its corners, swept the whole thing up into the air, twirled it several times above his white cap, and brought it down on the table without there being a rent in it. This procedure was repeated over and over again, whilst we watched spellbound. He furiously rolled the long, thin Turkish rolling-pin, then up would go the dough, kept upright by the swift rotation of his arms, and then down in one sweep. I was particularly impressed when looking at it, while it was in the air, to see that it was as transparent as gauze. Wrapped many times round minced meat in the sigara börek, or round grated kashar cheese in the ceviz börek, and cooked in deep fat, it is one of the superlative achievements of Turkish cooking.

FOAT TUGAY, *THREE CENTURIES*

Tepsi Boregi

Creamy Filo Cheese Pie

Serves 6–8 • This wonderful creamy Turkish pie is something between a savory flan and a cheese lasagna. The fillo turns into a soft, thin pasta, so don't expect it to be crisp and papery. It sounds complicated but it is quite easy, and you will be delighted by the lightness and the variety of flavors and textures.

- 7 ounces feta cheese
- 7 ounces cottage or farmer's cheese
- ½–¾ cup finely chopped dill
- ½ cup (1 stick) butter, melted
- 2¼ cups milk, warmed
- 4 eggs, lightly beaten
- 6 sheets fillo pastry
- 7 ounces Turkish kasseri cheese or mature cheddar, grated

For the filling, blend the feta cheese with the cottage or farmer's cheese and dill.

Mix the melted butter, milk, and eggs.

Use a rectangular baking dish or pan smaller than the sheets of fillo. Open the sheets only when you are ready to use them and keep them in a pile so that they do not dry out.

Lay a sheet in the greased baking dish or pan, fitting it into the corners and letting the edges come up the sides and overhang. With a ladle, pour a little of the milk-and-egg mixture (a little less than a sixth, as you will need enough for 6 layers with a larger amount for the last one, on top) all over the sheet and sprinkle with the grated kasseri or cheddar. Tear the second sheet into strips and lay them on top. Pour a little of the milk-and-egg mixture over the strips and sprinkle with the grated kasar or cheddar.

Lay the third sheet on top—as it is, without tearing it—and spread the cheese filling evenly on top. The fourth and fifth sheets must be torn into strips, and each layer sprinkled with the milk-and-egg mixture and the grated cheese. Fold the overhanging bits of fillo over the pie and lay the last sheet on top. Tuck it down into the sides and ladle the remaining milk-and-egg mixture over it.

Bake at 350°F for 30–45 minutes, until the top is golden brown. It puffs up and falls again when you cut it.

Serve hot, cut into squares.

Brik à l'Oeuf

Serves 1 • These Tunisian fried parcels in a crisp casing of *ouarka* (see page 125) are ubiquitous appetizers in North African restaurants. You can use fillo to make them, although it is not quite the same. They should be served immediately, as soon as they come out of the frying oil.

1 or 2 sheets fillo pastry
Vegetable oil for frying

FOR A TUNA FILLING

2 tablespoons chopped onion, fried
3 tablespoons mashed canned tuna
1 tablespoon chopped parsley
Salt and pepper
1 egg

FOR A CHEESE-AND-MUSHROOM FILLING

3 tablespoons grated cheese
3 or 4 mushrooms, sliced and sautéed
    lightly in butter or oil
1 tablespoon finely chopped flat-leaf
    parsley
Salt and pepper
1 egg

Spread 1 sheet of fillo out on a large plate or flat surface. If the fillo is of a very thin quality and the filling seems too wet and may result in a torn pastry, lay 2 sheets together one on top of the other.

Prepare one of the fillings. Mix the filling ingredients (except the egg) and place in a flat mound at one end of the sheet. Break the egg over the mixture without mixing it in. Fold the sheet over and over, folding in the sides and enclosing the filling in a neat, firm, but loose square parcel.

Drop the packet or *brik* into about ½ inch hot oil over medium heat. The oil must not be too hot or the pastry will burn before it is cooked inside. Turn it over as soon as it turns a light-brown color and fry the other side. Remove and drain on absorbent paper. The egg should be still runny. (It squirted out in my face once at a restaurant.)

Serve hot immediately, or keep warm in the lowest oven until ready to serve.

Sambousek bi Gebna

Little Cheese Turnovers

Makes about 35 • In Lebanon the turnovers with meat are the most prestigious, but we in Egypt always made cheese ones. No tea party was ever right without them. The recipe for the dough has been passed down in my family for generations as "1 coffee cup of oil, 1 coffee cup of melted butter, 1 coffee cup of warm water, 1 teaspoon of salt, and work in as much flour as it takes." We baked the pies, but it was also common to fry them in oil.

FOR THE DOUGH

½ cup sunflower or vegetable oil

½ cup (1 stick) butter, melted

½ cup warm water

½ teaspoon salt

About 3⅔ cups all-purpose flour

1 egg, lightly beaten with 1 teaspoon
  water, to brush on

Sesame seeds to sprinkle on (optional)

FOR THE CHEESE FILLING

1 pound crumbled or grated cheese such
  as feta, kashkaval, kasseri, or kefalotyri;
  try a half-and-half mixture of feta and
  cottage cheese (well drained) or the
  mixed Western-cheese variation given
  on page 131

2 lightly beaten eggs

White pepper

3–4 tablespoons chopped herbs such as
  flat-leaf parsley, mint, or dill

Make the dough. Heat the oil and butter in a small pan over low heat until the butter melts, then add the water and salt and beat well. Pour into a large mixing bowl.

Add the flour gradually—only just enough to have a greasy dough that holds together in a ball—stirring with a fork to begin with and then working it in with your hand. A few tablespoons more flour may be needed. The dough should be handled as little as possible, so stop mixing as soon as it holds together. Leave it to rest, covered in plastic wrap at room temperature, for 20 minutes. (Do not put it in the refrigerator: that will make it unworkable.)

This dough does not roll out very well. Take walnut-sized lumps, and roll each into a little ball. Flatten it as thinly as possible between the palms of your hands and pull it further into a round of about 4 inches in diameter.

Mix the filling ingredients and put a heaping teaspoon of the filling on half of each circle (1). Fold the other half over to make a half-moon shape and seal by pinching the edges firmly together. If you like, make the traditional wavy edge by pinching, folding, and twisting around the edge (2).

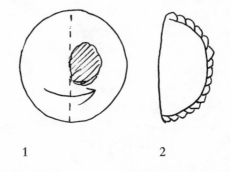

1   2

Arrange the pies on baking sheets (they need not be greased). Brush the surface of each pie with the beaten egg and, if you like, sprin-

(continued)

Sambousek bi Gebna (continued)

kle lightly with sesame seeds. Bake in a pre-heated 350°F oven for about 30 minutes, or until golden.

Serve the *sambousek* hot or cold, but they are best just out of the oven.

Variations

• Instead of baking, deep-fry in ½ inch vegetable oil. In this case, do not brush with the egg.

• You may use commercial frozen puff pastry (defrosted), but roll it out as thinly as you can.

Sambousek bi Lahm

Meat Turnovers

Makes about 25 • A Syrian and Lebanese specialty.

½ cup vegetable oil

½ cup warm water

½ teaspoon salt

2½ cups all-purpose flour

1 egg, lightly beaten with 1 teaspoon water

Meat filling with pine nuts (*tatbila*) (page 118)

A POEM ABOUT SAMBOUSEK

At a banquet given by the Caliph Mustakfi of Baghdad in the tenth century, a member of the company recited a poem by Ishaq ibn Ibrahim of Mosul describing sanbusaj (sambousek) as follows.

If thou wouldst know what food gives most delight,
Best let me tell, for none hath subtler sight.
Take first the finest meat, red, soft to touch,
And mince it with the fat, not overmuch;
Then add an onion, cut in circles clean,
A cabbage, very fresh, exceeding green,
And season well with cinnamon and rue;
Of coriander add a handful, too,
And after that of cloves the very least,
Of finest ginger, and of pepper best,
A hand of cumin, murri just to taste,
Two handfuls of Palmyra salt; but haste,
Good master, haste to grind them small and strong.
Then lay and light a blazing fire along;
Put all in the pot, and water pour
Upon it from above, and cover o'er.
But, when the water vanished is from sight

And when the burning flames have dried it quite,
Then, as thou wilt, in pastry wrap it round,
And fasten well the edges, firm and sound;
Or, if it please thee better, take some dough,
Conveniently soft, and rubbed just so,
Then with the rolling pin let it be spread
And with the nails its edges docketed.
Pour in the frying-pan the choicest oil
And in that liquor let it finely broil.
Last, ladle out into a thin tureen
Where appetizing mustard smeared hath been,
And eat with pleasure, mustarded about,
This tastiest food for hurried diner-out.

FROM MASUDI'S *MEADOWS OF GOLD*,
TRANS. BY ARBERRY IN
ISLAMIC CULTURE, 1939

In a large bowl, mix the oil, water, and salt, beating with a fork. Gradually work in enough flour to have a soft, malleable dough—stirring it in with the fork to begin with, then working it in with your hands. You may use it right away, or keep it for as long as a day, covered in plastic wrap. But it must be at room temperature, not chilled in the refrigerator.

The dough is very oily and must be rolled out without flouring the rolling pin or the work surface. These become oily and do not stick to the dough. Divide the dough into 4 pieces to make rolling easier. Roll out as thinly as you can, and cut into 4-inch rounds with a pastry cutter. Scraps can be immediately rolled into a ball and rolled out again, so you do not waste any part of the dough.

Put a heaping teaspoon of the filling in the center of one half of each circle. Fold the other half over to make a half-moon shape and seal by pinching the edges firmly together. If you like, make the traditional wavy edge by pinching, folding, and twisting around the edge. (See drawings on page 135.)

Arrange the pies on oiled baking sheets and brush the surface of each with the beaten egg mixed with a drop of water. Bake in a preheated 350°F oven for about 30 minutes, or until golden.

Pie Dough for Lahma bi Ajeen, Sfiha, and Fatayer

It is a bread dough made with olive oil.

1 teaspoon active dry yeast
Pinch of sugar
About 1 cup lukewarm water
3 cups bread flour
1 teaspoon salt
⅓ cup extra-virgin olive oil

Dissolve the yeast with the sugar in ½ cup of the warm water. Leave in a warm place for about 10 minutes, until it froths.

Sift the flour and salt into a large bowl and mix in the oil. Add the yeast mixture and, a little at a time, just enough of the remaining warm water so that the dough holds together in a ball. Begin by using a fork, then work it in with your hands. Knead vigorously for about 10 minutes, until the dough comes away from the sides of the bowl and is smooth and elastic.

To prevent a dry crust from forming on the surface, pour ½ tablespoon oil in the bottom of the bowl and roll the dough around in it to grease it all over. Cover the bowl with plastic wrap and leave in a warm place for about 1½ hours, until doubled in bulk.

Lahma bi Ajeen or Sfiha

Meat Tarts

Serves 3–6 • These famous "Arab pizzas" are traditionally made with bread dough rolled out extremely thin. Make them with the dough on page 137 and use one and a half times the amount of filling given here. Or use store-bought frozen pastry, as described below. It is not the same, but the result is equally delicious. Serve the tarts as an appetizer, or as a snack meal accompanied by thick strained yogurt and salad.

12 ounces frozen puff pastry, defrosted

1 egg white

Oil to grease the baking sheet

FOR THE FILLING

1 onion, grated or finely chopped in the food processor and drained of the juices

$\frac{1}{2}$–1 chili pepper, finely chopped

12 ounces ground lamb

4 ounces tomato paste ($\frac{3}{4}$ of a small can)

2 teaspoons sugar

2 tablespoons lemon juice or $1\frac{1}{2}$ tablespoons pomegranate concentrate

Salt and pepper

Cut the puff pastry into 6 pieces and roll each out thinly on a floured surface with a floured rolling pin, cutting the corners so as to make rounds of about 7 inches in diameter. (This pastry shrinks quite a bit, and the tarts will turn out much smaller when baked.)

Place the pastry rounds on oiled baking sheets or greaseproof or wax paper and brush the tops with half the egg white (this prevents the pastry from getting too soggy with juice). Bake them blind (without topping) in a preheated 450°F oven for 10 minutes, until they puff up and are golden. Take them out, turn them over, brush the other side with the remaining egg white, and return to the oven for another 8 minutes, or until this side is crisp and lightly colored. Let them cool.

Mix all the filling ingredients (make sure the onion is drained of its juices) and work very well with your hands to a soft, well-blended paste. Take lumps of the meat mixture and spread thickly over each pastry round.

Place the filled tarts in the hot oven and bake 15 minutes.

Serve hot.

Variations

• Omit the tomato paste and add $\frac{1}{3}$ cup chopped parsley and 3 tablespoons pine nuts to the filling.

• For delicious Lebanese *sfiha,* mix the meat and onion (strained of its juice) with $\frac{1}{2}$ cup yogurt, 2 tablespoons pomegranate concentrate, salt, pepper, and $\frac{1}{4}$ cup pine nuts, and omit the other filling ingredients.

Fatayer bi Sabanikh

Spinach Pies

Makes about 50 • These little triangular-shaped pies are a famous Lenten specialty of the Orthodox Christian communities of Syria and Lebanon. You can serve them hot or cold. They are meant to be tart and lemony. The filling must not be wet or the dough will get soft and will stick to the baking sheet and tear when it is baked. For this reason it is best to use frozen spinach, squeezed dry.

Pie dough (page 137)

FOR THE FILLING

2 pounds frozen leaf spinach, defrosted

¼ cup extra-virgin olive oil

1 onion or 6 scallions, finely chopped

4 tablespoons sumac

Juice of 1 lemon

1 cup pine nuts or coarsely chopped walnuts (optional)

Salt and pepper

Prepare the pie dough as described on page 137.

For the filling, put the spinach in a colander and press out the water, then squeeze the leaves between your palms to get rid of any remaining liquid. Coarsely chip the spinach and mix in a bowl with the rest of the filling ingredients.

Punch down and knead the risen dough briefly. Divide into 4 or 6 balls for easier handling. When rolling out one ball, keep the remaining ones wrapped in plastic.

Roll out each ball on a lightly floured sur-

(continued)

The Christian communities of Syria and Lebanon observe many fasts throughout the year during which they abstain from eating meat and sometimes also dairy foods. The Holy Eastern Orthodox Catholic Church prescribes weekly fasts on Wednesdays and Fridays, and commemorative fasts such as the fast of the Holy Apostles, the fast of Theotokos, of the beheading of Saint John the Baptist, of the Elevation of the Holy Cross, and the Eve of the Epiphany. The most important is during Lent, which begins seven weeks before Easter and commemorates the fast of Christ in the desert, when, according to the Scriptures, Satan appeared to tempt Him. The Passion-week fast commemorates His suffering and Passion.

The laws of abstinence oblige to either partial or complete abstinence. Meat may be taken only once, at the principal meal, or not at all, as on Fridays. During Lent, meat and dairy foods are prohibited. Vegetables, legumes, and grain, all cooked with olive oil—fava-bean salad, lentil soup, chickpeas and wheat, bulgur and tomatoes, eggplant stews—are famously known as Lenten dishes. Most prestigious among them are the pies that people make with bread dough and fillings such as spinach or chickpea, and tiny *zaatar*-covered bread rounds.

face with a floured rolling pin, and keep turning over the dough and dusting underneath with flour so that it does not stick. Roll out as thinly as possible (the dough is very elastic and springs back). Cut the sheet into 1½- to 2-inch rounds with a pastry cutter. Pick up the scraps, roll them into a ball, and roll out again to make more rounds, so as not to waste any dough. Take each round and roll out again, then pull out and stretch until it is paper-thin and about 3 to 3½ inches in diameter.

Another traditional way is to take walnut-sized lumps of dough, flatten them between your oiled palms, and pull and stretch the dough out as thinly as you can.

To make the pies, take each pastry round, lay it flat on one hand, and put a tablespoon of filling in the middle (1). Shape into the traditional 3-sided pyramid with a rounded base by lifting up 3 sides (with both hands) and bringing them together over the filling (2). Pinch the edges together, making thin, ridged joints in the shape of a 3-sided star and closing the pies (3). Place the pies on a lightly oiled baking sheet and press down a little to flatten their bases.

Bake in a preheated 450°F oven for 10 minutes, or until golden.

Fatayer bi Jibn

Cheese Pies

Make as the preceding recipe, *fatayer bi sabanikh,* but replace the spinach filling with 1 pound feta cheese mashed with a fork and mixed with a little pepper and 3 tablespoons extra-virgin olive oil.

Fatayer bi Labneh

Drained-Yogurt Pies

Make as the preceding recipe, *fatayer bi sabanikh,* but replace the spinach filling with yogurt that has been drained in a cloth until it is a soft creamy cheese (see page 112), mixed with salt, pepper, and a little grated onion.

Fatayer bi Hummus

Chickpea Pie

A Lebanese Lenten specialty is rounds of pie dough (page 137) rolled out thinly, with a handful of cooked chickpeas pressed in.

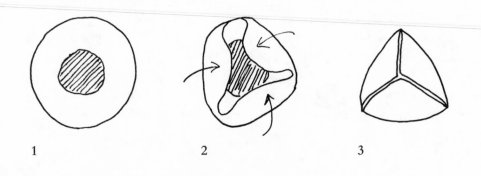

1   2   3

Ataïf bi Jibn

Pancakes Stuffed with Cheese

This is a specialty of Syria, Lebanon, and Egypt. Sweet *ataïf* (pancakes) are extremely popular stuffed with nuts and soaked with syrup). These savory ones are less common.

Prepare *ataïf*, following the recipe on page 444, adding a little salt to the batter instead of sugar.

Fill with a small slice of halumi cheese or mozzarella, or feta cheese crumbled with a fork and mixed with a few finely chopped chives or mint leaves.

Put a heaping teaspoon of filling in the center of each little pancake, on the uncooked side. Fold the pancake over the filling to make a half-moon shape and seal the edges by pinching them together hard with your fingers. The soft, moist dough will stick together.

Deep-fry in hot oil until golden and drain on paper towels.

Serve hot.

Arais

Bread Stuffed with Spiced Ground Meat

Serves 6 • Lebanese restaurants serve these cut in wedges as appetizers. A whole bread accompanied by a salad makes a good snack meal. Use a thin type of Arab or pita bread with a pouch.

6 thin pita breads
2 tablespoons vegetable oil
1 large onion, finely chopped
1½ pounds ground veal, beef, or lamb
1 chili pepper, finely chopped
Salt and pepper
½ teaspoon allspice
1 teaspoon cinnamon
2 teaspoons sumac or the juice of
    ½ lemon
A good pinch of cayenne
⅓ cup chopped flat-leaf parsley
4 tablespoons pine nuts, toasted
2 tablespoons melted butter or extra-
    virgin olive oil

Cut each pita on one side and open carefully without breaking the bread (warming it up makes this easier).

To make the filling, in a large skillet fry the onion in oil until golden. Add the meat and fry for about 10 minutes, stirring, crushing, and turning it over, until it changes color. Add the chili pepper, season with salt and pepper, and stir in the spices and parsley. Spread a sixth of the filling into each bread, then press it closed. Brush with melted butter or oil and place on a sheet of foil under the broiler. Broil, turning over once, until both sides are lightly colored.

Cut in half and then into wedges if serving as an appetizer. Serve hot with lemon wedges.

Soups

SHORBA

Soup is eaten for breakfast, lunch, or supper and also represents a meal in itself, accompanied by bread. Vendors sell soups from great cauldrons in the street in the very early hours on winter mornings to catch those who want to fill themselves up before getting to work. Some play a part in the rituals of religious festivals, and are known as festive or wedding soups, and there are famous Ramadan specials prepared during the Muslim fasting month.

Chicken Stock

Serves 6

1 chicken or 1 chicken carcass or
   enough wings and giblets for a
   good stock
1 large onion, quartered
2 carrots, cut into pieces
2 stalks celery with leaves
2 bay leaves
Bunch of parsley stalks
2 sprigs of thyme
Salt and pepper

Put all the ingredients for the stock in a large
saucepan and cover with about 2½ quarts (10
cups) water. Bring to the boil, remove any scum,
then reduce the heat and simmer for 1½ hours.

Ladle off any fat from the surface and strain
through a sieve, then return to the pan, taste,
and adjust the seasoning.

Meat Stock

Instead of the chicken, have a knuckle of veal
or lamb, or 1 or 2 marrow bones with ½
pound meat. Blanch the bones in boiling water
for 1–2 minutes, then throw the water out.
Then cook as above, with the same other ingredients, for 2 hours.

DUCK SOUP

A kinsman came to see Nasrudin from the country, and brought a duck. Nasrudin was grateful, had the bird cooked and shared it with his guest.

Presently another visitor arrived. He was a friend, as he said, "of the man who gave you the duck." Nasrudin fed him as well.

This happened several times. Nasrudin's home had become like a restaurant for out-of-town visitors. Everyone was a friend at some removes of the original donor of the duck.

Finally Nasrudin was exasperated. One day there was a knock at the door and a stranger ap-

peared. "I am the friend of the friend of the friend of the man who brought you the duck from the country," he said.

"Come in," said Nasrudin.

They seated themselves at the table, and Nasrudin asked his wife to bring the soup.

When the guest tasted it, it seemed to be nothing more than warm water. "What sort of soup is this?" he asked the Mulla.

"That," said Nasrudin, "is the soup of the soup of the soup of the duck."

SHAH, *THE EXPLOITS OF THE INCOMPARABLE MULLA NASRUDIN*

Hamud

Green Vegetable Soup with Garlic, Mint, and Lemon

Serves 6–8 • This tangy, aromatic soup was a family favorite in Egypt. The strong taste of lemon is the main feature. It was usually served over rice.

- 2 quarts chicken stock (see page 143) (or you may use 1 or 2 bouillon cubes)
- 3 leeks, cut into ³⁄₄-inch slices
- 1 head of celery with leaves, cut into ³⁄₄-inch slices
- 4 medium potatoes, peeled and diced
- Salt and white pepper
- 4 cloves garlic or more, chopped
- Juice of 1–3 lemons, to taste
- 1 teaspoon sugar, or more to taste
- 4 zucchini, cut into ¹⁄₂-inch slices
- 2 tablespoons dried mint

- About ²⁄₃–³⁄₄ cup (uncooked measure) plain cooked rice to serve with (optional) (See page 338)

Bring the stock to the boil in a pan. Put in the leeks, celery, and potatoes. Add salt, pepper, garlic, lemon juice, and sugar and simmer for about ¹⁄₂ hour.

Add the zucchini and mint and cook 15 minutes more.

Serve, adding rice if you like, in the soup plates.

Shorbat Tamatem

Tomato and Rice Soup with Mint and Cilantro

Serves 4 • With this fresh-tasting and aromatic Egyptian soup, it is best to cook the rice separately and add it just before serving, as it gets bloated and soft if it stands in the soup.

- ¹⁄₃ cup rice
- Salt
- 2 tablespoons olive oil
- 1 onion, chopped
- 2 cloves garlic
- 1 teaspoon tomato paste
- 2 pounds tomatoes
- 1–2 teaspoons sugar
- 2¹⁄₂ cups chicken stock (page 143) (or you may use 1 or 2 bouillon cubes)
- 2–3 tablespoons finely chopped cilantro
- 1 sprig of mint, finely chopped

Pour the rice into a pan of boiling salted water and cook for 18 minutes, or until tender, then drain.

Heat the oil in a large pan, add the onion, and fry until soft. Add the garlic and stir until the aroma rises, then stir in the tomato paste and take off the heat.

Cut the tomatoes in quarters and, without peeling them, blend to a cream in the food processor. Pour them into the pan.

Add sugar and the stock and cook for 15–20 minutes.

Just before serving, add the cooked rice and the chopped cilantro and mint.

Soupa Avgolemono

Egg and Lemon Soup

Serves 6 • In Greece it is made whenever chickens are boiled. In Egypt we called it *beid ab lamouna* and *shorba bel tarbeyah*. The stock can be prepared in advance, but the rest must be done at the last minute.

 2 quarts good chicken stock (see
 page 143)
 ½ cup long-grain rice
 Salt and white pepper
 3 tablespoons finely chopped flat-leaf
 parsley
 3 eggs
 Juice of 1 or 2 lemons

Bring the stock to the boil, add the rice, and cook for about 18 minutes, until it is tender. Season with salt and pepper and add the parsley.

When you are ready to serve, beat the eggs, add the lemon juice to them, and continue to beat until the mixture is pale and frothy. Add a ladle of hot stock and beat with a fork. Add a little more, then pour the mixture into the remaining broth, stirring vigorously. Heat through, stirring constantly, until it becomes very slightly creamy, but do not let it boil or the eggs will curdle (it must remain just below the boil). Remove the pan from the heat quickly. Taste, and add lemon and seasonings if necessary. The soup must be tart.

Serve immediately.

Variation

You can add vermicelli, pastina (tiny pasta grains), or tapioca instead of rice.

Moroccan Pumpkin Soup

Serves 6 • This delicate and beautiful soup is made with the large orange pumpkins that are sold cut up in large slices. Ask to taste a bit from an open one, as the taste varies. You will know if it is not very good.

 2½ pounds orange pumpkin
 3½ cups chicken stock (page 143) (or
 you may use 2 bouillon cubes)
 3½ cups milk
 Salt and white pepper
 2–3 teaspoons sugar, or to taste
 Cooked rice, ⅔ cup uncooked measure
 (optional)
 1 teaspoon cinnamon to garnish
 (optional)

Remove the peel, seeds, and fiber from the pumpkin and cut it into pieces. Put it in a large pan with the stock and the milk, season with salt, pepper, and sugar, and simmer for 15–20 minutes, until it is tender. Lift the pumpkin out, puree in a food processor, and return to the pan. Or mash the pumpkin in the pan with a potato masher.

Bring to the boil again, throw in the cooked rice, and simmer a minute more before serving. Add a little water if necessary to have a light creamy consistency.

Serve, if you like, with a dusting of cinnamon on each serving.

Melokheya

Serves 6–8 • *Melokheya* is Egypt's most popular national dish. It is an ancient peasant soup which is believed to be portrayed in pharaonic tomb paintings. It seemed to us as children that the fellahin (peasants) wore the same clothes, used the same tools, and repeated the same movements as did the figures working the land in pharaonic tomb paintings. Every peasant, however poor, had a little patch of ground for his own use, and in summer this was reserved exclusively for the cultivation of the deep-green *melokheya* leaf (*Corchorus olitorius*—in English, Jew's mallow). The women prepared the soup daily in large pots which they carried to the fields on their heads for the men to eat at midday. When the work was done and the men came home, they ate it again at dusk.

For many years, when we were relatively new in England, the leaves were very hard to find, and we hankered desperately for the soup. Some relatives of mine in Milan tried to grow the plant (it looks a bit like spinach) in the garden of their apartment building. After weeks of effort—getting the seeds (the same seeds were found in pharaonic tombs), planting them, watering, nurturing, harvesting—they invited a group of compatriots to eat the soup. The triumphant cook was horrified to find that the leaves she thought she had so lovingly raised were only local weeds. The *melokheya* had failed to grow.

Everybody from Egypt adores *melokheya,* which has a mucilaginous, glutinous quality imparted by the leaves. But be warned: it is an acquired taste. There are various ways of eating it in several stages, and each is something of a ritual. The soup may be eaten first with plain rice (that is how I like it—pure and simple), or with fried or toasted Arab bread; then with portions of the chicken or meat which was used for making the stock. Or you can serve it all together in many layers on the plate. In either case, it represents an entire meal. The layers may start with pieces of toasted bread at the bottom of the plate, but usually begin with rice, topped with a piece of chicken or meat, over which the soup is poured. Recently the Lebanese custom of sprinkling chopped onion steeped in vinegar on top has been adopted by some Egyptians.

In Egypt they use chicken, rabbit, goose, duck, or meat stock to make the soup. Many years ago I was employed in England to make the soup using a famous brand of bouillon cube for a television advertisement. Years later, when I went back to Cairo for the first time, I spied it being shown on television in a crowded café between episodes of "Dallas."

You are not likely to find fresh *melokheya,* but dried and frozen varieties are available from Middle Eastern stores. The frozen one is best. A lot of garlic is used in a sauce called *takleya* which goes in at the end, but it does not seem like too much when you eat.

A 3½-pound chicken

1 onion, peeled

6 cardamom pods (optional)

Salt and pepper

3 14-ounce packages frozen chopped *melokheya* leaves

FOR THE GARLIC SAUCE (TAKLEYA)

15–20 cloves garlic, or to taste, crushed

2–3 tablespoons coriander seeds, crushed in a mortar, or ground coriander

¼ teaspoon ground chili pepper, or more (optional)

3 tablespoons vegetable oil

Plain rice to serve with (page 338)

Put the chicken in a large saucepan with the onion and cardamom pods. Cover with water (about 3½ quarts) and bring to the boil. Remove any scum, season with salt and pepper, and simmer, covered, for 1 hour, or until the meat is very tender. Lift out the chicken, cut it into portions, and keep them warm, covered with a little stock. Discard the onion.

You should be left with about 3 quarts stock. Reduce it if necessary by boiling, or add more water. Put the *melokheya,* still frozen, into the simmering stock (this is according to the packet instructions). Let the ice melt entirely and simmer for another 10 minutes. Stir gently and take off the heat. Do not overcook, as the *melokheya* leaves could fall to the bottom, and they should stay suspended.

Prepare the *takleya* (the garlic sauce). Fry the garlic with the coriander and ground chili pepper in the oil (in Egypt *samna,* a clarified butter, is used), stirring well. When the sizzling garlic begins to color, pour it into the simmering soup, stir, and cook a further 1–2 minutes. Taste and adjust the seasoning.

Serve very hot with the rice and the chicken, heated through.

Garnishes and Variations

• Serve with 2 finely chopped mild red or white onions soaked in wine vinegar for 1 hour.

• For a "royal" *melokheya,* put a thin layer of Arab bread, lightly toasted and broken into pieces, at the bottom of the soup plates. Cover with a layer of rice, put a piece of chicken on top, pour *melokheya* over it all, and sprinkle with chopped onion soaked in vinegar (see preceding variation).

• You can add 2 or 3 ripe tomatoes, skinned and chopped.

• For the stock, instead of chicken, use 1½ pounds lamb, beef, or veal, preferably with 1 or 2 marrow bones.

• If you are using fresh *melokheya,* strip the leaves from the stalks, wash and drain them. Then chop by hand or in a food processor, add to the stock, and simmer for 5–10 minutes.

• If you are using dried *melokheya,* pulverize in the food processor. Throw a little hot water over the leaves. Let them swell until doubled in bulk, sprinkling with a little more water if necessary. Add to the stock and cook 15–20 minutes.

Ispanak Çorbasi

Spinach Soup

Serves 6–8 • The butter-and-flour thickening gives this Turkish soup a creamy texture, and the traditional egg-and-lemon finish gives a delicate tartness.

2 pounds fresh spinach or frozen chopped spinach, defrosted

2½ quarts meat or chicken stock (page 143) (or you may use 2 or 3 bouillon cubes)

1 large carrot, chopped

1 stalk celery, chopped

A few celery leaves, chopped

Salt and pepper

2 tablespoons butter

2 tablespoons flour

3 egg yolks

Juice of 1 lemon

If using fresh spinach, wash the leaves and put them in a pan over low heat, with the lid on. When they collapse into a soft mass, in 1–2 minutes, chop them in the food processor. If using frozen spinach, simply defrost.

Put the stock in the pan with the carrot and celery. Bring to the boil, add salt and pepper, and simmer for 20 minutes.

Melt the butter in a small pan. Add the flour, and stir vigorously over low heat for a few minutes. Beat in a ladle of the soup, then pour this back into the soup gradually, stirring constantly, and simmer over low heat for about 10 minutes. Stir in the spinach and cook about 7 minutes more. Just before serving, beat the egg yolks with the lemon juice in a bowl, then beat in a ladle of the soup. Pour this back into the soup gradually, stirring constantly. Bring the soup to just below boiling point and serve.

Havuç Çorbasi

Turkish Carrot Soup

Serves 6

1½ pounds carrots

2 quarts chicken stock (page 143) (or you may use 2 or 3 bouillon cubes)

Salt and pepper

1–2 teaspoons sugar

1–1½ teaspoons cinnamon

2 tablespoons butter

2 tablespoons flour

½ cup hot milk

3 egg yolks

Scrape, wash, and cut the carrots into medium pieces. Put them in a pan with the stock. Bring to the boil, add salt, pepper, sugar, and cinnamon, and simmer, covered, until the carrots are very soft. Blend to a cream in a food processor or blender.

Melt the butter in a separate pan. Add the flour, and stir for a few minutes over low heat. Add the milk, stirring vigorously, and cook, stirring, until the mixture thickens. Remove from the heat.

Just before serving, add the egg yolks one by one to the butter, flour, and milk mixture, beating vigorously. Then add this to the soup, mixing vigorously. Heat through, stirring constantly, until the soup thickens, but do not let it boil.

Remove from the heat at once, so that the yolks do not curdle, and serve immediately.

Shorbet Adds

Spiced Creamy Lentil Soup

Serves 6–8 • Lentil soup is an Egyptian favorite. You can buy it in the street from vendors. When I went back once during the fasting month of Ramadan, I was wandering through a long market street and stopped in a tiny café. There was only one table and I was the only customer, and all they had to offer was lentil soup. They must have been Copts. They served me in great style, offering me all kinds of extra garnishes—scallions, lemons, toasted pita croutons—rushing out to buy each one, after each new demand, from the stalls outside, then preparing them in front of me at the table.

There is no harm in making the soup in advance—even a day before.

1 large onion, chopped

3 tablespoons olive oil

3 cloves garlic, crushed

1–1½ teaspoons cumin

1–1½ teaspoons ground coriander

Pinch of ground chili pepper

1¾ cups split red lentils

Bunch of celery leaves, chopped

1 carrot, finely chopped

2 quarts chicken stock (page 143) (or you may use 2 or 3 bouillon cubes)

Salt and pepper

Juice of ½–1 lemon

TO GARNISH

1½–2 large onions, sliced

2–3 tablespoons extra-virgin olive oil

1–1½ pita breads to make croutons (optional)

3 lemons, quartered, to serve with

Soften the onion in the oil in a large saucepan. Add the garlic, cumin, coriander, and chili pepper and stir.

Add the lentils, celery leaves, and carrot, cover with stock, and simmer 30–45 minutes, until the lentils have disintegrated. Add salt and pepper, and water if the soup needs thinning. It should be quite thin, like a light cream. Stir in the lemon juice.

For the garnish, fry the onions in the oil, first covered, over low heat, stirring occasionally, then uncovered, over medium and high heat, stirring often, until crisp and very brown—almost caramelized.

Split and open out the pita breads and toast them in the oven or under the broiler, turning them over once, until they are crisp and lightly browned. Then break them into small pieces with your hands to make croutons.

Serve the soup very hot. Garnish each serving with a tablespoon of fried onions and pass the lemon wedges and croutons, if you like, for people to help themselves.

Shorbet Adds bil Hamud

Lemony Spinach and Brown Lentil Soup

Serves 6 • This is a very famous and very tasty Lebanese soup made with large brown lentils.

- 1 large onion, chopped
- 2 tablespoons olive oil
- 3 cloves garlic, finely chopped
- 1 cup large brown or green lentils (washed)
- 2 medium potatoes, diced
- 2 quarts water or chicken stock (page 143) (or you may use 2 or 3 bouillon cubes)
- 1 pound fresh spinach or frozen leaf spinach (defrosted)
- ¼ cup chopped cilantro
- Salt and pepper
- Juice of 1½ lemons, or more

In a large pan, fry the onion in the oil until soft and golden. Add the garlic and stir until it begins to color. Add the lentils and potatoes, and the water or stock, and simmer for 25 minutes, or until the lentils are tender.

If using fresh spinach, wash the leaves and put them in a pan with the lid on—and only the water that clings to them—over low heat, until the leaves collapse into a soft mass. Cut the cooked fresh or defrosted frozen spinach into thin ribbons with a knife.

Add the spinach and cilantro to the soup and season with salt and pepper. Stir well and add water, if necessary, to have a lighter consistency.

Cook a few minutes more and add lemon to taste (it should be tangy) before serving.

Variations

- For *adds bel shaghria*, add a handful of vermicelli, broken into small pieces in your hand, a few minutes before the end.
- For an alternative flavoring, fry 4 or 5 crushed garlic cloves in 2 tablespoons extra-virgin olive oil with 2 teaspoons ground coriander until the aroma rises. Stir this sauce, called *takleya*, into the soup just before serving.

Lablabi

Chickpea Soup

Serves 6–8 • This very popular Tunisian soup is eaten for breakfast. In poor families it serves as a meal during the day. Little cafés in popular areas serve it in the morning to people going off to work.

2 cups chickpeas, soaked overnight

2 quarts water

Salt

4 or 5 cloves garlic, crushed

1 teaspoon harissa (see page 464), or to taste (optional)

1–2 teaspoons ground cumin

6 slices day-old or very lightly toasted country bread

3–4 lemons cut in wedges

½ cup extra-virgin olive oil, or a bottle to pass around

Put the drained chickpeas in a pan with the water and simmer, covered, for 1½ hours, until the chickpeas are very soft, adding water to keep the chickpeas covered. Add salt, garlic, harissa, and cumin, and cook 20 minutes more.

Serve in individual soup bowls. Put a slice of toasted bread in each bowl and ladle the soup on top. Give people lemon wedges to squeeze over their bowls and pass round the bottle of olive oil for them to sprinkle on.

Shorbet Ful Nabed

Dried Fava Bean Soup

Serves 6–8 • This soup is popular in Egypt, where sick and convalescing people are encouraged to eat it to regain their health. It is plain but delicate in flavor, and highly nutritious, made with the same large fava beans as *ta'amia* (page 61), sold without their skins (they are a pale cream without their brown skins).

1¾ cups dried skinless split broad beans, soaked overnight

2 quarts chicken or meat stock (page 143) (or you may use 2 or 3 bouillon cubes), or water

4 or 5 cloves garlic, chopped

Salt and white pepper

4 tablespoons extra-virgin olive oil plus more to serve with

½ cup chopped flat-leaf parsley

2–4 lemons, quartered

Drain the beans and put them in a large saucepan with the stock or water. Add garlic and bring to the boil. Remove any scum and simmer, covered, for 2 hours, adding water if necessary, until the beans are so soft they fall apart. Then mash with a potato masher.

Season to taste with salt and pepper and stir in the oil. Bring to the boil again and add more water if necessary to thin the soup.

Serve with chopped parsley sprinkled over each individual bowl, and accompany with lemon quarters. Pass the olive oil around for people to dribble a little over their soup if they wish.

In Egypt, the soup is served with Arab bread to dip in it.

Cream of White Bean Soup

Serves 6–8 • Use dry white navy or haricot beans.

> 2 leeks
> 2 tablespoons vegetable or extra-virgin olive oil
> 1¾ cups white navy or haricot beans, soaked overnight
> 2 quarts meat or chicken stock (page 143) (or you may use 3 bouillon cubes)
> Salt and pepper

Cut off and discard the green parts of the leeks and wash the rest well, particularly in between the leaves. Cut into thin slices and sauté in oil in a large saucepan until soft.

Add the drained beans and the stock. Bring to the boil, remove the scum, cover, and simmer gently over low heat until the beans are very soft and almost falling apart, adding water if necessary. This may take 1½–2 hours.

Season to taste with salt and pepper, and simmer for a few minutes longer. Then blend to a puree in a food processor, return to the pan, add enough water if necessary to have a light, creamy texture, and bring to the boil again.

Serve hot.

Variations

• Add 2 skinned and chopped tomatoes and 1 tablespoon tomato paste at the start of the cooking. This gives the soup a soft-pink color.
• Add the juice of 1–2 lemons, and sprinkle chopped parsley and a little extra-virgin olive oil over each serving.

Shorbet Becellah

Yellow Split Pea Soup

Serves 6

1¾ cups yellow split peas (washed)

1 onion, chopped

1 stalk celery with leaves, chopped

2 quarts chicken or meat stock (page
  143) (or you may use 2 or 3 bouillon
  cubes) or water

Salt and pepper

2 teaspoons ground cardamom

Juice of ½–1 lemon

4 tablespoons finely chopped parsley

1 pita bread to make toasted croutons
  (optional)

Put the split peas in a pan with the onion and celery and cover with stock or water. Bring to the boil, remove the scum, and simmer gently, covered, until the peas are nearly disintegrating—from 1 to 1½ hours (after 25 minutes they are soft but still firm), adding water so as to have a light, creamy soup. Add salt, pepper, cardamom, and the lemon juice towards the end.

Serve hot. Garnish each serving with parsley and, if you like, with croutons.

For the croutons, split the pita bread and open it out. Toast it under the broiler, turning the pieces over once, until crisp and lightly browned. Then break them into little pieces with your hands.

Ashe Mâst va Khiar

Cold Yogurt and Cucumber Soup

Serves 6 • A refreshing summer soup from Iran.

1 quart plain whole-milk yogurt

⅔ cup sour cream

⅔ cup water

Salt and pepper

1 large cucumber, coarsely grated

4 or 5 scallions, finely chopped

6 ice cubes

A few sprigs of fresh mint, chopped

4 tablespoons black or golden raisins

Beat the yogurt and sour cream with the water. Add salt and pepper, cucumber, and scallions and stir well. Just before serving, put in the ice cubes and sprinkle with mint and raisins.

Yogurt Soups

Yogurt is a very ancient ingredient in the cooking of the Middle East. In certain soups, it is added at the end of cooking and just allowed to become hot, without boiling, so that there is no risk of curdling. Yogurt made from goat's milk does not curdle, but I don't much like the taste. When yogurt is called for in the actual cooking, precautions are taken to stabilize it so that it does not curdle (see page 113). Always use whole-milk yogurt.

Yayla Çorbasi

Yogurt Soup with Rice and Chickpeas

Serves 6 • In this lovely Turkish soup, the egg yolk and the flour prevent the yogurt from curdling. The rice is best cooked separately and added in before serving, as it gets bloated and mushy if left in the soup too long.

½ cup rice

Salt

5 cups chicken stock (page 143) (or you may use 2 bouillon cubes)

2 cups plain whole-milk or thick strained Greek-style yogurt

2 tablespoons flour

2 egg yolks

1½ tablespoons dried mint

Pepper

A 14-ounce can chickpeas, drained (optional)

Cook the rice in boiling salted water until tender, and drain.

Bring the chicken stock to the boil in a large pan.

In a bowl, beat the yogurt with the flour and egg yolks until well blended and add the mint, salt, and pepper. Pour this into the stock, beating vigorously, and bring to the boil, stirring constantly. Simmer over very low heat, until the soup thickens slightly.

Before serving, add the rice—and chickpeas, if you like—and heat through.

Variations

• Add a pinch of saffron pistils steeped in 2 tablespoons of hot water.

• An Iranian version adds ¼ teaspoon turmeric and a variety of chopped herbs, including parsley, tarragon, and chives, as well as shredded spinach.

• For a traditional optional garnish, heat 3 tablespoons butter or olive oil with 2 tablespoons dried crushed mint, and dribble a little of this over each serving. For another, heat the butter or oil with 2 teaspoons paprika.

A TALE OF GOHA

Goha was found by a friend squatting on the edge of a lake with a spoon and a pot of yogurt.

"What are you doing?" said the friend. Goha stirred a spoonful of thick yogurt in the water and said:

"I am turning the lake into yogurt."

Labaneya

Spinach Soup with Yogurt

Serves 6 • This is one of my favorite soups from Egypt.

> 1 pound fresh spinach or frozen leaf
>   spinach, defrosted
> 1 onion, chopped
> About 2 tablespoons sunflower oil
> 3 or 4 scallions, finely chopped
> 1/3 cup rice
> 1/4 teaspoon turmeric (optional)
> Salt and pepper
> 2 1/4 cups plain whole-milk yogurt
> 1 or 2 cloves garlic, crushed

Wash and drain the fresh spinach.

Sauté the onion in the oil in a large saucepan until soft and lightly colored. Add the spinach and put the lid on. Fresh spinach will crumple into a soft mass in a few moments. Cut the cooked fresh or defrosted frozen spinach up coarsely in the pan with a pointed knife.

Add the scallions and the rice and pour in 4 1/2 cups water. Add turmeric, if you like—it will give the soup a pale-yellow tinge and a faint tangy taste.

Season with salt and pepper, and simmer gently for about 18 minutes, until the rice is cooked. It should not be allowed to get too soft or mushy.

Beat the yogurt with the garlic and pour into the soup, beating vigorously. Heat through, but do not let the soup boil, or the yogurt will curdle.

Madzoune Teladmadj Abour

Armenian Yogurt Soup with Pasta

Serves 6 • A simple and delightful Armenian peasant soup.

> 1 large onion, chopped
> 2 tablespoons butter or vegetable oil
> 4 1/2 cups chicken stock (page 143) (or
>   you may use 2 or 3 bouillon cubes)
> 1–1 1/4 cups dry vermicelli, crushed into
>   small pieces in your hands
> Salt and white pepper
> 4 cups plain whole-milk yogurt
> 1/4 cup crushed dried mint

Sauté the chopped onion in the butter or oil in a large saucepan until soft. Add the stock and bring to the boil. Add the vermicelli and cook 5 minutes, until tender.

Just before serving, beat the yogurt. Pour into the soup gradually, beating vigorously, and heat to just below boiling. Do not allow the soup to boil, or it will curdle. Season to taste with salt and white pepper.

Serve, garnished with dried crushed mint.

Variations

• In another version of this soup, the yogurt is stabilized with eggs so that it can be cooked without curdling. Beat the yogurt with 2 lightly beaten eggs in a pan and bring to the boil slowly, stirring constantly in the same direction. Pour this into the stock with the vermicelli and simmer gently until the soup thickens a little.

• Instead of vermicelli use 1/2 cup pearl barley. Soak it overnight. Then drain, and simmer over low heat for 1 hour, or until the barley is swollen and soft. Continue as above. This is called *tanabour*.

Eshkeneh Shirazi

Persian Yogurt Soup with Walnuts and Fenugreek

Serves 6 • A specialty of the city of Shiraz. The herb fenugreek, called *shanbalileh,* gives the soup a very pleasant, slightly bitter flavor. It is not easy to find fresh. Chopped walnuts add texture.

3 tablespoons butter

3 tablespoons flour

4$\frac{1}{2}$ cups chicken stock (page 143) (or you may use 2 bouillon cubes)

Salt and pepper

$\frac{1}{2}$ cup walnut halves, chopped

4 tablespoons dried fenugreek leaves

3 cups plain whole-milk yogurt

Melt the butter in a large pan. Add the flour and stir over very low heat for a few minutes, until well blended. Pour in a ladle of stock, beating vigorously to keep lumps from forming. Add the rest of the stock gradually, stirring constantly. Season to taste with salt and pepper, and bring to the boil slowly, stirring often.

Add the walnuts and fenugreek and simmer, covered, for 15 minutes, until the soup thickens a little and has lost any floury taste.

Just before serving, pour the yogurt into the simmering soup, beating vigorously. Leave over low heat until it comes to just below boiling point, but do not allow the soup to boil, or it will curdle. Add a little salt and pepper, taking into account the saltiness of the stock.

Serve immediately.

Brudu bil Hout

Fish Soup with Tomatoes and Potatoes

Serves 4 • For this spicy and aromatic Tunisian soup, use any firm white fish, like cod or haddock, and serve it as a main course.

4 tomatoes, peeled and quartered

1 pound potatoes, peeled and quartered

4$\frac{1}{2}$ cups water

1 tablespoon tomato paste

$\frac{1}{4}$–$\frac{1}{2}$ teaspoon harissa (page 464), or good pinch of ground chili pepper and $\frac{1}{2}$ teaspoon paprika

$\frac{1}{2}$–$\frac{3}{4}$ teaspoon cumin

4 cloves garlic, chopped

Juice of $\frac{1}{2}$ lemon

Salt

3 tablespoons extra-virgin olive oil

1 pound white fish fillets, skinned

$\frac{1}{2}$ cup chopped flat-leaf parsley or cilantro

3 or 4 sprigs of mint, finely chopped

Put all the ingredients except the oil, fish, and herbs together in a pan. Simmer for 20 minutes, or until the potatoes are tender.

Stir in the oil and add the fish. Cook another 10 minutes. Then gently break up the fillets into smaller pieces, add the parsley or cilantro and the mint, and serve.

Shorbet Samak Beid ab Lamouna

Egg-and-Lemon Fish Soup

Serves 6 • You find the egg-and-lemon finish, also called *bel tarbeyah,* in all Middle Eastern countries. In Greece it is the famous *avgolemono.* Use skinned fish fillets—white fish such as cod or haddock—or have a mixture of seafood including peeled shrimp and, if you like, a handful of mussels (to clean and steam mussels, see page 198).

6 cups fish or chicken bouillon (use 2 fish or chicken bouillon cubes)

$\frac{1}{4}$ teaspoon saffron powder or threads or $\frac{1}{4}$ teaspoon turmeric (optional)

2 ounces vermicelli, broken into small pieces, or little pasta like orzo (they are called *lissan al assfour,* bird's tongues, in Arabic)

2 pounds skinned fish fillets, or $1\frac{1}{2}$ pounds fillets with $\frac{1}{2}$ pound shrimp and a dozen or so mussels

3 eggs

Juice of 1–2 lemons or 3–4 tablespoons white-wine vinegar

Salt and pepper

1 teaspoon cinnamon to garnish (optional)

Bring the stock to a boil in a large pan. Add the saffron, vermicelli, and fish fillets, cut into pieces, and cook 3–6 minutes, until the vermicelli is tender and the fish begins to flake. Add the seafood, if using, for the last 2–3 minutes of cooking.

In a bowl, beat the eggs with the lemon juice. Add a ladle of the liquid soup and beat well. Then pour the egg mixture into the soup and stir for a minute or so over low heat, until the soup thickens a little. Do not let it boil, or the eggs will curdle. Taste and add salt and pepper.

Serve at once, dusted, if you like, with cinnamon.

Variation

A Tunisian version has 1 tablespoon tomato paste, 2 large boiled potatoes cut into pieces, and 3 tablespoons chopped flat-leaf parsley or cilantro added to the stock.

Harira

Moroccan Bean Soup

Serves 10 • This is the much-loved national soup of Morocco. During the holy month of Ramadan, when Muslims fast between sunrise and sunset, the smell permeates the streets as every household prepares its own version to be eaten when the sound of the cannon signals the breaking of the fast at sunset. It is eaten with dates and honeyed cakes. A particular feature is the way it is given what is described in Morocco as a "velvety" touch by stirring in a yeasty batter or simply flour mixed with water.

2 marrow bones, washed (optional)

1 pound lamb or beef, cut into ½-inch pieces

1 pound small whole onions, peeled, or 2 large ones, coarsely chopped

1 cup chickpeas or beans (haricot, navy, or fava), soaked overnight

¾ cup large brown lentils, washed

1 pound ripe tomatoes, chopped

4 stalks celery with leaves, diced

1 tablespoon tomato paste

Meat Soups

Meat soups are almost like stews, substantial, with all kinds of legumes, grain, and vegetables. They are festive fare and in the home represent a meal in itself. Although, in the past, lamb and mutton were always used, beef and veal sometimes replace them today. Shoulder, breast, and especially lamb shank can be used, and beef round, chuck, or shin, the last of which gives a rich, gelatinous stock. If you are using veal, I recommend breast or shoulder, or knuckle (for its gelatinous quality). The meat is either left whole and allowed to soften and break up during the long cooking, or cut into cubes beforehand.

Marrow bones are commonly added. They are removed before serving, but the marrow is slipped into the soup, to be eaten with a piece of bread as a choice bit. In the Middle East, sheep's or calf's feet are added for their gelatinous quality.

When I was a child in Egypt, families gave their servants a daily sum with which to buy themselves, say, two piastres' worth of meat and 1 piastre's worth of vegetables. These were put in a large pot and left to cook over a very low flame on a Primus stove (*fatayel*) on the rooftops of the blocks of flats where servants' quarters were situated. Sometimes all the servants of one block pooled their purchases or money to make one large communal soup. The strong aromas entered the open windows of the flats below and enveloped the street. Employers defended themselves from the accusation that they ate well while their servants had only cheap food, by saying that the latter preferred their own. There was a great deal of truth in this, and I know many children who would sneak up to the roof terraces to share their servants' soups.

1 teaspoon pepper

½ teaspoon ground ginger

½ teaspoon saffron threads or powder

Salt

5 tablespoons all-purpose flour

¾ cup rice or crushed vermicelli
   (optional)

¾ cup chopped cilantro

⅓ cup chopped flat-leaf parsley

3 lemons, cut into wedges

Blanch the bones in boiling water for a few minutes and throw out the water. Put the meat and bones in a large pan with the onions and the chickpeas or beans. Cover with about 12 cups water and bring to the boil. Remove the scum and simmer, covered, for 1½–2 hours. Add the drained lentils and tomatoes, the celery and tomato paste, pepper, ginger, and saffron and simmer a further 15 minutes, adding water if necessary. Add salt when the lentils begin to soften. This part of the cooking can be done hours in advance.

In a small pan, beat 2 cups of cold water gradually and vigorously into the flour so as not to have any lumps. Add a ladle of broth from the soup and stir over low heat until the mixture begins to boil. Simmer for 10 minutes until it thickens.

If you are adding rice or vermicelli to the soup, it is best not to put it in long before serving, as it gets bloated and mushy. Stir in the rice and cook 15 minutes, or the crushed vermicelli and cook 5 minutes.

Pour the flour-and-broth batter into the soup, stirring vigorously. Add the chopped cilantro and parsley and cook a few minutes more, until the soup acquires a light, creamy texture.

Serve with lemon wedges.

Harira bel Djaj

Chicken and Chickpea Soup

Serves 10 • Another Moroccan soup, this one too makes a good meal to serve at a party.

A 3½-pound chicken

2 cups chickpeas, soaked in water overnight

1 large onion, coarsely chopped

5 tomatoes, peeled and chopped

Pepper

½–¾ teaspoon ground ginger

1 teaspoon cinnamon

Salt

4 ounces vermicelli, crushed into bits with your hand

½ cup chopped flat-leaf parsley

½ cup chopped cilantro

5 lemons, cut in wedges, to serve with

Put the chicken in a large pan with 3 quarts of water. Bring to the boil and remove the scum. Add the chickpeas, onion, tomatoes, and some pepper, and simmer, covered, for 1½ hours, until the chickpeas are soft. Add the ginger, cinnamon, and salt when the chickpeas begin to soften.

Lift out the chicken, remove the skin and bones, and cut up into small pieces. Return to the pan and add more water if necessary. Add the vermicelli, parsley, and cilantro and cook a few minutes until the vermicelli are tender.

Serve hot, accompanied by lemon wedges.

Variations

Here are two traditional ways of thickening the soup at the end if you wish:

• Just before serving, beat 3 eggs with a ladle of the broth from the soup, then pour this into the soup, stirring vigorously for a few seconds without letting the soup boil (or the eggs will curdle).

• Add 4 tablespoons flour mixed to a light cream with a few tablespoons cold water, and stir vigorously, then simmer for 5 to 10 minutes.

Ab Ghooshte Fasl

Iranian Bean and Vegetable Soup

Serves 6–8 • A measure of the importance of soups (*ash*) in Iran is that a cook is called an *ash-paz,* which means "maker of soup." This substantial soup with a great mix of beans makes a good winter meal. In Iran it is served with bread and bunches of fresh herbs such as cress, mint, cilantro, and also scallions, radishes, and pickles.

It is the type of soup you will find in the bazaar at the earliest hours of the morning, dished out for breakfast from huge cauldrons in which a sheep's head and feet have given their special richness, and where all the vegetables in season find their place.

$\frac{1}{3}$ **cup dried white haricot or navy beans, soaked overnight**

$\frac{1}{3}$ **cup yellow split peas, washed**

$\frac{1}{3}$ **cup black-eyed peas, washed**

$\frac{1}{3}$ **cup large brown lentils, washed**

1 pound lamb (shoulder or shank) or stewing beef, whole or in large pieces

1 large onion, thickly sliced

Salt and pepper

1 teaspoon cinnamon

$\frac{1}{2}$ **teaspoon turmeric**

$\frac{3}{4}$ **cup chopped flat-leaf parsley**

4 tomatoes, skinned

1 large eggplant, cubed

2 green bell peppers, cut into small pieces

4 small potatoes, peeled and halved

Put the drained beans and the washed peas and lentils in a large saucepan with the meat and onion and about 2 quarts of water. Bring to the boil, remove the scum, and simmer for an hour or more, until the meat and beans are very tender, adding salt, pepper, and spices when the beans have begun to soften.

Take out the meat, cut it up into small pieces, and put it back into the pan. Put in the vegetables and cook $\frac{1}{2}$ hour more, or until the vegetables are done, adding water if necessary.

Variation

You may add a handful of dried apricots or pitted prunes at the same time as the meat.

Dügün Çorbasi

Turkish Wedding Soup

Serves 8 • In this famous Turkish soup, the stock is thickened first with a butter-and-flour roux, and then again with an egg-and-lemon finish.

- 1 or 2 marrow bones, washed (optional)
- 1½ pounds lamb or beef, cubed
- 10 cups water
- 1 carrot
- 1 onion
- Salt and pepper
- 7 tablespoons butter
- ¼ cup flour
- 3 egg yolks
- Juice of 1 lemon
- 2 teaspoons paprika or ½ teaspoon chili-pepper flakes (optional)

Blanch the marrow bones, if using, in boiling water for a few minutes, and throw the water out. Put the meat and bones in a pan with the water and bring to the boil. Remove the scum, and add the carrot, onion, salt, and pepper. Simmer for 1½–2 hours, or until the meat is so tender it falls apart. Lift out the meat, bones, and vegetables. Cut the meat into small pieces and return to the pan. Push the marrow out of the bones into the pan.

In another pan, melt 4 tablespoons of the butter and stir in the flour. Add a ladle of the meat stock, stirring vigorously to keep lumps from forming. Bring to the boil, stirring constantly, then add another ladle of stock, and bring to the boil again, stirring. Pour into the soup pan, stirring vigorously, and simmer for at least 10 minutes.

Just before serving, beat the egg yolks and lemon juice in a small bowl, then beat in a ladle of the hot stock. Pour this into the simmering soup, stirring vigorously. Heat through, but do not let it boil, or the eggs will curdle.

Melt the remaining 3 tablespoons butter, stir in the paprika or chili-pepper flakes, and dribble a little over each individual serving.

WEDDING SONG

Your father, oh beautiful one!
Has so often screamed and shouted,
And lowered the price of your dowry,
And said, "My daughters are beautiful!"

MASPÉRO,
CHANSONS POPULAIRES

Shorbet el Fata

Bread Soup

Serves 6 • This Egyptian feast-day soup which is eaten seventy days after Ramadan is made of the leftover meat and bones of a sacrificial lamb. It is the custom to slay a lamb in the name of God, and to distribute the meat among the poor. The family of the donor must eat some of the lamb in order to benefit from the sacrifice, and this soup is a good way of doing so.

1 or 2 marrow bones (washed)

1 pound lamb, cubed

2 quarts water

Salt and pepper

⅓ cup rice, washed and drained

3 rounds small Arab or pita breads

2–4 cloves garlic, crushed

3 tablespoons butter or vegetable oil

3–4 tablespoons wine vinegar

3 tablespoons chopped flat-leaf parsley

Blanch the marrow bones in boiling water for a few minutes, then throw out the water. Put the meat and bones in a large pan with the 2 quarts water. Bring to the boil, remove the scum, add salt and pepper, and simmer for about 2 hours, until the meat is tender. Add water as necessary. There should be plenty of liquid.

Twenty minutes before serving add the rice, and continue to simmer until it is cooked but not mushy.

Split open the Arab or pita breads. Toast them under the broiler or in the oven until they are crisp and lightly browned. Arrange in the bottom of a soup tureen. Fry the crushed garlic in hot butter or oil until the aroma rises. Sprinkle with vinegar, bring to the boil, and pour over the toasted bread. Allow the toast to

become well soaked; then pour the soup over it and serve, garnished with parsley.

This method of serving soup over toasted and seasoned bread is a familiar one in the Middle East, and is also used with stews.

Armenian Meat Soup with Bulgur

Serves 6

1½ pound lamb shank or knuckle of veal

2 quarts cold water

1 carrot

1 onion

1 teaspoon ground cinnamon

Salt and pepper

½ cup bulgur (cracked wheat)

3 tablespoons finely chopped parsley to garnish

Put the meat in a large pan with the water and bring to the boil. Remove the scum. Add the carrot and onion, both whole, and the cinnamon. Season with salt and pepper, and simmer gently, covered, for 1½–2 hours, or until the meat is very tender, adding water as needed. Remove the vegetables. Lift out the meat, cut it up into pieces, and put it back in the pan. Add the bulgur and simmer for about 15 minutes, until it is tender. Add more water if the porridge becomes too thick. The bulgur will absorb a lot of liquid and expand considerably.

Serve garnished with parsley.

Egg Dishes

BEID

Eggs have a very important place in the Middle Eastern kitchen. In medieval times, they were used—poached or hard-boiled—as a garnish for various types of dishes, and this custom has continued to the present day. In Islamic Spain omelets were ubiquitous. Arab omelets are more like a flan or a cake, firm right through, and bursting with filling—not unlike the Spanish *tortilla,* to which they are related. They are very popular, served hot or cold, as an appetizer, a first course, a main dish, or a side dish. They are also picnic favorites. They are called *kuku* in Persia, *eggah* in Egypt, and pronounced *ajja* in other Arab countries.

Beid Masluq

Hard-Boiled Eggs with Cumin

Prepare hard-boiled eggs in the usual way. Peel them, cut them in half, and sprinkle with salt and ground cumin. Or serve whole, accompanied by a small bowl of salt mixed with about twice as much cumin to dip the eggs in. Serve as an appetizer.

Vendors sell the eggs in the street accompanied by little cornets of rolled-up newspaper filled with a thimbleful of seasoning—a mix of salt, cumin, and sometimes coriander—to dip in. In North Africa, the eggs are peeled, then gently simmered in water with a little saffron or turmeric and salt. This gives them a brilliant yellow color.

Beid bi Tom

Fried Eggs with Garlic and Lemon

Serves 3–6

2 tablespoons butter
2 cloves garlic, crushed
Juice of ½ lemon or 1 teaspoon sumac
6 eggs
Crushed dried mint to garnish

Melt the butter in a large skillet, or use 2 smaller ones. Add the garlic and lemon or sumac. Slide in the eggs, previously broken into a bowl, and continue to fry gently.

Rub some dried mint in the palm of your hand, letting it sprinkle over the eggs. When the whites are set, remove the pan from the heat, sprinkle lightly with salt, and serve.

Hard-Boiled Eggs

In Egypt, during the numerous festivals, such as the Mûlid el Nabi, which celebrates the birth of the Prophet, the pilgrimage to the sacred well of Zemzem, or the Cham el Nessim—a festival in honor of nature which originates in ancient Egypt and signifies "breathing the new fresh air"—people went out on picnics. They filled baskets with food and spent days and nights in public gardens or on visits to sacred places and the tombs of saints. They would settle down to enjoy the contents of their baskets while they listened to reciters of romances recounting the tales of *Abou-Zeyd, El Zahir,* and *Alf Leyleh wa-Leyleh (A Thousand and One Nights)*, and watched conjurers, buffoons, and dancers. Hard-boiled eggs—beautifully flavored and sometimes dyed red or yellow—have since time immemorial taken pride of place in the picnic baskets.

Çilbir

Poached Eggs with Yogurt

Serves 1–2 • This Turkish way of embellishing poached eggs is also good with fried eggs.

- 1 tablespoon vinegar to poach the eggs
- Salt
- 4 tablespoons plain whole-milk yogurt, at room temperature
- 1 small clove garlic, crushed (optional)
- 1 tablespoon butter
- ½ teaspoon paprika
- 2 eggs

Fill a pan with enough water to cover the eggs. Add vinegar and salt, bring to the boil, then reduce the heat to lowest.

Beat the yogurt with the garlic. Melt the butter with the paprika.

Break each egg into a cup and slide it into the pan of water. Cook for 1–2 minutes, until the whites have set. Lift out with a perforated spoon and serve at once.

Sprinkle with a little salt, pour 2 tablespoons of yogurt over each egg, and dribble butter and paprika over the yogurt.

Variation

For a Lebanese mountain dish, *beyd bi laban,* heat 2 tablespoons olive oil in a skillet, break in the eggs, and sprinkle with salt. Cook over low heat, stirring gently, to scramble them lightly. Before they set, when they are still runny, stir in 1 cup yogurt (at room temperature) and serve with bread.

Beid bi Khal

Scrambled Eggs with Vinegar

Serves 4 • In a skillet, soften 2 or 3 crushed garlic cloves over low heat in 2 tablespoons butter until they just begin to color. Beat 6 eggs lightly and season with salt and pepper. Pour into the pan and cook over gentle heat, stirring constantly. Add 2–3 tablespoons wine vinegar and stir to a creamy consistency.

Beid bi Tamatem

Eggs with Tomatoes

Serves 4

- 2 cloves garlic, crushed
- 1 tablespoon extra-virgin olive oil
- 1 pound tomatoes, peeled and chopped
- 1 teaspoon sugar
- Salt and pepper
- 2 tablespoons chopped mint leaves or flat-leaf parsley
- 4 eggs

In a large skillet, heat the garlic in the oil, then add the tomatoes, sugar, salt, and pepper.

Cook for 10 minutes and stir in the mint or parsley. Crack the eggs open and drop them whole into this sauce. Cook until they set.

Variations

- You may stir the eggs a little to have a creamy scramble.
- Fry 1 chopped onion in 2 tablespoons of oil till golden before adding the garlic.

Beid bi Gebna Maqli

Fried Cheese with Eggs

Serves 1 • This is usually prepared in individual portions in two-handled frying pans and served in the same pans straight from the fire. You can, of course, use one large frying pan, or as many as are convenient. In the Middle East, the hard, dry Greek cheeses kashkaval, kefalotyri, or kasseri and the white, firm, slightly rubbery halumi are used.

> 1 thick slice cheese
> Flour (optional)
> 1 tablespoon butter or extra-virgin olive oil
> Juice of ½ lemon (optional)
> 1 egg
> Salt and pepper

Some people dip the slice of cheese in flour before frying it, but this is not really necessary.

Fry the cheese in hot butter or oil. When it begins to melt, sprinkle with lemon juice if you like, and open the egg over it. Cook until the white sets. Sprinkle lightly with salt and pepper (taking into consideration the saltiness of the cheese), and serve piping hot.

Feta Cheese with Egg

Serves 1

> 1 clove garlic
> 1 teaspoon ground coriander
> 2 tablespoons extra-virgin olive oil
> 2 slices feta cheese
> 1 egg
> 1 tomato, chopped (optional)

In a small frying pan, fry the garlic with the coriander in 1 tablespoon oil for moments only, until the aroma rises.

Lay the slices of cheese on top and leave over medium heat until the cheese begins to fall apart. Break open the egg over it, and if you like, surround with chopped tomato.

Cook until the egg is done to your liking. My cousin Steve, who gave me this recipe, puts a lid on so that the top of the egg becomes opaque and misty. Eat with a dribble of the remaining oil.

One of a large variety of beliefs and practices connected with the "evil eye":

"When it has been proved that the evil eye has been given, steps may be taken to detect the guilty person. A common expedient is to hold an egg between the two palms and to press upon it as the name of each suspect is spoken. At the name of the guilty one the egg will break."

DONALDSON, *THE WILD RUE*

Shakshouka

Eggs with Bell Peppers and Tomatoes

Serves 4 • A dish of Tunisian origin that is eaten in most Middle Eastern countries, it makes an ideal snack meal. There are many versions. I like this one, called "nablia," which is a specialty of Nabeul.

> 2 red or green bell peppers, cut into ribbons
>
> 3 tablespoons vegetable or extra-virgin olive oil
>
> 3–4 cloves garlic, sliced
>
> 4 medium tomatoes, peeled and cut in quarters
>
> Salt and pepper
>
> 4 eggs

In a large skillet over medium heat, fry the peppers in the oil, stirring and turning them over, until they soften. Add the garlic, and when it just begins to color, add the tomatoes, salt, and pepper. Cook until the tomatoes soften.

Drop the eggs in whole, season again lightly with salt, and cook until the eggs set. Alternatively, you may stir the eggs gently and cook until creamy.

Serve hot with bread.

Variations

• In Tunisia they add ½ teaspoon harissa (see page 464), or ¼ teaspoon ground chili pepper and 1 teaspoon caraway seeds, or 1 preserved lemon peel (see page 459), cut into pieces, and 2 tablespoons capers.

• Add 3 medium-sized cooked potatoes, cut into pieces.

• Fry 2 sliced zucchini or 1 small eggplant, cut into cubes, at the same time as the peppers.

• Fry 1 sliced onion in the oil till golden, instead of the garlic.

Shakshouka with Merguez

Serves 4 • This makes a lovely snack meal. Merguez are spicy North African sausages. If you cannot find them, you can substitute hot Cajun or Creole sausages.

> 8 merguez sausages
>
> 3 tablespoons vegetable or extra-virgin olive oil
>
> 3 or 4 cloves garlic, chopped
>
> 1 pound tomatoes, peeled and chopped
>
> Salt and pepper
>
> 4 eggs

Fry the sausages in the oil in a large skillet, turning them over for 1–2 minutes. Add the garlic, and when the aroma rises, add the tomatoes. Sprinkle with salt and pepper and cook for about 15 minutes, until the sauce is reduced.

Break in the eggs and let them cook, whole, in the sauce.

Serve hot with good bread.

Variation

In Tunisia they add ¼–½ teaspoon harissa (see page 464) to the tomato sauce.

Fried Eggs with Chicken Livers

Serves 4

8 ounces chicken livers

2 tablespoons butter or vegetable oil

Salt and pepper

$1/2$ teaspoon ground cinnamon

4 eggs

Toss the chicken livers briefly in hot butter or oil in a large skillet over medium-high heat. Season with salt, pepper, and cinnamon. The livers must be brown outside but still pink and juicy inside and slightly undercooked.

Break the eggs over the livers, season lightly with salt and pepper, and cook until set. You can leave the eggs whole or scramble them slightly until creamy.

Cooking an Arab Omelet in the Oven

An Arab omelet, served hot or cold and cut into wedges or small squares, makes good party food. A large quantity can be baked in the oven, in greased oven dishes. The cooking time in a preheated 325°F oven varies from $1/2$ to 1 hour, depending on the size of the dish and the type of filling. The omelet should be firm, not runny, even in the center. Cover the dish with foil or a lid to begin with, then uncover for the final 15 minutes to allow the omelet to brown.

Eggah bi Bassal
Onion and Herb Omelet

Serves 2 • A simple and delicious snack, it can also be served as an elegant appetizer (see variation).

1 large onion, coarsely chopped

3 tablespoons vegetable or extra-virgin olive oil

4 eggs, lightly beaten

2 tablespoons chopped flat-leaf parsley

2 tablespoons chopped cilantro

1 tablespoon chopped mint

Salt and pepper

Fry the onion in 2 tablespoons of the oil until soft and golden. Mix with the eggs and the other ingredients.

Heat the remaining oil in a preferably non-stick frying pan. Pour in the egg mixture and cook over medium heat. As soon as the bottom sets, put under the broiler and cook the other side until the top is firm and lightly browned.

Serve hot or cold.

Variation

You can do tiny omelets like little pancakes to serve as finger food. Make a larger quantity and pour by the tablespoon, in batches, into the frying pan, turning over to brown the other side.

Eggah bi Gebna

Cheese Omelet

Serves 6 • This simple herby omelet is particularly delicious. Use a good-quality feta cheese, or try another cheese. It can serve as a main dish or an appetizer.

> 6 ounces feta cheese, mashed with a fork
> 8 eggs, lightly beaten
> 6 scallions, finely sliced
> 4 or 5 sprigs of mint, finely chopped
> 1 cup chopped flat-leaf parsley
> Pepper
> 3 tablespoons extra-virgin olive oil

Lightly beat together all the ingredients except the oil in a bowl.

Heat 2 tablespoons of the oil in a large nonstick skillet. When it begins to sizzle, pour in the egg mixture. Cook over low heat for about 10 minutes, or until the bottom sets.

Dribble the remaining oil over the top of the omelet and cook under the broiler for a few minutes, until lightly browned. Serve hot or cold, cut in wedges like a cake.

Eggah bi Betingan

Eggplant Omelet

Serves 2 • This is one of my favorites.

> 2 eggplants, weighing about 1 pound total
> 2 eggs, lightly beaten
> Salt and pepper
> Pinch of nutmeg
> 1 tablespoon vegetable oil

Roast the eggplants under the broiler and mash them in a colander so as to get rid of the juices (see page 63). Then beat with the eggs and add salt, pepper, and nutmeg.

In a preferably nonstick skillet, heat the oil and pour in the egg mixture. Cook for a few minutes on low heat, until the bottom begins to set and feels loose from the skillet when you shake the pan. Put under the broiler and cook until the top is firm and lightly colored. Alternatively, turn the omelet over by slipping it onto a plate and dropping it back, upside down, in the skillet to cook the other side.

Variations

• For 6 servings, fry 1 chopped onion in 2 tablespoons of oil till golden, add 5 peeled and chopped tomatoes, and cook for 15 minutes, until reduced to a thick sauce. Mix with the mashed eggplants and 4 eggs and proceed as above.

• For 6 servings, fry 1 chopped onion in 2 tablespoons vegetable or olive oil until golden, and add 2 crushed garlic cloves. Deep-fry briefly or broil 2 eggplants cut into cubes (see page 63). Drain on paper towels, then mix with 4 lightly beaten eggs, season with salt and pepper. Then proceed as above.

Eggah bi Kousa

Zucchini Omelet

Serves 2

3 zucchini (about 1 pound total)
Salt
1 large onion, chopped
3 tablespoons vegetable oil
2 eggs, lightly beaten
2 tablespoons chopped flat-leaf parsley
Juice of ½ lemon
Pepper
Pinch of nutmeg or allspice

Trim the zucchini and boil in salted water until very soft, then drain. Chop them and mash them to a pulp in a colander so as to get rid of the juices.

Fry the onion in 2 tablespoons of the oil until golden and mix with the zucchini, the eggs, and the rest of the ingredients except the remaining oil.

Heat the remaining oil in a preferably nonstick skillet and pour in the egg mixture. Cook over medium heat until the bottom sets. Then put under the broiler and cook until lightly browned and firm on top.

Serve hot or cold.

Variation

You can do tiny omelets like little pancakes to serve as finger food. Pour the mixture by the tablespoon in the skillet and turn over to brown the other side. Do them in batches.

Eggah bi Eish wa Kousa

Bread and Zucchini Omelet

Serves 6 • Serve this as a main dish with salads and yogurt.

1 medium-sized onion, chopped
3 tablespoons butter or vegetable oil
1 pound zucchini cut into ¼-inch slices
6 eggs
3 slices good country bread, crusts removed, soaked in a little milk or water
3 tablespoons chopped parsley
3 tablespoons chopped mint
Salt and pepper

In a large skillet, sauté the onion in 2 tablespoons butter or oil until soft and just beginning to color. Add the zucchini slices, and sauté, stirring and turning them over, until soft and lightly colored.

Beat the eggs and add the soaked bread, squeezed dry, crumbling it in your hand. Stir in the fried onion and the zucchini, and the chopped parsley and mint. Season lightly with salt and pepper and mix well.

Heat the remaining butter or oil in the cleaned skillet and pour in the egg mixture. Cook gently over very low heat for about 20 minutes, until the eggs are set. Dry and brown the top lightly under a broiler; or invert the omelet by slipping it first onto a plate and carefully dropping it back upside down into the skillet to cook the other side.

Eggah bel Kharshouf

Artichoke Omelet

Serves 2–4 • An elegant and tasty omelet. Use the frozen artichoke bottoms from Egypt which you can find in Middle Eastern stores, or hearts, which are more common in supermarkets.

7 ounces frozen artichoke bottoms or hearts (½ of 14-ounce package), defrosted
Salt
4 eggs
Pepper
1 clove garlic, crushed
A few sprigs of dill, finely chopped
A squeeze of lemon juice
1–2 tablespoons olive oil

Boil the artichoke bottoms or hearts in salted water to cover for a few minutes only, until tender, then drain. Chop and mash them, removing any tough fibers from the hearts.

Lightly beat the eggs with a little salt and pepper, the garlic, dill, and lemon juice, then mix in the mashed artichokes.

Heat the oil in a nonstick skillet, pour in the egg mixture, and cook over low heat with the lid on until the bottom sets. Put under the broiler and cook the top until lightly colored.

Serve hot or cold.

Variation

For a fava bean omelet, replace the artichoke bottoms with ½ pound fresh or frozen fava beans. I use a skinned frozen variety that you can find in Middle Eastern stores.

Eggah bi Korrat

Leek Omelet

Serves 4–6 • This is an Egyptian favorite.

1 pound leeks
3 tablespoons butter or extra-virgin olive oil
1 or 2 teaspoons sugar
Juice of ½ lemon
Salt and pepper
4 eggs

Trim off the roots of the leeks and cut off the tough green tops. Make a slash along the leeks to the center to be able to wash carefully between the leaves. Cut into thin slices. Put the leeks in a large pan with 2 tablespoons of the butter or oil. Add sugar, lemon juice, salt, and pepper. Put the lid on and let the leeks stew in their own juice for 20 minutes, or until very soft, stirring occasionally.

Beat the eggs lightly with a little salt, then stir in the leeks.

Heat the remaining butter or oil in the cleaned skillet and pour in the leek mixture. Cook, covered with a lid, over low heat until the bottom sets. Then put under the broiler to cook the top until firm and lightly colored.

Serve hot or cold.

Variation

Instead of sautéing, the leeks can be cut into large pieces, boiled in salted water until soft, and drained. Press the water out and chop in the food processor, then mix with the eggs.

Maacouda bi Batata

Potato and Parsley Omelet

Serves 4 • This Tunisian specialty is easy to make and quite delicious.

1 pound mealy potatoes, peeled
Salt
1 large onion, chopped
3 tablespoons vegetable or extra-virgin olive oil
3 eggs, lightly beaten
¼ cup chopped flat-leaf parsley
Pepper

Boil the potatoes in salted water, then drain and mash them. Fry the onion in 2 tablespoons of the oil till soft and golden, stirring occasionally.

Beat the eggs into the potatoes, then stir in the fried onion and the parsley, and season with salt and pepper.

Heat the remaining oil in a preferably nonstick skillet and pour in the potato mixture. Cook, covered, over low heat until the bottom sets. Then put under the broiler to cook the top until firm and lightly colored.

Serve hot or cold.

Variations

• For a Persian version, *kuku-ye sibzamini,* use 6 chopped scallions or a bunch of chives instead of the fried onions.
• For a potato *ojja,* fry the onion till golden, add 4 peeled and chopped tomatoes and the thinly sliced potatoes, and cook until the potatoes are soft. Then stir in the lightly beaten eggs and cook until set.

Tajin Sibnakh

Haricot Bean and Spinach Omelet

Serves 4 • In Tunisia, where egg dishes are ubiquitous, they call this a *tajin* because it is cooked in a clay dish of that name. It can be eaten hot or cold.

1 pound spinach
1 onion, chopped
2 tablespoons extra-virgin olive oil
2 teaspoons tomato paste
3 eggs
A 15-ounce can haricot or cannellini beans, drained
½ cup grated Gruyère cheese
Salt and pepper

Wash the spinach and only remove the stalks if thick and tough. Put the leaves in a large pan over low heat with the lid on and only the water that clings to them. They will crumple into a soft mass within a minute. Drain and press all the water out in a colander, then cut into ribbons.

Fry the onion in 1 tablespoon of the olive oil until golden, then stir in the tomato paste.

Lightly beat the eggs in a bowl. Add the spinach, onion, drained beans, and Gruyère. Season with salt and pepper and mix well.

Heat the remaining oil in a preferably nonstick frying pan and pour the mixture in. Cook over low heat, with the lid on, for 8–10 minutes, until the eggs set at the bottom. Then put under the broiler to dry and firm the top.

Kuku-ye Sabsi

*Spinach and Herb Omelet
with Walnuts and Raisins*

Serves 6 • The traditional Iranian New Year's
Day specialty is made with a number of green
herbs and leaves. Its greenness is a symbol of
fruitfulness in the coming year, bringing prosperity and happiness. Any favored herbs, such
as flat-leaf parsley, dill, chervil, tarragon,
chives, and cilantro, may be used.

6–8 eggs

4 ounces spinach, shredded

8 scallions, chopped

½–⅔ cup mixed chopped fresh herbs

3 tablespoons chopped walnuts
    (optional)

2 tablespoons raisins (optional)

Salt and pepper

2 tablespoons butter or vegetable oil

Lightly beat the eggs with the rest of the ingredients except the butter or oil.

Grease an ovenproof dish (about 10 inches)
with butter or oil and pour in the egg mixture.
Bake in a preheated 325°F oven for 45 minutes, covering the dish for the first 25 minutes,
until the eggs are firm with a golden crust on
top. Alternatively, cook the *kuku* in a large
preferably nonstick skillet. When the eggs have
set on the bottom, brown the top under a hot
broiler.

Serve hot or cold as a first course, accompanied by yogurt.

Variation

Use lettuce leaves instead of spinach, and barberries (a sharp red berry) instead of raisins,
and flavor with ½ teaspoon cinnamon and a
pinch of turmeric.

Eggah bi Sabaneh

Spinach Omelet

Serves 6 • Here is a simple Egyptian omelet
with a pleasant texture, to serve as a snack.

1 pound spinach, fresh or frozen

6 eggs

Salt and pepper

Pinch of nutmeg

A 15-ounce can chickpeas, drained
    (optional)

1½ tablespoons butter or vegetable oil

Wash the fresh spinach thoroughly and drain it.
Put it in a pan with no added water and the lid
on, and cook over low heat until the leaves
crumple to a soft mass. Drain and press the excess water out. Some people chop the leaves,
but I don't. If you are using frozen spinach,
allow to defrost, and press the water out.

Beat the eggs lightly with the spinach. Mix
well, adding salt, pepper, and nutmeg, and the
drained chickpeas if you like. Heat the butter
or oil in a preferably nonstick skillet and pour
in the egg mixture. Cook, covered, over low
heat until the bottom sets. Then put under the
broiler and cook until the top is firm and
lightly browned.

Serve hot or cold.

Variation

Add 3 peeled and chopped tomatoes, sautéed
in a little oil with 2 or 3 crushed garlic cloves.

Eggah bi Lahma

Meat Eggah

Serves 6 • This substantial omelet can be served as a main dish accompanied by salad.

    1 large onion, chopped
    4 tablespoons vegetable oil
    $\frac{1}{2}$ pound lean ground beef or veal
    Salt and pepper
    $\frac{1}{2}$ teaspoon allspice
    1 teaspoon cumin
    6 eggs
    $\frac{1}{4}$ cup chopped flat-leaf parsley
    1 large potato, chopped or grated
        (optional)

In a large, preferably nonstick skillet, fry the onion in 3 tablespoons oil until golden. Add the ground meat, crush it with a fork, and stir and turn it over for about 8–10 minutes, until it changes color, adding salt and pepper and the spices.

Beat the eggs lightly. Drain off any fat through a sieve from the meat and onion, then add them to the eggs along with the parsley. Add the potato, if you like, and mix well.

Heat the remaining oil in the cleaned skillet. Pour in the egg mixture, reduce the heat to as low as possible, and cover with a lid. Cook for about 20 minutes, until the eggs have set and only the top is still runny. Put the frying pan under a hot broiler until the top is firm and lightly browned.

Turn out and serve hot or cold, cut into wedges like a cake.

Variation

Use a boiled and mashed potato instead of a chopped or grated one.

Eggah bi Ferakh wa Rishta

Chicken and Pasta Cake

Serves 6 • Cardamom gives a delicate Arab touch to this substantial Egyptian omelet which can be served as a main dish.

    2 quarts chicken stock (see page 143)
        (or you may use 2 bouillon cubes)
    Salt
    12 ounces dry tagliatelle, broken with
        your hands into small pieces
    4 eggs, lightly beaten
    12 ounces cooked and boned chicken,
        cut into small pieces
    1 teaspoon cardamom seeds or powder
    Salt and pepper
    2 tablespoons butter or oil
    2 tablespoons chopped flat-leaf parsley

Bring the chicken stock to the boil, adding a little salt. Put in the noodles or tagliatelle and cook until only just tender, then drain.

Beat the eggs in a large bowl. Add the chicken, noodles, and cardamom seeds or powder. Season with salt and pepper, and mix well.

Heat the butter or oil in a large, preferably nonstick skillet. Pour in the egg mixture and cook over very low heat for about 25 minutes, or until it is set and only the top is runny. Dry and brown the top under a hot broiler. Turn out onto a serving dish, and serve garnished with chopped parsley.

Variation

Alternatively, you can bake the dish in a preheated 350°F oven for about 30–45 minutes, or until firm and lightly browned on top.

Ojja bil Merguez

*Scrambled Eggs with Potatoes
and Spicy Sausages*

Serves 6 • A hot and peppery Tunisian omelet.

- 3–4 tablespoons extra-virgin olive oil
- 4 medium potatoes, cubed or diced
- 1–2 tablespoons tomato paste
- ½ teaspoon harissa (see page 464), or 1 teaspoon paprika and a good pinch of ground chili pepper
- 4 cloves garlic, chopped
- 2 teaspoons crushed caraway seed
- 6 small merguez or other spicy sausages, sliced
- 6 eggs, lightly beaten
- Salt

Heat the olive oil in a large frying pan. Add the potatoes and sauté lightly. Add tomato paste, the harissa diluted in a drop of water or the paprika and chili pepper, the garlic, and the caraway seeds. Pour in just enough water to cover, and cook over low heat for about 10 minutes. Add the sausages and cook for a further 15 minutes. Let the liquid evaporate over high heat.

Pour in the eggs, add salt, and cook, stirring, until the eggs set to a soft, creamy consistency. Serve hot.

French-Style Omelets with an Oriental Flavor

Serves 2 • Make a plain French omelet with 4 eggs: Beat the eggs lightly, and season very lightly with salt and pepper. Heat a skillet (about 10 inches). Add a tablespoon of butter and shake the pan to allow it to run all over the base. When it starts to sizzle, but before it has had a chance to brown, pour in the eggs, stir a little, and when they start to set on the bottom, lift the edge up with a fork and tip the pan to allow the liquid from the top to run underneath. As soon as the eggs are no longer liquid but still very moist on top, remove the pan from the heat. Pour the prepared filling on one half of the omelet and fold the other half over the filling. Serve at once.

Fillings for a 4-Egg Omelet

Chicken Livers. Cut 3 chicken livers into small pieces, and sauté gently in a little butter for 2 or 3 minutes. Season to taste with salt, pepper, and a pinch of ground cinnamon.

Onions and Tomatoes. Sauté ½ chopped onion in 1 tablespoon vegetable oil until softened. Add 1 or 2 crushed garlic cloves. When the garlic just begins to color, add 3 skinned and chopped tomatoes. Season to taste with salt and pepper, or a pinch of ground chili pepper or chili flakes, and cook gently until the tomatoes are almost reduced to a pulp.

Spinach. Frozen spinach (defrosted), either leaf or chopped, will do. Fry 1 crushed garlic clove with ½–1 teaspoon ground coriander in 1 tablespoon butter or vegetable oil. Add about 2 ounces spinach and cook for a few minutes with the lid on until softened. Season with salt and pepper.

Fish and Seafood

SAMAK

"A remedy for a man who is 'tied' by his enemies, and made impotent. He must go to a quack, who will say: 'There is something written against you that has been eaten by a fish in the sea. I can release you from your trouble by obtaining the fish for a fee!' The quack finds a fish, writes a curse, perhaps on a piece of bread, puts it in the mouth of the fish, and delivers it to the patient. The latter will be cured."

FROM AN ANCIENT BOOK OF EGYPTIAN FOLK MEDICINE

One of my great-uncles was a kabbalist to whom people came with all kinds of problems, such as impotence and sickness. He cured them with amulets and tiny scrolls of paper which he hung round their necks. Sometimes he got a fish to swallow his magic words and threw it back into the water. In some parts of the Middle East, fish is still believed to have magical properties. Tunisians in particular—who are the greatest fish-eaters—believe it to be highly beneficial. The day after their wedding, couples are encouraged to step over a large fish as an assurance of happiness and a protection from evil. Today, the shape of a fish has become a symbol. Embroidered on material and carved in metal, it is believed to ward off the evil eye. In Egypt, one felt compelled to eat fish for the first meal in a new home. In Persia, fish is eaten on New Year's Eve to cleanse the people from evil, while Jews display the head alone in the center of the New Year table in the hope that Jews will always be at the "head."

The medieval cookery manual of al-Baghdadi gives a few recipes for fish, both fresh- and saltwater, but without specifying any varieties. Even today, recipes for fish can usually be applied to any of a number of varieties. When I ask what fish to use for a certain recipe, the answer is usually "Any fish you like" or "Any fish will do." Nevertheless, certain fish are more suitable for a particular dish and method of preparation, because of their size and firmness of flesh or oiliness and flavor.

Most of these dishes were, of course, originally evolved for fish from the Mediterranean and neighboring seas. Favorite fish are sea bass, called *loukoz,* which is the most prestigious and expensive; red mullet, called *barbunya* by the Turks and Sultan Ibrahim by the Arabs; sea bream or daurade, called *morgan* or *arous,* of which there are twenty-two species, big and small; sole, called *samak Moussa* after Moses (because of its thinness, it is said to have been cut in half when Moses separated the Red Sea). Other popular fish are gurnard or sea robin, John Dory, hake and tuna, monkfish, swordfish, sardines, anchovies, ray, skate, eels, whiting, mackerel and gray mullet, turbot, flounder and grouper, snapper, bluefish, and pompano. You can find most in America today, but you can anyway substitute fish from other seas. Freshwater fish like sturgeon, trout, salmon, eels, lampreys, and shad are also highly regarded.

The most common ways of cooking fish in the Middle East are to broil or roast it or to dip it in flour and deep-fry, and the usual dressing is lemon juice and a dribble of olive oil. But there are also many stunning special dishes. The only problem is that fish is usually overcooked. The cooking times I give are more in line with our tastes today.

Cleaning and Preparing Fish

Fishmongers clean and prepare the fish as you want it, but here is how to do it if you have to.

Snip off the fins with kitchen scissors. To remove the scales, hold the fish by the tail and scrape them off the wrong way with the blunt edge or the back of a knife or with a special fish-scraper. Do it over layers of newspaper or in the sink, as the scales fly. Rinse under cold water. Slit the belly from the head down and pull out the guts, then rinse the cavity. To skin a flat fish, make a cut across the skin just above the tail, ease it a little with a pointed knife, and pull it off.

It is customary in the Middle East to salt the fish about half an hour before cooking.

Samak Meshwi

BROILED FISH

A favorite Middle Eastern way of eating fish is barbecued over embers, but this can also be done indoors, over the heat of a pumice-stone rock grill or under an electric or gas broiler. Whole fish, steaks, and fillets are all excellent cooked quickly in the intense heat, before their juices have leached out and the flesh has dried up. They need only to be sprinkled with salt and brushed with oil before cooking, but you may like to try marinating in one of the marinades on the next page for $1/2$–1 hour. A larger whole fish should be slashed in 2 or 3 places on either side, in the thickest part, so that it cooks evenly. You may also stuff the belly with herbs and thin slices of lemon.

The grill must be well oiled and hot before the fish is placed on it, to prevent it from sticking. The fire must have died down to glowing embers, and a broiler must be turned on well in advance so that it is very hot. Flat fish and fillets should be placed near to the source of heat (2–3 inches away). Whole fish should be placed farther away; their skins will prevent them from drying out. But you can vary the distance depending on the size, to get a crisp, brown skin and tender juicy flesh. To find out if a fish is done, cut into the thickest part with a pointed knife. It is done when the flesh has turned opaque right through and when it begins to flake.

Serve grilled fish accompanied with lemon wedges and, if you like, one of the dressings or sauces on the following pages.

Marinades, Dressings, and Sauces for Broiled or Grilled and Fried Fish

Oil and Lemon Dressing

Serves 4 • This is the common all-purpose dressing for fish. It can also be used as a marinade.

Juice of 1 lemon
6 tablespoons extra-virgin olive oil
Salt and pepper
3 tablespoons finely chopped flat-leaf
   parsley to garnish

Mix the lemon juice, oil, salt, and pepper. Soak the fish in the marinade. Or pour over the fish when serving and garnish with parsley.

Tomato and Chili Dressing

Serves 4 • This is particularly delicious with grilled fish.

$3/4$ cup extra-virgin olive oil
4 tablespoons lemon juice
4 tomatoes, skinned and diced
$1/2$ red chili pepper, minced, or a pinch of
   ground chili pepper

Simply heat the oil with the lemon juice and tomatoes, adding the chili. Do not cook them.

Chermoula Sauce and Marinade

Serves 4 • This hot, spicy, garlicky mixture is the all-purpose, ubiquitous Moroccan sauce for fish. It goes on every kind of fish—fried, grilled, baked, and stewed. It is marvelous, and I strongly recommend it, but not for a fish with a delicate flavor.

Use half of it to marinate the fish in for $1/2$ hour before cooking, and pour the rest on as a sauce before serving.

$2/3$ cup chopped cilantro
4 cloves garlic, crushed
1 teaspoon cumin
1 teaspoon paprika
$1/4$–$1/2$ teaspoon ground chili pepper
   (optional)
6 tablespoons peanut or extra-virgin
   olive oil
Juice of 1 lemon or 3 tablespoons wine
   vinegar

Blend everything together in the food processor.

Tarator bi Tahina

Tahina Sauce for Fish

Makes about 3 cups • A ubiquitous sauce in Syria and Lebanon, served with fried and grilled fish as well as with cold fish.

1 cup tahina
1/4–1/2 cup lemon juice, or more
1–1 1/2 cups water
1/2 teaspoon cumin
Salt
2–4 cloves garlic, crushed
3 tablespoons chopped flat-leaf parsley
(optional)

Blend the tahina with the lemon juice and water in the food processor. The paste will stiffen at first and then become smooth. Add enough water to achieve a light cream. Add cumin, season to taste with salt, and beat in the garlic.

Pour over cold fish or serve in a separate bowl. Garnish with parsley, if you like.

Skordalia

Greek Garlic Sauce

Makes about 3 cups • You have to love garlic to appreciate this most ancient of sauces.

3 thick slices white country bread, crusts
removed, soaked in water
1/2 cup mashed potatoes
1/2 cup ground almonds
6–8 cloves garlic, crushed
1/3 cup white-wine vinegar
1 cup extra-virgin olive oil
A little salt

Squeeze the bread dry, put it in a food processor with the rest of the ingredients, and blend to a smooth, creamy paste.

Fish Kebab

Serves 4 • Although Turkey is surrounded on three sides by sea, it is not very strong on fish dishes. Seafood has not been part of the old Anatolian cooking traditions. Even in the coastal resorts, where seafood restaurants have mushroomed with the tourist trade, locals are not interested. The exceptions are Izmir and Istanbul, both famous for their fish markets and fish restaurants. The usual fare, like everywhere in the Middle East, is grilled or deep-fried fish. Swordfish kebab is a Turkish specialty, but other countries use other firm-fleshed fish, such as monkfish and tuna.

> 1½ pounds swordfish, tuna, or monkfish, cut into 1¼-inch cubes
>
> Bay leaves (about 20)
>
> 1 medium onion
>
> 6 tablespoons extra-virgin olive oil
>
> Juice of ½ lemon
>
> Salt and pepper
>
> 1 lemon, cut in wedges, to serve

Thread the fish cubes onto wooden or flat metal skewers, alternating with bay leaves. Liquidize the onion in the blender with the oil, lemon, salt, and pepper and marinate the fish on the skewers in this mixture for 20 minutes, leaving it, covered, in the refrigerator.

Cook over glowing embers or under the broiler for 4–6 minutes, turning the skewers a few times and brushing with the marinade.

Serve with lemon wedges.

Variations

• Marinate the pieces of fish, then thread them onto skewers with alternating pieces of bay leaf and slices of onion, pepper, and tomato, cut to the same size as the fish.

• Moroccans cut their fish into smaller cubes. For a Moroccan flavor, marinate in and dress with the *chermoula* sauce (page 180), omitting the cilantro.

• For an exciting sweet-and-sour flavor of Syria and Iran, marinate in a tamarind sauce. For this, boil 2 tablespoons tamarind paste with ⅓ cup water, stirring until the tamarind dissolves. Then beat in 3 tablespoons olive oil.

Grilled Tuna with Tomato and Caper Dressing

Serves 4 • Tuna is usually overcooked in the Middle East. But the best way of eating it is seared on the outside and raw on the inside, which makes it deliciously, meltingly tender. Otherwise it quickly dries out. It can be brushed with oil and cooked on the barbecue or under the broiler, but an easy and perfect way is to pan-grill it. The dressing is a glamorized version of the ubiquitous oil-and-lemon one. It is good with all kinds of fish.

8 tablespoons mild extra-virgin olive oil

4 tuna steaks

Salt and pepper

Juice of 1 lemon

2 tomatoes, diced

2 tablespoons capers, soaked to remove excess salt or vinegar (optional)

Film a grill pan or heavy nonstick skillet with oil. Put in the tuna steaks and cook over high heat for 1–2 minutes on either side, depending on their thickness. You should see the flesh still dark inside as it pales on the outside.

For the dressing, mix the rest of the ingredients with the remaining olive oil. Heat through to not-quite-boiling point and pour over the fish as you serve.

Variation

Add ¼ cup chopped cilantro, or 2 crushed garlic cloves and ¼–½ teaspoon harissa (page 464), to the dressing.

Levrek Izgarasi

Broiled Sea Bass with Raki

Serves 4 • I discovered it in Istanbul. I don't believe it is traditional, but the raki—the anise-flavored spirit—is a pleasing touch. You can use other fish too.

2 sea bass, each weighing about 1½ pounds

4 tablespoons extra-virgin olive oil

Salt and pepper

⅔ cup raki

2 lemons, cut in wedges, to serve

Slash the fish in 2 places in the thickest part on either side. Brush generously with oil and season with salt and pepper. Place on an oiled grill over glowing embers, or on a piece of foil in a heatproof dish under a preheated broiler. Cook for 8 minutes on either side.

Pour the raki over the fish at the table and light with a match. When the flames have died down, fillet the fish and place on 4 warmed plates.

Serve with lemon wedges.

Broiled Red Mullet Wrapped in Grape Leaves

Serves 6 • Red mullet is so highly rated it is called Sultan Ibrahim in the Arab world. In Turkey it is called *barbunya*. In this dish, which is simple to make and beautiful to offer, grape leaves keep the fish moist and impart a delicate flavor. You may use fresh or preserved leaves. If the grape leaves are fresh, scald them in boiling water for a moment or two, until they flop, then dip them quickly in cold water so as to preserve their color. If they are preserved in brine, soak them in hot water for ½ hour to remove the salt, changing the water once, then rinse them.

> 6 small red mullet, each weighing about
>   8 ounces
> 12 grape leaves
> Extra-virgin olive oil
> Salt
> 1½ lemons, cut in wedges

Ask the fishmonger to clean and scale the fish and to keep the heads on and give you the livers (they are a delicacy you can sauté and eat while you're cooking).

Place 2 grape leaves shiny side down on a plate so that together they are large enough to wrap up a fish. Brush with oil. Place a fish across the leaves, and sprinkle lightly with salt. Roll up into a parcel, folding down the top leaf so that the head sticks out. Repeat with the remaining fish and leaves.

Cook on a barbecue or under the broiler for about 4–5 minutes on each side.

Serve with lemon wedges.

Variations

• Stuff the cavities with 4 crushed garlic cloves mixed with ¼ cup chopped flat-leaf parsley.
• Sardines can be used instead of red mullet.

Roast Fish with Lemon and Honeyed Onions

Serves 2 • The honeyed onions make an enthralling accompaniment to a delicate fish.

> 2 whole sea bass, pompano, or red
>   snapper, weighing about 1 pound each
> 2 tablespoons extra-virgin olive oil
> Juice of ½ lemon
> Salt and pepper
> 1 lemon, cut into wedges, to garnish

FOR THE HONEYED ONIONS

> 1 pound onions, cut in half and sliced
> 4 tablespoons extra-virgin olive oil
> 2 tablespoons honey
> Juice of ½ lemon
> Salt and pepper

For the honeyed onions, cook the onions in the oil on very low heat, with the lid on, stirring occasionally, until very soft. Then remove the lid and cook, stirring, until the onions are golden. Add honey, lemon juice, salt, and pepper, and cook another 5 minutes.

Place the fish in a baking dish. Rub them with oil and lemon juice and season lightly with salt and pepper. Roast in a preheated 375°F oven for 15–20 minutes, or until done, then put under the broiler for 2 minutes, until the skin is crisp and brown. Serve with the reheated honeyed onions and lemon wedges.

Variations

• Add 2–3 tablespoons of black or golden raisins to the onions.
• A large, 3½-pound fish (to serve 6) can be covered with the cooked onion mixture (make 2 or 3 times the quantity) and baked at 425°F for about 30 minutes, by which time the onions will have turned into a golden crust.

Sultan Ibrahim Maqli

*Deep-Fried Red Mullet Stuffed
with Garlic and Parsley*

A street vendor in Cairo used to sell these wrapped in newspaper, to be eaten on the spot or carried home. Other small or medium-sized fish can be used in the same way.

Rub the fish with crushed garlic, salt, and pepper, and stuff them with finely chopped flat-leaf parsley mixed with a little crushed garlic. Lightly flour and deep-fry in very hot olive oil. Serve garnished with parsley and lemon wedges.

Samak Maqli

DEEP-FRIED FISH

Deep-frying in oil is the most popular way of cooking fish in the Arab world. The method—used for whole fish as well as steaks and fillets—was introduced to Spain and Sicily in the early Middle Ages by the Arabs.

Season the fish with salt inside and out and dredge with flour so that it is entirely, but lightly, covered (1 teaspoon ground cumin mixed with the flour gives a distinctive Arab flavor). You may also marinate the fish in one of the marinades given on page 180 for ½–1 hour, then dredge in flour.

Olive oil is the best oil for frying fish, because it can reach higher temperatures than other oils without deteriorating. Use the ordinary—not extra-virgin—oil, which is bland and mild. You can reuse it 4 or 5 times, but it must be filtered to remove impurities each time. Fry in oil deep enough to cover the fish entirely, in a pan large enough so that the oil does not boil over as it expands.

The oil must be very hot. Do not put too many pieces of fish in at the same time, or the temperature will drop considerably and the fish will be soggy instead of crisp. Cook fish of roughly the same size together, since different sizes need different cooking times and temperatures.

Put the fish in when the oil sizzles if you throw in a cube of bread. As soon as the fish is in, turn the heat up to maximum for a short time to make up for the heat lost. Then keep the oil at a constant, not-too-high temperature. Very small fish must be fried very quickly at a very high temperature. Larger fish take longer and need a lower temperature, so that they have time to cook inside before the skin gets burnt. Gently shake the pan occasionally, to prevent the fish from sticking, and turn over once, so that they are crisp and golden brown all over.

Lift out the fish and drain on paper towels. Serve garnished with chopped parsley and lemon wedges. You can also serve the fried fish with a dressing or sauce such as *chermoula* (page 180) or *tarator* (page 181).

Fried Marinated Fish Served Cold

Serves 8 • This makes an exciting cold first course or buffet dish. The fish is fried, then marinated in a beautifully flavored dressing. Make it at least an hour before you are ready to serve. You can use Mediterranean fish, such as bream, or any firm-fleshed fish, such as cod or haddock.

> 2 pounds fish fillets, skinned and cut into $1\frac{1}{2}$-inch pieces
> Flour
> Olive oil for frying

FOR THE MARINADE

> $\frac{3}{4}$ cup chopped cilantro
> 1 onion, finely chopped
> 1 chili pepper, finely chopped
> 2 cloves garlic, crushed
> 6–8 tablespoons extra-virgin olive oil
> Juice of $\frac{1}{2}$–1 lemon
> Salt

Roll the fish fillets in flour, turning to cover them lightly all over. Then deep-fry briefly in hot oil till golden, turning them over once. Drain on paper towels.

Mix the marinade ingredients and turn the fish in this mixture. Leave for at least an hour before serving cold.

Fish in a Hot Saffron and Ginger Tomato Sauce

Serves 2 • Fish cooked in tomato sauce is ubiquitous in the Middle East. This wonderfully flavored North African one may be used with all kinds of fish. Use whole fish such as red mullet, Caribbean goatfish, sea bass, or red snapper, or fillets such as haddock, cod, turbot, catfish, or salmon.

> 2 whole fish (about $\frac{3}{4}$ pound each) or about 1 pound fillets
> 3 cloves garlic, chopped
> 1 chili pepper, finely chopped
> 2–3 tablespoons extra-virgin olive oil
> 1 pound ripe tomatoes, peeled and chopped
> Salt and pepper
> $1\frac{1}{2}$ teaspoons sugar
> $\frac{1}{4}$ teaspoon crushed saffron threads or powdered saffron
> $1\frac{1}{4}$ inches fresh gingerroot, grated or crushed in a garlic press to extract the juice (do small pieces at a time)

Have the whole fish (if using) scaled and cleaned but leave the heads on.

In a frying pan, heat the garlic and the chili in the oil for moments only, until they soften. Add the tomatoes, salt, pepper, sugar, saffron, and ginger, and simmer 10 minutes.

Put the fish in the pan with the tomato sauce and simmer until done to your liking—about 3–6 minutes for fillets and about 6–10 minutes for whole fish (turning the whole fish over once), until the fish flakes but is still slightly underdone.

Pan-Cooked Fish with Preserved Lemon, Green Olives, and Capers

Serves 4 • Preserved lemon and olives are a favorite combination for fish dishes in Morocco and other North African countries.

2 tablespoons butter

2 tablespoons extra-virgin olive oil

1/3 teaspoon powdered ginger

1/4 teaspoon powdered saffron

4 fish steaks or fillets—you can use haddock, cod, turbot, hake, catfish, or salmon

Salt and pepper

1/2–1 preserved lemon (page 459), rinsed and cut into small pieces

12 green olives

2 tablespoons capers, soaked to remove their excess salt or vinegar (optional)

3 tablespoons chopped cilantro

Heat the butter with the oil in a large skillet and stir in the ginger and saffron.

Put in the fish. Sprinkle with salt and pepper and add the preserved lemon, green olives, capers, and cilantro. Cook at a high temperature very briefly first, to seal the fish, then lower the heat to finish the cooking until done to your liking, turning the fish over once. Fillets take 3–6 minutes, steaks about 6–8. The fish should flake but still be a little underdone.

Pan-Cooked Fish Fillet with Chermoula Sauce

Serves 4 • Pan-cooking with the famous marinade is the simplest and quickest way of preparing a Moroccan-style fish dish.

1/2 cup chopped cilantro

4 cloves garlic, crushed

1/2–1 teaspoon cumin

1 teaspoon paprika

1/4–1/2 teaspoon ground chili pepper (optional)

6 tablespoons extra-virgin olive oil

Juice of 1 lemon or 3 tablespoons wine vinegar

2 pounds fish fillets such as turbot, hake, or cod—skin on

For the *chermoula,* blend everything except the fish together in the food processor. Marinate the fish in half the quantity of sauce for 1/2 hour—setting aside the rest.

Put the fish in a large nonstick skillet filmed with oil over medium heat, skin side down, and cook, turning them over once, for 3–8 minutes, or until the fish flakes but is still a little underdone. If the fillets are thin, do not turn them over—they will cook through to the top.

Serve with the remaining sauce poured over.

Variation

For another *chermoula* (every town, every family, has its own special combination) mix: 1/2 cup chopped cilantro; 1/2 cup chopped flat-leaf parsley; 3 large garlic cloves, crushed; 1 1/2 teaspoons ground cumin; 1/2 teaspoon ground coriander; 1 1/2 teaspoons paprika; 1 good pinch of ground chili pepper; juice of 1 lemon or 4 tablespoons wine vinegar; and 2/3 cup extra-virgin olive or other oil.

Raya bel Batata

Skate with Cumin and Potatoes

Serves 4 • Small skate, tender enough to fry quickly, should be used for this Tunisian dish. The wings are bought already dressed from the fishmonger.

4 small wings of skate, weighing 2 pounds

4 cloves garlic, crushed in a garlic press

1½ teaspoons ground cumin

Salt

About ½ cup olive oil

1 pound potatoes, peeled, boiled, and sliced

Pepper

2 tablespoons capers

1 or 2 lemons, cut in quarters, to serve with

Cut the fish into pieces about 2 inches wide, cutting in between the long soft bones. Rub the pieces with a mixture of garlic, cumin, salt, and 3–4 tablespoons of the olive oil.

In a large frying pan, fry the fish pieces in batches in shallow oil, giving them about 4 minutes on either side, until the flesh begins to part from the bone. Remove to a baking dish.

Sauté the potatoes slowly in the same oil, adding salt and pepper and more oil, and turning them over, until they are tender.

Add the capers towards the end. Reheat the fish in a 400°F oven, covered with foil. Serve on a bed of the sautéed potatoes accompanied by lemon wedges.

Poached Fish with Saffron Vermicelli

Serves 4 • For this delightful and simple Moroccan dish, use fish fillets—monkfish or any firm-fleshed fish such as bream, turbot, haddock, cod—and have them skinned.

1½ pounds fish fillets, skinned

Salt

10 ounces dry vermicelli

Salt

½ teaspoon crushed saffron threads or powdered saffron

4–5 tablespoons extra-virgin olive oil

Pepper

4 tablespoons chopped parsley or cilantro

Poach the fish in barely simmering (not boiling) salted water for 5–10 minutes, until the flesh looks opaque when you cut into it.

At the same time, break the vermicelli in your hand into small pieces and cook in about 5 cups of boiling salted water with the saffron until just tender, stirring vigorously so that the vermicelli do not stick together. Drain, reserving about 1 cup of the saffron water to use as a sauce. (Keep the remainder if you like—there is very little left—to pour into a soup or a stew.) Beat the olive oil into the water, season with salt and pepper, and add the parsley or cilantro.

Serve the fish on a bed of vermicelli, with the sauce poured over.

Samak Tarator

Cold Poached Fish with Pine Nut Sauce

Serves 6 • *Tarator* is the name used in different countries for sauces made with a variety of nuts. This sharp, garlicky one with pine nuts belongs to Syria and Lebanon. In Egypt it was served at grand buffet parties, where whole fish were entirely covered with it. For this simpler version you may use any white fish—fillets or steaks.

6 fish steaks or fillets
Salt
Olive oil

FOR THE TARATOR SAUCE

1 slice white bread, crusts removed
1 cup pine nuts
Juice of 1–2 lemons
1 or 2 cloves garlic, crushed
Salt and white pepper
$\frac{1}{2}$ cup light sesame or sunflower oil

Season the fish with salt and bake in foil (see "To Cook Fish in Foil," at right).

For the sauce, soak the bread in water and squeeze dry. Put it in the food processor with the pine nuts, lemon juice, garlic, a little salt and pepper, and enough oil to have a cream the consistency of mayonnaise.

Variations

• Another way of making the sauce is to use fish stock instead of the $\frac{1}{2}$ cup oil.

• For a party dish, choose a large, delicate fish such as sea bass, hake, catfish, or salmon. Have it skinned and filleted and put the fillets together in a large piece of foil. Cook as described in "To Cook Fish in Foil," at right. Make 2–3 times the quantity of *tarator* sauce. Serve the fish cold, covered with the sauce, with the head and tail in place. The fish is usually decorated with a crisscross pattern, using fried pine nuts or flaked almonds. Alternative garnishes are: lemon slices, flat-leaf parsley, sliced green pickles, olives, radishes, and pieces of pimento.

To Cook Fish in Foil

In many Middle Eastern countries, home cooks used to send fish to be cooked, wrapped in newspaper, at the baker's oven. Now they cook it in foil. In this way the fish is steamed in its own juice and the flesh remains moist. It can be a whole large fish, or the fillets arranged in the shape of a fish with the head—if you want it for the presentation—wrapped separately. Brush a large sheet of foil generously with extra-virgin olive oil. Place the fish or fillets in the middle and sprinkle lightly with salt. Wrap in a loose parcel, twisting the foil edges together to seal it. Bake at 450°F—since the packet is sealed, there is no danger of even a fillet's drying out. The cooking time depends on the size of the fish. Test for doneness for a large fish after about 30 minutes. Cut down to the backbone at the thickest part and check that the flesh flakes away from the bone and has turned opaque right through. Fillets might be ready after 15–20 minutes.

Serve the fish hot or cold (let it cool in the foil) accompanied by a sauce.

L'Hout bel Shakshouka

Fish with Onions, Peppers, and Tomatoes

Serves 4 • Algerians serve deep-fried Dover sole over a bed of *shakshouka,* but other flat fish, such as lemon or gray sole or flounder, are excellent with the sautéed Mediterranean vegetables—and they can be broiled.

> 4 soles, or other flat fish, each weighing
>   about 12 ounces, skinned
> Salt
> 1 large onion, cut in half and sliced
> Extra-virgin olive oil
> 2 bell peppers, green or red—seeded and
>   sliced
> 1 or 2 cloves garlic, chopped
> 2 tomatoes, quartered
> Pepper
> Juice of 1 lemon

Season the fish lightly with salt.

Sauté the onion in the oil with the peppers, stirring occasionally, until the onion is golden and the peppers are very soft and lightly colored. Add garlic, and when the aroma rises, add the tomatoes. Sprinkle with salt and pepper and cook until the tomatoes have softened.

Brush the fish generously with olive oil and cook under a preheated broiler for 4 minutes on each side.

Serve the fish on a bed of the sautéed vegetables. Dribble on a little raw olive oil, and sprinkle with lemon juice.

Balik Pilaki

Cold Fish in Oil with Vegetables

Serves 6–8 • This Turkish specialty, popular throughout most of the Middle East, makes a good first course or cold buffet dish. Sliced swordfish is generally used, but most fish available in America are also suitable.

> 2 pounds fish: whole red mullet or
>   mackerel, or a piece of a larger fish,
>   sliced
> Olive oil
> 2 large onions, sliced
> 2 green peppers, seeded and sliced
> 2 cloves garlic, chopped
> 1 pound tomatoes, skinned and sliced
> ¼ cup chopped flat-leaf parsley
> 1 tablespoon tomato paste
> Salt and pepper
> About a dozen green or black olives,
>   pitted or not (optional)

Pan-fry the fish in a few tablespoons olive oil until lightly colored but not quite cooked inside, then lift out and reserve.

Clean the pan. Fry the onions in 3 tablespoons oil until soft and golden. Add the sliced green peppers and fry until soft and sweet. Add the chopped garlic and fry for a moment more. Finally, add the tomatoes, chopped parsley, and tomato paste diluted in about ½ cup water. Season to taste with salt and pepper, stir well, bring to the boil, and simmer for 15 minutes.

Lay the fish in the sauce carefully, so that the pieces are well covered, and cook for a further 5–10 minutes or until done, adding a little water if necessary. A few olives, blanched in boiling water to remove excess salt, can be added towards the end. Arrange the fish in a serving dish with sauce over it. Serve cold.

Yakhnit Samak bel Zafaran

Fish Stew with Onions and Saffron

Serves 4–6 • An old Arab dish, popular in Syria, Lebanon, and Egypt. It is very lemony, and sometimes saffron is replaced by turmeric. All kinds of fish can be used. Serve with plain rice, or rice with vermicelli (see page 340).

  2 onions, cut in half and sliced

  4 tablespoons vegetable or olive oil

  2–4 cloves garlic, crushed

  Juice of 2–3 lemons

  1/4 teaspoon crushed saffron threads or
    powdered saffron

  Salt and white pepper

  2 pounds skinned fish fillets or steaks

Fry the onions in 2 tablespoons of the oil till golden. Add the garlic, and just as it begins to color, add the lemon juice, the saffron, a little salt, and about 1 cup water. Simmer for 10–15 minutes.

Fry the fish pieces very briefly in a skillet filmed with oil over high heat, turning them over once, until lightly colored but still uncooked inside. Lift them out, drain on paper towels, and put them in the pan with the onion sauce.

Simmer, covered, over very low heat, so that the liquid barely trembles, until the fish is done—about 3 to 5 minutes for fillets, up to 10 minutes for steaks.

Variation

For *samak bi loomi,* a version from the Gulf States, use 3 tablespoons ground dried limes (see page 44) instead of lemon, turmeric instead of saffron, plus 1 teaspoon crushed cardamom seeds.

Tagen Samak bel Cozbara

Fish Stew with Tomatoes and Coriander Seed

Serves 4 • A favorite Egyptian flavoring is a mix of fried garlic and coriander. This dish is a specialty of Alexandria, where it is usually baked in a clay dish called a *tagen* (it is deeper than Moroccan tagines and with straight sides). You can make it with any white fish—steaks or fillets. Serve it with plain rice (page 338) or rice with vermicelli (page 340).

  1 1/2 pounds fish—fillets or steaks

  3 tablespoons vegetable oil

  Salt and pepper

  6 or 7 cloves garlic, crushed

  1–2 teaspoons ground coriander

  1 1/2 pounds tomatoes, peeled and
    chopped

  1–2 teaspoons sugar

In a large skillet, fry the fish briefly in the oil until lightly browned, but still uncooked inside, turning it over once and sprinkling with salt and pepper. Then lift it out.

Fry the garlic and the coriander together in the same oil over low heat for moments only, stirring, until the aroma rises. Add the tomatoes, stir in the sugar and a little salt and pepper, and cook for 15 minutes. Return the fish to the pan and cook for 2–5 minutes, or until it is done to your liking.

Variation

For *cozbareyet al samak,* cut the fish into chunks and fry briefly in oil. Lift out when it is done. In a small pan, heat 3 tablespoons olive oil with 5 or 6 crushed garlic cloves and 1–1 1/2 teaspoons ground coriander until the garlic begins to color. Pour over the fish.

Fish with Quinces

Serves 6–8 • Tunisia is famous for her fish dishes and her fish couscous. Here is one of the prestigious dishes which can be served with couscous. Prepare couscous as in the recipe on page 375 so that it is ready at the same time.

4 or 5 cloves garlic, chopped

3 tablespoons olive oil

2 pounds tomatoes, peeled and chopped

Salt

2 teaspoons sugar

1 or 2 chilies, cut open and seeded

1½ inches fresh gingerroot

½ teaspoon crushed saffron threads or powdered saffron

¼ cup raisins

2 or 3 quinces, peeled and sliced (2 if very large)

2 pounds fillets of bream or other fish, such as cod or haddock

Fry the garlic in the oil until it only just begins to color. Add the tomatoes, salt, and sugar, and put in the chilies. Peel and grate the ginger, or cut it into small pieces and crush it in a garlic press to extract the juice over the pan. Add the saffron and the raisins and simmer over low heat. Put in the quinces as you peel them so that they do not turn brown. They are a very hard fruit, and you need a large strong knife to cut them.

Cook, covered, for 15 to 30 minutes, or until the quinces are tender. The time varies depending on the size, quality, and ripeness of the fruit. Remove one or both of the chilies when you think the sauce is hot enough. Five to 10 minutes before serving, add the fish, and simmer until the flesh begins to flake. Serve the fish stew and the couscous in separate dishes.

Stewed Eel with Onions, Honey, and Raisins

Serves 6 • A specialty of the port of Salé, this is one of the rare fish couscous dishes of Morocco. The eel is usually cooked in a saffron broth, but I prefer to sauté the eel and serve it with a small portion of couscous (see page 375). The honeyed onions beautifully complement the delicate flavor of this fish. Have the eel skinned (the skin is tough and inedible) and cut into pieces or filleted by the fishmonger.

2 pounds eels

2 pounds onions, cut in half and sliced thinly

5 tablespoons vegetable or extra-virgin olive oil

1 teaspoon cinnamon

¼ teaspoon crushed saffron threads or powdered saffron

1–2 tablespoons honey

Juice of ½–1 lemon

¾ cup raisins

Salt and pepper

3 tablespoons butter

Sprinkle the eels with a little salt.

Put the onions with 4 tablespoons oil in a large pan. Cook with the lid on over very low heat, stirring occasionally, until soft (they will stew in their own juice). It will take a long time because of the quantity. Take the lid off and cook, stirring often, until lightly golden. Add the cinnamon, saffron, honey, lemon juice, raisins, and a little salt and pepper. Stir well, and cook gently for 5 minutes.

In a large skillet, sauté the eel in butter and the remaining tablespoon of oil, sprinkling with salt and pepper, until just cooked through. Serve on a bed of onions with couscous.

L'Hout Hraimy

Peppery Hot and Garlicky Fish

Serves 6 • A North African—particularly Libyan—specialty. Algerians call the piquant sauce *chetitha*. The dish is not for everybody, and it is not for a delicate fish.

  1 whole head of garlic
  2 teaspoons tomato paste
  ⅓ cup vegetable oil
  1 teaspoon paprika
  1 teaspoon cumin (optional)
  1 teaspoon harissa (page 464) or
    ¼–½ teaspoon ground chili pepper
  Salt
  Juice of 1 lemon
  2 pounds fish fillets or steaks

Peel the garlic and puree in a blender. Put it in a large skillet with the tomato paste and stir in the oil and the rest of the ingredients except the fish. Add 1 cup water, bring to the boil, and simmer 5 minutes. Put in the fish and cook over low heat for 3–10 minutes, turning over once, until the fish is cooked, adding a little water if it is too dry.

Serve hot.

Psari Plaki

Baked Fish

Serves 6 • In Egypt we called it *poisson à la grecque*. All kinds of fish can be cooked in this way—small ones whole, and large ones cut into steaks. Serve hot or cold with good bread and a salad.

  6 fish steaks, about 1 inch thick
  Salt and pepper
  Juice of ½–1 lemon
  2 onions, sliced
  ¼ cup extra-virgin olive oil
  3 cloves garlic, chopped
  1 pound tomatoes, peeled and quartered
  1 cup dry white wine
  ¼ cup chopped flat-leaf parsley

Arrange the fish in a baking dish. Season with salt and pepper and sprinkle with lemon juice.

Fry the onions in 2 tablespoons of the oil until golden. Add the garlic, and as soon as it begins to color, add the tomatoes and the wine. Season with salt and pepper and simmer for about 20 minutes. Add the parsley, and pour over the fish.

Sprinkle on the remaining oil and bake in a preheated 325°F oven for 20 minutes, or until the fish is opaque right through and flakes when you pierce it with a knife.

Variations

• Bake a large whole fish such as bass, red snapper, gray mullet, bluefish, or pompano in the same way. Bake at 425°F for about 30 minutes, basting with the sauce occasionally.

• Add sliced or cubed potatoes to the tomato sauce.

Tajen Samak bi Tahina

Fish Baked in Tahina Sauce

Serves 6 • This is very popular in Syria and Lebanon and can be served cold with salads such as tabbouleh (page 76) or hot with rice.

> 2 pounds fish fillets, skinned and cut into
>   6 pieces
> Salt
> 2 large onions, cut in half and thinly
>   sliced
> 2–3 tablespoons extra-virgin olive oil
> 1 cup tahina
> ½–⅔ cup lemon juice, or to taste
> 1 cup water, or more as required
> ¼ cup chopped flat-leaf parsley
> 2 or 3 lemons, cut in wedges, to serve
>   with

Season the fish with salt.

In a large pan, sweat the onions in 2–3 tablespoons oil with the lid on over very low heat, stirring occasionally, until soft and just beginning to color.

Beat into the tahina the lemon juice and enough water to obtain a light creamy consistency (it will stiffen at first, before becoming smooth and runny). Add salt to taste.

Spread the onions on the bottom of a baking dish, lay the fish on top, and pour the sauce all over the fish. Bake in a preheated 400°F oven for 20–30 minutes, or until the fish flakes easily. Serve sprinkled with parsley.

Variation

Some fry the fish very briefly first, in shallow oil over high heat, so that it is lightly browned but not yet cooked inside, then bake it with the onions and the sauce for a further 10 minutes.

Shad Stuffed with Dates

Serves 6 • This freshwater fish, found in the Sebou River, is popular in Morocco. It is fat but rather full of bones, and its delicate flesh is said to be at its best soon after spawning upriver. In America it is sold already boned, which makes stuffing easy. Dates are stuffed with rice and blanched almonds, and they, in turn, provide the stuffing for the fish.

> ¼ cup finely chopped blanched almonds
> 2–3 tablespoons cooked rice
> 1 teaspoon sugar
> ½ teaspoon ground cinnamon plus
>   ¼ teaspoon to garnish (optional)
> Pepper
> ¼ teaspoon ground ginger
> 1–2 tablespoons butter
> 8 ounces fresh dates (dried ones will do,
>   but choose soft, juicy ones)
> A 3-pound boned shad
> Oil
> Salt
> ½ onion, finely chopped

Mix together the chopped almonds, rice, sugar, cinnamon, and a pinch each of pepper and ginger, and knead with a little butter to hold everything together.

Pit the dates and stuff them with the almond-rice mixture.

Rub the fish all over with oil, salt, pepper, and a little ground ginger. Open up the 2 top fillets and arrange the stuffed dates down the center, then replace the top fillets. Place the fish on a large, well-oiled sheet of foil and sprinkle with the finely chopped onion. Wrap the fish up neatly and seal the edges of the foil firmly. (The foil allows you to omit sewing up the fish.) Lay the parcel on a large baking pan.

Bake in a preheated 350°F oven, about 15 minutes per pound, or until the flesh begins to flake when you cut into the thickest part with a pointed knife. Then unwrap the foil and place the fish under the broiler to become crisply golden. Serve dusted with cinnamon if you like.

Sayyadiah

Fish with Rice

Serves 8–10 • This is a very popular Arab dish. There are white and brown versions, which depend on whether you let the onions go brown or not. Use skinned fillets of fish such as bream, turbot, haddock, cod, or halibut.

Vegetable oil

4 or 5 large onions, sliced

Salt

1 teaspoon ground cumin or allspice

2 pounds skinned fish fillets

Juice of 1/2–1 lemon

1 pound long-grain rice, washed

In a large saucepan, fry the onions in 2 or 3 tablespoons oil over very low heat, with the lid on, until soft and transparent but still white, stirring occasionally. Let them get dark brown if you want a brown *sayyadiah*. Add about 5 cups water and simmer until the onions have nearly melted. You can leave the onions as they are, or blend them to a pulp with some of the liquid.

Return them to the pan, and season with salt and cumin or allspice. Add the fish and simmer for about 4–8 minutes, until cooked but still firm. Skim off the scum as it rises to the surface.

Remove the fish and keep hot. Retain about 4 cups of the onion stock to cook the rice in. Pour the remaining stock into another pan and add lemon juice to taste, to make a sauce.

Throw the washed and drained rice into the first portion of boiling stock. Let it boil vigorously for a minute, then reduce the heat, cover the pan, and simmer gently, undisturbed, until the rice is tender, about 15–20 minutes.

Just before serving, reheat the fish in the sauce. Serve the rice heaped in a mound on a large serving dish. Arrange the pieces of fish over or around it, and pour the hot, lemony sauce over the whole dish.

Variations

• For an elegant presentation, press the fish, then the rice over it, into an oiled mold. Heat through in the oven before turning out carefully. Garnish with 1/2–1 cup lightly fried pine nuts and/or split blanched almonds.

• Here is an Egyptian version. Color and soften the onions, then fry the fish briefly with the onions so that it is still uncooked inside. Make a stock with the bones, head, and trimmings of the fish, simmered with 1 stalk celery, 1 onion, and 1 carrot. Strain through a fine sieve. Cook the rice as above, in 1 1/2 times its own volume of stock. Mix the cooked rice with the fish and onions in a baking dish. Garnish with lightly fried pine nuts and moisten with a little of the stock, considerably reduced. Bake in a preheated 300°F oven for 15–20 minutes.

Koftet el Samak

Fried Fish Balls

Makes 40–50 small balls • You can serve these Egyptian fish balls as mezze or finger foods at a party. Use any white fish, such as cod, haddock, bream, whiting, or hake.

> 2 pounds skinned fish fillets
>
> 2 eggs
>
> 2 teaspoons salt
>
> ½ teaspoon pepper
>
> 2 teaspoons ground cumin
>
> 2–4 cloves garlic, crushed
>
> ⅔ cup fine breadcrumbs or matzo meal
>
> ½ cup finely chopped flat-leaf parsley or cilantro (optional)
>
> Flour
>
> Oil for deep-frying

Cut the fish fillets into pieces and finely chop them in the food processor for 5 seconds.

Beat the eggs lightly and add salt, pepper, cumin, and garlic. Mix with the fish and add the breadcrumbs or matzo meal. Work very well with your hands into a stiff paste. Wet your hands and take lumps of paste and roll them into balls the size of large marbles. Pour plenty of flour on a plate and roll the fish balls in it, covering them lightly with flour.

Deep-fry briefly in hot oil until browned all over, turning them over once. Drain on paper towels and serve, preferably hot.

Variations

• Instead of cumin, add 1 teaspoon ground coriander, ½ teaspoon ground ginger, and ¼ teaspoon cayenne or ground chili pepper.

• A Gulf States version has 3 tablespoons ground dried limes (see page 44), 1 teaspoon turmeric, and ½ teaspoon cumin as flavoring.

Sardines in the Algerian Manner

Serves 6 • This is quite a lot of work, as fishmongers don't usually bother to scale sardines, but it makes a very tasty mezze.

> 2 pounds fresh sardines
>
> 3 teaspoons ground cumin
>
> 2 or 3 cloves garlic, crushed
>
> ½ teaspoon ground chili pepper
>
> Salt
>
> 2 eggs, beaten
>
> Flour or fine dry breadcrumbs
>
> Olive oil for deep-frying

Wash and scale the sardines and remove heads and tails. Slit them open down one side only, and remove their backbones. Dip the sardines, open side down, in a mixture of ground cumin, garlic, ground chili pepper, and salt. Stick the sardines together in pairs, open sides together, trapping the seasonings between them.

Dip the pairs in beaten egg, then in flour or breadcrumbs. Deep-fry in hot oil, being very careful not to let the pairs separate. Drain on paper towels and serve hot.

Variation

For a Moroccan version with a mashed-potato stuffing: mash 1 pound boiled potatoes and mix with ½ cup chopped flat-leaf parsley, ½ cup chopped cilantro, and 3 beaten eggs. Add salt and pepper, 1 teaspoon cumin or 1 teaspoon cinnamon, 1 teaspoon paprika, and a pinch of chili pepper. Take a lump the size of a small egg. Roll it into a long oblong and press between 2 sardines. Dip in flour and deep-fry quickly in hot oil, then drain on paper towels.

Shrimp and Tomato Pilaf

Serves 6–8 • This can be served as a first course or a main dish. It has a deliciously fresh tomato flavor with a touch of cinnamon.

1½ pounds tomatoes

1 large onion, chopped

3 tablespoons extra-virgin olive oil

4 cloves garlic, chopped

½ chili pepper, finely chopped

2 chicken bouillon cubes

2 cups American long-grain rice

Salt and pepper

2 teaspoons sugar

1 teaspoon cinnamon

1¼ pounds peeled cooked large shrimp

2 lemons, cut into quarters, to serve with

Peel the tomatoes and liquefy them in the food processor, then measure their volume. It should add up to a little more than 2¼ cups.

Fry the onion in the oil till soft and lightly colored. Add the garlic and the chili and stir until the aroma rises.

Add the liquid tomatoes and just enough water to make up 4½ cups with the tomatoes. Stir in the crumbled bouillon cubes and bring to the boil. Add the rice, salt and pepper, sugar, and cinnamon. Stir well and cook, covered, on low heat for 15–20 minutes. The rice should be tender but still a little moist. Fold in the shrimp gently and heat through with the lid on. Serve hot, accompanied by lemon wedges.

Spicy Shrimp

Serves 2 • A Moroccan way with shrimp that is quick to do and really delicious. If you buy the shrimp frozen, let them thaw in the refrigerator before peeling.

2 cloves garlic, crushed

3 tablespoons sunflower or extra-virgin olive oil

1 teaspoon paprika

¾ teaspoon cumin

¼ teaspoon ground ginger

A good pinch of cayenne or ground chili pepper

½ pound large fresh or frozen shrimp, peeled

Salt

2–3 tablespoons chopped cilantro or parsley

Heat the garlic in the oil until the aroma rises. Stir in the spices and throw in the shrimp. Season with salt, add the cilantro or parsley, and fry quickly, stirring, for about 5 minutes, until the shrimp turn pink.

Mithia Krassata

Mussels in White Wine

Serves 4–6 • A Greek way of cooking mussels.

4 pounds mussels

3 cloves garlic, crushed

3 tablespoons extra-virgin olive oil

2 cups dry white wine

3 tablespoons chopped flat-leaf parsley

Scrub the mussels, pull off the beards, and wash in several changes of cold water. Test to see if they are alive: discard any which are broken or too heavy or too light, or which do not close when they are tapped or dipped in cold water.

In a very large pan, heat the garlic in the oil. As soon as the aroma rises, add the wine. Simmer for 10 minutes, until it is reduced to about 1 cup—it acquires a delicious mellow flavor.

Put in the mussels and, with the lid on, put them on very high heat for 1–2 minutes, until they open. Take off the heat, discard any which remain closed, and serve the mussels in their shells sprinkled with parsley. Pour over them the wine-and-mussel liquor left in the pan, through a sieve lined with cheesecloth to catch any sand.

Scallops with Tamarind

Serves 4 • You can buy tamarind paste (page 46) from Middle Eastern stores. Serve the scallops as an appetizer accompanied with a leaf salad.

1 tablespoon tamarind paste

3 tablespoons water

4 tablespoons mild extra-virgin olive oil

12 sea scallops

Salt

In a little pan, heat the tamarind and water, stirring, until the tamarind dissolves, and let it cool. Then beat in the oil.

Wash the scallops and pull away the intestinal thread. Cook them in a greased frying pan for 30–40 seconds on each side, sprinkling with a little salt.

Serve hot with a drizzle of the tamarind dressing on each.

Variation

Another dressing for scallops is 3 tablespoons extra-virgin olive oil and 1 teaspoon cinnamon.

To Clean and Prepare Squid

Pull the head away from the body pouch and discard the soft innards, which come out with it. Discard the insides of the pouch—the ink sac, if any, the icicle-shaped transparent cuttlebone, and the soft innards. Keep the tentacles in their bunches but remove the eyes and the small round cartilage at the base of the tentacles by cutting with a sharp knife just above the eyes (be careful that ink doesn't squirt out at you from the eyes). Rinse thoroughly.

Kalamarakia Yemista

Stuffed Squid

Serves 6 • This Greek dish takes time and effort but is something special to offer at a dinner party. Serve with rice or with mashed potatoes (see page 297).

2 pounds small squid (about 14 baby squid)

4 tablespoons olive oil

3 tablespoons pine nuts

⅔ cup short-grain rice

3 tablespoons raisins

Salt

1 large onion, chopped

2 cloves garlic, chopped

1 pound tomatoes, peeled and chopped

1 cup dry white or red wine

2 teaspoons sugar

¼ teaspoon ground chili pepper (optional)

3 tablespoons chopped flat-leaf parsley

Clean and prepare the squid as described in box on page 198.

Heat 2 tablespoons of the oil in a small pan. Add the pine nuts, and stir so that they are lightly colored all over. Stir in the rice and raisins, and add a little salt and 1 cup water. Stir and simmer over low heat for 10 minutes, until the water is absorbed. Fill each squid about two-thirds full only, to allow the rice to expand. Secure the openings with toothpicks.

For the sauce: Fry the onion in the remaining 2 tablespoons of oil until golden. Add the garlic and cook, stirring, until it begins to color. Add the tomatoes, wine, sugar, salt, and chili pepper if using. Simmer, uncovered, for 15 minutes.

Lay the squid in a single layer in an oven dish, pour the sauce over them, and place the clusters of tentacles at the top end of each squid. Cover with foil and bake in a preheated 400°F oven for 15–30 minutes, depending on the size of the squid.

Serve hot, sprinkled with parsley.

Squid with Garlic and Chilies

Serves 4

1½ pounds small squid

3 tablespoons olive oil

3 cloves garlic, chopped

2 red chilies, seeded and finely chopped

Salt and pepper

3–4 tablespoons chopped cilantro

1 lemon, cut in wedges, to accompany

Clean and prepare the squid as described in the box on page 198. Cut the body pouches in rings.

Heat the oil in a large frying pan. Put in the garlic and chilies and the squid. Season with salt and pepper and sauté briefly, turning over the pieces, for 2–3 minutes only.

Sprinkle with cilantro and serve hot with lemon wedges.

Octopus Cooked in White Wine

Serves 6 • This is served as an appetizer in Greece. The wine gives it a special flavor.

- 1 small octopus, weighing about 2 pounds
- 1 cup dry white wine
- 2 tablespoons white-wine vinegar
- 2 teaspoons sugar
- Salt and pepper
- 5 tablespoons extra-virgin olive oil
- 3 tablespoons chopped flat-leaf parsley

Octopus is usually sold cleaned and tenderized. But here is how you clean it if you have to do it yourself: Cut partway through the muscle which unites the tentacles to the inside of the head and discard all the contents of the head cavity. This involves pulling or cutting out the ink sac, the hard oval "beak," and the gelatinous innards. Turn the head inside out and wash well under running water. Squeeze or cut out the eyes and any cartilage. Remove any scales which may be left on the suckers and wash the octopus thoroughly.

Blanch the octopus for 5 minutes in boiling water, then drain. Put it in a saucepan with the wine, vinegar, sugar, salt and pepper, and just enough water to cover. Simmer over very low heat for about 1–1½ hours, until tender, adding water to keep it covered. Lift out the octopus and reduce the sauce.

Cut the octopus into 1-inch slices, and mix with the sauce and the olive oil.

Serve cold, sprinkled with parsley.

Ritza

SEA URCHINS

Hunting for *ritza* (the Greek name for sea urchins) is a favorite pastime in Alexandria. It was a great joy to swim out to the rocks, and dive into the sea to discover hosts of dark-purple-and-black spiky, jewel-like balls clinging fast to the rocks. We would wrench them away and take them back to the beach in net bags. We cut a piece off the top, squeezed a little lemon over the soft, salmon-colored flesh, and scooped it out with a piece of bread.

Sea urchins are available in good fish markets in New York and sometimes elsewhere in the United States. You can bring them home fresh and eat them in the same way.

Uskumru Dolmasu

Stuffed Mackerel

Serves 6 • A Turkish delicacy. A humble fish for a regal occasion. The skin of the fish is stuffed with its own flesh mixed with a rich filling. It is rolled in beaten egg, then in flour and breadcrumbs, and deep-fried in olive or nut oil. It is quite a bit of work but is delicious eaten hot or cold, as an entrée or as a main dish.

6 small mackerel

2 eggs, lightly beaten

Fine dry breadcrumbs

Oil

FOR THE STUFFING

1 large onion, finely chopped

Olive oil

4 ounces shelled walnuts, ground or pounded

2 ounces shelled hazelnuts, ground or pounded

2 ounces raisins

2 teaspoons mixed spices (a mixture of allspice, cinnamon, nutmeg, cloves, and pepper)

Salt

½ cup each of chopped parsley and fresh dill or chervil

Clean the fish and cut off their heads, but do not cut the bodies. Snap the backbones off near the tail. Rub the skins to loosen them and to soften the flesh. Then, using your hands, rub and squeeze the fish, starting from the tail, forcing the flesh and bones out of the loosened skin as though emptying a tube of paste. This is quite easily done, as the skin is very strong. Any tears in the skin can be mended by sewing them up with a needle and thread. Another good method for emptying the fish skins is to loosen them as above, then, holding the backbone firmly where it shows at the head, to pull the skin down, turning it inside out. Proceed as above. Remove the bones carefully and break up the flesh for the stuffing.

Prepare the stuffing. Fry the onions until soft and golden in 2 tablespoons oil. Add the nuts, raisins, spices, and salt to taste, and mix well. Add the fish and fry for 3 minutes longer. Stir in the chopped parsley and dill or chervil, and remove from the heat.

Fill the fish skins tightly with this mixture, closing the openings by sewing them up carefully. Dip in beaten egg and then in breadcrumbs. Fry in hot oil until golden brown and cooked through.

Serve hot or cold.

Fessih

SALTED AND DRIED FISH

Ever since ancient times, salted and dried fish has been known in all parts of the Middle East. This was originally done to preserve the fish so that it could be stored and taken on long journeys, or sent to regions far away from the coast. Today, it is prepared in this way because people like it. The fish is washed and cleaned and split open. It is salted inside and out and left to dry in the hot sun. In Egypt it is the specialty of Sham el Nessim, the national holiday when everyone goes picnicking.

Poultry

TOUYOUR

In the villages of most Middle Eastern countries, where it requires an *eid el kibir,* or a very important feast, to kill a lamb, poultry is the usual festive dish. Geese, ducks, hens, or fat chickens are the traditional festival queens. Often the birds are boiled first to provide the legendary wedding or other festive soups and, in Egypt, the *melokheya* (page 146). Sometimes the birds are filled with rich stuffings. They are cooked in an extraordinary variety of ways, and beautifully flavored and decorated following ancient traditions. Egyptians like to point to the tomb paintings which show that their ancestors in pharaonic times cooked geese and ducks and pigeons.

Maxime Rodinson, in his description of the manuscript of the *Kitab al Wusla il al Habib,* found in Syria, which is believed to have been written in the thirteenth century, notes over five hundred recipes for chicken, of which he has unfortunately fully translated and explained only a few. Among them are:

- Minced chicken and lamb rissoles
- Stuffed boned chicken

- Chicken with vinegar

- Chicken boiled with crushed chickpeas

- Chicken with lemon or pomegranate sauce

- Chicken with rhubarb or quinces

- Chicken with hard-boiled egg yolks and herbs

- Chicken with pistachio nuts; with hazelnuts, walnuts, almonds, or poppy seeds; with parsley, oranges, or rose jam; with plum jelly, yogurt, or mulberries

- Chicken with chickpeas, onions, and cinnamon, or spiced rice

- Chicken with pistachios, perfumed with rose water and musk

- A loaf of bread stuffed with chicken

The luscious ingredients in the recipes are echoed in the dishes of today—in the fruit stews of Morocco, the walnut and hazelnut sauces of Turkey and Syria, and the chickpeas, onions, and lemons of Egypt.

I*n his* **Kitab al-Ifadah wa'l-l'Tibar,** *written in 1204 after a visit to Egypt, Abd al Latif al-Baghdadi gives a description of the food of the time:*

As for the stews of the Egyptians, those which are sour or ordinary have nothing in particular, or very little, different from those used elsewhere, but on the contrary, their sweet stews are of a singular kind, for they cook a chicken with all sorts of sweet substances. Here is how they prepare the food: They boil a fowl, then put it in a julep, place under it crushed hazelnuts or pistachio nuts, poppy seeds, or purslane seeds, or rose hips, and cook the whole until it thickens. Then they add spices and remove it from the fire.

These stews are surnamed fistakiyyeh *(pistachio),* bondokiyyeh *(hazelnut),* khashkhaschiyyeh *(poppy), or* wardiyeh *(rose hip) or* sitt alnoubeh *(purslane, called "Nubian woman" because of its black color). There are many skillful ways of preparing this kind of food which would entail too great detail to describe.*

ZAND AND VIDEAN,
THE EASTERN KEY

Hamam Meshwi

*Broiled Mediterranean Pigeons,
Squabs, or Poussins*

Serves 2–4 • One of the happiest memories of my childhood in Cairo is the outings in the company of several uncles, aunts, and cousins to an old restaurant called Le Café des Pigeons on the way to the Pyramids, where we feasted on charcoal-broiled baby pigeons. Huge platters, piled high with halved pigeons sprinkled with lemon juice and parsley, were brought to us in the ancient gardens of the restaurant, overgrown with jasmine and bougainvillea. The birds were so young and tender we could eat them bones and all.

Mediterranean pigeons are like squabs. You can also use poussins (small spring chickens) in the same way. They are best grilled over dying embers, where they acquire a most seductive flavor and aroma, but you can also cook them indoors, over the heat of a pumice-stone rock grill or under the broiler. Serve them with salad and pita bread.

2 Mediterranean pigeons, squabs, or
 poussins
$1/4$ cup chopped flat-leaf parsley

FOR THE MARINADE

Juice of 1–$1^{1/2}$ lemons
1 onion, liquefied in a blender or food
 processor
2 or 3 cloves garlic, crushed (optional)
3 tablespoons olive oil
Salt and pepper

Cut the pigeons, squabs, or poussins in half down the breastbone and through the back with kitchen shears or a bread knife. Cut the wing and leg joints just enough to pull them a little apart, so that the halves lie flat and cook more evenly. Or cut the birds into quarters. Refrigerate for about an hour, turning the pieces over at least once.

Place the marinated pieces on an oiled grill over glowing embers which are no longer smoking. Cook, basting with the marinade, and turning over once, for about 15 to 20 minutes, or until the pieces are brown all over but still tender and juicy inside. Test one piece by cutting it with a knife. The juices should not be pink.

Serve sprinkled with chopped parsley.

Variations

• Turks like to flavor this with a little cinnamon instead of the garlic and lemon.
• Brushing with melted butter instead of the marinade produces a very succulent result.
• A delicious variation is to marinate the chicken pieces for as long as possible in yogurt flavored with crushed garlic, salt, and pepper. Sometimes dried crushed mint is added, and a little paprika is mixed with the yogurt to give the chicken an appetizing red color. The yogurt does not contribute very much to the flavor, but serves to tenderize the flesh of the chicken.

Pigeons or Squabs
with Dates

Serves 4 • The combination of chicken or meat with dates is very ancient in the Arab world. This recipe is inspired by a Moroccan one. I made it with baby partridge, which was delicious. You could also use small guinea hens or poussins. Use soft dried dates.

2 inches fresh gingerroot, grated, or crushed in a garlic press to extract the juice

2 cloves garlic, crushed

4 tablespoons extra-virgin olive oil

Juice of 1 lemon

Salt and pepper

2 tablespoons honey

4 young Mediterranean pigeons, squabs, or small poussins

10 ounces dates, pitted (Tunisian or Californian dates)

1 teaspoon ground cinnamon

¼ cup toasted sesame seeds (optional)

Mix the ginger and garlic with the olive oil and half the lemon juice. Add salt and pepper and 1 tablespoon honey and beat well. Turn the birds in this marinade, and leave them in for ½ hour. Arrange on a baking dish, breast side down, and roast in a preheated 425°F oven for about 15 minutes. Turn them over and roast for another 10 minutes, or until they are done to your taste.

Put the dates in a pan and only just cover with water. Add cinnamon and the remaining honey and lemon and cook for 10 minutes, until the dates are soft and have absorbed the flavors. Serve the dates in the center and the pigeons around, and sprinkle all over with sesame seeds, if you like.

About Pigeons in Egypt

Raising pigeons is one of the passions of Egypt. People raise them for eating and also as carrier and racing pigeons. All the villages along the Nile have tall, conical pigeon towers, and in Cairo you see small dovecotes perched on balconies and hanging out of windows. At night you hear people whistling and calling back their flocks, for fear that a neighbor should entice them away.

In spring and summer, Cairo markets are full of tiny live pigeons (they are eaten when they are about four weeks old). There is even one market devoted to the merchandising of pigeons alone.

Saman bi Einab

Quails with Grapes

Serves 4 • A wonderful dish. Even those who think it is not worth cooking quail because the birds are too small think this is delightful. In Morocco, ground ginger is used, but with fresh ginger it is particularly delicious. I peel and cut the root into pieces and squeeze them through a garlic press to obtain the juice. But if you are used to grating ginger, do that.

8 quails

3 tablespoons sunflower or vegetable oil

5–6 tablespoons butter

Salt and pepper

3 inches fresh gingerroot, or to taste, grated, or crushed in a garlic press to extract the juice

3 cloves garlic, crushed

1 pound large seedless white grapes, washed and drained

Quails are often sold with some remaining feathers, which need to be pulled or burnt off.

In a large skillet, heat 1 tablespoon of the oil with the butter. Put in the quails and sauté briskly over medium heat for about 8 minutes, turning to brown them lightly all over, and adding salt, pepper, and ginger. Add the garlic, and cook moments more, until the aroma rises, then take off the heat.

Put the grapes with the remaining oil in a saucepan. Sprinkle with a little salt, and cook, with the lid on, over low heat for about 20 minutes, or until the grapes are soft, stirring occasionally. Add them to the quails in the frying pan and cook for about 10 minutes, or until the quails are done to your liking.

Serve hot.

THE QUAILS

The Khoja shot a large number of quails, which he dressed and put on to stew. He clapped the lid on the saucepan and went out to invite his friends to dinner, wishing to give some of them who were always questioning his skill an agreeable proof of it.

While he was out, another man came and carried off the cooked quails, putting live quails in their place.

The Khoja's friends arrived, the saucepan was brought out, and the Khoja proudly took the cover off; the quails flew out with a flutter and disappeared. The Khoja stared in amazement, and then ejaculated:

"Oh Lord! granted that Thou hast restored the quails to life and made the dear little creatures happy again, how about my butter, salt, pepper, herbs, cooking expenses, and all my hard work? Who is going to pay for them?"

BARNHAM, TRANS.,
TALES OF NASR-ED-DIN KHOJA

Bata wal Safargal

Roast Duck with Quince

Serves 4 • On a visit to Egypt, a hostess who invited me for dinner told us how she had run after the ducks that had escaped as she carried them home. There are many dishes of duck and chicken with quince in the Arab world. This one has the flavors of Morocco. The quince slices acquire a wonderful caramelized taste when they are fried.

> 1 duck, weighing about 5 pounds
> 1 tablespoon vegetable oil plus more for frying quince
> Salt and pepper
> 2 medium-sized quinces (or 1 very large one), weighing about 1 pound
> 1 teaspoon ground ginger
> 1 teaspoon cinnamon
> Juice of 2–2½ lemons or more
> 3 tablespoons honey

Rub the duck with 1 tablespoon of the oil and season with salt and pepper. Prick the skin with a fork in several places, so that the melted fat can ooze out. Put it, breast side down, on a rack in a roasting pan in a preheated 400°F oven for about 2 hours, turning it over after an hour, until the skin is crisp and brown and the flesh still soft and juicy. Pour out the fat as it is released (at least twice).

Cook the quinces at the same time as the duck. Wash and scrub them and wrap each one in a piece of foil. Put them in an oven dish or on a baking sheet, and place them under the duck, where the oven is a little less hot. A large quince can take up to 1½ hours to bake, medium ones about 1 hour (the time depends on their size and ripeness). Take them out when they feel a little soft when you press.

When cool enough to handle, cut them into quarters and cut away the hard cores, then cut each quarter into 2 slices—or 3 slices if the quince is large. (Do not peel them.) Keep aside.

When the duck is almost ready, fry the quince slices in shallow oil until brown (this gives them the delicious caramelized taste), then lift them out and drain on paper towels.

Prepare a sauce. Pour off all but 2 tablespoons of fat from the roasting pan, add a few tablespoons of water, and set the pan over high heat. Scrape up the browned bits, and stir in the ginger and cinnamon, the lemon juice and honey. Let it bubble up.

Serve the duck with the sauce poured over, accompanied by the fried quince. It's great.

Siman Meshwi

Broiled Quail

Serves 6 • Every year, migrating quails fly over the Mediterranean to Alexandria. Hundreds of the small birds fall, exhausted, on the dunes of the beaches of Agami, to be caught in large nets and collected in baskets. They are plucked and cleaned and marinated in a rich sauce, then grilled on the beaches over numerous little fires. Now quail farms are an important part of the local economy. Broiled quail are also a specialty of Lebanese restaurants, where they are served as mezze. The flavorings here are those of Alexandria.

6 quails
5 tablespoons extra-virgin olive oil
Salt
½ teaspoon ground cumin
½ teaspoon ground coriander
½ teaspoon ground cardamom
1 onion, blended to a cream in a food processor
Pinch of cayenne pepper or ground chili pepper
2 tablespoons finely chopped flat-leaf parsley to garnish
2 lemons, cut into wedges, to serve with

Wash the quails. You may need to singe some stray feathers. Using kitchen shears or a serrated knife, cut the birds open along the breastbone, then pull them out and flatten them as much as you can so that they cook evenly.

Mix the remaining ingredients except the parsley and lemon, and turn the birds in this marinade. Leave for 1 hour before cooking over glowing embers or under a hot broiler for 5–6 minutes, until browned all over but still juicy inside. Turn over once, leaving them longer with the bone side towards the fire, and be careful not to overcook.

Serve sprinkled with parsley, accompanied with lemon wedges.

Variation

For a Lebanese flavor, marinate in a mixture of olive oil with the juice of 1 lemon, 2 crushed garlic cloves, and salt and pepper.

Hamam Mahshi bil Burghul

Pigeon, Squab, or Poussin Stuffed with Bulgur, Raisins, and Pine Nuts

Serves 6 • In Cairo a few years ago, I was invited to dinner by a woman who was living alone in the family villa after her parents had died. While she spent a month in hospital with her sick mother, squatters had built dwellings in the large garden. By now it was a few years since they had settled in, and she couldn't get them out because of delays in the legal process. But I think she was lonely and had got used to them and was not trying too hard. The squatters had built a clay oven, and a dovecote where they kept pigeons; and chickens were running around. They grew all kinds of vegetables and herbs and gave her some of the produce. She watched their daily antics, noting that, while they quarreled all the time, the pigeons were loving and faithful towards each other. While her cook was preparing stuffed pigeons and minty broad beans with artichoke hearts for us, we watched the squatters cook their pigeons on the grill together with slices of eggplant and onion. Her recipe is one of my favorites. You will need the coarse bulgur, available from Greek and Middle Eastern stores. For a large and varied meal, you can serve half a bird per person. There is a large amount of stuffing because people like to have more on the side.

Stuffed pigeon is one of the delicacies of Egypt, which you serve, as they say, "if you really want to show somebody you love them." The stuffing is most commonly rice or *ferik* (young green wheat), but bulgur is an easier and delicious alternative.

1 large onion

Juice of 1 lemon

6 tablespoons sunflower or vegetable oil

Salt and pepper

1½ teaspoons ground cardamom

1½ teaspoons cinnamon

¾ teaspoon allspice

6 baby Mediterranean pigeons, squabs, or small poussins

FOR THE STUFFING

4½ cups chicken stock (page 143) (or you may use 2 chicken bouillon cubes)

1 pound coarse-ground bulgur (cracked wheat)

Salt and pepper

1½ teaspoons cinnamon

⅔ cup pine nuts

5 tablespoons butter or vegetable oil

¾ cup black or golden raisins, soaked in water for 15 minutes

For the marinade, put the onion, cut in pieces, the lemon juice, oil, salt and pepper, cardamom, cinnamon, and allspice in a blender or food processor and liquidize. Marinate the birds in this mixture for ½ hour.

For the stuffing, bring the stock to the boil in a pan, then add the bulgur, salt, pepper, and cinnamon. Stir and cook, covered, over very low heat for about 15 minutes, or until the liquid is absorbed and the grain is tender.

Fry the pine nuts in 1 tablespoon of the butter or oil, stirring and turning them, until lightly browned. Add the pine nuts, the drained raisins, and the remaining butter or oil to the cracked wheat in the pan, and mix well.

Spoon some of the stuffing into each of the birds so that the cavity is only three-quarters full, leaving room for the bulgur to expand. Secure the openings with toothpicks. Spread each bird with some of the marinade mixture and arrange in a baking dish, breast side down. Roast in a preheated 350°F oven for 25 minutes, then turn over and roast for 20 minutes more, or until they are golden brown and the juices no longer run pink when you cut in the thick part of a thigh.

At the same time, reheat the remaining bulgur stuffing in a baking dish in the oven, covered with foil, for 15–20 minutes.

Variation

For a Turkish stuffing, have 1 fried chopped onion and 1 cup coarsely chopped walnuts instead of raisins and pine nuts, and flavor the bulgur with 1 teaspoon cinnamon and ½ teaspoon allspice.

Frakh Ma'amra

*Mediterranean Pigeons or Squabs
Stuffed with Couscous*

Serves 4 • Many years ago, hearing of her prestigious cooking, I went to see a woman in Casablanca. She received me in a pale-blue kaftan on a patio with turquoise-and-cobalt mosaics. She explained that her family was from Fez and that her cooking was Fassi, which is reputedly the most refined regional cuisine of Morocco. She had three cooks working for her, but when she had guests, even only one or two, she said she spent at least six hours cooking in the kitchen herself. I asked if there were ways of shortening the cooking times. She said no. Her daughter, who was studying law in the States, interrupted: "Yes, there are shortcuts, you don't *have* to take that long." Her mother was deeply offended. Were all those years that she had spent in the kitchen to please her family a waste, then? Were all her efforts to make things exquisite of little value?

We cannot, of course, aspire to the extraordinary refinements of the grand family kitchens of Morocco, but we can achieve quite delicious results without much trouble. One of the recipes the lovely lady gave me was for pigeons stuffed with couscous. When she had a party, she prepared a huge mountain of couscous and covered it with little pigeons, shining and golden in their honey sauce.

This is an extremely easy version of the grand dish. Using quick-cooking couscous makes it easy. You can double the number of pigeons for a dinner party, but then you will need more large saucepans.

FOR THE STUFFING

2 cups quick-cooking couscous
Salt
1–2 tablespoons superfine sugar
3 tablespoons vegetable oil
1 tablespoon cinnamon
1–2 tablespoons orange-blossom water
3 tablespoons raisins, soaked in warm
  water for 10 minutes
1 cup blanched almonds
2 tablespoons butter

4 Mediterranean pigeons or squabs
3 tablespoons butter or sunflower oil
1½ large onions, finely chopped or
  grated
2 cloves garlic, crushed
2 teaspoons cinnamon
¼ teaspoon ginger
½ teaspoon saffron powder
Salt and plenty of pepper
2 tablespoons honey

To prepare the stuffing, moisten the couscous with 2 cups of warm salted water. Stir well, so that it is evenly absorbed. After about 10 minutes, stir in the sugar, 2 tablespoons of the oil, the cinnamon, and the orange-blossom water, and rub between your hands so as to break up any lumps. Add the drained raisins. Fry the almonds in the remaining oil, coarsely chop them and stir them into the couscous.

Fill each pigeon or squab with about 3 tablespoons stuffing. They should not be too

Mahshi bel Loz

*Mediterranean Pigeons or Squabs
Stuffed with Meat and Pine Nuts*

tightly packed, or the stuffing may burst out. Sew up the skin at both ends with cotton thread (or use toothpicks to secure), and reserve the remaining stuffing.

In a wide and heavy saucepan, put the 3 tablespoons butter or oil, the onions, garlic, cinnamon, ginger, saffron, and salt. Add about 1¼ cups water and the stuffed pigeons or squabs.

Simmer gently, covered, for about 30 minutes, until the birds are tender, adding more water if necessary and turning them over at least once, ending up breast down, so that they are well impregnated with the sauce. Lift one out (to make a little room) and stir in the honey. Then return the squabs to the pan and continue to cook until the flesh is at melting tenderness.

At the same time, heat the remaining stuffing in a baking dish, covered with foil, in a 400°F oven for about 20 minutes. Then stir in the butter.

To serve, make a mound of the stuffing and place the birds on top.

Serves 4 • An Egyptian delicacy.

FOR THE STUFFING

1 large onion, chopped
2 tablespoons vegetable oil
¾ pound ground beef
Salt and pepper
¾ teaspoon cinnamon
3 tablespoons pine nuts

4 small Mediterranean pigeons or squabs
2 onions, grated or finely chopped
4 tablespoons vegetable oil
½ teaspoon ground cardamom
1 teaspoon cinnamon
Juice of 1 lemon
Salt and pepper

For the stuffing, fry the onion in the oil until golden. Add the meat, break it up with a fork, and stir, turning it over, for 2–3 minutes, until it changes color. Add salt and pepper, cinnamon, and pine nuts, and stir well.

Stuff the birds with this, and close the openings with toothpicks.

In a large pan or casserole, heat the onions in the oil until golden, and stir in the cardamom and cinnamon. Put in the pigeons or squabs, half-cover with water, and add lemon juice, salt, and pepper. Cook, covered, for ¾–1 hour, turning the birds over once, until they are very tender. Uncover towards the end to reduce the sauce, and serve hot.

Shish Taouk

Chicken Kebab

Serves 4 • Grilled chicken on skewers is part of the Arab kebab-house and restaurant trade. The flavoring here is Lebanese. Look at the variations for alternatives, and be careful not to overcook, as chicken pieces dry out quickly. Leg meat remains juicier than breast meat.

4 boned and skinned chicken fillets— breasts or legs

4 tablespoons extra-virgin olive oil

2–4 cloves garlic, crushed

Juice of ½ lemon

Salt and pepper

OPTIONAL GARNISHES

4 tablespoons chopped flat-leaf parsley

1 lemon, quartered

1 mild red onion, finely sliced

2 teaspoons sumac to sprinkle on

Cut the chicken into 1-inch pieces. Mix the oil, garlic, lemon juice, salt, and pepper and leave the chicken in this marinade for ½ hour or longer, turning the pieces over once.

Thread onto flat-bladed skewers and cook over the glowing embers of a charcoal fire or under the broiler for 6–10 minutes, until lightly browned, turning the skewers over once, and brushing with the marinade.

Serve on a bed of parsley, with lemon wedges and sliced onion. Sprinkle if you like with sumac (in which case, do not use the lemon wedges).

Variations

• For a Turkish marinade, liquidize in a food processor 1 onion with 4 tablespoons olive oil, 1 teaspoon cinnamon, salt, and pepper.

• For a Moroccan flavor, use as a marinade ¼ teaspoon ginger, 1 teaspoon paprika, a good pinch of ground chili pepper, and salt mixed with 4 tablespoons extra-virgin olive oil. Serve sprinkled with chopped cilantro.

• For an Iranian version, turn the chicken pieces in 4 tablespoons melted butter mixed with ¼ teaspoon saffron powder, the juice of ½ lemon, and some salt.

THE ROAST CHICKEN

The Khoja sat under a tree eating some roast chicken.

A man came up to him and said, "How nice! I should like some of that. Please give me a bit."

"I am very sorry, brother," answered the Khoja. "It isn't mine. It is my wife's chicken."

"But you are eating it," said the man.

"Of course," said the Khoja. "What else can I do? When she gave it to me she said, 'Eat it.'"

BARNHAM, TRANS.,
TALES OF NASR-ED-DIN KHOJA

Fish Kebab with rice (page 182)

Fried Marinated Fish (page 186)

Fish in a Hot Saffron and Ginger Tomato Sauce (page 186)

Quails with Grapes (page 206)

Chicken with Tomatoes and Honey (page 219)

Kofta with Tomato Sauce and Yogurt (page 239)

Lamb Tagine with Peas, Preserved Lemon, and Olives (page 250)

Artichokes, Fava Beans, and Almonds (page 283)

Djaj fil Forn

Roast Chicken with Lemon and Garlic

Serves 4 • *Djaj* is the Arabic word for chicken; *ferakh* is an Egyptian term. Every day, the trams and buses coming into the towns from the villages are crowded with peasants carrying crates of live, cackling poultry. The chickens are killed and plucked at the market or poultry shops. This is a simple and homely but delicious Egyptian way of cooking the birds.

    A 3½–4-pound chicken
    2 tablespoons mild extra-virgin olive oil
    Juice of ½ lemon
    Salt and pepper
    2 cloves garlic, crushed

Rub the chicken with a mixture of olive oil, lemon juice, salt, pepper, and garlic. Put it breast side down in a roasting pan in a preheated 350°F oven, so that the fat runs down and prevents the breast from drying out.

Roast for 1¼ to 1½ hours, until well browned, turning the chicken breast side up about midway through. Test for doneness by cutting into a thigh with a pointed knife. The juices should run clear, not pink.

Variations

• Rub the chicken with a mixture of 2 tablespoons olive or sunflower oil, 1 teaspoon cinnamon, ½ teaspoon allspice or ground cardamom, salt, and pepper.
• Add 2 teaspoons ground cumin to the original marinade.
• Liquidize in a blender or food processor 1 quartered onion, 2 tablespoons olive oil, and 1 tablespoon sumac, and rub the chicken with this mixture.

Chicken Sofrito

Serves 4 • The chicken acquires a delicate, tangy flavor and pale-yellow tinge. It was a regular dish in my parents' home. Serve it hot with potatoes or with rice; as part of a cold buffet meal; or for a cold family meal in summer, accompanied by salads.

    2 tablespoons vegetable oil
    Juice of ½–1 lemon
    ½ teaspoon turmeric
    Salt and white pepper
    4 cardamom pods, cracked
    A 3½–4-pound chicken

Put the oil and lemon juice in a large saucepan or casserole with a lid, along with a cupful of water, the turmeric, salt, white pepper, and cardamom pods. Bring to the boil, then place the chicken in the pan. Cover and cook over very low heat, turning the chicken over frequently, and adding another cupful of water as the juices are absorbed. Continue cooking for about 1½ hours, until the chicken is very soft and tender. Adjust the seasoning and serve.

If serving cold, lift out the chicken, divide it into joints, remove the larger bones and skin, and arrange in a serving dish. If you prefer an absolutely clear jelly, skim any fat off the surface of the sauce, and use paper towels to remove the last traces. Pour over the chicken and allow it to become quite cold, covered, in the refrigerator. On cooling, the sauce will become a pale, lemony jelly and the chicken will be a very delicate off-white.

Ferakh bel Tamatem

Sautéed Chicken Breasts with Tomatoes

Serves 4 • This is a quick and simple way of cooking chicken.

1 tablespoon butter

1 tablespoon sunflower or vegetable oil

4 boned chicken breast halves, with or
    without skin

Salt and pepper

4 cloves garlic, crushed

1 pound tomatoes, peeled and cut into
    small pieces

1–2 teaspoons sugar

$^1/_2$ teaspoon cinnamon

Heat the butter with the oil in a skillet. Put in the chicken breasts, season with salt and pepper, and brown them lightly on both sides.

Add the garlic, tomatoes, sugar, and cinnamon. Cook for 15–20 minutes, or until the chicken is done but still juicy.

A TALE OF GOHA

He was stopped at the gates of the town by the Turkish police, who asked what he fed his chickens. "Wheat," said Goha. The police then demanded to see his receipt for the taxes paid on the wheat he had used. Not having heard of, or paid, any taxes on wheat, Goha was dragged off to the qadi (magistrate) and forced to pay a fine of five piasters, more than half of what he expected to get for his chickens.

The next time he journeyed to the soukh, he declared that he had fed the chickens on barley, to escape the fine. It turned out that barley, too, was taxable, and he was fined again.

The incident was repeated several times. Goha tried chickpeas, millet, and beans, but it turned out that all of these were taxable. Finally, in desperation, having been stopped yet again by the police and asked what his chickens had been fed on, he replied, "Oh! I just give each one a maleem (farthing) a day and tell him to buy what he likes!"

In Egypt, it is common practice for peasants and vendors to push a large handful of corn down the birds' throats before killing them, so that they weigh more.

Tabaka Piliç

Chicken with Plums

Serves 6 • A Turkish dish of Georgian origin. Georgia borders on northwestern Turkey and is famous for plum trees and plum sauces. The traditional way to make this dish is to cut the chicken all the way down the back with kitchen shears or a bread knife, open it out, and cut away the bones. You season the flesh inside with crushed garlic, salt, and pepper, then close the chicken up, flatten it with a weight, and cook it in a pan gently in some butter for about 40 minutes, turning it over once. But I find it is easier and equally good to use chicken fillets.

6 boned and skinned chicken fillets
  (a mix of breasts and legs)
2 tablespoons butter
1 tablespoon vegetable oil
Salt and pepper
2 or 3 cloves garlic, chopped
6 large or 12 small plums

FOR THE SAUCE

4 tablespoons plum jam
1 tablespoon red- or white-wine vinegar
1 clove garlic, crushed
Pinch of chili-pepper flakes or ground chili pepper

In a large skillet, sauté the chicken pieces in a mixture of butter and oil over very low heat for about 15–20 minutes, until they are no longer pink inside when you cut in with a knife. Sprinkle with salt and pepper, and turn the pieces over at least once, adding garlic towards the end.

Put in the plums and cook briefly, turning them over, until they soften a little. Their skins will tear, but it doesn't matter.

For the sauce, heat the plum jam with the vinegar in a small saucepan, stir in the garlic and chili flakes or chili pepper, and cook for a few moments longer.

Serve the chicken pieces with the sauce poured over, garnished with the plums.

Ferakh bel Hummus

Chicken with Chickpeas

Serves 4–6 • This was a family favorite that my mother often made.

1 onion, finely chopped
2 tablespoons vegetable oil
³⁄₄ teaspoon turmeric
A 3¹⁄₄–4-pound chicken
1¹⁄₄ cups chickpeas, soaked overnight
Juice of 1 lemon, or more to taste
2–4 cloves garlic, crushed
Black pepper or a pinch of cayenne or ground chili pepper
Salt

Fry the onion in the oil in a large saucepan until golden, then stir in the turmeric.

Put in the chicken and turn it until it is yellow all over. Add 2½ cups water, the drained chickpeas, lemon juice, garlic, and pepper. Bring to the boil and simmer, covered, for 1 hour or longer, until the chicken is very tender, the chickpeas are soft, yellow, and lemony, and the liquid is reduced. Turn the chicken occasionally and add aadd water so that there is plenty of liquid sauce. Add salt when the chickpeas have softened.

Adjust the seasoning and cut up chicken.

Of Moroccan Chicken Tagines and Qdras

The word "tagine"—the name of the Moroccan round clay cooking pot with the pointed cone-shaped lid, and also that of the food cooked in it—has become so glamorous and prestigious in our Western world, and so misused in restaurants in Morocco, that it has come to mean any kind of stew. The clay tagine, cooking ever so gently and ever so slowly over a brazier (*kanoun*) of constantly replenished embers, diffuses the heat all round the pot and produces at the end a much-reduced unctuous sauce sizzling with oil or butter (usually clarified).

But for parties and great occasions, it has never been possible to cook in tagines, because they don't contain all that much. The cooking is done in the large pot which forms the bottom part of the couscous steamer, called *qdra*. You can see some huge ones for sale and hire in the markets. The old ones, in copper, are being repaired; the new ones are in aluminum and in stainless steel.

More than twenty years ago, when I was traveling in Morocco, I visited the hotels where they were just beginning to serve Moroccan food rather than French. In the kitchen of one of the grandest, where the cooks were all women, the man who supervised them said that they were trying to transpose home cooking to a commercial kitchen but that it was very difficult to mass-produce and get the same results as in the home. This applied also to the long-cooked dishes which they could not prepare in the tagines. They cooked them in large pans and brought them to the table in little individual tagines beautifully decorated with blue, green, turquoise, and yellow arabesques. And now people at home also find it more convenient to cook in saucepans. The result may not be the same, but it can be a very good approximation if you cook slowly and reduce the sauce until it is rich and unctuous. Now that you can purchase beautifully decorated tagines in America, you may be tempted to serve in them.

The word *qdra*—the name of the giant pots—also came to mean the kinds of dishes with noble ingredients that are cooked in a *qdra* for the grand parties of the royal city of Fez, the ingredients being chickpeas, almonds, *smen* (clarified butter), onions reduced to melting softness, and saffron. The poor man's *qdra,* referred to as *marqa,* are the stews cooked in the countryside in ordinary saucepans and the stews sold by vendors in the streets and in the souks. These are cooked in peanut oil, and turmeric is used instead of saffron.

Djaj Qdra Touimiya

Saffron Chicken with Chickpeas and Almonds

Serves 4–6 • In this delicately flavored and scrumptious Moroccan *qdra,* the long-cooked almonds should become very soft.

As so often in Moroccan cooking, one onion is cooked first with the meat or chicken, and when these are nearly done, the remaining onions are added. The first onion is used to add flavor to the meat, and it practically melts and disappears into the sauce. The onions added later keep their shape and add body to the sauce.

A 3½–4-pound chicken

2 tablespoons butter

3 medium onions

¼ teaspoon crushed saffron threads or powdered saffron (optional)

1 teaspoon ground cinnamon, or more

Pepper

½ cup chickpeas, soaked overnight, or a 1-pound can of chickpeas

¾ cup blanched almonds

Salt

¼ cup chopped flat-leaf parsley

Juice of ½ lemon

Put the chicken, butter, and 1 onion, finely chopped, in a large pan, and cover with water. Add saffron, cinnamon, and pepper. Bring to the boil, add the soaked chickpeas (if using canned ones, they go in later) and the almonds, and simmer for about 1½ hours, until the chickpeas are soft and the chicken is very tender, adding salt when the chickpeas begin to soften, and more water if necessary. Lift out the chicken and cut into serving pieces.

Add the rest of the onions, finely chopped, the parsley, and canned chickpeas if using, and boil slowly for about 15 minutes, or until the onions are soft and the sauce considerably reduced. Return the chicken pieces to the sauce to heat through.

To serve, arrange the chicken pieces on a serving dish, cover with chickpeas and almonds and the sauce, and squeeze lemon juice over the dish.

Variations

• Dried black-eyed peas, or haricot or navy beans, can be used instead of chickpeas, or all three can be cooked together.

• *Djaj qdra bel looz* (chicken with almonds) has twice the amount of almonds and no chickpeas.

Djaj Mqualli

Chicken with Preserved Lemon
and Olives

Serves 4 • The last time I ate this famous Moroccan dish was in a restaurant in Paris where there was an evening of Arab poetry and tales accompanied by musicians. It was not the best example of the dish, but I always find it enjoyable. I love the special flavor of preserved lemons. At every vegetable market in North Africa, and now also in the south of France, you can see stalls laden with huge piles of soft lemons oozing with juice beside several varieties of olives. The two are often used together. The pulp of the preserved lemon is discarded, and the skin alone is used. The word *mqualli* alludes to the way the chicken is cooked, with oil and only a little water.

A 3½–4-pound chicken

3 tablespoons peanut or vegetable oil

1 large onion, grated or very finely chopped

2 or 3 cloves garlic, crushed

¼ teaspoon crushed saffron threads or powdered saffron

½–¾ teaspoon ground ginger

1½ teaspoons cinnamon

Salt and pepper

Peel of 1 or 2 preserved lemons (see page 459), rinsed and cut in quarters

12 green or pale-brown olives, soaked in 2 changes of water for ½ hour

Put the chicken in a large saucepan with all the ingredients except the preserved lemons and olives.

Half-cover with water and simmer, covered, turning the chicken over a few times, and adding water if necessary, for about 1½ hours, or until the chicken is so tender that the flesh pulls off the bone and the liquid is reduced to a thick unctuous sauce.

Throw the lemon peel and drained rinsed olives into the sauce for the last 15 minutes of cooking. Some like to add the peel at the very end; some like to chop part of it up to flavor the sauce. Cut the chicken into serving pieces and serve hot, with the sauce poured over.

RIDDLE:
Our black servant is green.
Her children are born white and
then grow black. Who is she?

ANSWER:
An olive tree.

Djaj Matisha Mesla

Chicken with Tomatoes and Honey

Serves 4 • This Moroccan tagine is one of my favorites. The chicken cooks in the juice of the tomatoes, which reduces to a sumptuous, thick, honeyed, almost caramelized sauce. And it looks beautiful too.

A 3½–4-pound chicken, cut into quarters

3 tablespoons peanut or vegetable oil

1 large onion, grated

2 pounds tomatoes, peeled and cut into pieces

Salt and plenty of pepper

½ teaspoon ground ginger

2 teaspoons ground cinnamon

½ teaspoon crushed saffron threads or powdered saffron

2 tablespoons clear honey (Moroccans use up to 4 tablespoons)

¾ cup blanched almonds, coarsely chopped, toasted under the broiler or fried in oil

2 tablespoons sesame seeds, toasted

Put all the ingredients except the honey, almonds, and sesame seeds in a large pan. Cook gently, covered, turning the chicken occasionally, for about 1¼ hours, or until the flesh is so tender it can be pulled off the bone easily.

Remove the chicken, and continue to cook the sauce over medium heat until reduced to a thick, sizzling cream. Stir as it begins to caramelize, and be careful that it does not stick or burn. Now stir in the honey, return the chicken pieces to the sauce, and heat through. Serve hot, covered with the sauce and sprinkled with the almonds and sesame seeds.

Djaj bel Loz

Chicken with Almonds and Honey

Serves 8 • A magnificent dish, and a stunning example of the way Moroccans mix savory and sweet. Chicken pieces are first stewed with lemon juice and saffron, then baked with a topping of almonds and honey.

2 large onions, chopped

4 tablespoons peanut or vegetable oil

1 teaspoon ground ginger

1½ teaspoons cinnamon

2 3½–4-pound chickens, cut into quarters

Salt and pepper

½ teaspoon powdered saffron

Juice of ½–1 lemon

1½ cups blanched almonds, coarsely ground

1 tablespoon rose water

4–5 tablespoons honey

In a large pan, cook the onions in the oil over low heat with the lid on until they soften, stirring occasionally. Stir in the ginger and cinnamon and put in the chicken. Cover with water, add salt and pepper, saffron, and lemon juice, and simmer, covered, for 30 minutes. Taste and adjust the seasonings (the sauce should be quite salty), and move the pieces so that the top ones go to the bottom.

Lift the chicken pieces out and arrange them in a large, shallow baking dish. Remove the skin if you like, and pour the sauce over.

Mix the ground almonds with the rose water and honey. Spread this paste over the chicken pieces and bake in a 350°F oven for about 30–45 minutes. The flavor, with the melting honey, is divine. Serve hot.

Jaj bel Lissan al Assfour

Chicken with Pasta

Serves 6 • This Syrian dish is made with a type of pasta called *lissan al assfour* (bird's tongues) which looks like large grains of rice. It cooks in the sauce from the chicken and acquires a rich, spicy flavor and light-brown color. You will find it in Middle Eastern stores as well as in the pasta section of supermarkets, where it is called "orzo." An apricot sauce, *salsat mishmisheya,* sometimes accompanies the dish (see variations).

1 large onion, chopped

2 tablespoons sunflower oil

1 chicken, about 3½ pounds

4 cloves garlic, sliced

2 teaspoons cinnamon

1 teaspoon crushed cardamom seeds

½ teaspoon ground ginger (optional)

Salt and pepper

Juice of ½ lemon

2 cups orzo

2 tablespoons butter

In a pan large enough to contain the chicken, fry the onion in the oil until soft. Put in the chicken, and pour in 4½ cups of water (it will not cover the chicken entirely). Add garlic, cinnamon, cardamom, ginger if you like, salt, and pepper. Simmer for 1–1½ hours with the lid on, until the chicken is so tender the meat falls off the bone, turning the chicken over once halfway through. Take out the chicken, and when it is cool enough to handle, remove the skin and bones.

Bring the sauce to the boil, add the lemon juice, and throw in the pasta. Cook for 8–10 minutes, or until tender, adding boiling water—about 1 cup—if necessary, and more salt and pepper.

Stir in the butter and put the chicken pieces back into the pan, over the pasta. Heat through before serving. The pasta becomes soft rather than *al dente.*

Variations

• Dry vermicelli (*shaghria* in Arabic), crushed into 1-inch pieces with your hands, can be used instead of the orzo. They will need less cooking time—about 5–6 minutes.

• For the apricot sauce to accompany, simmer ½ pound tart, unsweetened dried apricots in water until soft. Add the juice of ½ lemon if you prefer a sharper taste. When the apricots are soft, crush them with a fork and continue to simmer until reduced to a soft puree, or puree to a cream with the liquid in a food processor. Serve hot or cold in a separate bowl.

• In Morocco, they boil a chicken, lift it out of the broth, and cut it up, then cook broken vermicelli in the broth. They serve the chicken covered and concealed by the vermicelli and garnished with sprinklings of ground cinnamon in a pattern of lines.

Tagine T'Faia

*Tagine with Hard-Boiled Eggs
and Almonds*

Serves 4–6 • In Morocco they say that this dish, like many others, was brought back from Andalusia by the Moors after the Reconquista.

- 1 chicken, weighing about 3½ pounds, cut into 4–6 pieces
- 3 tablespoons butter or vegetable oil
- Salt and pepper
- ½ teaspoon ground ginger
- About ¼ teaspoon powdered saffron
- 2 onions, finely chopped
- 3 tablespoons finely chopped flat-leaf parsley
- 6 hard-boiled eggs
- ⅔ cup blanched almonds, or more

Put the chicken pieces in a large pan with 2 tablespoons of the butter or oil, salt, pepper, ginger, saffron, onions, and parsley. Cover with water, bring to the boil, and simmer gently, half covered, for ¾–1 hour, or until the chicken has absorbed the taste of the ginger and saffron and is well cooked, and the sauce is reduced.

Heat 3 tablespoons of water with a pinch of powdered saffron. Shell the hard-boiled eggs and roll them in the saffron water to color them all over. Fry the blanched almonds in the remaining butter or oil, shaking the pan and turning them over, until lightly colored.

Arrange the chicken in a serving dish and pour the sauce over it. Arrange the eggs on top, between the pieces of chicken, and garnish with fried almonds.

Yogurtlu Basti

Chicken with Spiced Yogurt

Serves 4 • A Turkish dish in which yogurt, an important feature in Turkish cooking, is flavored with cardamom and ginger.

- 2 cups plain whole-milk yogurt
- 1 teaspoon ground cardamom, or the seeds, crushed
- 1½ inches fresh gingerroot, grated, or crushed in a garlic press to extract the juice
- 1 large onion, chopped
- 2 tablespoons olive oil
- A 3½-pound chicken, cut into quarters, or 4 chicken fillets
- Salt and pepper
- ¼ cup blanched almonds, toasted and coarsely chopped

In a bowl, mix the yogurt with the cardamom and ginger and let them infuse while you cook the chicken.

In a large skillet, fry the onion in the oil till soft. Add the chicken pieces and sauté until the onions are golden and the chicken pieces lightly browned. Add salt and pepper and a cup of water, and cook over low heat—12 minutes for breast meat, 20 minutes for dark—until the chicken is very tender and the sauce reduced, turning the chicken pieces over and adding a little water if it becomes too dry.

Remove the pan from the heat and stir in the yogurt. Serve sprinkled with almonds.

Fattet Jaj

Fatta with Chicken

Serves 8 • This multi-layered dish is complex and time-consuming, and I don't expect many people to attempt it. But it is very important in the Arab world, especially in Syria and Lebanon. And it is one of those recipes which bring me a flood of memories. I had received a letter from a woman I did not know in Beirut saying that she would like to meet me and that she had recipes for me. It was the late Josephine Salam. On our first meeting—at Claridge's tearoom, where a band played Noël Coward tunes—she brought me a bottle of orange-blossom water and a copper pan. She volunteered to come to my house and show me how to make *fattet jaj*. I got the ingredients, and we made so much that we had to call in the neighbors to eat. I saw her for many years after that, and we had many meals together. It was the time of the civil war in Lebanon, and I received through her an ongoing account of everyday life in the ravaged city. Her daughter Rana has become a conceptual artist. For her thesis at the Royal College of Art in London, she asked me to give a lecture on the history of Middle Eastern food. She filled the college with hangings announcing the event, with my portrait painted on by a cinema-poster painter in Egypt. She laid out foods and spices as in a souk, put on a tape of Egyptian street sounds and music, and offered Arab delicacies.

4 cups thick Greek-style drained yogurt, at room temperature

4 cloves garlic, crushed

1 chicken, about 3½ pounds

Juice of 3 lemons

1 teaspoon ground cardamom

5 or 6 small pieces of mastic (page 44), pulverized with a little salt (optional)

Salt and pepper

1 large onion, finely chopped

4 tablespoons vegetable oil

1 pound lean ground beef

1 cup basmati or long-grain rice (washed if basmati)

1 teaspoon ground cinnamon

Fatta

A number of Arab dishes go under the name *fatta,* which describes the manner of breaking crisp toasted Arab bread into pieces with your hands. They all have in common a bed of toasted bread soaked in a flavorsome stock, and also a topping of yogurt. The fillings in between vary. The most common is with chickpeas (page 333); another is with eggplants (page 314). A special favorite is with chicken, meat, and rice. They are considered family food and are not usually offered to guests, but if you go by the delight with which they are described, they are more popular than party dishes.

1 teaspoon allspice

3 very thin pita breads or 2 ordinary pitas

Vegetable oil for frying

¼–⅓ cup pine nuts

Pour the yogurt into a bowl and beat in the garlic. Let it come to room temperature.

Wash the chicken. Put it in a large pot and cover with water. Bring to the boil, and remove any scum. Add the lemon juice and cardamom, mastic if you like, salt, and pepper, and cook until the chicken is very tender and almost falls off the bones—1 to 1½ hours. Lift out the chicken, remove the skin and bones, and return the chicken pieces to the stock. Bring it to the boil again when you are ready to serve.

In the meantime, make the *hashwa* or filling: Fry the onion in 3 tablespoons of the oil until it is golden brown, stirring occasionally. Add the ground meat and cook, crushing and stirring it, until it has changed color, then add the rice and continue to stir. Add cinnamon and allspice, salt and pepper, and 1¾ cups water. Cover the pan and reduce the heat to a minimum. Cook gently over low heat for about 20 minutes, until the rice is done.

Open out the pita breads. Toast them in the oven or under the broiler until they are crisp and only lightly browned. Then break them up into pieces in your hands and spread them at the bottom of a deep serving dish.

Work quickly to assemble the dish when you are ready to serve, so that all the layers, apart from the yogurt, are hot. Cover the toasted bread with the rice-and-meat *hashwa*. Lay over this the chicken pieces, and pour over

enough of the flavorsome stock to soak the bread thoroughly. Cover entirely with the yogurt, and sprinkle the top with the pine nuts lightly fried in a drop of oil.

Serve at once.

Note: If you want to prepare this in advance, assemble the layers in a large ovenproof dish, cover it with foil, and heat it up in the oven before serving.

Variation

Instead of toasting the bread, Josephine cut it into triangles, deep-fried them in oil until crisp and brown, and then drained them on paper towels.

ARAB SAYING:
"Eat and praise your host."

Madzounov Manradzo

*Bulgur and Meat Dumplings with
Chicken and Yogurt*

Serves 8 • Armenian dishes are humble and rustic. This one is a party dish which combines everyday ingredients in a complex way. The serving is something of a ritual.

A 3½–4-pound chicken

½ cup chickpeas, soaked overnight

Salt and pepper

1 cinnamon stick

1 onion

1½ cups fine- or medium-ground bulgur (cracked wheat)

¾ pound finely ground beef or lamb

2 egg yolks

1 tablespoon cornstarch

4 cups plain whole-milk yogurt, at room temperature

3 tablespoons melted butter

1 tablespoon dried mint

Put the chicken in a large pan with the drained chickpeas. Cover with 3 or more quarts of water, add the cinnamon stick, and bring to the boil. Remove the scum and simmer, covered, for about 1¼–1½ hours, until the chicken and the chickpeas are very tender. Add salt and pepper when the chickpeas have begun to soften.

Make the dumplings. Finely chop the onion in a food processor. Rinse the bulgur and drain, squeezing out the excess water, then add the bulgur to the chopped onions in the food processor, along with the meat and a little salt and pepper. Blend to a soft paste. Rub your hands with oil. Take lumps of the paste and roll into small walnut-sized balls. Arrange them on a plate.

Pour off the chicken stock into another pan, leaving just enough to keep the chickpeas and chicken moist. Lift out the chicken, remove the skin and bones, and cut it into pieces, then return the pieces to the pan with the chickpeas.

Drop the dumplings into the stock and simmer for about 15 minutes. Lift them out with a slotted spoon and keep aside in the pan with the chicken and chickpeas.

Reduce the stock to about 4 cups. Mix the egg yolks with the cornstarch in a large bowl to a smooth paste, and beat in the yogurt (the yolks and cornstarch will prevent it from curdling when it cooks). Beat in a ladle of the hot stock, pour this into the pan with the simmering stock, and stir constantly over low heat until the mixture begins to boil and thickens very slightly (it will be quite soupy).

Before serving, add the chicken, chickpeas, and dumplings, drained of their stock, and heat through.

Serve in soup plates with the melted butter and mint dribbled over the top.

Djaj Mahshi bel Hashwa

*Chicken with Rice, Ground Meat,
and Nut Stuffing*

Serves 6 • Chicken with rice-and-ground-meat stuffing or *hashwa* is a classic festive dish of the Arab world. The old way was to boil the stuffed chicken first, then briefly roast it to give it a golden color. These days it is more common to cook the stuffing separately and to roast the chicken. For a large party you can make double the quantity, shape the stuffing in a mound in a large round oven dish, cover it with the cut-up pieces of chicken, then heat it through, covered with foil, before serving.

1 chicken, 3½–4 pounds
1 teaspoon cinnamon
1 teaspoon ground cardamom
Salt and pepper
2 tablespoons sunflower or vegetable oil

FOR THE STUFFING

¾ pound ground lean beef or lamb
2 tablespoons oil
Salt and pepper
1 teaspoon cinnamon
1 teaspoon cardamom seeds, crushed
¾ cup long-grain rice
1½ cups chicken stock (page 143) (or you may use 1 bouillon cube)
½ cup split blanched almonds or coarsely chopped pistachios
⅔ cup pine nuts, lightly toasted

Wash the chicken and rub it with a mixture of cinnamon, cardamom, salt, pepper, and oil. Place the chicken, breast side down, in an oven dish and roast in a preheated 350°F oven for 1–1½ hours, or until the skin is well browned but the chicken is still juicy inside, turning it over halfway through.

For the stuffing, fry the ground meat in the oil, crushing it, turning it over, and breaking up any lumps, until it changes color. Add salt and pepper, cinnamon, and the cardamom seeds, and stir well. Add the rice, mix very well, and pour in the stock. Cook with the lid on, over very low heat, for 20 minutes, or until the rice is very tender. Stir in the almonds or pistachios and the pine nuts.

Serve the chicken with the stuffing.

Morg Tu Por

Chicken Stuffed with Dried Fruits

Serves 6 • I have also made this Persian stuffing for Christmas turkey, using twice the amount.

1 chicken, about 3½–4 pounds
1 onion, finely chopped
Butter or vegetable oil
½ pound prunes, soaked, pitted, and chopped
½ pound dried apricots, soaked and chopped
⅓ cup raisins
2 apples, peeled, cored, and chopped
Salt and pepper
1 teaspoon ground cinnamon

Clean and wash the chicken. Fry the chopped onion in 2 tablespoons butter or oil until soft and golden. Add the chopped fruits and the raisins and sauté gently for a few minutes. Season to taste with salt, pepper, and cinnamon.

Stuff the chicken with some of this mixture, and secure the opening with a toothpick or sew it with thread. Rub the chicken with salt, pepper, and the remaining butter or oil, and place it breast side down in a baking dish. Put the rest of the stuffing in another oven dish and cover with foil. Roast the chicken in a preheated 325°F oven for about 1½ hours, turning the chicken over after 40 minutes. Bake the remaining stuffing for the last 30–40 minutes.

Serve the chicken surrounded with the extra stuffing, accompanied by rice.

Variation

You may add ¾ cup coarsely chopped walnut halves and ⅓ cup barberries (see page 43) to the stuffing.

Boned Stuffed Chicken with Veal and Pistachios

Serves 8 or more • This was a regular at my aunt Régine's dinner parties. It is similar to dishes featured in medieval manuals. The French would call it a galantine.

  1 chicken, about 3½ pounds
  4 tablespoons vegetable oil
  Salt and pepper
  1½ pounds ground veal
  ½–⅔ cup very coarsely chopped
     pistachio nuts
  Juice of ½ lemon

Clean and wash the chicken, and cut off the wing tips and leg ends to make the removal of the skin possible. Singe the chicken over a flame to loosen the skin from the flesh. Carefully pull the skin right off, as though undressing the chicken, taking care not to tear it, starting from the neck and pulling it off the legs last. It will come right off with the occasional help of a pointed knife. Wash the skin, turn it right side out, and put it aside.

Cut the skinned chicken into quarters, put them in a saucepan, and cover with water. Add 2 tablespoons of the oil, season with salt and pepper, bring to the boil, and simmer gently until the chicken is very tender—about 30–45 minutes. Remove from the heat and let it cool in the stock. Drain and keep the stock.

Bone the chicken, discarding nerves and tendons, and grind or chop the meat finely. Put it in a large bowl, mix in the ground veal, and season with salt and pepper. Knead very well, then add the pistachio nuts and work them into the mixture.

Using a needle and strong thread, sew up all but the largest vent in the chicken skin and darn any holes. Stuff the skin carefully with the chicken-and-veal mixture, and re-form as nearly as possible in its original shape. Sew the opening tightly.

Heat the remaining oil in a large pan, put in the stuffed chicken, and turn to brown it lightly all over. Add the lemon juice and about half a ladle of the stock. Simmer gently, covered, for about 1 hour, turning the chicken over, and adding more stock, half a ladle at a time, if it becomes dry. At the end of the cooking time, the veal should be well cooked and almost blended with the chicken, and the sauce much reduced. Remove from the heat and allow to cool overnight in its own sauce.

Serve cold. Traditionally, the chicken is served already cut in thick slices, but I think it looks rather beautiful with its subdued boneless shape, served whole and sliced at the table.

Variation

A version said to be for lazy cooks is just as delicious, though not as dramatic. Cook the chicken as in the recipe for *sofrito* (page 213), adding just a pinch of turmeric or none at all. When cool, skin it and remove the bones and tendons. Grind or chop the flesh and mix it with the ground veal, 1 egg, and a handful of chopped pistachios. Knead thoroughly and roll into a thick sausage shape. Sauté in 2 tablespoons hot oil, turning it until golden all over. Add water, a little at a time, as it becomes absorbed, and simmer gently, covered, until well cooked, turning it over once. Allow to cool in its sauce for several hours before serving. Serve cut in slices.

Fesenjan e Ordak

Duck with Walnut and Pomegranate Sauce

Serves 4 • *Fesenjan* is a famous Persian sauce for rice with stewed duck. I love the sauce, which has a special sweet-and-sour flavor from pomegranate molasses (*rob-e nar*), but I don't like stewed duck, so I roast the duck instead.

1 duck, weighing about 5 pounds

3 tablespoons vegetable oil

Salt and pepper

2 large onions, chopped

1½ cups walnuts, finely chopped

4 tablespoons sour-pomegranate syrup (molasses or concentrate)

1–2 tablespoons sugar, or to taste

1 cup chicken stock (page 143) (or you may use ½ bouillon cube)

Rub the duck with 1 tablespoon of the oil and season with salt and pepper. Prick the skin with a fork in several places so that the melted fat can ooze out. Put it breast side down on a rack in a baking dish in a preheated 400°F oven. Cook for about 2 hours, until the skin is crisp and brown and the flesh still juicy, turning the duck over so that it is breast side up after an hour. If you don't have a rack, you can lay the duck straight in the dish, but you must pour out the fat as it is released—at least twice.

For the sauce, in a pan fry the onions in the remaining 2 tablespoons of oil until golden brown, stirring occasionally. Add the walnuts and stir for 1–2 minutes. Stir in the pomegranate syrup and the sugar, and pour in the stock. Stir well, and simmer for 15–20 minutes, until the sauce is thick.

Carve the duck and serve the pieces on plain rice. Pour the sauce on top.

GEESE AT AKSHEHIR HAVE ONLY ONE LEG

One day the Khoja cooked a goose and took it as a present to Tamerlane. On the road he could not restrain his appetite and ate one of the legs. On arrival at the palace he presented his offering in due form, but Tamerlane noticed that there was one leg short and asked him where it was. The Khoja replied, as cool as a cucumber, that all the geese at Akshehir had only one leg. "If you don't believe me, look at those geese standing over there by the fountain!"

It was quite true. The geese were all standing on one leg, sound asleep in the sunshine, the other leg tucked up and their heads sunk in their breasts.

Tamerlane looked out of the window and saw that they really had only one leg.

Now, it chanced to be the moment for changing the palace guard. The band struck up. The roll of the big drum and skirl of pipes made the welkin ring. The geese soon found their second legs and ran off helter-skelter, trying to escape. Tamerlane saw them and at once called the Khoja to the window saying, "You are a liar. You see they all have two feet."

"Yes," replied the Khoja, "and if you had the noise of those drum-sticks ringing in your ears you would grow four legs."

BARNHAM, TRANS.,
TALES OF NASR-ED-DIN KHOJA

Deek Mahshi

Roast Turkey with Meat, Nut,
and Rice Stuffing

Serves 8–10 • In the Middle East, turkeys range freely and are small and tough, more like game birds, so they are usually stewed, which makes the flesh tender and moist. In America, roasting is best for the birds.

A 10-pound turkey

Juice of 1 lemon

Salt and pepper

2 tablespoons vegetable oil

FOR THE STUFFING

2½ tablespoons vegetable oil

1 pound lean ground lamb or beef

1½ cups mixed whole nuts: blanched almonds, pistachios, and pine nuts

2 cups long-grain rice

⅓ cup raisins (optional)

Salt and pepper

1 teaspoon ground cinnamon

¼ teaspoon ground allspice

3 cups water

Wash the turkey and rub it inside and out with lemon juice and a little salt.

Prepare the stuffing. Heat 2 tablespoons of the oil in a large pan. Add the ground meat and fry, crushing and turning it over with a fork, until it changes color. Fry the nuts in the remaining ½ tablespoon of oil in a skillet, beginning with the almonds (pine nuts take moments only), stirring. Add them to the meat with the rice and the raisins. Season with salt, pepper, cinnamon, and allspice and mix well. Add the water, bring to the boil, then simmer, covered, over low heat for 20 minutes.

Stuff the turkey loosely with this mixture, and sew the openings tightly with strong thread. Put any extra stuffing in a baking dish and cover with foil to reheat before serving. Truss the bird, sprinkle with salt and pepper, and rub with oil. Put it breast side up in a large roasting pan and cook in a preheated 425°F oven for ½ hour.

Now turn the turkey breast side down, reduce the oven temperature to 350°F, and cook for 1½ hours. Then turn the turkey breast side up again and cook a further ½–1 hour, until it is crisp and brown and the juice runs clear when you cut into a thigh with a pointed knife.

Put the extra stuffing to heat through in the oven during the last 20 minutes. The turkey may either be served whole, with the extra stuffing on the side, or carved into pieces and arranged over the stuffing in a large platter.

Variation

The turkey can be boned before stuffing: Cut the skin and flesh of the bird along the spine all the way down from the neck. Starting from the neck, strip and cut away the flesh from the carcass as close to it as possible, using a very sharp knife, taking care not to damage the skin, and pushing the flesh back as you cut. Break the shoulder and leg joints. Carefully remove the carcass all in one piece. Pack very loosely with stuffing and sew up neatly, re-forming the bird as far as possible in its original shape. In this way it will take more stuffing. The legs and wings remain unboned and help to keep the shape of the turkey firm.

Meat Dishes

LOUHOMAT

In Arab literature and folklore, meat dishes have always been labeled the food of the rich and aristocratic, in contrast with the filling dishes of beans, lentils, and wheat which are the diet of the poor. Many stories and proverbs illustrate this distinction. Here is an old Egyptian tale of the Mamluk period by Ahmad ibn al Hajjar, in which the various foods are personified and their status is defined, from a book about the pleasant war between mutton and the refreshments of the market:

> King Mutton reigns over a large and powerful people, comprising mainly different types of meats. He hears of the power of a rival, King Honey, who has been crowned by the poor, and who reigns over vegetables, fruits, sweets, fish, dairy dishes, and the refreshments of the market. King Mutton sends his ambassador, Mutton's Tail (alya), to King Honey, demanding that he surrender his kingdom and pay tribute. King Honey refuses and calls his troops together, but the ambassador has taken advantage of his stay in the kingdom to debauch and corrupt the officers of rank, in particular, the Sugar, the Syrup, the Clarified Butter, and others, to whom he has promised important positions at the court of his master. Thus, because of their treachery, the

battle between the two armies is easily won by the troops of King Mutton, and even the reinforcements of fruits sent to help the broken army of King Honey are of no avail.

Most Arab meat recipes, medieval as well as modern, simply call for meat—meat with lentils, meat with yogurt, and so on—without specifying what kind of meat or any particular cut. This is because, in the past, only mutton and lamb were eaten, apart from occasionally kid and very rarely gazelle or camel. Cattle were seldom raised, because of the lack of humidity and grazing land, except for a water buffalo called *gamoussa* mainly used to work in the fields, or for the rich milk which produces the famously thick cream of the region. Cattle brought from elsewhere had to travel a long way across whole countries to reach the Middle East, and by the time they got to their destination, their flesh was tough and inedible unless ground. Today, beef and veal are gradually becoming more popular. Al-

---

Kharouf Meshwi
WHOLE ROAST LAMB

Whole lamb roasted on a spit or in the baker's oven is a festive, ceremonial repast prepared for parties, festivals, and large family gatherings. Roast baby lamb stuffed with rice mixed with nuts and raisins (*qouzi mahshi*) is cooked in the same way and served on a huge tray, surrounded by mountains of the stuffing. When I was a girl at the wedding of one of my cousins, they served baby lambs made to look like miniature camels, their boneless backs shaped into humps.

Although the poor can rarely afford meat, there is one day at least when all are assured of eating it. This is at the Eid-el-Kurban (also called Eid-el-Kibir in Egypt), on the tenth day of the last month of the Muhammadan year, a festival in commemoration of Abraham's sacrifice of Ismail. (In Islamic lore he offered Ismail; in Jewish lore it was Isaac.) By

ancient custom, well-to-do families sacrifice a sheep or lamb on this day. The victim must be fat, young, and unblemished. The eyes of the animal are blackened, a piece of confectionery is placed in its mouth, and its head is turned towards Mecca. The words "In the name of God" are spoken as the animal is slain. It is roasted on a spit, and the meat is distributed to the poor. These offerings are also made after a death or a birth, and on other important occasions such as moving house, the start or end of a long journey, or the arrival of an important guest. In Cairo, our balcony overlooked a street where, on several occasions, I watched the roasting of a ceremonial lamb, accompanied by wailing and singing. The smell penetrated my bedclothes and wardrobe, and remained with me through the night.

---

though mutton and lamb remain the most widely used and favored meats, imported beef and veal quite often replace them, the dishes otherwise remaining unchanged.

The most popular way of cooking meat is to broil or roast it. The word *meshwi* in Arabic covers all types of meat—large joints, chops, small skewered pieces, or a whole animal—broiled or roasted over a fire. It is the celebratory food of the Arab world, the street food, and the main fare of the restaurant trade which developed as kebab houses.

Another way of cooking meat which is both common and prestigious is in a stew—*yakhni* to Syrians and Lebanese, "tagines" to North Africans, and *khoresht* to Iranians. For those who can afford meat, a stew accompanied by rice or bulgur or by bread represents the main everyday meal. But stews can also reach extraordinary heights of sophistication to be the grand festive foods prepared for wedding parties and great occasions.

A medieval Arab cookery manual gives a method of barbecuing a sheep adopted from the Crusaders. It was pierced with a rod and held between two poles. Fires were lit on either side, with the result that roasting was quicker and more even. A nineteenth-century Turkish manual by a certain Sidqi Effendi gives instructions for roasting a lamb in the open. A hole is dug in the ground and filled with charcoal. The lamb is rubbed with salt, pepper, and onion juice, a wooden or metal rod is pushed right through the lamb from breast to hindquarters, and the legs are trussed together.

In North Africa, people light small fires in their courtyards and sit around them while a joint of lamb is turned on a spit, helping themselves to slices of meat as it becomes deliciously brown and tender. In Turkey, *döner kebab* is an old classic of the kebab houses. Slices of tender lamb, marinated for several hours in a mixture of oil, salt, pepper, and onion juice with the addition, sometimes, of herbs such as parsley, wild marjoram, or mint, are threaded and packed tightly, with a few pieces of fat squeezed between them, onto a rotating vertical spit. The spit turns automatically and slowly close to a hot charcoal fire. Gas and electric heat are also used. Slices are cut off as the meat acquires a warm brown glow. In restaurants this is done in full view of the diners. The ubiquitous *döner kebab* (*shawarma* in Arabic) now well known in Europe and America is a sad version of the real thing, with poor meat—often compressed ground meat—excessive fat, and uninspired flavoring.

Another Middle Eastern way of cooking a whole lamb or joints of meat is in a deep cylindrical pit dug in the ground, called *tandir*. A wood fire is lit at the bottom, the lamb is placed on hot stones, and the mouth of the hole is sealed. When the meat is taken out it is so meltingly tender you can pull it apart with your fingers.

In his *Isret Name,* the sixteenth-century Turkish poet Revani describes a stew as "a saint who makes his prayer rug float upon the water," comparing the pieces of meat floating in the rich sauce to the prayer rugs on which the saints of old were supposed to traverse rivers.

Stews are among the finest features of Middle Eastern cooking. It is here, most of all, that you find the great similarities to dishes recorded in Arabic culinary manuscripts of the tenth to the fourteenth centuries. Thirty-five years ago, when I first came across these manuscripts, I was struck by the likeness to the modern recipes I was collecting. There was the same combination of ingredients, the same pairing of vegetables or fruits with meat, the same blends of aromatics, and methods of cooking—cutting the meat into cubes or grinding it and rolling it into little balls before sautéing and stewing. Echoes of the old dishes, a legacy of ancient Persia, can be found all over the Middle East, but most remarkably, and in a stunning number of dishes, along the route charting the Arab conquering armies from Baghdad across North Africa through Tunisia and Morocco on their way to Spain. It was thrilling to discover that a high culinary art had been passed down over the centuries, and that you could still find remnants of it in Tunis and Fez. I was so excited by recipes written in Baghdad in 1226 by a certain Muhammad ibn Hassan ibn Muhammad ibn al-Karim al-Katib al-Baghdadi, who claimed to love eating above all pleasures, that I cooked them all. It felt as though I was re-creating the Thousand and One Nights in my kitchen.

On the practical side, while you need prime cuts of meat for broiling or roasting, cheaper cuts, especially fatty ones, are best for stews. The lengthy cooking makes the meat deliciously tender. Although the cooking time is long, the labor is simple, and stews are the kind of thing that you can prepare in advance. And they can always be extended for the unexpected guest—according to tradition, simply by adding water. Nineteenth-century cookery manuals often state that the amounts given will serve a certain number of people, but that you can add water if a friend should arrive. Traditionally, in many countries, stews were cooked in the gentle all-round heat of a clay dish over the fire, as for the tagines of North Africa, or in the public baker's oven or the outdoor clay oven such as the *tagen* of Egypt. Nowadays most people use heavy-bottomed saucepans or casseroles.

Meatballs and ground-meat dishes are another very popular and prestigious feature of Middle Eastern cooking. The advantage here is in the flavoring, with the aromatics being incorporated into the meat.

ARAB SAYING:
"One's eating shows one's love."

Fakhda Mahsheya

Roast Leg of Lamb with Ground Meat, Rice, and Nut Stuffing

Serves 6 • The grandest Arab meal is a whole stuffed baby lamb. A succulent leg accompanied by the traditional stuffing called *hashwa* is a representative of that ideal. The meat is cooked gently, for a long time, to such melting tenderness that you can pull morsels off with your fingers.

1 leg of lamb

4 cloves garlic, cut into slivers

2 tablespoons vegetable oil

Salt and pepper

FOR THE STUFFING (HASHWA)

1 pound ground beef

4 tablespoons sunflower oil

1¼ cups long-grain rice

Salt and pepper

2 teaspoons cinnamon

½ teaspoon allspice

2 cups meat or chicken stock (page 143) (or you can use a bouillon cube), boiling hot

¼ cup split almonds

⅓ cup pistachios

¼ cup pine nuts

Make slashes into the meat with a sharp-pointed knife and insert the pieces of garlic. Rub the meat all over with oil, salt, and pepper and put it in a roasting pan in a preheated 400°F oven. For rare meat roast 12 minutes per pound plus 20 minutes more; for medium-rare, roast 16 minutes per pound plus 20 minutes more; for well-done, roast 20 minutes per pound plus 20 minutes more. The Middle Eastern way is well-done.

Prepare the stuffing. In a large pan, fry the meat in 2 tablespoons of the oil, turning it constantly and breaking up lumps, until it has changed color. Add the rice, and stir well for a few minutes. Then add salt, pepper, cinnamon, and allspice. Pour in the boiling stock, mix well, and simmer, covered, for 20 minutes, or until the rice is tender, adding a little stock or water if it becomes too dry.

Fry the mixed nuts in the remaining oil until they just begin to color, and mix them into the rice before serving.

Let the meat rest in the turned-off oven with the door open for 15 minutes before carving. Serve accompanied with the stuffing.

Variations

• Add to the stuffing 1 teaspoon cardamom, and pinches of ground cloves and nutmeg.

• Add ¼ cup raisins to the stuffing.

Dala' Mahshi

Stuffed Breast of Lamb

Serves 6–8 • This is an old family favorite which I recommend if you don't mind taking time and trouble. You may substitute for the apricot sauce a sauce made with sour cherries. Serve with extra stuffing.

2 whole large breasts of lamb
Oil
Salt and pepper
½ pound dried apricots—a tart, natural (not sweetened) variety, soaked in water to cover for 1 hour

FOR THE STUFFING AND SIDE DISH

2 medium-sized onions, chopped
2–3 tablespoons vegetable oil
½ pound ground beef
2 cups long-grain rice
¼ cup chopped flat-leaf parsley
Salt and pepper
¾ cup pine nuts or chopped walnuts
¾ cup currants or raisins (optional)

Ask the butcher to chine the meat and to cut a pouch between the skin and the ribs—or do the latter yourself with a long, sharp knife.

Prepare the stuffing. In a large saucepan, fry the onions in the oil until golden. Add the ground beef and fry, crushing and turning it over with a spoon, until browned. Stir in the rice, add parsley, salt, and pepper, and mix well. Pour in 3¼ cups water. Cover the pan and simmer undisturbed over low heat for 20 minutes, or until the water has been absorbed and the rice is tender but still firm. Let it cool, then mix in the nuts and, if you wish, the currants.

Stuff the pouches with the rice mixture, and put the extra stuffing in an oven dish, covered with foil. Rub the breasts with oil, salt, and pepper, and put them in a roasting pan. Set uncovered in an oven preheated to 425°F, then reduce immediately to 325°F and roast for about 1 hour, or until the meat is well cooked and browned on the outside. Put the extra stuffing in for the last 20 minutes to heat through.

Put the apricots in a small pan with enough of their soaking water to cover. Bring to the boil and simmer, uncovered, for about 20 minutes, until the apricots are very soft and the liquid is reduced. If you like, blend to a cream in the food processor.

A few minutes before serving, pour off the excess fat from the roasting pan. Turn the oven up to 450°F. Pour the apricot sauce over the lamb and glaze in the oven for 5 to 7 minutes. Do not leave in the oven too long, as the apricots burn easily.

Variations

• Instead of roasting, the stuffed breasts may be braised on top of the stove. First they are seared in hot butter or oil until browned all over, then the apricots and their water are added, and the lamb is simmered gently for about 1 hour, or until it is very tender and the sauce is reduced. The breasts must be turned over and water added as required.

• Make a sauce with ½ pound pitted dried sour cherries instead of the apricots.

Leg of Lamb with Onions, Potatoes, and Tomatoes

Serves 6 • My aunt Latifa and uncle Mousa lived in a villa in a suburb of Cairo. It was large and housed their extended family. There was no oven. Much of the cooking was done over a *mangal* (portable outdoor grill) and a Primus oil heater, and trays were sent off daily to the baker to be cooked in the bread oven. This dish was sent to the baker.

1 leg of lamb (about 4 pounds)

3 or 4 cloves garlic, slivered

Salt and pepper

1½ pounds potatoes, thickly sliced

2 large onions, sliced

1 pound tomatoes, sliced

2 teaspoons dried *rigani* (wild marjoram) or oregano (optional)

Pierce the leg of lamb all over with the point of a sharp knife and insert the slivers of garlic at different depths. Rub generously with salt and pepper.

Put the prepared lamb, fat side up, in a large baking dish or roasting pan, and surround it with the sliced potatoes, onions, and tomatoes. Pour in ½ cup water, and sprinkle if you like with a little *rigani* or oregano.

Preheat the oven to 425°F. Put in the leg of lamb and reduce the heat immediately to 325°F. Roast for about 2½ hours, or until done to your liking, basting occasionally with the pan juices.

Turn the vegetables over once during the cooking so that they cook evenly in the juices from the joint, and pour off excess fat. The joint should be very tender and juicy, and the vegetables quite soft. I like them practically dis-integrating, but if you prefer them to be rather more firm, add them to the roast after about half an hour's cooking, when the meat has already released some fat. Baste the vegetables when you baste the meat, and moisten occasionally with a little water if necessary.

Let the meat rest in the turned-off oven with the door open for 15 minutes before serving. Remove the lamb to a board—it makes carving easier.

Variation

You can of course cook the leg of lamb without the vegetables. Here is a sauce which you can pour on each serving as you hand it out: fry a handful of blanched, slivered almonds in a drop of oil till golden, add the defatted juices from the pan and a little water, and stir in 2 tablespoons black or golden raisins.

Shish Kebab

Grilled Meat on Skewers

Serves 6 • Meats grilled on skewers have become the best-known Middle Eastern foods as the standard fare of Lebanese, Turkish, and Iranian restaurants abroad. They are a symbol, in particular, of Turkish food. Turks say that this way of cooking meat was created during the conquering era of the Ottoman Empire, when Turkish soldiers, forced to camp out in tents for months on end, discovered the pleasures of eating meat grilled out of doors on wood fires.

Twenty years ago, on a gastronomic visit to Turkey, I went with an interpreter on an arranged tour of kebab houses in Istanbul. At every stop I was invited to eat. It became a grand marathon—*une grande bouffe*. At the fifth establishment they opened the refrigerated room and showed me all the prize cuts, which were later presented to me straight from the fire on a gigantic plate. As well as the kebabs and ground-meat *kofta kebab* on skewers, there were small lamb chops, kidneys, slices of calf's liver, beef steaks, *sucuk* (spicy beef sausages), and pieces of chicken. It was a gourmand's dream, but for a woman already satiated from eating elsewhere and afraid of giving offense, it was a nightmare.

In Greece and Turkey, alternating pieces of onion, tomato, and bell pepper are threaded onto the skewers in between the cubes of meat. This looks good, but it is not a good idea, as the meat and vegetables take different times to cook and the meat becomes wet and does not get properly seared. So, if you must have roasted vegetables, have them on another skewer, or straight on the grill. In some countries, lumps of fat are pressed between pieces of meat to keep them from drying out as the fat melts.

> 2 pounds boned leg of lamb
> 2 large onions, liquidized in the food processor
> ⅔ cup extra-virgin olive oil
> Salt and pepper

Cut the meat into 1-inch cubes. Prepare a marinade by mixing the onion juice with the oil, salt, and pepper and soak the meat in this

---

*I*t was common for people to buy a live sheep at the market, and to keep it for a few days in the kitchen before killing it. A tale of Goha illustrates this custom.

One day, Goha took his small son to the market with him to buy a sheep. Now, it is well known that the value of a sheep depends on the amount of fat which it stores in its tail. At the souk, Goha proceeded to feel, and weigh in his hands, the tails of the sheep, one after another, until his son asked:

"Father, why do you do that?"

"I must do so before I decide which sheep to buy," Goha replied.

A few days later, while sitting waiting for the evening meal, the little boy turned to his father and said:

"Father, our neighbor was here today. I think he wants to buy my mother!"

for at least 1 hour (Iranians and Turks marinate overnight), keeping it covered in the refrigerator, and turning the pieces over at least once.

Thread the pieces of meat onto 6 skewers, preferably the flat, wide type, so that the meat does not slide.

Grill over charcoal or wood embers, making sure that the fire has stopped smoking. Place the skewers 3 inches from the fire on a well-oiled grill. Or broil under a preheated gas or electric broiler. Cook for about 7–10 minutes, turning over once, until the meat is well browned on the outside but still pink and juicy inside.

Ways of Serving

Serve the kebabs on top of a thin Arab flatbread over sprigs of flat-leaf parsley or chervil; or inside a pita bread topped with a salad of finely chopped raw tomato, cucumber, and onion with herbs.

Alternatively, place the skewers on a bed of rice or bulgur.

In Iran the rice is garnished with an egg yolk presented on the half-shell. The yolk is then stirred into the rice at table. This is *chello kebab.* The Turks serve kebabs with yogurt as a sauce.

Other Popular Marinades

- For a Greek one, blend in the food processor 2 onions, 2 tomatoes, ⅔ cup extra-virgin olive oil, the juice of 1 lemon, 2 teaspoons dried *rigani* (wild marjoram), salt, and pepper.
- For a marinade inspired by Sidqi Effendi's nineteenth-century Turkish cookery manual, blend to a cream ⅔ cup olive oil, 2 onions, 1 teaspoon ground cinnamon, salt, and pepper.

- For another Turkish marinade, blend 1¼ cups yogurt, 1 onion, salt, and pepper.

Additions

- At the same time, broil quartered onions and tomatoes and sweet peppers cut into 1-inch pieces threaded on skewers.
- Broil whole medium-small eggplants at the same time, turning them until they are soft inside, and serve them cut open. In some Turkish restaurants in London's famously Turkish Stoke Newington district, they thread thick slices of eggplant between pieces of meat, and the eggplants have time to roast and become deliciously tender.
- In Lebanon they thread cherry tomatoes and pickling onions between the pieces of meat.
- Lamb cutlets, or chops, and filet of beef can be marinated and grilled or broiled at the same time so as to have a mix of meats.

By reason of the sweet smiles
of the salt cellar of her mouth, blood flows
from the heart as from a salted kebab.

KANJU 'L ISHTIHA
(THE TREASURE OF THE APPETITE)
by Abu Ishaq of Shiraz,
the sixteenth-century Persian poet of food

Kofta Meshweya

Grilled Ground Meat on Skewers

Serves 4 • In Egypt this is the favorite kebab. It is also mine. I love the soft, moist texture of the meat, and the flavors of parsley and onion. The traditional way of preparing it is to chop all the main ingredients by hand, then to chop them together. They still do this in restaurants (where it is called *kofta kebab* or *kofta alla shish*)—but you can achieve good results with the blade of the food processor if you do each ingredient separately. For a moist, juicy *kofta* you need a good amount of fat. Most of it will melt away in the heat of the broiler. You will need skewers with a wide, thick blade to hold the ground meat and prevent it from rolling around. If you find it difficult, you can always shape the meat into burgers (see variations).

1½ pounds lamb from the shoulder, with some fat

Salt and pepper

½ cup chopped flat-leaf parsley

2 medium onions, grated or very finely chopped

Cut the meat in chunks, then blend in the food processor to a soft paste, adding salt and pepper. Put it in a bowl with the parsley and the onions—drained of juices—and knead well with your hand until well blended.

Divide the meat into 8 balls and wrap each one around a skewer, pressing firmly so that it holds together in a long, flat sausage shape. Place the skewers on an oiled grill over a fire, or on a rack under the broiler, and cook for 5–8 minutes, turning over once or more, until lightly browned.

Serve with warmed pita bread or on top of those very thin Arab flatbreads or with rice or bulgur.

Accompaniments

• Slice 1 large onion thinly and sprinkle generously with salt. Leave for 30 minutes, until the juices run out and it loses its strong flavor. Then rinse and drain and sprinkle with 1 tablespoon sumac.

• Serve on a bed of chopped flat-leaf parsley and mint mixed with 1 thinly sliced onion and sprinkled with 1 tablespoon sumac.

• Serve with chopped flat-leaf parsley and diced lemon (the lemon is peeled and cut into tiny cubes).

• Serve with 8 or more broiled cherry tomatoes.

• Roast 4 long, mild green peppers (you find them in Middle Eastern stores) until softened.

• In Turkey they serve *kofta kebab* on a bed of yogurt beaten with a sprinkling of salt, pepper, and chopped parsley and mint, and topped with chopped tomatoes.

Variations

• Use chopped fresh mint as well as parsley.

• Add to the meat mixture 1 teaspoon cinnamon and ½ teaspoon allspice.

• Add to the meat ½ teaspoon cumin and ½ teaspoon ground coriander seed.

• Add ½ teaspoon red-pepper flakes or a pinch of chili pepper.

• Instead of pressing the meat on skewers, you can make it into hamburgers and grill them or cook them in a pan filmed lightly with oil.

• Cut long, thin eggplants into 1½-inch slices and thread them in between lumps of *kofta*. The skin protects the flesh from drying out. This is a specialty of Aleppo.

Yogurtlu Kebab

Kofta with Tomato Sauce and Yogurt

Serves 4 • Hardly any dishes were invented by restaurant chefs in Turkey, but this one was, by a man called Iskander; that is why it is also known as *Iskander kebab*. It made its appearance in the 1920s, after the Ottoman Empire had crumbled and Turkey became a republic. The cooks who had worked in the palace kitchens and in the homes of the aristocracy (much of the aristocracy moved to Egypt) became unemployed and looked for ways to survive. Many of them opened restaurants—*lokandesi* and kebab houses.

This dish has remained a mainstay of Turkish kebab houses, where it is sometimes served dramatically in a dome-shaped copper dish—the type that was used at the palace. On one level it reflects the preponderance of yogurt in the Turkish kitchen. I serve it in deep individual clay bowls which can be kept hot in the oven. It is a multi-layered extravaganza. There is toasted pita bread at the bottom. It is covered by a light sauce made with fresh tomatoes, topped by a layer of yogurt. This is sprinkled with olive oil which has been colored with paprika and with pine nuts. Skewers of grilled ground meat *kofta* or small burgers (as in this recipe) are laid on top. The tomato sauce and the meat must be very hot when you assemble the dish. The yogurt should be at room temperature.

❧

RIDDLE:
It is red like blood;
it burns like fire. What is it?

ANSWER:
Red pimento.

☙

FOR THE TOMATO SAUCE

1 pound tomatoes, peeled and chopped

4 tablespoons olive oil

Salt and pepper

1 teaspoon sugar

1 thin pita bread

Ground-lamb *kofta* mixture, as in preceding recipe (page 238), with the same amount of meat

2½ cups plain whole-milk or thick strained yogurt (see page 110), at room temperature

1 teaspoon paprika

2–3 tablespoons pine nuts, toasted or not

2 tablespoons finely chopped flat-leaf parsley to garnish (optional)

Put the tomatoes in a pan with 1 tablespoon of the oil, salt, pepper, and sugar, and cook over medium heat until they soften.

Toast the pita bread until it is crisp, then break it into small pieces.

Shape the ground-lamb *kofta* into 12 or 16 small burgers. Cook them under the broiler, turning them over once, until they are brown outside but still pink inside.

In each individual bowl, put a quarter of the toasted bread, cover with a quarter of the tomato sauce, and top with a layer of yogurt. Mix the paprika with the remaining oil and dribble over the yogurt, then sprinkle with pine nuts. Arrange the meat burgers on top. If you like, garnish further with chopped parsley.

Brochettes de Kefta

Ground Meat Kebabs

Serves 8, with 16 skewers • Moroccans call their diminutive kebabs *brochettes,* in the French manner. The streets of Fez are dotted with little braziers of glowing charcoal over which turn wood or metal skewers heavy with tiny pieces of meat, liver, or *kefta,* enveloping passersby with their irresistibly enticing aromas. Many spices are used in the *kefta,* but so discreetly that you can hardly guess what has gone in.

> 2 pounds lamb, finely ground
>
> 2 onions, grated
>
> 3 tablespoons chopped flat-leaf parsley
>
> 3 tablespoons chopped cilantro
>
> 1/4 teaspoon ground cumin
>
> 1/4 teaspoon ground coriander
>
> 1/4 teaspoon ground ginger
>
> 1/4 teaspoon cinnamon
>
> Salt and pepper
>
> 1/4 teaspoon ground chili pepper (optional)

Mix finely ground meat with onions, herbs, and seasonings, and knead vigorously until very smooth and pasty. Wet your hands and divide the meat into 32 egg-sized lumps. Press them firmly around small, square-bladed skewers, two on each skewer, and form into thin sausage shapes. Cook over charcoal or under the broiler for 4–5 minutes, until done, turning over once. Be careful not to overcook, as the meat dries out quickly. Serve at once with bread.

Variations

• For a minty *brochette,* mix the meat and onion with 3 tablespoons chopped cilantro, 3 tablespoons chopped mint, 2 teaspoons ground cumin, salt, and pepper.

• When serving, dribble 4 tablespoons extra-virgin olive oil mixed with the juice of 1/2–1 lemon over the *brochettes.*

Brochettes and Souk Cuisine— Street Food in Morocco

An exciting part of visiting Morocco, as with many other Arab cities, is the street food. In every town, in the souk, in the old medinas, in the squares where weekly markets set up, at bus stops on intercity roads, there are street vendors. From tiny cafés and boutiques as small as a cupboard, from carts or stands or sometimes an upturned box with a chair for customers, they offer their specialties—boiled-carrot salad with cumin, *harira,* spicy little snails, *brochettes de kefta,* sweet fritters.

Place Djemaa-el-Fna in Marrakesh is magical. During the day, musicians and dancers from the mountains, snake charmers, fire eaters, letter writers, storytellers have possession of the huge square. As the sun begins to fall, the entire space is taken over by hundreds of cooks setting up stands and trestle tables, starting charcoal fires. Their clients sit on benches around each stand. All night long they serve up soup accompanied with dates, calves' feet with chickpeas, and sheep's heads from huge pots. Stews smell of turmeric; fried fish of cumin and cilantro; chicken of preserved lemon. Cooking aromas mingle in the smoke of the famous *brochettes* cooking over charcoal.

Arni Tou Hartiou

*Lamb with Grape Leaves Baked
in Fillo Parcels*

Serves 6 • This is a version, using fillo pastry, of a Greek dish of lamb baked in parchment packets.

24 grape leaves, fresh or preserved in
    brine
1 piece of boned leg of lamb (about
    2 pounds)
4–5 tablespoons olive oil
Juice of ½ lemon
¾ cup red wine
Pepper
2 cloves garlic, crushed
2 teaspoons *rigani* (wild marjoram) or
    oregano
2 tablespoons butter, melted
6 sheets fillo pastry
Salt

If you are using fresh grape leaves, blanch them for a few seconds in boiling water, until they become limp and their color changes. If you are using leaves preserved in brine, soak them in boiling water for 1 hour to remove their saltiness, changing the water at least once. Rinse and drain well.

Cut the meat into 6 fat slices.

In a bowl, mix the oil, lemon juice, wine, pepper, garlic, and oregano or marjoram, and turn the pieces of meat in this marinade. Leave in a cool place for ½ hour or longer.

When you are ready to cook, brush each sheet of fillo very lightly with melted butter. Place 2 grape leaves on each, side by side towards the middle of a long edge. Lay a piece of meat over them, sprinkle with very little salt, and cover with 2 more grape leaves.

Fold the fillo over and over the meat and leaves, wrapping them up in a loose package. Repeat with the rest of the fillo, meat, and leaves. Brush the top of each packet lightly with melted butter and place on an oven rack.

Bake in a preheated 325°F oven for about 30 minutes, by which time the meat should be done and the fillo lightly colored. You will have to cut into one piece to make sure that it is done to your liking. Serve the packets as they are, crisp and hot.

Variations

• Sprinkle the meat with ½ pound grated cheese. Kefalotyri is used in Greece, but mature cheddar is an acceptable alternative.
• In a Turkish version called *Ali Pasha kebab*, meat is stewed with 1 chopped onion and 2 peeled and chopped tomatoes, until the meat is tender and the liquid has dried out, before it is wrapped in fillo and baked. The result is wonderfully moist, tender meat.

Kuzu Kapama

Lamb with Scallions and Herbs

Serves 6 • A Turkish specialty. The meat becomes so tender you can pull pieces off with your fingers.

- 1 leg of young, tender lamb (about 4 pounds)
- 2 large bunches of scallions, chopped
- 1 bunch of fresh dill or chervil, finely chopped
- 1 large onion, quartered
- 1 cup water
- 2 tablespoons oil
- Salt and pepper

Clean the leg of lamb and remove excess fat. Put it in a saucepan or casserole with the scallions, herbs, and onion. Add water and oil, and season with salt and pepper. Cover and simmer gently for about 2½–3 hours, or until very tender, turning the lamb over occasionally, and adding a little more water as necessary.

Choua

Moroccan Steamed Lamb

Serves 6 • The popularity of tagines means that they have eclipsed other methods of cooking in Morocco, such as steaming, where the meat becomes very tender and succulent. Serve *choua* with mashed potatoes and with vegetables such as zucchini or eggplants.

- 2 pounds leg or shoulder of lamb, cut into ¾-inch cubes
- Salt
- 1 teaspoon ground cumin

Sprinkle lamb lightly with salt and cumin. Steam over boiling water for about 2 hours, or until the meat is tender and juicy. In the past, steaming was done in a pot sealed with paste, but today a hermetically sealed double steamer can be used instead.

Laban Ummo

Meat Cooked in Yogurt

Serves 6 • Recipes for meat cooked in yogurt abound in medieval Arabic cookery manuals, where the dish was called *madira*. As early as the tenth century, the Arab writer Badia'z Zaman wrote a tale entitled "Al Madirya" about the dish. Such dishes are still popular in the Arab world. The name of this Lebanese version, which means "his mother's milk," implies that the meat of a young animal is cooked in its own mother's milk. It can be made with chunks of meat or lamb shanks. Serve with plain rice (page 337) or rice with vermicelli (page 340).

2 pounds lean lamb, preferably leg, cut into 1½-inch cubes

Salt and white pepper

1 pound pearl or small onions, peeled

5 cups plain whole-milk yogurt or, preferably, strained Greek-style yogurt

1 egg white or 1 tablespoon cornstarch

3 cloves garlic, crushed or finely chopped (optional)

1 tablespoon dried crushed mint (optional)

Put the meat in a large pan and cover with water. Bring to the boil, remove any scum, and add salt and pepper. Cook with the lid on for 1 hour.

Add the onions and cook for ½ hour more, or until the meat is very tender and the onions are soft, adding water to keep the meat covered at first and letting it reduce, uncovered, so that most of it has evaporated at the end and there is hardly any broth left.

Prepare the yogurt by mixing with egg white, or the cornstarch dissolved in a little water, following the directions for stabilizing yogurt on page 113, to prevent it from curdling during cooking. Add it to the cooked meat, stir in the garlic if using, and simmer gently, uncovered, for 10 to 15 minutes, adding a little salt. Stir in the mint, if using, towards the end.

Some cooks pass round a little bowl of dried mint for people to help themselves if they wish.

Variations

• Use 6 small lamb shanks instead of the cubed meat, and cook them until they are so tender that the meat falls off the bone.

• For an Egyptian version, add 5 cardamom pods to the meat and onions from the beginning. Just before serving, fry 4 crushed garlic cloves with 1 tablespoon ground coriander in 2 tablespoons butter or oil, until the garlic just begins to color, and pour over the meat and yogurt as you serve.

• A Turkish version has a large bunch of chopped dill added towards the end of the cooking.

Mozaat

Veal Shank with Potatoes

Serves 6 • The particular quality of this stew, which I hated as a child, lies in its texture. The knuckle or shin of veal (we called it *bitello,* from the Italian *vitello*) contains the large leg-bone and marrow. The connective tissue turns into gelatin while the meat becomes juicy and succulent. In Egypt, the potatoes were sliced and fried in oil before going into the stew, but I prefer to omit the frying.

> 2 pounds shin of veal (shanks) in large
>   pieces with bone
> 3 tablespoons vegetable oil
> Salt and pepper
> Juice of $\frac{1}{2}$ lemon
> $\frac{1}{2}$ teaspoon turmeric (optional)
> $1\frac{1}{2}$ pounds potatoes, cut into thick
>   slices, or small peeled new potatoes

In a large pan, sauté the meat in hot oil, turning to brown the pieces all over. Season with salt and pepper, add lemon juice and, if you wish, turmeric. Half-cover with water. Simmer, covered, for $1\frac{1}{2}$ hours, or until the meat is very tender and the sauce rich and reduced, adding a little more water as it becomes absorbed, and turning the meat over occasionally.

Add the potatoes and more water to cover them, and cook for 30 minutes, until they are tender and have absorbed the rich flavors of the sauce. Serve hot.

Variation

Add 9 frozen artichoke bottoms (a 14-ounce package), defrosted, for the last 20 minutes of cooking, and use fewer potatoes.

Hünkâr Beğendi

Lamb Stew with Creamy Eggplant Sauce

Serves 6 • This dish is uniquely Turkish, and was developed in the Ottoman palace kitchens. A current legend surrounding the name of the dish, which means "sultan's delight," places it in 1869, when the Sultan Abdul Aziz entertained Empress Eugénie, wife of Napoleon III, in his white rococo palace of Beylerbey, on the Asian side of the Bosporus. The Empress was ecstatic about the creamy eggplant sauce which served as the bed for a stew and asked for the recipe to be sent to her cooks. The Sultan's cook explained that he could not give the recipe, because he "cooked with his eyes." Serve it with rice.

FOR THE STEW

> 1 large onion, cut in half, then in slices
> 3 tablespoons vegetable oil
> $1\frac{1}{2}$ pound lamb cut into $\frac{3}{4}$-inch cubes
> 2 cloves garlic, chopped
> 1 pound tomatoes, peeled and chopped
> 1 teaspoon sugar, or to taste
> Salt and pepper

FOR THE EGGPLANT CREAM SAUCE

> 3 pounds eggplants
> Juice of $\frac{1}{2}$ lemon
> 4 tablespoons butter
> 3 tablespoons all-purpose flour
> 2 cups hot milk
> Salt and white pepper
> $\frac{1}{4}$ teaspoon grated nutmeg (optional)
> $\frac{1}{2}$ cup grated kasseri or cheddar cheese

For the lamb stew, fry the onion in the oil until soft. Add the meat and garlic and cook, turning the meat, until lightly browned all over. Add the tomatoes, sugar, salt, and pepper. Cover with water and simmer, with the lid on, for 1–1½ hours, until the meat is very tender, adding water if it becomes dry, and letting the liquid reduce at the end.

For the sauce, prick the eggplants with a pointed knife so that they do not burst in cooking. Put them on a sheet of foil on a baking sheet and roast them in the hottest oven for about ½ hour, turning them on their side (not right over) until they feel very soft when you press them. Peel carefully. Then drop them in a bowl of water with the lemon juice and leave for 15 minutes, to keep their flesh white.

Melt the butter in a saucepan, add the flour, and stir over very low heat for about 2 minutes, until well blended. Remove from the heat and add the milk gradually, beating vigorously all

the time. Season with salt and white pepper, add nutmeg, if you like, and cook over low heat, stirring constantly, for about 15 minutes, until the milk sauce thickens.

Drain the eggplants in a colander and press out as much of the water and juices as possible. Chop them with a pointed knife in the colander, then mash them with a fork. Mix with the milk sauce, beating vigorously until well blended. Return to the heat, add the grated cheese, stir until melted, taste, and add salt and pepper. (The traditional way is to add the eggplants first, before the milk, but I find it easier to make the béchamel-type sauce first and then incorporate the eggplant.)

Serve the stew with the eggplant cream sauce in a ring around it.

HÜNKÂR BEĞENDI—SULTAN'S DELIGHT

Emine Foat Tugay writes about this Turkish dish in her book Three Centuries. She calls it "Sultan's Pleasure," but these days it is usually referred to in English as "Sultan's Delight."

Hünkâr beğendi is a purée of eggplant, with small pieces of meat cooked in butter and tomato juice placed in the center. As in the salad, the eggplant is cooked on a hot baking tin, peeled, and mashed. A little melted butter is poured over it just before serving. The dish derives its name from a legend. Once upon a time a sultan went out hunting. Whilst pursuing his quarry, he penetrated into a large forest, and soon lost sight of both the game and his attendants. He wandered about till nightfall, getting farther and farther into unknown country until, hungry and exhausted, he at last saw a light in the distance. Filled with hope, the sultan urged his weary horse towards it till he came to the house whence the light

had proceeded. Here he was hospitably received, and his host immediately sent word to the cook to prepare a meal. It was late, dinner was over long since, and all that remained in the kitchen were some scraps of meat and a few eggplants. The cook, being a resourceful man, cut up the meat and put it in a pot, the vegetables he threw on the hot cooking range, and mashed them. The result was a steaming dish, of which the sultan ate every morsel. Replete and rested he sent a purse filled with gold to the cook and asked the name of the dish, never having eaten it before. He was told that the cook had invented it on the spot, whereupon the sultan declared that henceforth it should be called Sultan's Pleasure.

Veal Chops in Tomato Sauce

Serves 2 • A quick and simple dish to be served with rice, bulgur, or potatoes, or with bread.

- 2 tablespoons vegetable oil
- 2 loin veal chops
- 1 onion, sliced
- 1 or 2 cloves garlic, chopped
- 3 ripe tomatoes, skinned and chopped
- 1 teaspoon sugar, or to taste
- Salt and pepper
- 1 tablespoon chopped flat-leaf parsley

Heat the oil in a skillet, and sauté the chops very briefly to brown them lightly on both sides. Remove them from the pan.

Fry the onion in the same oil until golden. Add the garlic and stir until the aroma rises. Then add the tomatoes and season with sugar, salt, and pepper.

Return the chops to the pan and cook gently, turning them over once, for about 10 minutes, or until the meat is tender and the sauce is rich, adding a drop of water if it becomes too dry. Serve with chopped parsley on top.

⋆⋆⋆

ARAB PROVERB:
"God loveth those who are content."

⋆⋆⋆

Lahma bi Ma'ala

Meat in the Skillet

Serves 6 • A homely Egyptian dish using beef. Serve with rice or potatoes.

- 1 pound onions, coarsely chopped
- 2–3 tablespoons vegetable oil
- 2 pounds best stewing beef, chuck or top rump, cut into 1¼-inch cubes
- Salt and pepper
- 1 teaspoon ground allspice
- 1 pound tomatoes, skinned and chopped
- 2 tablespoons tomato paste
- ⅓ cup chopped flat-leaf parsley

In a large skillet, fry the onions in the oil, over low heat, until golden, stirring occasionally. Add the meat, and turn the pieces to brown them all over. Add salt, pepper, and allspice, the tomatoes and tomato paste, and water barely to cover.

Simmer gently for 1½–2 hours, until the meat is very tender, covered to begin with, adding a very little water from time to time and letting it reduce at the end. Add parsley towards the end.

Variations

• For a Moroccan flavor, season with ½ teaspoon cumin, ¼ teaspoon ginger, ½ teaspoon allspice, and a good pinch of chili powder.

• For the Tunisian *mirmiz,* fry a sliced green bell pepper, cut into ribbons with the onions, and put in a small hot dried chili pod or two.

• Add a 14-ounce can of chickpeas or navy beans, drained, towards the end.

A TALE OF GOHA

Goha hadn't eaten meat for several weeks and had worked up a great desire for it, so he sold an old pair of shoes and a hat and gave the money to his wife, saying: "Today I want a good stew with meat. Put in whatever vegetable you like, but there must be meat. Here's ten piastres, go and buy a rotl of mutton." He went off to work, happy with the thought of the marvelous stew. On her way to the butcher the wife stopped at the spice merchant's and could not resist buying some perfume with the money she had in her pocket. When Goha came home beaming all over, she put the pot of stew in front of him and served him a large plateful. He ate it all, finding beans, lentils, chick-peas, potatoes, macaroni, rice, eggplants, and okra, but no meat. He served himself again, fished around in the pot, but still found no meat. He asked his wife: "Where's the meat?" "Oh!" she said. "I went to the neighbor's to borrow some spices and when I came back the cat had eaten the meat."

Goha got up, looked around the flat, saw the cat, took hold of him, tied him up, and put him on the scales. He weighed just over a rotl. "If this is the cat where's the meat, and if this is the meat where's the cat?"

TOLD BY AN ALGERIAN TROUBADOUR
IN THE SOUTH OF FRANCE

THE STEAM FROM A MEAT STEW

A poor man at Akshehir found a crust of dry bread and was thinking how he could find something to give it a relish when he passed by a cook's shop and saw a saucepan of meat sizzling and boiling on the fire. It gave out a delicious odor.

He went up to the saucepan and began breaking off little bits of bread, holding them in the steam until they became quite soft, and then he ate them.

The Cook looked on with astonishment at this very odd way of making a meal, and for some time said nothing, but no sooner had the poor man finished, than he caught hold of him and demanded payment.

The man protested that he had really had nothing from the Cook, and refused.

It happened that our Khoja was Cadi [judge] of Akshehir at the time, and when the Cook brought the man before him he heard the charge in the ordinary course. Taking two coins from his pocket, he said to him, "Now listen to this," and he began to shake the coins and make them rattle. "All the satisfaction you get will be the sound of these coins."

The Cook cried out in amazement, "But, your Honour, what a way to treat me!"

"No!" said the Khoja. "It is a perfectly just settlement of the claim. A man who is so mean as to ask for payment for the steam of his meat will get the sound of these coins and nothing more."

BARNHAM, TRANS.,
TALES OF NASR-ED-DIN KHOJA

Bamia Matbookha

Meat and Okra Stew

Serves 6 • This is a common and much-loved dish of Egypt. You also find it in other countries. Use small okra—they are much nicer than the tougher large ones—and serve with rice or bulgur. Traditionally, okra is put in to cook at the same time as the meat, so that it becomes extremely soft and falls apart, but these days it is not uncommon to add it at a later stage, so that it remains firm. That is the way I like it.

1¾ pounds small young okra (called *bamia* in Egypt)

3 tablespoons sunflower or vegetable oil

2 large onions, chopped, or ¾ pound baby onions, peeled

2 cloves garlic, chopped

1 teaspoon ground coriander

1¾ pounds beef, lamb, or veal stew meat, cut into 1¼-inch cubes

1 pound tomatoes, peeled and sliced

1–1½ tablespoons tomato paste

Salt and pepper

Juice of 1 lemon

Wash the okra and trim the stem ends, cutting round the cap to form a little cone.

Heat the oil in a large pan and fry the onions until soft and golden. Start on low heat with the lid on, then uncover and turn up the heat to medium. Add the garlic and coriander and put in the meat. Turn the pieces until they change color all over.

Add the tomatoes, cover with water, and stir in the tomato paste. Season with salt and pepper, stir well, and simmer over low heat for 1–1¼ hours. Stir in the okra, adding water if necessary, and cook for 20 minutes, or until the meat and okra are tender and the sauce is reduced.

Add lemon juice and serve hot with rice.

Variations

• In the Said, in Upper Egypt, they boil the meat (about half the quantity) first in water, then lift the pieces out and cook the okra in the stock along with 2 cups tomato juice and 2 small chopped chili peppers. When the okra is very soft, they mash it with a fork (you can use a food processor). They put the meat back in the pan with the mashed okra and add a sauce called *takleya* made by frying 5 crushed garlic cloves with 1 teaspoon ground coriander in 2 tablespoons oil until the garlic is golden. The dish is quite soupy.

• For an Iraqi version, add 2 dried limes (see page 44) from the start. Crack them open with a hammer before you put them in, or pierce them with a skewer when they have softened in the stew. Omit the fresh lemon juice. The dried limes give a distinctive and delicious flavor.

• A Syrian version adds 2 tablespoons pomegranate syrup (molasses or concentrate) in mid-cooking. Omit the lemon juice.

• For a Turkish version, add 2 tablespoons wine vinegar.

Lahma bi Betingan

Meat and Eggplant Stew

Serves 6 • Also called *buraniya,* this is one dish where I prefer to broil or grill the eggplants instead of frying them, before putting them in the stew. Serve with rice or bulgur or with bread.

2 onions, chopped

Vegetable oil

2 or 3 cloves garlic, chopped

1½ pounds lamb, beef, or veal, cut into cubes

3 tomatoes, skinned and quartered

Salt and pepper

Juice of ½ lemon

1 teaspoon cinnamon

½ teaspoon allspice

3 medium eggplants

3 tablespoons chopped flat-leaf parsley

Fry the onions in about 2 tablespoons oil until soft and golden. Add the garlic, then add the meat and brown it well. Add the tomatoes and seasonings: salt, pepper, lemon juice, cinnamon, and allspice. Cover with water, stir well, and bring to the boil. Simmer gently, covered, for about 1½ hours, until the meat is very tender, adding water to keep it covered.

Cut the eggplants into ½-inch-thick slices and brush them generously with oil. (You do not need to peel the eggplants, because the peels will soften later, in the stew.) Cook them under the broiler or in a grill pan, turning them over once until lightly colored. (See page 290 about treating eggplants.) Cut them in half and add them to the stew. Simmer, covered, for ½ hour, adding the parsley towards the end.

Variations

• For a Tunisian version, add 1 cup dried chickpeas, soaked overnight and drained, at the same time as the meat. Add ½ teaspoon harissa (page 464) or a good pinch of ground chili pepper. Other spices can be cinnamon and nutmeg.

• For a Moroccan taste, change the spices to 1 teaspoon ground ginger, 1 teaspoon cinnamon, and ¼ teaspoon powdered saffron.

• In Turkey, roasted bell peppers, quartered, are added in with the eggplants.

Cuts of Meat for Stews

Favorite cuts of meat for stews and long, slow cooking are: shoulder of lamb, because of the melting tenderness given by the fat content; neck filet; lamb knuckle or shanks on the bone, because the melting connective tissue gives a rich gelatinous quality; and the best end of neck cutlets. Preferred beef cuts are brisket, chuck, and blade; and for veal they are knuckle, shanks, and breast.

Pssal ou Loubia

*Spicy Sausages and Meat with
Haricot or Navy Beans*

Serves 6 • They call it the Tunisian cassoulet.

- 3 tablespoons vegetable oil
- 3 onions, chopped
- 6 cloves garlic, chopped
- 1 pound shoulder of lamb or stewing beef, cut into 6 pieces
- ½ pound merguez (Tunisian sausages) or chorizo, cut into pieces
- 1 cup white haricot or navy beans, soaked overnight
- 3 tomatoes, peeled and chopped
- 1 teaspoon cinnamon
- 1 teaspoon ground coriander
- Pepper and salt

Heat the oil in a large pan, and fry the onions until lightly colored. Add the garlic and stir until the aroma rises. Put in the meat and the merguez and turn them to brown them lightly all over.

Add the drained beans, the tomatoes, cinnamon, coriander, and pepper. Pour in about 7 cups water and cook, covered, over very low heat for 1½ hours. Add salt and simmer another ½ hour, adding a little water if necessary and reducing the sauce towards the end.

Serve hot.

Lamb Tagine with Peas, Preserved Lemon, and Olives

Serves 6–8 • Here is another Moroccan tagine. Buy the peas fresh and young, in the pod, when you can. Some supermarkets sell fresh shelled ones that are young and sweet, and frozen baby peas—*petits pois*—are also perfect to use.

- 2 pounds leg or shoulder of lamb, trimmed of excess fat and cut into cubes
- 2 tablespoons vegetable oil
- 1 onion, chopped
- Salt and pepper
- 1 teaspoon ground ginger
- A good pinch of chili powder or chili flakes (optional)
- ¼ teaspoon powdered saffron
- 4 cups shelled fresh peas or frozen *petits pois*, defrosted
- 2 tomatoes, peeled and chopped
- Peel of 1 preserved lemon, or more (see page 459), cut into pieces
- 12 green olives

Put the meat in a large pot with the oil, onion, salt and pepper, ginger, chili if using, and saffron. Cover with water and cook, covered, for 1–1½ hours, until the meat is very tender, adding water to keep it covered in its sauce.

Add the peas, tomatoes, preserved lemon peel, and olives and cook, uncovered, a few minutes longer, until the peas are tender and the sauce is reduced.

Serve hot with bread or couscous.

Moroccan Cooking and Tagines

Moroccan cooking is the most refined in North Africa and one of the most exquisite in the Middle East. It has come to be appreciated in America in great part through Paula Wolfert's splendid book *Couscous and Other Good Food from Morocco*. Like the rest of North Africa, Morocco was invaded by the Arabs in several waves, beginning in the seventh century and until the fourteenth. The country benefited from the dynamic civilization of the Islamic Empire. It inherited more directly than any other Muslim country the high culinary culture of medieval Baghdad, which was itself heavily influenced by Persian cooking traditions. To these it added its own indigenous Berber traditions and a unique legacy from Spain.

The Arabs invaded Spain with Berber foot soldiers in 711. They conquered half the country, which became known by the Arab name of Al Andalus, and they remained in the south for almost eight hundred years. For two centuries, from the eleventh to the thirteenth, the ruling dynasties, the Almoravids and the Almohads, were Berber. A vast Berber Empire, with Marrakesh as the capital, spread through Spain, Tunisia, and Algeria, and south into Senegal. For centuries there was constant cultural exchange between the countries, and when the Moors were finally expelled from Spain in 1492 and moved to North Africa, they brought with them an art of living, an exuberant life style and dishes. All these foreign influences come together in the high culinary culture which evolved as court cuisines in the royal kitchens of the great dynasties of Morocco—the Almoravids, the Almohads, the Merinids, the Saadians, and the Alaouites.

The tagines, which marry meat with vegetables or with fruit, the savory with the sweet, and an extraordinarily delicate blend of spices, are part of that bourgeois high cuisine. The name "tagine" derives from the clay pot with conical lid in which stews are traditionally cooked slowly over a fire. These days, while the stews may be finished off and presented in tagines, they are more practically cooked in large copper, aluminum, or stainless-steel pots (you see them for rent and for sale in the souks) and also in pressure cookers, which have taken the country by storm. The result is not the same as the long, slow cooking over a constantly replenished wood fire in the low, diffuse heat of a clay pot, which produces at the end a rich, reduced sauce, unctuous with fat and sometimes also with honey.

The meat commonly used for tagines is the shoulder of lamb. If you find the shoulder too fat, trim off the fat or use other cuts. Tagines are served with bread, not with couscous. In Paris, North African restaurants sometimes accompany them with couscous.

Marquit Quastal

Lamb Tagine with Chestnuts

Serves 6–8 • This Tunisian dish, more commonly made with dried chestnuts, is more to my taste with fresh and even frozen ones. While Tunisia has been sympathetic to Western ideas, and although it was subjected to a massive immigration of French and Italian peasants when it became a French protectorate, it has sustained Arab cooking in its most ancient form. This beautiful and fragrant stew is an example.

1 large onion, chopped

4 tablespoons butter or olive oil

2 cloves garlic, chopped

2 pounds lamb (preferably shoulder), trimmed of excess fat and cut into 1½-inch pieces

Salt and pepper

1 teaspoon ground ginger

1 teaspoon cinnamon

1½ pounds chestnuts, fresh or frozen (defrosted)

1–2 tablespoons honey (optional)

Fry the onion in the butter or oil until it begins to color. Add the garlic and meat and turn to brown it all over. Add salt and pepper, ginger, and cinnamon. Cover with water and simmer, covered, for 1½ hours, or until the meat is very tender, adding water to keep it only just covered and letting it reduce towards the end so that the sauce is rich and unctuous.

To peel the fresh chestnuts, make a slit on one side with a sharp, pointed knife and cook under the broiler, turning them over once, until they are browned and the skins come off easily. Peel them when cool enough to handle but still hot. Fifteen minutes before the end of cooking, add them to the meat and stir in the honey if using. If using frozen chestnuts, defrost them thoroughly before putting them into the stew, and simmer 10 minutes. Serve hot.

Variation

For a tagine with chickpeas, raisins, and chestnuts, add 1 cup cooked canned chickpeas and 2 tablespoons raisins at the same time as the chestnuts. You could also add 1 tablespoon rose water.

Lamb Tagine with Artichokes and Fava Beans

Serves 8 • This Moroccan tagine is easy to make with the frozen artichoke bottoms from Egypt and frozen skinned fava beans (both really good) available in Middle Eastern stores.

2 pounds shoulder of lamb, cut into large pieces

2 onions, sliced

4 tablespoons butter or vegetable oil

Salt and pepper

1 teaspoon ginger

$\frac{1}{2}$ teaspoon saffron

Two 14-ounce packages frozen artichoke bottoms, defrosted

Two 7-ounce packages frozen skinned fava beans, defrosted

Juice of $\frac{1}{2}$–1 lemon

$\frac{1}{2}$ cup chopped cilantro leaves

1 preserved lemon peel (page 459), cut into strips (optional if garnish)

Put the meat with the onions, butter or oil, salt, pepper, ginger, and saffron in a pan and cook, turning over the meat, for about 5 minutes. Cover with water and simmer, covered, for $1\frac{1}{2}$ hours, or until the meat is very tender, adding water if it becomes too dry. Remove the lid and reduce the sauce at the end.

Add the artichoke bottoms, fava beans, and lemon juice and cook 10 minutes, until the artichokes are tender. Add the cilantro and cook 1 or 2 minutes more.

Serve hot, garnished if you like, with the preserved lemon peel.

Variation

For an Egyptian beef stew with fresh green fava beans: Sauté 1 pound fresh or frozen (and defrosted) beans in 3 tablespoons vegetable oil with 1 pound cubed stewing beef until lightly browned. Add 2 whole garlic cloves, 1 teaspoon ground coriander, salt, and pepper, and cover with water. Simmer, covered, for about $1\frac{1}{2}$ hours, or until the meat is very tender.

Tagine Barkok

Lamb with Prunes

Serves 6 • *Tagine barkok,* made with or without honey, is one of the most popular fruit tagines of North Africa. It is eaten with bread. Restaurants in Paris accompany it with couscous and bowls of boiled chickpeas and boiled raisins (see page 377).

- 2 pounds shoulder of lamb, cubed and trimmed of excess fat, or cut into 6 pieces
- 3 tablespoons vegetable oil
- ¾ teaspoon ground ginger
- ¼ teaspoon powdered saffron
- 2 teaspoons ground cinnamon
- Salt
- ½ teaspoon pepper
- 1 large onion, finely chopped or grated
- 2 cloves garlic, chopped
- 12 ounces California pitted prunes, soaked for 1 hour
- 1–3 tablespoons honey (optional)

OPTIONAL GARNISHES

- 3 tablespoons lightly toasted sesame seeds
- ½–1 cup lightly toasted blanched almonds, left whole or coarsely chopped

Put the meat in a pan with the oil, ginger, saffron, half the cinnamon, the salt, pepper, onion, and garlic. Cover with water and simmer gently, covered, for 1½ hours, until the meat is very tender, adding a little water as required to keep the meat covered.

Add the prunes and the remaining cinnamon and cook 30 minutes, until the liquid is reduced to a thick, unctuous sauce. Stir in the honey, if using, and cook 10 minutes more.

Garnish, if you like, with toasted sesame seeds and almonds.

Variation

Put the almonds in with the meat from the start of the cooking; they will come out very soft.

Sweet Tagines

Tagines of meat with fruit—a legacy of Baghdad from the time of Harun-al-Rashid—are celebratory dishes cooked for happy occasions. Prunes, apricots, dates, quinces, raisins, gooseberries, apples, and pears are used, and the usual spices are ginger and cinnamon, often with lots of black pepper to mitigate the sweetness. There is also sometimes honey, which you might find strange but enjoyable. You have to be very careful with your dosage of honey. Start with a tiny bit and add more to taste.

Mishmishiya

Tagine of Lamb with Apricots

Serves 6–8 • The dish derives its name from the Arabic word for apricot—*mishmish*. Only a tart natural—not sweetened—dried or semi-dried variety will do. Fresh apricots may also be used, in which case they should be added at the end and cooked for a few minutes only, so that they don't fall apart. The reason why there is fresh gingerroot rather than the ground spice which is usual in Morocco is that the recipe comes from Paris. Serve with bread.

2 large onions, chopped

2 tablespoons vegetable or extra-virgin olive oil

1½ teaspoons cinnamon

½ teaspoon cumin

Good pinch of ground chili pepper, to taste

2 pounds leg or shoulder of lamb, trimmed of excess fat

Salt and plenty of pepper

1½ inches fresh gingerroot, cut into slices

3 cloves garlic, crushed

1 pound dried apricots

A 14-ounce can chickpeas, drained (optional)

Fry the onions gently in the oil until soft.

Stir in the cinnamon, cumin, and chili powder, and put in the meat. Turn the pieces over, add salt and pepper, ginger, and garlic, and cover with about 2¼ cups water. Simmer, covered, for 1½ hours, turning the meat over occasionally, and adding water if necessary.

Add the apricots and cook for ½ hour more, adding water if necessary.

Add the drained chickpeas, if using, 10 minutes before the end.

Variations

• An alternative combination of flavorings is ½ teaspoon coriander, ¼ teaspoon ground cloves, and 1 teaspoon rose water. Also, ¼ cup raisins may be added.

• Here is the *mishmishiya* in al-Baghdadi's thirteenth-century cookery manual as translated by Arberry (see appendix): "Cut fat meat small, put into the saucepan with a little salt, and cover with water. Boil and remove the scum. Cut up onions, wash, and throw in on top of the meat. Add seasonings, coriander, cumin, mastic, cinnamon, pepper and ginger, well ground. Take dry apricots, soak in hot water, then wash and put in a separate saucepan, and boil lightly; take out, wipe in the hands, and strain through a sieve. Take the juice, and add it to the saucepan to form a broth. Take sweet almonds, grind fine, moisten with a little apricot juice and throw in. Some color with a trifle of saffron. Spray the saucepan with a little rosewater, wipe its sides with a clean rag, and leave to settle over the fire; then remove."

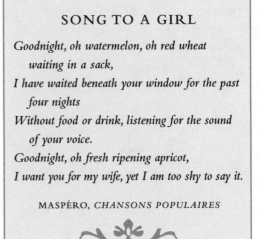

SONG TO A GIRL

Goodnight, oh watermelon, oh red wheat
waiting in a sack,
I have waited beneath your window for the past
four nights
Without food or drink, listening for the sound
of your voice.
Goodnight, oh fresh ripening apricot,
I want you for my wife, yet I am too shy to say it.

MASPÉRO, *CHANSONS POPULAIRES*

Rutabiya

Tagine of Meat with Dates

Serves 6 • *Rutab* is the Arabic word for dates. You might find this dish too sweet. In Morocco it is made with fresh Tafilalet dates, but you may use the Tunisian or the moist dried California ones available in America. Serve with bread.

2 pounds lamb, trimmed of excess fat
Salt and plenty of pepper
¼ teaspoon powdered saffron
½ teaspoon ginger
2 teaspoons cinnamon
4 tablespoons oil
2 large onions, finely chopped
1–2 tablespoons honey (optional)
¼–½ pound fresh or moist dried
    Tunisian or California dates, pitted
½–¾ cup blanched almonds, left whole
    or coarsely chopped, toasted or fried
    in oil
3 tablespoons sesame seeds, toasted

Cut the meat into 6 pieces and put it in a pan. Add salt, pepper, saffron, ginger, 1 teaspoon of the cinnamon, and the oil and onions. Cover with water and simmer, covered, for 1½ hours, or until the meat is very tender, adding water to keep the meat covered, and turning the pieces over.

Add the honey, if you like, and the remaining cinnamon and cook until the sauce is reduced, turning the pieces of meat over. Add the dates and cook 10–15 minutes more.

Serve sprinkled with almonds and sesame seeds.

Safardjaliya

Tagine of Lamb with Quince

Serves 6 • This is a Moroccan version of a dish you find in many Middle Eastern countries. Serve with bread.

2 pounds shoulder of lamb, cut into large pieces

2 onions, sliced

4 tablespoons butter or vegetable oil

Salt and plenty of pepper

1 teaspoon ginger

1/2 teaspoon saffron

2 pounds quinces

Juice of 1/2 lemon plus 1 optional lemon

1 teaspoon cinnamon

3–4 tablespoons honey

Put the meat with the onions, butter or oil, salt, pepper, ginger, and saffron in a large pan and cook, turning over the meat, for about 5 minutes. Cover with water and simmer, covered, over low heat for 1 1/2 hours, or until the meat is very tender, adding water if it becomes too dry. Remove the lid at the end to reduce the sauce.

Wash and scrub the quinces. Have ready a pan of boiling water with the juice of 1/2 lemon. Cut the quinces into quarters (you will need a big strong knife and plenty of force, as they are very hard). Do not peel them, but cut away the blackened ends, and drop them at once into the acidulated boiling water (the lemon stops them from going brown). Simmer for 15–30 minutes, until tender. The time varies greatly, and you must watch them, as they can fall apart very quickly. They should not be too soft. Drain, and when cool enough to handle, cut out the cores.

Put them in the pan with the meat, flesh side up. Sprinkle with cinnamon and pour a little honey on each. Squeeze the extra lemon, if using, over the stew. Cook for 5 minutes, then turn the quinces over and cook a few minutes more.

Variations

• A Lebanese version is flavored with 1 teaspoon cinnamon and 1 teaspoon crushed cardamom seeds instead of the spices used above. Small meatballs—made with 1/2 pound ground beef or lamb blended to a paste in the food processor with 1 grated onion and 1 cup bulgur—are sometimes added.

• Instead of the quinces, pears or sharp green apples, peeled and quartered and sautéed in butter or oil or a mixture of both, may be added to the stew towards the end of the cooking.

• Chicken is also cooked with quinces in the same way as lamb.

ARAB PROVERB:
"A guest is the captive of the whole quarter."
(Said to a guest who declines the invitation of his host's friends.)

Lamb with Apples and Cherries

Serves 6 • This is a Persian stew which is a sauce for plain rice. You will find many more Persian sauces with meat in the rice chapter. Use dried pitted sour cherries.

2 pounds lean lamb, cubed

2 tablespoons vegetable oil

$\frac{1}{2}$ cup yellow split peas

Salt and pepper

$1\frac{1}{2}$ cups dried pitted sour cherries

1 tart apple, peeled, cored, and diced

Lemon juice (optional)

In a large pan, brown the meat in the oil until lightly colored all over. Add the yellow split peas and water to cover, and season with salt and pepper. Bring to the boil and skim off any scum. Cover the pan and simmer for about $1\frac{1}{2}$ hours, or until the meat is very tender.

Add the cherries, diced apple, lemon juice (if the fruits are not tart), and a little more water if necessary. Cook for a further $\frac{1}{2}$ hour and serve hot.

COOKING BY CANDLE

Nasrudin made a wager that he could spend a night on a nearby mountain and survive, in spite of ice and snow. Several wags in the teahouse agreed to adjudicate.

Nasrudin took a book and a candle and sat through the coldest night he had ever known. In the morning, half-dead, he claimed his money.

"Did you have nothing at all to keep you warm?" asked the villagers.

"Nothing."

"Not even a candle?"

"Yes, I had a candle."

"Then the bet is off."

Nasrudin did not argue.

Some months later he invited the same people to a feast at his house. They sat down in his reception room, waiting for the food. Hours passed.

They started to mutter about food.

"Let's go and see how it is getting on," said Nasrudin.

Everyone trooped into the kitchen. They found an enormous pot of water, under which a candle was burning. The water was not even tepid.

"It is not ready yet," said the Mulla. "I don't know why—it has been there since yesterday."

SHAH, *THE EXPLOITS OF THE INCOMPARABLE MULLA NASRUDIN*

Lahma bel Karaz

Meatballs with Sour Cherries

Serves 6–8 • This is an old family recipe which originates in Syria. It is easy to make now that dried pitted sour cherries are available. We used to have to pit them. Serve it with rice or, as was usual in the old days, on miniature pita breads split in half, soft side up.

1½ cups dried pitted sour cherries

1½ pounds lean ground lamb or veal

Salt and pepper

¼ teaspoon grated nutmeg

¼ teaspoon ground cloves

1 teaspoon ground cinnamon

Vegetable oil

1 large onion, chopped

Juice of 1 lemon

Miniature "picnic" rounds of pita bread
    to serve on (optional)

Soak the sour cherries in water to cover for ½ hour.

Put the meat in a bowl. Add salt, pepper, nutmeg, cloves, and cinnamon, and knead vigorously to achieve a soft, pasty texture. Roll into balls the size of fat marbles and fry briefly in shallow oil, turning them and shaking the pan until they change color all over. You will have to do them in batches. Lift them out with a slotted spoon. They should be pink and underdone inside.

In a large saucepan, fry the onion in 2 tablespoons oil till soft and golden, add the cherries with their soaking water and the lemon juice, and simmer for 10 minutes. Add the meatballs and cook gently for 5–10 minutes, turning them until they are cooked through and have absorbed the cherry juices.

Serve the meatballs with their sauce on little rounds of pita bread split in half and arranged on a large flat platter. Or serve with plain rice.

Variations

• Prepare a tomato sauce: Fry a chopped onion with 2 chopped garlic cloves in 2 tablespoons oil. Add 4 peeled and chopped tomatoes, 1 tablespoon tomato paste, and a little water. Add the cherries and meatballs and simmer until the meatballs are tender.

• For another Syrian version, blend half the soaked cherries with the soaking water in the food processor and add 1–2 tablespoons pomegranate syrup (concentrate or molasses).

Meat Pie with Mashed Potatoes

Serves 6–8 • I love this Arab equivalent of shepherd's pie.

2³⁄₄ pounds mealy potatoes

Salt

6–8 tablespoons butter, cut into pieces

³⁄₄ cup milk

FOR THE FILLING

2 onions, chopped

4 tablespoons vegetable oil

2 pounds ground lamb or beef

Salt and pepper

1¹⁄₂ teaspoons cinnamon

¹⁄₂ teaspoon allspice

¹⁄₂ cup pine nuts

3 tablespoons raisins (optional)

Peel and boil the potatoes in salted water until done. Drain, mash them, and stir in the butter and milk. Season with salt and beat well.

For the filling, fry the onions in 3¹⁄₂ tablespoons of the oil, stirring occasionally. Start on very low heat with a lid on until they are soft, then let them color with the lid off. Add the ground meat, salt, pepper, cinnamon, and allspice, and cook, crushing and turning the meat over, for 10 minutes. If you like, strain off the fat.

Heat the pine nuts in about ¹⁄₂ tablespoon of oil in a skillet, shaking the pan to brown them lightly all over, then stir them into the meat mixture. If you like, stir in the raisins.

Spread a layer of meat filling at the bottom of a large baking dish (about 14¹⁄₂ by 10¹⁄₂ inches), cover with a layer of mashed potatoes, and press down to flatten. Bake in a preheated 400°F oven for 30 minutes, or until lightly browned.

Batoursh

Ground Meat with Eggplants and Yogurt

Serves 4–6 • This intriguing layered dish with a delicious mix of textures and flavors is a specialty of the city of Hama in Syria.

3 eggplants, weighing about 1¹⁄₂ pounds

4 tablespoons vegetable or extra-virgin olive oil

2 onions, chopped

1 pound ground lamb or beef

Salt and pepper

¹⁄₄ cup pine nuts

2 cups plain whole-milk or thick strained yogurt (see page 110), at room temperature

3 tablespoons tahina (sesame paste) (optional)

2 cloves garlic, crushed

Cook the eggplants under the broiler or roast them in the oven, then peel, chop, and mash them to a puree (see page 63). Beat in 2 tablespoons of the oil.

Fry the onions in the remaining oil in a large skillet until soft. Add the ground meat, salt, and pepper and cook, crushing the meat and turning it over, for about 8 minutes, until it changes color. Add the pine nuts and cook 5 minutes more. Set aside, and reheat just before serving.

Beat the yogurt with the tahina, if using, and garlic.

To serve, spread a layer of the eggplant puree (warm or at room temperature) at the bottom of a serving dish. Pour the yogurt on top, and cover with the hot ground meat and pine nuts.

Moussaka

Serves 6–8 • This famously Greek dish is to be found throughout the Arab world without the creamy topping. Broiling or grilling instead of frying the eggplants makes for a lighter and lovelier moussaka. This one is made up of a layer of eggplants, a layer of meat and tomatoes, and a layer of cheesy white (béchamel-type) sauce. Serve with salad and yogurt.

FOR THE MEAT AND TOMATOES

2 onions, thinly sliced or chopped

3 tablespoons vegetable oil

1½ pounds ground lamb or beef

Salt and pepper

2 teaspoons cinnamon (optional)

5 large tomatoes, peeled and chopped

2 teaspoons sugar

½ teaspoon chili-pepper flakes (optional)

3 tablespoons chopped flat-leaf parsley

FOR THE WHITE SAUCE TOPPING

4 tablespoons butter

4 tablespoons flour

2½ cups hot milk

Salt and pepper

Pinch of grated nutmeg

2 eggs

½ cup grated cheddar

3 eggplants (about 1½ pounds total), left unpeeled, cut crosswise in ⅓-inch slices

Vegetable or olive oil

Fry the onions in the oil in a large skillet or saucepan until golden. Add the ground meat and stir, crushing it with a fork and turning it over, until it changes color. Add salt, pepper, cinnamon if using, tomatoes, sugar, and chili flakes if you like. Stir well, and cook until the liquid has almost disappeared, then mix in the parsley.

Prepare a white sauce: Melt the butter in a pan. Add the flour and stir over low heat for a few minutes, until well blended. Add the hot milk a little at a time, stirring vigorously each time, until it boils, taking care not to allow lumps to form. Simmer over low heat, stirring occasionally, until the sauce thickens. Add salt and pepper and a pinch of nutmeg. Beat the eggs lightly, beat in a little of the white sauce, then pour back into the pan, beating vigorously. Do not allow the sauce to boil again. Add the cheese and mix well until melted.

Brush the eggplant slices generously with oil and broil or grill them, turning them over once, until lightly browned. Line the bottom of a large baking dish (about 14½ by 10½ inches) with half the slices. Spread the meat on top, and cover with the remaining eggplant slices. Pour the white sauce all over.

Bake, uncovered, in a preheated 400°F oven for about 45 minutes, until golden.

Serve hot, straight from the dish. It can also be cooked in small individual clay bowls, the layers repeated in the same way.

Koukla

Meatballs

Serves 4 or more • From the Greek word for "doll," these Greek meatballs make lovely finger food, as good cold as they are hot.

1 slice white bread, crusts removed

1 pound lamb, beef, or veal

1 egg

¼ teaspoon ground allspice or ¾ teaspoon ground cinnamon

Salt and pepper

3 tablespoons chopped flat-leaf parsley

Vegetable oil for shallow frying

Soak the bread in water and squeeze dry. Put the meat in the food processor with the bread, egg, allspice or cinnamon, salt, and pepper, and blend to a soft homogenous paste. Add parsley, and process very briefly to amalgamate it.

Wet your hands with water and roll the meat paste into marble-sized balls, and deep-fry in hot oil for a few minutes, until cooked through and a rich brown color. Drain on paper towels.

Variation

For an alternative Arab flavor, use 1 teaspoon cumin and ½ teaspoon coriander and, if you like, a pinch of ground chili pepper, instead of allspice or cinnamon.

About Meatballs

In America, meatballs have a low prestige rating, perhaps because they invoke the spaghetti and meatballs of the poor Sicilian immigrants when they first arrived. It is the Arabs who brought meatballs to Sicily, and in the Arab world meatballs are highly regarded and considered refined and sophisticated. This is partly because they require labor. In the old days, the meat was chopped by hand or put through a grinder two or three times, then pounded with a pestle and mortar until it was a smooth, soft paste. Nowadays, those who have one use a food processor to obtain a soft, pasty texture. But if you have a good butcher who can give you fine ground meat, all you have to do is knead it a little with your hands to turn it to the required paste. Meatballs always used to be fried in shallow oil before they were stewed, but now many people broil or bake them briefly in a hot oven.

Armenian Kofta with Mashed Potato, Pine Nuts, and Raisins

Serves 4

1 mealy potato, weighing about
   12 ounces
Salt and pepper
$\frac{1}{4}$ cup pine nuts
Vegetable oil for frying
1 pound ground lean lamb or veal
1 small egg, lightly beaten
$\frac{1}{4}$ cup black or golden raisins
Flour

Peel and boil the potato in salted water until tender, then drain. Put it back in the pan, mash it, and dry it out thoroughly over medium heat.

Fry the pine nuts in a drop of oil, shaking the pan to brown them lightly all over.

Mix the ground meat with the mashed potato and add the egg, salt, and pepper. Knead vigorously by hand until well mixed and smooth. Work the pine nuts and raisins into the meat-and-potato mixture.

Shape into walnut-sized balls and flatten them slightly. Dip them in flour to coat them lightly all over, and deep-fry in medium-hot oil, turning them over once, until crisp and brown.

Meatballs with Eggplant Sauce

Serves 6 • A delicious Turkish specialty to be served hot with rice or bulgur.

4 eggplants, about 2 pounds total
1$\frac{1}{2}$ pounds ground lamb or beef
2 eggs, lightly beaten
3 tablespoons dry fine white
   breadcrumbs or matzo meal
$\frac{3}{4}$ teaspoon ground cumin
$\frac{3}{4}$ teaspoon ground allspice
Salt and pepper
Sunflower or vegetable oil
1 large onion, chopped
2 or 3 cloves garlic, finely chopped
1 large beefsteak tomato, peeled and
   finely chopped

Roast, peel, and mash the eggplants as described on page 63.

For the meatballs, put the ground meat, eggs, and breadcrumbs in a bowl with the cumin, allspice, salt, and pepper and knead with your hands to a soft paste. Or blend in the food processor. Shape the mixture into small balls and fry in shallow oil over medium heat, turning them until they are colored all over. Remove, and drain on paper towels.

In another large frying pan, fry the onion in 3 tablespoons oil until soft and golden. Add the garlic and stir until it begins to color, then add the tomato, salt, and pepper and cook for a few minutes, until reduced. Add the mashed eggplants, season again with salt and pepper, and cook gently, stirring, for about 8 minutes, until much of the liquid has disappeared. Drop in the meatballs and simmer for 5–10 minutes.

Tagine Kefta Mkawra

Tagine of Meatballs in Tomato Sauce with Eggs

Serves 6 • This is one of my favorites. You will need a large shallow pan that can go to the table. In Morocco the cooking is finished in a wide earthenware tagine which goes on top of the fire. Serve it with plenty of warm bread.

FOR THE MEATBALLS

1½ pounds ground lamb or beef

1 onion, very finely chopped

3 tablespoons finely chopped flat-leaf parsley

Salt and pepper

Pinch of ground chili pepper, to taste

1 teaspoon cinnamon

½ teaspoon ground ginger

1 teaspoon ground cumin

Vegetable oil for frying

FOR THE TOMATO SAUCE

2 onions, chopped

2 tablespoons olive oil

2 cloves garlic, crushed

1½ pounds tomatoes, peeled and chopped

1–2 teaspoons sugar

Salt

1 small chili pepper, seeded and chopped (optional)

3 tablespoons chopped flat-leaf parsley

3 tablespoons chopped cilantro

6 eggs

For the meatballs, mix all the ingredients together except the oil and knead into a soft paste. Roll into marble-sized balls and fry them very briefly in batches in shallow oil, shaking the pan to color them all over. Lift out with a slotted spoon and drain on paper towels.

In a large shallow pot which you can bring to the table, prepare the sauce. Fry the onions in the oil till soft. Add the garlic, tomatoes, sugar, salt, and chili pepper if you like, and simmer for 20 minutes, until reduced. Add parsley, cilantro, and the meatballs, and cook 5 minutes.

Just before serving, break the eggs carefully over the sauce, leaving them whole, and cook until the whites have set.

Daoud Basha

*Meatballs with Pine Nuts and
Tomato Sauce*

Serves 6 • The dish takes its name from the Ottoman pasha who administered Mount Lebanon in the nineteenth century. Serve with rice or mashed potatoes. The meatballs are usually fried, then cooked in a tomato sauce, but baked this way they have a light, fresh flavor.

1½ pounds ground lamb

2 onions, grated or finely chopped

Salt and pepper

1 teaspoon cinnamon

½ teaspoon allspice

⅔ cup pine nuts

½ cup raisins (optional)

Vegetable oil

2 pounds tomatoes, peeled

2 teaspoons sugar

3 cloves garlic, crushed (optional)

In a bowl, mix the ground lamb with the onions, salt and pepper, cinnamon, and allspice, and work to a paste with your hand. Roll into balls the size of small walnuts. Make a hole in each ball with your finger and stuff in a few pine nuts—and raisins if you wish. Then close the hole. Alternatively, and more easily, work the pine nuts and raisins into the meat paste, then roll it into balls.

Put a little oil in a soup plate and roll the meatballs in it. Then put them in a baking dish and bake in a preheated 400°F oven for 15–20 minutes, until their color changes.

Cut the tomatoes up and liquidize them in the food processor or blender. Add a little salt and pepper, the sugar, and the garlic, and pour over the meatballs. Bake for another 35 minutes, turning the meatballs over once.

Serve hot.

Variations

• Add the juice of 1 lemon and a good pinch of chili flakes to the sauce.

• Another way is to peel and chop the tomatoes, fry the garlic in 2 tablespoons oil in a large saucepan for a moment or two, until the aroma rises, then add the tomatoes, salt, pepper, and sugar and simmer 10 minutes. Bake the meatballs on their own as described above for 15 minutes, then add them to the tomato sauce and simmer for 20 minutes more, or until the sauce is reduced and the meatballs are very tender.

Kofta bel Sabanekh
wal Hummus

Meatballs with Spinach and Chickpeas

Serves 6 • This is common throughout the Middle East.

1½ pounds ground lean beef, lamb, or veal

1 onion, grated or finely chopped

Salt and pepper

Vegetable oil

1 pound fresh spinach or frozen chopped spinach

1 tablespoon butter

A 14-ounce can chickpeas or two, drained

2–4 cloves garlic, crushed

2 teaspoons ground coriander

Put the ground meat and onion in a bowl. Add salt and pepper, mix well, and work with your hand to a soft paste. Roll into walnut-sized balls and fry briefly in shallow oil, in batches, turning them so that they are brown all over but still pink inside. Drain on paper towels.

Wash the fresh spinach leaves thoroughly, and remove stems only if they are thick. Put them in a large pan with the butter, and no extra water, over low heat for a minute or so with the lid on, until the leaves crumple into a soft mass. (If using frozen spinach, defrost it and heat it in the pan with the butter until it is soft.) Cut up the spinach very roughly with a pointed knife in the pan, add the drained chickpeas, season with salt and pepper, and stir well.

Put in the meatballs, stir, and cook with the lid on. In Egypt it was usual to cook a further ½ hour, adding a little water, until the meatballs were very soft. I like the meat to be still a little pink inside, so I cook for 5 minutes only.

The particular refinement of this dish comes from a fried mixture called *takleya* added in at the end. Fry the garlic in 2 tablespoons oil with the coriander until the mixture smells sweet. Stir this in at the end of the cooking.

Serve with rice.

Variations

• A Turkish way of eating this is smothered in yogurt mixed with crushed garlic and a little salt, pepper, and dried crushed mint. The whole is decorated with a sprinkling of scarlet paprika. In this case, omit the *takleya* at the end.

• A variation from Iran is *khoresh sak,* a spinach-and-orange sauce served with rice. The juice of 1 lemon and 2 oranges is mixed with 1 tablespoon flour and cooked with the meat and spinach for 20 minutes. In this case, add only crushed garlic fried in butter, without coriander, at the end.

Blehat Lahma bi Beid

*Meat Rolls Stuffed with
Hard-Boiled Eggs*

Serves 8

3 slices white bread, crusts removed

2 pounds ground beef or lamb

2 egg whites

1 teaspoon ground cinnamon

$\frac{1}{2}$ teaspoon grated nutmeg

Salt and pepper

1 onion, finely chopped

2 tablespoons finely chopped flat-leaf
parsley (optional)

4 hard-boiled eggs, shelled

Flour

Vegetable oil

$\frac{1}{3}$ cup tomato paste

3 bay leaves

1 stalk celery with leaves, chopped

Soak the bread in water and squeeze dry. Put it in the food processor with the meat, egg whites, cinnamon, nutmeg, salt, and pepper and process to a soft paste. Then mix in the onion and the parsley, if using.

Divide the meat mixture into 4 equal parts and shape each portion round a hard-boiled egg, making 4 oval rolls. Pat and press the meat firmly round the eggs so that the rolls do not come apart during cooking.

Flour the rolls and fry briefly in hot shallow oil, turning them, until lightly browned all over.

In a large pan, make a sauce by mixing the tomato paste with about $1\frac{1}{4}$ cups water. Add the bay leaves, celery, salt, and pepper. Bring it to the boil and simmer for a few minutes. Then put in the meat rolls and simmer gently for about 20 minutes, until they are well done and the sauce has reduced.

Lift the rolls out very carefully. Serve them sliced, hot or cold, with the sauce poured over.

Variation

A Persian version is made by adding about $\frac{1}{3}$ cup yellow split peas, boiled until soft and drained, to the meat mixture, and embedding a few soaked pitted prunes next to the hard-boiled eggs.

Kofta Mabrouma

Meat Rolls with Pine Nuts

Serves 6 • This is a specialty of Aleppo in Syria, where it is traditionally baked in a round tray and served on a round dish, with the rolls arranged in a coil.

2 pounds lean ground lamb or beef

2 medium onions, grated

2 eggs, lightly beaten

Salt and pepper

$\frac{2}{3}$ cup pine nuts

3 tablespoons vegetable oil

Chopped flat-leaf parsley and slices of
lemon to garnish

Mix the meat with the grated onions and the eggs, add salt and pepper, and knead vigorously by hand until soft and pasty. *(continued)*

Kofta Mabrouma (continued)

Divide the meat mixture into 6 lumps. Roll each into a long cigar-shaped roll, then flatten into a thin rectangle. You can do this by placing the rolls between 2 sheets of wax paper and flattening with a rolling pin.

Put a row of pine nuts along one of the longer sides of each rectangle, about ¼ inch from the edge, and roll up into a fat sausage, starting from the edge lined with pine nuts.

In an oiled round tart pan or oven dish, arrange the rolls end to end and brush with oil. Bake in a 350°F oven for about ¾ hour, or until well browned.

Serve garnished with parsley and lemon slices.

Kibbeh

Kibbeh is the national dish of Syria, Lebanon, and Jordan. Iraq boasts dozens of different *koubba,* and you find them in Turkey and Cyprus. There are innumerable versions of this family of dishes, which epitomize the food of the "Fertile Crescent." *Kibbeh* is said to have been mentioned in ancient Assyrian and Sumerian writings and to have been served by King Ashur Nassir Bal II. Daily life once revolved around its preparation, and in some places, it still does. The pounding of the meat and wheat in a stone or metal mortar with a heavy metal pestle is a dramatic ritual. It is the sound that was instantly provoked by the arrival of an unexpected guest or a ring of the doorbell, a sound that wakened one in the morning and lulled one to sleep in the afternoon. I know of no other dish whose preparation is enveloped by such mystique. Some women are known to have a special "hand" or "finger" for making *kibbeh.* This knack is envied by other women, and especially by their husbands. One is said to be favored by the gods if one is born with a long finger, which makes the shaping of beautiful long torpedo-shaped *kibbeh* easier. Today the food processor and a special machine which takes care of the whole process, from meat grinding to stuffing, have changed people's lives in the cities if not the villages.

There are countless versions of *kibbeh,* some widely known throughout the Middle East, others less common or belonging to one particular community. It always involves a mixture of minced lamb, grated onion, and fine-ground bulgur (cracked wheat, or *burghul,* in Arabic) pounded to a paste. Eaten raw, it is called *kibbeh nayyeh.* The same paste can be fried or grilled. In *kibbeh bil sanieh,* a layer of ground-meat filling is sandwiched between two layers of *kibbeh* and baked in the oven. Stuffed *kibbeh* are hollow oval or long torpedo-shaped shells of the same paste filled with a ground-meat filling and deep-fried.

Small *kibbeh* dumplings are added to vegetable stews, or are cooked in yogurt, pomegranate juice, or sesame meal mixed with bitter-orange juice.

Kibbeh Nayyeh

Raw Kibbeh

Serves 8–10 • Serve as an appetizer accompanied, if you like, with a sauce called *keema,* the recipe for which follows this one.

FOR THE KIBBEH MIXTURE

1 large onion, peeled

Salt and pepper

¾ cup fine-ground bulgur

1 pound lean, tender lamb from the leg, trimmed of all fat and cut in cubes

Iced water

TO GARNISH AND ACCOMPANY

Extra-virgin olive oil

A few mint leaves

Bunch of scallions

Small romaine-lettuce leaves

Puree the onion in a food processor, adding a little salt and pepper. Rinse the bulgur in a sieve under cold running water and squeeze out the excess moisture. Add it to the onion, blend thoroughly, and pour out of the work bowl.

Now process the meat to a soft paste, adding a little salt and pepper. Add the onion-and-bulgur mixture and process again, adding a little iced water gradually (start with ¼ cup), just enough to achieve a soft paste. Continue to process, in batches if you like, or knead with your hands to a smooth, elastic, doughy consistency. Chill in the refrigerator.

Serve chilled, spread thinly on a flat glass or china serving plate. Drizzle generously with oil and garnish with a few mint leaves.

Accompany with trimmed scallions and a bowl of small romaine lettuce, and serve with Arab bread.

Variations

• You may like to spice the *kibbeh* mixture with 1 teaspoon cumin, 1 teaspoon coriander, 1 teaspoon cinnamon or ½ teaspoon allspice, and a good pinch of ground chili pepper or cayenne. I have become very fond of that. You can also have a squeeze of lemon juice over the top with the olive oil.

• Another way of serving *kibbeh nayyeh* is to roll the meat mixture into small, thin fingers and place each one in the cup of a small romaine or Bibb lettuce leaf. Sprinkle with olive oil and lemon juice, or with tamarind diluted in a little water, and garnish with chopped scallions and a dusting of paprika or ground chili pepper.

• Proportions of meat and wheat can be varied, and quantities reversed.

• A marvelous spicy version from Gaziantep, in southeastern Turkey, called *çiğ köfte* is so full of wheat and has so many spices that you can hardly tell the raw-meat content. Pour boiling water over 1¼ cups bulgur and soak for ½ hour. Drain, press all the excess water out, and mix with 2 grated onions. Blend ½ pound lean lamb to a paste in a food processor. Add the bulgur and grated onions and the following: 1 tablespoon tomato paste, 1 teaspoon salt, 1 teaspoon paprika, ½ teaspoon ground chili pepper or cayenne, ½ teaspoon cumin, ½ teaspoon coriander, ½ teaspoon cinnamon, ¼ teaspoon allspice, and ¼ cup finely chopped flat-leaf parsley. Blend to a homogenous paste. Serve spread on a dish sprinkled with parsley and lemon juice, or rolled into little balls.

Keema

A Sauce for Kibbeh Nayyeh

Serves 8–10 • A popular way of serving *kibbeh nayyeh*, which makes it more of a grand dish, is with this ground-meat sauce. Veal is popularly used.

- 1 pound onions, chopped
- 2 tablespoons vegetable oil
- 1 pound lean ground veal
- 1/2 cup pine nuts
- Salt and pepper
- Juice of 1 lemon

Fry the onions in the oil over low heat until golden. Add the ground veal and fry, crushing the meat with a fork and turning it over, until it changes color. Add the pine nuts. Season to taste with salt (about 1 teaspoon) and pepper, and add a little water to moisten. Simmer gently until the meat is well cooked and soft and the liquid is reduced. Some people prefer to fry the pine nuts lightly on their own and add them just before serving.

Sprinkle with lemon juice and serve in a separate bowl with the *kibbeh nayyeh*.

Kibbet Lahem

Kibbeh Dumplings

These little balls of meat and bulgur are poached in soups, in yogurt, and in meat stews with okra, eggplants, zucchini, quinces, and sour cherries. They should be cooked until they are very soft. Make a *kibbeh* mixture as in the method for *kibbeh nayyeh* (page 269) but using 1 1/2 cups bulgur. Process to a soft doughy paste. Wet your hands and roll into 3/4–1-inch balls.

Kibbeh bil Sanieh

Meat and Bulgur Pie in a Tray

Serves 10 • This is good hot or cold. Serve with yogurt and salads.

FOR THE SHELL

- 1 1/4 cups fine-ground bulgur
- 1 large onion, quartered
- 1 pound lean lamb
- 1 1/2 teaspoons salt
- 1/4 teaspoon pepper
- 1 teaspoon cinnamon
- 2–3 tablespoons vegetable oil

FOR THE HASHWA (FILLING)

- 1 large onion, chopped
- 3 tablespoons vegetable oil
- 1 1/2 pounds ground lamb, beef, or veal, preferably a little fatty, cut into pieces
- Salt and pepper
- 1 teaspoon cinnamon
- 1/2 teaspoon allspice
- 3/4 cup pine nuts

For the shell, rinse the bulgur in a sieve in cold running water under the tap and drain. Puree the onion in a food processor. Add the meat and salt and pepper and blend to a paste. Remove the paste from the processor and mix with the bulgur and cinnamon, then process, in batches, to a soft well-blended paste, adding iced water gradually by the tablespoon (start with 2–3) to achieve a smooth elastic consistency.

For the filling, fry the onion in the oil till soft. Add the ground meat, salt, pepper, cinnamon, allspice, and pine nuts and fry for 10 minutes, turning and crushing the meat with a fork, until it changes color.

To assemble the pie, grease a large round or

rectangular (10-by-14-inch) shallow baking pan with oil. Press half the shell paste evenly on the bottom of the tin, about ¼ inch thick. Spread the filling on top and cover with the rest of the paste. This last layer of shell needs to be built up gradually. Wet your hands, take large lumps of the paste, flatten them between your palms, and lay them on top of the filling until it is entirely covered. Patch up any holes and press down firmly with your hands. An alternative way of doing the top crust is to place the ball of meat-and-bulgur mixture between 2 sheets of plastic wrap or wax paper and to flatten it out with a rolling pin. Take the top sheet off and turn out quickly over the pie.

With a pointed knife, cut crisscrossing straight or diagonal parallel lines right through to the bottom, making square or diamond shapes, and also run the knife round the edges. Brush or sprinkle the top with 2–3 tablespoons oil and bake in a preheated 375°F oven for 40 minutes, until golden brown.

Variations

- In the filling, instead of pine nuts have ¾ cup mixed coarsely chopped walnuts and pistachios.
- Add 2 tablespoons pomegranate syrup (concentrate or molasses) and 1 tablespoon sumac to the filling.
- Flavor the shell with 2 teaspoons cumin and ¼ teaspoon hot cayenne pepper instead of cinnamon.
- Add 4 tablespoons tomato paste to the shell mixture. It is used both for the taste and for the "meaty" red color it lends.
- Add 4 tablespoons each of soaked currants and chopped walnuts to the filling and omit the pine nuts.

Kibbeh Makli Mahshieh
Stuffed Fried Kibbeh

Serves 6 • These are the most prestigious and popular *kibbeh*. The preparation requires skill and application. The art lies in making the outer shells as long (at least that is what we thought in Egypt, for I know now that the Lebanese prefer a small, oval, stocky shape) and as thin as possible. The crisp, light, tasty shells should crack to divulge a juicy, aromatic meat filling. Serve hot or cold with tahina cream salad (page 67), baba ghanouj (page 65), and other salads.

FOR THE KIBBEH SHELL

1¼ cups fine bulgur
1 small onion, quartered
1 pound lean tender lamb
Salt and pepper

FOR THE MEAT FILLING OR HASHWA

1 medium onion, finely chopped
2 tablespoons oil
½ pound lean ground beef
Salt and pepper
½ teaspoon allspice
½ teaspoon cinnamon
⅓ cup pine nuts, lightly toasted
Sunflower or light vegetable oil for
  frying

For the shell, soak the bulgur in cold salted water for 10 minutes, then wash in a sieve under cold running water and drain. Squeeze excess water out. Puree the onion to a paste in the food processor. Add the lamb, salt, and pepper and process to a soft paste. Take out the meat and mix with the bulgur. Process the

(continued)

mixture in two batches until it is blended to a soft, smooth, doughlike paste. You may need to add a tablespoon or two of cold water. Leave it to cool, covered, in the refrigerator. This will make it less sticky and easier to work.

For the filling, fry the onion in the oil till soft. Add the beef and cook, stirring and crushing it with a fork, until it changes color. Season with salt, pepper, allspice, and cinnamon and stir in the pine nuts.

To shape and stuff the *kibbeh,* keep wetting your hands with cold water. Take a lump of *kibbeh* paste the size of a small egg and roll into an oval shape. Holding it in your left hand, make a hole in one end with the index finger of your right hand. Use your cupped left hand to pat the paste around the finger and work it into a long, slim oval shell. Opening and closing your hand, pressing the paste with your finger towards your palm, and slipping the shell round and round, clockwise, enlarge the hole and make the shell as thin as possible (less than ¼ inch). Patch any holes with a wet finger.

Fill each shell with about 1 tablespoon of filling. Wet the open rim and pinch it closed. Taper the ends to achieve a slim oval shape. British soldiers in the Middle East during the Second World War used to call these *kibbeh* "Syrian torpedoes," and I think that describes their shape rather well.

Leave the *kibbeh* covered in the refrigerator until you are ready to cook them.

Deep-fry the *kibbeh* in hot vegetable oil for 5–10 minutes, until a rich, dark brown color, and drain on paper towels. Or, if you prefer, bake them: Put them on a greased oven sheet, brush all over with oil, and bake in a preheated 375°F oven for about 30–40 minutes, or until well browned.

Serve very hot. These *kibbeh* can be prepared ahead and fried just before serving, or fried and warmed up again in a covered dish in the oven.

Variations

- To the shell mixture add ½ teaspoon of allspice and 1 teaspoon of cinnamon, or ½ teaspoon ground coriander and 1 teaspoon of cumin.
- Add 2 tablespoons pomegranate syrup (concentrate or molasses) and 1 tablespoon ground sumac to the filling.
- For another Syrian filling, try a mixture of yogurt cheese, chopped walnuts, and pomegranate seeds.
- A Turkish version called *içli köfte* has ¾ cup mixed chopped walnuts and pistachios instead of pine nuts in the filling, and a good pinch of ground chili pepper.
- If you find the making of long torpedo shapes difficult, make the easier Lebanese egg-shaped ones.
- Small egg-shaped stuffed *kibbeh,* poached in boiling water for 5–7 minutes, are thrown into meat stews with eggplants, zucchini, artichokes, quinces, and sour cherries.
- A fried *kibbeh* with the same filling, sold in Cypriot stores in London, has the following meatless dough for a shell: Wash 1½ cups fine ground bulgur in a fine-meshed sieve and squeeze it dry. Mix with 1 cup all-purpose flour, 1 tablespoon oil, and a little salt. Knead vigorously for 15 minutes, adding enough water to achieve a smooth paste. It has a tendency to break as it is handled, and must be carefully patched. Some people add 2 tablespoons tomato paste (to give the color of meat) and 1 teaspoon cumin.

Potato Kibbeh

Serves 8 • For a grander presentation, people make potato croquettes with the ingredients, using the ground meat and nuts as a filling and sometimes dipping in beaten egg and flour before deep-frying. But it is far simpler and just as good to make it in a baking dish. It makes a delicious and filling dish for a large group.

FOR THE SHELL

2 cups bulgur, coarse-ground

1½ pounds mealy potatoes

Salt and pepper

4–6 tablespoons butter, cut into pieces

3 eggs, lightly beaten

A good pinch of nutmeg

½ teaspoon allspice

FOR THE FILLING

1 large onion, chopped

3 tablespoons oil

1½ pounds ground lamb or beef

2–3 tablespoons currants

2–3 tablespoons pine nuts or chopped
  walnuts

1 teaspoon cinnamon

Salt and pepper

Soak the bulgur in hot water for 20 minutes, or until it softens, then drain and squeeze out the excess water. Peel and boil the potatoes in salted water till soft, then drain and mash well. Add the butter, eggs, spices, salt, and pepper and beat well. Add the bulgur and mix thoroughly.

To make the filling, fry the onion in oil till golden. Add the meat and continue to fry, stirring, crushing, and turning it over until it changes color. Add the currants, nuts, cinna-mon, salt, and pepper, and cook a few minutes more. Drain off any fat if you like.

Spread half the potato-and-bulgur mixture on the bottom of a large (14-by-10-inch) baking dish. Cover with the meat filling and top with the remaining potato-and-bulgur mixture. An easy way is to wet your hands and take lumps of the mixture, then press it between your palms and lay the flattened pieces on top of the filling. Build up a crust that covers all the filling.

Bake in a 375°F oven for about 35–45 minutes, or until the top is slightly browned.

Kibbeh Labanieh

Kibbeh Cooked in Yogurt

Serves 6–8 • Because of its whiteness, this is a festive dish served on the New Year to augur a year full of happiness. It is served hot with rice in winter, and cold in summer.

Stuffed *kibbeh* (page 271), uncooked

FOR THE YOGURT SAUCE

1 quart plain whole-milk yogurt
Salt
1 tablespoon cornstarch or 1 egg white
3 or 4 cloves garlic, crushed
2 tablespoons crushed dried mint
3 tablespoons butter or olive oil

Pour the yogurt in a large pan. Add salt. Stabilize it with cornstarch or egg white as described on page 113, so that it can cook without curdling. Bring it to the boil, add the *kibbeh* uncooked, and simmer for about 20 minutes. Fry the crushed garlic and crushed dried mint in hot butter or olive oil. Pour this over the yogurt when serving.

Serve hot or cold, with plain rice.

Variations

• Instead of stuffed *kibbeh,* you may use the *kibbeh* dumplings on page 270.
• Add the crushed garlic raw to the yogurt and garnish the dish with crushed dried mint.
• Cooked rice is sometimes added to the yogurt in the pan and simmered for a minute or so before serving.

Kouneli Stifatho

Rabbit and Onion Stew

Serves 4–5 • *Stifatho* is a Greek dish also made with beef. Serve it with rice or potatoes.

1½ pounds small pickling or pearl
   onions
5 tablespoons olive oil
1 rabbit, cut into serving portions
¼ cup red-wine vinegar
2 cups dry red wine
4 tomatoes, peeled and chopped
Salt and pepper
2 teaspoons sugar
4 cloves garlic, chopped
2 bay leaves
6 peppercorns
5 cloves
½ teaspoon allspice

To peel the onions more easily, throw them into a pan of boiling water and boil for a few minutes, until the skins loosen. Peel as soon as they are cold enough to handle. Put them with 2½ tablespoons of the oil in a large skillet and cook over medium heat, shaking the pan to color them lightly all over.

In a large pan, sauté the rabbit pieces in the remaining oil, turning to brown them on all sides. Pour in the vinegar and wine, the sautéed onions, and all the remaining ingredients. Add water barely to cover and simmer, covered, for about 1 hour, until the rabbit and onions are very tender. Alternatively, bake at 350°F in a covered casserole for 2–2½ hours.

Arnavut Ciğeri

Albanian-Style Liver

Serves 6 • Serve with potatoes.

1 onion, cut in half and thinly sliced
Salt
1½ pounds calf's or lamb's liver
1½ tablespoons paprika
Flour
Olive oil
2–3 tablespoons finely chopped parsley
   to garnish

Sprinkle the onion with salt and leave for an hour to soften and lose its strong taste. Drain the juices released.

Cut the liver into strips 1 inch thick and remove any tough sinews or skin. Sprinkle with 1 tablespoon paprika and toss well, then roll in flour, shaking to separate all the pieces of liver.

Heat a little oil in a frying pan and fry the liver briefly over medium-high heat, stirring and turning the pieces, until browned all over but still pink and juicy inside. Remove from the pan and drain on paper towels. Sprinkle with a little salt.

Mix the remaining ½ tablespoon paprika with a little of the frying oil and dribble over the liver. Serve garnished with parsley and the softened onions.

Liver with Vinegar

Serves 3–4 • This Lebanese specialty is served as an appetizer, but it is also good as a main course accompanied by mashed potatoes. Calf's liver has a better flavor and texture, so use it if you can.

1 pound calf's or lamb's liver, cut in thin
   slices
2 tablespoons butter
1 tablespoon extra-virgin olive oil
Salt and pepper
2 cloves garlic, crushed
1½ teaspoons crushed dried mint
   (optional)
¼ cup wine vinegar

If serving as an appetizer, cut the liver slices into 1½-inch pieces, but leave the slices whole if serving as a main dish.

Sauté the liver in a mixture of butter and oil over medium heat very briefly, for a minute or so, adding salt and pepper and turning the pieces over, until lightly colored but pink inside. Remove from the pan and put aside.

Add crushed garlic and mint, if you like, and when the aroma rises, stir in the vinegar. Return the liver to the pan and cook ½ minute more, turning the pieces over. The liver should still be a little pink inside.

Variations

• A different sort of tartness can be obtained by sprinkling with 1 tablespoon ground sumac instead of adding vinegar.

• Fry 1 sliced onion in the butter and oil until soft, before adding the liver.

Kidneys with Lemon

Serves 6 • Serve with salad.

- 6 calf's or 12 lamb's kidneys
- 2 tablespoons butter
- Salt and black pepper
- Juice of 1 lemon, or more
- 3–4 tablespoons finely chopped flat-leaf parsley

Remove the outer skins of the kidneys (and the fat if they are enclosed in it). Cut lamb's kidneys in half and calf's kidneys into walnut-sized pieces, and cut out as much of the fatty, gristly cores as possible.

Sauté in hot butter for 3–4 minutes, until firm and lightly browned all over but still pink and juicy inside, adding salt and pepper. Take care not to overcook, as kidneys become tough. Sprinkle with lemon juice, and serve garnished with parsley.

Kidneys in Tomato Sauce

Serves 6 • Serve with mashed potatoes.

- 6 calf's kidneys or 12 lamb's kidneys
- 2 onions, sliced
- 2–3 tablespoons vegetable oil or butter
- 2 cloves garlic, chopped
- 6 tomatoes, peeled and chopped
- Salt and black pepper

Remove the outer skins of the kidneys (and the fat if they are enclosed in it). Cut lamb's kidneys in half and calf's kidneys into walnut-sized pieces, and cut out as much of the fatty, gristly cores as possible.

In a large skillet, fry the onions in oil or butter until golden. Add the garlic and the kidneys, and sauté, turning them over, for 3–4 minutes, until lightly browned all over but still pink and juicy inside.

Remove the kidneys from the pan. Add the tomatoes, and season with salt and pepper. Cook gently for about 10–15 minutes. Return the kidneys to the pan and heat through before serving.

Kawareh bi Hummus

Calf's Feet and Chickpeas

Serves 6 • This dish is loved all over the Middle East and in the Balkans for its rich, gelatinous texture. It is sometimes served as a soup. Christians also use pig's trotters. Serve with bread and a light salad.

2 calf's feet

3 tablespoons vegetable oil

Pepper

1 teaspoon turmeric

1½ cups chickpeas, soaked overnight

Salt

Wash and scrape the calf's feet thoroughly. Blanch them in boiling water until a scum has formed. Throw out the scum and the water.

Heat the oil in a large saucepan and turn the feet in it for a minute or so. Add pepper and turmeric, and the drained chickpeas. Cover with water, bring to the boil, and simmer gently for about 4 hours, until the meat is practically falling off the bones. Add salt when the chickpeas are tender.

Bone the feet if you wish, and return the meat to the pan.

Variations

• Instead of chickpeas, add 1½ pounds cubed or thickly sliced potatoes about 20 minutes before the end of the cooking time.

• *Hergma,* a Moroccan variation, is spiced with ½ teaspoon ground ginger, 1 teaspoon paprika, and ½ teaspoon ground chili pepper or cayenne, instead of turmeric. A cup of cooked rice is added at the end.

• A custom in my family was to add 6 eggs in their shells. They were parboiled separately in water first, to cleanse the shells, then put in at the start of cooking, at the same time as the chickpeas. Before serving, you might like to peel the eggs and return them to the pot to heat through.

• A Turkish version called *fasulyeli paça* is made with white haricot or navy beans instead of chickpeas, and turmeric is not used.

Yogurtlu Paça

Sheep's Feet with Yogurt

Serves 6 • A delicious Turkish dish—the rich meat is offset by the cool yogurt.

6 sheep's feet
Rind of ½ lemon
2 large cloves garlic
Salt and pepper
6 thin slices bread, crusts removed, toasted

FOR THE GARNISH

2 cups plain whole-milk yogurt
2 cloves garlic, crushed
Salt and white pepper
3 tablespoons butter
1 teaspoon paprika

Scrub the feet thoroughly. In a large pan, blanch them in boiling water for 5 minutes and throw out the scum with the water.

Cover with fresh water, and add the lemon rind, garlic, salt, and pepper. Bring to the boil and simmer for 3–4 hours, until the meat is practically falling off the bones.

Lay the slices of toast in one layer in a large shallow ovenproof dish, and moisten well with stock from the feet. Extract the feet and bone them, arranging the meat on top of the soaked toast. Sprinkle on more stock if the dish seems too dry (reserving some for the garnish), cover, and keep warm, or reheat when ready to serve.

Prepare the garnish when ready to serve. Beat the yogurt with a few tablespoons of stock, the garlic, salt, and white pepper. Melt the butter in a small saucepan and add paprika.

Remove the dish from the oven and serve smothered with the yogurt and sprinkled with a trickle of red paprika butter.

Mokh Mazlouk

Brains with Garlic and Turmeric

Serves 6

3 sets calf's brains or 6 sets lamb's brains
1 tablespoon wine vinegar
2–3 tablespoons vegetable oil
2 cloves garlic, crushed or halved
1 stalk celery, thinly sliced (optional)
½ teaspoon turmeric
Juice of ½ lemon, or more
Salt and pepper
3 tablespoons finely chopped parsley

Soak the brains in water acidulated with a little vinegar for 1 hour. Carefully peel off the thin outer membranes and connective tissue enclosing them. Wash under cold running water and drain well. Separate each brain into 2 or 4 parts, depending on whether lamb's or calf's brains are used.

In a pan, heat the oil with ½ cup water, the garlic, sliced celery if used, turmeric, and lemon juice. Add a little salt and pepper and simmer for a minute or two—or for about 15 minutes if celery is used, to allow it to soften. Poach the brains gently in this barely simmering liquor for 10–15 minutes, taking care not to break them. They will be tinged a beautiful yellow by the turmeric. Add a little water if the sauce evaporates too quickly.

Serve the brains in their sauce, sprinkled with finely chopped parsley.

Variation

Instead of turmeric, add 1 teaspoon ground cumin to the sauce, or ½ teaspoon ground cardamom seeds.

Sautéed Sweetbreads with Lemon and Cinnamon

Serves 4 • In the Middle East it is the more available lamb's sweetbreads (sweetbreads are the thymus gland) that are used, but calf's sweetbreads are much more delicate, with an unusual creamy-tender texture. You must start the initial preparation a few hours before you want to cook them, as they need lengthy soaking.

- 1 pound calf's sweetbreads
- 1 onion, thinly sliced
- 3 tablespoons butter
- ¼ teaspoon cinnamon
- Juice of ½ lemon

Soak the sweetbreads in lukewarm water for 2–3 hours to remove any traces of blood, changing the water twice. Rinse them and remove the tough outer membrane and any bits of fat, but leave the inner membrane intact so that the sweetbreads don't disintegrate. Put them in a pan of lightly salted water, bring slowly to the boil, and simmer 3 minutes; this firms them up. Lift them out with a slotted spoon and plunge them into cold water. Drain and dry them, and pull off any gristle.

Fry the onion in the butter in a large skillet, over low heat, until soft.

Slice the sweetbreads and put them in the skillet. Dust lightly with cinnamon and cook the slices for 1 minute on each side.

Squeeze lemon juice over them and serve.

Vegetables

KHODAR

Vegetables and legumes have had an important place in a part of the world where much of the population was composed of impoverished peasants who could rarely afford meat—maybe once a week, or sometimes only on festive occasions. Vegetables are much loved and hold a dignified, sometimes splendid position in the hierarchy of food, representing both everyday and celebratory foods, in turn appetizers, pickles, salads, main and side dishes, as well as integral partners in meat and poultry dishes. You find the same vegetables in all the countries of the Middle East. When the Arabs began their thrust into the region in the seventh century, extending the Islamic domain across the Middle East and North Africa, they spread the cultivation of spinach, eggplants, artichokes, squashes, and fava beans. They also spread ways of cooking and combining them.

The new crops from the New World of the Americas—tomatoes, peppers, potatoes, sweet potatoes, Jerusalem artichokes, corn, beans, and pumpkins—which had been brought to Spain and Portugal by the Conquistadors in the sixteenth century, arrived very late in the Muslim Orient. Most were adopted in the Arab world as late as the nineteenth century, when that world became fascinated with things European. The new vegetables were integrated into the old dishes and were also used in new ways that quickly became typical of the particular area. The tomato arrived in the late nineteenth century and had a dramatic effect, revolutionizing the cuisines of the area. It was introduced in Aleppo in 1851, where it was called *franji,* which means "French," as everything that came from Europe was then called. In Egypt it was introduced in 1880, and in Algeria in 1910. Nowadays there is hardly a dish in Algeria which does not include a tomato or tomato paste. Middle Eastern cuisines today seem inconceivable without the tomato, which has a very important place. One way of cooking almost all vegetables involves a tomato sauce with onions or garlic, the origin of which is the Spanish *sofrito.* In the past that sauce was reduced until it was thick and jammy and strong-tasting, but these days many people cook it for less time and it has a lighter, fresher taste.

Of the many different categories of vegetable dishes, there are those that are deep-fried, either with or without batter; those cooked in tomato sauce; those cooked in butter and served hot; and those cooked in olive oil and served cold. Turkey has a famous range of dishes called *zeytinyagli,* which means they are cooked in olive oil. There are famous couplings with legumes like lentils, chickpeas, and beans; layered gratins with cheese and eggs; and endless varieties of stuffed vegetables. Those who are interested in vegetarian dishes will also find some in other chapters, such as those on appetizers, eggs, rice, and bulgur.

Certain vegetarian dishes are associated with Christian communities because of the fasts prescribed by the Eastern Orthodox Churches, the Roman Catholic and Armenian Churches, and the Coptic Church of Egypt. Until a few decades ago in Syria and Lebanon, Christians felt obliged to abide by the strict dietary rules laid down by their church. These rules prohibited all foods derived from animals, including dairy products, for forty days before Christmas and Easter, and fifteen days before the Assumption of the Virgin Mary, as well as on every Wednesday and Friday in the year. Nowadays restrictions have generally been dropped, and those who can afford to, eat meat every day, be it in very small quantities in a stew or a stuffing. But many of the old meatless dishes are still characterized as the Lenten dishes and part of the cooking traditions of the Christians of Syria, Lebanon, and Greece and of the Copts of Egypt.

Artichokes and Preserved Lemons with Honey and Spices

Serves 4–6 • This is good hot or cold, as a first course. The Moroccan play of flavors, which combines preserved lemon with honey, garlic, turmeric, and ginger, makes this a sensational dish. I make it with the frozen Egyptian artichoke bottoms that I find in Oriental stores. If you want to use fresh ones, see the box below to prepare them.

3 cloves garlic, crushed
3 tablespoons extra-virgin olive oil
¼–½ teaspoon powdered ginger
Pinch of turmeric
Juice of 1 lemon
1½–2 tablespoons honey
Peel of 1½ preserved lemons (page 459), cut into strips
1 pound (1½ packages) frozen artichoke bottoms
Salt

Heat the garlic in the oil for a few seconds only, stirring. Take the pan off the heat and add the ginger, turmeric, lemon juice, honey, and preserved lemons. Put in the artichoke bottoms and add a little more than a cup of water and some salt. Cover, and simmer for about 15 minutes, or until the artichokes are tender, turning them so that every part gets to cook in the liquid, and adding a little water if necessary. Remove the lid to reduce the sauce at the end.

To Prepare Artichoke Hearts or Bottoms

Have ready a bowl of water acidulated with the juice of ½ lemon or 2–3 tablespoons vinegar to drop the artichokes into as soon as they are prepared so that they don't discolor.

TO PREPARE BABY-ARTICHOKE HEARTS with small globe artichokes, pull off the tough outer leaves so that you are left with the pale inner heart. With a small sharp knife, peel the stems and trim them, leaving about 1 inch. Slice off the spiky tops and cut the artichokes in half from tip to stalk. Then scoop out the chokes with a pointed spoon. Drop into the acidulated water.

TO PREPARE BOTTOMS OF LARGE ARTICHOKES, cut off the stems at the base and trim off all the leaves and any hard bits around the base with a sharp knife. Remove the chokes with a pointed knife. Drop into the acidulated water.

Kharshouf bel Ful wal Loz

Artichokes, Fava Beans, and Almonds

Serves 4 • The Copts of Egypt observe a long and arduous fast during Lent—El Soum el Kibir—when they abstain from every kind of animal food, such as meat, eggs, milk, butter, and cheese, and eat only bread and vegetables, chiefly fava beans.

Artichoke hearts and fava beans in oil is a favorite Lenten dish, also popular with the Greeks of Egypt. These two vegetables are partnered in every Middle Eastern country, and indeed all around the Mediterranean, but this dish with almonds is uncommon and particularly appealing.

You can find frozen artichoke hearts and bottoms from Egypt that are difficult to tell from fresh ones, and frozen skinned fava (or broad) beans in Middle Eastern stores. But if you want to use fresh ones, see the box on the opposite page for preparing artichoke hearts or bottoms. If your fava beans are young and tender, you do not need to skin them.

- 1 tablespoon flour or cornstarch
- 1¼ cups water
- 2–3 teaspoons sugar
- Juice of 1 lemon
- 3 sprigs of dill, chopped
- 1 or 2 cloves garlic, crushed or finely chopped
- Salt
- 3–4 tablespoons mild extra-virgin olive oil
- A 7-ounce package frozen skinned fava (broad) beans, defrosted
- A 14-ounce package frozen artichoke hearts or bottoms, defrosted
- ⅓ cup blanched almonds

In a small bowl, mix the flour or cornstarch with a tablespoon or two of the water to a smooth paste and pour into a pan with the rest of the water. Add sugar, lemon juice, dill, garlic, and a little salt and bring to the boil, stirring vigorously so that the flour does not go lumpy. Simmer for about 10 minutes, then beat in the oil.

Put in the fava beans, artichoke bottoms, and almonds and cook gently for 15–20 minutes, or until the vegetables are tender and the sauce is reduced.

Serve hot or cold as a first course. An attractive way is to spoon the broad beans and almonds into the artichoke cups.

Variation

Use young garden peas or *petits pois* instead of fava beans.

Ful Ahdar bel Laban

Fava Beans with Yogurt

Serves 6 • Fava beans are the most important vegetable of Egypt. Buy young, tender ones in their season. If they are very young, you can cook them in their pods, which you cut into pieces. Some supermarkets sell young fava beans already shelled in packets, which do not need to be skinned. Older beans have tough skins as well as tough pods. The skinned frozen ones you can buy in Middle Eastern stores are particularly good.

 1 pound fresh shelled fava beans
 Salt
 1–2 tablespoons extra-virgin olive oil
 2 cloves garlic, crushed
 2 cups plain whole-milk yogurt, at room
  temperature
 Pepper
 2 teaspoons dried mint (optional)

Boil the beans in salted water until tender, and drain. Heat the oil in the pan and add the garlic with the beans. Stir over low heat until the aroma rises. Mix the yogurt with a little salt and pepper—and the mint, if you like.

Serve the beans with the yogurt poured over.

Variations

• You may pour the yogurt into the pan with the beans. Stir over low heat, but do not let it boil, or the yogurt will curdle.

• For *ful ahdar bel cosbara,* omit the yogurt and add the juice of ½ lemon and 4 tablespoons chopped cilantro to the beans.

Spinach with Raisins and Pine Nuts

Serves 4 • This makes a good side dish. The Arabs brought it all the way to Spain and Italy.

 1 pound spinach
 1 medium onion, chopped
 2 tablespoons extra-virgin olive oil
 Salt and pepper
 2 tablespoons pine nuts
 2 tablespoons raisins, soaked in water for
  15 minutes

Wash the spinach, and remove stems only if they are thick and tough. Drain, and press the excess water out. Put the leaves in a pan with the lid on. Cook over low heat for moments only, until they crumple to a soft mass. They will steam in the water that clings to them.

In another pan, fry the onion in the oil till golden. Stir in the pine nuts and let them color lightly. Add the spinach and the drained raisins. Season with salt and pepper, and cook, stirring, for a minute or so. Serve hot.

Sabanekh bel Hummus

Spinach with Chickpeas

Serves 6 • The combination of spinach with chickpeas is common throughout the Middle East, but the flavors here are Egyptian. You may use good-quality canned chickpeas. It is good served with yogurt.

$^{1}/_{2}$ cup chickpeas, soaked overnight, or a
    14-ounce can cooked chickpeas
Salt
2 pounds spinach
4–6 cloves garlic, chopped
1$^{1}/_{2}$ teaspoons ground coriander
3 tablespoons extra-virgin olive oil
Pepper
Juice of 1 lemon (optional)

If you are using the dried and soaked chickpeas, drain and boil them in fresh water for 1$^{1}/_{4}$ hours, or until very tender, adding salt when they begin to soften.

Wash the spinach and remove stems only if they are thick and tough, then drain well.

In a large pan, fry the garlic and coriander in the oil, stirring, until the aroma rises. Pack in the spinach without adding any water, cover with a lid, and put over low heat until the leaves crumple to a soft mass. Add the drained chickpeas—cooked or canned—season with a little salt and pepper, mix very well, and cook a few minutes more. If there is too much liquid, reduce a little on high heat.

Serve hot or cold, with a squeeze of lemon if you like.

Variations

• Fry 1 large chopped onion in 3 tablespoons olive oil. Add 2 medium peeled and chopped tomatoes and 1 teaspoon sugar and cook until reduced, then stir in the cooked spinach and the chickpeas.

• White haricot or navy beans may be used instead of chickpeas.

Sabanekh bel Tamatem wal Loz

Spinach with Tomatoes and Almonds

Serves 4 • Spinach, like most vegetables in the Arab world, is also cooked with tomatoes. Almonds are a special touch.

1 pound spinach
1 onion, coarsely chopped
2$^{1}/_{2}$ tablespoons vegetable or extra-virgin
    olive oil
2 tomatoes, peeled and chopped
Salt and pepper
$^{1}/_{3}$ cup blanched almonds, toasted or
    fried (optional)

Wash the spinach, and remove stems only if they are hard and thick. Put it in a pan with the lid on and no extra water over low heat. Cook for moments only, until the leaves crumple in a soft mass.

Fry the onion in 2 tablespoons of the oil until soft and golden. Add the tomatoes, salt, and pepper and cook until reduced a little. Stir in the spinach. Fry the almonds in the remaining oil and stir them in. Serve hot.

Spinach with Garlic and Preserved Lemon

Serves 4 • A North African dish which can be served hot as a side dish or cold as a salad.

- 1 pound spinach
- 3 cloves garlic, chopped
- 3 tablespoons vegetable or extra-virgin olive oil
- Salt
- ¼ teaspoon ground chili pepper
- Peel of ½ preserved lemon (page 459), chopped

Wash the spinach, and remove stems only if they are hard and thick. Drain, and press the excess water out.

Heat the garlic in the oil in a large pan. When the aroma rises, put in the spinach with no extra water. Cook over low heat with the lid on, until the leaves crumple in a soft mass. Add salt, chili pepper, and preserved lemon, stir well, and cook for a few minutes more.

Serve hot or cold.

Aloo Sfenaj

Spinach and Prunes with Beans

Serves 6 • A Persian dish.

- 2 pounds spinach
- 1 large onion, coarsely chopped
- 2–3 tablespoons vegetable oil
- ¼ teaspoon turmeric
- 1 teaspoon cinnamon
- ⅔ cup pitted prunes
- ½ cup black-eyed peas or red beans, soaked for 1 hour, or 1 pound canned
- Salt and pepper

Wash the spinach and drain. Remove the stems only if they are tough.

Fry the onion in the oil in a large pan until golden. Stir in the turmeric and cinnamon and add the prunes and drained peas or beans. Cover with water, and cook about ½ hour, or until the peas or beans are soft.

Pack the spinach in the pan, cover with a lid, and cook until it crumples to a soft mass. Add salt and pepper, stir, and mix well, and cook for 5 minutes more.

Hindbeh wa Bassal

Curly Chicory with Onions

Serves 6 • Chicory is one of the vegetables be-lieved to have been eaten in ancient Egypt. It has a pleasant, slightly bitter taste when it is cooked. In this Lebanese mountain dish, wild chicory is used.

   1 large head of chicory or frisée (about
      1 pound)
   Salt
   1 large onion, sliced
   6 tablespoons extra-virgin olive oil
   4 cloves garlic
   A 15-ounce can chickpeas, drained
      (optional)
   Pepper
   2 lemons, cut in quarters

Trim off the stem end of the chicory and wash the leaves. Boil in salted water for 5–10 min-utes, until soft, then drain thoroughly, and press the excess water out. Cut the leaves up into medium pieces.

   Fry the onion in 2 tablespoons of the oil in a large pan until quite brown, stirring occasion-ally. Add the garlic, and when the aroma rises, stir in the chicory and the chickpeas, if using. Add salt and pepper, and cook for a few min-utes longer.

   Stir in the remaining oil and serve, hot or cold, with the lemon quarters.

Kousa Mabshoura

Zucchini with Onions, Garlic, and Mint

Serves 6–8 • This is as good cold, when it is served as an appetizer with bread, as it is hot as a side dish. It is the kind of thing people make with the leftover insides of hollowed-out zuc-chini when they stuff them.

   2 pounds zucchini, cut into large pieces
   3½ cups chicken stock (page 143) (or
      use 2 bouillon cubes)
   2 onions, chopped
   4 tablespoons extra-virgin olive oil
   4 cloves garlic, crushed
   2 tablespoons chopped mint leaves
   Salt and pepper
   1 lemon, cut into wedges (optional)

Boil the zucchini in the stock for about 15 minutes, or until soft. Drain, mash, and chop them in a colander to get rid of the excess liq-uid (drink the stock—it has a lovely vegetable flavor).

   In a large frying pan, fry the onions in 2 ta-blespoons of the oil until golden. Add the gar-lic, and stir until it just begins to color. Add the zucchini, mint, salt, and pepper and cook, stir-ring and mixing well, for about 5 minutes.

   Stir in the remaining oil and serve hot or cold with lemon wedges.

Variation

Stir in 2 cups natural or thick Greek-style strained yogurt before serving, or pass the pot round for people to help themselves.

Kousa Makli

Fried Zucchini Slices

Serves 4 • Some people like to dip the zucchini slices in flour, which is supposed to seal them so that they absorb less oil, but it makes little difference. One popular way of serving them is accompanied with yogurt, or with a tomato sauce (page 464).

> 4 zucchini, cut lengthwise into slices
>   about ⅓ inch thick
> Flour (optional)
> Salt
> Vegetable or olive oil for frying

If you like, dip the zucchini slices in flour seasoned with a little salt, turning to cover them lightly all over. I leave this procedure out.

Heat enough oil in a large pan to cover the bottom amply, and fry the slices until golden, turning over once. Drain on paper towels. Sprinkle with salt if you haven't used the flour seasoned with salt.

Variations

• For *kousa makli bel khal,* fry the zucchini without coating them in flour and serve sprinkled with a little wine vinegar.

• For *kousa ateh,* sauté round slices in 3 tablespoons extra-virgin olive oil with 3 or 4 chopped garlic cloves and 1–2 tablespoons dried mint.

Kousa bi Gebna

Zucchini Gratin with Cheese

Serves 6–8 • This is a family dish we all loved. My mother accompanied it with yogurt. The fried onions and large amount of sharp cheese lift the usually somewhat insipid taste of zucchini.

> 1 large onion, chopped
> 2 tablespoons vegetable oil
> 2 pounds zucchini, cut into ½-inch slices
> Salt
> 3 eggs, lightly beaten
> 2 cups shredded mature cheddar cheese
> White pepper
> Pinch of grated nutmeg

Fry the onion in oil till soft and golden. Poach the zucchini in salted water for a few minutes, until only just tender, and drain.

In a bowl, mix the eggs and cheese, add pepper and nutmeg, and fold in the onions and zucchini.

Pour into a greased ovenproof dish and bake in a preheated 350°F oven for about 30 minutes, or until firm and lightly browned.

Serve hot or cold.

About Eggplants

The appearance of this vegetable, shiny and purple-black, attractive though it is, has stirred the imagination of people in the Middle East, who have ascribed to it, in turn, gentle virtues and malicious magical powers. It is recommended, for instance, in some parts, not to grow eggplants in one's garden in case an evil one should spring up bearing the curse of female infertility.

Despite these attributed powers, eggplants are easily the favorite vegetable in every Middle Eastern country. In most countries, they are available in abundance throughout the year, either home-grown or imported from a neighboring country where the seasonal crop comes at a different time. In Turkey alone it is claimed there are a hundred ways of cooking them. You will find many more recipes with eggplants in different chapters of the book.

There are different types of eggplants: small and round, large and round, long and thin, and small and thin. The color varies from mauve with sparks of violet, to blue-black, and one variety is opaline white. All should be shiny and firm. The smaller ones are used for stuffing.

About Salting Eggplants

The most common way of cooking eggplants is to simply fry the slices. The trouble is that they absorb too much oil. They simply soak it up, which, to our tastes today, is less appealing than it once was. Another old problem—that eggplants can occasionally be excessively bitter—is now almost nonexistent. I have only once ever had an eggplant which was unpalatable because of its bitterness. The natural, slightly bitter taste is part of the appeal.

In every Middle Eastern country, the age-old custom is to salt the eggplants to rid them of their bitter juices, and this is also supposed to make them absorb less oil when they are fried. There are two traditional ways of salting. One is to soak the peeled or sliced eggplants in very salty water (with a plate on top to hold them down) for $1/2$–1 hour. The other is to sprinkle the slices with plenty of salt and leave them in a colander to degorge (sweat) their juices for $1/2$–1 hour, then rinse and dry them on paper towels.

Lately, I have experimented with batches of eggplants to see if salting really makes a difference. It did not make any difference to the taste, but it did make some, though not much, difference to the amount of oil absorbed. Even if they have been salted, eggplants absorb a lot of oil when they are fried. Briefly frying in very hot oil seals them to a degree. They may also absorb a little less oil when they are coated in batter as fritters. But that is not enough to make a difference.

Nowadays many people prefer to broil or grill eggplants, in which case salting is not really necessary. Although this is not the best way for every dish, it is a perfectly good alternative to frying on many occasions.

Fried, Broiled, Grilled, or Roasted Eggplant Slices

Two or three eggplants weighing about 1½ pounds total serve 6 people as a mezze or as an accompaniment to poultry or meat. Cook them in one of the following ways to serve hot or cold. Slices are generally about ⅓ inch thick.

TO FRY

Slice the unpeeled eggplants. Salt them for ½ hour, rinse them, and pat them dry with paper towels. Deep-fry in about ⅓ inch very hot vegetable or bland olive oil until browned and soft when you prick them with a fork, turning them over once. Drain on paper towels.

As fritters in a light batter: For the batter, pour ¾ cup sparkling water gradually into ¾ cup all-purpose flour, whisking vigorously, then beat in 2 tablespoons vegetable oil and a little salt. Leave for ½ hour, then beat an egg white until stiff and fold it into the batter. (A Tunisian batter is 2 eggs beaten with 3 tablespoons flour.) Dip the eggplant slices in the batter and deep-fry till crisp and golden and soft within, turning over once. Drain on paper towels.

TO BROIL

Peel the eggplants, then slice (they should be peeled because the skins remain tough when they are broiled). Brush the slices generously with vegetable or olive oil and cook on the barbecue or under the broiler for 6–8 minutes, turning over once.

TO GRILL

Peel the eggplants, then slice (they should be peeled because the skins remain tough when they are grilled). Brush the slices generously with vegetable or olive oil and cook on an oiled grill for 6–8 minutes, turning over once.

TO ROAST

Peel the eggplants, then slice them (they should be peeled because the skins remain tough when they are roasted). Place the slices on a piece of foil and brush generously with vegetable or olive oil. Cook in a preheated 475°F oven until lightly browned and soft inside.

Betingan Meshwi bel Dibs al Rumman

Roasted Eggplants with Pomegranate Syrup

Serves 4 • The best eggplants to use for this are white-fleshed with no seeds.

4 medium-small eggplants

3 tablespoons pomegranate syrup (molasses or concentrate)

6 tablespoons extra-virgin olive oil

Salt

Pinch of ground chili pepper

¼ cup finely chopped flat-leaf parsley

Roast the eggplants whole in the oven or under the broiler, turning them over, until they feel very soft when you press.

Mix the rest of the ingredients together as a dressing.

To serve, cut the eggplants in half lengthwise and pour the dressing over the flesh.

Variation

Use 2 tablespoons balsamic or wine vinegar instead of pomegranate syrup.

Ma'loubet el Betingan

Eggplant and Rice Mold

Serves 6–8 • *Ma'louba* means "upside down" in Arabic. This is a layered meat, vegetable, and rice dish which is turned out upside down like a cake without disturbing the layers. A special wide pan with short straight sides is used to cook it. The eggplant is normally fried first, but broiling in this case does not impair the flavor. It is famously a Palestinian dish. The rice absorbs the meat sauce and the flavor of the eggplants and becomes soft and brown. Serve it with yogurt.

> 2 onions, chopped
>
> Vegetable oil
>
> 1 pound lamb or beef, cut into ³⁄₄-inch cubes
>
> Salt and pepper
>
> 1 teaspoon cinnamon
>
> ¹⁄₂ teaspoon allspice
>
> 2 pounds eggplants, cut into ¹⁄₃-inch-thick slices
>
> 2 cups long-grain or basmati rice, washed
>
> ¹⁄₂ cup toasted pine nuts, to garnish (optional)

In a large pan (at least 10 inches wide), fry the onions in 3 tablespoons oil over very low heat, with the lid on, until soft. Add the meat and brown it all over. Cover with water, add salt, pepper, cinnamon, and allspice, and cook for about 1 hour, or until the meat is tender, adding water to keep it covered.

Meanwhile, arrange the eggplants on a baking sheet, brush both sides generously with oil, and sprinkle very lightly with salt. Broil under a preheated broiler, turning over once, until lightly browned on both sides.

In the pan, off the heat, put a layer of eggplant slices on top of the meat. Pour half the rice evenly over them and sprinkle with a little salt. Arrange a second layer of eggplant slices and pour the remaining rice all over them. Sprinkle with a little salt and add enough water to just cover the rice. Do not stir, and cover with a lid. Bring to the boil, then simmer on the lowest possible heat for about 20 minutes, or until the rice is tender, adding water if it becomes too dry. Leave to rest and keep hot for 20 minutes before serving.

Place a large round serving platter on top of the pan and quickly turn upside down, tapping the bottom of the pan, so that the contents come out undisturbed. Garnish, if you like, with pine nuts.

Variations

- Add 4 peeled and chopped tomatoes to the meat.
- For *ma'loubet al arnabeet,* use fried cauliflower florets (page 296) instead of eggplants.
- For *ma'loubet al bamia,* use 1¹⁄₂ pounds boiled okra instead of eggplants.
- *Recipes from Baghdad* (see bibliography) gives a recipe for a *maklouba* with 1 pound fresh or frozen chestnuts instead of eggplants. Make a gash in the skin on the flat side of each chestnut and broil them under a preheated broiler until the skins loosen. Peel as soon as they are cool enough to handle.

Whole Roasted Peppers with Yogurt and Fresh Tomato Sauce

Serves 6 • Bell peppers change in color as they ripen from olive, pale, and bright green to vivid yellow and red. The red ones are the ripest and sweetest. In Turkey they are roasted or deep-fried whole and served hot as a first course accompanied with yogurt or with a tomato sauce. There is no need to peel them. A long, pointed, piquant (but not hot) variety is also prepared in the same way.

6 fleshy bell peppers
2 cups plain whole-milk or thick Greek-style strained yogurt

FOR THE TOMATO SAUCE

3 cloves garlic, chopped
1–2 tablespoons extra-virgin olive oil
1½ pounds tomatoes, peeled and chopped
1 tablespoon sugar
Salt
A good pinch of ground chili pepper or flakes
2 tablespoons vinegar

Put the bell peppers on a piece of foil on a baking sheet and roast in a preheated 350°F oven for ¾–1 hour, until soft and browned in parts, turning them over once.

For the tomato sauce, heat the garlic in the oil, stirring for a few seconds only, until the aroma rises. Add the tomatoes, sugar, salt, and chili pepper, and cook, stirring occasionally, for about 20 minutes, until reduced and thick. Add the vinegar towards the end. Serve the peppers whole. Do not peel them. Pass around the yogurt and the tomato sauce for people to help themselves.

Variations

• Mix 1–2 crushed garlic cloves with the yogurt and add a little salt.
• Small eggplants, one for each person, can be roasted whole at the same time and served with the peppers.

Roasted Tomatoes

Serves 4–8 • Moroccan *tomates confites* have a deliciously intense flavor. Serve them hot or cold with grilled meat or fish or as an appetizer.

8 ripe plum tomatoes
Olive oil
Salt and pepper
2 tablespoons sugar

Cut the tomatoes in half lengthwise. Brush an oven dish or baking sheet (or a piece of foil) with olive oil and place the tomatoes on it, cut side up. Sprinkle each with salt, pepper, and sugar (sprinkle the sugar with your fingers) and cook in a 275°F oven for 3½–4 hours, until shriveled and shrunken. Serve them hot or cold, cut side up, on a flat platter.

Bamia bel Banadoura

Okra in Tomato Sauce

Serves 4–6 • Okra is one of the most popular vegetables in the Middle East. Cooked this way, it may be served cold as a salad, or hot with rice, or as a side dish with meat or chicken.

- 1 pound okra, preferably small young ones
- 1 large onion, cut in half and sliced
- 3 tablespoons sunflower or extra-virgin olive oil
- 2 cloves garlic, chopped
- 1 pound ripe tomatoes, peeled and chopped
- Salt and pepper
- Juice of ½ lemon (optional)
- 1–2 teaspoons sugar
- A small bunch of flat-leaf parsley or cilantro, chopped

With a small, sharp knife, cut off the stems and trim the caps of the okra and rinse well. Fry the onion in the oil till golden. Add the garlic, and fry for moments only, until the aroma rises. Now add the okra and sauté gently for about 5 minutes, turning over the pods.

Add the tomatoes, salt, pepper, lemon, and 1 teaspoon of the sugar and simmer 20 minutes, or until the okra is tender and the sauce reduced. Taste, and add more sugar if you like. Stir in the parsley or cilantro and cook a minute more.

Variation

From the start add 1 or 2 dried limes (see page 44), cracked open with a hammer or pierced with a skewer when they have softened, or 2–3 teaspoons of dried ground limes, instead of the lemon juice.

Bamia bel Takleya

Okra with Garlic and Coriander

Serves 4–6 • *Takleya* is the name of the fried garlic-and-coriander mix which gives a distinctive Egyptian flavor to a number of dishes. It goes in at the end. In Upper Egypt they chop up and mash the okra when it is cooked. Serve hot as a side dish with meat or chicken.

- 1 pound okra, small young ones
- 1 onion, chopped
- 3 tablespoons vegetable or extra-virgin olive oil
- Salt and pepper
- Juice of ½–1 lemon (optional)
- 5 cloves garlic, finely chopped
- 1½–2 teaspoons ground coriander

With a small, sharp knife, cut off the stems and trim the caps of the okra, then rinse well.

Fry the onion in 2 tablespoons of the oil till golden. Add the okra and sauté gently for about 5 minutes, stirring and turning over the pods. Barely cover with water (about 1½ cups), add salt and pepper, and simmer for about 20 minutes, or until tender. Add the lemon juice, if using, towards the end and let the sauce reduce. (The lemon juice is usually added when the dish is to be eaten cold.)

For the *takleya,* heat the garlic and coriander in the remaining oil in a small pan, stirring, for a minute or two, until the garlic just begins to color. Stir this in with the okra and cook a few minutes more before serving hot.

Variation

For *bamia makli,* sauté the okra in olive oil for 8 minutes, turning the pods over, then add 4 or 5 crushed garlic cloves and 4 tablespoons chopped cilantro, and cook a few moments more.

Green Beans in Tomato Sauce

Serves 6 • Use olive oil and add lemon juice if you want to eat this cold.

 1 onion, coarsely chopped

 3 tablespoons vegetable or extra-virgin olive oil

 4 cloves garlic, finely chopped

 1 pound ripe tomatoes, peeled and chopped

 1 pound green snap beans, topped and tailed and cut into 2 or 3 pieces

 Salt and pepper

 1 teaspoon sugar

 Juice of ½ lemon (optional)

Fry the onion in oil till soft and golden. Add the garlic, and when the aroma rises, add the tomatoes and beans. Season with salt, pepper, and sugar, add water if necessary to cover the beans, and lemon juice if using, and simmer 15–20 minutes, or until the beans are tender and the sauce reduced a little.

Tbikhit Qra

Pumpkin and Chickpeas

Serves 6 • Combinations of fresh and dry vegetables are called *tbikha*s in North Africa. All kinds of vegetables—peppers, carrots, turnips, cardoons, spinach—are cooked together with chickpeas and dried beans. This dish can be made hot and peppery with harissa, but it is very good without.

 1-pound piece orange pumpkin

 1 large onion, cut in half and sliced

 4 tablespoons olive oil

 4 medium tomatoes, peeled and chopped

 1–2 teaspoons sugar

 Salt and pepper

 ½ teaspoon harissa (optional) (page 464)

 A 1-pound can chickpeas, drained

 3 tablespoons chopped flat-leaf parsley (optional)

Peel the pumpkin, remove any pips and fibrous bits, and cut the flesh into pieces.

Fry the onion in the oil till golden, stirring occasionally. Add tomatoes, sugar, salt, pepper, and harissa if using, and stir well. Add the chickpeas and pumpkin. Moisten with 4–5 tablespoons water and simmer, with the lid on, for about 20 minutes, or until the pumpkin is tender, adding parsley towards the end. The pumpkin releases plenty of its own water, but if it becomes too dry, add a little more during the cooking. Serve hot.

Variation

Add 1 red pepper, cut into ribbons, to fry with the onions.

Korrat

Leeks

Serves 6 • Onions and leeks have been known in Egypt since ancient times. Romans regarded Egyptian leeks as the best. According to legend, the Emperor Nero was fond of them. This is an Egyptian way of preparing them. Serve cold as a salad or an appetizer, or hot as an accompaniment to meat or chicken.

> 2 pounds leeks
> 2 or 3 cloves garlic, crushed
> 1 tablespoon sugar
> 4 tablespoons vegetable or extra-virgin olive oil
> Juice of 1 lemon
> Salt

Wash the leeks carefully to remove any soil nestling between the leaves. Trim the root ends and cut off the tough green part of the leaves. Cut the rest into 2-inch pieces.

Fry the garlic and sugar in hot oil for moments only, until the sugar becomes slightly caramelized. Add the leeks and turn them, over moderate heat, to color them lightly. Sprinkle with lemon juice, add salt, and barely cover with water. Stew gently over very low heat until the leeks are tender and the liquid is reduced.

Serve hot or cold.

Arnabeet bel Lamoun

Cauliflower with Olive Oil and Lemon

Serves 4

> 1 cauliflower
> Salt
> 2 tablespoons extra-virgin olive oil
> 1 clove garlic (optional)
> Juice of 1 lemon
> Pepper

Wash and trim the cauliflower and cut it into florets. Boil in salted water until just tender, then drain.

Heat 2 tablespoons extra-virgin olive oil in a pan. Some like to soften a little crushed garlic in the oil. Add the lemon juice, salt, and pepper and turn the cauliflower in this over low heat. It will absorb the oil and lemon.

Some serve it with *tarator bi tahina* (page 65).

Arnabeet Makli

Deep-Fried Cauliflower

Fried cauliflower is very popular in the Arab world. There are several ways of doing it.

Wash the cauliflower and separate into florets. Briefly poach in salted water until slightly tender. Drain and allow to dry well. Then deep-fry in about 1 inch of vegetable or olive oil till golden, and drain on paper towels. Alternatively, dip in one of the batter mixtures given for fried eggplants on page 290 and deep-fry until golden, turning over once. Another way is to roll the florets in beaten egg, and then in flour or breadcrumbs. Deep-fry in very hot oil until crisp and golden. Drain on paper towels.

Serve hot or cold, with yogurt.

Egyptian Cauliflower Fritters in Tomato Sauce

Wash, separate into florets, boil, dip in batter, and deep-fry a cauliflower, as directed in preceding recipe. Both the egg-and-flour and the batter methods are suitable.

Prepare a tomato sauce in a large saucepan. Fry 2 garlic cloves in about 2 tablespoons oil until golden. Add 3–4 tablespoons tomato paste diluted in 1 cup water, 3 tablespoons chopped parsley, and salt and black pepper to taste. Simmer for 10–15 minutes.

Drain the deep-fried florets, and drop them into the tomato sauce. Simmer for about 25 minutes, until the cauliflower is very soft and the sauce is much reduced.

Jazar bi Zeit

Carrots in Oil

Serves 4 • A North African way of cooking carrots.

> 1 pound carrots, peeled and cut into ½-inch-thick slices
> Salt
> 2 cloves garlic, mashed or chopped fine
> 1 tablespoon dried mint
> 2 tablespoons extra-virgin olive oil

Put the carrots in a pan and barely cover with water. Add salt and simmer, covered, for 20 minutes, or until tender. Uncover to let the liquid reduce.

Add garlic, mint, and olive oil, and cook a few minutes more.

Serve hot or warm.

Variation

A Tunisian version calls for 1 tablespoon tomato paste in the cooking water.

Mashed Potatoes with Olive Oil and Parsley

Serves 6 • This Tunisian way with potatoes is as good hot as it is cold. Sweet potatoes can be used in the same way. Although in the Arab world potatoes never had the importance they acquired in Europe, and they never replaced grain, they are treated in a most delicious way. You must try the variations belonging to various countries which follow. Serve hot or cold with grilled or roasted meats and chicken. Some can also be served cold as appetizers.

1½ pounds mealy potatoes

Salt and pepper

6 tablespoons extra-virgin olive oil

4 tablespoons chopped flat-leaf parsley

Peel and boil the potatoes in salted water until soft. Drain, keeping about ½ cup of the cooking water.

Mash the potatoes and beat in the olive oil. Add salt and pepper to taste and enough of the cooking water to have a soft, slightly moist texture. Then stir in the parsley.

Variations

• Fold in 3 tablespoons capers, soaked in water then drained and squeezed, or 5 chopped scallions.

• Fold in some chopped black or green olives—about 12.

• Add ¼–½ teaspoon turmeric to the cooking water, or ½ teaspoon harissa (page 464) at the end.

• Add ½ teaspoon cumin, ½ teaspoon paprika, 3 tablespoons chopped cilantro, and the juice of ½ lemon or the chopped peel of ½ preserved lemon (page 459).

• With sweet potatoes, add 1 teaspoon ground ginger to the cooking water, then pinches of powdered saffron, cumin, and chili when you mash the potatoes. Use chopped cilantro instead of parsley, and if you like add ½ preserved lemon peel, chopped.

• A spiced baked-potato puree comes from Algeria: Peel, boil, and mash 2 pounds of potatoes, then mix with 3 large eggs. Season with salt and pepper, 2 teaspoons cumin, 1 tablespoon paprika, and, if you like, ½ teaspoon chili pepper, and stir in ½–¾ cup chopped parsley or cilantro. Pour into a baking dish and bake at 400°F for 25 minutes.

Batata Melousseh bi Senobar

Mashed Potatoes with Butter and Pine Nuts

Serves 6–8

2 pounds mealy potatoes

Salt

6 tablespoons butter

⅓–½ cup milk

Pepper

1 teaspoon cinnamon

1 large onion, coarsely chopped

2 tablespoons oil

3 tablespoons pine nuts

Peel the potatoes and boil in salted water till tender. Mash them, beat in butter and milk, and season with salt, pepper, and cinnamon. Fry the onion in oil till golden, add the pine nuts, and let them brown.

Serve the mashed potatoes hot, spread flat on a platter, with the onion and pine nuts on top.

Batata Harra

Sautéed Potatoes with Garlic, Chilies, and Cilantro

Serves 4 • An Arab way.

1 pound waxy new potatoes

Salt

3–4 tablespoons extra-virgin olive oil

3 or 4 cloves garlic, chopped

1 or 2 chilies, chopped, or a good pinch of chili flakes

3–4 tablespoons chopped cilantro or flat-leaf parsley

Boil the potatoes in salted water until tender, then peel and cut into slices or quarters. In a skillet, heat the oil, add the garlic, chilies or chili flakes, and potatoes, and sauté, turning the potatoes over and sprinkling on a little salt, until crisp and golden.

Add the cilantro or parsley and stir.

Variation

For a spiced new-potatoes dish: Put 1 pound baby potatoes, unpeeled and washed, in a saucepan with 2–3 tablespoons olive oil and 5 whole peeled garlic cloves. Only just cover with water. Add salt and pepper, 1 teaspoon paprika, a pinch of dried red-pepper flakes or 1 or 2 small chili peppers, $\frac{1}{2}$–$\frac{3}{4}$ teaspoon ground cumin, and $\frac{1}{2}$–$\frac{3}{4}$ teaspoon coriander. Simmer gently until the potatoes are tender. Reduce the liquid over high heat at the end, and stir in 4 tablespoons chopped cilantro or flat-leaf parsley.

Baked Potatoes and Tomatoes

Serves 6 • You need waxy new potatoes for this. Large ones can be quartered, baby ones can be left whole or cut in half. I don't bother to peel the very small ones. Serve hot or cold.

1 pound tomatoes, peeled and cut into pieces

2 teaspoons sugar

Salt

$\frac{1}{4}$–$\frac{1}{2}$ teaspoon ground chili pepper or flakes

8 cloves garlic, peeled and left whole

4 tablespoons extra-virgin olive oil

2 pounds waxy new potatoes, peeled and quartered or cut in half

$\frac{1}{4}$ cup chopped flat-leaf parsley

Put the tomatoes in a baking dish. Sprinkle with sugar, salt, and chili pepper. Add the rest of the ingredients, mix well, and sprinkle in a little more salt. Bake in a preheated 375°F oven for 50–60 minutes.

Variations

• There is a similar dish in Morocco called *batata hzina,* which means "sad potatoes." Add $\frac{1}{2}$ teaspoon cumin and $\frac{1}{2}$ teaspoon ginger to the above. Sweet potatoes are treated in the same way.

• For a Turkish dish for 6, fry 2 chopped onions in 2 tablespoons extra-virgin olive oil till soft. Add 2 more tablespoons oil and mix with $1\frac{1}{2}$ pounds new potatoes, peeled, boiled, and quartered. Add 4–6 chopped garlic cloves, 1 teaspoon cumin, the peeled and chopped tomatoes, a handful of black olives, 3 sprigs oregano, and $\frac{1}{2}$–1 teaspoon dried red-pepper flakes. Bake 45–60 minutes at 400°F.

Spicy Mashed Sweet Potatoes with Raisins

Serves 6

2 pounds sweet potatoes

Salt

6 tablespoons butter

Pepper

½ teaspoon ginger

1 teaspoon cinnamon

2 tablespoons black or golden raisins, soaked in water for 15 minutes

Peel the sweet potatoes and cut them into pieces. Boil in salted water for about 15–20 minutes, until soft. Drain and mash with a fork. Add butter, salt and pepper, ginger, and cinnamon, and beat well. Then add the drained raisins.

Sweet Potatoes Moroccan Style

Serves 6 • I like the surprising blend of sweet potato with ginger and chili pepper.

2 onions, chopped

2 tablespoons vegetable or extra-virgin olive oil

2 cloves garlic, crushed

3 tomatoes, peeled and chopped

½ teaspoon ginger

2 pounds sweet potatoes, peeled and cut into 1-inch cubes

Pinch of ground chili pepper (optional)

Salt

Fry the onions in the oil till soft. Add garlic, and when the aroma rises, add the tomatoes and ginger.

Put in the sweet potatoes and add 1½ cups water—or enough to half-cover the potatoes. Add chili pepper and salt. Cook, uncovered, for 15 minutes, or until the potatoes are tender and the liquid has almost disappeared, turning the potatoes over.

Serve hot or cold.

Turnips with Dates

Serves 2–4 • Cooked vegetables are not highly considered in Iraq, where they usually only find a place in a pot with meat, but turnips are treated with special respect. One way of dealing with young turnips is to peel and boil them in salted water, then press them under a weight to squeeze out some of the water, and serve them with a dusting of sugar. A special flavor is obtained when a little date syrup, called *dibbis* (see page 43), is stirred into the cooking water.

Lately, I have tried sautéing sliced turnips with fresh dates and found it very pleasant to serve as a side dish with meat or chicken.

You may use a moist variety of California dried dates.

1 pound young white turnips, peeled and sliced
2 tablespoons butter
Salt and pepper
6 moist dried dates, pitted and cut into small pieces

Boil the turnips in salted water until only just tender and drain.

Heat the butter in a skillet and sauté the turnips until they begin to color. Season with salt and pepper, add the dates, and cook through, shaking the pan and stirring.

TURNIPS ARE HARDER

The Mulla one day decided to take the King some fine turnips which he had grown.

On the way he met a friend, who advised him to present something more refined, such as figs or olives.

He bought some figs, and the King, who was in a good humour, accepted them and rewarded him.

Next week he bought some huge oranges and took them to the palace. But the King was in a bad temper, and threw them at Nasrudin, bruising him.

As he picked himself up, the Mulla realized the truth. "Now I understand," he said; "people take smaller things rather than heavy ones because when you are pelted it does not hurt so much. If it had been those turnips, I would have been killed."

SHAH, *THE EXPLOITS OF THE INCOMPARABLE MULLA NASRUDIN*

Tartoufa bel Banadoura

Jerusalem Artichokes in Tomato Sauce

Serves 6 • A disadvantage of these root vegetables is that they provoke wind. But they do have a delicious flavor. Smoother, less knobbly varieties available today are easier to peel.

2 pounds Jerusalem artichokes
1 onion, finely chopped
2 cloves garlic, halved
3 tablespoons olive oil
3 tomatoes, peeled and chopped
2 tablespoons tomato paste
1 teaspoon sugar, or to taste
3 tablespoons finely chopped flat-leaf
   parsley
Salt and pepper
Juice of ½ lemon (optional)

Peel the Jerusalem artichokes.

Fry the onion and garlic in olive oil until soft and golden. Add the Jerusalem artichokes and roll them in the oil by shaking the pan. Add the tomatoes, the tomato paste, a little sugar, parsley, salt and pepper, and the lemon juice if using. Stir well, and add just enough water to cover. Simmer gently for ½ hour, or until the Jerusalem artichokes are tender and the sauce is reduced. Add more water during cooking if necessary, and reduce it at the end.

Terbiyeli Kereviz

Celeriac with Egg and Lemon Sauce

Serves 4 • This Turkish specialty, usually served hot, is also good cold. The only problem is the peeling, or, rather, the cutting away of the skin, which is covered in soil.

1 celeriac, weighing about 1 pound,
   peeled and cut into ¾-inch cubes
Juice of 1 lemon
Salt
1 teaspoon sugar
2 egg yolks

Put the celeriac in a pan and cover with water. Add the juice of ½ lemon, some salt, and the sugar, and simmer, covered, for 20–30 minutes, until tender.

Just before serving, beat the egg yolks with the remaining lemon juice, and pour into the pan, beating vigorously. Do not let it boil, or the eggs will curdle. As soon as the sauce has thickened slightly, serve immediately.

Celeriac in Olive Oil

Serves 4 • We made this in Egypt.

1 celeriac, weighing about 1 pound
2 tablespoons extra-virgin olive oil
Juice of ½ lemon, or more to taste
¼ teaspoon turmeric (optional)
Salt and pepper
Pinch of sugar, or as much as 1 teaspoon

Peel the celeriac and cut into ¾-inch cubes. Sauté gently in the olive oil until lightly colored. Add a little water, barely to cover, and stir in lemon juice, turmeric, salt, pepper, and sugar. Simmer about 25 minutes, until the celeriac is tender and the liquid is considerably reduced.

Eat hot or cold.

Roasted Mixed Vegetables

Serves 6 • This is one of my favorite ways of cooking vegetables for a dinner party. You can do most of it in advance and put them in the oven again ½–¾ hour before serving.

3 eggplants (about 1¼ pounds total)
4 red bell peppers
8 small–medium white or red onions
4 tablespoons extra-virgin olive oil
Salt and pepper

Put all the vegetables, whole and unpeeled, on a sheet of foil on a baking sheet in a preheated 400°F oven. Roast for 1 hour, or until all the vegetables are soft—the eggplants should be very soft and the skin of the peppers blackened and blistered.

When cold enough to handle, peel the vegetables (for peeling peppers, see page 84). Press the eggplants very gently in a colander to remove some of their juices, and cut into large pieces. Cut each pepper into 4 strips. Cut the onions in half.

Put all the vegetables in a baking dish and sprinkle with oil, salt, and pepper. Mix gently and roast at 400°F for a further ½ hour, or until nicely browned.

Serve hot.

Turlu

Winter Vegetables Pot

Serves 6 • *Turlu* is a Turkish dish of mixed seasonal vegetables cooked in olive oil. The winter *turlu* consists of root vegetables and beans.

1 onion, cut in half and sliced

½ cup extra-virgin olive oil

2 medium waxy new potatoes, peeled and quartered

1 medium celeriac, peeled and cubed

1 large carrot, scraped and sliced

5 scallions, chopped

2–4 large cloves garlic, or more

Salt and pepper

1 teaspoon sugar

A 1-pound can white haricot beans, drained

3 tablespoons finely chopped parsley

In a large pan, fry the onion in half the oil until golden. Add the other vegetables and the garlic, and barely cover with water. Add salt and pepper and the sugar and bring to the boil. Simmer until all the vegetables are well cooked and the liquid is reduced to a sauce. Add the beans and the remaining oil and cook a few minutes more.

Serve hot, garnished with chopped parsley.

Spicy Root Vegetables

Serves 6–8 • A Tunisian way of cooking winter vegetables. It can be eaten hot or cold.

1 celeriac

3 carrots

3 turnips

1 small sweet potato

½ pound Jerusalem artichokes

5 tablespoons vegetable or extra-virgin olive oil

½ teaspoon turmeric

2 teaspoons caraway seeds

Salt and pepper

A good pinch of ground chili pepper, or to taste

Juice of ½ lemon

Peel and dice all the vegetables and put them in a pan with the rest of the ingredients.

Half-cover with water and cook on low heat with the lid on for 20 minutes, or until the vegetables are done, turning them over so that they are all in the water for some of the time. (They will also cook in the steam.)

Remove the lid and reduce the liquid to a sauce.

Tbikha of Turnips with Spinach and Chickpeas

Serves 6 • A *tbikha* is a Tunisian dish which mixes fresh vegetables with pulses such as chickpeas and dried fava beans.

- 1 large onion, chopped
- 3 tablespoons extra-virgin olive oil
- 2 cloves garlic, crushed
- 1 tablespoon tomato paste
- 1 teaspoon sugar
- 1 pound (about 5 small) turnips, peeled and quartered or cut in half
- Salt and pepper
- A ½-pound can cooked chickpeas or fava beans, drained
- 1 teaspoon harissa (page 464) (optional)
- 1 pound spinach, washed, with only heavy, tough stems removed

In a large saucepan, fry the onion in the oil till golden. Add the garlic, and when the aroma rises, stir in the tomato paste and the sugar.

Put in the turnips and barely cover with water. Add salt and pepper, stir well, and simmer for 20 minutes, or until the turnips are tender and the liquid is much reduced. Put on high heat if necessary to evaporate it.

Add the chickpeas or fava beans and stir in the harissa if using. Pack the spinach on top and put the lid on. When the leaves crumple to a soft mass, mix well and cook a few minutes more.

Durra
Grilled Corn on the Cob

Walking along the *corniche* or waterfront in Alexandria, one is irresistibly lured by the smell of corn grilled over charcoal. Vendors sit behind little braziers filled with glowing coals, fanning the flames furiously, or letting the sea breeze do it for them.

Remove the leaves or husks. Place the cobs on a charcoal grill, not too close to the fire. Turn them constantly. The grains will become flecked with black charred spots, but inside they will be soft and milky.

RIDDLE:
*Beaded, her head is high
and she sleeps in a shawl.
Guess who she is.*

ANSWER:
A corn cob.

Stuffed Vegetables

Dolma to the Turks, *dolmathes* to the Greeks, *dolmeh* to the Iranians, and *mahshi* to the Arabs, stuffed vegetables are the great party pieces and festive dishes of the Middle East. Every country has developed its own versions, leaving them whole and hollowing them; making a slit or cutting them in half; and stuffing them with a variety of fillings.

The origin of stuffed vegetables is not certain, though both the Turks and the Greeks claim them as their creation. They do not appear in the early Arab manuscripts, but they were known at the time of the Ottoman Empire, and were famously served at the banquets of the Sultans. They are likely to have developed as part of a court cuisine, in the palace kitchens, where teams of skilled and dedicated cooks strove to excite the curiosity and titillate the palates of a rich and powerful leisured class.

Today people of modest means can usually afford stuffed grape leaves and vegetables. They count their own time as cheap and spend it lavishly on hollowing and wrapping and making elaborate fillings. It satisfies the wish to give of yourself by taking trouble, as well as the need to impress by culinary expertise. It is the kind of cooking, like little pies and pastries, that people do in company with relatives and friends, which is associated with good times and fun in the kitchen.

In the past, stuffed vegetables were fried gently in oil or *samna* (clarified butter) before being stewed, or they were sent in large trays to be cooked in the baker's oven. Today the tendency is to make dishes lighter, and frying is usually omitted.

A man carried seven eggs in the fold [pocket] of his robe.

He met another man in the street and said to him:

"If you can guess what I have in the fold of my robe, I will give you these eggs, and if you can tell me how many there are, I will give you all seven."

The other thought for a while and said:

"I don't understand, give me another clue."

The man said:

"It is white with yellow in the middle."

"Now I understand," exclaimed the other. "It is a white radish that has been hollowed and stuffed with a carrot!"

A man told this anecdote to a group of people. When he had finished, one of his audience asked, "But tell us, what was there in the fold of his robe?"

CHRISTENSEN,
CONTES PERSANS

What is more natural than a
white radish stuffed with a carrot?

Classic Vegetable Fillings

A great variety of vegetable fillings exist. Vegetables with a meat filling are meant to be eaten hot, those with a meatless filling are usually cooked in oil and eaten cold. In Turkey these are called *yalangi dolma* or "false *dolma*," because of the lack of meat. The following are the fillings most widely used. Quantities are enough to stuff about 2 pounds of vegetables, but this varies according to the size of the vegetables and the amount of pulp scooped out.

Meat Filling

To fill about 2 pounds of vegetables • It is called *sheikh el mahshi* and also *tatbila*. The word *sheikh* implies that it is the grandest since it is all meat.

2 tablespoons vegetable oil

1 onion, finely chopped

12 ounces lean ground lamb or beef

Salt and pepper

$1/2$ teaspoon ground cinnamon or
    $1/4$ teaspoon ground allspice

$1/3$ cup pine nuts (optional)

Heat the oil in a frying pan. Add the onion and fry gently until soft and transparent. Add the meat, sprinkle with salt, pepper, and cinnamon or allspice, and stir, crushing the meat with a fork and turning it over, until it changes color. Moisten with a few tablespoons of water and cook gently for about 10 minutes, until the meat is tender.

Fry the pine nuts, if using, in a skillet in a drop of oil, shaking the skillet until lightly browned all over, and stir into the meat.

Meat and Rice Filling

To fill about 2 pounds of vegetables • This is the most common filling and is called *hashwa*. If the vegetables are going to be stewed, the filling can be mixed raw. If the vegetables are going to be baked, the filling must be cooked first, because the rice needs liquid. Short-grain or round rice is used because it is sticky and binds the filling.

1 onion, finely chopped (optional)

2 tablespoons vegetable oil

$1/2$ pound lean ground lamb or beef

$1/3$ cup short-grain or round rice, washed
    and drained

1 tomato, peeled and chopped (optional)

3 tablespoons finely chopped parsley
    (optional)

Salt and pepper

$1/2$ teaspoon ground cinnamon or
    $1/4$ teaspoon ground allspice

If the vegetables are going to be stewed, put all the ingredients together in a bowl and knead well by hand until thoroughly blended. Do not fill the vegetables more than three-quarters full, to allow for the expansion of the rice.

If you will be baking the vegetables in the oven, the filling must be cooked. Fry the onion in 2 tablespoons of oil till soft, add the ground meat, and stir gently, crushing and turning it over, until it changes color. Add the rest of the ingredients, mix well, cover with $3/4$ cup water, and simmer for 18 minutes, or until the rice is done.

Rice Filling

To fill about 2 pounds of vegetables • This meatless filling is for vegetables to be eaten cold. These are usually cooked with olive oil. If the vegetables are to be stewed, the rice is used raw; if they are baked, it has to be cooked.

3/4 cup short- or medium-grain rice
1 tomato, peeled and chopped
1 large onion, finely chopped
1/4 cup finely chopped flat-leaf parsley
Salt and pepper
1/2 teaspoon ground cinnamon or
    1/4 teaspoon ground allspice (optional)

If the vegetables are to be stewed, mix all the ingredients together in a bowl, kneading well by hand until thoroughly blended. When filling the vegetables, allow room for the rice to expand.

Use boiled rice and pack the vegetables a little more tightly if they are to be baked.

Variation

Usual additions are: 2 tablespoons finely chopped fresh dill or mint or 1 tablespoon dried, and 5 finely chopped scallions.

A Rice and Chickpea Filling

To fill about 2 pounds of vegetables • This too is for vegetables to be eaten cold.

2/3 cup cooked chickpeas (you may use canned ones)
1/2 cup short- or medium-grain rice
2 tomatoes, peeled and chopped
1 large onion, finely chopped
Salt and pepper
1/4 cup chopped fresh mint
1/2 teaspoon ground cinnamon or
    1/4 teaspoon ground allspice

Crush and mash the chickpeas and mix with the rest of the ingredients. Work well with your hand.

Cook the rice if you are going to bake rather than stew the vegetables.

About Vegetable Djinns

There was in the past—and in some places there still is today—a belief in the existence of numerous spirits or djinns who inhabit both things and people. Folktales give a fascinating picture of foods inhabited by djinns—vegetable djinns, rice djinns, meat djinns, chickpea djinns. These spirits are seasoned and spiced, and given piquant, naughty, or gentle personalities.

Eggplants Stuffed with Meat and Rice

Serves 6 • These can be baked, or cooked in a pan with water or stock. They are often cooked with other vegetables stuffed with a similar filling, and sometimes placed in a meat stew.

12 small (3½–4½-inch) or 6 medium
    (6-inch) long and slim eggplants
Meat-and-rice filling (page 306)
4 tablespoons vegetable oil
Salt and pepper
Juice of 1 lemon

Cut off the stem ends of the eggplants and reserve. Soften the pulp by rolling them on the table and pressing them with the palm of your hand. Hollow them, using an apple corer or a special tool for hollowing vegetables (you find them in Arab markets). Insert the corer through the cut end and push it as far as possible, making sure that you don't break through the other end, and twisting it to loosen the pulp and pull it out. Repeat to make a reason-

A TRUE ARTIST IN THE KITCHEN

Our chef, who had already served my mother before she was married, was very old and wished to retire and settle in his village. His second assistant, a young man named Mustafa, who had been with the old man ever since he began as a scullery-boy, asked to be kept on in the house. My father had already noticed him as being intelligent and singularly gifted as a cook. He therefore gave him the chance to show his mettle and promoted him to be head chef. Mustafa was an apt pupil, and as my father had himself explained to him the finer points of preparing both Turkish and European food, he soon excelled in both. He remained with my parents for many years, till his abominable temper, which apparently grew worse in the same ratio as his cooking approached the summit of culinary perfection, forced them to dismiss him in 1909. He used to vent his ill-humor on the cooking of the servants' food, which finally became quite uneatable, and in the end neither complaints nor his master's sharp reprimands had any lasting effect.

He was still with us when in 1908 we went for part of the summer to Ostend, and was summoned to cook for us there. The family spent a few days at Brussels and accordingly Mustafa was put on the Brussels coach of the Orient Express at Istanbul. We were rather anxious about him since he had never been abroad and spoke nothing but Turkish. However, he arrived safely and was met at the station by my mother's French and Turkish maids. Having acquired a smattering of each other's languages, each was capable of understanding what the other said. They took him to a pension where he was to spend a night before going with us to Ostend, and told him about the hours of meals and how to ask for anything he might need. The next morning, when the French maid went to fetch Mustafa, the proprietor of the pension met her in the hall and said that having abruptly left his seat at dinner, Mustafa had hurriedly gone to his room and locked his door. He had not answered when the proprietor went up to ask whether anything was

ably large hole. (Use up the discarded flesh for another dish.)

Prepare the filling in a bowl, using raw rice.

Stuff the eggplant shells three-quarters full with the filling, to allow room for the rice to expand. Close them with the reserved "corks."

Put the oil in a large saucepan. Place the eggplants in it, packed close and in layers. Add enough water, mixed with salt, pepper, and lemon juice, barely to cover them. Cover with a lid, and cook over gentle heat for 40 minutes, or until the eggplants and the filling are tender. Remove the lid at the end so that the water, if any is left, evaporates.

Serve hot.

---

wrong, nor had he come out for breakfast. The maid knocked at Mustafa's door until he cautiously opened it to ascertain who she was, and admitted her. Asked whether anything was the matter, he exploded and shouted that they had given him HAM at dinner. Horrified by the sight of "unclean" meat, he had sought the sanctuary of his room, where at least he was spared from further abominations. The only thing he wanted was to leave this house of perdition as soon as possible. The maid soothed him as best she could and took him to our hotel. The shock of this experience lasted all through our sojourn at Ostend, and during the whole time he was there he never ate or drank anything outside our house.

In his kitchen Mustafa was a true artist, and even invented a form of dolma *which I have never eaten since he left. He lightly boiled leeks, carrots, and celery, just enough to soften them, and peeled them into thin layers. These he cut into squares, placed some spiced minced meat in the center, and folded each piece into a small triangle. He then neatly arranged the different vegetables in layers in a cooking pot with a rounded bottom, and cooked them in broth. Before serving up he would reverse the pot on to a round dish, where the little dolmas formed an appetizing mound. He was the only cook I ever met who had the skill and patience for this work.*

In those days every vegetable was skillfully laid out in a cooking pot, with a few pieces of meat cut small, and sliced tomatoes at the bottom, if cooked with butter, or a whole onion when with oil, and then the finished product served reversed in a dish. The appearance of the little shapes thus turned out was most attractive. No self-respecting chef would ever have served up his vegetables in any other form. Owing to the great expenditure of time which was required for the preparation of such dishes, this kind of elaboration is no longer practiced.

FOAT TUGAY, *THREE CENTURIES—
FAMILY CHRONICLES OF TURKEY
AND EGYPT* (1963)

Imam Bayildi

*Cold Stuffed Eggplant with
Onions and Tomatoes*

Serves 6 • This famous Turkish dish is served as a cold appetizer or first course. Conflicting stories are told about the origin of its name, which means "the Imam fainted." Some say it came about when an imam (Muslim priest) fainted with pleasure on being served it by his wife. Others believe that the Imam fainted when he heard how expensive the ingredients were, and how much olive oil had gone into the making. The dish is part of the range of *zeytinyagli* (cooked in olive oil) dishes Turkey is famous for. It can be cooked in a saucepan or in the oven.

6 small (3½–4½-inch) long and thin
   eggplants
Salt
⅓ cup extra-virgin olive oil
1 cup good-quality tomato juice
1 teaspoon sugar, or more
Juice of 1 lemon

About Stuffing Eggplants

Small eggplants (3½–4½ inches long) are usually stuffed whole, although medium-sized ones can also be used. The usual way to stuff them whole is to cut a slice off the stem end just below the hull and reserve it to use as a "cork" and to scoop out some of the pulp with a small knife or a pointed spoon. (Use the discarded pulp for another dish.) Rolling the eggplant on the table and pressing it with the palm of your hand facilitates this. The eggplants are stuffed, and closed with the reserved "corks." They are placed upright in a large pan, packed tightly with the "cork" ends facing upwards, and cooked in stock or tomato juice which is poured over to almost cover them. Zucchini and small bell peppers, stuffed with the same filling, are sometimes cooked together in the same pot with the eggplants.

A Turkish way is to leave about ½ inch of the stalks on, remove the hulls, and peel off ½-inch-wide strips lengthwise, leaving alternating strips of bare flesh and shiny peel. This ensures that the eggplants keep their shape, while the peeled strips allow the bitter juices to escape after sprinkling with salt. A deep slash is made along the center, right through the eggplant, to within ½ inch of each end, and the filling is pressed into this slash.

A third way, used when the eggplants are baked, is to cut the eggplants in half lengthwise. In this case the eggplants can be a little larger. They are peeled or not, and a bit of the pulp is scooped out to hold the filling.

1½ large onions, cut in half and sliced thinly

2–3 tablespoons extra-virgin olive oil

5 cloves garlic, chopped

1 cup chopped flat-leaf parsley

4 tomatoes, peeled and chopped

Salt

Trim the stalk ends of the eggplants (you may leave the stalk). Peel off ½-inch-wide strips of skin lengthwise, leaving alternate strips of peel and bare flesh. Make a deep cut on one side of each eggplant lengthwise, from one end to the other, but not right through, so as to make a pocket. Soak the eggplants in water with 1 tablespoon of salt and leave for 30 minutes, then drain and dry them.

For the filling, soften the onions gently in the oil, but do not let them color. Add garlic and stir for a moment or two, until the aroma rises. Remove from the heat and stir in the parsley and tomatoes. Season to taste with salt, and mix well.

Stuff the eggplants with this mixture and place them tightly side by side, with the opening on top, in a wide, shallow pan. Pour over them the oil and enough tomato juice to cover, mixed with a little sugar, salt, and the lemon juice. Cover the pan and simmer gently for about 45 minutes, or until the eggplants are soft and the liquid is much reduced.

If you want to bake the stuffed eggplants instead, arrange them in a baking dish, cut side on top, with the rest of the ingredients poured over. Cover with foil and cook in a preheated 400°F oven for 1 hour, or until soft.

Allow to cool before arranging on a serving dish. Serve cold.

Variations

• Some cooks fry the eggplants very briefly first in olive oil.

• If the eggplants are too large for 1 person, cut them in half and make the slash into the cut side.

• For zucchini *imam bayildi,* hollow 2 pounds zucchini by scooping out their centers from the stem end, using an apple corer (see page 315), taking care not to pierce them right through. Stuff with the above filling and set the zucchini in layers, side by side, on a bed of tomato slices in a large pan. Pour over them about ⅓ cup extra-virgin olive oil mixed with a teaspoon of sugar and a little salt. Cover the vegetables with water and simmer, covered, over low heat, for ½ hour, or until soft.

Karniyarik

Eggplants with Meat Filling

Serves 6 • These eggplants—the Turkish name means "slashed belly"—represent a main dish to be served hot with a rice or bulgur pilaf. The Syrian and Lebanese version is with the meat filling on page 306.

> 6 medium (6-inch) thin and long
>   eggplants
> Salt
> Vegetable oil
> 2 onions, chopped
> ¾ pound ground beef or lamb
> 1 tablespoon tomato paste
> 2 large tomatoes, one peeled and
>   chopped, the other cut into 6 slices to
>   garnish
> Salt and pepper
> 1 teaspoon cinnamon
> ½ teaspoon allspice
> ¼ cup chopped flat-leaf parsley
> 1 cup good-quality tomato juice

Trim the caps and leave the stems on the eggplants. Peel ½-inch strips off the skins lengthwise, leaving ½-inch stripes of skin. Soak in water with 1 tablespoon salt and leave for 30 minutes, then drain and dry them. Fry them very briefly in hot shallow oil, 2 or 3 at a time in a skillet, turning to brown them lightly all over, then drain on paper towels.

For the filling, in another skillet heat 2–3 tablespoons fresh oil, and fry the onions until soft. Add the meat and cook for about 10 minutes, crushing the meat with a fork and turning it over, until it changes color. Add the tomato paste and tomatoes, salt and pepper, cinnamon,

and allspice. Stir well, and simmer for about 10 minutes, until the liquid is reduced.

Place the eggplants side by side in a single layer in a baking dish. With a sharp-pointed knife, make a slit in each one, lengthwise, along one of the bare strips on the top, without reaching the 2 ends (up to about 1 inch from each end). With a dessert spoon, open out the slits and push open the flesh on the sides to make a hollow pocket.

Fill each eggplant with some of the filling, and garnish with a slice of tomato placed on top. Pour the tomato juice into the dish, cover with foil, and bake in a preheated 350°F oven for about 40 minutes, or until the eggplants are soft.

Variations

• For Syrian and Lebanese *sheikh el mahshi betingan,* use 6 medium eggplants with the meat filling on page 306. The juice of 1 lemon may be added to the liquid in the baking dish.
• It is also common to cut the eggplants in half lengthwise and bake them with the filling spread all over the cut sides.

SYRIAN SAYING:
*"The woman killed herself
with work, yet the feast lasted
only one day."*

Sweet-and-Sour Stuffed Eggplants

Serves 6 • A Persian filling of meat and rice with yellow split peas is cooked in a sweet-and-sour sauce and served hot with plain rice.

12 small (3½–4½-inch) or 6 medium
   (6-inch) long and slim eggplants
3–4 tablespoons vegetable oil
⅔ cup wine vinegar
⅓ cup sugar
¼ teaspoon powdered saffron

FOR THE FILLING

⅓ cup yellow split peas
⅓ cup rice
Salt
1 medium-sized onion, finely chopped
2 tablespoons vegetable oil
½ pound lean ground lamb or beef
Pepper
3 tablespoons finely chopped parsley
3 scallions, finely chopped (optional)
½ teaspoon ground cinnamon
Pinch of grated nutmeg

Cut off the stem ends of the eggplants, and hollow them using an apple corer or a special tool for hollowing vegetables (you find them in Arab markets). Push the corer into the pulp as far as possible, making sure that you don't break through the other end, twisting it to loosen the pulp and pull it out. Repeat to make a reasonably large hole. (Use up the discarded flesh for another dish.)

Prepare the filling. Cook the yellow split peas and the rice in unsalted water for about 18 minutes, adding salt towards the end, when the split peas have softened. Sauté the onion in the oil until soft. Put the onion and the rest of the filling ingredients in a bowl. Mix well, and work with your hand until thoroughly blended. Stuff the eggplants with this mixture so that they are almost full.

Pack the eggplants in a large pan and arrange side by side, in 2 or 3 layers on top of each other. Barely cover with water mixed with the oil. Simmer gently, covered, for about ½ hour. Mix the vinegar with the sugar and saffron, pour over the vegetables, and continue to cook gently, covered, for another ½ hour.

Nasrudin and a friend went to an eating-house and decided, for the sake of economy, to share a plate of eggplants.

They argued violently as to whether they should be stuffed or fried.

Tired and hungry, Nasrudin yielded and the order was given for stuffed eggplants.

His companion suddenly collapsed as they were waiting, and seemed in a bad way. Nasrudin jumped up.

"Are you going for a doctor?" asked someone at the next table.

"No, you fool," shouted Nasrudin. "I am going to see whether it is too late to change the order."

SHAH, *THE EXPLOITS OF THE INCOMPARABLE MULLA NASRUDIN*

Fattet al Betingan Mahshi

Stuffed Eggplants with Toasted Bread,
Tomatoes, and Yogurt

Serves 6 • This Syrian and Lebanese dish, for which the city of Damascus is famous, is complex and requires time, but it is not difficult and it has dramatic appeal, with different layers of texture and flavor. There are those who prefer deep-frying the stuffed eggplants and the bread, and those who stew the eggplants in tomato sauce and toast the bread instead of frying. I have tried both ways and found them both delicious. A little sour-pomegranate concentrate gives a brown color and sweet-and-sour flavor to the tomato sauce.

Vegetable oil

12 ounces ground beef or lamb

Salt and pepper

1 teaspoon cinnamon

$^1\!/_4$ teaspoon allspice

$^1\!/_2$ cup pine nuts

6 small eggplants ($3^1\!/_2$–$4^1\!/_2$ inches long), weighing about $1^3\!/_4$ pounds

2 pounds tomatoes, peeled and chopped

2 teaspoons sugar

$1^1\!/_2$ tablespoons pomegranate concentrate or molasses (optional)

2 pita breads

2 cups plain whole-milk yogurt or $1^1\!/_2$ cups thick, drained yogurt at room temperature

2 cloves garlic, crushed (optional)

For the eggplant stuffing, heat 2 tablespoons oil in a skillet. Put in the meat and cook for about 10 minutes, adding salt, pepper, cinnamon, and allspice, and crushing the meat with a fork and turning it over until it is cooked and the liquid has evaporated.

In a small skillet, fry the pine nuts in a drop of oil, shaking the pan to brown them lightly all over. Stir half the pine nuts into the meat.

Wash and dry the eggplants and hollow them out with a corer (see page 315). Fill them with the meat-and-pine-nut mixture. (Use the eggplant flesh for another dish.)

Make the tomato sauce in a wide pan or baking pan. Put in the tomatoes with the sugar, a little salt and pepper, and, if you like, the pomegranate concentrate. Stir well and simmer for 5 minutes. Put in the eggplants, and simmer over low heat for 45 minutes, or until the eggplants are very soft, turning them over once.

Open out the pita breads, cutting around them with scissors or a serrated knife, and separating them into halves. Toast them under the broiler until they are crisp and lightly browned.

Mix the yogurt with the garlic, if using.

Just before serving, assemble the different components in a wide and deep serving dish. Break the toast into small pieces with your hands into the bottom of the dish. Take the eggplants out of the tomato sauce, and pour the tomato sauce over the toast, which will become soft and bloated. Pour the yogurt all over, and arrange the stuffed eggplants on top. Then sprinkle with the remaining pine nuts.

Variations

• Instead of cooking the eggplants in the tomato sauce, fry them in enough medium-hot oil to half-cover them, turning to cook them all over. The skins (there is no bare flesh) stop them from absorbing the oil. Lift them out and drain on paper towels.

• Mix 2 tablespoons tahina paste with the yogurt.

Eggplants Stuffed with Rice

Serves 6 • Serve cold as a first course.

> 12 very small (3–3½-inch) eggplants
> Rice filling or rice-and-chickpea filling
> (page 307)
> ½ cup extra-virgin olive oil
> ½ pound tomatoes, thinly sliced

Cut off the stem ends of the eggplants and reserve to use as "corks." Hollow them, using an apple corer or a special tool for hollowing vegetables (you find them in Arab markets). Insert the corer through the cut end and push it in as far as possible, making sure that you don't break through the other end, and twisting it to loosen the pulp and pull it out. Repeat to make a reasonably large hole. (Use up the discarded flesh for another dish, such as a stew or a salad.)

Prepare one of the fillings in a bowl, using raw rice. Stuff the eggplants only three-quarters full, to allow the rice to expand. Close the openings with the reserved "corks."

Heat 2 tablespoons of the olive oil in a large saucepan. Cover the bottom of the pan with a layer of sliced tomatoes and arrange the stuffed eggplants in layers on top. Cover with another layer of tomato slices, and pour the remaining olive oil all over. Add water to cover the vegetables, and simmer over very low heat, covered, for 30–45 minutes, or until the eggplants and their fillings are cooked, adding a little more water if necessary. The liquid should be very much reduced by the end of cooking. Remove the lid to evaporate it if necessary.

Allow to cool in the saucepan, and turn out onto a serving dish.

Variation

In the rice-and-chickpea filling, the chickpeas may be replaced by chopped walnuts.

Mahshi Kousa
Zucchini Stuffed with Meat and Rice

Serves 6–8 • Stuffed zucchini was one of our everyday dishes in Cairo. When my parents settled in London, my mother searched for a long time for a proper zucchini corer but in the end settled for an apple corer to do the job. In the past it was customary to fry the zucchini in butter until lightly colored before stewing, but it is usual now to omit this step. The most common filling is the meat-and-rice one called *hashwa* (page 306).

> 2 pounds small or medium-sized
> zucchini
> Meat-and-rice filling (without the
> onions) (page 306)
> 1 or 2 tomatoes, sliced
> 2 tablespoons tomato paste
> Juice of 1½ lemons
> 2–4 cloves garlic
> Salt
> 1 teaspoon crushed dried mint

Wash the zucchini and slice off the stem end. With a long, narrow apple or vegetable corer (they are long and thin and you find them in Arab markets), make a hole at this end of each vegetable and scoop out the pulp, being careful not to break the skin and not to break through the other end, which must remain closed. This is done by digging in gently and giving a sharp quick twist before pulling out the pulp. It is a skill that is acquired with a little practice. Keep the pulp for a stew or salad.

Prepare the filling in a bowl. Fill each zucchini two-thirds full only, to allow room for the rice to swell. There is no need to block the openings. *(continued)*

Lay a few thin slices of tomato in the bottom of a large, deep saucepan. Place the stuffed zucchini side by side in layers on top of the tomatoes. Mix the tomato paste with 1¼ cups water and the juice of 1 lemon and pour over the zucchini. Add more water if necessary to cover the zucchini. Cover the saucepan and simmer very gently for about 45 minutes, or until the zucchini are soft.

Crush the garlic cloves with a little salt. Mix with the mint and the remaining lemon juice, sprinkle over the zucchini, and continue cooking for a few minutes longer. The mint is added at the end, because prolonged cooking tends to spoil the taste.

Variations

• For Syrian stuffed zucchini with tamarind, add 2–3 tablespoons tamarind paste (see page 46) and 2 tablespoons sugar to the 1¼ cups water and bring to the boil, stirring, until the tamarind is dissolved.

• Iranians favor the filling with yellow split peas on page 313, and serve the zucchini topped with yogurt.

• For *mahshi cousa bi banadoura,* cook the zucchini in the following tomato sauce: Fry 1 large chopped onion in 2 tablespoons vegetable oil until golden. Add 2 crushed garlic cloves, and when it begins to color add 1 pound peeled and chopped tomatoes, season to taste with salt and pepper, and simmer gently for 10 minutes.

Mahshi Kousa bel Laban

Stuffed Zucchini Cooked in Yogurt

A delicious version, to be served hot with plain rice or with *roz bil shaghria* (rice with vermicelli, page 340).

Prepare stuffed zucchini as in the preceding recipe for *mahshi kousa,* using the meat-and-rice filling. Arrange them in a saucepan, and only just cover with water. Bring to the boil and simmer gently, covered, for about 30 minutes, until the water is absorbed and the zucchini are nearly done, adding a little more water if necessary.

Stabilize about 1 quart yogurt for cooking (page 113) so that it does not curdle.

Crush 3 garlic cloves with a little salt. Add about 1 teaspoon crushed dried mint, and mix well. Fry this mixture in 1 tablespoon butter for moments only, until it begins to color, and stir into the yogurt. Pour this over the zucchini and simmer, covered, for about 20 minutes longer.

Serve hot.

Mahshi Kousa bel Mishmish

Stuffed Zucchini with Apricots

This was a family favorite.

Soak 1½–2 cups dried apricots of a tart, natural variety for 1 hour.

Prepare and stuff zucchini as in the basic recipe for *mahshi kousa* on page 315, using the meat filling (without rice) on page 306.

Drain the apricots, reserving the soaking water. Cut them open without separating the halves completely. Arrange a layer of fruit halves over the bottom of a large saucepan. Place a layer of stuffed zucchini side by side over the apricots, and cover them with a second layer of apricots. Continue with alternate layers of vegetables and fruit, ending with a layer of fruit.

Mix the water in which the apricots have been soaked with 3 tablespoons extra-virgin olive oil and the juice of 2 lemons and pour into the pan. Add water if necessary, barely to cover the vegetables. Cook, covered, over very low heat for about 1 hour, until the stuffed zucchini are soft, adding water a ladle at a time, as the liquid in the pan becomes absorbed.

Peppers Stuffed with Rice

Serves 6 • Serve cold as a first course. Choose peppers that can stand on their bases.

1 large onion, finely chopped
6 tablespoons extra-virgin olive oil
1¼ cups short-grain or risotto rice
Salt and pepper
1–2 teaspoons sugar
3 tablespoons pine nuts
3 tablespoons currants
1 large tomato, peeled and chopped
½ teaspoon cinnamon
¼ teaspoon allspice
2 teaspoons dry mint
3 tablespoons chopped dill or parsley
Juice of 1 lemon
6 medium green or red bell peppers

Fry the onion in 3 tablespoons of the oil until soft. Add the rice and stir until thoroughly coated and translucent. Pour in 2½ cups water and add salt, pepper, and sugar. Stir well, and cook 15 minutes, or until the water has been absorbed but the rice is still a little underdone. Stir in the pine nuts, currants, tomato, cinnamon, allspice, mint, dill or parsley, lemon juice, and the rest of the oil.

To stuff the peppers, cut a circle around the stalk end and set aside to use as caps (with the stalk). Remove the cores and seeds with a spoon, and fill with the rice mixture. Replace the caps. Arrange side by side in a shallow baking dish, pour about ¾ inch of water into the bottom, and bake at 375°F for 45–55 minutes, or until the peppers are tender. Serve cold.

Variation

Stuff the peppers with meat or meat-and-rice filling, page 306, and serve hot.

Tomatoes Stuffed with Herbed Rice

Serves 4 • You can serve these hot or cold.

1 medium onion, chopped

3 tablespoons extra-virgin olive oil

1½ teaspoons tomato paste

⅔ cup short-grain or risotto rice

1⅓ cups water

Salt and pepper

1 tablespoon chopped mint

1 tablespoon chopped dill

2 tablespoons chopped parsley

Juice of ½–1 lemon or 1 tablespoon sumac

¼ teaspoon allspice

1 teaspoon cinnamon

4 firm, large (beefsteak) tomatoes or 10 small tomatoes

For the filling, fry the onion in 1 tablespoon of the oil till golden. Stir in the tomato paste and the rice. Add the water, salt, and pepper, stir well, and simmer for 12 minutes, or until the water is absorbed. Mix in the mint, dill, parsley, lemon juice or sumac, allspice, cinnamon, and the remaining oil.

Cut a small circle around the stalk and cut out a cap from each tomato. Remove and discard (or save for another dish) the pulp and seeds with a pointed teaspoon. Fill with the rice stuffing and replace the caps. Arrange in a shallow baking dish and bake in a preheated 350°F oven for 20–30 minutes, until the tomatoes are soft, keeping watch so that you can remove them if they start to fall apart.

Variations

A Lebanese version has 2 tablespoons pomegranate syrup and ¼ cup chopped walnuts in the rice filling. Another has 3 tablespoons chopped hazelnuts and 3 tablespoons raisins. For these, use the master recipe, omitting the herbs and the sumac.

Tomatoes Stuffed with Roast Peppers, Tuna, Capers, and Olives

Serves 6 • This version of the Tunisian *meshweya* (page 85) can be served hot or cold. I prefer it cold.

4 red bell peppers

Salt

3 tablespoons extra-virgin olive oil

¾ cup flaked canned tuna

2 tablespoons capers

¼ cup chopped black olives

Peel of ½ preserved lemon (page 459), chopped

2 tablespoons chopped flat-leaf parsley

6 large tomatoes

For the filling, roast and peel the peppers (see page 84), remove the seeds, and cut into strips about ¾ inch wide. Mix with the rest of the ingredients except the tomatoes.

Cut a small circle around the stalk of each tomato and cut out a cap. Remove the pulp and seeds with a pointed teaspoon. Fill with the roast-pepper mixture and replace the caps. Arrange in a shallow baking dish and bake in a preheated 350°F oven for 20–30 minutes, or until the tomatoes are a little soft, keeping watch so that they do not fall apart.

Variation

In Tunisia they may add 1 or 2 garlic cloves, 1 minced hot chili pepper, and 1 teaspoon of *tabil* (page 48).

Sheikh el Mahshi Banadoura

Tomatoes Stuffed with Ground Meat, Currants, and Pine Nuts

Serves 4–8 • This is to be served hot.

8 medium tomatoes

1 onion, chopped

3 tablespoons sunflower oil

½ pound lean ground lamb or beef

Salt and pepper

1 tablespoon currants or raisins

2 tablespoons pine nuts or coarsely chopped walnuts

½ teaspoon cinnamon

½ teaspoon allspice

3 tablespoons finely chopped flat-leaf parsley

Cut a circle around the stalk end of the tomatoes and cut out a cap from each. Remove the pulp and seeds with a pointed teaspoon.

Fry the onion in oil till golden. Add the meat, salt, and pepper. Turn the meat over and squash it with a fork until it changes color. Stir in the currants or raisins and the pine nuts or walnuts, and add cinnamon, allspice, and parsley.

Fill the tomatoes with this and cover with their tops. Put them close to each other in a baking dish and bake in a preheated 350°F oven for about 30 minutes, or until the tomatoes are soft, being careful that they do not fall apart.

Variation

Dilute 2 tablespoons tomato paste in about ⅔ cup water. Season with salt and pepper, and add 4 tablespoons oil and the chopped tomato pulp. Pour over the stuffed tomatoes before baking.

Mahshi Kharshouf

Stuffed Artichoke Bottoms with Meat and Pine Nuts

Serves 4 • This old classic is prestigious in the Arab world. In Egypt, during their season, artichokes were sold by vendors who brought crates to the kitchen door, and our cook pared the bottoms. Nowadays I use frozen artichoke bottoms that are so good you cannot tell they are not fresh. Look for them (a flat-cup variety) as produce of Egypt in Middle Eastern stores.

1 onion, chopped

2 tablespoons sunflower oil

2 tablespoons pine nuts

10 ounces ground veal, lamb, or beef

2 tablespoons finely chopped flat-leaf parsley

Salt and pepper

¼ teaspoon allspice

½ teaspoon cinnamon

1 small egg, lightly beaten

A 14-ounce package frozen artichoke bottoms (about 9), defrosted, or 9 or 10 fresh ones (see page 282 for preparation)

Juice of ½–1 lemon

1 tablespoon olive oil

Fry the onion in the oil till golden. Add the pine nuts and stir till lightly colored. Mix the raw meat, flat-leaf parsley, salt and pepper, allspice, cinnamon, and egg, and knead to a soft paste with your hands. Then work in the onions and pine nuts.

Take lumps of the meat mixture and fill the artichoke bottoms, making little mounds. Place them in a shallow baking dish.

Mix the lemon juice with the olive oil and about 1 cup water and pour into the dish. Bake in a preheated 350°F oven for 30 minutes, until the meat is done.

Serve hot or cold.

Variations

• You may add ¼ teaspoon turmeric to the water in the baking dish.

• For an alternative filling: Mix the ground beef with 1 egg and 2 slices white bread, crusts removed, soaked in water and squeezed dry. Add salt and pepper, ½–1 teaspoon thyme, and a pinch of nutmeg, and knead well.

• A Tunisian version of the filling is ground veal with 2 tablespoons finely chopped onion, salt, and pepper, mixed with 1 lightly beaten egg.

Mahshi Bassal bel Tamarhendi

Onion Rolls Stuffed with Meat in Tamarind Sauce

Serves 4–6 • This elegant dish with an exquisite sweet-and-sour caramelized flavor is a specialty of Aleppo in Syria. The onion layers are used to make little rolls around a filling. In Egypt we soaked the tamarind pods and used the filtered juice. Now I find that the Indian tamarind paste obtainable from Middle Eastern stores is perfectly good to use.

2 large mild onions

1 pound lean ground lamb or beef

Salt and pepper

1 teaspoon cinnamon

$\frac{1}{2}$ teaspoon allspice

3 tablespoons finely chopped flat-leaf parsley

$1\frac{1}{2}$ tablespoons tamarind paste (page 46)

$1\frac{1}{2}$ tablespoons sugar

3 tablespoons sunflower oil

Peel the onions and cut off the ends. With a sharp knife, make a cut on one side of each, from top to bottom, through to the center—and no farther. Throw into a big pan of boiling water and boil for 10–15 minutes, until they soften and begin to open so that each layer can be detached. Drain, and when cool enough to handle, separate each layer carefully by easing your fingers inside each. If they don't detach easily you may have to throw the onions back into boiling water after one or two have been removed.

For the filling, knead the ground meat with the salt, pepper, cinnamon, allspice, and pars-

ley. Put a walnut-sized lump into each curved onion layer and roll up tightly. Line the bottom of a wide, shallow pan with discarded bits of onion (this is to protect the rolls). Pack the stuffed onion rolls tightly on top.

Melt the tamarind paste and 1 tablespoon of sugar in about $\frac{3}{4}$ cup boiling water and pour over the onions, adding more water to cover if necessary. Place a plate on top to hold the onions and simmer, covered, on very low heat, adding more water as required, for about 45–60 minutes, until they are very soft and the water is absorbed.

Now arrange the rolls in one layer on a flat, heatproof serving dish, sprinkle the top with the remaining sugar, and caramelize under the grill. It gives them a warm, wrinkly look. They are best served hot but are also very good cold.

Variations

• For Saudi Arabian onion rolls, stuff the onion layers with the following meat-and-rice filling: Fry $\frac{1}{2}$ pound ground meat in 2 tablespoons vegetable oil, crushing and turning it over, until it changes color. Add $\frac{1}{2}$ teaspoon ground cinnamon or $\frac{1}{4}$ teaspoon ground allspice and $\frac{1}{2}$ cup American rice, and barely cover with water. Simmer for 18 minutes, or until the rice is done.

• Instead of the tamarind sauce, pour over the rolls a mixture of water—just enough to cover—with 2 tablespoons oil and 1–2 tablespoons vinegar. Finish them in the oven to dry them out a little and give them a nice wrinkly look.

Mahshi Bassal

Stuffed Onions with Meat Filling

Serves 4–8

4 large Spanish onions, peeled
Meat filling (page 306)
2 tablespoons tomato paste
Salt and pepper

Boil the onions whole in water for 30 minutes, until they are tender, and drain. When they have cooled a little, cut in half crosswise and remove the centers, leaving a shell of about 3 layers and patching any little holes left at the bottom with pieces of onion.

Prepare the filling and stuff the onions with it. Place them side by side in a baking dish. Mix 1 cup water with the tomato paste, add salt and pepper, and pour into the bottom of the dish. Bake in a preheated 400°F oven for 40–50 minutes.

An ancient Persian remedy: *"A cold may be cured by throwing an onion on a neighbor's house—the neighbor will get the cold."*

It was also believed that "A person must not eat a raw onion on Friday, or the angels will not remain with him." Nevertheless, "He who eats onions for forty-one days will become a hadji, *or pilgrim, to Mecca."*

DONALDSON, *THE WILD RUE*

Persian Sweet-and-Sour Stuffed Cabbage Rolls

Serves 6 • This is sometimes made with lettuce leaves.

1 medium-sized white Dutch or Savoy cabbage
1¼ cups rice
½ cup yellow split peas
1 large onion, finely chopped
Vegetable oil
1 pound ground beef
½ teaspoon turmeric
Salt and pepper
½ tablespoon tomato paste
¼ cup chopped flat-leaf parsley
⅔ cup wine vinegar
2 tablespoons sugar

To detach the cabbage leaves, cut a deep cone into the core at the stem end with a pointed knife and plunge the whole cabbage into boiling salted water. This will soften and loosen 1 or 2 layers of leaves. Detach these, and plunge again into boiling water to detach more leaves, and continue until all of the leaves are separated. Cut very large leaves in half, but leave small ones whole.

Prepare the filling. Wash the rice and cook in boiling water until it is almost tender—about 10 minutes—then drain. Boil the split peas separately until tender. Fry the onion in 3 tablespoons oil until soft and transparent. Add the meat and turmeric and season to taste with salt and pepper. Cook, stirring, until the meat changes color, then remove from the heat and add the rice and split peas, tomato paste, parsley, and more salt and pepper. Mix well.

Lay the cabbage leaves on a plate one at a time. Shave off the thickest part of the hard rib if necessary. Put a heaping tablespoon of the mixture at the bottom of each leaf, bring the sides up over it, and roll up into a bundle. Put a little oil at the bottom of a heavy pan, cover with a few broken leaves to protect the others from burning, then arrange over them rows and layers of stuffed cabbage rolls.

Mix the vinegar with an equal quantity of water, stir in the sugar, and pour over the rolls.

Put a plate over them, cover the pan, and cook gently on a very low flame for ¾–1 hour, until rolls are very tender and the liquid has been absorbed, adding water if necessary.

Serve hot or cold.

Sweet-and-Sour Flavors

Reading about ancient, pre-Islamic Persia of the Sassanid period and its dualist Zoroastrian religion, based on the confrontation of the two forces of good and evil, I was struck by the similarity between the early philosophy and the principles of harmony which Persians applied to their food. The Zoroastrian belief is that their god Ahouramazda created the world. The spirit of creation which pulled matter out of nothing awoke a force of resistance, giving birth to a spirit of evil, Angromainyous, whose creative and malicious urge was to destroy the harmony of the universe. In this religion, creation could only exist in the equilibrium of the opposing forces which it had aroused.

It is this equilibrium, poised between the vinegar and the sugar, pairing opposite flavors and textures, meat with fruit, sweet with sour, savory with sweet and spicy, strong with mild, which the Persians of the Sassanid period reflected in their dishes, and which you find in Iranian dishes today. Many of these were adopted by the Caliphs of Baghdad, and spread throughout the Islamic world.

During the same period, parts of India adopted a version of the Zoroastrian religion—the Parsees of today, but with one god of creation, and without a necessary enemy or evil force. Northern Indian food is not unlike Persian food, but it lacks the particular harmony through opposites which the Persian dishes have.

It is also interesting to compare the Middle Eastern "sweet and sour" to that of China. The Chinese have a predilection for sweet and sour, and harmony through opposites, and their early religion was also based on opposing forces of good and evil.

Mahshi Coromb

Stuffed Cabbage Leaves

Serves 6

1 medium-sized white Dutch or Savoy
   cabbage
Salt
Meat-and-rice filling (page 306)
Juice of 1 lemon
Pepper

Cut a deep cone into the core at the stem end
with a pointed knife and plunge the whole
cabbage into boiling salted water to soften and
loosen 1 or 2 layers of leaves. Detach these and
plunge again into boiling water to detach more
leaves. Continue until all of the leaves are separated. Cut very large leaves in half, but leave
small ones whole.

Prepare the filling, leaving it uncooked.

Lay the cabbage leaves on a plate, one at a
time. Shave off the thickest part of the hard rib
flat with a knife. Put a heaping tablespoon of
filling on each leaf, near the stem end, and roll up
loosely, tucking in both sides to enclose the filling. The parcel must be loose, to leave room for
the rice to expand without tearing the leaves.

Line a large saucepan with torn or unused
leaves to prevent the stuffed leaves from sticking to the bottom. Set the stuffed leaves on top
of them in layers, packing them tightly. Cover
with water and lemon juice mixed with a little
salt and pepper. Cover the pan and cook very
gently for ¾–1 hour. Serve hot.

Variations

- Cover with tomato juice instead of the water.
- Tuck 6 or 7 whole garlic cloves in between
the stuffed leaves.
- Add 1 tablespoon dried mint or 3 of
chopped fresh dill to the sauce at the end.

Mahshi Korrat

Stuffed Leek Rolls with Tamarind

Makes about 22 • This version with tamarind is
from Aleppo. Serve hot or cold, as a first course
or part of a buffet meal.

4 very fat leeks
Salt and pepper
1 pound ground beef
1 teaspoon cinnamon
¼ teaspoon allspice
⅓ cup vegetable oil
1½ tablespoons tamarind paste (see
   page 46)
1½ tablespoons sugar

Cut the hard green ends off the leeks, so that
you have white cylinders about 6 inches long.
With a sharp knife, make a slit very carefully
along one side of each leek, through to the
center but no farther. Boil the leeks in salted
water till softened. Drain and cut a slice off the
root end, freeing the layers from each other.
You will have wide rectangular strips.

Season the ground meat with salt, pepper,
cinnamon, and allspice and work to a soft paste
with your hands. Put about 1 heaping tablespoon filling in a line along the larger side of a
rectangle, leaving about 1 inch at each end, and
roll up like a long thin cigar. Continue with all
the leaves. When they get too narrow, put 2 together to make a roll.

Heat the oil in 2 large skillets. Put in the
rolls, side by side, and sauté gently for a few
minutes, until lightly colored all over, turning
them over once. Dilute the tamarind paste and
sugar in a little hot water and pour over the
rolls. Add more water—enough to cover them.

Cook, covered, over very low heat for ½–¾
hour. Remove the lids towards the end to reduce the sauce if necessary.

Mahshi Qarah

Stuffed Pumpkin

Serves 6–8 • The round, sweet orange-fleshed pumpkins are the ones to use for this dish. The amount of stuffing you need depends on the size of the pumpkin. If you wish to make it without meat, increase the quantity of rice.

- 1 pumpkin, about 9 inches in diameter
- 1 medium onion, finely chopped
- 2 tablespoons vegetable oil
- ½ pound ground meat—lamb, beef, or veal
- ½ cup short- or medium-grain rice, cooked
- 2–3 tablespoons pine nuts
- 2–3 tablespoons black or golden raisins
- Salt and pepper
- 1 teaspoon cinnamon or ½ teaspoon allspice

Wash the pumpkin and, with a strong sharp knife, cut out a round lid around the stalk end of the pumpkin and lift it out. Scrape inside and remove the seeds and loose fibers.

Make the filling. Fry the onion in the oil till soft. Add the meat and continue to cook, crushing it with a fork and stirring until it changes color. Add the rest of the ingredients (the pine nuts may be toasted or fried till lightly colored) and fill the pumpkin. Put the lid on, place it on a baking sheet, and bake for at least an hour in a 375°F oven, until it feels soft when you press.

Bring to the table and serve hot, cut into generous slices, each topped with stuffing.

Variations

- Replace the rice filling with bulgur pilaf with raisins and pine nuts (page 368).
- Sprinkle a little sugar inside to sweeten the flesh before filling the pumpkin.

Mahshi Safargel

Stuffed Quinces

Serves 4 • This is exquisite and also very easy. The quinces are hard and take a long time to cook before you can even cut them up and stuff them, but you can bake them hours— even a day—in advance. I use very large quinces, weighing a pound each. Serve as a hot first course.

- 2 large quinces (1 pound each)
- 1 medium onion, chopped
- 1½ tablespoons vegetable oil
- 3 tablespoons pine nuts
- 7 ounces lean ground lamb or beef
- Salt and pepper
- 1 teaspoon cinnamon
- ¼ teaspoon allspice

Wash the quinces and rub off the light down that covers their skin in patches. Put them on a piece of foil on a baking sheet and bake in a preheated 325°F oven for 1½–2 hours, until they feel soft when you press.

For the stuffing, fry the onion in the oil until soft. Add the pine nuts and stir, turning them over, until golden. Put the raw ground meat in a bowl and add salt, pepper, cinnamon, and allspice. Mix and work well to a smooth paste with your hand. Add the fried onion and pine nuts and work them into the paste.

When the quinces are cool enough to handle, cut them open lengthwise. Remove the cores with a pointed knife and discard them. With a pointed spoon, scoop out about a third of the pulp and mix it into the meat stuffing. Heap a quarter of this mixture into each quince half and press it down.

Put the 4 stuffed quince halves on the baking sheet and bake at 350°F for another ½ hour. Serve hot.

Beans, Chickpeas, Lentils, and Other Legumes

Since ancient times, dishes based on legumes such as chickpeas, beans, and lentils have been looked down on as the food of the poor. In literature, proverbs, and songs they are constantly referred to as the food of the poor or the food of the mean. They have even been included as such in the *Kitab al Bukhala* (*Book of Misers*) by the writer al-Jahiz (775–868). But regardless of the stigma, these usually peasant dishes are nevertheless loved by everybody. Numerous jokes are told about Arab dignitaries who, when served with French *haute cuisine* or cosmopolitan food in hotels or at banquets, long for the *ful medames* (page 328) or chickpeas and spinach which they can tell that the servants are eating from the aromas wafting up from the kitchens.

A little dull at times, but more often used in exciting combinations with other ingredients and deliciously flavored with spices, garlic, onions, and herbs, legumes are also important for their nutritive value. By themselves, they can be eaten cold as mezze or salads, or hot as vegetable side dishes. Cooked with meat, vegetables, rice, and pasta, they add body and texture to many wonderful winter stews.

Many vegetarian dishes which use legumes are known as the Lenten dishes of the Christian communities and are associated with the austerity month, which falls at the end of winter. For Muslims, they are the substantial winter foods on which people survive.

EGYPTIAN PROVERB:
*The man of good breeding eats beans
and returns to his breeding.*

Zeytinyagli Barbunya

*Borlotti Beans with Onions and
Tomatoes in Olive Oil*

Serves 6 • Beans cooked in olive oil and eaten at room temperature are a Turkish staple. The mottled pink borlotti beans (they are called *barbunya,* which is also the name for red mullets) are a special treat. The Turkish ones obtainable here need to be picked over for foreign matter. There are also good-quality canned varieties which you can use.

1½ cups borlotti beans, soaked overnight

1 large onion, sliced

6 tablespoons extra-virgin olive oil

3 cloves garlic, chopped

1 pound tomatoes, peeled and chopped

1 tablespoon tomato paste

1–2 teaspoons sugar

Good pinch of ground chili pepper or
 flakes

Salt

Bunch of dill, chopped

¼ cup chopped flat-leaf parsley

Drain the beans, and boil them in fresh, unsalted water for 30 minutes.

Fry the onion in 2 tablespoons of the oil until soft and golden, stirring occasionally. Add garlic and stir for a minute or so. Then add the tomatoes and cook gently until reduced to a pulp. Stir in the tomato paste, sugar, and chili pepper or flakes. Put in the drained beans and cover with about 2¼ cups water. Cook, covered, for 1 hour, or until the beans are tender (the time varies quite a bit), adding salt when they begin to soften, and more water as the mixture becomes dry. Add dill and the remaining oil, and cook for a few minutes more.

Stir in the parsley and leave to cool in the pan.

Variation

Use haricot or butter beans instead of borlotti beans. At a pinch, for an instant dish, you may use good-quality canned beans.

Ful Medames

Egyptian Brown Fava Beans

Serves 6 • The traditional Egyptian breakfast of dried fava beans is also the national dish, eaten at all times of the day, in the fields, in village mud-houses, and in the cities. Restaurants serve it as a mezze, and it is sold in the streets. Vendors put the beans in large, round, narrow-necked vessels, which they bury through the night in the dying embers of the public baths.

Ful medames is pre-Ottoman and pre-Islamic. It is probably as old as the Pharaohs. According to an Arab saying: "Beans have satisfied even the Pharaohs." Egyptians gleefully tell you that the little brown beans have been found in pharaonic tombs and have been made to germinate. There are fields of them, and promotional explanations on fake papyrus by the Ministry of Agriculture. Of course, they could have been put there by tomb robbers.

There are many types of dried fava beans—small, middle-sized, and large, all of which can be used—and there are very good-quality canned ones. Most expatriates are happy with canned ones, which they improve on with flavorings and trimmings. These need to be turned into a pan with their juice and cooked for 15 minutes.

Dealing with Legumes

Legumes (or pulses) once needed to be picked over and cleaned of little stones and impurities. A few of the packaged ones still do, and they usually need to be washed. Some need soaking in plenty of cold water for a few hours or overnight, which helps to soften them and shortens the cooking time. Brown fava beans, navy beans, and chickpeas need lengthy soaking and cooking. In the past, chickpeas were soaked with a pinch of bicarbonate of soda, which left a slightly peculiar taste, and still required prolonged cooking. And it was often necessary to remove their tough outer skins—a long and tedious operation. The ones sold today are of a superior, skinless quality. It is necessary only to soak them in plain cold water for two hours or overnight. A way of reducing the soaking time is to put the beans or chickpeas in a pan full of cold water, bring them to the boil, and leave them to soak in the water for 1 hour.

Brown or green lentils, yellow split peas, and black-eyed peas do not need soaking and require much less cooking time, while red lentils disintegrate very quickly. The time required to cook different types of legume varies according to their age or time in storage. The older they are, the longer they take to cook.

Salt should not be added at the start of cooking legumes, as it does not allow them to soften. It should be added when they have begun to soften.

2 cups small Egyptian fava beans (*ful medames*), soaked overnight (and left unpeeled)

Salt

⅓ cup chopped flat-leaf parsley

Extra-virgin olive oil

3 lemons, quartered

Salt and pepper

4–6 cloves garlic, crushed

Chili-pepper flakes

Cumin

As the cooking time varies depending on the quality and age of the beans, it is good to cook them in advance and to reheat them when you are ready to serve. Cook the drained beans in a fresh portion of unsalted water in a large saucepan with the lid on until tender, adding water to keep them covered, and salt when the beans have softened. They take 2–2½ hours of gentle simmering. When the beans are soft, let the liquid reduce. It is usual to take out a ladle or two of the beans and to mash them with some of the cooking liquid, then stir this back into the beans. This is to thicken the sauce.

Serve the beans in soup bowls sprinkled with chopped parsley and accompanied by Arab bread.

Pass round the dressing ingredients for everyone to help themselves: a bottle of extra-virgin olive oil, the quartered lemons, salt and pepper, a little saucer with the crushed garlic, one with chili-pepper flakes, and one with ground cumin.

The beans are eaten gently crushed with the fork, so that they absorb the dressing.

Optional Garnishes

- Peel hard-boiled eggs—1 per person—to cut up in the bowl with the beans.
- Top the beans with a chopped cucumber-and-tomato salad and thinly sliced mild onions or scallions. Otherwise, pass round a good bunch of scallions and quartered tomatoes and cucumbers cut into sticks.
- Serve with tahina cream sauce (page 65) or salad (page 67), with pickles and sliced onions soaked in vinegar for 30 minutes.
- Another way of serving *ful medames* is smothered in a garlicky tomato sauce (see page 464).
- In Syria and Lebanon, they eat *ful medames* with yogurt or feta cheese, olives, and small cucumbers.

Variations

- A traditional way of thickening the sauce is to throw a handful of red lentils (¼ cup) into the water at the start of the cooking.
- In Iraq, large brown beans are used instead of the small Egyptian ones, in a dish called *badkila,* which is also sold for breakfast in the street.

RIDDLE:

It is divided into two equal parts and covered by a strong skin. Praised be God, who made it! And how do Arabs call it?

ANSWER:

El ful.

Lentils in Butter

Serves 6 • A good partner to omelets, little spicy sausages, and fried or broiled eggplant.

2½ cups large green or brown lentils, washed
1 onion, chopped
1 tablespoon vegetable oil
2 cloves garlic, chopped
Pepper
1 teaspoon ground cumin
Salt
2 tablespoons butter
Juice of ½ lemon (optional)

In a large saucepan, fry the onion in the oil until soft and golden, stirring occasionally. Add the garlic and stir until it just begins to color.

Add the lentils, pour in about 2½ cups water, and bring to the boil. Add pepper and cumin, and simmer gently, covered, for about 20–30 minutes, until the lentils are tender, adding salt when they begin to soften. Add more water as it becomes absorbed and let it reduce at the end.

Serve with the butter stirred in until melted, and a squeeze of lemon if you like.

❧

To dream of eating beans forebodes quarrelling and discord.

EGYPTIAN DREAM BOOK, 1231

❧

Adds bel Tamatem
Lentils in Tomato Sauce

Serves 4 • This is good hot or cold, with plenty of raw olive oil.

2 cloves garlic, crushed
3–4 tablespoons extra-virgin olive oil
3 medium tomatoes, peeled and chopped
1 cup large green or brown lentils, washed
Salt and pepper
1 teaspoon sugar
¼ cup chopped flat-leaf parsley

Heat the garlic in 1 tablespoon of the oil for a moment or two, until the aroma rises. Add the tomatoes and cook for 3 minutes. Then add the lentils and about 1 cup water. Stir and simmer, covered, over low heat for 20 minutes, or until the lentils are tender, adding salt, pepper, and sugar when they begin to soften.

Before serving, add parsley and stir in the remaining oil.

THE YOUNG GIRL'S SONG

By my father's life! By my father's life!
I will not have the poor man!
He wakes me in the morning and says,
He wakes me in the morning and says,
"Pound the lentils early!"
By my father's life! By my father's life!
I will have the rich man!
He wakes me in the morning and says,
He wakes me in the morning and says,
"Pound the pastry with fat!"

MASPÉRO, *CHANSONS POPULAIRES*

Shula Kalambar

Lentils with Spinach

Serves 6 • A lentil-and-spinach dish was prepared in medieval Persia to heal the sick. For the cure to be effective, the ingredients had to be bought with money begged in the streets. Here is a modern version.

1½ cups large green or brown lentils, washed

Salt

1 pound fresh spinach or frozen leaf spinach

2 tablespoons butter or olive oil

2 or 3 cloves garlic, crushed

½ teaspoon ground coriander

½ teaspoon ground cumin

Pepper

Boil the lentils in water for about 20 minutes, or until very tender, adding salt when they begin to soften, then drain.

Wash and drain the spinach and remove any hard stems. Put it in the pan with the lid on over very low heat for a minute or two, until the leaves crumple into a soft mass. They will steam in the water that clings to them. If using frozen spinach, defrost. Cut the spinach leaves into ribbons.

Heat the butter or oil in the pan. Add the garlic with the coriander and cumin and stir for a moment or so, until the aroma rises. Now put in the lentils and spinach, add pepper, stir very well, and cook for a few minutes more.

A TALE OF GOHA

Goha invited a friend to his house. No sooner had he placed a plate piled high with food before him than the man had eaten it all up. Several times he rushed to fetch more beans, more rice, and more chickpeas, which he had prepared for his own lunch and for next day's as well. Each time the man emptied the plate and waited for more. Finally, there was nothing left in the house to eat. Then the man remarked that he was on his way to the doctor because he was suffering from loss of appetite. Appalled, Goha begged him to stay away when he had recovered it!

Chickpeas with Turmeric

Serves 6 • In Morocco it is poor food eaten hot with bread. A grander version with saffron is served as a first course. You may use canned chickpeas. The same can also be done with white cannelini beans, dried or canned.

    2 tablespoons vegetable or olive oil
    1 large onion, chopped
    3 cloves garlic, crushed
    ½ teaspoon turmeric
    1½ cups chickpeas, soaked overnight, or
        two 15-ounce cans chickpeas, drained
    Salt and pepper
    1 cup chopped cilantro or flat-leaf
        parsley

Heat the oil in a large pan and fry the onion until golden. Add the garlic and stir for a moment or two. Stir in the turmeric and add the drained soaked chickpeas. Cover with water and simmer for 1¼ hours, or until the chickpeas are very tender, adding salt and pepper when they have begun to soften, and water to keep them covered. Reduce the liquid at the end so that you have a thick sauce.

If using canned chickpeas, drain them and add ½–1 cup water and cook for about 20 minutes, to allow them to absorb the flavors.

Stir in the cilantro or parsley and cook 5 minutes more.

Variations

- Use ½ teaspoon crushed saffron threads or powder instead of the turmeric.
- Add the juice of 1 lemon.
- Cannelini beans, dried and soaked overnight, or canned ones, drained, can be used in the same way as chickpeas.
- For different, spicy chickpeas, omit the turmeric and add ½ teaspoon cinnamon, 1 teaspoon cumin, and ¼ teaspoon ground chili pepper.
- For another Moroccan version, omit the turmeric, put a chili pepper in the cooking water, season with salt and pepper when the chickpeas have already softened, and add chopped cilantro at the end, when the water has almost evaporated.

Chickpeas

These hard, round, corn-colored peas with an earthy flavor are the most common legumes in the Middle East. You will find recipes including them all over this book. Mashed and smoothly pureed, they are a base for salad dips. Whole, they combine well with chicken, meat, and vegetables. Mixed with rice and vermicelli or bulgur or in a stew destined for couscous, they provide excitement in texture and flavor. Once upon a time you had to peel them. Today they come to us skinless.

Fattet Hummus

Chickpeas with Yogurt and Soaked Bread

Serves 4–6 • A number of popular Lebanese dishes which go under the name of *fatta* (see page 222) involve yogurt and a bed of soaked toasted or fried bread. This one is served for breakfast accompanied by scallions and green peppers cut into strips.

¾ cup chickpeas, soaked in cold water
    overnight
Salt
2–2½ cups Greek-style thick drained
    yogurt or plain whole-milk yogurt
3 cloves garlic, crushed
Pepper
2 pita breads

TO GARNISH

1–2 tablespoons dried mint leaves
3–4 tablespoons pine nuts
1 tablespoon butter or vegetable oil
Good pinch of ground chili pepper or
    flakes (optional)

Drain the chickpeas and simmer in fresh water to cover until they are really very soft, usually well over an hour, adding salt only when they are nearly done.

Beat the yogurt with the garlic and pepper.

Open out the pita breads and leave them for a few minutes in a very hot oven, or turn them under the broiler until they are crisp and very lightly browned. Then break them up with your hands into the bottom of a serving dish. Pour the chickpeas and some of their cooking water over the bread, soaking it thoroughly, keeping out a few chickpeas to decorate the dish.

Pour the yogurt mixture over the chickpeas.

To garnish, crush the mint leaves over the top. Fry the pine nuts in the butter or oil until they are a light brown. Sprinkle these and the extra chickpeas over the yogurt. Some people like to sprinkle on hot ground chili pepper or chili flakes.

Serve at once, while the chickpeas are hot and the rest is lukewarm.

Variations

• A Damascus version called *tasseia* has the chickpeas crushed with a pestle and mortar and mixed with 2–3 tablespoons tahina, the juice of ½ lemon, and 1 crushed garlic clove. You can put this in a blender with a little of the cooking liquor. Squeeze a little lemon juice in the chickpea water before sprinkling over the bread, spread the mashed chickpea cream over the top, and cover with yogurt, then garnish as before.

• Instead of toasting the bread, some people like to cut it into triangles and deep-fry them in hot oil, then drain the pieces on paper towels and carry on as above.

• An old version of this dish is made with lamb's trotters, which give a deliciously rich flavor and texture to the stock.

Rice

ROZ

Rice is the grand prestigious dish, the festive dish that has pride of place at banquets and on all celebratory occasions. In the cities, for those who can afford it, it is also an everyday family dish. Rice was first introduced in the marshlands of the area through Persia from India, and was spread by the Arabs as far as Sicily and Spain. By the tenth century it had become an important basic food in the Middle East. In many countries today it forms the main part of the meal, with small amounts of meat and vegetables as garnish or accompaniment. It is *roz* to the Arabs and *pilav* to the Turks. Iranians call it *chelow* when it is plain, and *polow* when combined with other ingredients. In the Arabian Gulf they have taken to an Indian way of making it and call it *biriyan*.

Plain rice is served with stews, grilled meats, and salads, and it is also accompanied by sauces. It is sometimes colored yellow with saffron or turmeric, or red with tomatoes, and it can be garnished with nuts. It is molded into various shapes for presentation, a favorite being a ring. Rice is also cooked with other ingredients, such as vegetables, fruit, nuts, meat, chicken, and fish. In Middle Eastern tradition, it is served at the same time as all the other dishes, to be chosen first or last, to each individual's taste. Some people claim that they cannot taste anything without eating rice at the same time. In families where the Western style of serving three courses has been adopted, rice is often served at the end of the meal, accompanied by a special sauce, or by part of the main dish which has been set aside to be savored with it. In Turkey it is sometimes served at the end of the meal to accompany dried fruit in syrup (see Khoshaf, page 409).

Many different types of rice exist. It is grown in Iran, Iraq, Syria, Egypt, and Turkey. Varieties of long-grain, usually those grown locally, are generally used for savory rice dishes. Short-grain (also known as "pudding" rice) and medium-grain (risotto rice) are used for stuffing vegetables or for puddings, because they stick together in the stuffing and become creamy quickly when cooked in milk. The special appeal of long-grain lies in its ability to be tender while remaining firm and separate. The finest-quality long-grains are cultivated in Iran, where there are at least six different and particularly fragrant varieties. The most prestigious, which are used for very special occasions because they are very expensive, are the black-tailed *domsiah,* the imperial-court *darbari,* and the amber-scented *ambar-bu.* Then come *sadri,* which is the most commonly used; the dagger-shaped *khanjari;* and the sweet *shikari.* In Turkey, *bersani* is the rice commonly used, although *kulakli,* which is grown in small quantities near the Syrian border, is considered the best of the home-grown. In Egypt, *rashidi* rice is the most appreciated. None of these are available in America. American long-grain and the prestigious basmati, which is closest to the third quality of Persian rice and is the most widely favored rice in the Middle East for its wonderful flavor and aroma, are fine alternatives. Originally from India and Pakistan, basmati is now also grown in Texas.

About Cooking Rice

Ways of cooking rice vary from one country to another. Plain rice is cooked in water with salt, or in stock. A good amount of fat—either butter or oil—is involved in the cooking or added in at the end.

Different types of rice require different quantities of water and cooking times. Each batch of rice harvested, even from the same fields, differs in the amount of water it needs. When households buy it in large sacks, the first dish made from the opened sack ascertains the amount of water required. In Egypt, the newly harvested local rice requires the same volume of water as of rice. If the rice is a year old, more water is needed.

As a rule, 1 cup of long-grain rice, including basmati, absorbs about $1\frac{1}{2}$ cups of water—or a little more. In some cases—and for those who prefer a softer, moist rice—twice the volume of water is used. Americans are used to twice the volume, but if you want rice to have a more Middle Eastern texture, try the proportions in the recipes that follow.

The practice in the Middle East has always been to wash the rice, and in some countries also to soak it for between half an hour and overnight. When rice used to come in burlap sacks it had to be cleaned of stones and roughage and sometimes small insects as well, and it had to be washed in several changes of water. The packaged rice available today is perfectly clean, and modern milling usually makes washing unnecessary. Some imported rice needs to be washed to be rid of the starchy powder which causes it to be slightly sticky when cooked. American long-grain does not need washing, but basmati usually does. To wash the rice, pour warm water over it in a bowl, stir well, and leave to soak for a few minutes. Pour into a fine-meshed sieve or a small-holed colander and rinse under cold running water until the water runs clear. Then drain.

The preparation of rice is enveloped by great mystique in all the Middle Eastern countries, and although it is extremely simple, various methods exist. There are regional ways, and every family cherishes secret rituals, refusing to believe that it is possible to achieve success without them. Tastes also vary. Some prefer a dry rice with firm and separate grains, others would like it softer and a little moist.

By some Middle Eastern standards, 2 cups of rice feeds 2 people, but by Western standards, it is enough for 6. This also varies depending on whether it is to be a side dish or main course.

If you want to reheat the rice before serving, it is best to do so in the oven in a baking dish, covered with foil, as rice tends to burn at the bottom of the pan when it is dry.

Ways of Cooking Plain Rice

A Syrian Way

Serves 4–6

2 cups long-grain or basmati rice

3 cups water

Salt

4 tablespoons butter or vegetable oil

Wash the rice, if basmati, in warm water, then rinse, and drain. American long-grain does not need washing. Bring the water to the boil in a pan with a little salt to taste. Throw in the drained rice, bring to the boil again, and boil vigorously for 2 minutes. Cover the pan with a tight-fitting lid and cook over very low heat, undisturbed, for about 20 minutes, until the water has been absorbed and the rice is cooked. It should be tender and separate, with little holes all over the surface. Turn off the heat, and allow the rice to rest for 5 minutes.

Melt the butter in a saucepan and pour it evenly all over the rice. Let it rest again, covered, for 5 minutes longer, until the melted fat has been absorbed by the rice. It tastes better with butter, but you may use oil instead.

❧

An Egyptian riddle describes the manner of serving rice at the end of a meal:

QUESTION:
Why is rice like a shaouish *(policeman)?*

ANSWER:
It is brilliantly white like the shaouish's *uniform in the summer, and it arrives at the end like the* shaouish *when everything (i.e., the trouble) is over.*

A Lebanese Way

The ingredients and quantities (to serve 4–6) are the same as above.

Wash the rice if basmati, and drain well. It is not necessary to wash American long-grain. Put the 3 cups of water, salt, and 4 tablespoons butter in a saucepan, and bring to the boil. Throw in the rice and boil vigorously for 2 minutes. Cover the pan tightly and cook over very low heat, undisturbed, for about 20 minutes, until the rice is tender and fluffy, and little holes have appeared all over the surface. Turn off the heat and allow to rest for 10 minutes before serving.

A Turkish and Egyptian Way

In Turkey it is *sade pilav;* in Egypt it is *roz mefalfel.* The ingredients and quantities are the same as in the first recipe. Turks always use butter and plenty of it for rice to be eaten hot, and use olive oil when it is to be eaten cold. Butter is truly wonderful with rice, but some people today have turned to using a bland vegetable or seed oil, sunflower oil being the most common.

Wash the rice if basmati and drain well.

Heat the butter or oil in a saucepan. Throw in the rice and stir gently for a minute or two, until the grains are translucent and well coated with fat. Add the water (or use stock—a bouillon cube will do at a pinch) and salt. Bring to the boil vigorously, then cook gently over very low heat, tightly covered and undisturbed, for about 20 minutes, until the rice is tender and the characteristic little holes have appeared on the surface. Never stir while it is cooking. Allow to rest, covered, for 10 minutes before serving. *(continued)*

A Persian Way for Chelow or Steamed Plain Rice

As with her art of miniature painting and poetry, Persia has carried the preparation of rice to extraordinary heights of refinement. In Iran today, whereas bread is the daily staple, rice is the occasional prestige food for most of the population. It is said that no other country prepares rice in the same perfectionist manner. The result is a light, separate, and fragrant grain.

The principle is to parboil the rice briefly until it is only half cooked, then to strain it and finish the cooking in dry heat, so that it continues to cook in its steam. Although this preparation may sound complicated, it is not so, and the result is so exquisite that it is well worth trying. You will understand the importance of rice in Iranian life and the national pride in making it to perfection.

You must use basmati, which is the closest to Iranian rice. In Iran, according to tradition, they start the preparation the day before, soaking the rice overnight in water with plenty of salt, but the basmati we get today cooks perfectly well without soaking. If you soak it overnight it falls apart when you cook it.

It is good to use a heavy-bottomed nonstick pan.

For 6 people, wash 1 pound (2¼ cups) basmati rice in a few changes of lukewarm water, then under the cold tap in a small-holed colander or large strainer.

Fill a large, preferably nonstick, pan with about 2 quarts water, add 3 tablespoons salt, and bring to the boil. Sprinkle the drained rice in gradually and let it boil vigorously for about 6–10 minutes. Test a grain of rice by biting it. When it is just a little underdone—it must be slightly harder than you would like to eat it—drain quickly in the colander or strainer and rinse in lukewarm water.

Put 2 tablespoons butter or vegetable oil in the pan and mix in 2 spatulas of rice. Pour in the rest of the rice and mix in 2–4 more tablespoons butter or oil. Stretch a clean dishcloth across the top of the pan, put the lid on top, and lift the corners of the cloth up over it. (In Iran they use a lid made of raffia covered by a removable cloth called a *damkoni*.)

Put the rice on high heat for a few minutes, until it is hot enough to steam, then leave it to steam over very low heat for 20–30 minutes, until the grains are tender and separate. The cloth will absorb the excess steam. If you are not using a nonstick pan, to release the crispy bottom of the rice put the pan briefly on a cold surface or dip it in cold water.

The crisp, golden-brown crust that forms at the bottom is considered a delicacy to be offered first to guests. It is called *tah dig*.

A beautiful way to serve—easily done with a nonstick pan—is to turn the rice out like a cake. It will have a beautiful golden crust.

If you are not using a nonstick pan, remove the crust with a spatula and serve separately.

Variations

• For a yellow saffron garnish, crush ½ teaspoon saffron threads with the back of a teaspoon and let it infuse in ¼ cup boiling water, mix with a ladle of cooked rice, and sprinkle over the rice when serving.

• Put thin slices of fried bread or raw potato at the bottom of the pan when steaming, with the rice on top, and serve them in the same way as the crispy rice *tah dig*.

• Another way of producing a golden-crust *tah dig* is to mix 1 small egg with 2 tablespoons plain yogurt and ½ tablespoon water infused with ¼ teaspoon crushed saffron. Mix this with a ladle of cooked rice and spread over the hot butter or oil at the bottom of the pan.

• Served without a sauce, as an accompaniment to shish kebab, plain white rice is eaten with a generous lump of butter and, traditionally, with raw egg yolks served in eggshells. One yolk is poured over each individual portion of rice and then stirred into it, making a glistening, creamy sauce. This is in the tradition of the cookshop or restaurant and not part of domestic home cooking.

• Bowls of sumac are put on the table for people to help themselves.

• A special electric rice-cooker is now widely used in Iran and throughout the Middle East. It regulates itself and makes the cooking of rice very easy with good results, though not quite as good as the traditional way; and it produces a crispy golden crust at the bottom. It is available in America. Read the instructions that come with it before you use it.

Quick and Easy Boiled and Steamed Rice

Serves 6 • The following method, a simplification of the Persian one, is the one I mostly use today. It works well with all types of rice, because the grain can absorb as much water as it needs.

2 cups long-grain or basmati rice
Salt
4–6 tablespoons butter or vegetable oil

Wash the rice, if basmati, in warm water and drain. American long-grain does not need washing. Bring a large pan of salted water to

the boil. Pour in the rice and cook over high heat for about 10–12 minutes, until the rice is still slightly underdone. Then drain quickly.

In the same pot, heat half the butter or oil. Pour in the rice, add the remaining butter or oil and a little salt, and stir gently. Cover with a tight-fitting lid and steam on very low heat for 20 minutes, or until the rice is tender.

Rice with Chickpeas

Prepare plain rice in any of the above ways. At the same time, sauté 1 chopped onion in 2 tablespoons butter or oil until softened. Add drained chickpeas from a 15-ounce can and cook, stirring, until heated through. Stir into the rice. In Turkey this is *nohutlu pilav*. It features famously in Ottoman folklore. At the Palace of Topkapi, in the time of Mehmed the Conqueror, a little gold ball in the shape of a chickpea would be embedded in the rice, creating excitement among the guests, who all hoped to be the happy recipients (unless they broke a tooth).

Roz bil Shaghria

Rice with Vermicelli

Serves 4–6 • This is the most popular everyday Arab rice dish. It is eaten on the second night of the Muslim New Year "so that one's employment may be prolonged and multiplied" like the vermicelli broken into little bits; or, as some say, "so that one may be prolific and beget many children." Serve with a yogurt-and-cucumber salad, such as the one on page 70.

³⁄₄ cup dry vermicelli broken into 1-inch pieces in your hand
2 tablespoons vegetable oil
1½ cups long-grain rice
3¼ cups boiling water or chicken stock (page 143) (or you may use a bouillon cube)
Salt
2 tablespoons butter

In a saucepan, fry the vermicelli in the oil over medium heat until lightly golden, stirring so that they color evenly. Watch them, as they brown very quickly.

Add the rice and stir until the grains are coated. Then pour in the boiling water or stock, add salt, and stir well. Cook, covered, over low heat for about 20 minutes or until the rice is tender and the water absorbed.

Stir in the butter, and serve hot.

Variations

• Add a handful of boiled or canned and drained chickpeas at the same time as the water.
• Fry 1 chopped onion in the oil till transparent, then add the vermicelli.
• You can toast the vermicelli under the broiler or in a dry skillet instead of frying it.

Pilaf with Currants and Pine Nuts

Serves 6 • Many dishes standardized in the courtly kitchens of Constantinople during Ottoman rule spread throughout the Empire. This is one of the classics that you find in all the cities that were once outposts of the Empire. It is good to serve with meat or chicken.

1 large onion, chopped
3 tablespoons sunflower oil
²⁄₃ cup pine nuts, toasted
2 cups long-grain rice
3 cups chicken stock (page 143) (or you may use 1½ bouillon cubes)
1 teaspoon ground allspice
1 teaspoon cinnamon
Salt and pepper
3 tablespoons currants
6 tablespoons butter, cut into pieces

In a large pan, fry the onion in the oil until soft and golden. Add the pine nuts and stir until lightly colored. Add the rice and stir over moderate heat until well coated in fat.

Add the stock and stir in the allspice, cinnamon, salt and pepper, and the currants. Bring to the boil, then simmer, covered, over low heat for 20 minutes, or until the rice is tender.

Stir in the butter and serve hot.

Variation

For Turkish *iç pilav*, sauté ½ pound diced liver—chicken livers or lamb's liver—in 1 tablespoon butter until it changes color, adding salt, pepper, and ¼ teaspoon of the allspice. Fold into the rice with 3 tablespoons finely chopped fresh dill when the rice has cooked for 15 minutes, and leave, covered, over very low heat for 10 minutes more.

Tomatoes Stuffed with Ground Meat, Currants, and Pine Nuts (page 319),
and Stuffed Artichoke Bottoms with Meat and Pine Nuts (page 320)

Sweet Jeweled Rice (page 350)

Bulgur Pilaf with Tomatoes and Eggplant (page 368)

Couscous with Squabs and Almonds (page 381)

Orange Slices in Orange Syrup (page 406)

Quinces Poached in Syrup (page 412)

Almond Snake (page 433)

Almond Fingers (page 434) and Ma'amoul (page 438)

Roz bel Zafaran

Spiced Saffron Rice

Serves 6 • Yellow rice is a festive, celebratory dish, prepared for its delicate flavor and decorative quality, and in the hope that its color will bring joy and happiness. This spiced version is particularly delicious.

> 2 cups basmati or long-grain rice
>
> 3 cups chicken stock (page 143) (or you may use a bouillon cube)
>
> 1 teaspoon cardamom seeds (Indian stores sell them out of the pod)
>
> 6 cloves
>
> 3 cinnamon sticks, about 3 inches long
>
> 1/2 teaspoon powdered saffron or saffron threads
>
> Salt and pepper
>
> 4 tablespoons butter or vegetable oil

Wash the rice, if basmati, in warm water, and rinse in a small-holed colander in cold water under the tap.

In a pan, bring the stock to the boil with the cardamom seeds, cloves, and cinnamon sticks and simmer for 10 minutes. Add the saffron and a little salt and pepper and pour in the rice. Let it come to the boil again and stir well, then lower the heat to a minimum and cook on low heat, with the lid on, for about 20 minutes, until little holes appear on the surface and the rice is tender.

Stir in the butter, cut into pieces, or the oil.

Serve the rice hot, in a mound, or press in a mold and heat through in the oven before turning it out.

Variations

• Serve sprinkled with a mixture of lightly toasted pine nuts and coarsely chopped almonds and pistachios, or throw these into the bottom of the mold, if using one, before pressing in the rice, so that they come out on top when you turn out.

• Add 3 tablespoons currants at the same time as the rice.

• Garnish, if you like, with 1 chopped onion fried till golden, or 3 tablespoons raisins soaked in boiling water for a few minutes and 3 tablespoons flaked or chopped almonds toasted under the broiler or fried in 2 tablespoons oil.

• For rice with turmeric—referred to as "Oriental saffron" and used as an alternative—substitute 1/2 teaspoon turmeric for the saffron.

Rice to Accompany Fish

Serves 6 • The traditional Arab rice for fish is pale yellow with saffron and garnished with pine nuts. Turmeric, the "Oriental saffron," sometimes replaces the expensive spice. Here the grains become softer and less separate with more water than in other rice dishes, and olive oil is often used.

½ **cup vegetable or extra-virgin olive oil**

¼ **teaspoon saffron powder or threads or**

   ¼ **teaspoon turmeric**

2 **cups long-grain rice**

Salt and pepper

2 **onions, sliced into half-moon shapes**

½ **cup pine nuts**

Heat 2 tablespoons of the oil in a pan. Stir in the saffron and throw in the rice. Sprinkle with salt and pepper and stir well over medium-high heat until the rice acquires a transparent yellow glow. Add 4 cups boiling water, cover the pan, and simmer very gently, undisturbed, for about 20 minutes, until the rice is tender and the water has been absorbed. Stir in 4 more tablespoons of oil.

Fry the onions in the remaining 2 tablespoons of oil, stirring occasionally, until very soft and more brown than golden. Add the pine nuts, and stir until golden.

Serve the rice in a mound, garnished with the pine nuts and onions.

Rice with Pine Nuts, Pistachios, and Almonds

This is an elegant and decorative way of serving rice at a party.

Prepare plain or saffron rice, cooking in water or chicken stock, following one of the recipes at the beginning of this chapter.

Chop ½–¾ cup mixed pistachios and blanched almonds coarsely, and fry them with ½ cup pine nuts in a little oil until just golden. Or use only one or two kinds of nuts.

Just before serving, spread the nuts evenly over the bottom of an oiled ring mold large enough to hold all the rice. Press the rice over the nuts tightly and turn out onto a heated serving dish. This traditional ring shape is common for rice. In this case, it will be crowned by the assortment of nuts.

An advantage is that you can pack the rice and nuts into the oiled mold in advance and keep it warm in a low oven, ready to be unmolded just before serving.

Sabzi Polow

Rice with Herbs

Serves 6 • Iranians have a predilection for fresh herbs, which they use in huge quantities. This traditional Iranian New Year's dish consists of rice cooked with a variety of fresh herbs. Their greenness is believed to ensure a happy and "green" year ahead. The herbs are chosen according to individual taste and mood, and to what is available. Favorite Iranian herbs include tarragon, chives, flat-leaf parsley, dill, fenugreek, and cilantro. Choose 3 or 4 or use them all, but try to use fresh ones.

    2 cups basmati rice
    Salt
    A huge bunch (2 cups) of mixed herbs,
        including tarragon, chives, flat-leaf
        parsley, cilantro, and dill, finely
        chopped
    6 scallions, finely chopped
    6 tablespoons butter or 4 tablespoons
        vegetable oil

Wash the rice in warm water and drain.

Bring plenty of salted water to the boil. Pour in the rice and boil for about 12 minutes, until the rice is still slightly undercooked. Throw in the herbs and scallions and drain at once. The herbs will cling to the rice.

In the same pot, heat half the butter or oil. Pour in the rice, and add the remaining butter or oil and some salt. Stir gently, cover with a tight-fitting lid, and steam for 15–20 minutes over very low heat.

Variation

You may prefer to mix in the herbs at the end, when the rice has been steamed.

Ispanakli Pilav

Rice with Spinach

Serves 4 • Rice dishes feature in a big way in miniatures depicting the feasts and banquets of the Turkish Ottoman Sultans, and one researcher found mentions of 100 in the archives of Topkapi in Istanbul. Yogurt makes a good accompaniment to this simple and delightful one.

    1 pound fresh spinach
    1 large onion, chopped
    4 tablespoons extra-virgin olive oil or
        vegetable oil
    1½ cups long-grain rice
    2¼ cups water or chicken stock (page
        143) (or you may use a bouillon cube)
    Salt and pepper

Wash and drain the spinach, and remove only tough stems. Cut it coarsely or leave it whole.

Fry the onion in 2 tablespoons of the oil in a large pan till soft.

Add the rice and stir well. Then add the water or stock, salt and pepper, and the spinach. Stir and cook, covered, on very low heat for about 18–20 minutes, or until the rice is tender. Stir in the remaining oil.

Serve hot or cold. Accompany with yogurt, beaten, if you like, with crushed garlic.

The Halicis of Turkey

In all the years that I have been researching food around the world, I have never come across anyone as passionately and selflessly committed to recovering and upholding the culinary heritage of a country as is Nevin Halici of Turkey. She made the first extensive study of the regional foods of Turkey, recording other information, such as the occasions on which dishes are served and what they mean, and allusions to the way of life in each region. She taught cooking in a girls' school, and had been asked to give demonstrations to chefs of some of the big hotels whose management wanted to introduce regional dishes. (Most of the cooks in Turkey come from the region of Bolu and have a historical connection with the old Ottoman palace. They are trained in a particular Istanbul style, and regional foods are unknown to them.)

More than twenty years ago chance took me to Konya, in Central Anatolia, where I met the Halici family. There was a food symposium (in Turkish) and a cooking competition between neighboring villages. The Halicis, headed by Feyzi Halici (a poet and onetime senator), had organized it. They owned a carpet shop and were also in charge of the Culture and Tourism Association.

Their activities included the Mevlana Festival of Whirling Dervishes, the troubadour and rose festivals, horse races, pigeon competitions, the national javelin games, folk poetry and music, and Koran reading competitions.

I asked them if they would consider doing an international food symposium. A few months later I received a letter asking for a list of people who might be interested in attending such an event. It turned out to be the most fantastic, magical affair. Starting with a stay at the Pera Palas in Istanbul, we were invited to travel around the country and taste all manner of foods, many of which were unknown even to the Turkish gastronomes traveling with us. We heard scholarly lectures about the history of Turkish food; we visited palace kitchens and food bazaars and went to see artisans at work. We were invited into people's homes and such places as a factory where the workers had brought dishes from home for a banquet. Other entertainments were belly dancing and sword dancing and whirling dervishes. Feyzi and Nevin Halici invited people from all over the world to biennial food congresses from 1986 until 1994, when the congresses stopped for lack of funds.

Domatesli Pilav

Tomato Pilaf

Serves 4 • A more common version of the tomato pilaf which spread throughout the old Ottoman lands is made exclusively with tomato paste, but this one has a marvelous fresh flavor and delicate salmon color.

- 1¼ cups basmati or long-grain rice
- 1 onion, chopped
- 2 tablespoons vegetable oil
- 2 cloves garlic, crushed
- 1 tablespoon tomato paste
- 1 pound ripe tomatoes, peeled and chopped
- Salt and pepper
- 2 teaspoons sugar

If using basmati, wash the rice in warm water and rinse under the cold tap. American long-grain does not need washing.

Fry the onion in the oil until soft and golden. Add the garlic, and when the aroma rises, stir in the tomato paste and add the tomatoes. Season with salt, pepper, and sugar and cook 20 minutes.

Throw in the rice, and add enough water to cover the rice by about ¾ inch. Bring to the boil and simmer, covered, over low heat for about 20 minutes, until the rice is tender and the water absorbed, adding a little water if it becomes too dry.

Balkabagi Pilav

Pumpkin Pilaf

Serves 4 • The success of this Turkish pilaf depends on the flavor of the orange-fleshed pumpkin, which varies. (It should be sweet-tasting.) I prefer the dish without the raisins.

- 1 pound orange pumpkin (weight with seeds and stringy bits removed)
- 1 onion, chopped
- 2 tablespoons sunflower oil
- 1½ cups basmati or long-grain rice (washed if basmati)
- 2 cups chicken stock (page 143) (or you may use 1 bouillon cube)
- 1 teaspoon cardamom seeds
- 1 teaspoon ground cinnamon
- Salt and pepper
- 1 tablespoon raisins (optional)
- 3 tablespoons butter

This very large type of pumpkin is often sold by the slice. Cut the peel off, and cut it up into ⅔-inch cubes.

Fry the onion in the oil till golden. Add the rice, and stir until the grains are covered in oil. Add the pumpkin and pour in the stock. Add the cardamom seeds, cinnamon, salt, pepper, and raisins if using, and stir well. Simmer, covered, on low heat until the rice and pumpkin are tender.

Stir in the butter, and leave for a few minutes with the lid on before serving.

Roz bel Ful Ahdar

Rice with Fava Beans

Serves 6 • In Egypt this is prepared in the spring, when fava beans are very young and tender. It is served hot as an accompaniment to meat, or cold with yogurt and a salad. Egyptians do not remove the skins of the beans.

> 1 pound fresh shelled or frozen fava
>   beans
> Salt
> Vegetable oil
> 1 large onion, finely chopped
> 3 cloves garlic, crushed
> 1 teaspoon ground coriander
> 2 cups basmati or long-grain rice (wash
>   if using basmati)
> Pepper
> 3 cups water

Boil the beans in salted water for a few minutes, until they are tender, then drain.

Heat 3 tablespoons oil in a pan and fry the onion until soft and golden. Add the garlic and coriander and stir for a moment or two. Then add the drained beans and sauté a little, stirring and turning them over.

Add the rice, and stir until transparent. Add salt and pepper and pour in the water. Bring to the boil and simmer over low heat, covered, for about 20 minutes, until the rice is tender.

Variations

• Omit the coriander and stir into the cooking water 1½ cups chopped fresh dill and ¼ teaspoon saffron powder or crushed threads.

• Another prestigious dish is rice with artichokes. Use a 14-ounce package of frozen and defrosted artichoke hearts or bottoms, cut into quarters, instead of fava beans.

Roz bel Balah

Rice with Dates

Serves 6 • An Arab dish often served with grilled fish.

> 2 cups basmati or long-grain rice
> ⅔ cup blanched almonds, halved
> 5 tablespoons butter or oil
> 3 tablespoons black or golden raisins
> ⅔ cup coarsely chopped California dates
> Salt

If using basmati, wash in warm water and rinse under the cold tap. American long-grain does not need washing.

In a skillet, fry the almonds in half the butter or oil until just golden. Add the raisins and the dates, and stir gently over moderate heat for a few minutes more.

Bring a large pot of salted water to the boil and throw in the drained rice. Boil for 10 minutes, until not quite tender, then drain.

Melt a tablespoon of butter in the pan. Return the rice and stir in the date-and-almond mixture and the remaining butter or oil. Cover with a tight-fitting lid, and steam over very low heat for about 20–30 minutes, until the rice is tender.

Variation

For rice with date syrup (*dibbis*), called *mhammar* in the Gulf States, boil the rice in salted water for 10 minutes, then drain. Heat 1 tablespoon butter at the bottom of the pan and pour the rice back in. Add 2 tablespoons butter, ½ cup date syrup, ½ teaspoon saffron powder, 1 teaspoon ground cardamom, salt, and pepper. Stir well. Put the lid on and leave to steam, covered, over low heat for 20 minutes. You will find date syrup (*dibbis*) in Middle Eastern stores.

Labnieh

Rice with Yogurt

There is a dish of rice cooked in yogurt which has been stabilized so that it doesn't curdle (see page 113), but it is simpler and just as good to pour yogurt over plain rice. Everyone likes this, and Arab doctors prescribe it for people with stomach troubles.

For 6, cook 2 cups of rice using one of the methods on pages 337–339. Beat 2 cups of plain whole-milk yogurt at room temperature in a bowl with 1 tablespoon dried mint, 2 crushed garlic cloves, and a little salt and white pepper. Pour some over each portion of steaming hot rice as you serve.

I also like it plain, without mint or garlic.

"Honor to rice;
let burghul *go hang itself!"*

—an old Lebanese saying
originating from the time
when rice was a delicacy and
was rapidly eclipsing burghul,
until then considered the staple
food of the Lebanon.

Roz bi Dfeen

Rice with Meat and Chickpeas

Serves 6 • This homely dish is a favorite in Syria and Lebanon. Good-quality canned chickpeas will do. If you are using them, drain a 14-ounce can and put them in with the rice.

> 1 pound small pearl or pickling onions
>   or shallots, peeled
> 3 tablespoons butter or vegetable oil
> 1 pound lean beef or lamb, cut into
>   small cubes
> 1/3 cup chickpeas, soaked overnight
> Pepper
> 1 teaspoon ground cumin or cinnamon
> Salt
> 2 cups long-grain rice

To peel the onions more easily, blanch them first in boiling water.

Sauté the onions in the butter or oil in a large, heavy saucepan, stirring and shaking the pan, until golden. Add the meat and stir, turning the pieces over, until browned.

Add the soaked and drained chickpeas, and cover with water. Add pepper and cumin or cinnamon, and simmer gently, covered, for about 1½ hours, or until the meat is very tender and the chickpeas are soft, adding water if necessary, and salt when the chickpeas have begun to soften.

Add enough more water to make the liquid up to about 3 cups. Bring to the boil again, throw in the rice, mix well, and simmer, covered and undisturbed, for about 20 minutes, or until the rice is tender, adding more water if it appears too dry.

Turn off the heat, and allow to rest for a few minutes before serving.

Tavuklu Pilav

Chicken Pilaf

Serves 6 • There is something very comforting about this homely Turkish pilaf in which the rice is cooked in the broth of the chicken. For an Arab version with pine nuts, flavored with cinnamon and cardamom, see the variation.

A 3½–4-pound chicken

Salt and pepper

2 bay leaves

1 sprig of thyme or oregano

2 cups long-grain rice

Put the chicken whole in a large pot. Cover with water, season with salt and pepper, and add 2 bay leaves and the thyme or oregano. Bring to the boil and simmer, covered, for about 1 hour, until the chicken is very tender.

Lift the chicken out, and when it is cool enough to handle, cut into 6 serving pieces. If you like, remove skin and bones. Keep warm in a little of the broth to prevent it from becoming dry. Then cut the rest of the meat into small pieces to be mixed in with the rice.

Measure the remaining broth. If there is more than about 4½ cups, reduce by vigorous boiling. If there is less, add water until you have 4½ cups. Set aside 1½ cups as sauce. Return the small chicken pieces to the 3 cups of stock in the pan. Throw in the rice, stir, and bring to the boil, then reduce the heat and simmer gently, covered and undisturbed, for 20 minutes, until the rice is tender.

To serve, reheat the reserved chicken portions, heap the rice on a large, flat serving dish, and arrange the chicken portions on top. Pass around the 1½ cups of broth for everyone to pour on as a sauce.

Variation

For the Arab *roz bi jaj* (rice with chicken), the stock is perfumed with 1 teaspoon ground cinnamon and 1 teaspoon cardamom seeds. The rice is cooked in the broth with small pieces of chicken, as described above; ⅓ cup blanched almonds and about 2–3 tablespoons pine nuts are lightly fried in oil and arranged at the bottom of an oiled ring or pyramid-shaped mold. The cooked rice is pressed over them, then the mold is turned out onto a serving dish and surrounded by serving pieces of chicken.

Another presentation is to line the mold first with a layer of nuts, then with the boned chicken, and to pack the rice in over the meat. Inverted, this looks beautiful too.

Seleq

Lamb with Rice Cooked in Milk

Serves 8 • Rice cooked in milk for a very long time, until it is a soft cream, is a specialty of Saudi Arabia. It serves as a bed for lamb, often a whole animal, presented on a tray with melted clarified butter trickled on top. It is said that in the city of Taif they make it better than in Jedda or Medina. It is similar to a medieval dish featured in al-Baghdadi's manual (see appendix). Serve with a cucumber, lettuce, and tomato salad. Some people accompany it with honey, to be stirred into each portion separately.

> 1 leg of lamb (about 4 pounds), trimmed of excess fat, boned, and cut into 8 pieces
> 2 onions, finely chopped
> Salt and pepper
> 5 cups milk
> 4 cups long-grain rice
> ¾ cup (1½ sticks) butter, melted

Put the meat with the onions in a large pan. Cover with water, and add salt and pepper. Bring to the boil, remove any scum, and simmer for 2 hours, or until the meat is very tender. Lift out the meat and keep warm with a little broth poured over it.

Add water to the broth in the pan if necessary to bring the volume up to 7 cups. Add the milk and bring to the boil. Then throw in the rice and cook very gently, covered, for about 30 minutes, or until it is very tender and creamy. Adjust the seasoning.

Serve on a large tray with melted butter poured over the rice and the meat arranged on top.

Variations

• Here is a Moroccan way of cooking rice in milk: Boil 1 pound long- or medium-grain rice in plenty of salted water for 10 minutes and drain. Then cook in 5 cups milk to which have been added 3 cinnamon sticks, 3 or 4 grains mastic (pulverized by grinding with a pestle and mortar), 2 tablespoons orange-blossom water, and salt to taste. Simmer gently until all the liquid has been absorbed. Serve in a large dish with a meat stew on top.

• Egyptians do a rice similar to the Moroccans', flavoring it only with cinnamon and a touch of nutmeg.

Kuzu Pilav

Lamb Pilaf

Serves 6 • A popular Turkish pilaf.

3 tablespoons butter or oil
1 large onion, finely chopped
1 pound lean lamb, cut into small pieces
Salt and pepper
1 teaspoon ground cinnamon
2–3 tablespoons tomato paste
3 tablespoons finely chopped flat-leaf
  parsley
2 cups long-grain rice

Heat the butter or oil in a large, heavy-bottomed saucepan, and fry the onion until golden. Add the meat and brown it gently all over. Season with salt, pepper, and cinnamon. Cover and cook the meat and onions over low heat in their own juices for 10 minutes.

Stir in the tomato paste and add water to cover. Sprinkle with finely chopped parsley, bring to the boil, and simmer gently for 1½ hours, until the meat is very tender and the sauce reduced, adding more water if it becomes too dry.

Bring up the liquid left in the stew to about 3–3½ cups by adding water. Stir in the rice, bring to a vigorous boil, then simmer gently over very low heat, covered and undisturbed, for about 20 minutes, or until rice is soft, adding more water if it appears too dry.

Variations

• Add a tablespoon each pine nuts and raisins to the simmering stew.
• Add a sliced sweet pepper and 2 tomatoes, peeled and cut into pieces, to the meat, and cook 5 minutes before adding the tomato paste and water.

Djavaher Polow

Sweet Jeweled Rice

Serves 6 • This Iranian rice, a festive dish served at weddings, is as sumptuous as you get. You can see by its appearance why it is called "jeweled." Iranian and Middle Eastern stores sell barberries (sour berries called *zereshk*), sugared orange peel, and slivered almonds and pistachios. Dried pitted sour cherries and cranberries can be found in some supermarkets.

2 whole chicken breasts, boned and
  skinned
6 tablespoons butter or vegetable oil
Salt
2 cups basmati rice
⅓ cup dried pitted sour cherries
⅓ cup dried cranberries
⅓ cup barberries
¼ teaspoon saffron powder or crushed
  saffron threads
¼ cup candied orange peel (see note,
  page 352) or coarse-cut orange
  marmalade, chopped (optional)
½ cup split blanched almonds
⅓ cup coarsely chopped or slivered
  pistachios

Sauté the chicken breasts in 2 tablespoons of the butter or oil, turning them over once and sprinkling lightly with salt, until lightly browned but still juicy inside. Cut each half breast into about 6 slices.

Wash the rice in warm water and rinse in a colander under the cold tap. Soak the sour cherries, cranberries, and barberries in water for 15 minutes.

Throw the drained rice in plenty of boiling salted water in a large (9–10-inch) preferably nonstick pan and boil for about 10 minutes, until partly cooked and still a little firm, then drain.

Heat 2 tablespoons butter or oil in the bottom of the pan and stir in the saffron. Spread alternate layers of rice, chicken pieces, and the rest of the ingredients, ending with rice and sprinkling lightly with salt. Add the remaining butter (cut in little pieces) or oil over the top at the end.

Put the lid on and steam on the lowest heat for about 20–30 minutes, or until the rice is tender.

For serving, see box below.

Variations

• Instead of the sour cherries and cranberries, have chopped dried apricots and chopped dates, or raisins.

• If you use a nonstick pan, you can turn the rice out like a crusty golden cake.

Serving Persian Polows

Exquisite layered rice dishes—combinations of meat, vegetables, fruit, and nuts with herbs and spices—are the jewels in the crown of Persian gastronomy. They are part of the grand princely cuisine created in the sixteenth century, in the Safavid period, and are still today the festive, celebratory dishes served on very special occasions. Many of the polows you are offered in Iranian homes today could have come straight out of a compilation of recipes by one Ostad Nurollah, a professional cook in Shah Abbas' reign at the end of the sixteenth century.

The rice is first parboiled and drained while still underdone, then layered with other ingredients and steamed over low heat for 20–30 minutes.

To turn out the rice easily, the bottom of the pan is placed in cold water for a minute. The pan is inverted over a large platter and the ingredients gently mixed. The crusty bottom, considered a delicacy, is served on a separate plate. Two or three tablespoons of rice, colored with a little saffron powder mixed with boiling water, are a usual garnish sprinkled on top.

With the coming of nonstick coatings, a version of the rice dishes which comes out looking like a cake with a golden crust has become very popular and is easy to produce. It is thrilling to break into the crisp shiny brown crust to find the sparkling white or saffron-yellow grains encrusted with bits of spiced meat, vegetables, fruit, and nuts tumbling out.

Shirini Polow

Sweet Rice with Carrots and Orange Peel

Serves 6 • Candied tangerine or orange peel is the sweet element in this festive Persian rice with carrots. Persian shops sell the candied peel, as well as slivered almonds and pistachios. To make the candied peel yourself, see the recipe that follows this one.

- 2 cups basmati rice
- 2 whole chicken breasts, skinned and boned
- 7 tablespoons melted butter or vegetable oil
- Salt and pepper
- ½ teaspoon good-quality powdered saffron or crushed saffron threads
- 2 cups carrots cut into thin 1-inch strips
- ¾ cup candied tangerine or orange peel (recipe follows)
- 1 cup blanched almonds or pistachio nuts, chopped

Wash the rice in warm water and rinse in a colander under the cold tap.

Sauté the chicken in 3 tablespoons of the butter or oil with salt and pepper and ¼ teaspoon of the saffron for about 15 minutes, until the chicken is tender but still pink and juicy, turning the pieces to color them lightly all over. Then cut into small pieces.

Sauté the carrots in the same butter or oil for 10 minutes, or until tender, stirring and adding salt and a few tablespoons water.

Boil the rice in a large (9–10-inch) heavy-bottomed preferably nonstick pan for about 10 minutes, until still a little underdone, and drain quickly. Add the remaining ¼ teaspoon saffron to 2 tablespoons of the butter or oil and mix into the rice in the colander. Pour the 2 re-maining tablespoons butter or oil in the bottom of the pan and sprinkle alternate layers of rice and chicken with carrot, candied peel, and nuts in the pan, starting and ending with a layer of rice. (You should have 3 layers of rice.)

Stretch a clean cloth over the top of the pan, put the lid on, and steam over very low heat for 20–30 minutes. The cloth will absorb the steam and help the rice to retain its fluffiness.

For serving, see box on page 351.

Candied Orange Peel

To make candied peel, use the peel of 3 or-anges with as much of the white pith removed as possible. Slice peel into thin strips and make a note of the weight. Simmer without sugar in about ½ cup water until soft. Then add sugar equal to the measured weight, and cook until the water is reduced and the strips of peel are sweet. The peel of bitter oranges is particularly good to use for this dish.

Geisi Polow

Rice with Lamb and Apricots

Serves 6 • Apricots have a particular affinity with lamb. The early Arab Abbasid dynasty, centered in Baghdad, adopted the combination from the old Persian Empire that preceded it and created a series of dishes on the theme which they called *mishmishiya* (see page 255), *mishmish* being the Arab word for "apricot." Apricot is still a favorite partner to lamb in modern Iran. The rest of the Middle East has adopted it to a lesser degree. You need a tart, natural variety of apricots, not a sweetened one.

> 2 cups basmati rice
> 6 tablespoons melted butter or vegetable oil
> 1 onion, finely chopped
> 1 pound lean lamb, cut into small cubes
> Salt and pepper
> ½ teaspoon ground cinnamon
> ¼ teaspoon allspice
> ¾–1 cup tart dried apricots, cut in half
> 2 tablespoons black or golden raisins

Wash the rice in warm water and rinse in a colander under the cold water tap.

Heat 2 tablespoons of the butter or oil in a pan and fry the onion until golden. Add the meat and sauté gently, turning the pieces to brown them all over. Add salt and pepper, cinnamon, allspice, apricots, and raisins. Cover with water and simmer, covered, over low heat for 1–1½ hours, until the meat is very tender and has absorbed the sweet-and-acid flavors of the fruit, adding water as required. Reduce the liquid at the end.

Boil the rice in a large (9–10-inch), heavy-bottomed, preferably nonstick pan for about 10 minutes, until still a little underdone. Then drain, and mix with 2 tablespoons butter or oil.

Pour the remaining butter or oil in the bottom of the pan and mix in a ladle of rice. Arrange alternate layers of rice and meat with apricot sauce, starting and ending with a layer of rice. Cover and steam gently over very low heat for 20–30 minutes, until the rice is tender. A cloth stretched underneath the lid will absorb the steam and make the rice fluffier.

For serving, see box on page 351.

Variations

• You may use 4 boned and skinned portions of chicken, cut into small pieces, instead of meat. They will need only about 20 minutes' cooking before being added to the rice.
• Boil the apricots and raisins separately, in water to cover, for 10 minutes. And arrange them in a layer on top of the meat.
• Add ¼ teaspoon good-quality saffron powder or crushed threads to the melted butter before you mix it into the rice.

Albalou Polow

Rice with Sour Cherries

Serves 6 • I was served this exciting dish by Iranian friends who live near me in London. As the golden crust was broken, the rice, stained patchily with red cherry juice, tumbled out with little meatballs and cooked cherries. Fresh sour cherries are used in Iran in their short season. They are pitted or not, and cooked with sugar until they are jammy. I use dried pitted sour cherries without sugar, with delicious results.

2 cups basmati rice

1½ cups pitted dried sour cherries

1 pound ground lamb or beef

1 onion, grated

Salt and pepper

¾ teaspoon cinnamon

⅓ cup melted butter or vegetable oil

3 tablespoons slivered or chopped almonds

3 tablespoons slivered or chopped pistachios

2–3 tablespoons sour-cherry syrup or jam

Wash the rice in warm water and rinse in a small-holed colander or large strainer under the cold-water tap.

Soak the sour cherries in water to cover for 15 minutes. (If they are of a moist variety they don't need soaking.)

Put the ground meat and grated onion in a bowl and add salt, pepper, and cinnamon. Mix well and knead to a soft paste. Roll into balls the size of large cherries. Fry them briefly in 2 tablespoons of the butter or oil over medium heat in a large skillet for about 10 minutes, turning them or shaking the pan, to brown them all over.

Toss the drained rice into a large (9–10-inch), heavy-bottomed, and preferably non-stick pan of boiling salted water and boil for about 10 minutes, until partly cooked and still a little firm. Then drain quickly.

Heat 2 tablespoons of the butter or oil in the bottom of the pan and mix with a ladle of the rice. Spread alternate layers of rice and meatballs, then drained cherries, beginning and ending with rice. (You should have 3 layers of rice.) Pour the remaining butter or oil all over. Steam, with the lid on, over very low heat for about 20–30 minutes, until the rice is tender.

For serving, see box on page 351. Garnish with the slivered or chopped almonds and pistachios and a dribble of sour-cherry syrup or jam.

Variations

• Use 1 pound of fresh sour cherries, pitted or not.
• Mix ¼ teaspoon good-quality saffron powder or crushed threads with 1 tablespoon hot water and stir into the butter or oil.

Teheran Zereshk

Rice with Chicken and Barberries

Serves 6 • Sour little red berries called barberries (*zereshk* in Persian) and yogurt give this chicken-and-rice dish an exciting flavor and texture. The woman who wrote out this recipe for me more than thirty years ago added a comment that it was the most famous and traditional of Iranian dishes.

2 cups basmati rice

2 whole chicken breasts, boned and skinned

6 tablespoons butter or vegetable oil

Salt and pepper

1½ cups yogurt

1 egg, lightly beaten

¼ teaspoon powdered saffron or crushed saffron threads

⅓ cup dried barberries

Wash the rice in warm water and rinse in a colander under the cold water tap.

Sauté the chicken pieces in 2 tablespoons of the butter or oil until tender, adding salt and pepper and turning them over once. Then cut each piece into 6 slices.

Mix the yogurt and the egg in a large bowl. The egg prevents the yogurt from curdling. Add salt and pepper and the saffron mixed with 2 tablespoons boiling water. Beat well. Put the pieces of chicken in, and turn them so that they are well coated with the mixture. Then lift them out onto a plate.

In a large (9–10-inch), heavy-bottomed, preferably nonstick pan, boil the rice in plenty of salted water for about 10 minutes, until it is still a little underdone, then drain quickly. Mix half the rice with the yogurt mixture.

Heat 2 tablespoons of the butter or oil in the bottom of the pan. Cover the bottom and sides with the rice-and-yogurt mixture to form a kind of inner mold. Put a layer of chicken pieces in this mold, sprinkle with a few barberries, and cover with a layer of plain rice. Repeat, making sure that there is always the wall of yogurt-and-rice mixture on the sides, until the ingredients are finished. Using a piece of plastic wrap, press gently down all over. Put the lid on and cook for about 30 minutes on very low heat.

To serve, turn out onto a serving platter. If the sides are not detached from the pan, cut around them with a pointed knife. The outside should be a crisp brown crust, and the beautiful yellow and white layered inside crumbly. If you are not using a nonstick pan, dipping the bottom into cold water will help you to turn out the rice.

Variation

You can use a nonstick oven dish or pot and bake the layered rice, covered, in a preheated 350°F oven for 1–1½ hours.

THE FEAST OF TANTALUS

One of the notables invited the Khoja to Iftar.* He went to ask him quite early in the day, then took him round from one mosque to another until he became desperately hungry.

As they entered the dining-room he saw stuffed turkey, baklawa, and cakes on the sideboard and felt that he could hold out no longer. As they took their places his mouth began to water.

First some excellent tripe soup was served, and the host with great ceremony proceeded to taste it.

"Drat the man!" he cried. "Kiaya!† come here at once! How often have I bid you tell the cook not to put garlic into the soup? Take it away at once!"

The Khoja looked after it wistfully and gently tightened his belt.

Then turning to him his host remarked, "It is quite impossible to make these cooks understand. They will do as they like, whatever you say to them."

A chorus of voices answered, "They will indeed."

At this moment the turkey was put on the table. It was done to a turn and smelt delicious. The stuffing was made of raisins, rice, and pistachios, and there was so much of it that it went all over the dish.

The host took a small piece, but he had no sooner done so than he cried out furiously, "Aga, come here! Did I not tell you the other day to see that the rascal does not use spice? Do you do this on purpose? Thirty years you have been in my service and yet you allow this to go on! God pay you out for this! Take it away!"

Out went the turkey, and the poor Khoja heaved a deep sigh as he saw his sheet-anchor disappear.

Then a eunuch brought in the baklawa, but the host scowled at him and said, "You stupid Arab! Do hungry people begin with sweets? Away with it!"

As the whip fell on his shoulders, the poor fellow let the dish fall and bolted from the room.

The Khoja, seeing all these tempting dishes carried out one after the other, took his spoon and catching hold of a dish of pilaf which was on a side-table, began to devour it.

"Hullo! what are you doing there, Khoja?" cried the host.

"Oh! sir," said the Khoja, "do give me a chance before you condemn it to the same fate as the others. Let me have a little talk with my old friend the Pilaf—ask how he is and find out what he has inside him! Never mind me!"

At this the guests began to roar with laughter. The dishes were then brought in again, they set to work in earnest and made a merry meal.

BARNHAM, TRANS.,
TALES OF NASR-ED-DIN KHOJA

---

* Iftar is the breaking of the month's fast on the eve of the Bairam. It is also applied to the breaking of the fast every evening.
† Kiaya: head servant, butler, or major-domo.

Addas Polow

Rice with Lentils and Dates

Serves 6 • This exquisite and elegant Persian rice can also be made with chicken.

2 cups basmati rice

½ cup butter or vegetable oil

1 onion, chopped

1 pound lamb or beef, cut into ¾-inch cubes

Salt and pepper

1 teaspoon cinnamon

¼ teaspoon allspice

1 cup brown or green lentils, rinsed

½ teaspoon good-quality powdered saffron or crushed saffron threads diluted in ¼ cup hot water

½ cup black or golden raisins

1 cup pitted dates, split in half or coarsely chopped

⅓ cup blanched almonds (optional)

Wash and drain the rice.

Heat 2 tablespoons of the butter or oil in a skillet, and fry the onion until golden. Add the meat and sauté, stirring and turning the pieces, until browned all over. Cover with water, add salt and pepper, cinnamon, and allspice, and simmer for 1 hour, or until the meat is tender and the liquid absorbed.

Boil the lentils in water for about 20 minutes, until done, adding salt when they begin to soften. Then drain.

Now boil the rice in a heavy-bottomed, preferably nonstick pan for 10 minutes, until not quite tender and still a little underdone. Drain the rice. Melt 2 tablespoons of the butter in the bottom of the pan, then stir in 2 tablespoons of the saffron water and about a third of the rice.

Spread half the meat on top, then sprinkle on half the lentils, raisins, dates, and almonds if using. Cover with a layer of rice and the remaining meat, lentils, raisins, and dates, and finish with the rice that is left. Melt the remaining butter, stir in the remaining saffron water, and pour all over. Cook, covered, on very low heat for 20–30 minutes.

To serve, see box on page 351.

Havij Polow

Rice with Carrots

Serves 6 • This lovely Persian *polow* is served with lamb meatballs buried in the rice (see note), or as an accompaniment to a roast leg of lamb (see page 233).

- 2 cups basmati rice
- 1 onion, finely chopped
- $1/3$–$1/2$ cup butter or vegetable oil
- $1\frac{1}{2}$ pounds carrots, coarsely grated or cut into little sticks
- 1–2 tablespoons sugar, or more (optional)
- 1 teaspoon ground cinnamon (optional)
- Salt
- 1 tablespoon rose water

Wash the rice in warm water and rinse in a colander under the cold water tap.

Fry the onion in 2–3 tablespoons of the butter or oil until soft and golden. Add the grated carrots and sauté gently for 10 minutes. Add sugar and cinnamon and cook 3–4 minutes longer.

Boil the rice in salted water in a large (9–10-inch), heavy-bottomed, preferably non-stick saucepan for about 10 minutes, until not quite tender and still a little underdone. Drain and mix with the remaining butter or oil, keeping aside 2 tablespoons. Heat the 2 tablespoons butter or oil in the bottom of the pan, then spread alternate layers of rice and sautéed carrots, starting and ending with a layer of rice. Sprinkle rose water over the top and cook over very low heat for about 30 minutes. The rose water, a relic of early-medieval times, gives a subtle perfume to the dish.

To serve, see box on page 351.

Note: For meatballs, season $1\frac{1}{2}$ pounds ground lamb with salt, pepper, and 1 teaspoon cinnamon. Mix well and knead until smooth and pasty. Shape into marble-sized balls and fry in a little oil for about 8–10 minutes, turning them over, until browned all over but still pink and juicy inside.

Almond Sauce for Rice

Serves 4 • An exquisite specialty of Damascus in Syria to serve over $1\frac{1}{2}$ cups rice, cooked by any method for plain rice (pages 337–339).

- $1/2$ cup ground almonds
- $2\frac{1}{2}$ cups chicken stock (page 143)
- Salt and white pepper
- 2 cloves garlic, crushed
- 2 tablespoons chopped flat-leaf parsley plus 2 tablespoons to garnish
- $1/2$ teaspoon sugar
- Juice of 1 lemon, or more
- Pinch of turmeric (optional)

Mix the almonds and cold stock together in a saucepan. Bring to the boil, season to taste, and add all the other ingredients. A pinch of turmeric may be used to give the sauce an attractive pale-yellow color. Simmer gently, stirring occasionally, for 20–30 minutes, until the mixture thickens and the ingredients have blended to give a rich, flavorsome sauce.

Serve ladled over rice, with a sprinkling of chopped parsley.

Variation

Add some chicken, cut into small pieces, and 2 tablespoons pine nuts.

Roz ou Hamud

Rice with Hamud Sauce

Serves 6 • This rice with a delicious lemony vegetable sauce called *hamud* is much loved in Egypt. Use chicken giblets or a chicken carcass to make a rich stock. It is also acceptable to use bouillon cubes. Serve this to accompany chicken dishes.

2 cups long-grain rice

1 turnip, cut into pieces

1 large potato, cut into small pieces

2 stalks celery with leaves, chopped

2 leeks, thinly sliced

2 or 3 zucchini, thinly sliced

2 quarts chicken stock (page 143)

Salt and pepper

4 cloves garlic, chopped

Juice of 1–2 lemons, to taste

2 tablespoons chopped fresh mint

2 tablespoons chopped flat-leaf parsley

Prepare plain rice according to one of the recipes on pages 337–339.

Put all the vegetables in a pan with the stock. Bring to the boil and remove any scum. Add salt, pepper, garlic, and lemon juice. (Start with the lesser amount of lemon juice and add more later.) The sauce is meant to be very tart.

Simmer gently, covered, for about 45 minutes, until the potato has practically disintegrated and the other vegetables are extremely soft, adding water if necessary. Add the mint and parsley towards the end. Serve, pouring the sauce over each portion of rice with a ladle.

Variation

Put 6 chicken wings, or 1 or 2 breast halves, in with the vegetables. Remove skin and bones and cut up into small pieces before serving.

A TALE OF GOHA

One day Goha went to the market. He stopped to gaze into the window of a restaurant where pilafs, stews, chickens, fish, and other appetizing dishes were displayed. As he stood there enjoying the delicious aromas which reached him through the open door, the head cook hailed him:

"Come in, sir, and make yourself at home!"

Believing that he was being invited as a guest, Goha accepted. He sat down and ate as much as he could of all the dishes, filling his pockets with pilaf to take home to his son. But as he got up to leave, the head cook called out:

"Pay me! You have eaten ten piasters' worth of food!"

"But I haven't any money," Goha replied. "I thought I was your guest."

The head cook dragged Goha before the Emir, who ordered him to be driven through the streets sitting backwards on a donkey as a punishment. As he proceeded through the town in this manner, followed by a train of jeering onlookers, some of them even playing music on pipes and drums, a friend saw him and exclaimed:

"What are you doing, Goha? Why are they treating you in this manner?"

"I was served good pilaf for nothing, with extra thrown in for my son," replied Goha. "And now I am having a free donkey ride with free music as well!"

Persian Khoresht-ha

SAUCES FOR RICE

Of all the favorite Persian dishes, the most common and most representative are the combined rice dishes, or *polow,* and the sauces, or *khoresht-ha,* that are served over white rice or with nan bread, and represent a main dish. It is in these dishes, most of all, that the refined knowledge and experience of centuries have crystallized to give the exquisite combinations of meat with vegetables, fruits, nuts, herbs, and spices.

Khoresht-ha are, by English standards, stews rather than sauces. A great variety of ingredients are used to make them. Meat and poultry are cut into smallish pieces. Vegetables are diced, sliced, or left in larger pieces. Fruits are sliced and cut, nuts chopped, and dried beans soaked. Fresh herbs are used. Delicate spices are used in small quantities—the sauces are never hot, peppery, or strong. Occasionally, a drop of rose water is added. Sweet-and-sour pomegranate syrup is a favorite flavoring. The ingredients are usually sautéed in butter or oil, then water is added, never very much, and they are left to cook slowly and gently for a long time, until the juices and flavors blend.

These sauces vary from family to family and according to which ingredients are in season. In the summer, all the local vegetables find their way in. As they become more scarce, apples and quinces appear, and when they, too, disappear in the winter, their place is taken by nuts and dried fruits. Since the stews contain both meat and vegetables, they can be served as meals in themselves with rice. In modern Iran they are often preceded by an omelet. The traditional meat in Iran was always lamb—leg or shoulder, or lamb shanks—but these days, especially in expatriate communities, people also use beef or veal and chicken. The usual fat is butter or rendered lamb fat. I love the flavor, but, because I have been used to cooking with oil, I find that lighter and the result equally delicious.

Khoresht-e Ghormeh Sabzi

Herb Sauce

Serves 6 • This is one of the most popular sauces in Iran and a favorite of mine. Dried limes and the herb fenugreek give it a unique and delicious bitter-sour taste. Flat-leaf parsley, chives, and in some versions dill and cilantro complete the symphony of flavors. Fresh fenugreek can be found in Iranian and Oriental stores in the summer, and packets of dried fenugreek leaves are available the year round. Only a little is used, because it is very powerful. The dried limes can be found in Oriental and Indian stores in various forms, whole, broken into pieces, and powdered. To make them yourself, see page 44. If you can't find the powdered one, add an extra whole one. Serve with plain rice steamed in the Persian manner (page 338) or the quick and easy boiled and steamed rice (page 339).

- 1 large onion, finely chopped
- 6 tablespoons vegetable oil
- 1½ pounds beef or lamb, cut into ¾–1-inch cubes
- 4 dried limes (page 44)
- 1 tablespoon ground dried lime (see above)
- Salt and pepper
- 2 leeks, green part included, chopped
- 8 scallions, green part included, chopped
- 1 cup chopped flat-leaf parsley
- ½ cup chopped cilantro (optional)
- ¼ cup chopped dill (optional)
- ¼ cup chopped fresh fenugreek leaves or 2 tablespoons dried leaves
- A 1-pound can red kidney beans or black-eyed peas, drained

Fry the onion in 2 tablespoons of the oil till soft. Add the meat and turn the pieces until browned all over. Add about 4 cups of water, to cover. Bring to the boil and remove the scum, then turn down the heat. With the point of a knife, make little holes in the dried limes and put them in, as well as the ground dried lime. Add salt and pepper.

As soon as you have put the meat in, prepare the green vegetables and herbs. Chop the leeks and scallions finely in the food processor. Then chop the rest of the herbs. My impulse is usually to put the herbs in at the last minute, but in this recipe it is quite different. They are sautéed first, then cooked with the meat for a long time. Heat the remaining 4 tablespoons oil in a large pan and put all the vegetables and herbs in together. Sauté, stirring often, over medium heat for about 15 minutes, until they begin to darken. Then add to the meat (if you are using dried fenugreek leaves, put them in at this stage) and simmer for about 1½–2 hours, until the meat is very tender.

Add the kidney beans about ½ hour before the end of the cooking. As the limes soften, squeeze them with a spoon on the side of the pan so that they absorb the liquid and cease to float on the surface.

Serve very hot over plain white rice.

Khoresht-e Gheimeh

Yellow Split Pea Sauce

Serves 6 • This Persian sauce is exquisite, with delicate spicing and dried lime as the dominant flavor. Serve it with plain rice prepared in the Persian manner (page 338) or the quick and easy boiled and steamed rice (page 339).

> 1 large onion, chopped
> 2–3 tablespoons vegetable oil
> 1½ pounds lamb or beef cut into 1-inch cubes
> 4½ cups water
> ½ teaspoon turmeric
> 1 teaspoon cinnamon
> ¼ teaspoon nutmeg
> Pepper
> 4 dried limes (page 44)
> ¾ cup yellow split peas, soaked in water for 1 hour
> Salt

In a large pan, fry the onion in the oil until soft. Add the meat and sauté, turning to brown it all over. Add the water and bring to the boil.

Remove the scum and add turmeric, cinnamon, nutmeg, and pepper. Pierce a few little holes in the dried limes with a pointed knife and put them in.

Simmer for 1 hour, then add the drained split peas and cook ½–1 hour more, or until the meat and split peas are very tender, adding salt towards the end and more water, if needed, to keep the meat covered.

Variation

The rice and sauce are also served topped with fried diced potatoes. These are added in the pan, at the end of cooking, to sit on the surface of the stew and soak up some of the sauce.

Khoresh Bademjan

Eggplant Sauce

Serves 4–6 • Chicken may be used instead of meat. Serve with plain rice steamed in the Persian manner (page 338) or the quick and easy boiled and steamed rice (page 339). The eggplants are usually deep-fried, but in this instance it is as good to broil or grill them, as they get stewed as well. If you don't fry them, it is not really important to salt them (see page 289).

> 1 large onion, chopped
> Vegetable oil
> 1 pound lean lamb or beef, cubed
> 2 dried limes (page 44), cracked or pierced with the point of a knife, or the juice of 1 lemon
> 3 tomatoes, peeled and chopped
> Pepper
> ½–1 teaspoon turmeric (optional)
> ½ teaspoon ground cinnamon
> ¼ teaspoon grated nutmeg
> ⅓ cup yellow split peas
> Salt
> 6 small eggplants (3½–4 inches long), peeled and cut in half lengthwise

Fry the onion in 2 tablespoons oil in a large saucepan until golden. Add the meat and brown it on all sides. Add the dried limes or lemon juice, and tomatoes. Cover with 2½ cups water and add pepper, turmeric, cinnamon, and nutmeg.

Simmer gently for 1 hour, then add the split peas and cook for 20 minutes. Season with salt when the split peas have begun to soften, and add more water occasionally, if needed to keep the meat covered.

Brush the cut side of the eggplants generously with oil and cook them, on the cut side only, under the broiler or on the grill until browned. They do not need to be entirely cooked, as they will cook further in the stew.

Add them to the stew, and cook, covered, for 30 minutes longer, or until the eggplants are very soft.

Variations

- Fry 1 small chopped onion in 2 tablespoons oil until golden. Add 2 tablespoons dried crushed mint and 2 crushed garlic cloves. When the garlic just begins to color, pour over the sauce at the end, as a garnish.
- If you can get hold of unripe grapes, put them into the stew instead of the dried limes.

Khoresht-e Rivas

Rhubarb Sauce

Serves 4–6 • Serve this Persian sauce, which has an unusual tart flavor, with plain rice steamed in the Persian manner (page 338) or the quick and easy boiled and steamed rice (page 339).

4 tablespoons butter or vegetable oil
1 onion, finely chopped
1 pound lean stewing beef or lamb, cubed
Salt and pepper
½ teaspoon cinnamon
¼ teaspoon allspice
1 pound fresh rhubarb stalks
Juice of ½ lemon
½ cup chopped flat-leaf parsley
¼ cup chopped fresh mint

Heat 2 tablespoons of the butter or oil in a large saucepan and fry the onion until golden. Add the meat and sauté, turning the pieces, until browned all over. Cover with water and add salt, pepper, cinnamon, and allspice. Bring to the boil and simmer for 1½ hours, until the meat is very tender, adding water to keep the meat covered.

Trim the rhubarb stalks and cut them into 2-inch lengths. Sauté in the remaining butter or oil for a few minutes, then sprinkle with lemon juice and cook for a few minutes longer. Add to the meat sauce with the parsley and mint and simmer for 10 minutes.

Khoresht-e Sib

Apple Sauce

Serves 4–6 • Serve with plain rice steamed in the Persian manner (page 338) or the quick and easy boiled and steamed rice (page 339).

- 1 onion, finely chopped
- 4–5 tablespoons butter or vegetable oil
- 1 pound lamb or beef, cut into cubes
- Salt and pepper
- 1 teaspoon cinnamon
- 4 tart cooking apples
- Juice of 1 lemon, or more

Fry the onion in 2 tablespoons of the butter or oil in a large saucepan until soft and golden. Add the meat, and turn to brown it all over. Add salt, pepper, and cinnamon. Cover with about 2½ cups of water. Bring to the boil, remove any scum, and simmer gently for 1½ hours, or until the meat is very tender, adding water as needed to keep the meat moist.

Peel and core the apples and cut into thick slices. Sauté gently in the remaining butter or oil in a large skillet until lightly colored all over. Add to the meat stew with the lemon juice. Cook for a further 5 minutes, or until tender. Do not allow the apples to disintegrate, unless you prefer to mash them to a puree with a fork.

Serve with plain rice.

Variation

You can add ⅓ cup split peas to the stew ½ hour before the end of the cooking, and chicken can be used instead of meat.

Khoresht-e Holu

Peach Sauce

Peaches are much loved in Iran and are used in cooking. Prepare this sauce as in the preceding recipe, using either meat or chicken, and substituting 4–5 large, slightly unripe peaches or nectarines, preferably not-quite-ripe ones, for the apples. To peel them easily, first plunge them in boiling water for moments only. Then peel, remove the pits, and slice them or cut them into largish pieces. Sauté briefly in butter or oil, and add them to the sauce with ½ cup chopped flat-leaf parsley and 3 tablespoons chopped fresh mint. Simmer for a further 5 to 10 minutes. Here again, lemon juice and cinnamon are the flavoring. Some people like to add about 1–2 tablespoons sugar.

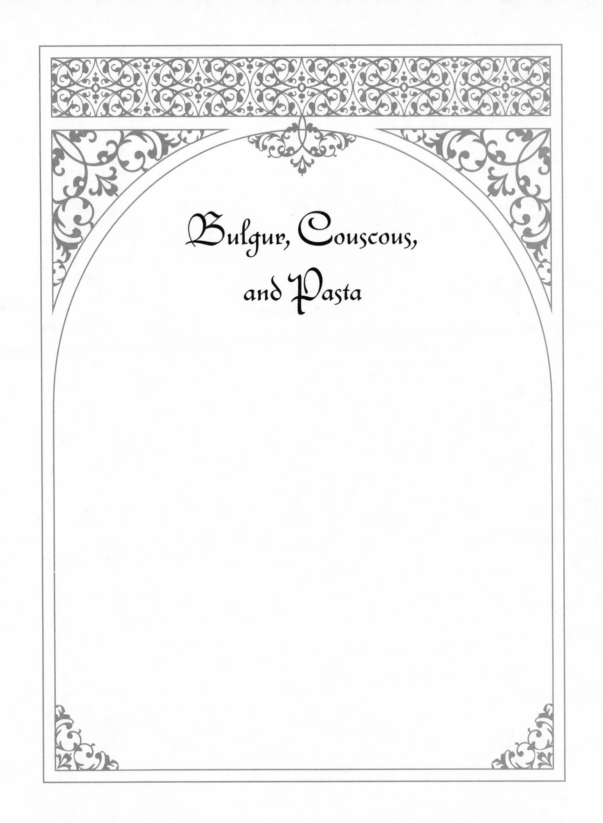

Bulgur, Couscous, and Pasta

Bulgur

Cracked Wheat

Cracked wheat—*burghul* in Arabic, *bulgur* in Turkey, and *pourgouri* in Cyprus—is the rural staple of the Arab world and Turkey. In the countryside it takes the place of rice as an accompaniment to all kinds of dishes. It is whole wheat kernels that have been boiled, then dried and ground. In the old days in rural areas, before mechanization, and still today in some parts, it is made collectively. The men harvest the wheat. The women separate the grain from the chaff. They wash the grain and boil it for hours in huge pots until it splits, then dry it in the sun, spread out on large sheets laid out on the flat roofs of houses or in the fields. When it is dry and hard, it is taken to be ground in a stone mill. Bulgur is now manufactured in the United States. Three types of grind—coarse, medium, and fine—can be found in Middle Eastern stores, but the medium one is the most widely available.

Bulgur is usually washed before cooking. Pour cold water over it in a bowl. Stir well, then rinse in a small-holed colander under the tap. However, when I have omitted washing, I have not detected much difference in the final dish.

Plain Bulgur Pilaf

Serves 6–8 • Coarse-ground bulgur is used to make pilaf. About one and a half times the volume of water or stock is needed to cook it. This quick and easy dish is an ideal alternative to rice or potatoes. You may well want to adopt it as an accompaniment to stews, grills, and indeed to all foods that are usually coupled with rice. It is tastier when real chicken or meat stock is used (see page 143), but you can use bouillon cubes, and water alone will do very well.

4$\frac{1}{2}$ cups water or stock (or you may use 2 bouillon cubes)

3 cups coarse-ground bulgur, washed in cold water and drained

Salt and pepper

4–5 tablespoons butter, cut into small pieces, or vegetable oil

Bring the water or stock to the boil in a large pan and pour in the bulgur. Add salt and pepper (taking into account the saltiness of the stock) and cook, covered, over low heat for 10–15 minutes, until it is tender and all the liquid is absorbed, adding a little water if it becomes too dry.

Stir in the butter or oil and leave off heat, covered, for 15 minutes, to allow the wheat to swell and become tender before serving.

Variations

• For a grand and delicious pilaf, stir in 2–3 tablespoons toasted pine nuts or slivered almonds and 2 tablespoons raisins when you pour in the bulgur.

• For *burghul bil shaghria,* use half the amount of bulgur with $\frac{1}{2}$ pound dry vermicelli broken into small pieces in your hands and toasted in a dry frying pan or under the broiler, stirring often, until browned.

Bulgur Pilaf with Chickpeas

Serves 8 • This is filling comfort food which fits easily with other dishes. You find it in Turkey and in Arab countries.

4$\frac{1}{2}$ cups water or chicken or meat stock (page 143) (or you may use 2 meat or chicken bouillon cubes)

3 cups coarse-ground bulgur, washed in cold water and drained

4 tablespoons butter or sunflower oil

A 14-ounce can chickpeas, drained

Salt and pepper

Bring the stock to the boil. Pour in the bulgur and cook, covered, on low heat for about 15 minutes, or until the water is absorbed and the grain is tender.

Stir in the butter or oil, the chickpeas, and salt and pepper, and heat through.

Variation

Garnish with 1 large sliced onion fried in oil till caramelized and brown.

Bulgur Pilaf with Raisins and Pine Nuts

Serves 6–8 • This grand bulgur pilaf spread throughout the countries that were part of the Ottoman Empire. It is used as a side dish and a stuffing.

4½ cups chicken stock (page 143) (or you may use a bouillon cube) or water

3 cups (1 pound) coarse-ground bulgur, washed in cold water and drained

Salt and pepper

½ cup pine nuts

4–5 tablespoons butter or vegetable oil

⅓ cup black or golden raisins, soaked in water for ½ hour

Bring the water or stock to boil in a pan. Add the bulgur, salt (taking into account the saltiness of the stock), and pepper and stir, then cook, covered, on very low heat for about 15 minutes, or until the liquid is absorbed and the grain tender. Turn off the heat and leave, covered, for 10 minutes, or until the grain is plump and tender.

Fry the pine nuts in a tablespoon of the butter or oil, shaking the pan until golden. Stir it into the bulgur with the remaining butter or oil and the drained raisins and heat through.

Burghul bi Banadoura

Bulgur Pilaf with Tomatoes

Serves 6–8 • Tomatoes give this pilaf a wonderful fresh flavor. It can be eaten hot as a side dish or cold as a mezze. If it is to be eaten cold, you might like to use a mild-tasting olive oil.

1 large onion, chopped

5 tablespoons vegetable or extra-virgin olive oil

3 cups coarse-ground bulgur, washed in cold water and drained

1 pound tomatoes, peeled and chopped

2 teaspoons tomato paste

2 teaspoons sugar

Salt and pepper

1 teaspoon allspice

1½ cups water

Fry the onion in 2 tablespoons of the oil till golden. Add the bulgur and stir well.

Add the tomatoes, tomato paste, sugar, salt, pepper, allspice, and water. Stir and cook, covered, over very low heat for 15 minutes, adding a little water if too dry, or letting it evaporate uncovered if too wet. Leave to rest, covered, for 10 minutes, or until the grain is plump and tender, then stir in the remaining oil.

Variation

Fry 2 medium eggplants, cut into 1-inch cubes, in shallow oil until lightly browned all over and soft inside. Drain on paper towels and fold gently into the bulgur.

Burghul bi Jibn wal Batinjan

Bulgur with Cheese and Eggplants

Serves 4–6 • This Syrian recipe which combines bulgur with eggplants and the salty, chewy halumi cheese makes a lovely vegetarian main dish.

1 eggplant, weighing about ¾ pound, cut into 1-inch cubes

Salt

1½ large onions, sliced

Vegetable oil

2 cups coarse-ground bulgur, washed in cold water and drained

3¼ cups boiling water or chicken stock (page 143) (or you may use a bouillon cube)

Pepper

7–9 ounces halumi cheese, cubed

Sprinkle the eggplant generously with salt and leave in a colander for ½ hour to degorge its juices. Then rinse, and dry with paper towels.

Fry the onions in 2 tablespoons oil till golden. Add the bulgur and stir. Pour in the boiling water or stock, season with salt and pepper, and stir well, then cook on very low heat, with the lid on, for about 15 minutes, or until the water has been absorbed and the cracked wheat is tender.

Fry the cubed eggplant briefly in hot oil, turning the cubes so that they are lightly colored all over. Lift out, and drain on paper towels.

Stir 4 tablespoons oil into the bulgur. Add the cheese and the eggplant and gently fold them in. Heat through with the lid on until the cheese is soft. Serve very hot.

Burghul bi Dfeen

Bulgur with Meat and Chickpeas

Serves 6 • A very old Arab dish. It is good to serve yogurt with it.

12 pearl or pickling onions, peeled

Vegetable oil

1 pound lean lamb or beef, cut into ¾-inch cubes

⅔ cup chickpeas, soaked in cold water overnight

5 cups water

Pepper

1 teaspoon cinnamon

1 teaspoon allspice

Salt

2 cups coarse- or medium-ground bulgur

4–6 tablespoons melted butter (optional)

Fry the onions in 2–3 tablespoons oil, shaking the pan to brown them lightly all over. Add the meat and sauté, turning the pieces over, until browned.

Add the drained chickpeas and cover with water. Add pepper, ½ teaspoon cinnamon, and the allspice and simmer, covered, until the meat and chickpeas are very tender, about 1–1½ hours. Add salt when the chickpeas have softened.

Add the bulgur, stir well, and cook, covered, for about 15 minutes, until all the liquid has been absorbed, adding a little water if it seems too dry. Let sit, covered, for about 15 minutes, while the grain becomes swollen and tender. It is usual to pour melted butter into the pan before serving, but you may leave this out.

Serve sprinkled with the remaining cinnamon.

Etli Bulgur Pilavi

Bulgur Pilaf with Meat

Serves 6 • This old Turkish classic is a meal in itself, to be accompanied by a salad.

- 2 onions, chopped
- 6–8 tablespoons butter or vegetable oil
- 1/2 pound lean lamb or beef, cut into 2/3-inch cubes
- Salt and pepper
- 3 large tomatoes, peeled and chopped
- 1 1/2 tablespoons tomato paste
- 2 cups coarse- or medium-ground bulgur, washed in cold water and drained

In a large saucepan, fry the onions in 2–3 tablespoons of the butter or oil until golden. Add the meat and sauté over moderate heat for a few minutes, turning to brown the pieces all over. Season with salt and pepper and stir in the tomatoes and tomato paste. Cover with water and simmer gently, covered, for 1–1 1/2 hours, or until the meat is tender, adding water to keep the meat covered but letting it reduce towards the end.

Add the bulgur and about 2 cups boiling water—assuming there are about 2 cups of liquid sauce already in the pan. Add more if there is not. Add salt, stir well, and cook, covered, over low heat for about 10–15 minutes, or until the liquid has been absorbed, adding a little water if it seems too dry. Let stand for a further 15 minutes, while the grain becomes swollen and tender. The bulgur should be plump and soft. Stir in the remaining butter or oil before serving.

Variations

- Substitute 2 chicken joints (1 thigh and 1 breast half, for instance) for the meat. Cook for about 30 minutes, then remove skin and bones and cut up the chicken into small cubes.
- Add 1/2 cup chopped flat-leaf parsley. Mix it in at the end.

Tagen Ferakh bel Ferik

Baked Chicken with Green Wheat

Serves 4–6 • This Egyptian village dish usually made with pigeons (*hamam*) is just as good, and easier to make, with a good corn-fed chicken. *Ferik* is young green wheat which has been harvested before it is ripe and set alight between layers of straw. The moist young kernels are separated from the charred chaff and straw by threshing, then washed and dried and coarsely ground. There is a pleasant roughness and a lingering smoky flavor about this grain. You will find it (also spelled *frika*) in Middle Eastern stores. It needs to be washed in 2 or 3 changes of water.

A 3½-pound chicken
1 medium onion, peeled and left whole,
    and 1 large onion, chopped
Salt and pepper
1 teaspoon ground cardamom
1½ teaspoons cinnamon
¼ teaspoon allspice
4 tablespoons butter or vegetable oil
2 cups *ferik,* washed

Put the chicken in a pan with the whole onion and cover with water. Bring to the boil and remove the scum. Add salt, pepper, cardamom, cinnamon, and allspice, and simmer for 1 hour.

In another pan, fry the chopped onion in 2 tablespoons of the butter or oil until soft. Add the drained *ferik* (green wheat) and stir for 1–2 minutes. Pour in 1 cup of the chicken broth, stir well, and cook for 5 minutes, until the water is absorbed. Then stir in the remaining butter.

Lift out the chicken, cut it into pieces, and arrange in a baking dish. A clay one with straight sides, called a *tagen,* is used in Egypt.

Spread the wheat on top. Reduce the chicken broth remaining in the pan and boil it down to about 1½ cups. Pour 1½ cups of broth over the wheat, cover with foil, and cook in a preheated 350°F oven for about 30 minutes.

Variation

For *hamam bel ferik,* use 4 baby squabs instead of the chicken, and leave them whole.

Ferik

Green Wheat

Serves 4 • Ferik (also spelled *frika*), or green wheat, which is very common in the Egyptian countryside, makes a good side dish. It has a wonderful earthy texture and an unusual smoky flavor. (See the introduction to the preceding recipe.)

1 cup *ferik*
1½ cups water
Salt
2 tablespoons butter

Wash the *ferik* in 2 or 3 changes of water, then rinse in a colander.

Bring the water with salt to the boil in a saucepan. Add the *ferik*, bring to the boil again, and cook, covered, over low heat for about 15 minutes, or until the grain is tender, adding a little water if it is too dry.

Stir in the butter and leave, covered, for about 10 minutes before serving.

Kesksou

Couscous

Couscous is the staple food and national dish of the Maghreb—the North African countries of Morocco, Tunisia, Algeria, and Libya. The processed grain is durum hard-wheat semolina which has been ground a little coarsely, then moistened and coated or "rolled" in flour (usually durum flour). The resulting granules are cooked by steaming. (Other grains—barley, corn, and millet—are also used, to make different kinds of couscous.) The name also refers to dishes based on the grain—soupy stews with meat, chicken, or fish and vegetables, over which the grain is steamed.

According to French statistics, couscous has become the dish most commonly eaten outside the home in France today. They call the phenomenon "*la conquète de la France par le couscous*" (the conquest of France by couscous). It happened as a result of the great waves of "Pieds Noirs" (returning settlers from the old French colonies) and North African immigrant workers who have come to France since the colonies gained independence. To French people, couscous is the cheap filling meal you can get in the small corner restaurant. Because the greater number of immigrants are from Algeria, it is an Algerian type of couscous, with tomato paste and plenty of peppery harissa (page 464), that has emerged as the standard, with the usual kind of transformations that occur when dishes move to a new country and from the home to the café. The famous *couscous royal* with different meats, some boiled, some grilled, and the *couscous merguez* with spicy sausages, have nothing to do with dishes in North Africa.

In North Africa, couscous is served on great occasions both happy and sad—at funerals and at weddings. It is a celebratory dish served at the end of great feasts to make sure that no one could be left hungry. Usually it is the musicians and the tolbas, the men who come to pray in expectation of a good meal, who get to eat it. At home, it is the traditional Friday meal, into which goes any vegetable left over from the week's provisions. And it is the food sent to the mosque to be distributed to the poor.

Couscous is associated with the indigenous Berbers, who call it *kesksou*. No written reference was made of it until the thirteenth century, at the time when the Almohad dynasty ruled Andalusia and all of North Africa, when it featured prominently in culinary manuscripts of both the Maghreb and Spain. The special type of durum wheat which is used originated in Ethiopia and was supposedly introduced in the region by the Arabs by the tenth century. But it is in the Berber lands, where steaming in a clay colander placed over a steaming pot was an age-old practice, that the special way of rolling the grain and cooking it over a stew was developed. A few couscous dishes have been adopted by other Arab countries, such as Egypt and Lebanon, where they call it *maghrebia* (perhaps because the word *cous* in Arabic is an unmentionable part of the female anatomy), but these dishes are very different from the ones of North Africa.

Until not very long ago, in North Africa, every family bought its wheat at the market and took it to the local mill to be ground to the degree of fineness they preferred. Back home, the grain went through a process of rolling with fine flour. Large amounts were prepared to be stored, or for occasions such as a wedding or a circumcision or a return from a pilgrimage to Mecca. Women from the family and neighbors got together to do it. The preparation took hours, but it was a day of fun and rejoicing, when the women gossiped and laughed and sang. When the rolled grain was to be stored so that it could keep, it was steamed for about twenty minutes, then dried out in the shade in the open for two days on sheets laid out on rooftops. Nowadays very few women roll their own grain, even in the country-side. The process has been industrialized, and they buy it ready-rolled and partially precooked, or an instant (precooked) variety which they can get in three different grades: fine, medium, and large. Those who will only have the homemade cous-cous for a special event call professional artisans—Berber women or dadas (see page 125)—to the house to make it.

Traditionalists and purists find the commercial instant or quick-cooking variety unacceptable, even offensive. It certainly does not have the special quality of the real thing, used as soon as the grain has been rolled, but I suspect they are also mourning the loss of an old culture and the rituals that accompany it. The instant or quick-cooking couscous is used in many North African restaurants in Paris and by busy families in France as well as in Algeria, Tunisia, and Morocco, and it is that which you will find in your supermarket and specialty store. If you treat it in the best possible way—and it can also be the easiest way—it will give you very good results. The aim is to make it swell and become extremely light and airy, each grain soft, delicate, velvety, and separate from its neighbor.

There are many regional and seasonal versions of the dish. Every family makes couscous in their own special way, and every time it is made, it is different. It can be very simple, with the grain and one vegetable alone, or it can be quite grandiose, with baby pigeons sitting on a mountain of grain with a scattering of almonds and raisins.

The soup or stew is generally made with meat, usually lamb, or chicken, and a number of vegetables. Chickpeas are often added, and sometimes raisins too. The broth may be colored red with tomato paste or yellow with saffron or turmeric. Many spices are used, but sparingly, so that one can hardly define each individual aroma.

In Algeria and Tunisia a fiery sauce is prepared separately with some of the broth mixed with harissa or with ground chili pepper. This sauce is served beside the couscous for those who wish to be "inflamed and intoxicated." In Morocco stews are light, with a delicate and aromatic blend of flavorings. In Tunisia and Algeria, where the meat, and sometimes the vegetables too, are first braised in butter or oil, they are heavier and more strongly flavored. Tunisians like their stews hot and peppery. Algerians often add tomato paste.

Couscous has become very fashionable in America these days. It is used by chefs in all kinds of inventive ways. For people at home it can be the easiest thing to prepare in advance and to serve at a large dinner party. It is quite spectacular, and there is something about the dish that inspires conviviality. For those who have been to North Africa, it evokes the extraordinarily exotic charms of the Maghreb.

How Couscous Is Rolled by Hand

Processing couscous requires experience, skill, and patience. A few handfuls of semolina (medium-ground durum wheat) are spread in a wide, round, shallow wooden or clay dish. The semolina is sprinkled with a little cold salted water and rolled with the fingers of an open hand so that it is moistened evenly. Then it is rolled with a circular clockwise movement with the fingers and palm of the hand, as it is sprayed with repeated sprinklings of flour (usually fine durum flour) and salted water, until the semolina granules are evenly coated with flour to form tiny balls. Up to a pound of flour can be used to coat a pound of semolina. The rolled granules are shaken through two or three sieves with different-sized holes (the first with larger holes) to sort them by size, and lastly through a very fine sieve to eliminate the excess flour. Larger granules are enlarged with more rolling in flour and used separately as a type of pasta called *berkoukes* or *mhammas*.

Cooking Couscous

Steaming Traditional Couscous

The traditional method of cooking couscous (the "real thing," not the quick-cooking variety) is by steaming over a watery stew or over water. The method calls for delicate handling. Bad handling will result in a lumpy and rather stodgy couscous.

The grain must cook only in the steam. It must not touch the broth throughout the steaming. The *couscoussier,* the pot traditionally used, is made of glazed earthenware or tinned copper, and, more recently, of aluminum or stainless steel, and has two parts—the bottom is a large round pot in which the stew is cooked, the top consists of a colander to hold the couscous. If you cannot get an authentic *couscoussier,* you can improvise with a metal colander with small holes that fits snugly over a large pan. It is important that steam can escape only from the top, so seal the join with a band of wet cloth (it is most effective if the wet cloth is steeped in a flour-and-water paste) or with aluminum foil.

When the stew in the bottom part of the *couscoussier* is well on the way (about 1 hour before the end of cooking), start preparing the grain. Wash 3 cups couscous in plenty of water and drain in a sieve. Put in a wide bowl and let the grain absorb the moisture for 10 minutes. Then rub between your hands to break up any lumps and to air the grain. Turn it into the sieve part of the *couscoussier,* sprinkling the grain lightly in layers and not pressing it down. Do not cover the sieve with a lid. After the couscous begins to give off steam, continue to steam for 15 minutes.

Now turn the couscous out back into the bowl. Sprinkle 1 cup of cold water mixed with 1 teaspoon salt over the couscous, then turn and rake the grain with a serving spoon, and, when it is cool enough to handle, rub it between the palms of your hands to break up any lumps and separate and air the grains. The water will make the grains swell. Leave the couscous for 10 minutes, then sprinkle on more water (about 1 cup), until it becomes swollen and tender. Return to the top of the *couscoussier,* and when the steam emerges, let it steam for a further 10 minutes.

Turn out the couscous again. Rub 2 tablespoons vegetable oil in with your hands, and air the grain again. Steam a third time, for 5 minutes. (This can be done much later, just before serving.)

Stir in 2 tablespoons butter, cut into pieces.

The grain can also be steamed over boiling water.

Note: When using instant quick-cooking couscous, the method is the same but the repeated steaming time is very much reduced, and most people usually steam only twice instead of three times.

Cooking with Commercial Quick-Cooking Couscous

The commercial varieties of couscous we get in the U.S.A. are industrially precooked and instant. They are the "medium"-sized granules, which are best for ordinary couscous dishes. A "fine" size is used for the sweet couscous *seffa* that you will find in the dessert chapter (page 422), but the "medium" will also do.

I visited a couscous factory in Sfax during an Oldways International Symposium in 1993 which took us on a fabulous gastronomic tour of Tunisia. We were received with welcoming banners, and offered a tasting of dozens of

(continued)

sumptuous couscous dishes—both savory and sweet—and a demonstration by women in Berber dress of the old ancestral ways of rolling couscous by hand. When the owner of the factory showed me around the plant, I asked him what the best way to use his product was, since packages sold abroad gave different instructions. He said that, although steaming is a ritual and part of the culture of North Africa, which the people are used to and hold on to (they steam everything, including vermicelli and rice), you could just as well add water and heat up the precooked couscous in the oven or a microwave.

I know from hearing home cooks complain about their failures trying to steam precooked couscous that you are more likely to have success by simply heating it up in the oven, for example. I want couscous to be easy and trouble-free, so that people will adopt it. Couscous should be the easiest thing for you to make, but there is an art, even with the instant variety, to achieving a light, airy, separate, and digestible grain. Follow the instructions below for an easy way of preparing quick-cooking couscous in the oven and you will get good results.

An Easy Way of Preparing Quick-Cooking Couscous in the Oven

This is how I make couscous. It is very simple, and you can hardly fail, but there is an art to doing it well.

A package of couscous weighing 500 grams contains 3 cups, while a 1-pound package contains only 2¾ cups, so you had better measure it, as the weight varies depending on the brand. A foreign brand is likely to be 500 grams.

In North Africa 6 cups usually serve 6–8 people, but for us 3–4 cups are ample.

Put the couscous in a wide oven dish so that the grains are not squashed on top of each other. I use a large round clay dish, in which I also serve. Gradually add the same volume (3 cups for 3 cups of grain) of warm salted water (with ½–1 teaspoon of salt), stirring all the time so that it is absorbed evenly. Keep fluffing up the grain with a fork and breaking up any lumps (as the grains stick together). After about 10–15 minutes, when the grain is plump and tender, mix in 3 tablespoons vegetable oil and rub the grain between your hands above the bowl, to air it and break up any lumps.

Put the dish, uncovered (I used to cover it with foil, but now I find that leaving it uncovered keeps it fluffier), in a preheated 400°F oven and heat through for 15–20 minutes, until very hot. After about 10 minutes, fluff it up again with a fork. (Smaller quantities can be heated, covered, in a microwave oven.)

Before serving, work in 3 tablespoons butter or vegetable oil and break up any lumps very thoroughly.

Other common package instructions recommended by manufacturers:

1. For 2 people, boil 1 cup salted water in a saucepan. Remove from the heat, add 1 tablespoon oil and 1 cup couscous, and mix. Allow the couscous to expand for 5–7 minutes, then add a knob of butter and separate the grains with a fork. Reheat for a minute over low heat while continuously stirring, or place for 1 minute in a microwave oven.

2. For 5–6 people, use 3 cups couscous. Empty the box into a dish and moisten with lukewarm water mixed with ½–1 teaspoon salt. Allow 10 minutes for the couscous to puff up before steaming in a *couscoussier*. As soon as the steam has penetrated through the couscous, empty into a dish and toss with butter or oil.

Serving Couscous

The traditional way to serve couscous is in a wide, round, slightly deep dish. Shape the grain in a mound or a cone with a hollow at the top. Lay the meat in the hollow and the vegetables on top or on the sides. Pour 1 or 2 ladles of broth over it all. Bring the rest of the broth to the table separately. By tradition, couscous is a communal dish, and the old way was for everyone to eat with one hand from the serving dish, from the side in front of them. Nowadays it is eaten with a spoon. The meat is supposed to be so tender that you don't need to cut it with a knife. On grand occasions the mound of couscous is garnished with boiled chickpeas, raisins, and fried blanched almonds, as well as sprinklings of confectioners' sugar and ground cinnamon for decoration.

Another way of serving, which has been adopted in France and which you might find more practical, is to serve in separate dishes: the grain on its own, the broth with the meat and vegetables in a separate bowl. Serve in soup plates, the grain on the bottom with the meat and vegetables and the broth ladled on top. If you like, pass around a peppery sauce made by adding harissa (page 464) or ground chili pepper to a few ladles of the broth.

Variations to the Grain

- For saffron couscous, add ¼ teaspoon powdered saffron to the water before moistening the couscous.
- Serve the grain mixed with hot cooked or canned chickpeas, heated through, and raisins, boiled in a little water and then strained.

Garnishes

- Sprinkle the grain with cinnamon and confectioners' sugar and whole or chopped toasted blanched almonds, making a design with lines of cinnamon fanning down like rays from the top.
- Decorate with walnut halves and raisins.

Side Dishes

- For caramelized onions, cook 2 pounds sliced onions in about 4 tablespoons sunflower oil, with the lid on, over very low heat, stirring occasionally, for 20–30 minutes, until very soft. Then cook uncovered until they are really very brown, stirring often. Stir in 2 tablespoons sugar and 1 teaspoon cinnamon and cook a few minutes more.
- Simmer ½ pound raisins in water to cover for about 10 minutes, until soft, and serve them in a bowl.
- Soak ½ pound chickpeas for at least 1 hour, then drain and simmer in fresh water for 1½ hours, or until very tender, adding salt when they begin to soften. Serve them hot in a bowl in their cooking water.

Kesksou Bidaoui bel Khodra

Berber Couscous with Seven Vegetables

Serves 10 • This is the most famous Moroccan couscous, which you can improvise around. It can be made with lamb or chicken or with a mix of the two. In local lore, the number seven has mystical qualities. It brings good luck. Choose seven vegetables out of those listed—onions and tomatoes do not count as vegetables but as flavorings, so choose seven more. It is a long list of ingredients, but the making of the dish is simple—a matter of throwing things into a pot—and it feeds a big party. The soup or stew can be prepared well in advance, and so can the grain.

FOR THE GRAIN

5 cups couscous

5 cups warm water

1–2 teaspoons salt

4 tablespoons vegetable oil

4 tablespoons butter or more oil

FOR THE STEW

3 pounds lean lamb or beef, cut in large pieces, or 1½ pounds meat and 1 chicken, cut into pieces

2 large onions, quartered, then cut in thick slices

1¼ cups chickpeas (soaked overnight) or a 1-pound can, drained

3 tablespoons sunflower oil

Pepper

½ teaspoon saffron powder or threads

Salt

4 or 5 tomatoes, quartered

1 pound carrots, cut in half lengthwise or into thick pieces

1 pound turnips, peeled and quartered, or left whole if baby ones

1 small or ½ large white cabbage, cut into chunks

1 pound zucchini, cut into big pieces

½ pound fresh shelled or frozen fava beans

2 fennel bulbs, quartered

1 pound orange pumpkin, peeled and cut into pieces

½ pound eggplant, cut into pieces

2 green peppers, cut into ribbons

2 chili peppers

1 cup chopped cilantro

1 cup chopped flat-leaf parsley

2 teaspoons harissa (page 464), or 2 tablespoons paprika and 1 teaspoon ground chili pepper, or more to taste

Prepare the couscous as described in "An Easy Way of Preparing Quick-Cooking Couscous in the Oven" (page 376), using the quantities given in the ingredients list above; do not add the final butter till ready to serve.

Put the meats in a large pan with the onions and the drained chickpeas. If you are using canned ones, leave them out now and put them in towards the end of the cooking. Cover with about 3 quarts water, add the oil, pepper, and saffron, and simmer, covered, for 1 hour. Add salt, the tomatoes, carrots, and turnips, and cook for ½ hour more, or until the meats are very tender.

Add the remaining ingredients except the harissa and more water—you need to have plenty of broth—and cook a further ½ hour.

Make a hot, peppery sauce to accompany. Take 3 ladles of broth from the stew and stir in the harissa or the paprika and ground chili pepper—enough to make it very strong and fiery.

To serve, pile the couscous onto a large round dish. Add butter or more oil and work it into the grain as it melts. Shape it into a mound with a pit or crater at the top. Arrange the meat at the top and the vegetables down the sides, and pour a little broth all over.

Serve the broth in a separate bowl. Pass the broth and the hot, peppery sauce round for people to help themselves.

A French way of serving is to present the couscous separately, and the meat and vegetables with the broth in a large bowl.

Variations

- You may add ⅓ cup raisins or pitted dates towards the end.
- Other possible flavorings are ½ teaspoon ground ginger, 1½ teaspoons cinnamon, and 1 teaspoon coriander.
- Algerians put in runner beans and green peas.

FROM COUSCOUS TO A LOAF OF BREAD

A man one day brought home some meat to his wife for dinner. She took semolina and began to make couscous. Only . . . she put so much water in that the grain grew to the size of mhammas.* Her husband watched her in silence.

"My dear, wouldn't you rather have some good mhammas?" she asked him.

"Why not?" he replied.

Quickly she added more water to the grains, so they got sticky and formed a dough. The man watched her without saying a word.

"My dear, wouldn't you prefer bread?"

"Why not?"

Quickly she kneaded the dough . . . and made a fine loaf. When she put it in front of him he shouted:

"By my forebears! if you don't immediately change this loaf into couscous, you won't spend one more night under this roof!"

And he repudiated her.

NACER KHEMIR, STORIES FROM
OUM EL KIR—CONTES D'UNE MÈRE

---

* Mhammas *is a soft, pastalike grain.*

Kesksou Tfaya

Couscous with Honeyed Caramelized Onions and Raisins

Serves 6 • The special feature of this dish is the exquisite mix of honeyed caramelized onions and raisins called *tfaya* which is served as a topping of the long-cooked, deliciously tender meat. The broth which moistens the grain is the meat broth. A sprinkling of fried or toasted almonds is an optional garnish.

FOR THE GRAIN

4 cups couscous

4 cups warm water

$\frac{1}{2}$–1 teaspoon salt

3 tablespoons vegetable oil

3 tablespoons butter or extra oil

2 pounds lamb, cut into large pieces

$2\frac{1}{2}$ pounds onions

Salt and pepper

$\frac{3}{4}$–1 teaspoon ginger

$2\frac{1}{2}$ teaspoons cinnamon

4 cloves

$\frac{1}{2}$ teaspoon saffron threads or powder

2 tablespoons butter

1 tablespoon extra-virgin olive oil

2 tablespoons honey

1 cup raisins, soaked in water for 20 minutes

1 cup almonds

Prepare the grain as described in "An Easy Way of Preparing Quick-Cooking Couscous in the Oven" (page 376), using the quantities given in the ingredients list above.

Prepare the meaty stew or soup. In a large pan, put the meat and about $\frac{1}{2}$ pound of the onions, coarsely chopped, and cover with about $1\frac{1}{2}$ quarts water. Bring to the boil and remove the scum. Add salt, pepper, the ginger, 1 teaspoon of the cinnamon, and the cloves and simmer for $1\frac{1}{2}$ hours. Add the saffron and more water to keep the meat well covered (there should be a lot of broth) and simmer for $\frac{1}{2}$ hour more. The meat should be so tender you could pull it apart with your hands.

For the honeyed onion *tfaya,* cut the remaining onions in half and slice them. Put them in a pan with about 1 cup water. Put the lid on and cook, covered, over low heat (they will steam) for about $\frac{1}{2}$ hour, until the onions are very soft. Remove the lid and cook until the liquid has evaporated. Add the butter and oil and cook until the onions are golden. Stir in the honey and the remaining $1\frac{1}{2}$ teaspoons cinnamon, the drained raisins, and a pinch of salt and cook 10 minutes more, or until the onions caramelize and become brown.

Toast the almonds in a dry frying pan or fry them in a drop of oil until golden, turning them over. Coarsely chop about half of them.

To serve, make a mound of couscous and make a hollow in the center. Moisten with a ladle of the meat broth. Put the meat in the hollow and cover with the onion-and-raisin *tfaya.*

Sprinkle with a mixture of chopped and whole toasted or fried blanched almonds, and serve the broth separately. Alternatively, you might prefer to serve everything separately, or straight into soup plates.

Couscous with Squabs and Almonds

Serves 6 • In Morocco, they make this elegant couscous with small Mediterranean pigeons, but squabs and small poussins will also do.

6 small squabs or poussins

3–4 tablespoons butter or vegetable oil

1 pound onions, chopped

1 pound pearl or pickling onions, peeled

Salt and pepper

$1/2$–1 teaspoon saffron threads

1 teaspoon ground ginger

$1^{1}/2$ cups blanched almonds

$3/4$ cup black or golden raisins (optional)

Large bunch of cilantro, chopped

FOR THE GRAIN

4 cups couscous

4 cups warm water

$1/2$–1 teaspoon salt

3 tablespoons vegetable oil

3 tablespoons butter or extra oil

Put the squabs in a very large saucepan with the butter or oil and both the chopped and the pearl or pickling onions (an easy way to peel the pearl or pickling ones is to blanch them first in water, which loosens their skins).

Cover with a little more than 2 quarts water. Add salt, pepper, saffron, ginger, almonds, and raisins, and cook, covered, for 45–60 minutes, turning the squabs over, until they are very tender, adding the cilantro towards the end.

At the same time, prepare the grain as described in "An Easy Way of Preparing Quick-Cooking Couscous in the Oven" (page 376), using the quantities given in the ingredients list above.

Before serving, break up any lumps very thoroughly and work in the 3 tablespoons of butter or extra oil. Shape into a mound and arrange the squabs on top. Fish out the onions, almonds, and raisins with a perforated spoon and scatter them around the squabs. Serve the broth separately.

Variation

If you like, make a hot sauce to pass around for people to help themselves if they want to: pour 2 ladles of the stock into a bowl, and mix in 1 teaspoon harissa or more to taste (see page 464), or 1 teaspoon paprika and $1/3$ teaspoon ground chili pepper.

Couscous with Lamb and Prunes

In Moroccan restaurants in Paris a popular item on the couscous menu is a tagine of lamb with prunes (see page 254) served with couscous. It is quite delicious. Prepare the couscous as described in "An Easy Way of Preparing Quick-Cooking Couscous in the Oven" (page 376). In bowls, as side dishes, they also give you boiled chickpeas and boiled raisins (page 377). It is a wonderful combination.

Kesksou bel Hout wal Tomatish

Couscous with Seafood and a Fresh Tomato Sauce

Serves 6 • You can use any firm white fish, such as cod, bream, hake, or haddock, for this Algerian couscous.

FOR THE GRAIN

3 cups couscous

3 cups warm water

$\frac{1}{2}$–1 teaspoon salt

3 tablespoons extra-virgin olive oil

3 tablespoons butter or extra oil

3 cloves garlic, finely chopped

2 tablespoons extra-virgin olive oil

$1\frac{1}{2}$ pounds large ripe tomatoes, peeled and chopped

Salt and pepper

2 teaspoons sugar

$1\frac{1}{4}$ inches fresh gingerroot, grated, or crushed in a garlic press to extract the juice

Pinch of chili flakes or powder (optional)

A 14-ounce can chickpeas, drained

$1\frac{1}{2}$ tablespoons raisins (optional)

$1\frac{1}{2}$ pounds fish steaks or fillets, skinned

$\frac{1}{2}$ pound large shrimp, shelled

$\frac{1}{3}$ cup chopped flat-leaf parsley

$\frac{1}{3}$ cup chopped cilantro

Prepare the grain as described in "An Easy Way of Preparing Quick-Cooking Couscous in the Oven" (page 376), using the quantities given in the ingredients list above, and olive oil instead of vegetable oil.

Sauté the garlic in the oil for a few seconds. Add the tomatoes, salt, pepper, sugar, ginger, chili if using, chickpeas, and raisins if using, and simmer 15 minutes.

Put in the fish and cook 3–4 minutes. Add the shrimp and cook 3–4 minutes more, or until the fish flakes when you cut into it. Add the parsley and cilantro towards the end.

Serve hot, poured over the hot couscous.

Variations

• For a hot Tunisian version, add 1 teaspoon or more harissa (page 464) to the sauce and omit the chili pepper.

• Garnish with 8 green or black olives.

Couscous with Fish, Tomatoes, and Quinces

Serves 6 • Tunisia is famous for fish couscous. This uncommon one is elegant and aromatic, with the mingled scents of saffron and quince. Have the fish cleaned and left whole. It is usually steamed in a separate steamer, but it is better to bake it in foil in the oven, which is a way of steaming it.

FOR THE GRAIN

3 cups couscous

3 cups warm water

1/2–1 teaspoon salt

3 tablespoons extra-virgin olive oil

2 tablespoons butter or extra olive oil

3 quinces

3 tablespoons olive oil

1 pound large ripe tomatoes, peeled and chopped

1 teaspoon sugar

Salt and pepper

1/4–1/2 teaspoon saffron threads or saffron powder

1 fish such as sea bass, red snapper, or porgy, weighing about 3 pounds, or 2 smaller ones

Prepare the grain as described in "An Easy Way of Preparing Quick-Cooking Couscous in the Oven" (page 376), using the quantities given in the ingredients list above, and olive oil instead of vegetable oil.

Cut the quinces in half and trim off the darkened ends. This fruit is very hard, so use a large strong knife to press down on them. Put them in a pan, cover with water, and simmer about 20 minutes, until just tender. Strain and keep the cooking water. Cut into quarters and remove the cores and pips.

In a large skillet, heat 2 tablespoons oil, put in the tomatoes and add the sugar, salt, pepper, and saffron. Cook until the tomatoes soften and fall apart. Put in the quinces and add 2 ladles of the quince water. Simmer until the quinces are very tender. This is the sauce.

Brush a large sheet of foil (or 2 if you are cooking 2 fish) generously with oil. Place the fish in the middle and sprinkle lightly with salt. Wrap in a baggy parcel, twisting the foil edges together to seal it. Bake at 450°F. The cooking time depends on the size of the fish. Test for doneness for a large fish after about 30 minutes, for smaller ones after 20 minutes. Cut down to the backbone at the thickest part and check that the flesh flakes and has turned white and opaque right through.

Serve the couscous in a large round dish. Put the fish in the middle and the sauce around it.

Kesksou bel Hout
wal Batata

Couscous with Fish and Potatoes

Serves 6 • This Algerian couscous is like a fish soup served over the grain. Small fish are left whole and large ones are cut into steaks, but I prefer to use fillets, because it is unpleasant to deal with fish bones here. Use firm white fish such as turbot, bream, cod, haddock, and monkfish.

FOR THE GRAIN

3 cups couscous

3 cups warm water

$^1/_2$–1 teaspoon salt

6 tablespoons extra-virgin olive oil

2–2$^1/_2$ pounds fish fillets

Salt and pepper

2 onions, cut in half and sliced

2 tablespoons extra-virgin olive oil

5 cloves garlic

1 teaspoon cumin

1 tablespoon harissa (see page 464) (optional)

4 tomatoes, peeled and chopped

1 pound waxy new potatoes, cut in half, or quartered if large

1 teaspoon sugar

Prepare the grain as described in "An Easy Way of Preparing Quick-Cooking Couscous in the Oven" (page 376), using the quantities given in the ingredients list above, and using olive oil instead of vegetable oil or butter.

Season the fish with salt and pepper and leave, covered, in the refrigerator while you prepare the soup.

In a large pan, fry the onions in the oil till they just begin to color. Add the garlic and fry for a minute. Then stir in the cumin and the harissa, if using. Put in the tomatoes and potatoes. Cover with about 1 quart water and add sugar, salt, and pepper.

Simmer until the potatoes are tender. Then add the fish and cook 4–10 minutes, until the flesh begins to flake when you cut into it.

Serve the grain with the fish on top and the broth in a separate bowl.

Couscous with Peas

Serves 4 • This is one of very few traditional couscous dishes using one vegetable alone. Another is with fava beans. You can also mix peas and very young, tender fava beans together. As there is no broth, the grain needs plenty of butter (you could use vegetable or olive oil instead). Tiny young fresh peas are sold podded in packages in some supermarkets. Otherwise, frozen *petits pois* will do.

- 2 cups couscous
- 2 cups warm water
- 1/2–1 teaspoon salt
- 1 tablespoon vegetable oil
- 4–6 tablespoons butter, cut into small pieces
- 1/2–1 pound fresh peas or frozen *petits pois*

Put the couscous in an oven dish and add the salted water gradually, stirring so that it gets absorbed evenly. After about 15 minutes, when the grain has become plump and almost tender, add the oil and rub the grain between your hands to air it and break up any lumps.

Heat the couscous through in a pan, covered with a lid, so that it steams. As it is a small quantity, it is all right to do it in a saucepan, but you must be careful not to let it burn. Add a drop of water if it seems too dry.

Cook the peas in salted water for minutes only, until they are just tender.

Before serving, break up any lumps in the couscous and stir in the butter and the peas.

A Festive Meal in a Traditional Moroccan Home

You are always received with effusive warmth. As you enter the hallway you may step on a soft carpet of rose petals. The walls of the living area are covered with brilliantly colored hangings. Placed against them are low sofas covered with embroidered cushions. The meal is on the patio. This inner courtyard is lined with turquoise-and-cobalt mosaics. Water trickles from a fountain. The scent of jasmine and fruit trees hangs in the air. A band plays Andalusian music. The tables are large brass trays on low folding legs. You sit on cushions around them.

Dishes follow one another. A multitude of appetizers—pickles; spiced vegetables; fried fish in a sauce with cumin, chili, and cilantro; pastry cigars filled with chopped meat or with prawns; then pigeon pie or stuffed baby pigeons cooked in a saffron-and-ginger honey sauce; followed by a tagine of lamb, accompanied with various vegetable salads. And at the end, couscous, mountains of it, crowned with meat cooked to melting tenderness and vegetables pressed down the sides.

Then platters of fruit, followed by mint tea served with almondy pastries. You might be worried about how much food is left uneaten. But the next day family, friends, and neighbors have their feast; and what is left—every bit of it—is eaten by the cooks, staff, and helpers. That is part of the ritual.

Pasta

Rishta, Shaghria, Lissan al Assfour

Pasta was known in ancient Persia and is featured in medieval Arab cookery manuals in Syria and Baghdad. The name *rishta* (*rishteh* in Iran and *erizte* in Turkey)—meaning "thread" in Persian—is used for tagliatelle-type noodles. Other traditional Arab pastas include vermicelli, called *shaghria,* and one that looks like fat grains of rice and is called *lissan al assfour,* which means "bird's tongues" in Arabic and is known as orzo in the U.S. Like rice, pasta escaped the stigma of being a filling dish for the poor. Instead, it is considered grand, and is served on special occasions. In all the recipes, you can use commercial dry tagliatelle, tagliolini, vermicelli, and orzo.

Very few people make pasta at home anymore, except for when they make the pasta for stuffed dumplings such as *manti* (page 390).

The usual way with the long dry commercial pasta—tagliatelle, tagliolini, and vermicelli—is to break it up into small (about 1-inch) pieces and, often, to toast it or fry it first before boiling in water.

Rishta bi Adds

Noodles with Lentils

Serves 6 • An Arab dish and a Lenten specialty.

2 onions, finely chopped
2 tablespoons vegetable oil
2 or 3 cloves garlic, crushed
1 teaspoon ground coriander
1 cup brown or green lentils, washed
Salt
½ pound dry commercial tagliatelle,
 broken into 1-inch pieces in your hand
4 tablespoons butter
Pepper

Fry the onions in the oil until soft and golden. Add the garlic and coriander, and continue to fry gently, stirring, until the garlic begins to color.

Boil the drained lentils in plenty of unsalted water for 15–20 minutes, until tender. Add salt, throw in the tagliatelle, and boil vigorously until the pasta is done *al dente*.

Drain quickly, stir in the butter and the fried onions, sprinkle with pepper, and mix well. Serve very hot.

Variation

Sometimes red lentils are used. In this case they are cooked separately in about 2½ cups water and allowed to disintegrate to a puree.

Rishta bi Adds wa Tamatem

Noodles with Lentils and Tomatoes

Serves 4–6

1 large onion, coarsely chopped
2 tablespoons vegetable oil
1 pound ripe tomatoes, peeled and cut
 into pieces
Salt and pepper
1 teaspoon sugar
1 cup green or brown lentils, washed
7 ounces fettucine or tagliatelle
2 tablespoons butter
1 tablespoon dried mint

In a large pan, fry the onion in the oil till golden. Add the tomatoes, season with salt, pepper, and sugar, and turn off the heat. Heat through when you are ready to serve.

Boil the lentils in plenty of water for about 20 minutes, until tender. Add salt and the pasta, and boil vigorously until done *al dente*. Drain quickly, pour into the pan with the onion and tomatoes, and heat through.

Heat the butter with the mint until it sizzles and pour over the dish before serving.

Rishta bi Betingan

Pasta with Eggplants

Serves 6–8 • The eggplants are usually fried, but for those who want to broil them, that too can be done, as they are then cooked further in a tomato sauce.

> 2 pounds eggplants, sliced
> Salt
> 1 large onion, chopped
> Vegetable oil
> 3 cloves garlic, chopped
> 2 pounds tomatoes, peeled and chopped
> 1 teaspoon cinnamon
> $\frac{1}{4}$ teaspoon nutmeg
> $\frac{1}{4}$–$\frac{1}{2}$ teaspoon ground chili pepper or flakes
> 1 pound tagliatelle
> $\frac{1}{3}$ cup grated Parmesan or Gruyère (optional)

Sprinkle the eggplant slices, if you like, with salt, and leave them in a colander for at least $\frac{1}{2}$ hour to allow the bitter juices to drain. Rinse, drain, and pat dry with paper towels.

Fry the onion in 2 tablespoons oil until soft and golden. Add the garlic and stir for a moment or two. Then add the tomatoes, cinnamon, nutmeg, salt, and the chili pepper or flakes.

Fry the eggplant slices very briefly in about $\frac{1}{2}$ inch of very hot oil, turning them over once until lightly colored, then drain on paper towels. Alternatively, brush the slices with oil and broil them under a preheated broiler, turning them over, until lightly browned. They can be slightly undercooked. Add the eggplants to the tomato sauce and cook for 10 minutes more.

Boil the tagliatelle in salted water until slightly underdone and drain.

Grease a large baking dish. Fill it with alternating layers of pasta and the eggplant mixture, starting and finishing with a layer of pasta and keeping a little of the sauce to pour over the top. Sprinkle, if you like, with grated cheese.

Bake in a 350°F oven for 20–30 minutes. The pasta will absorb the flavors of the sauce.

Lissan al Assfour bel Goz

Pasta with Walnuts

Serves 4 • In Egypt, little "bird's tongues" pasta that looks like large grains of rice (called orzo in the U.S.) is used. An alternative is broken vermicelli. The pasta is fried or toasted before being cooked in stock. Be sure the walnuts are fresh.

> 1 cup orzo
> About 3 cups chicken or meat stock (page 143) (or you may use 1–1½ bouillon cubes)
> Salt and pepper
> 2 tablespoons extra-virgin olive oil
> 1 cup chopped walnuts

Toast the little pasta in a skillet, shaking the pan, to brown them lightly all over. Add stock a cup at a time and a little salt (take into consideration the saltiness of the stock or bouillon), and cook about 15 minutes, until tender. There should be just a little liquid left as the sauce.

Serve in a shallow dish, sprinkled with olive oil and topped with the nuts.

Rishta bi Laban wa Bassal

Tagliatelle with Yogurt and Fried Onions

Serves 4 • A large amount of fried onions makes this refreshing Syrian pasta particularly tasty.

> 3 large onions, cut in half, then into thick slices
> 3–4 tablespoons extra-virgin olive oil
> 3 cloves garlic, crushed
> 14 ounces tagliatelle
> Salt
> 1 quart plain whole-milk yogurt at room temperature
> 1 teaspoon sumac

In a large saucepan, fry the onions in the oil, covered, over very low heat, until golden, stirring every so often. Add the garlic and cook moments more, until it begins to color. Turn off the heat. Heat through when you are ready to serve.

Boil the tagliatelle in salted water until done *al dente.*

Beat the yogurt with a little salt. Serve the tagliatelle directly on the plates. Pour the yogurt on top and sprinkle with fried onions and a dusting of sumac.

Manti

Turkish Meat Dumplings in Yogurt Sauce

Serves 8–10 • *Manti,* a specialty of Kayseri, are said to have been brought to Turkey from China by the Tartars. I first saw them being prepared in a hotel in Izmir twenty years ago. I was accompanied by Nevin Halici, a cooking teacher, culinary historian, and ethnographer, who was then researching the regional foods of Turkey. She was going from village to village, knocking on people's doors and attending the traditional lunches where women cook together. The second time I saw the little dumplings being made was in a hotel in San Francisco, where at the invitation of the Institute of Food and Wine she was cooking a Turkish meal for almost a hundred people. She shaped the dumplings into tiny, open-topped, moneybag-like bundles, baked them for 20 minutes, poured chicken broth over them, and put them back in the oven again until they softened in the broth.

The following recipe is for the easier version, like ravioli, which many Turkish restaurants make today. It is really delicious and quite different from any Italian dish. They call it *klasik manti,* and often cook it in chicken broth (see variation), which is particularly delicious.

FOR THE FILLING

10 ounces lean ground lamb
1 medium onion, grated
2 tablespoons finely chopped flat-leaf parsley
1/4 teaspoon salt
1/4 teaspoon pepper

FOR THE PASTA

2 cups all-purpose flour
1/4 teaspoon salt
1 egg, lightly beaten
About 1/2 cup water

FOR THE SAUCE AND GARNISH

1 quart thick strained yogurt, at room temperature
4–5 cloves garlic, crushed
1/2 cup (1 stick) butter, for the garnish
1 teaspoon crushed dried mint or 1 teaspoon chili flakes, for the garnish
Salt

To make the filling, put all the ingredients in a bowl, mix well, and work to a paste with your hand.

To make the pasta dough, put the flour, salt, and egg in another bowl, and mix well. Gradually add the water, working it in with your hand until the mass holds together. Add a little flour if too sticky, or a drop of water, if necessary. Knead for 10 minutes, until the dough is smooth and elastic, adding a little flour if too sticky. Divide the dough into 2 balls. Wrap each in plastic wrap and leave to rest at room temperature for 30 minutes.

Roll out the first ball of dough as thinly as possible (to about 1/16 inch thick) with a floured rolling pin on a floured surface, or use a pasta machine. If rolling by hand, lift the dough occasionally and dust with flour underneath so that the sheet of dough does not stick.

To make the *manti,* cut the sheet of dough into strips 1 1/4 inches wide, then cut across the strips to make 1¼-inch squares. Place a tiny amount of filling—about ½ teaspoon—in the middle of each square (using half the filling for the first sheet of dough). Fold the pasta over the filling so that 2 opposite corners meet, making a triangle. Press the edges very firmly together to seal them. (If they don't stick, wet around the edges with a finger dipped in water.) Place the *manti* on a floured baking sheet or tea towel, making sure they do not touch.

Repeat with the remaining ball of dough and the other half of the filling.

For the yogurt sauce, beat the yogurt with the garlic.

To make the garnish, heat the butter, and when it sizzles, add the mint or chili flakes.

Bring a large pan of salted water to a boil (or use 2 pans so as not to crowd the *manti*). Lower the heat to a simmer and cook for about 2 minutes, or until the *manti* are tender, then drain.

Serve hot with yogurt poured over each serving and a dribble of melted butter and mint or chili flakes on top.

Variations

• Use chicken broth (page 143) instead of water, or add 2–3 bouillon cubes to the cooking water.

• A fresh tomato sauce may be used as a topping instead of the melted butter and mint or chili flakes. Sauté 1 chopped clove garlic very briefly in 2 tablespoons vegetable oil, add 1 pound peeled and chopped tomatoes, salt, and a good pinch of chili flakes, and cook until the tomatoes have softened.

Shaghria bi Laban wa Snobar

Vermicelli with Yogurt and Pine Nuts

Serves 4 • People used to make 1-inch-long vermicelli by rolling tiny pieces of dough between their fingers. Make it by breaking dry vermicelli in your hand.

14 ounces dry vermicelli, broken with your hand into 1-inch pieces
2 chicken bouillon cubes
Salt
2 cups plain whole-milk yogurt, at room temperature
2 or 3 cloves garlic, crushed (optional)
⅔ cup pine nuts
1 tablespoon vegetable oil

Cook the vermicelli in plenty of boiling water with the crumbled bouillon cubes until just tender, then drain. You may not need to add salt to the water, because of the saltiness of the cubes.

For the sauce, mix the yogurt with the garlic and a little salt.

For the topping, fry the pine nuts in the oil, shaking the pan, until lightly colored all over.

Serve the vermicelli with the yogurt poured over and sprinkled with the pine nuts.

Variation

Instead of the pine nuts, heat 4 tablespoons olive oil with 2 teaspoons paprika and dribble over the yogurt.

Madzounov Champra Porag

Pasta and Meatballs with Yogurt

Serves 6 • This Armenian specialty makes a hearty main dish. It has a pure and fresh quality and is an entirely different experience from eating an Italian or Asian pasta dish.

  1 pound ground lamb or beef
  1 medium onion, finely chopped or
    grated
  Salt and pepper
  1 teaspoon cinnamon
  1 chicken bouillon cube
  3/4 pound pasta shells or other small
    pasta shapes
  1 egg, lightly beaten
  1 quart plain whole-milk yogurt

TO GARNISH

  4 tablespoons butter
  4–5 cloves garlic, crushed
  3 tablespoons crushed dried mint

Mix the ground meat and onion and add salt, pepper, and cinnamon. Work to a soft paste with your hands and roll into 3/4-inch balls. Bring to the boil, with the bouillon cube, enough water to cover the meatballs. Drop them in and poach them for about 15 minutes.

Cook the pasta in boiling salted water until done *al dente.*

Beat the egg into the yogurt (so that the yogurt doesn't curdle; see page 113) and season with salt and pepper. Slowly bring to the boil, stirring every so often. Add the drained meatballs and drained pasta and heat through.

For the garnish, melt the butter, and stir in the garlic and the mint. Let it bubble for a moment only. The garlic should not fry.

Serve hot with the garnish dribbled on top.

Lissan al Assfour bel Lahm

Bird's Tongues with Meat Stew

Serves 6 • This is a meat stew with pasta. I am assured that it only tastes right if small Italian pasta called "orzo," which look like tiny bird's tongues or largish grains of rice, are used. In Egypt, families used to make the pasta themselves with flour and water, rolling tiny bits of dough into little ovals between their fingers. A friend recalls spending hours doing this with her brother every Sunday as a small child.

  2 or 3 onions, sliced
  3 tablespoons vegetable oil
  2 pounds lamb or beef, cubed
  Salt and pepper
  1–1 1/2 teaspoons cinnamon
  3/4 pound orzo
  Grated Parmesan cheese (optional)

In a large pan, fry the sliced onions in oil until soft and golden. Add the cubed meat and turn to brown it all over. Season with salt, pepper, and a little cinnamon. Add water to cover and cook, covered, for about 1 1/2–2 hours, or until the meat is very tender, adding water if it becomes dry.

Add the pasta, cover with water, and cook for a further 20 minutes, or until the pasta is tender. Add more water if necessary. Quite a bit of sauce must be left at the end of cooking.

Serve with grated Parmesan cheese—an Italian influence in Egypt.

Breads

KHUBZ

In the Middle East, bread really is the staff of life. The region is famous for its many types of flatbreads: leavened and unleavened, with or without a pocket, thick and thin like a cloth. They are baked over a domed metal sheet, in clay-lined ovens called *tannour,* and in wood-fired baker's ovens. The most common type of Arab bread—now ubiquitous in America as pita—is round, flat, and leavened, with a hollow pouch running right through. It is made with various qualities of wheat flours. A coarse whole-wheat flour makes a dark, earthy bread with a strong taste; a refined unbleached white flour results in a softer white bread. Even the outer crust is not crisp but soft, while the inside is chewy, and good for absorbing sauces. In Egypt they believe that the same bread was made in pharaonic times. Wall paintings in tombs and clay models depict what seems to be its making. Although bread is available commercially everywhere in towns, many people still prefer to make their own in an outdoor clay-lined brick oven or send it to be baked in the communal oven.

Commercial Pita

Many shops and supermarkets in America now sell pita bread in different shapes (round and oval) and sizes, and different degrees of thinness, and specialist bakeries produce refined varieties.

The bread becomes dry and hard very quickly, but it is easy to resuscitate. To do so, wet it briefly under the cold-water tap and heat under the broiler or in the oven. To keep many loaves hot, put them in the oven, packed together in silver foil. Pita freezes very well. Put loaves in the freezer as fresh as you can. Transfer them straight from there to the oven or the grill.

The religious and superstitious feeling attached to bread is stronger in some countries than in others. To some it is, more than any other food, a direct gift from God. An invocation to God is murmured before kneading the dough, another before placing it in the oven. A hungry man will kiss a piece of bread given to him as alms. A piece of bread found lying on the ground is immediately picked up, kissed, and respectfully placed on a wall or a table. At a gastronomic conference in Istanbul, I will always remember the look of horror on the Turks' faces when one of the foreign contributors placed a piece of bread under the leg of a wobbly table to steady it. They all swooped to retrieve it.

Bread is eaten with every meal and with every type of food. It is used instead of a fork—people break off a piece and double it over to enclose and pick up a morsel—or to dip in a sauce or cream salad, held delicately between the thumb and the first two fingers. In the street, pocket bread is cut in half and the pocket is filled with hot foods and salads. The bread is also toasted and broken into pieces and used as croutons or as a base for various dishes, such as *fatta* (page 222), *fattoush* (page 74), and in soups and stews. Some people, my father among them, claim that they cannot truly savor a sauce, or anything in fact, without a piece of bread.

Toasted Croutons and Fried Bread

To make toasted croutons, open out pita or other flat Arab breads, splitting them in half, and put them straight on the shelves of the hottest oven, or under the broiler, until crisp and lightly browned. Break into small pieces by crushing in your hands.

Serve in a pile to accompany soup, or to line the bottom of a salad bowl to absorb the dressing (in which case they become pleasantly soft and soggy).

Deep-fried pita bread is as tasty as it is rich. Cut the bread into triangles with scissors, open them out, and drop into very hot oil. Use this to garnish salads and cold vegetable dishes. Many dishes called *fatta* (page 222), after the manner of breaking the bread, make use of these croutons.

Khubz Abbas

In Iraq, ground meat is mixed into the bread dough before it is baked.

A note in *Recipes from Baghdad* (see appendix) says: "A vow to make *khubz Abbas* as a thanks offering on the fulfillment of one's wish is generally taken at the time of acute anxiety, such as the illness of a beloved relative. In the event of recovery this savory bread is prepared in vast quantities. Hot melted butter is also poured over rounds of plain *khubz* which are then sprinkled with sugar. The rounds of bread are arranged in great piles and are distributed in hundreds to the poor."

Khubz

Arab Bread—Pita

Makes 16 8-inch breads • The flatbread with a pouch which we know as pita is *khubz*, which means "bread," in the Arab world. In Egypt, *eish baladi* (*eish* means "life" and *baladi* means "local") is made with a mix of whole-wheat and unbleached white flour, while the one made with white flour is called *eish shami* (*shami* means "Syrian"). The bread is round and 8 inches in diameter.

- 1 tablespoon active dry yeast (or 1 package)
- 2½ cups lukewarm water
- ¼ teaspoon sugar
- About 6 cups unbleached white bread flour or unbleached all-purpose flour
- 1½–2 teaspoons salt
- 3 tablespoons vegetable or extra-virgin olive oil

In a large bowl, dissolve the yeast in ½ cup of the warm water. Add the sugar, and when it begins to froth (this will be proof that the yeast is still active), stir in the remaining water. Add 3 cups of the flour, 1 cup at a time, gradually, stirring vigorously. Let this sponge rest for 10 minutes, or until it froths.

Stir in the salt and 2 tablespoons of the oil and mix well. Add the remaining flour gradually, a little at a time (you may need less), until you have a dough that holds together in a ball. Knead well by hand in the bowl, or on a floured board, for about 10 minutes, until it is smooth, shiny, and elastic and no longer sticks to your fingers, dusting with a little flour occasionally if it is too sticky.

Put the remaining tablespoon of oil in the

(continued)

bottom of the bowl and roll the ball of dough around to grease it all over. This will prevent the surface from becoming dry and crusty. Cover with plastic wrap and leave in a warm place free of drafts for about 2 hours, until doubled in bulk.

Preheat the oven set at the maximum, 500°F temperature for at least 20 minutes, and place a large baking sheet in the hottest part.

Punch the dough down and knead again for a few minutes, then divide in half. Divide the first half into 8 lumps. Flatten each one on a lightly floured surface with a rolling pin sprinkled with flour, into rounds between ⅛ and ¼ inch thick and about 7–8 inches in diameter. Dust with flour and lay the rounds on a cloth sprinkled with flour. Arrange them 1 inch apart, so that they do not touch as they grow. Cover with another lightly floured cloth, and leave to rest and rise again for about 20 minutes at room temperature.

When the bread has risen again, place 2 rounds at a time on the hot baking sheets sprinkled lightly with flour, and bake for 3–5 minutes, or until they puff up like balloons and are slightly brown on top.

Wrap the breads together in a cloth while still hot, or put them in a plastic bag to keep them soft and pliable, while you bake the remaining breads and repeat with the second half of the dough.

Note: You can make the bread under the broiler. Place it far enough underneath so that it does not touch the broiler when it puffs up (it will burn). Turn over as soon as it balloons, and leave only a minute longer.

Variations

- To make *eish baladi,* use whole-wheat bread flour or a half-and-half mixture of unbleached white and whole-wheat bread flours. (Whole-

wheat alone doesn't allow the bread to rise enough.)

- To make *khubz sarj,* which means "bread cloth" and is used to roll up food in, you need a convex (dome-shaped) metal plate heated over a fire (an open fire or a gas fire). With a rolling pin, roll the balls of dough as thin as you possibly can without making any holes, on a floured cloth. When the dome is hot enough, carefully place the sheet of dough on it. To do this, lift up the dough by rolling it up on the rolling pin and then gently unrolling it over the dome. When bubbles appear, in about 3–5 minutes, the bread is ready.
- For *mafrooda* of the Gulf States, make the same dough as for *khubz,* using white flour or a mix with whole-wheat. Roll out the rounds and prick them all over with a fork so as not to have a pouch. Bake quickly without letting them rise.
- Iranian breads called *nane lavash* (a very large one) and *taftoon* are leavened flatbreads without a pouch. They are pricked all over with a fork and pressed down on the baking sheet or griddle with a cushion to prevent the bread from puffing up. They are baked 3 minutes on one side, until the dough bubbles, then turned over and cooked on the other side for 2 minutes more.
- An excellent snack can be made with the above recipe by making a depression in the flattened dough and breaking an egg into it before it goes in the oven. Sprinkle with salt and pepper. The egg will set firm as the bread bakes.
- To make olive bread, work black olives, pitted and chopped, into the dough, and prick all over with a fork so as not to have a pouch.

Mana'eesh or Fatayer bi Zaatar

Thyme Breads

Makes about 18 5-inch breads • These very thin, soft breads, which you can roll up, are like Bedouin skillet breads. They work very well for me in a skillet, and I finish them under a broiler, but you can also bake them. For the topping, you can buy ready-made *zaatar* mixtures, which contain thyme and the tangy spice sumac, in Middle Eastern stores. You need only add olive oil. But it is easy enough to make your own *zaatar* mix at home. My favorite is simply thyme and sesame seeds with salt and olive oil. The quantities here make for a richer than usual topping. Serve the breads for breakfast, with labneh (see page 112), as a snack with a salad, or as an appetizer, cut into wedges.

½ recipe Arab bread dough (page 395)

FOR THE ZAATAR TOPPING

½ cup dried thyme

½ cup sesame seeds

3 tablespoons powdered sumac (optional)

¾ cup extra-virgin olive oil

Salt to taste

Follow the instructions for making the bread dough.

Mix the topping ingredients into an oily paste.

After you have punched the dough down, divide into 3 or 4 balls and roll out one ball at a time, wrapping the remaining ones in plastic wrap. Roll out on a floured surface, with a floured rolling pin, to about ¼ inch thickness. Cut into 2½-inch rounds with a pastry cutter. Pick up the scraps, roll into balls, and flatten again to make more rounds. Now roll out each round as thinly as possible (the dough is very elastic and springs back), lifting it up, dusting the surface with flour, and turning the round over so that the dough does not stick. Then pull and stretch the dough with your hands until it is paper-thin and about 5–6 inches in diameter.

Preheat the broiler. Lightly oil a skillet and place it over high heat. Taking one round of dough at a time, spread about 1½ tablespoons of *zaatar* paste over its surface with your hand. When the skillet is very hot, turn the heat down as low as possible; then gently pick up the dough and lower it in. Cook for 2 minutes over low heat in the skillet, then put under the broiler (about 3 inches from the heat) for about 1 minute, until the top is browned. Continue with the remaining rounds of dough and *zaatar* paste, rubbing the skillet with an oiled paper towel between rounds.

Alternatively, if you want to bake the breads, place on lightly greased baking sheets, spread the paste over each round, and bake in a preheated 450°F oven for 5–10 minutes, or until lightly browned.

Place in plastic bags (with toppings facing each other) to keep them soft. They keep for several days and also freeze well.

Serve hot or warm.

Variations

• For a hot chili bread, instead of *zaatar* use as a topping ½ cup olive oil mixed with 4 tablespoons dried chili flakes.

• For chickpea breads, *fatayer bi hummus,* a Lebanese Lenten specialty, press into the dough a handful of cooked chickpeas before baking. Omit the topping.

Semit

Bread Rings Covered with Sesame Seeds

Cairo vendors sell these bread rings covered with sesame seeds from large baskets, or sometimes threaded onto long wooden poles. They often sell them with *zaatar* (page 47) or *do'a* (page 55) to dip in. In summer, they cry their wares at the entrances of open-air cinemas, or carry them round the tables and across the rows of chairs, chanting "*Semit! Semit!*" The audience eagerly collect provisions to last them through the performance: rings of *semit,* cheese, salted grilled melon seeds or *leb,* peanuts, and Coca-Colas. They while away the time as they wait for darkness to fall and the film to start by eating and chatting; or they watch the children running up and down the aisles, and dancing on the cinema stage to popular Arab and Greek tunes. (We danced when we were children.)

You can make excellent *semit* at home. Make an ordinary bread dough. After its first rising, knead and divide the dough in 2. Roll each piece backwards and forwards between the palms of your hands until the dough forms a long, fat, evenly thick rope about 22 inches long. Place both ropes on oiled baking sheets in the form of rings, pinching the ends and sticking them together. Cover the breads with a cloth and leave to rise in a warm place for 20–30 minutes. Brush them with an egg beaten with 2 tablespoons water, and sprinkle with 4 tablespoons sesame seeds. Bake in a preheated 425°F oven for the first 10 minutes, then reduce the heat to 325°F, and bake for a further 15–20 minutes, or until the rings are golden and sound hollow when tapped.

Bread in the Moroccan Medina

In the old days in the Medina people sent their bread to be baked at the communal oven, the same oven which heated the water for the *hammam,* the public bath next door. Nowadays many families have a metal gas oven special for baking bread, but in the poor quarters they still have their bread baked communally. Children rush through the streets balancing large wooden trays or flat wicker baskets on their heads. On the trays are rounds of flattened dough laid on a cloth, and covered by another cloth. At the bakery, the children stand close to the oven, watching where their bread is put down so as not to lose it among the other loaves. Families often mark their loaves with a pinch, or brand it with a sign drawn with a stick, in order to be able to recognize and claim their own when it comes out. The baker knows the tastes of each family, who likes it brown and crusty, who likes it pale and soft.

An indication of the importance of bread is the enormous and glamorous bread baskets. My Moroccan friend Fatima left me her bread basket when she left London for Saudi Arabia. It is huge, with a pointed hat and a red leather band. My grandchildren hide in it.

Semolina Aniseed Bread

Makes 2 9-inch loaves • There are many North African semolina breads. I love this crusty, crumbly one with a rich aniseed flavor.

1½ tablespoons active dry yeast

About 1½ cups lukewarm water

Pinch of sugar

3 cups fine semolina

3½ cups unbleached white bread flour

¾ cup vegetable or olive oil

1 teaspoon salt

2 eggs

1½–2 tablespoons green aniseed

2 tablespoons sesame seeds

1 egg yolk

Dissolve the yeast in ¾ cup of the warm water and add a pinch of sugar. Leave for 10 minutes, until it froths.

In a large bowl, mix the semolina and flour, add the oil and salt, and mix well. Beat the whole eggs lightly with the aniseed and sesame, and blend into the flour mixture. Add the yeast mixture and work it in well with your hand. Then add the remaining water, working it in gradually, adding just enough to have a ball of dough that holds together. (You may need to add more water, but the dough must not be too wet.)

Knead the dough vigorously in the bowl or on a board for 10 minutes, until smooth and elastic. Pour a little oil in the bottom of the bowl and roll the dough in it to grease it all over. Cover the bowl with plastic wrap, and leave in a warm place for 2 hours, until doubled in bulk.

Punch the dough down and divide in 2. Knead each piece for a minute and roll into a ball. Flatten each ball into a round about 9 inches in diameter and ¾ inch thick, and place on baking sheets that have been oiled and lightly dusted with cornmeal or semolina. Brush the tops with egg yolk mixed with 1 tablespoon water. Leave uncovered at room temperature for 30–45 minutes to rise again.

Bake in a preheated 400°F oven for 30 minutes, until it is brown and sounds hollow when you tap the bottom.

Variation

An Algerian version adds the zest of 1 orange or 2 teaspoons dried ground orange zest.

Matlouk

Plain Semolina Bread

Makes 1 9-inch loaf • In Algeria they sometimes bake it on a griddle or skillet, but that didn't work well for me.

1 tablespoon active dry yeast
1 cup lukewarm water
Pinch of sugar
½ teaspoon salt
3 cups fine semolina
1 egg yolk

Dissolve the yeast in half the water and add a pinch of sugar. Leave to rest for 10 minutes, until it froths.

In a bowl, sprinkle the salt over the semolina and add the yeast mixture. Work it in with your hand and add the remaining water gradually, adding just enough so that the dough sticks together in a ball. Pour a drop of oil in the bottom of the bowl and turn the dough in it so that it is greased all over.

Knead vigorously for 10 minutes in the bowl or on a board. Then roll into a ball and flatten with your hands into a round about 9 inches in diameter. Place it on an oiled baking sheet lightly dusted with cornmeal or semolina. Cover with a cloth and leave in a warm place for 1½ hours, until doubled in bulk.

Brush the top with egg yolk mixed with 1 tablespoon water and bake in a preheated 400°F oven for 30 minutes, or until the bread is brown and sounds hollow when you tap the bottom.

Tsoureki

Sweet Greek Easter Bread

Makes 3 large breads • There are many feast days in the Greek Orthodox calendar which are marked in the kitchen. Easter is the most important. The date is movable, fixed on the first Sunday following the full moon of the spring equinox, but generally falling within the first half of April.

Houses are whitewashed and decorated with lilac, clothes are made, and new shoes are bought. There is much activity in the kitchen, for the feast also marks the breaking of forty days' Lenten fast and a complete fast on Good Friday. Solemn candlelit processions are followed by national rejoicing to celebrate the Resurrection. Paschal Lambs are roasted on spits in gardens and open spaces, and the innards are used for mayeritsa soup, which is finished with the favorite egg-and-lemon mixture. Hard-boiled eggs are dyed red, a color supposed to have protective powers, and polished with olive oil, and a sweet braided bread is adorned with them.

2 tablespoons active dry yeast
½ cup warm water
¾ cup sugar
1 cup (2 sticks) unsalted butter
5 eggs
1¾ cups warm milk
10 cups flour
Oil
2 egg yolks
Sesame seeds (optional)
Split almonds (optional)
Hard-boiled eggs dyed red (optional)
  (see Note)

Kahk

Savory Bracelets

Dissolve the yeast in the warm water, adding 1 teaspoon of the sugar, and leave in a warm place for 10 minutes, until it bubbles.

In a large mixing bowl, beat the remaining sugar and butter to a light cream, then beat in the eggs, one at a time. Slowly pour in the warm milk and the yeast mixture, beating well.

Add the flour gradually, a little at a time, mixing well after each addition, using enough to form a soft dough. Knead the dough until it is smooth and elastic (at least 10 minutes by hand), adding flour if it is too sticky. Oil the top with your hands, cover with a damp cloth, and leave in a warm place for 1–2 hours, until it has doubled in bulk.

Punch the dough down, knead again, oil the top, and let it rise once more. When it has risen a second time, punch down again and divide in 9 equal parts. Roll each part into a long strand, about 1½ inches thick and 18 inches long, pulling to stretch it farther. Join 3 strands together and braid. Do the same with the other strands. Place the braided loaves on well-oiled baking sheets. Brush the loaves with the egg yolks mixed with 1 tablespoon water. If you like, sprinkle with sesame seeds, press in a few split almonds, and push 1 or 2 eggs into the braiding in each loaf.

Set aside to rise in a warm place for 40 minutes.

Meanwhile, preheat the oven to 375°F. Bake about 50 minutes, or until the loaves are lightly browned and sound hollow when tapped. Place on a rack to cool.

Note: To dye hard-boiled eggs, leave them in a bright-red food coloring until the intensity of the color is strong enough. Drain, and when they are dry, make them shine by rubbing them gently with an oiled paper towel.

Makes about 46 • Three recipes for "*ka'ak*" are given in the medieval *Kitab al Wusla il al Habib* (see appendix). Here is my mother's. It makes rather a large quantity, but they keep for a long time in a box. My mother kept a biscuit tin permanently full of them. She said she used margarine rather than butter because it did not become rancid if you kept the *kahk* a long time.

> 1 tablespoon active dry yeast
> About 2 cups lukewarm water
> Pinch of sugar
> 1 cup (2 sticks) margarine or butter
> 6 cups bread flour
> 1–1½ tablespoons salt (or less)
> ½–1 tablespoon ground cumin
> ½–1 tablespoon ground coriander
> 1 egg, lightly beaten with 2 tablespoons water
> Sesame seeds
> Vegetable oil

Dissolve the yeast in a little of the warm water. Add a small pinch of sugar and let it stand in a warm place for about 10 minutes, until it begins to bubble. Melt the margarine or butter and let it cool.

Put the flour in a large bowl. Add salt, cumin, and coriander to taste (I prefer the larger quantity of spices given), mixing them in well. Work in the melted butter or margarine and the yeast mixture. Add the remaining warm water gradually, working it in, adding just enough to make a stiff dough that holds together in a ball. Knead vigorously for about 10 minutes, until smooth, shiny, and elastic.

Take walnut-sized lumps of dough and roll

(continued)

them into thin cigarette shapes about 4 inches long. Bring the ends together and press them firmly against each other to make little bracelets. Paint their tops with the egg mixed with water, using a pastry brush or a piece of cotton. Dip the egg-coated surface in a plate containing sesame seeds. Some will stick.

Place the bracelets on oiled baking sheets and allow them to rest and rise in a warm place for 2 hours.

I am told that a good way of knowing when the bracelets are ready for the oven is to put a small lump of dough in a glass of water when it is first made. It will sink to the bottom, but then it will slowly rise again. When this happens, the rest of the dough is ready for baking.

Bake the bracelets in a preheated 350°F oven for 20 minutes. Lower the heat to 300°F and bake for 1 hour longer. Then leave them to dry out for up to 2 or 3 hours in the lowest (225°F) oven, until they are firm and crisp right through and a pale-golden color. Let them cool before you put them in a box.

Note: Some people allow the dough to rise once in the large bowl first. Pour 1 tablespoon oil in the bottom of the bowl and turn the dough around in it to grease it all over. Cover the bowl with plastic wrap and leave in a warm place for 1–2 hours, until the dough has doubled in bulk. Punch down and knead again for a minute or so before shaping the little bracelets. Brush with egg and dip in sesame seeds. Place them on baking sheets and let them rise again for 20 minutes.

Variations

• We sometimes vary our *kahk* by sprinkling with *mahlab* (the ground kernel of a type of black cherry) as well as sesame seeds.

• Moroccans add ½ teaspoon allspice and a pinch of chili pepper to the dough.

Desserts, Pastries, and Sweetmeats

HALAWEYAT

Throughout the Middle East, the usual conclusion to a meal is fruit. The pastries, puddings, jams, and preserves which have given the region its reputation for a sweet tooth are prepared to mark special occasions and to entertain guests, at different times of the day, when they are served with coffee or tea. Pastries are symbols of generosity and friendship, happiness, rejoicing, and success. Quantities are made regularly and stored away, ready for the casual caller and the unexpected guest, who, by convention, expects and enjoys a warm, enthusiastic welcome at any time of the day. He or she will invariably be received, even at an awkward time, with the famous Oriental hospitality, the ingrained courtesy and decorum that have been rooted deeply by centuries of custom. Sweet delicacies will be pressed upon them with a Turkish coffee or a mint tea.

Besides spontaneous calls, there are special occasions when visiting is obligatory. A new arrival in town, a return home from a trip, a sickness, a death, a birth, a circumcision, a wedding, and the innumerable Muslim festivals, the *mûlid*s, all set the pastry-making and -eating rituals in motion. Certain occasions call for a particular sweet. Beautifully colored and decorated pastries and confectionery, sweet-scented creams, and delicately fragrant dried-fruit salads are made days in advance and served to commemorate or celebrate an event, as symbols of joy or sadness.

Muslim festivals sometimes last for as long as ten days—ten days of continuous merry-making. Nearly every week brings some excitement and has some saint to be honored, some memory to be cherished, or some rite to be performed. The first ten days of the sacred Moharram, the opening month of the year, are holy. The passion play of Hasan and Husein follows, performed in reverence to the memory of the martyrs. In the second month, caravans of pilgrims returning from Mecca are welcomed with picnic celebrations. In the third month comes the Rabi el Awal or Mûlid el Nabi, the festival of the Prophet's birth. Then come the Mûlid el Bulak, the feast of the Lady Zeinab, and the feast of the "miraculous ascent"—the visit to paradise. After the great fast of Ramadan follow the Id es-Saghir and the visiting of cemeteries. There are also the processions of Kisweh, of the Holy Carpet, and that of the Mahmal, the Ark of the Covenant.

In Egypt, many of the festivals are not based on either the Muslim or Coptic religions, but derive from ancient Egyptian pagan rites and customs. People want to enjoy themselves, and any occasion is a pretext for fun, for laughter and merry-making, for dancing and singing in the streets. Fire eaters and magicians perform, Kara Guz (the Egyptian Punch and Judy) stands appear. Children tie colored papers to their bicycle spokes, young girls put on dresses in fabulous colors—sugar pink, scarlet, orange, mauve, lilac, and acid green—young men wear Western pajamas in the street. It is a time for buying from street vendors brilliantly colored syrups and sweet pastries made with nuts, honey, and sugar and colored yellow, pink, and green for joy and happiness.

At one particular festival, the day of the sacrifice of the bride of the Nile (the Bent el Nil), we used to buy a large sugar doll painted in many different colors, with red lips and pink cheeks, and dressed in frilled and pleated multicolored tissue and silver papers. To my mother's horror, I once ate the whole doll, licking and chewing it for a month, undressing it and dressing it again after every repast.

For me, sweets are associated with feelings of well-being, warmth, and welcome, of giving and receiving, of crowds of people smiling, kissing, hugging, and showering hospitality. I remember how hard it was to refuse, when visiting our many relatives and friends, the delicacies and pastries that were forced upon us, after our mother had impressed on us that we should not take more than three stuffed grape leaves, two *kahk,* and two *ma'amoul,* because it was discourteous to be too eager and it might appear that we were not properly fed at home.

Pastries are sold in shops that specialize. They are also made at home. Housewives pride themselves on making a perfect *konafa* or the lightest fillo pastries, and will rarely divulge their secrets of success to anyone but their daughters. Or they *may* give the recipe under pressure, but with one deliberate mistake, so as to ensure failure when a rival attempts it.

It is customary during periods of general festivity for every housewife to prepare mountains of assorted pastries on large trays, to be sent to relatives and friends. She duly receives as many in return. On important family occasions, relatives and friends come, days before the party, to help the hostess prepare a large variety of delicacies. Sometimes an itinerant cook is called in to make one or two specialties for which she is famous, and then moves on to another house to make the same dish again. We always knew beforehand if we were to be served Rachèle's *ataïf* or Nabiha's *karabij* or *konafa à la crème,* and we could rejoice at the thought.

⊱✤⊰

ARAB SAYING:
"He who fills his stomach with melons is like
him who fills it with light—
there is baraka *(a blessing) in them."*

⊱✤⊰

Fruit

In the traditional Arab house with an interior garden, there are always fruit trees, and the scent of their blossoms is one of the pleasures. It is from the Persians that the Arabs absorbed their love of fruit trees and the notion that paradise was an orchard.

There are figs, prickly pears, apricots, dates, grapes, physalis (cape gooseberries), melons and watermelons, mangoes and guavas, custard apples and pomegranates, peaches, plums, cherries, medlars and bananas, apples and pears, tangerines and oranges.

For a party, make a beautiful arrangement with a selection of fruits—some left whole, some peeled and cut up.

Another tradition is to offer dried fruit and nuts or fruit preserves with coffee.

Rose-Scented Fruit Salad

Peel where necessary and cut up a variety of fruits, such as melon, mango, bananas, oranges, apples, pears, apricots, nectarines, strawberries, seedless grapes, kiwis, cherries, and pineapple.

Sprinkle with a mixture of sugar, lemon juice, and rose water. To serve 6, you may like 4–6 tablespoons sugar, the juice of 1 lemon, and 1–2 tablespoons rose water. Leave to macerate for at least an hour before serving, turning over the fruit a few times. The sugar will draw out their juice to form a fragrant syrup.

Orange Slices in Orange Syrup

Serves 4 • The orange zest and the orange-blossom water give a delicate fragrance to the syrup.

The zest of 2 oranges
2 cups freshly squeezed orange juice
$\frac{1}{2}$ cup sugar
1 tablespoon orange-blossom water
6 oranges

Grate the zest, and put it in a pan with the orange juice and sugar. Bring to the boil, and stir until the sugar has dissolved, then add the orange-blossom water.

Peel the oranges so that no pith remains, and cut them into thick slices. Put them in a serving bowl and pour the orange syrup on top.

Serve cold.

RIDDLE:
*She is the beautiful daughter
of a handsome man. Her beauty is
that of the moon. Her children
are in her bosom, and her
dwelling is high. Who is she?*

ANSWER:
An orange.

Kaymakli Kayisi Tatlisi

Apricots Stuffed with Cream

Serves 4–6 • You need to use large dried apricots for this famous Turkish sweet. The cream used in Turkey is the thick *kaymak* made from water buffaloes' milk (see box below). The best alternatives are clotted cream and mascarpone.

½ pound large dried apricots, soaked in
    water for 1 hour or overnight

1¼ cups water

1¼ cups sugar

1 tablespoon lemon juice

1 tablespoon rose water

1 cup *kaymak,* clotted cream, or
    mascarpone

3 tablespoons finely chopped pistachios

Drain the apricots. Make a syrup by boiling the water with the sugar and lemon juice. Add the rose water and the apricots and simmer for 10–15 minutes, then leave to cool.

Make a slit along one side of each apricot and stuff with a little of the cream or mascarpone.

Arrange on a dish and serve sprinkled with chopped pistachios.

Eishta or Kaymak

THICK CREAM

The rich *gamoussa* (buffalo's) milk of the Middle East yields, when it is boiled, a cream which rises to the top and is so thick it can be cut with a knife. It is *eishta* in Arabic and *kaymak* in Turkish. Every family collects layers of this cream whenever the milk is boiled, to eat with bread and honey or jam for breakfast, or with a variety of pastries. A substitute, though not as splendid, can be made with a mix of heavy cream and milk.

Stir 4½ cups milk with 1½ cups heavy cream. Pour into a wide, shallow dish. Use the widest available, to give the cream the greatest possible surface. Bring to the boil slowly and simmer gently over very low heat, so that it barely trembles, for about 1½ hours. Turn off the heat and let stand for 7 hours before putting in the refrigerator. Chill overnight before using. A thick layer of cream will have formed on the surface of the milk. Using a sharp-pointed knife, detach the edges of the cream from the pan and transfer to a flat surface or a large plate. Cut into squares.

Lay the cream flat on pastries or curl it into little rolls.

Ordinary thick clotted cream, mascarpone, and whipped double cream are good enough substitutes.

Bademli Kayisi

Baked Apricots Stuffed
with Almond Paste

Serves 6 • The special appeal here is the contrast between the tartness of the apricots and the sweetness of the almond paste.

13 large ripe but firm apricots
1 cup blanched almonds
$\frac{1}{2}$ cup superfine sugar
3 tablespoons rose water

Make a slit in each apricot and remove the pit.

Blend the almonds, sugar, and rose water to a soft paste in the food processor. Take lumps the size of a small walnut and roll them into balls. Push them into the apricot slits, and press the apricots to squeeze the filling gently.

Arrange the stuffed fruits on a heatproof dish and bake in a preheated 350°F oven for about 20 minutes, or until they have softened a little. Keep an eye on them, and remove if they start to fall apart too quickly.

Serve hot or cold.

Khoshaf bil Mishmish

Macerated Apricots and Nuts

Serves 6 • This delicately fragrant sweet is an old Syrian specialty of Ramadan, the Muslim month of fasting, when it is eaten to break the daily fast. It keeps very well for days, even weeks, covered with plastic wrap in the refrigerator.

1 pound dried apricots
3 cups water
$\frac{1}{4}$ cup raisins (optional)
$\frac{1}{4}$ cup blanched almonds
2 tablespoons pine nuts
2 tablespoons coarsely chopped
   pistachios
1 tablespoon rose water
2 tablespoons sugar (optional)

Soak the apricots in the water overnight.

Drain and reserve the soaking water. Take a dozen of the apricots and blend to a light puree with the water in a food processor. Return to the remaining apricots in a serving bowl and stir in the rest of the ingredients.

Serve chilled.

Khoshaf el Yameesh

Macerated Dried Fruit and Nut Salad

Serves 6 • A mixed dried fruit salad with nuts is a favorite in Egypt during Ramadan, the month-long fast, when Muslims fast during the day and eat after sunset. All through the day, people, hungry and listless, are hardly able to work, and dream of what they would like to eat. At nightfall, when the sky is a cherry red, the cannons boom through the cities signaling the end of the fast, and the muezzins sing it out from all the minarets. The silent city suddenly comes alive with the clatter of spoons and plates, glasses and jugs, and with the sound of relieved hunger and laughter, of music and merry-making. The longed-for dishes wait on tables, trays, and the floor, piled high with *ful medames, falafel,* and *bamia,* meatballs and kebabs, *khoshaf* and apricot cream (following recipe).

Every family has its favorite combinations of dried fruits.

- 1½ pounds mixed dried fruit: dried apricots, prunes, pitted sour cherries, and raisins
- ½ cup blanched almonds, halved
- ½ cup blanched pistachio nuts or pine nuts or a mixture
- ⅓–1 cup sugar
- 1 tablespoon rose water
- 1 tablespoon orange-blossom water

Wash the fruits if necessary, and put them all in a large bowl. Mix with the nuts and cover with water. Add sugar to taste, and rose and orange-blossom water.

Let the fruits soak for at least 48 hours. The syrup becomes rich with the juices of the fruit and acquires a light-golden color.

Variations

• A less common version is to add dried figs and peaches, and a few fresh pomegranate seeds. Their luminosity brings out the rich orange, mauve, and brown of the fruit, and the white and green of the nuts.

• Some people dissolve *amareldine* (sheets of dried, compressed apricot) in the water to thicken and enrich it. Putting 3 soaked apricots through the food processor with a little water will achieve the same effect.

• Instead of macerating, you can cook the fruit with the nuts and almonds. Simmer gently for about ½ hour. It becomes a compote.

Amareldine Matboukh

Apricot Cream

Serves 6 • Another Ramadan specialty in Egypt is a cream made of sheets of dried pressed apricots (*amareldine*) soaked, then boiled in water. I was in Cairo during the Ramadan month a few years ago and saw hundreds of bowls of this tart-tasting fruit cream offered free at street parties. The sheets of *amareldine* available these days do not have the pure taste they once had—perhaps due to preservatives. It is better to use natural dried apricots. Pistachios or almonds and thick cream are optional embellishments. Sometimes cornstarch is used to give the cream the texture of jelly. For this, see the variation.

- 1 pound dried natural unsweetened apricots
- 3 cups water
- 1 tablespoon orange-blossom or rose water, or to taste
- Juice of $\frac{1}{2}$ lemon
- 1–2 tablespoons sugar, or to taste
- $\frac{1}{2}$–$\frac{3}{4}$ cup coarsely chopped pistachios or almonds
- 1 cup whipped heavy cream or yogurt to serve with

Soak the apricots overnight in the water to cover. Put them through a blender or food processor, with enough of their soaking water to have a thick puree, adding orange-blossom water, lemon juice, and sugar to taste. If you like, stir in half the pistachios or almonds. Otherwise use them all as a garnish.

Serve chilled, sprinkled with the remaining pistachios or almonds, accompanied by whipped heavy cream or yogurt.

Variation

For Syrian *muhallabeya amareldine*, which has a jellylike texture: Dissolve 2 tablespoons cornstarch in $\frac{1}{2}$ cup water and add it to the apricot puree in a pan. Bring to the boil slowly, stirring constantly, then simmer, stirring, until the mixture thickens. Stir in the almonds and pistachios and pour into a bowl. Serve chilled.

Prunes Stuffed with Walnuts in Orange Juice

Serves 6–8 • We used to soak the prunes overnight in tea to make pitting easier. Now pitted ones are available, but stuffing them still takes time. I watch television or listen to music while I do this. I prefer the dessert without the cream topping. Either way, it keeps very well for days.

    1 pound pitted prunes (the moist
        California or French type)
    1¼ cups walnut halves
    2 cups freshly squeezed orange juice

FOR THE OPTIONAL TOPPING
OR ACCOMPANIMENT

    1¼ cups heavy cream
    2 tablespoons sugar
    1 tablespoon rose or orange-blossom
        water

Make the hole in each prune a little wider with your finger and stuff each with a walnut half. Put them in a pan, cover with orange juice, and simmer over low heat for 20–30 minutes, or until they are soft, adding a little water if they become too dry. Serve chilled as they are, or with the topping.

For the optional topping, whip the cream until it thickens, and add sugar and rose water. Pour all over the prunes and chill together before serving, or pass round in a bowl for people to help themselves.

Variation

Instead of orange juice, use a half-and-half mixture of water and red wine. This was done in Jewish households.

Visneli Ekmek Tatlisi

Stewed Cherries on Bread

Serves 8 • I love this simple Turkish sweet, which is also made with apricots (see variation). I use a brioche-type bread for the base.

    8 large slices bread, about ½ inch thick
    2 pounds sour cherries or black cherries
    12 ounce jar of morello or black-cherry
        jam
    Juice of ½–1 lemon
    1¼ cups *kaymak* (page 407) or clotted or
        extra-thick heavy cream, mascarpone,
        or thick strained yogurt to serve with

Trim the crusts off the bread and toast the slices in the oven until lightly golden. Wash and drain the cherries and remove the stems.

Put the jam in a large pan with ⅔ cup water and bring to the boil (you may use a "reduced-sugar" jam). Add the cherries and lemon juice, and simmer gently for 20 minutes, or until the cherries are soft. Let them cool, and strain the juice into a bowl.

Arrange the toasted bread on a flat serving platter and ladle a little juice over each piece, soaking the bread so that it is soft but not so that it falls apart. Top with the stewed cherries and serve with the cream.

Variation

A similar sweet is made with apricots. Pit 2 pounds apricots, put them, a jar of apricot jam, the juice of ½ lemon, and ⅔ cup water in a large saucepan. Cook, stirring, for a few minutes, until the apricots begin to soften, and continue as above.

Quinces Poached in Syrup

Serves 4–8 • You will find quinces in Middle Eastern grocers from October until February and longer. Large ones can weigh as much as 1 pound. Try the variation too. I love it.

> 2 large or 4 small quinces, weighing
> about 2 pounds total
> Juice of $\frac{1}{2}$ lemon
> 1 cup sugar
> $\frac{2}{3}$ cup *kaymak* (page 407), clotted cream,
> mascarpone, or heavy cream

Wash the quinces and scrub to remove the light down that covers their skin in patches. Cut them in half through the core, but do not peel them. The fruit is extremely hard, so you will need a strong knife and a lot of strength. You do not need to core them, and the pips are important, as they produce a wonderful red jelly. Cook the quinces as soon as they are cut, as the flesh discolors quickly.

Have ready a pan of boiling water—about 3–4 cups—with the lemon juice and sugar. Put in the fruit, cut side down, and simmer until the fruit is tender and the syrup turns into a reddish jelly. The time varies greatly, from 20 to 60 minutes, for the fruit to be tender, and the syrup can take more than an hour to turn into a reddish jelly. You have to watch the fruit so that it does not fall apart. If it becomes tender too quickly, lift out, reduce the syrup by simmering, then return the fruit to the pan and cook until the syrup becomes reddish and thick. The thickened syrup has a hardening effect and prevents the fruit from falling apart.

Arrange the quince halves, cut side up, on a serving dish, and pour the syrup on top. It will turn into a jelly when it cools. Serve chilled or at room temperature with dollops of *kaymak,* clotted cream, mascarpone, or whipped heavy cream.

Variation

This roast caramelized quince is wonderful and easy. Bake the quinces whole, in a 375°F oven, for about $1\frac{1}{2}$–2 hours (the time varies depending on their size and ripeness), or until they feel soft. Cut them in half through the core and put them, cut side up, in a shallow baking dish. Put a sliver of butter and sprinkle 2 tablespoons of sugar on top of each half. Put under the broiler for a few minutes, until the sugar has turned a dark brown and filled the kitchen with a sweet smell.

Pumpkin Dessert

Serves 4 • A much-loved Turkish dessert. You can find the large orange-fleshed pumpkins sold in slices in Middle Eastern and Indian stores.

> 1 pound pumpkin (weight without
> stringy parts and seeds)
> $\frac{1}{4}$–$\frac{1}{2}$ cup sugar
> 1 cup finely chopped walnuts
> $\frac{1}{2}$–$\frac{3}{4}$ cup *kaymak* (page 407) or clotted
> cream (optional)

Cut off the rind, remove the pips, and cut away the stringy bits. Cut the pumpkin into pieces of about $1\frac{1}{4}$ inches. Put them in a wide saucepan with about $\frac{1}{2}$ cup water and cook with a tight lid on (so that they steam) over low heat for about 15 minutes, or until tender. The pumpkin will release its own juice.

Add the sugar, and simmer, uncovered, for 10 minutes, or until the sugar has melted and the syrup is reduced, turning over the pumpkin.

Serve cold, sprinkled with chopped walnuts. If you like, accompany with *kaymak* or clotted cream.

Moz wal Balah

Date and Banana Dessert

Serves 6 • This is something we used to make in Egypt. Use a moist variety of dried dates.

4 or 5 bananas
½ pound pitted dates, fresh or dried
1¼ cups light cream

Arrange alternate layers of thinly sliced bananas and halved dates in a serving bowl. Pour cream all over and chill for a few hours before serving. The cream will soak into the fruit and give it a soft, slightly sticky texture.

Yogurt with Honey

Serves 2 • Yogurt with honey is eaten for breakfast and as a dessert. Choose a scented honey. Adding ginger is unusual but delicious.

1¼ inches fresh gingerroot (optional)
1¼ cups plain whole-milk or thick
  Greek-style drained yogurt
1½ tablespoons honey, or more to taste

Peel and grate the ginger, or cut it into pieces and press them in a garlic press to extract the juice over the yogurt, if you like. Add the honey and stir.

Variations

• Yogurt with rose-petal jam, which you'll find in Middle Eastern stores, makes a simple and delicious dessert.
• Fruit preserves such as quince, apricot, or sour-cherry may be used instead of honey.

Sholezard

Saffron Rice Pudding

Serves 6 • This intriguing rice pudding made with water—not milk—called *zerde* in Turkey and *sholezard* in Iran, has a delicate flavor and pretty, jellylike appearance.

⅔ cup short-grain or round rice
6 cups water
1 cup sugar
¼ teaspoon saffron threads or good-
  quality powder
1 tablespoon cornstarch
3 tablespoons rose water (optional)
2 tablespoons raisins
2 tablespoons slivered or chopped
  pistachios
2 tablespoons slivered almonds

Boil the rice in the water for about 30 minutes, then add the sugar.

Mix the saffron with 1 tablespoon boiling water and stir it in. Dissolve the cornstarch in 3–4 tablespoons cold water and pour into the pan, stirring vigorously. Continue to stir for a few minutes, until the liquid part thickens, then simmer on low heat for 30 minutes.

Add the rose water and stir in the raisins, pistachios, and almonds.

Let it cool a little, then pour into a glass bowl.

Variations

• Add 1 teaspoon cardamom seeds with the rice from the beginning.
• Serve with a dusting of cinnamon.

Muhallabeya

Milk Pudding

Serves 6 • This is the most common and popular Arab dessert. It is a milky cream thickened by cornstarch or rice flour (in the old days the rice was pulverized with a pestle and mortar). In Lebanese restaurants it is usually made with cornstarch; at home rice flour is used, or a mixture of both. In Turkey they call the cream *sutlage*.

2–3 tablespoons cornstarch

4 tablespoons rice flour

5 cups milk

½ cup sugar, or more to taste

1 tablespoon orange-blossom or rose water

½ cup chopped almonds and pistachio nuts to decorate

Mix the cornstarch and rice flour with about ½ cup of the cold milk, making sure that you break up any small lumps. Bring the rest of the milk to the boil and add the cornstarch-and-rice-flour mixture, stirring constantly with a wooden spoon.

Keep over low heat and stir constantly, until you feel a slight resistance as you stir. Continue to cook gently over low heat for 15–20 minutes, until the cream thickens more, stirring occasionally and being careful not to scrape the bottom of the pan (the cream burns slightly at the bottom and if it is scraped it will give a burnt taste to the pudding). Add sugar towards the end. Stir in orange-blossom or rose water, and cook a minute more. Let the cream cool a little before pouring into a glass serving bowl or small individual ones.

Chill before decorating (it firms up when it chills) with a pattern of chopped almonds and pistachios.

Variations

• Omit the cornstarch and use 6 tablespoons of rice flour.

• Pour a honey syrup over the cold *muhallabeya*. For the syrup: Bring to the boil 3 tablespoons honey with ½ cup water. Stir well, and add 1 tablespoon orange-blossom or rose water. Let it cool, and pour over the cold, firmed cream. It will seep in gradually.

• It can also be decorated with crystallized rose petals or violets.

• An Algerian touch is to add the grated zest of 1 lemon to the cream, and to garnish with a dusting of cinnamon.

• For a stiffer cream that can be molded, increase the amount of rice flour to up to ⅔ cup. Pour into oiled individual molds and turn out just before serving, then decorate with nuts.

• When a bowl of *muhallabeya* is garnished very lavishly with mounds of chopped nuts of different kinds (it can be done in a gorgeous pattern), it is called, with intended irony, "dish of the poor"—*keshk el fu'ara*.

Milk Puddings

The Middle East possesses a wide range of milky puddings made with whole rice, rice flour, or cornstarch, each with a subtle difference in texture and taste. The addition of flavorings such as orange-blossom or rose water, mastic, cinnamon, and cardamom; the incorporation of ground almonds, raisins and nuts, and traditional decorations transform humble ingredients into exquisite exotic desserts.

TURKISH SWEETS IN OTTOMAN TIMES

Of the sweets, some, like the talash tatlisi, a brittle hollow roll which melted in the mouth and was garnished with kaymak, the Turkish cream, have now disappeared entirely. The hurma tatlisi (date sweet), so-called because it had the shape of a ripe date, and both crisp and melting, is also hardly ever seen nowadays. The sweets which are easier to make still survive. Among the desserts made with milk, the most deceptive under its bland appearance is the tavuk gögsü, or breast of chicken. The white flesh of chicken wings was beaten to an absolutely smooth pulp. Not one little solid piece was allowed to remain. The pulp was then cooked with milk, sugar, and a little powdered sahleb root, till it became a thick mass. Poured into a dessert dish, its surface was garnished with powdered cinnamon. Tavuk gögsü had a delicious flavor and when it was properly made the presence of meat was quite imperceptible. My parents sometimes had it served when they had foreign guests. They always liked it and could hardly believe that they had been eating camouflaged chicken. This dish is also dying out for lack of chefs who can make it. There are of course several simpler milk puddings, which it would take too long to describe in detail. My favorite dessert boasted the name of keshkül-ü-fukara, or bowl of the pauper. Long ago dervishes and holy men, who called themselves "the paupers of God," went begging food from house to house. Everyone gave a little piece of what they had, until finally the bowl was filled with many different kinds of food. The name was applied to the dessert, which is made from the juice and flesh of coconuts and milk of almonds, because its surface was covered with little mounds of different kinds of very finely chopped nuts. Walnuts, hazelnuts, almonds, green pistachios, and the snow-white flesh of the coconut formed a pleasing pattern, satisfying both to the eye and to the palate.

FOAT TUGAY,
THREE CENTURIES

Keşkül

Almond Pudding

Serves 6 • This Turkish cream with ground almonds is one of my favorite milk puddings.

- ³⁄₄ cup blanched almonds
- 4¹⁄₂ cups whole milk
- 4 tablespoons rice flour
- ³⁄₄ cup sugar
- A few drops of almond extract
- 2 tablespoons finely chopped pistachios to garnish

Grind the almonds in the food processor (the texture is best if you do not use commercially ground ones).

Bring the milk to the boil and take off the heat.

In a small bowl, mix the rice flour to a paste with 4–5 tablespoons cold water, making sure there are no lumps. Pour this into the milk, stirring vigorously with a wooden spoon, and cook—stirring constantly and always in the same direction, to keep lumps from forming—for about 15 minutes, or until the mixture begins to thicken.

Add the sugar and ground almonds and continue to cook on the lowest possible heat, stirring occasionally, for 20 minutes, or until the consistency is that of a thin porridge. Always stir in the same direction, and do not scrape the bottom of the pan, as the bottom tends to stick and burn a little, and you do not want to scrape up any burnt bits. Stir in the almond extract and pour into a serving bowl or individual bowls. Let the cream cool before sprinkling on the pistachios. Serve chilled.

Saffron Caramel Cream

Serves 6 • A friend described the flavors of a pudding she tasted in an Iranian restaurant, and I applied them to the classic *crème caramel*. It is magnificent.

- 2¹⁄₂ cups whole milk
- ¹⁄₂ cup sugar plus 4 more tablespoons to make the caramel
- A pinch of saffron threads
- ¹⁄₄ teaspoon cardamom seeds
- 2 tablespoons rose water
- 4 eggs, lightly beaten

Scald the milk with the ¹⁄₂ cup sugar, the saffron, and the cardamom and let it cool to lukewarm. Add the rose water, and gradually beat in the eggs.

Heat the remaining 4 tablespoons sugar in a small pan until it melts and becomes dark brown. Add 4 tablespoons water. The liquid caramel will harden and then melt and bubble. Pour into a mold (a ring or round mold about 1 quart). Turn the mold around so that the liquid caramel reaches and covers every part. Use a spoon to help spread it up the sides. Heating the mold in the oven beforehand will keep the caramel (which hardens as it cools) runny for longer. If you use a pan as mold, you can prepare the caramel straight in it.

Let the caramel cool before pouring in the milk mixture slowly (too much force will disturb the caramel). Place the mold or can in a pan of water and bake in a 350°F oven for about 1–1¹⁄₂ hours, or until the custard has set.

Chill before turning out. Run a pointed knife around the edges of the mold, place a serving dish on top, and turn upside down.

Balouza

Scented Jelly

Serves 6 • It looks like white opaline encrusted with little stones. When it is served, it trembles like a jelly. It is customary for an admiring audience to compliment a belly dancer by comparing her tummy to a *balouza*.

- ½ cup cornstarch
- 4 cups water
- ½ cup sugar, or to taste
- 3 tablespoons orange-blossom or rose water
- ½ cup coarsely chopped blanched almonds or pistachio nuts

Mix the cornstarch to a smooth paste with a little of the water in a large pan. Add the rest of the water and the sugar, and stir vigorously with a wooden spoon until dissolved. Bring to the boil slowly, stirring constantly, then put on the lowest heat and simmer gently, still stirring continually, until the mixture thickens.

To test if it is ready, dip a spoon in the hot cream and see if it clings and coats the spoon. Another test is to drop ¼ teaspoon of it onto a cold plate—if it remains a solid little ball and does not flatten out, it has thickened enough.

Stir in orange-blossom or rose water and continue to cook for 1–2 minutes more. Add the chopped nuts, stir well, and pour into a glass bowl. Serve chilled. It will set firmly.

Variations

• You can make this not too sweet (with less sugar) and add a spoonful of rose-petal or quince jam to each serving.

• For *balouza muhallabeya,* a creamier, less firm version, use milk instead of water. Leave out the nuts and use them as garnish instead. Flavor if you like with ½ teaspoon mastic, pounded or ground to a powder with a pinch of sugar. Chill and decorate with chopped blanched almonds or pistachios, or with both. This is the pudding you will usually find in Lebanese restaurants today.

RIDDLE:
A sparkling saber, so sweet to pull out. The kings of the East and the kings of the West cannot put it back into its sheath. What is it?

ANSWER:
Milk.

Balta or Hetalia

Serves 6 • This is Syrian and beautiful, like white blossoms and brown leaves floating in a pure scented stream, but it is not to everybody's taste.

1 recipe *balouza* (preceding recipe)

FOR THE SYRUP

2¼ cups cold water

½ cup sugar, or more to taste

1 tablespoon orange-blossom or rose water, or to taste

½ cup black or golden raisins

½ cup split blanched almonds

¼ cup chopped pistachio nuts

Prepare the *balouza* and pour into a moistened square or rectangular dish (about 8 or 9 inches), so as to have a thick layer. Cool, then chill in the refrigerator. When it has set into a firm jelly, cut it into 1-inch squares with a knife.

Prepare the syrup, which is not cooked, straight into a large glass serving bowl: Pour in the water and add sugar and a little orange-blossom or rose water, and stir until the sugar has dissolved. Taste again, and add sugar if it is not sweet enough, or water if it is too sweet. Stir in the raisins, the almonds, and the pistachios.

Turn out the squares of *balouza* and drop them into the syrup. Stir gently and serve.

Roz bi Haleeb

Rice Pudding

Serves 6 • Mastic, the resin from the lentisk tree, a native of the Greek island of Chios, gives this homely pudding an intriguing and, to me, very delicious flavor. (Lebanese pronounce it *miskeh,* and some restaurants wrongly call it "musk.") It is bought in small translucent grains or crystals. You have to pound or grind them to a powder with a pinch of sugar.

1 cup short-grain or round rice

1¼ cups water

5 cups whole milk

¾ cup sugar, or to taste

1 tablespoon orange-blossom or rose water

¼ teaspoon powdered mastic

Boil the rice in the water for 8 minutes. Add the milk and simmer over very low heat for 30–45 minutes, stirring occasionally to make sure that the bottom does not stick and burn.

When the rice is very soft and the milk is not entirely absorbed, add the sugar and stir until dissolved. Add orange-blossom or rose water and the mastic, and stir vigorously. Cook for ½ minute longer, and pour into a serving bowl. The pudding should be creamy. If it is dry, add a little milk.

Serve hot or cold.

Variations

• Garnish, if you like, with chopped nuts, or top with fruit preserves or fruits poached in syrup.

• Pour the pudding into a baking dish and bake at 350°F for 30 minutes, until a brown crust forms.

Om Ali

Egyptian "Bread-and-Butter" Pudding

Serves 8 • The name means "Ali's mother," and it is the most popular sweet in Egypt. I had never heard of it when I lived there, but now it is everywhere. People in Cairo say it arrived in the city from the villages of Upper Egypt, but there it is said to be from Cairo. One joker explained that it was a bread pudding introduced by a Miss O'Malley, an Irish mistress of the Khedive Ismail. Go and believe him! People find all sorts of ways of making it—with pancakes, with thinly rolled-out puff pastry, with pieces of bread, and with fillo pastry. Fillo gives the most appealing texture, and it is good to bake the pastry initially rather than fry it in butter as is usual in Egypt.

> 6 sheets of fillo
>
> 6–8 tablespoons butter, melted
>
> ⅔ cup black or golden raisins
>
> 1 cup mixed whole or slivered blanched almonds, chopped hazelnuts, and chopped pistachios
>
> 5 cups whole milk
>
> 1¼ cups heavy cream
>
> ½–⅔ cup sugar
>
> 1–2 teaspoons cinnamon (optional)

Leave the sheets of fillo in a pile to keep them from drying out. Brush each one with melted butter and place them on top of each other on a buttered baking sheet.

Put the buttered fillo sheets in a preheated 350°F oven for about 10 minutes, until they are crisp and the top ones are very slightly colored.

When cool enough to handle, crush the pastry with your hands into pieces into a baking dish, sprinkling raisins and nuts in between the layers.

Bring the milk and cream to the boil in a pan with the sugar, and pour over the pastry. Sprinkle, if you like, with cinnamon, and return to the oven. Raise the heat to 425°F and bake for about 20–30 minutes, or until slightly golden.

Serve hot.

Variations

• You may bake the pudding in individual clay bowls, as they do in Egyptian restaurants.

• A Moroccan version has the boiling milk and cream poured onto crisp, fried paper-thin pastry broken into small pieces. It is eaten like a cereal with nuts and raisins without further baking.

Shaghria bi Laban

Vermicelli with Milk

Serves 4–6 • Vermicelli broken into 1-inch pieces, or pasta which looks like large grains of rice, called *lissan al assfour* or "bird's tongues," and orzo in the U.S., is used. Both of these types of pasta were made at home by rolling the dough between two fingers, but now they are available commercially.

In Egypt it is a breakfast dish, served sprinkled with nuts and raisins. Chopped bananas are sometimes also added. The pasta is usually fried until it is golden brown and then boiled. In North Africa, where they steam the pasta without first frying it, it is served as a dessert.

The mastic must be pounded or ground to a powder with a pinch of sugar.

- 4 cups whole milk plus more to serve with
- 9 ounces dry vermicelli or "bird's tongues" pasta
- ⅓–1 cup sugar, to taste
- 2 tablespoons orange-blossom or rose water
- 3–4 grains of mastic, ground to a powder (optional)
- 1 cup chopped mixed nuts (walnuts, hazelnuts, almonds, pistachios)
- ¼ cup raisins

Bring the milk to the boil in a pan and drop in the pasta. If using vermicelli, crunch into 1-inch pieces in your hand.

Simmer for about 5 minutes, until the pasta begins to soften. Then add the sugar, flower water, and mastic if using. Cook until the pasta is tender and most of the milk absorbed. Eat hot, sprinkled with nuts and raisins. Add more hot milk if necessary. It should be quite soupy.

LULLABY FOR A SON

After the heat and after the bitterness, and after the sixth of the month,
After our enemies had rejoiced at her pain and said, "There is a stone in her tummy!"
The stone is in their heads! And this overwhelms them.
Go! Oh bearer of the news! Kiss them and tell them, "She has borne a son!"

FROM MASPÉRO,
CHANSONS POPULAIRES

LULLABY FOR A NEWBORN GIRL

When they said, "It's a girl!"—that was a horrible moment.
The honey pudding turned to ashes and the dates became scorpions.
When they said, "It's a girl!," the corner stone of the house crumbled,
And they brought me eggs in their shells and instead of butter, water.
The midwife who receives a son deserves a gold coin to make earrings.
The midwife who receives a son deserves a gold coin to make a ring for her nose.
But you! Oh midwife! Deserve thirty strokes of the stick!
Oh! You who announce a little girl when the censorious are here!

FROM MASPÉRO,
CHANSONS POPULAIRES

Ashura

Wheat or Barley with Nuts

Serves 12 • An Egyptian breakfast of boiled whole wheat, with hot milk poured over and sprinkled with sugar called *belila*, is turned into a celebratory dish on the 10th of Moharram (the first month of the Muslim calendar), when it is embellished with a flower fragrance and with nuts. Unless it is very young, wheat remains chewy even after lengthy cooking, so I use barley, which is less common but softens relatively quickly.

- 2 cups whole barley or wheat, washed and soaked overnight
- 1 cup sugar, or to taste
- 2 cups milk
- 2 tablespoons orange-blossom or rose water

TO GARNISH

- ½ cup pistachios, coarsely chopped
- ½ cup blanched almonds, coarsely chopped
- ¼ cup pine nuts
- ¾ cup raisins, soaked in water and drained (optional)
- 1 teaspoon cinnamon

Simmer the drained barley or wheat in plenty of fresh water for about 1 hour, or until the grain is very tender. Barley takes 20–30 minutes, wheat 1–2 hours. Drain, and pour into a large serving bowl or individual bowls.

Boil the sugar with the milk until the sugar has dissolved. Stir in the flower water. Pour over the grain, and serve, hot or cold, garnished with the nuts and with raisins if you like, and dusted with cinnamon.

Variation

The Turkish *asure,* prepared on the first day of Moharram, is an extraordinary dish in the number of its ingredients. In Turkey it also commemorates Noah's salvation from the Flood. According to legend, Noah made *asure* when the Flood subsided from everything that remained of foodstuffs at the bottom of sacks. The usual ingredients today are chickpeas, haricot beans, fava beans, whole wheat, black and golden raisins, dried figs, dried apricots, dates, hazelnuts, walnuts, almonds, and pomegranate seeds. *Asure* is a pudding with a creamy base of milk and sugar thickened with cornstarch and flavored with rose water and cinnamon. I have eaten it, but I have never made it myself.

Seffa

Sweet Couscous

Serves 6–8 • Fine-grained sweet couscous, called *seffa* in Morocco and *mesfouf* in Tunisia, is served hot, accompanied by cold milk or buttermilk. I like to eat it for breakfast. There are many versions.

Dried fruit such as dates and raisins, and nuts such as almonds, walnuts, and pistachios, can be added, and the grain can be flavored with orange-blossom water or with cinnamon, honey, or sugar. A particularly wonderful version is with fresh grapes. The most common, *seffa be zbib,* is with large black or golden raisins. *Seffa be tamr* is with dates and walnut halves. There is also one with pomegranate seeds.

Here is a basic *seffa/mesfouf* followed by possible garnishes. Serve it in bowls and pass round a jug of hot milk to pour over.

3 cups fine or medium couscous

3 cups warm water

$\frac{1}{2}$–1 teaspoon salt

2 tablespoons vegetable oil

Sugar, to taste

1–2 tablespoons orange-blossom water (optional)

6–8 tablespoons butter

Confectioners' sugar to decorate

Ground cinnamon to decorate

Pot of honey to pass round

Prepare couscous as described in "An Easy Way of Preparing Quick-Cooking Couscous in the Oven" on page 376, using the amounts of couscous, water, salt, and oil called for in the above list.

Before serving, break up any lumps very thoroughly, add sugar to taste, and, if you like, orange-blossom water, and work in the butter.

Mix in one of the garnishes that follow, leaving some aside to decorate the dish.

Serve in a round, shallow dish. Shape into a cone. Dust the pointed top with confectioners' sugar and draw lines down the sides with cinnamon. Decorate further with the bits of garnish that have been left aside.

Serve in soup bowls. Accompany with bowls of sugar, cinnamon, and honey for people to help themselves if they want to, and with a jug of hot milk.

Possible Garnishes

• $\frac{1}{2}$ cup raisins soaked in water for 15–20 minutes, then drained

• $\frac{1}{2}$ pound dates and 1 cup chopped walnut halves (keep a few whole to decorate)

• $1\frac{1}{2}$ cups mixed chopped lightly toasted nuts, including pistachios, walnuts, and hazelnuts, and $\frac{1}{2}$ cup black or golden raisins

• Plenty of fresh grapes

• The fresh pink seeds of 2 pomegranates

• 1 cup blanched almonds, lightly toasted or fried in a drop of oil till golden, and coarsely chopped

• For a Tunisian version, make a syrup by boiling $\frac{3}{4}$ cup water with $1\frac{1}{4}$ cups sugar and the juice of $\frac{1}{2}$ lemon. Pour half of it over the cooked grain and heat in the oven for 15 minutes. Serve with the rest of the syrup poured over and a sprinkling of chopped pistachio nuts.

Jellatys and Granitas in Egypt

Italian and French ice creams such as *sfogliatella, cassata,* and *café liégeois* were made in masterly fashion in Egypt, but there were specialists who excelled in famously Middle Eastern ice creams such as *dondurma kaymakli,* a milk ice cream with a chewy texture and mastic flavor, and wonderfully fruity granitas. (Sicilians say they learned how to make granitas from the Arabs who occupied the island in the early Middle Ages, but in Egypt ice creams were called *jellaty* after the Italian word *gelati.*)

Ice creams were served in every café in Cairo and Alexandria. Groppi's, the Café Paradis, the Sans Souci, Cecil's, and the Beau Rivage were famous all over the world for theirs. I have many happy childhood memories of long, hot afternoons spent eating ice creams. In the evenings, for a special family treat, we were taken before or after or instead of the cinema to eat them in an open-air café. We almost invariably met numerous relatives, friends, and acquaintances. Tables were joined together as parties grew to swallow up the whole café. The fragrance of the ice creams made with ripe fruit mingled with that of the jasmine necklaces which vendors brought round the tables, their arms heavy with rows of the little white flowers. People also made ices at home, in a bucket with a churn surrounded by a freezing mixture of crushed ice and salt.

Basic Method for Making Granitas with Fruit

Blend the fruit to a light, creamy pulp, adding sugar to taste. Pour into ice-cube trays, cover with plastic wrap, and let the pulp freeze hard for 6 hours or overnight in the freezer. Put the frozen cubes, in batches, in the food processor and turn them into a very fine, soft, frothy slush. Pour into a serving bowl and return to the freezer, covered with plastic wrap. Take the granita out 15 minutes before serving.

Melon Granita

Serves 6 • Buy very ripe melons with a sweet fragrance that you can smell from a distance.

2 medium melons

Juice of 1 lemon

³/₄ cup sugar, or to taste

¹/₂–1 tablespoon orange-blossom water, to taste

Cut open the melons. Peel and remove the seeds. Cut the flesh into pieces and blend in the food processor—with the lemon juice, sugar, and orange-blossom water—to a liquid pulp. You should have about 6 cups. The amount of sugar depends on how sweet the melons are. Continue following the "basic method" (page 423).

Apricot Granita

Serves 8

2 pounds ripe apricots

1 cup sugar, or more to taste

³/₄ cup water

Juice of ¹/₂ lemon

Wash the apricots and remove stones and stems.

Put the sugar in a pan with the water and lemon juice and bring to the boil (this amount of sugar gives a tart, not-too-sweet taste). Simmer 5 minutes and let it cool.

Turn the apricots to a paste in a blender or food processor. Add the syrup and blend to a cream.

Continue as in the "basic method" (page 423).

Lemon Granita

Serves 6

4 cups water

1¹/₄ cups sugar

1 tablespoon orange-blossom water

1¹/₄ cups lemon juice

The grated rind of 1 lemon (optional)

Boil the water and sugar together for a few minutes, stirring, until the sugar has dissolved. Cool, and add orange-blossom water and lemon juice.

Stir well, and continue as in the "basic method" (page 423).

Orange Ice Cream

Serves 6 • This wonderful ice cream is quite different from the usual orange granita. Make it a day before you want to serve it.

8 egg yolks

¹/₂ cup sugar

2¹/₄ cups freshly squeezed orange juice

Beat the egg yolks with the sugar to a pale, thick cream.

Bring the orange juice to the boil in a pan, then pour it gradually over the egg yolks, beating vigorously all the time. Pour back into the pan and stir constantly and vigorously over the lowest heat, without letting it boil, until the mixture thickens to a very light custard. Let it cool.

Line a mold with plastic wrap, and pour in the orange custard. Cover with plastic wrap and put in the freezer.

Take the ice cream out of the freezer 15 minutes before you are ready to serve. Remove the plastic wrap on the top, turn out on a serving plate, and remove the remaining plastic wrap.

Dondurma Kaymakli

Sahlab Ice Cream

Serves 14 or more • The brilliant white milk ice cream with a chewy texture of my childhood was made with *sahlab* (also known as *salep*; see page 46), the ground root tuber of a member of the orchid family, and mastic, a hard resin exuded from the lentisk tree. It has become something of a mythical ice cream, as it can no longer be found in Turkey, Lebanon, Syria, and Egypt, countries that used to make it. *Sahlab* is very expensive, and what you buy is often adulterated. Be careful not to use too much mastic, as the taste would become unpleasant.

2 tablespoons powdered *sahlab*

4 cups milk

1$\frac{1}{3}$ cup heavy cream

1$\frac{1}{2}$ cups sugar

$\frac{1}{4}$ teaspoon mastic

1 tablespoon orange-blossom water

Chopped pistachio nuts to garnish

Dissolve the powdered *sahlab* in about 1$\frac{1}{2}$ cups of the milk. Put the rest of the milk in a saucepan together with the cream and sugar, and bring to the boil. Add the milk-and-*sahlab* mixture gradually, beating with an electric beater. Simmer very gently over low heat for about 20–30 minutes, stirring constantly with a wooden spoon.

Crush and pulverize the mastic by pounding with a pinch of sugar, and stir into the milk mixture. Add orange-blossom water, mix well, and cook for a moment more.

Pour into a wide dish (about 11 inches) lined with plastic wrap, and cover with wrap. Put in the freezer overnight or days ahead.

At any point after the mixture has frozen hard, remove from the freezer, turn it out of the dish, and blend in batches in a food processor. The longer you blend, the whiter it will get and the more chewy and elastic the texture. Pour into a mold lined with plastic wrap and cover with wrap. Put in the freezer again for at least 1 hour.

Take the ice cream out of the freezer 10–15 minutes before serving. Serve sprinkled with pistachio nuts.

Note: Mastic mixed with a little candle wax is the local chewing gum in Egypt.

Dairy Ice Cream with Mastic and Rose Water

Serves 6 • This is a modern version of *dondurma kaymakli* without *sahlab*. Mastic and rose water give it an exotic allure. The mastic, a resin exuded from the lentisk tree, is sold in small, hard, translucent lumps, like crystals. It must be pounded or ground to a fine powder with a pestle and mortar, together with a pinch of sugar.

> 4 egg yolks
> ½ cup sugar
> 1¼ cups light cream
> 1–2 tablespoons rose water, to taste
> ¼ teaspoon pulverized mastic
> 1¼ cups heavy cream

Beat the egg yolks and sugar to a thick, pale cream in a bowl. Bring the light cream to the boil and gradually pour over the yolk mixture, beating all the time.

Put the bowl in a pan of boiling water, or in the top of a double boiler, and stir or lightly beat until the mixture thickens into a custard. Add the rose water, sprinkle the mastic over the whole surface (if it falls in one place, it will stick together in a lump), and stir thoroughly.

Beat the heavy cream until firm and fold it into the cooled custard.

Pour into a mold lined with plastic wrap and cover with more plastic wrap. Freeze overnight. Take out of the freezer 10–15 minutes before serving.

Variation

You can cheat and use store-bought dairy ice cream. Leave to soften slightly, and gently mix in the flavorings (some ice creams collapse if you beat vigorously or blend in a food processor), then put back into the freezer.

The Khoja had been invited out, and sat with the guests chatting and chewing mastic gum, when a servant came in to say that dinner was ready.

As the guests rose to go into the dining-room the Khoja took the mastic out of his mouth and stuck it on the tip of his nose.

When they asked him why he did it, he answered, "Poor people should always keep an eye on their property."

BARNHAM, TRANS.,
TALES OF NASR-ED-DIN KHOJA

Booza al Fusduk

Pistachio Ice Cream

Serves 8–10 • This is not an old, traditional ice cream but one developed by Egyptian expatriates in Europe with traditional ingredients and flavorings. It is very rich. Some Indian and Middle Eastern stores sell blanched and slivered or ground pistachios. If they are not available, you will have to buy shelled pistachios and blanch them for a few moments in boiling water to detach their skins, then peel them (a time-consuming labor), and grind them. Use 1 cup shelled pistachios to obtain 1 cup ground ones.

6 egg yolks

1⅓ cups sugar

2½ cups light cream

2–3 tablespoons rose water, to taste

1 cup ground pistachios

Beat the egg yolks and sugar to a thick, pale cream. Bring the light cream to the boil in a pan and gradually pour over the yolk mixture, beating all the time. Pour the mixture back into the pan, place it in another pan of boiling water, and stir until the mixture thickens into a custard.

Add the rose water and fold in the ground pistachios. Let it cool, then pour into a bowl lined with plastic wrap. Cover with plastic wrap and freeze overnight.

Turn out 10–15 minutes before serving.

Note: Some people cheat and use store-bought vanilla ice cream. Mix in rose water and pistachios and freeze again.

Booza al Loz

Almond Ice Cream

Serves 8 • This too is modern.

¾ cup blanched almonds

1¼ cups milk

1¼ cups heavy cream

4 egg yolks

¾ cup sugar

2–3 tablespoons orange-blossom water

3 drops of almond extract

Grind the almonds. Put them in a pan with the milk and cream and bring to the boil.

Beat the egg yolks with the sugar to a pale, light cream. Gradually pour the hot milk-and-almond mixture into the yolks and sugar and continue to beat until well blended. Return this to the pan, and stir constantly over very low heat until the mixture thickens to the consistency of custard, but do not let it boil, or the yolks will curdle.

Add the orange-blossom water and the almond extract (pour the drops into a spoon first, as it is easy to pour too much and then the taste would be nasty). Let it cool. Pour into a bowl lined with plastic wrap, cover with plastic wrap, and freeze overnight.

Turn out 10–15 minutes before serving.

Pastries

Atr

Sugar Syrup

A traditional and constant feature of Middle Eastern sweets and pastries is the sugar syrup which is used both in making them and to bathe, soak, or sprinkle on many of them.

It is either thin and liquid, or thick and treacly, and scented with rose water or orange-blossom water or both. It can be made in advance and stored for many weeks, even months, in a glass jar, ready to be used. The following quantities give the most common thickness.

    2 cups sugar

    1 cup water

    ½ tablespoon lemon juice

    1–2 tablespoons or more rose water or
      orange-blossom water, or both

Bring sugar, water, and lemon juice to the boil. (The lemon juice is to prevent the syrup from crystallizing when it is cold.) Lower the heat, and simmer gently for 8–10 minutes, or until the liquid has thickened enough to coat a spoon. Stir in the rose or orange-blossom water and simmer for a minute or so.

Notes: Quantities of sugar and water can be varied according to the degree of thickness required for the syrup. You can also determine the thickness by the cooking time. The longer it is simmered, the more it is reduced, the thicker it will be. It is only when the syrup has cooled that you can really know how thick it is (it appears thinner when hot). If it is not right, it can be thickened by further cooking, or thinned by adding a little water and simmering again.

If used heavy-handedly, this syrup will give pastries the rather sickly-sweet stickiness which characterizes badly made pastries in pastry shops.

When a syrup is used for pastries, it is added only when they are already baked, fried, or cooked. It is added *very cold* to the *hot* pastries. (The opposite view, that the syrup must be poured hot, has many adherents, but we in Egypt always held firmly to our own.) Either it is poured over them as they come out of the oven, or the pastries themselves (such as *luqmat el qadi*) are dropped into it for a few minutes, then lifted out, richly saturated.

*Arab saying condemning
an ostentatious wedding:
"The bride is a frog but
the wedding is a cyclone."*

THE KHOJA'S FEIGNED ASSAULT ON HIS WIFE

Behold the Khoja in a violent passion with a big stick in his hand rushing after his wife and shouting, "I have had enough of you! I'll give you a good thrashing and pay you for all the annoyance you have caused me these thirty years! Then go and complain to anyone you wish!"

His wife ran along screaming, "Help! Good people of Mohammed! This fellow has gone mad again. Save, oh, save me!"

There happened to be a wedding at a house close by, and the guests, hearing the cries, rushed out into the street and carried the Khoja's wife into the harem for safety. They then turned to the Khoja and begged him to be quiet, saying, "We all know how foolish women can be; but is this a nice thing for you to do?—for you are a man of culture and you would be the first to find fault with us if we were to do it."

While they were trying to pacify him, the owner of the house came forward and said, "My dear Khoja, let me profit by this unpleasant business to ask you a favor. Of course I was rude not to have invited you to our party. It was partly because it was for young people and I was afraid you might find it tiresome, but I am so delighted to have this opportunity. Please do us the honor of joining us for a while and let us hear what it was all about."

Though these words served to calm the Khoja to a certain extent, he was still growling with indignation when he entered the house.

As the wedding breakfast was ready, the guests took their places. The Khoja at once began to describe how the quarrel had arisen and kept them all in a roar of laughter.

Just then some baklawa was brought in. The Khoja ate from the dish which was placed before him with the greatest relish, while he continued his description of the quarrel, and then wound up by saying, "Lucky woman! Lucky rascal! So she took refuge here, did she? If I could have got hold of her I would have given her ear a twist like this," said he, twirling the dish of baklawa round towards himself, which made the people laugh again.

"Ha! ha!" they said, "you can't help joking even when you are angry!"

After trying a variety of delicacies, the guests left the table and coffee was served.

The Khoja then made a humorous speech to those present. He said, "Our good neighbor here gave a wedding party, but did not invite us. As I found out that he was going to have some nice things to eat and especially my favorite dish baklawa, my wife and I thought the matter over and we got up this little pantomime so as to get our share. As for my little wife, I am really very fond of her. God bless her! Would you mind sending someone into the harem to let her know that I am waiting? We must be off, but I hope you will go on enjoying yourselves."

He left them marveling at this very ingenious trick he had played them.

BARNHAM, TRANS.,
TALES OF NASR-ED-DIN KHOJA

Baklawa

Makes about 50 pieces • The finest-quality sheets of fillo are best to use for *baklawa*.

FOR THE SYRUP

2¹⁄₂ cups sugar

1¹⁄₄ cups water

2 tablespoons lemon juice

2 tablespoons orange-blossom or rose water

1 pound fillo (about 24 sheets)

³⁄₄ cup (1¹⁄₂ sticks) unsalted butter

3–3¹⁄₂ cups (1 pound) pistachio nuts or walnuts, ground medium-fine

Prepare the syrup first. Dissolve the sugar in the water with the lemon juice and simmer a few minutes, until it thickens enough to coat a spoon. Add orange-blossom or rose water and simmer for ¹⁄₂ minute. Allow to cool, then chill in the refrigerator.

In a greased baking pan, a little smaller then the sheets of fillo, lay half the sheets, one at a time, brushing each with melted butter and letting the edges come up the sides of the tray or overhang.

Spread the nuts of your choice evenly over the sheets. Then cover with the remaining sheets, brushing each, including the top one, with melted butter. With a sharp knife, cut diagonal parallel lines 1¹⁄₂–2 inches apart into diamond shapes right through to the bottom.

Bake the *baklawa* in a preheated 350°F oven for 30–35 minutes, or until it is puffed up and golden. Remove from the oven, and pour the cold syrup over the hot *baklawa* along the slashed lines. The amount of syrup called for is the usual one. If you prefer to use less, pour on three-quarters or half the amount, and let people help themselves to more if they wish to.

When cool and ready to serve, cut the pieces of pastry out again and lift them out one by one onto a serving dish, or turn the whole pastry out (by turning it upside down onto a large sheet and then turning it over again on the serving dish) and cut out again along the original lines.

Variations

- Use vegetable oil instead of butter if you like.
- *Kul-wa-shkur* ("eat and thank") is filled with ground blanched almonds mixed with half their weight in sugar. In this case, use half the amount of syrup.
- In Iraq and Iran, they flavor the almond with 1 tablespoon ground cardamom. Sometimes the amount of filling goes up to 2 pounds almonds.
- In Greece, they stir a spoonful or two of honey into the syrup.
- When using walnuts, you can mix 2 teaspoons cinnamon into the filling.
- For a cream-filled Turkish *muhallebili baklava,* bring to the boil 3¹⁄₂ cups milk. Mix ¹⁄₂ cup rice flour with ¹⁄₂ cup cold milk to a paste. Add this to the boiling milk, stirring vigorously, and continue to cook over very low heat, stirring constantly, until the mixture thickens. Simmer for about 15 minutes, adding about ¹⁄₃ cup sugar towards the end. Let it cool before using as a filling instead of the nuts.

About Baklawa and Konafa

All over the Middle East, *baklawa* and *konafa* are present at every party and served at every occasion. No bakery or café could be without them. They even go in donkey carts on those national day-long picnics to the cemeteries, filling the huge baskets alongside the pickles, bread, lettuce, and falafel (page 61). They are part of the celebrations of rejoicing with the dead; tokens of love for the departed, who are believed to come out from the tombs to play on the seesaws and swings, and to enjoy the merry dancers, musicians, jugglers, and *gala-gala* men (magicians) with their relatives.

The pastries are not mentioned in medieval Persian or Arab works, and seem to have made their appearance in the region during the time of the Ottoman Empire. They are the best-known Middle Eastern pastries abroad. Unfortunately, they are known at their worst, because, as with all food prepared commercially in a foreign country, they are invariably degraded. The cooking fats used are the cheapest, peanuts are sometimes used instead of pistachios, walnuts, or almonds, and too much syrup is used to give them a longer shelf life.

THE "POISONED" DISH OF BAKLAWA

In view of the high character and learning of the Khoja, the notables of Akshehir were anxious that their boys should profit by his instruction and appointed him head master of the town school.

One of the notables whose boy attended the school examined him on the lessons he was preparing. The boy answered his questions so well that his father was highly delighted and, calling a servant, bade him take the Khoja a present of a tray of baklawa.

It came just when lessons were going on, and the Khoja wondered how he could prevent the boys getting hold of it. He himself had been called away suddenly to attend a funeral, so, as he could do nothing with it till he came back, he called up the head boys and said to them, "I am putting this tray on the shelf here. Be careful you don't touch it. I don't quite trust the man who sent it, for we were once on very bad terms. Most likely there is something poisonous in it, and if so, it is not a mere practical joke, but a crime he has committed. Mind, it is your own look-out; but if you all die of poison, I shall be held responsible, and you will cause me to be thrown into prison and rot there."

When the Khoja had gone, the head boy, who happened to be his nephew and knew that this was only humbug, took the tray down from the shelf, sent for his particular chums, and tried to persuade them to join him in eating it.

(continued)

The "Poisoned" Dish of Baklawa (continued)

The boys cried, "No! It is poisoned. The Khoja said so. We won't touch it. We don't want to die."

"It is a trick, boys. Just see me eat it! Now you can't say anything after that," said he, as he took some.

"All right," said the others; "but what answer are we to give the Khoja?"

"You leave that to me," said he. "I have got an answer ready that will quiet him. Now then, let us polish off the baklawa."

Feeling more at ease, the boys at once set to work and made a clean sweep of it, shouting and laughing as they did so.

That rascal of a nephew must have made his plans ever since the baklawa arrived, for no sooner had they finished eating it than he ran into the Khoja's room, caught hold of a penknife on the inkstand and broke it. At that moment the Khoja came in, and seeing the penknife, asked angrily who had broken it.

The boys all pointed to his nephew as the culprit.

"What did you do this for?" he demanded. "Do you want me to break your bones for you?"

The boy pretended to cry and said, "My pen broke. I tried to mend it with your penknife and broke the knife. Then I said to myself, 'How ever can I look Uncle in the face? What answer can I give him? If he comes in now, he is sure to give me such a thrashing that he will break every bone in my body. It were far better to die than bear such torture,' said I. Then I began to think what was the best way to kill myself. I did not think it nice to throw myself down the well, because it would make it smell. Then I suddenly remembered the baklawa on the shelf which you told us was poisoned. I took down the tray, and first I repeated the words of our Creed, 'There is no God but God, and Mahomet is his prophet'; then I said good-bye to my schoolfellows and sent word to my father and sister and to my poor mother who had been angry with me. I begged them all to forgive me, and then saying 'Bismillah!'★ I shut my eyes and swallowed the baklawa. I did not forget to clean up the tray with my fingers, but . . . I am sorry to say . . . such is my unhappy lot . . . I did not die . . . I could not die!"

The poor Khoja, though exasperated at the loss of his favourite dish and the breaking of the penknife, which had been a present from his father, could not help exclaiming, "My lad, I am amazed that at your age you should have thought of such a clever plan. I am always ready with an answer whatever I am asked, but you will soon be able to give me points. It is quite clear that this is hereditary in our family."

BARNHAM, TRANS.,
TALES OF NASR-ED-DIN KHOJA

★ In the name of God.

M'hencha

Almond Snake

Serves 30–40 • This Moroccan pastry is a very long coil (hence the name *m'hencha,* meaning "snake") of fillo pastry filled with a ground-almond paste. It is stunning to look at and exquisite. I give very large quantities, because it is the thing to make for a grand occasion, but of course you can make it smaller and reduce the quantities. The flavor is better if you grind the blanched almonds yourself rather than use commercially ground ones.

FOR THE FILLING

7½ cups (3 pounds) ground almonds

5 cups (2 pounds) superfine sugar

2 tablespoons ground cinnamon

Just under 1 cup orange-blossom water

A few drops of almond extract
(optional)

FOR THE PASTRY

1 pound fillo pastry

½ cup (1 stick) butter, melted

2 egg yolks for glazing

TO GARNISH

Confectioners' sugar

1 tablespoon cinnamon

Mix all the filling ingredients and work into a paste with your hands.

Open out the sheets of fillo when you are ready to use them, and keep them in a pile so that they do not dry out. Brush the top one lightly with melted butter. Take lumps of the almond paste and roll into fingers about ¾ inch thick. Place them end-to-end in a line all along one long edge of the top sheet of fillo, making one long rod of paste. Roll the sheet of fillo up over the filling into a long, thin roll, tucking the ends in to stop the filling from oozing out.

Lift the roll up carefully with both hands and place it in the middle of a sheet of parchment paper or a greased sheet of foil on the largest possible baking sheet. Very gently, curve the roll like a snail. To do so without tearing the fillo, you have to crease the pastry first like an accordion by pushing the ends of the roll gently towards the center with both hands.

Do the same with the other sheets until all the filling is used up, rolling them up with the filling inside, curving the rolls, and placing them end to end to make one long tight coil.

Brush the top of the pastry with the egg yolks mixed with 2 teaspoons water and bake in a 350°F oven for 30–40 minutes, until crisp and lightly browned.

Serve cold, sprinkled with confectioners' sugar and with lines of cinnamon in the shape of the spokes of a wheel. Cut the pastry as you would a cake, which will give you pieces of varying sizes. It is very rich, and some will only want a small piece.

Variation

For a pistachio *m'hencha,* use ground pistachios instead of almonds. Although less common, this too is fabulous!

Assabih bi Loz

Almond Fingers

Makes about 30 • These exquisite and delicate Arab pastries are family favorites. They are extremely easy to make, and delightfully light. They feature in medieval manuscripts as *lauzinaj,* which were fried and sprinkled with syrup, rose water, and chopped pistachios. In North Africa they are deep-fried, but we have always baked them.

2⅓ **cups ground almonds**

½ **cup superfine sugar, or to taste**

3 **tablespoons orange-blossom water**

½ **pound fillo-pastry sheets**

6 **tablespoons unsalted butter, melted**

Confectioners' sugar to sprinkle on

Mix the ground almonds with the sugar and orange-blossom water.

Cut the sheets of fillo into 4 rectangular strips about 12 by 4 inches (the size of sheets varies so it is not possible to be precise) and pile them on top of each other so that they do not dry out. Brush the top one lightly with melted butter.

Put 1 heaping teaspoon of the almond mixture at one of the short ends of each rectangle, or take a small lump and press it into a little sausage in your hand. Roll up into a small cigar shape, folding the longer sides slightly over the filling midway. (See drawings.)

Place on a buttered baking sheet and bake in a preheated 325°F oven for 30 minutes, or until lightly golden.

Serve cold, sprinkled with confectioners' sugar.

Variations

• Other delicious fillings are ground pistachios flavored in the same way, with sugar and orange-blossom water; or chopped walnuts mixed with sugar and either a tablespoon of ground cinnamon or the grated zest of an orange and 3 tablespoons fresh orange juice.

• You may deep-fry the pastries instead of baking them, in not very hot oil and for only a very short time, until lightly colored. Drain on paper towels and dust with confectioners' sugar. Serve hot or cold.

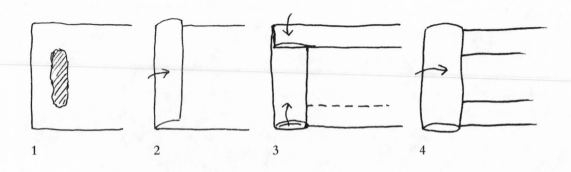

1   2   3   4

Kaab el Ghzal

*Pastry Crescents Filled
with Almond Paste*

Makes 24–26 • These most famous of Moroccan pastries are best known abroad by their French name, *cornes de gazelle* or gazelle's horns. Stuffed with ground-almond paste and curved into horn-shaped crescents, they are ubiquitous wedding-party fare. I have eaten some with a very thin hard crust, and some with a thicker, crumbly crust. This one, made with eggs rather than butter, is thin and crisp.

FOR THE PASTRY

3 cups all-purpose flour

2 eggs, lightly beaten

$\frac{1}{2}$ cup vegetable oil

6–8 tablespoons fresh orange juice, or as required

FOR THE FILLING

$3\frac{1}{4}$ cups ground almonds

1 cup sugar

1 egg, lightly beaten

1 egg yolk

The zest of 1 lemon or 1 orange

1–2 drops of vanilla extract or almond extract (optional)

For the pastry, mix the flour with the eggs and the oil very thoroughly. Then bind with just enough orange juice to hold it together in a soft malleable dough. Wrap in plastic and leave to rest for $\frac{1}{2}$ hour.

Mix the filling ingredients to a soft paste.

Divide the pastry dough into 4 for easier handling, then roll out into sheets as thinly as possible (about $\frac{1}{8}$ inch) on a floured surface, with a floured rolling pin. Cut into 4-inch squares. Take a walnut-sized lump of almond paste and shape into a sausage about $4\frac{1}{2}$ inches long, fatter in the middle and tapering off towards the ends. Place it in the middle of a square, diagonally, on the bias, about $\frac{1}{3}$ inch from the corners. Fold the dough over the filling (a wide-bladed knife helps to lift the dough) and roll up, then very gently curve into a crescent, turning the ends away from the point in the middle. Repeat with all the pastry squares and the rest of the paste.

Arrange on oiled baking sheets and bake in a preheated 375°F oven for 30 minutes. The crescents should not turn brown, but only just begin to color. They will be soft. Do not try to move them until they are cool and firm.

Dip in confectioners' sugar so that they are entirely covered.

Variation

Some people cut the pastry into rounds, place a line of filling in the middle, and fold the pastry over the filling to make a half-moon shape. They pinch the edges together, trim some of the excess rounded edge, and curve the pastries slightly into a crescent.

Konafa

Serves 12 • Called *knafe* by Syrians and Lebanese and *kadaif* by Greeks and Turks, the dough for this pastry that looks like soft white uncooked shredded wheat or vermicelli can be bought in Middle Eastern stores. There are several traditional fillings. The one with nuts is what you find in Arab pastry shops. The one with cream is my favorite. The one with the cheese is the easiest. The last two are meant to be served hot. They make a marvelous after-dinner dessert and teatime pastry. The quantities given below for the syrup are the usual large amount. You can pour only half over the pastry and serve the rest separately for those who want more.

FOR THE SYRUP

2¼ cups sugar

1¼ cups water

2 tablespoons lemon juice

2 tablespoons orange-blossom water

FOR THE CREAM FILLING

⅔ cup rice flour

5 cups milk

4 tablespoons sugar

⅔ cup heavy cream

FOR THE PASTRY

1 pound *konafa* pastry (*kadaif*)

1 cup (2 sticks) butter, melted

⅔ cup pistachios, coarsely chopped, to garnish

Make the syrup first. Boil the sugar, water, and lemon juice for 8–10 minutes, then add the orange-blossom water. Let it cool, then chill in the refrigerator.

For the filling, mix the rice flour with enough of the cold milk to make a smooth paste. Bring the rest of the milk to a boil. Add the rice flour paste, stirring vigorously with a wooden spoon. Leave on very low heat and continue to stir constantly until the mixture thickens. Continue cooking over very low heat for 15–20 minutes (it will thicken more), stirring occasionally without scraping the bottom of the pan, so as not to pick up any burnt bits. Add the sugar and stir well. Let it cool before adding the heavy cream and mixing well.

Put the *konafa* pastry in a large bowl. Pull out and separate the strands as much as possible with your fingers so that they do not stick together too much. Pour the melted and slightly cooled butter over it and work it in very thoroughly with your fingers, pulling out and separating the strands and turning them over so that they do not stick together and are entirely coated with butter.

Spread half the pastry at the bottom of a 12-inch round pie pan. Spread the cream filling over it evenly, and cover with the rest of the pastry. Press down and flatten with the palm of your hand. Bake in a 350°F oven for about 45 minutes. Then raise the temperature to 425°F for about 15 minutes, until the pastry colors slightly.

Just before serving, run a sharp knife round the pie to loosen the sides, and turn out onto a large serving dish. Pour the cold syrup all over the hot *konafa* and sprinkle the top lavishly with chopped pistachios.

Alternatively, you can pour only half the syrup before serving, and pass the rest around in a jug for people to help themselves to more.

Notes: If you want to brown the top of the pie (though that is not usual, some like to do it), run the pan over a burner before turning it out. In the trade, *konafa* is cooked over a fire, then turned upside down from one tray into an identical tray and cooked on the other side. In this way the pastry is browned on both sides.

You can also make 2 small pies, and one can go in the freezer before baking, for another time.

Variations

- For a cheese filling for *konafa bi gebna,* which is also served hot with the syrup poured over, use homemade *gebna beida* (the "white cheese" on page 113) or a mix of 1 pound ricotta with 1 pound grated or chopped mozzarella. There is no added sugar. The cheese used in the Arab world, called *akaoui,* is only slightly sharp and salty, but the *akaoui* sold abroad is far too salty and needs to be soaked in water to remove the salt (it is also extremely expensive). This too is served hot with syrup poured over.

- For a nut filling, spread 1 pound chopped walnuts, almonds, or pistachios. (If you are using walnuts, mix them with 1 teaspoon cinnamon.) Pour the cold syrup over the pastry as it comes out of the oven. This nut pastry is served cold.

- *Konafa* can also be made into small, individual rolled pastries. This is the form in which they are most commonly sold in pastry shops. The threads of dough are wrapped around a filling of chopped or ground walnuts, chopped pistachios, or ground almonds to which a little sugar and some rose water have been added. One way of making them is to lay a flat bundle of threads of dough moistened with melted butter on a clean surface. Lay a flat rod or a wide skewer along it diagonally. Arrange the filling over the rod or skewer, then roll or flap the threads of dough tightly round the rod. Slip the rod out carefully, leaving the filling inside the roll. Arrange the rolls on baking sheets and bake as described above. Then pour cold syrup over them as they come out of the oven. Cut into individual portions and serve cold. One traditional way of baking the rolls is to arrange them in a spiral in a round baking tin.

- *Konafa bil assal* is plain fried or baked *konafa* (without a filling) served with clear honey poured over and topped with thick cream or with chopped nuts. Alternatives to the Arab cream called *eishta* (page 407) are clotted cream and mascarpone.

Ma'amoul

Date- or Nut-Filled Pastries

Makes about 40 • These glorious pastries have a melt-in-the-mouth shell and a variety of fillings of dates or nuts—walnuts, pistachios, or almonds. See the variations for these. My mother always had a biscuit tin full of them to offer with coffee. In Syria and Lebanon they make them with semolina instead of flour.

An uncle told us of a baking competition organized by a dignitary in Aleppo many years ago. The maker of the best *ma'amoul* would get a prize, the equivalent of about two pounds, to be paid by the dignitary. Hundreds of *ma'amoul* poured into his house, certainly more than two pounds' worth, and enough to keep him eating happily for months.

FOR THE DATE FILLING

1 pound pitted dates

About ½ cup water

3 cups all-purpose flour

1 cup (2 sticks) unsalted butter, cut into pieces

2–3 tablespoons orange-blossom or rose water

4–5 tablespoons milk

Confectioners' sugar to sprinkle on

Prepare the filling. Cut the dates up into pieces. Put them in a saucepan with the water and cook over low heat, stirring, until they turn to a soft paste. Let it cool.

Put the flour in a bowl and work the butter in with your fingers. Add orange-blossom or rose water and the milk—only just enough, if any, for the dough to hold together—and work until it is soft, malleable, and easy to shape.

Take a walnut-sized lump of dough. Roll it into a ball and hollow it out with your thumb. Pinch the sides up to make a pot shape. Fill the hole three-quarters full with the filling and bring the dough up over the opening to close into a ball. Flatten the filled balls slightly.

Place the pastries on a large baking tray. Make little decorations in the tops of the pastries with tweezers, or make little dents with the points of a fork. (This will help the confectioners' sugar to cling after they are baked.) Bake in a preheated 325°F oven for 20–25 minutes. Do not let the pastries become brown, or they will be hard and their taste will be spoiled. While they are still warm, they appear soft and uncooked, but on cooling they become firm.

When cool, dust the pastries with confectioners' sugar. They will keep for a long time in a tightly closed tin.

Variations

• The following three nut fillings are considered the grandest, and they really are delicious. Use them instead of the date filling:

2½ cups finely chopped walnuts mixed with 4 tablespoons sugar, 1 teaspoon cinnamon, and the grated rind of ½ orange

2½ cups ground pistachio nuts mixed with 4 tablespoons sugar and 1 tablespoon rose water

2½ cups ground almonds mixed with 4 tablespoons sugar and 2 tablespoons rose or orange-blossom water.

• An easier version of the date-filled *ma'amoul* is a date roll. Divide the dough into 4 parts. Roll out and flatten each part into a rectangle 2 inches wide. Spread the date paste over each rectangle thinly and roll up lengthwise into a fat sausage shape. Cut diagonally into 1¼-inch sections. Prick the tops with a fork so that they will hold the sugar better. Bake as above and, when cool, roll in confectioners' sugar.

Karabij

Makes about 40 • A specialty of Aleppo in Syria, karabij consists of small round *ma'amoul* (see preceding recipe) filled with pistachios or walnuts, bathed in a brilliant white cream called *naatiffe*. The cream, which has a unique flavor and texture, is made with what we called "*bois de Panama*" and affectionately in Arabic *erh el halawa* or "soul of the sweet." It is the wood of a South American tree belonging to a species called saponaria, which produces a thick white foam when it is boiled in water. The root of a plant commonly known as soapwort, which produces the same kind of foam (they are both used as a shampoo to wash carpets and textiles), can also be used.

1 recipe *ma'amoul* (preceding recipe) filled with 1 recipe nut filling (see variations to *ma'amoul* recipe)

FOR THE NAATIFFE CREAM

2–3 ounces *bois de Panama*
1¼ cups sugar
1 tablespoon lemon juice
1 tablespoon orange-blossom water
Whites of 3 large eggs

Prepare the *ma'amoul* dough exactly as described in the basic recipe but leave out rose or orange-blossom water and use water rather than milk to bind it. Fill the *ma'amoul* with nut filling and shape them into little balls. Do not flatten them, and do not decorate their tops. Bake as directed and cool.

Prepare the cream. Pulverize the dried pieces of *bois de Panama* (the wood we had at home was white, but I have seen some darker ones). Soak it for several hours in 1¼ cups water. Transfer to a very large saucepan together with the soaking water, and boil until the mixture has thickened and is reduced to about a quarter of the original volume. Take care while doing this, as the mixture foams and rises considerably. Strain through fine muslin. You will be left with about ¼ cup.

Heat the sugar with ½ cup water until dissolved. Bring to the boil and add lemon juice. Simmer until thickened. Add the orange-blossom water, and remove from the heat. Add the hot solution of *bois de Panama* (off the heat, as otherwise it will foam up and overflow), stirring vigorously with a fork. Then leave to cool.

Whisk the egg whites until very stiff. Add the heavy syrup mixture gradually, little by little, beating vigorously all the time. The mixture will foam and expand into a thick, shiny, white, elastic cream. This is the *naatiffe*.

Dip each *ma'amoul* in this cream, making sure it is well coated. Arrange them all in a pyramid in a serving dish, and pour the rest of the cream over them.

Makroud

*Semolina Pastries Stuffed
with Date Paste*

Makes about 35 • Although not my favorite pastry, *makroud* is very popular in North Africa, especially in Tunisia, which is a land of dates. The pastries are usually deep-fried in oil, then dipped in warm honey. I prefer the lighter baked version.

  6 cups medium-ground semolina

  1³⁄₈ cups (2³⁄₄ sticks) unsalted butter,
    melted

  6 tablespoons orange-blossom water

  ³⁄₄–1 teaspoon salt

  2 pounds dried dates (a soft, moist kind),
    pitted

  2 tablespoons vegetable oil

  2 teaspoons cinnamon

  ¹⁄₄–¹⁄₂ teaspoon ground cloves

  A pot of honey (about 1 pound)

For the semolina dough, mix the semolina with the melted butter, 4 tablespoons of the orange-blossom water, and a little salt. Then add just enough water—about 1 cup—to make the paste hold together in a soft, malleable ball. You can do this in a food processor. Leave to rest, wrapped in plastic wrap, for 15 minutes.

For the filling, put the dates in a pan with the oil, cinnamon, cloves, and the remaining orange-blossom water. Add ¹⁄₂–1 cup water (you need very little if the dates are moist, more if they are a very dry variety) and simmer until the dates are soft and the water has evaporated. Blend to a soft paste in the food processor.

Divide the semolina pastry in half. Roll out one half into a square or rectangle ¹⁄₄ inch thick. You do not need to flour the surface or the rolling pin—the pastry will not stick, as it is very greasy. Carefully lift the sheet of pastry onto a baking sheet (it does not need greasing) with the help of a large spatula or by rolling it round the rolling pin. If it tears, it does not matter—simply stick the pieces together on the baking sheet. (You can roll the pastry out on a plastic sheet, which makes it easier to transfer to a baking sheet.)

Spread the date filling evenly all over the pastry.

Roll out the remaining pastry in the same way, and place it on top of the date paste. With a sharp-pointed knife, cut into lozenges: first cut parallel lines 1¹⁄₂–1³⁄₄ inches apart, then cut parallel lines diagonally across. Bake in a preheated 350°F oven for 45–50 minutes.

Heat the honey in a pan. As the pastry comes out of the oven, dip the lozenges briefly, a few at a time, in the honey, turning them over once. Then place on a serving dish.

Ghorayebah

Butter Cookies

Makes about 50 • These are delightful meltingly soft cookies. You must also try the variation with ground hazelnuts.

> 2 cups (4 sticks) unsalted butter
> 1¼ cups superfine sugar
> 4 cups all-purpose flour
> Blanched almonds or pistachio nuts to decorate

Cream the butter and beat it until it becomes white. Add the sugar, beating constantly for about 5 minutes, until it is a smooth cream. Add flour gradually, working it in by hand. Although no liquid is added, this makes a very soft dough. If the dough is too soft, add a little more flour.

Take walnut-sized lumps, roll them into balls, and flatten them slightly. Place them on a baking sheet a little apart from each other, as they spread slightly. Stick a blanched almond or pistachio on top of each one.

Bake in a 325°F oven for 20–30 minutes. Do not let the *ghorayebah* overcook. They must remain very white: they taste quite different if they are even slightly brown. Let them cool before you try to move them.

Variations

- An exquisite variation is to replace ½ cup of the flour with ½ cup ground hazelnuts.
- You can flavor the dough with a grating of nutmeg, or 1–2 teaspoons of cinnamon or ground cardamom.
- Another traditional shape for *ghorayebah* is little bracelets. Roll the dough into 4-inch-long sausage shapes about ½ inch thick, and bring the ends together to make bracelets. Decorate with split almonds or pistachios.

Basbousa bel Goz el Hind

Semolina and Coconut Pastry

Serves 8–10 • Some years ago, when a block of flats crumbled in the suburbs of Cairo, a newspaper jokingly asked people to save any leftover *basbousa* to rebuild it.

FOR THE SYRUP

> 1½ cups sugar
> ½ cup water
> 1 tablespoon lemon juice

> ½ cup (1 stick) unsalted butter
> 2 cups semolina
> 1 cup superfine sugar
> ¾ cup desiccated coconut
> ½ cup all-purpose flour
> ⅔ cup milk
> 1 teaspoon baking powder
> A few drops of vanilla extract

Prepare the syrup first by boiling the sugar and water with the lemon juice for about 7 minutes, until it is thick enough to coat a spoon. Allow to cool, and chill.

Melt the butter in a large saucepan. Add the remaining ingredients and beat well with a wooden spoon until thoroughly mixed. Pour the mixture into a large buttered oven dish or baking pan, making a thin layer. Flatten out as much as possible. Bake in a preheated 350°F oven for about 20–30 minutes. Look at it after 20 minutes to see if it has cooked enough. It should be crisp and a rich gold.

Cut into squares or lozenge shapes as soon as it comes out of the oven, and pour the cold syrup over the hot *basbousa*.

Serve hot or cold.

Basbousa bel Laban Zabadi

Semolina Pudding with Yogurt

Serves 6 • *Basbousa* is a popular Egyptian pastry, also called *helwa,* which means "sweet."

FOR THE SYRUP

1$\frac{1}{2}$ cups sugar

$\frac{1}{2}$ cup water

Juice of $\frac{1}{2}$ lemon

8 tablespoons (1 stick) unsalted butter

$\frac{1}{2}$ cup blanched almonds

$\frac{2}{3}$ cup yogurt

1 cup sugar

1$\frac{1}{2}$ cups semolina

1 teaspoon baking powder

1 tablespoon vanilla sugar or a few drops of vanilla extract

1–1$\frac{1}{2}$ cups *eishta* (page 407), clotted cream, or mascarpone, to serve with (optional)

Make a syrup by boiling the sugar, water, and lemon juice for 5–8 minutes, until it thickens enough to coat a spoon. Let cool, then chill.

Melt 6 tablespoons of the butter. Toast the blanched almonds under the broiler or in a dry skillet and chop them finely.

Beat the yogurt with the sugar in a large mixing bowl. Add the melted butter and all remaining ingredients except the cream and the 2 tablespoons unmelted butter. Beat well until thoroughly mixed. Pour into a large, rectangular, buttered baking pan and bake in a preheated 375°F oven for $\frac{1}{2}$ hour.

Pour the cold syrup over the hot *basbousa* as soon as it comes out of the oven. Cut into lozenge shapes and return to the oven for a further 3 minutes.

Before serving, melt the remaining 2 tablespoons of butter, pour over the pastry, and spread with *eishta* (the rich cream from water buffalo's milk), clotted cream, or mascarpone.

THE NATIONAL DISH HELWA

One day he was chatting with some friends, when the conversation turned upon the national dish, helwa.

"Some years ago," said the Khoja, "I wanted to make some helwa flavored with almonds, but I could never manage to do it."

"That is very odd. It is not difficult at all. Why couldn't you make it?" they asked.

"Well," said he, "when there was flour in the larder there was no butter, and when there was butter there was no flour."

"Oh, nonsense, Khoja! Do you mean to say that all that time you could not find both?"

"Ah, yes," he answered, "it did happen once, but then you see I was not there to make it."

BARNHAM, TRANS.,
TALES OF NASR-ED-DIN KHOJA

Basbousa bel Loz

Semolina Pastry with Almonds

Serves 6

3 cups water

2 cups sugar

1 teaspoon lemon juice

1 cup blanched almonds

²/₃ cup butter

1 cup semolina

To garnish: whole blanched almonds,
eishta (the rich cream from water
buffalo's milk, page 407), or clotted or
whipped heavy cream

Bring water, sugar, and lemon juice to the boil
in a pan. Simmer for 8 minutes.

Chop the almonds finely and fry them in
the hot butter together with the semolina until
they are a beautiful golden color.

Add the hot syrup slowly, stirring constantly, over low heat until the mixture thickens. Remove from the heat and cover the pan.
Let it cool a little.

Pour into individual greased molds and flatten out on top. Turn out immediately and
serve warm. Decorate each portion with an almond or a dollop of cream.

Sambousek bel Loz

Almond Rissoles

These Syrian pastries are prepared with the
dough given under savory *sambousek bi gebna*
on page 135, using a little sugar instead of salt,
and a filling of 2 cups ground almonds mixed
with ¾–1 cup superfine sugar and 2 tablespoons orange-blossom water.

Take walnut-sized lumps of dough, roll each
into a little ball and flatten as thinly as possible
between the palms of your hands, then pull it
further into a round of about 4 inches in diameter. Put a heaping tablespoon of filling in the
center of each. Fold in half, making a half-
moon shape, then pinch and fold the edges
firmly in a sort of festoon.

Deep-fry the pastries in hot oil until golden
brown, and drain on paper towels. Or, better
still, paint their tops with lightly beaten egg
yolk and bake in a preheated 350°F oven for ½
hour, until golden.

Iraqis flavor the filling with 1 teaspoon
ground cardamom.

Ataïf

Arab Pancakes

Makes about 30 tiny open pancakes or about 12 large stuffed pancakes • *Ataïf* are dearly loved all over the Arab world. They were favorites of the Caliph Mustakfi of Baghdad in the tenth century. At a lavish banquet in his honor, a poem written by a certain Mahmud ibn Husain al-Kushâjim extolling the merits of *ataïf* was recited. Basically pancakes dipped in syrup, they are sprinkled with pistachios and eaten with thick cream or, more grandly, they are stuffed with chopped nuts or with cheese. The stuffed ones are my favorites.

They are eaten during festivals, especially during the month of Ramadan, when they are sold in the street. They are the sweets of happy occasions such as weddings. Once upon a time, in Egypt, on the day of betrothal, a string of camels or donkeys brought the bride's furniture and belongings to the house of the bridegroom, while he gave a farewell "stag" banquet complete with dancers and singers. The young bride had a ritual bath and was then conducted to her new home by a colorful procession headed by buffoons and musicians, dancers, jugglers, sword swallowers, and fire eaters. These were followed by lavishly decorated donkey carts. A first cart carried a coffeemaker with pots and cups and a fire, making coffee for well-wishers. A second carried makers of *ma'amoul* and trays covered with these pastries to distribute. A third carried pancake makers, handing out *ataïf* to passersby. When the bride arrived at the house, she sat down with her guests to a feast where hundreds of these delicacies were consumed.

Families nowadays usually buy their *ataïf* ready-made from bakeries, and then stuff them and soak them in syrup. But the batter is easy enough to make at home. Several people I know always make it themselves. None have scales, nor do they measure quantities. They just look at the batter and add more water or more flour if they think it requires it. An aunt who lives in California and who has never ceased to cook in the Oriental manner uses a well-known pancake mix, which is very acceptable.

FOR THE BATTER

- 1½ teaspoons active dry yeast
- 1 teaspoon sugar
- 1½ cups lukewarm water
- 1⅓ cups all-purpose flour

FOR THE SYRUP

- 2½ cups sugar
- 1¼ cups water
- 1 tablespoon lemon juice
- 1–2 tablespoons orange-blossom or rose water
- Vegetable oil

For the batter, dissolve the yeast with the sugar in ½ cup of the water. Let it stand in a warm place for 10 minutes, or until it froths. Put the flour in a large bowl. Add the yeast mixture and the remaining water gradually, beating vigorously, to make a creamy, lump-free batter. Cover the bowl with plastic wrap, and leave in a warm place for about 1 hour. The soft, almost liquid batter will rise and become bubbly and a little elastic.

To make the syrup, bring the water to the boil with the sugar and lemon juice and simmer for 10 minutes, until it is thick enough to coat the back of a spoon. Then stir in the orange-blossom or rose water and simmer for a few seconds more. Allow to cool, then chill in the refrigerator.

When the batter is ready, rub a nonstick skillet with oil (use a paper towel) so as to grease it with a very thin film. Heat the skillet until it is very hot, then reduce the heat and keep it at medium.

TO MAKE TINY OPEN ATAÏF

Pour the batter by the tablespoon into the skillet, making several small rounds that are not touching, in the pan. As little holes appear on top and the pancakes come away from the pan easily and become golden on the bottom, turn and do the other side. Drop them into the syrup when they are done.

To serve, arrange in one layer on a flat serving dish. Spread with about ½ pound thick cream. In the Middle East the cream made from buffalo's milk called *eishta* is used (see page 407), but you may use clotted cream or mascarpone or whipped heavy cream.

Sprinkle on about 1¼ cups chopped pistachios or almonds, or spread a teaspoonful of rose-petal jam over the cream (this is popular at weddings). For a party, make a mound with several layers of pancakes, each spread with cream and rose-petal jam or sprinkled with chopped pistachios or almonds.

TO MAKE STUFFED ATAÏF

This is one of my favorite Arab sweets. Pour ½ ladle of batter into the oiled skillet over medium heat, tilting the pan a little to allow it to spread. It will not spread out too much and will remain in a small, round, fattish shape. Fry one side of the pancake only—this is very important. The other side must remain uncooked and moist, so that its edges can be stuck together. When the pancakes lose their whiteness and little holes appear, and as they become detached from the pan, lift them out and pile them up on a plate ready to be stuffed.

Put a heaping tablespoon of stuffing (see below) in the middle of each pancake, on the uncooked side. Fold the pancakes in half over the filling to make a half-moon shape, and close the pastries by pinching the edges firmly together to seal them and trap the filling.

Deep-fry, a few at a time, in medium-hot oil about 1 inch deep, until pale brown, turning them over once. Lift them out with a perforated spoon and drain on paper towels. Then dip them, while still hot, in the above syrup.

Serve hot or cold. You can make them in advance and reheat them, covered, in the oven. For those who have a sweet tooth, serve them with more syrup poured over.

Filling for Ataïf bi Loz— Pancakes Stuffed with Walnuts

Mix 2 cups coarsely ground or chopped walnuts, 3 to 4 tablespoons sugar, and 2 teaspoons ground cinnamon. They are divine.

Filling for Ataïf bi Gebna— Pancakes Stuffed with Cheese

In the Middle East a slightly salty and sharp cheese called *akaoui* is used. Alternatives are ricotta, mozzarella, and even a slightly salted halumi (soak the cheese in several changes of water to remove the salt). A good combination is ¾ pound of a half-and-half mixture of mozzarella and ricotta, blended to a paste in the food processor. Dip the hot pancakes in syrup and serve hot. Mozzarella and halumi become hard and rubbery when they are cold.

Taratir-at-Turkman

Pastry Ribbon Fritters

Taratir-at-turkman means "bonnets of the Turks." There are very old recipes for these little pastries. The quantities make a large number, but they keep very well in a tin.

5 egg yolks

½ teaspoon salt

3 tablespoons superfine sugar

2 tablespoons brandy

5 tablespoons plain whole-milk yogurt

About 3 cups all-purpose flour

Oil for deep-frying

Confectioners' sugar

Place the egg yolks in a large mixing bowl. Add salt and beat until thick and lemon-colored. Add the sugar and brandy, and continue beating. Add the yogurt and mix well. Sift in the flour, stirring with a wooden spoon to begin with, and then working the dough by hand. Add just enough flour to have a dough that sticks together in a ball. Knead vigorously in the bowl or on a floured board for 10–15 minutes, until the dough is smooth and elastic and begins to blister. Cover with plastic wrap and leave to rest for about ½ hour.

Divide into 2 pieces to roll out more easily. Roll out each piece as thinly as possible on a lightly floured surface, with a floured rolling pin. Cut into ribbons about ¾ inch wide, then divide into 3-inch strips. Make a 1-inch-long slit down the center of each strip and pull one end through. Alternatively, tie the strips in knots, which is easier.

Deep-fry a few at a time in oil—medium-hot and 1½ inches deep—until the pastries are puffed and just golden, turning them once. Lift out with a perforated spoon. Drain on paper towels and sprinkle with confectioners' sugar.

Siphnopitta

Honey and Cheese Cake

Serves 6–8 • A Greek Eastertime specialty, especially renowned on the island of Siphnos. Mizithra, a soft, fresh, unsalted cheese made from sheep's milk, is used there, but a bland, unsalted curd or cream cheese may be substituted.

1 cup (2 sticks) unsalted butter, chilled

1⅔ cups flour

½ teaspoon salt

1 pound fresh ricotta cheese

4 eggs

½–⅔ cup honey, to taste

2 teaspoons cinnamon

To prepare the pastry shell, work the chilled butter into the flour mixed with salt with your hands, or use a food processor, mixing in short pulses. Gradually add 3–4 tablespoons water, just enough to make the dough hold together in a soft ball. Handle it no further, wrap it in plastic wrap, and chill for about 30 minutes.

Line a deep 10-inch pie pan with the dough by patting it out with the palm of your hand (it is easier than trying to roll out this rich dough). Bake in a preheated 350°F oven for 10 minutes. Mix the cheese, eggs, honey (start with the lesser quantity and taste before you add more, as it might be too sweet for you), and 1 teaspoon of the cinnamon. Blend well.

Let the empty baked shell cool before filling. (If it is hot it will disintegrate.) Pour the cheese mixture gently all over the pastry base and return to a preheated 375°F oven for about 35 minutes, until it is firm and the top golden.

Dust with the remaining cinnamon and let it cool before serving.

Zalabia or Luqmat el Qadi

Little Round Fritters in Syrup

Serves 6–8 • A recipe is given in al-Baghdadi's medieval cookery manual for these crisp little golden balls soaked in scented syrup or honey, bearing the same name, *luqmat el qadi,* which means "judge's mouthfuls." In Egypt they are known as *zalabia,* in Lebanon they are known as *aweimat.* The Greeks have a similar sweet called *loukoumades.* They are street food. Vendors deep-fry them and throw them into a syrup. During festivals they are sometimes colored bright yellow or red for joy and happiness and sold sprinkled with sugar and cinnamon. For parties they are served piled in a pyramid on a platter, held together by a sticky syrup.

FOR THE SUGAR SYRUP

5 cups sugar

2 cups water

Juice of ½ lemon

1 tablespoon rose or orange-blossom water

FOR THE BATTER

1 package or 2 teaspoons active dry yeast

Pinch of sugar

3 cups lukewarm water

3⅓ cups unbleached white bread flour or all-purpose flour

½ teaspoon salt

Vegetable oil for deep-frying

Make the syrup first. Put the sugar, water, and lemon juice in a pan and simmer for 10–15 minutes, until it is thick enough to coat a spoon. Add the rose or orange-blossom water and simmer a few moments longer, then chill.

For the batter, dissolve the yeast with the sugar in about ½ cup of the warm water and let stand 10–15 minutes, until it froths. Put the flour in a large bowl and mix in the salt and the yeast mixture, then stir in the remaining water gradually and beat vigorously for about 10 minutes, until smooth and elastic. Cover with plastic wrap and leave to rise in a warm place for at least 1 hour, then beat the batter once more and let it rise again.

Make the fritters in batches. Pour little balls of batter by the teaspoon or tablespoon (they can be small or large) into 1½ inches sizzling but not-too-hot oil, and fry until puffed up, crisp, and golden, turning them to brown them all over. You may find it easier if you dip the spoon in oil, so that the batter rolls off easily. Lower the heat a little, so that the fritters have time to get done inside before they are too brown. The batter is light and produces irregular, rather than perfectly round, shapes. If the oil is not hot enough to begin with, the batter tends to flatten out.

Lift the fritters out with a slotted spoon, drain on paper towels, and dip them in the cold syrup for a few seconds, or let them soak up the syrup for longer. They are at their best hot, but are also good cold.

Variations

• In North Africa, they pour the batter through a funnel in the shape of a coil—they call it a rose.

• Instead of sugar syrup, make a honey syrup by heating up honey with about half the volume of water.

• Instead of soaking in syrup, sprinkle with confectioners' sugar and cinnamon.

Polenta Annabi

Polenta Fritters

Serves 8 • Algerian polenta fritters are soft and creamy inside and crisp and golden outside. They are eaten hot, but you can prepare them in advance and reheat them. They are delicious.

4½ cups milk

1¼ cup sugar

Few drops of vanilla extract

The grated rind of one lemon

1½ cups quick-cooking cornmeal (polenta)

6 tablespoons butter, cut into pieces

5 eggs, lightly beaten

¾ cup raisins

Flour

Vegetable oil for deep-frying

Confectioners' sugar to sprinkle on

In a saucepan, bring the milk to the boil with the sugar, vanilla extract, and grated lemon rind. Stir in the cornmeal and keep stirring with a wooden spoon for 5–10 minutes.

Take off the heat, add the butter and eggs, and beat vigorously with the spoon until they are amalgamated with the polenta into a soft creamy mass. Add the raisins, and mix well. Then pour into a wide, oiled dish and let it cool.

When the polenta has firmed, take lumps the size of small tangerines and pat them into round, not-too-flat cakes. Put some flour on a plate and turn the polenta cakes in this to cover them all over.

Deep-fry in batches in 1½ inches hot oil until golden, turning them over once. Serve hot, dusted with a little confectioners' sugar.

Variation

For a polenta cake, pour the polenta mixture into an 11- or 12-inch oiled oven dish or tart pan and bake in a 350°F oven for 25 minutes, then put under the broiler until golden. Serve hot or cold, dusted with confectioners' sugar. Cut into wedges.

Sfendj

Doughnut Rings

Makes about 20 • In North Africa, *sfendj,* also called *khfaf,* are sold by street vendors. People buy them for breakfast. They can be plain or with raisins. Eat them hot as soon as they are done or reheat in the oven. Serve them with honey or dusted with sugar.

1 package or 2 teaspoons active dry
   yeast

About 1¼ cups lukewarm water

Pinch of sugar

3 cups unbleached white bread flour

½ teaspoon salt

3 tablespoons raisins (optional)

Oil for frying

Confectioners' sugar to sprinkle on or
   honey to serve with

In a large bowl, dilute the yeast in about ½ cup of the warm water with a pinch of sugar and leave to rest until it froths.

Put the flour in a bowl and mix in the salt. Pour in the yeast mixture and just enough of the remaining water to have a dough that holds together in a ball. Knead vigorously for 10 minutes, until the dough is smooth, shiny, and elastic. Add the raisins, if you like, and work them evenly into the dough. Pour 1 tablespoon oil into the bowl and turn the dough around in it to grease it all over. Cover the bowl with plastic wrap and leave in a warm place for about 2 hours, or until doubled in bulk.

Heat about 1½ inches oil in a large pan or deep skillet until it sizzles when you throw in a piece of bread.

Punch down the dough and knead for ½ minute. Oil your hands. Take lumps the size of an egg and roll into balls. Flatten each between your hands and make a hole in the middle with your finger. Enlarge the hole by pulling out the dough to make a ring, or twirl it around your finger.

Lower the rings gently into the oil, a few at a time, and lower the heat to medium. The dough will puff up at once. Turn the rings over once, and cook until crisp and golden. Drain on paper towels and serve sprinkled with confectioners' sugar or accompanied by a bowl of honey.

Eish es Seray or Ekmek Kadaif

Palace Bread

Serves 8–10 • When I was a girl I could die for this. I hardly ever make it now, but I was very happy to find it again in Istanbul. This is a sweet of Turkish origin which was very popular in Egypt. Some bakeries and cafés always had a large tray full of the rich, translucent, golden-ocher bread soaked in honey and syrup. Numerous recipes exist, and of course the texture and taste depend on the bread and the honey used. Use a fragrant honey like Hymettus or acacia.

3¾ cups sugar

1¼ cups water

1 tablespoon lemon juice

⅔–1¼ cups honey

1–2 tablespoons rose water

A large round loaf of white or whole-
    wheat bread

1½ cups *eishta* (see page 407), clotted
    cream, or mascarpone

¼ cup chopped pistachios (optional)

Make a thick syrup. Bring to the boil the sugar and water with the lemon juice. Simmer 10 minutes, until it thickens. Stir in honey and rose water and simmer for 2 minutes longer. You can darken the syrup to a rich deep brown (the traditional color for this sweet) by melting 2 tablespoons sugar in another pan until it is a dark-brown caramel and stirring it into the hot syrup.

Cut a slice about ¾ inch thick horizontally right across the loaf of bread, and cut away the crust around it, so as to obtain one large soft crustless disk of bread. Dry out in a very low oven until slightly colored. Then moisten with water.

Pour the syrup into a wide, shallow round pan which will hold the whole crustless disk of bread. Bring the syrup to the boil. Place the bread in it and simmer very gently, squashing and pressing it down with a wooden spoon to help it absorb the syrup better. Cook for about ¾ hour, adding water if it becomes too sticky, until the bread is entirely soaked through and is soft, rich, and heavy.

Turn out onto a round serving platter and allow to cool.

Spread with a thick layer of cream or mascarpone and sprinkle, if you like, with chopped pistachios.

Serve very small portions, as *eish es seray* is extremely rich and nobody can eat too much of it.

Variations

- Individual slices of bread can be used in the same way as the single large disk of bread and simmered until soaked through and very soft.
- In the Lebanon the syrup is scented with the grated zest of an orange.

Sweetmeats

Among Middle Eastern pastries, there are some very small delicacies which are easy to prepare in large quantities, and which make lovely sweetmeats to serve at large parties or after dinner with coffee. Several are made with ground almonds. There are also apricot drops, dates and walnuts stuffed with ground almonds, caramelized hazelnuts, pistachios, and walnuts.

Various recipes exist for almond paste. Some date back to medieval times. All are still very popular today. Many are traditionally cut into lozenge shapes. It is believed that the word "lozenge" is derived from these Arab sweets made with almonds, the word for which is *loz* in Arabic.

ARAB PROVERB:
*"A year in which there are plenty of almonds and
dates increases prosperity and life."*

Orass bi Loz

Almond Balls

Makes 22–24 balls

2 cups ground almonds

1 cup superfine sugar

1 or 2 drops of almond extract
(optional)

About 3 tablespoons rose or orange-
blossom water

12 blanched almonds or pistachio nuts to
garnish (optional)

Confectioners' sugar to roll the balls in
at the end

Mix the ground almonds and sugar in a bowl. Add the almond extract if you wish (I prefer it without), and rose or orange-blossom water, and work well with your hands. The mixture will seem dry at first, but the almonds will release enough oil to bind the mixture. Knead to a soft doughy paste.

Shape into 1-inch balls (the size of large marbles) and roll in confectioners' sugar. Decorate each ball, if you like, with a split almond or pistachio stuck on top.

Variations

• Instead of 1 cup superfine sugar, use 2 cups confectioners' sugar.

• Do the same recipe with ground pistachio nuts instead of almonds and stick a whole pistachio on the top. These green balls are heavenly.

• Stuff the almond balls with chopped pistachios. This is really superb. Make a little hole in each almond ball with your finger and fill it with chopped pistachios mixed with sugar.

Close the hole over the pistachios and shape into a ball again. Roll the balls in confectioners' sugar and place them in small paper cases. Decorate the top of each ball with a whole or half pistachio which has been stripped of its thin skin to make its greenness apparent.

• In Iraq, almond paste, colored yellow with moistened saffron powder, is flattened in a tray, cut into lozenges, and covered with gold-leaf paper. Thus adorned, it is sent to friends by a bride's family to celebrate her wedding.

ARAB WISDOM:
"When I go to my house after a day of labor, the food tastes good to me though it be cheap. Does, then, the richest merchant in the city enjoy his quail and duck and partridges more than I enjoy my bread and dates? And can man be happier than I with my wife, for if there be not love, what pleasure has a man in a woman?"

Kahk bi Loz

Almond Bracelets

Use a paste similar to that given for almond balls (preceding recipe). Mix 1 pound (5 cups) ground almonds with 1 pound (2½ cups) confectioners' sugar. Add the white of 1 small egg, stiffly beaten, and just enough orange-blossom water to make a firm, dryish paste. (For a paste made with 2½ cups ground almonds, use only half a small egg white and do not be tempted to use more.)

Knead the paste well, and roll into thin sausages about 5 inches long. Bring the ends together and flatten them, making bracelets the size of small napkin rings. Decorate, if you like, with a few blanched almonds. Arrange on cookie sheets lined with baking paper.

Bake in a preheated 400°F oven for about 10 minutes. The bracelets must not be allowed to color. They will be soft while hot but become firm on cooling. Lift carefully when they have cooled.

Variation

For almond macaroons, roll into walnut-sized balls, flatten them slightly, and stick a blanched almond in the middle of each.

Almond Bracelets

Almond bracelets are favorites at engagement and wedding parties. They are also served at the ritual bath of a young bride. Although this ceremony is still common in rural districts, the custom is fast disappearing from modern town weddings.

The bride goes to the public bath accompanied by her female relatives and friends. She walks with a woman at each side, under a canopy of silk borne by four men. Married women head the procession, followed by young, unmarried girls. The bride walks behind. At the bath, she washes in scented water, watched by all the women and girls. A feast follows. While the guests are entertained by female singers, large trays piled high with pastries are passed round. No feast of this type could be without the traditional *kahk bi loz.*

Among the songs sung at the bath, one goes as follows:

Shimmering, shimmering, little lettuce heart, shimmering!
Oh my little brother, she is white, and her whiteness is tinted with pomegranate!
Oh my little brother, she is white, and her whiteness is seductive!

On such occasions the relatives try to assess if the girl will make a good wife and if she will be able to bear children easily. Remarks abound on the width of her hips and the size of her breasts.

Tamr bi Loz

Stuffed Dates

Makes about 50 • In North Africa the almond stuffing is colored green to give the semblance of pistachios, which are considered grander. You can of course use real pistachios.

1½ cups ground almonds or pistachios

½ cup superfine sugar

2–3 tablespoons rose water or orange-blossom water

1 pound dried dates (the soft California or Tunisian ones)

Mix the ground almonds or pistachios and sugar in a bowl, and add just enough rose or orange-blossom water to bind them into a firm paste. Put in less than you seem to require, as, once you start kneading with your hands, the oil from the almonds will act as an extra bind. Alternatively, you can start with blanched almonds or pistachios and blend all the ingredients except the dates to a paste in a food processor.

Make a slit on one side of each date with a pointed knife and pull out the pit. Take a small lump of almond or pistachio paste, pull the date open wide, press the paste in the opening, and close the date only slightly over it, so that the filling is revealed generously. They keep well for weeks.

Halawa Tamr

Date and Walnut Drops

Makes about 50 • Blend in a food processor and reduce to a paste 1 pound dried pitted dates (of the soft, moist variety), then work in 1 pound coarsely chopped walnuts. Shape into marble-sized balls and roll in confectioners' sugar. They keep well for weeks and are good to serve with coffee.

Variation

For an Algerian version with dried figs, blend in the food processor 1 pound dried figs, 1 pound pitted dates, 2 tablespoons honey, and 1 tablespoon aniseed, then work in ½ pound coarsely chopped nuts. Shape into marble-sized balls and roll in confectioners' sugar.

THE DATE STONES

The Khoja was eating dates, and his wife noticed that he did not take out the stones.

"It seems to me that you are not taking out the pits," said she.

"Of course not," said he. "When I bought them the greengrocer did not allow for the pits when he weighed the dates. Had he thrown them away, he could not have sold his dates; and as I paid cash down, do you think I am going to throw them into the street? Not I! Whoever told you I was so wasteful? I paid for them, have eaten them and found them very good, so that is enough!"

BARNHAM, TRANS.,
TALES OF NASR-ED-DIN KHOJA

Halawa Mishmish

Apricot Balls

Makes about 50 • Use a natural, tart variety of dried apricots, not the sweetened or honeyed ones; they must also be soft. These keep well for weeks and are good to serve with coffee.

1 pound dried apricots

Confectioners' sugar

About 25 shelled pistachios to decorate

Do not soak or wash the apricots, or you will produce a cream. Put them as they are in the food processor and blend them to a smooth paste, adding a very little water, by the teaspoon if necessary. Wash your hands and, wetting them or greasing them with a little oil so that the paste does not stick, take little lumps of paste and roll into marble-sized balls. Roll them in confectioners' sugar and press half a pistachio on the top of each.

Variations

• Mix ½ cup coarsely chopped pistachios with 2 tablespoons of sugar. Make a small hole in the center of each apricot ball, put in a little of the filling, close the hole again, and roll in confectioners' sugar.

• Work ½ cup coarsely chopped pistachios into the apricot paste with your hands.

A PERSIAN TALE

A peasant went into town. As he walked through the bazaar, he came across a confectionery shop with all sorts of brightly colored confectionery displayed on the street. The owner of the shop sat on the doorstep.

The peasant went up to him, pointed two fingers at his eyes and said:

"Hou!"

The confectioner asked him why he had done that.

"I thought you were blind and could not see me!" came the reply.

"But I am not blind!" said the confectioner.

"Then how," asked the peasant, "if you can see, can you resist eating your sweets?"

CHRISTENSEN, *CONTES PERSANS*

Stuffed Walnuts

Makes 20

1⅓ cups ground almonds

⅔ cup superfine sugar

2–3 tablespoons orange-blossom water,
   or more

20 shelled walnuts or 40 walnut halves

⅔ cup sugar

Make a firm paste by mixing the ground almonds, superfine sugar, and orange-blossom
water and kneading it with your hands. Take
about 1 heaping teaspoon of the paste and press
it between 2 walnut halves. Place these on an
oiled surface (a marble slab, a plate, a pastry
sheet will do).

Make some caramel by heating and stirring
the sugar until it melts and turns a light-brown
color. Pour a little over each walnut. When it is
cold and hard, it will hold the walnut halves together. Place in little paper cases to serve.

Caramelized Nut Clusters

Caramelized almonds, hazelnuts, and pistachio
nuts were among the range of confectionery
sold on the beaches of Alexandria when I was a
child. Young vendors paced the sands carrying
confections and sweetmeats in large, flat wicker
baskets, chanting "*Fresca!*" (I wonder if it originated from the Italian, meaning "fresh.") They
balanced the baskets on their heads, resting
them on a coiled piece of soft cloth, and sometimes carried a second basket perched on one
hip and held at the other side by an out-
stretched hand. Their chant was echoed by that
of other vendors, singing, "*Casquette, baranet,
pantofla, pastillia, chocolat!*" ("Caps, hats, slip-
pers, pastilles, chocolate!"), or "*Gazouza,
gazouza!*" ("Fizzy lemonade!"). Some sold
salted roasted peanuts and pistachios as well as
confectionery, and gambled these in games of
odds-and-evens with their customers.

To make nut clusters, put about 3⅓ cups
whole hazelnuts, almonds, or pistachio nuts
(blanched or not) together in little heaps on an
oiled marble slab or on a large oiled plate. Melt
2¼ cups sugar over very low heat, stirring constantly. Allow the caramel to become light
brown, then pour it over the nut clusters. As it
cools, the caramel will harden and hold the
nuts together.

Alternatively, and more simply, the nuts or
almonds can be thrown into the hot, light-
brown caramel and stirred until they are all well
coated. Pour the whole onto an oiled slab or
plate. When it has hardened, crack it into
pieces.

A less common variation is to simmer the
nuts in honey instead of caramel until the mixture thickens. Sesame seeds are sometimes used
in this manner.

Pickles and Preserves

MEKHALEL

Food preservation is a particularly important problem in hot countries, especially in isolated, nonagricultural areas. The processes used today by families, grocers, and street vendors are those inherited from their ancestors of the ancient Oriental and classical civilizations, who had an even greater need for careful preservation in the days before easy transport, refrigerators, canning, and freezing. Although pickling was originally devised as a method of preservation, the result is so delicious that pickles are now prepared for their own sake, to be served as mezze or to accompany main dishes. They are usually eaten as soon as they are ready, and the pickling solutions contain less salt and vinegar than they would if they were made to last, which makes them more appealing.

Pickles are prepared in their season, and also throughout the year, since even when the vegetables are not in season in one area, it is now generally possible to import them from a neighboring country. Every home has its *martaban,* or jars filled with various pickles, ready for eating at all times of the day.

My father has told me he remembers that when he was a child visiting relatives in Syria the women of the family devoted their time to pickling and to making jams and syrups whenever they had no parties, feasts, or other household activities to occupy them. Large glass jars were filled with turnips, onions, cucumbers, lemons, cauliflower, eggplants, and peppers. The family could hardly wait to start eating them, and often did so before the pickles were quite ready. A visit to the cellar or store cupboard to see how they were maturing and mellowing to soft pinks, saffrons, mauves, and pale greens was a mouth-watering expedition.

Grocers in the Middle East prepare their own pickles. It was customary in the past, and still is today, for them to offer customers a taste of their newly mellowed pickles as well as a sample of their cheeses and jams. This custom may have been motivated by the hope that the customer would not be able to resist taking some home; but any ulterior motive was well concealed behind a heart-warming affability and generosity. Some "*Roumi*" (Greek) grocers in Egypt would even insist on offering a second helping, regardless of whether there appeared to be any intention on the customer's part to buy.

A relative of my father's was known to go from one grocer to another, tasting here and there, a little of everything, dipping a large finger into a new batch of jam or honey, until he had satisfied his appetite. No shopkeeper ever begrudged him, since they all regarded "tasting" as a traditional and obligatory duty. They may even have been secretly flattered that this fat man visited them so often.

Restaurants like to display a vividly colorful assortment of pickles, sometimes placing them on their windowsills to lure customers in. Pickle jars are also a feature of the street. Squatting on the pavements of busy streets, vendors sell homemade pickled turnips swimming in a pink solution, or eggplants looking fiercely black and shiny in enormous jars. Passersby dip their hands in, searching for the tastiest and largest piece, and savor them with bread provided by the vendor, soaking it in the pink salt-and-vinegar solution or the seasoned oil. Some can only afford to dip their bread in the pickling liquor and sit in the sun, rapturously savoring the treat. When the pickles are finished, the vendor sometimes sells the precious liquor as a sauce for rice.

Hamad M'Rakad

Preserved Lemons

Preserved lemons lend a unique and distinctive flavor to North African dishes. You find the softened lemons in jars, or sold loose in street markets. They are now also common fare in the south of France. You can make them yourself. They take about 4 weeks to mature and can last a year. When they are ready to use, the pulp is scooped out and thrown away—only the skin is eaten. You can use small limes with thin skins, or ordinary lemons with thick ones.

There are three common ways of making them.

Lemons Preserved in Salt and Lemon Juice

In this method, which is considered most prestigious and gives the best results, no water is used. You will need $\frac{1}{3}$ cup salt for 1 pound lemons. This works out at about 4 tablespoons salt for 4 lemons.

> 4 lemons (choose them with thick skins)
> 4 tablespoons sea salt
> Juice of 4 more lemons, or more

Wash and scrub the lemons. The classic Moroccan way is to cut each lemon in quarters but not right through, so that the pieces are still attached at the stem end, and to stuff each with plenty of salt. Put them in a glass jar, pressing them down so that they are squashed together, and close the jar. Leave for 3–4 days, by which time the lemons will have released some of their juices and the skins will have softened a little. Press them down as much as you can and add fresh lemon juice to cover them entirely. Close the jar and leave in a cool place for at least a month, after which they should be ready. The longer they are left, the better the flavor. (If a piece of lemon is not covered, it develops a white mold which is harmless and just needs to be washed off.)

Before using, rinse to get rid of the salt and scoop out and discard the pulp.

Lemons Pickled in Brine

This is the same procedure as above, but instead of adding lemon juice, cover the lemons with brine made by adding 2 tablespoons salt to warm water. Lemons prepared this way take longer to mature. Some people pour a little oil on top as a protective film.

Lemons Boiled in Brine and Preserved in Oil

This quick, unorthodox method gives very good results in 4 days, and the lemons last for months.

With a sharp knife make 8 fine—superficial, not deep—incisions into the lemon skin, from one end of the lemon to the other. Put the lemons in a large pan with salted water (about 8 tablespoons salt for 8 lemons) to cover. Put a smaller lid on top of them to keep them down as they float, and boil for about 25 minutes, or until the peels are very soft. When cool enough to handle, scoop out the flesh, pack the skins in a glass jar, and cover with olive or vegetable oil. They are ready to use after 4 days, or even sooner.

Torshi Left

Pickled Turnips

Makes 2 quarts • The most popular pickle of the Arab world is turnips turned pink with cherry-colored beet juices. Huge jars of these pickles adorn the streets and decorate the windows and counters of cafés and restaurants. In Egypt the turnips are pickled in brine alone, or with just a little added vinegar. They are ready to eat within 4–6 days and should be eaten within 6 weeks.

2 pounds small white turnips
1 raw or 2 cooked beets, peeled and cut into slices
3¾ cups water
3 tablespoons salt
3–4 tablespoons red- or white-wine vinegar

Peel the turnips and cut them in half or quarters. Pack the pieces in a clean 2-quart jar interspersed with slices of beet.

Boil the water with the salt and vinegar, and let it cool a little before pouring over the turnips and closing the jar.

Store in a warm place or at room temperature for 6 days, until mellowed, then keep in the refrigerator.

Variations

• Put 4 peeled garlic cloves in with the turnips.
• Put 1 or 2 chili peppers in the jar.
• A medieval recipe for *lift mukhalal muhalla* from al-Baghdadi gives directions for turnips pickled in vinegar, sweetened with honey, perfumed with aromatic herbs, and tinted with saffron.

Torshi Arnabeet wa Koromb

Pickled Cauliflower and Red Cabbage

Makes 2 quarts • This pickle turns a deep purple with the juice from the red cabbage. You can also use white cabbage and color the pickle with a few slices of raw or cooked beet.

1 young white cauliflower
½ red or white cabbage
1 small dried chili pepper (optional)
About 4 cups water
1 cup white-wine vinegar
3 tablespoons salt

Wash the cauliflower and separate it into florets. Cut the cabbage into thick slices in one direction, and then again thickly in the other direction. Leave it in chunks; do not shred it or take the leaves apart. Pack into a 2-quart glass jar, arranging alternate layers of cauliflower and cabbage chunks. If you like, bury a chili pepper among the vegetables.

Bring the water and vinegar to the boil with the salt and let it cool a little, then pour over the vegetables. Close tightly, and store in a warm place. The pickle will be ready in a week and should be eaten within 6 weeks. It keeps longer if stored in the refrigerator.

LEBANESE SAYING:
*"Her face is whiter
than the inside of a turnip."*

Torshi Khiar

Pickled Cucumbers

Makes 2 quarts

2 pounds small pickling cucumbers

4 cloves garlic, peeled

A few celery leaves or a few sprigs of
   fresh dill or 1 teaspoon dill seed

3 or 4 black peppercorns

3 or 4 whole coriander seeds

4 cups water

½ cup white-wine vinegar

3 tablespoons salt

Scrub the cucumbers well and pack them in a
2-quart glass jar with the whole garlic cloves,
celery leaves, sprigs of dill, or dill seed, peppercorns, and coriander seeds distributed at regular intervals.

Bring the water and vinegar to the boil with
the salt and pour over the vegetables. Close the
jar tightly with a glass top if possible, and leave
in a warm place to soften and mellow.

The pickle should be ready in 10 days. It
will not keep for longer than about 6 weeks
unless stored in the refrigerator.

Torshi Betingan

Pickled Eggplants

Makes 2 quarts

2 pounds very small, long, thin eggplants
   (3–4 inches long)

Salt

4 or 5 cloves garlic, finely chopped

1 or 2 small dried chilies, finely chopped

2½ cups water

1¼ cups white-wine vinegar

Wash the eggplants. Do not peel them, but
make a small slit lengthwise in each one. Poach
them in boiling salted water for 5–10 minutes,
until softened, weighing the eggplants down
with a small, heavy lid. Drain, and when
cooled, press gently to squeeze the water out.

Mix the chopped garlic and chilies and stuff
the eggplants with this mixture through the
slits. Arrange them in layers in a glass jar.

Put the water, 1½ tablespoons salt, and the
vinegar in a pan and bring to the boil, then
pour over the eggplants. Close the jar tightly.
The pickle will be ready to eat after 4 days and
will keep up to 2 months or longer in the refrigerator.

SELLING PICKLES

Once the Khoja started to sell pickles. He
bought the entire stock-in-trade of a man,
including his donkey. He started on his rounds,
crying, "Pickles for sale!" but when they came to
the crowded part of the town and to the house of a
former customer, the donkey would begin to bray so
loudly that the Khoja could not make himself
heard, and was obliged to hold his tongue.

One day in a crowded thoroughfare the Khoja
was just preparing to cry, "Pickles!" when the donkey got the start of him and began to bray. Then he
lost his temper and said, "Look here, mate, are you
selling them, or am I?"

BARNHAM, TRANS.,
TALES OF NASR-ED-DIN KHOJA

Torshi Meshakel

Mixed Pickles

Makes 2 quarts

2 small pickling cucumbers, left whole

1 large carrot, thickly sliced

1 small cauliflower, separated into florets

1 sweet green pepper, seeded, cored, and thickly sliced

½ pound small white turnips, peeled and quartered

3 cloves garlic

½ raw beet, peeled and cut into medium-sized pieces (optional)

1 or 2 small dried chili peppers

A few sprigs of fresh dill and 2 teaspoons dill seed

3 cups water

1 cup white-wine vinegar

4 tablespoons salt

Wash and prepare the vegetables and pack them tightly in glass jars with the garlic cloves, beet, chili peppers, and dill divided between them.

Boil the water, vinegar, and salt and pour over the vegetables. Prepare and add more liquid if this is not enough to cover them. Seal tightly, and store in a warm place. The pickle should be ready in about 2 weeks, and keeps 2 months if stored in the refrigerator. The vegetables will be soft and mellow, and tinted pink by the beet. The beet can be omitted if you prefer the vegetables in their natural colors.

Lamoun Makdous

Pickled Lemons in Oil

It is also good made with fresh limes.

Scrub lemons well and slice them. Sprinkle the slices generously with salt and leave for at least 24 hours on a large plate set at an angle, or in a colander. They will become soft and limp, and lose their bitterness. Arrange the slices in layers in a glass jar, sprinkling a little paprika between the layers. Cover with olive, nut, or a light vegetable oil.

Close the jar tightly. After about 3 weeks the lemons should be ready to eat—soft, mellow, and a beautiful orange color.

My mother accidentally discovered a way of speeding the process when left with dozens of lemon wedges which had been used to garnish a large party dish. She put them in the freezing compartment of her refrigerator to keep them until she was ready to pickle them. When she sprinkled the frozen lemons with salt, she found that they shed a large quantity of water and softened in just over an hour. They were ready for eating after only a few days in oil and paprika.

Mekhalel Betingan

Vinegared Eggplants in Olive Oil

Makes 2 quarts • This easy pickle makes a ready delicious mezze.

> 2 pounds eggplants
> Salt
> 1¼ cups red- or white-wine vinegar
> 6 cloves garlic, finely chopped or
>   crushed
> 1 tablespoon crushed dried oregano
> Olive oil

Peel and slice the eggplants. Arrange them in a sieve or colander, sprinkling each layer with salt. Leave for ½ hour to allow the bitter juices to drain away. Rinse off the salt, then poach the slices for 5–10 minutes in boiling vinegar with enough added water to cover, until soft.

Drain well, and arrange the slices in layers in a glass jar, putting a little crushed garlic and oregano between the layers. Fill the jar with oil and close it tightly.

The eggplants will be ready after about a week and will keep several months.

There is a superstitious belief in some Middle Eastern countries that certain types of eggplant bring the curse of infertility. Women are sometimes afraid to use a particularly black one or an oddly mauve one. On the other hand, a walk through a field of eggplants is sometimes prescribed as a cure for female sterility. For many years the head gardener at the Ezbekieh Gardens in Cairo derived a small income from a patch of eggplants by charging women a fee to walk through it.

Betingan Makdous

Stuffed Eggplant Pickle in Oil

Makes 2 quarts • This popular Lebanese pickle is served as a mezze. Make sure the walnuts have a fresh taste.

> 2 pounds small, thin eggplants
>   (3–4 inches long)
> Salt
> 1 cup finely chopped walnuts
> 1 small chili, finely chopped
> 4–6 cloves garlic, crushed
> Olive oil

Trim the stem end of the eggplants and pierce the skin in a few places with a pointed knife. Poach in salted water for 10–15 minutes, or until soft, weighing the eggplants down with a small, heavy lid. Drain, and when they are cool, very gently squeeze to get rid of the water.

Mix the walnuts with the chili and garlic and add a little salt. Cut a slit lengthwise down the middle of each eggplant but not right through, leaving the ends so as to form a pocket. Stuff with the walnut mixture.

Put the eggplants in a colander over a bowl, with a plate and weight on top, and leave overnight for water to drain. Transfer carefully to a jar, and cover with oil. They should be ready in a few days, and they keep for a month in the refrigerator.

Felfel bi Zeit

Bell Peppers in Oil

Bell peppers marinated in olive oil are one of my favorite pickles. Roast and peel fleshy red bell peppers (see page 84). Put them in a jar and cover with olive oil. You may add a little salt, lemon juice, and crushed garlic. Moroccans add a touch of ground chili pepper.

Harissa

Chili Paste

Makes ³⁄₄–1 cup • This famous and formidable chili paste goes into many North African, especially Tunisian, dishes. It keeps very well for many weeks in the refrigerator if covered with oil. You can now find it store-bought more easily, including some homemade-type artisanal varieties.

> 2 ounces dried hot red chili peppers
> (stems and seeds removed)
> 4 cloves garlic, peeled
> 1 teaspoon ground caraway
> 1 teaspoon ground coriander
> ¹⁄₂ teaspoon salt
> Extra-virgin olive oil

Soak the chili peppers in water for 30 minutes, until soft. Drain and pound with the garlic, spices, and a little salt with a pestle and mortar, or blend in a food processor, adding just enough oil, by the tablespoon, to make a soft paste.

Press into a jar and cover with oil.

Salsat al Banadoura

Tomato Sauce

Serves 6 • Although this is not a pickle, I am including the recipe because it is a very useful sauce to have at hand when required, and it can be prepared in advance and stored in jars. It keeps for months if the surface remains covered with a film of oil.

> 1 large onion, finely chopped
> Olive oil
> 4 cloves garlic, peeled
> 2 pounds tomatoes, peeled and quartered
> Salt and pepper
> 1–2 teaspoons sugar
> 2 teaspoons crushed dried oregano

Fry the onion until soft and golden in 3 tablespoons oil in a large saucepan. Add the whole garlic cloves and fry for a few minutes longer, until lightly colored.

Add the tomatoes, salt and pepper, and the sugar. Sprinkle with oregano, and cook gently over low heat, squashing the tomatoes with a wooden spoon, until softened. Then cover the pan and simmer very gently for 1 hour, or until the tomatoes are reduced to a thick jammy sauce.

Remove the garlic cloves and pour the sauce into a glass jar. Pour a thin layer of oil over the surface, cover the jar tightly, and store in the refrigerator.

Variation

A Moroccan version adds ¹⁄₂ teaspoon cinnamon and ¹⁄₂ teaspoon powdered ginger.

Jams and Fruit Preserves

MURABBIYAT

Like pastries, jams remind me vividly of my childhood, of visiting relatives, of sitting on low sofas surrounded with bright silk and velvet cushions. My father's sisters, whom we visited regularly, were always fragrant with their favorite homemade soaps perfumed with violets, rose water, orange blossom, and jasmine. Their homes were intoxicating with the frankincense which they used in every room, as well as musk and ambergris, and the jasmine, orange blossom, and rose petals which were left soaking in water in little china or crystal bowls.

Candied orange peel, quince paste, coconut, fig, date, rose, tangerine, and strawberry jams would be brought in as soon as we arrived, together with pyramids of little pastries, to the accompaniment of tiny tinkling silver spoons, trembling on their stands like drops on a chandelier. Delicately engraved and inlaid silver trays carried small crystal or silver bowls filled with shiny jams: orange, brilliantly white, mauve, rich brown, deep rose, or sienna red. They were arranged around the spoon stand, next to which was placed a glass of water, ornate with white or gold arabesques.

As coffee was served, the trays were brought round to each of us in turn, for us to savor a spoonful of each jam with one of the little spoons, which was then dropped discreetly into the glass of water. At our beautiful aunt Régine's we would be served the best date jam in existence; our favorite rose jam was made by our gentle aunt Rahèle; and Camille made an inimitable sour-cherry jam.

These jams and preserves can be eaten with bread or savored on their own with coffee or a glass of ice-cold water. They can also be served as a ready dessert with thick cream, or as an accompaniment to rice pudding.

Naring

Bitter Orange Peel in Syrup

This is one of the most popular and exquisite preserves. As the peels keep well in the refrigerator, you can collect them gradually. Choose thin-skinned oranges, preferably the bitter Seville type. Rub very lightly with a fine grater to remove their shine and some of their bitterness, being careful not to grate too deeply. Then, with a sharp-pointed knife, cut 6 deep lines in the peel from end to end and pull off the peel in 6 strips.

> 2 pounds orange peel
> 2 pounds sugar
> 4½ cups water
> Juice of ½ lemon

Boil the peel in water for about ½ hour, until soft. Drain. If using the peel of ordinary oranges, soak in fresh cold water for a day, changing the water once or twice if possible. If using bitter orange peel, it should be left to soak for 4 days, and the water should be changed twice a day.

If the peel is very pithy, scrape some of the white pith away with a spoon, to make it less pasty. Roll the strips of peel up one by one, and thread them onto a thick thread, like beads on a necklace, to prevent them from unrolling.

Make a syrup in a large pan. Boil the sugar and water with the lemon juice, and simmer until the sugar has melted. Drop the necklace in and simmer for about 1 hour, until the peel has absorbed the syrup thoroughly. Lift out, remove the thread, and drop the peel rolls into a clean glass jar.

If the syrup is not thick enough, boil vigorously to reduce it until it coats the back of a spoon. Cool slightly, and pour over the orange peel to cover it completely. Close the jar tightly. It should last for months.

Serve the rolls of peel either with some of their syrup, or drained and rolled in granulated sugar like crystallized fruits.

Tangerine Jam

This magnificent jam makes a delicious ready dessert that can be served with thick cream.

> 2 pounds tangerines
> 2 pounds sugar

Cut the tangerines in half. Squeeze out the juice and keep, covered, in the refrigerator.

Remove the thin membranes which separate the segments and fibers inside the peel. Then simmer the peels in water for about 7–10 minutes until soft. Drain, cover with a fresh portion of cold water, and soak for 12 hours or overnight, changing the water once or twice if possible, to get rid of all the bitterness.

Drain the peel and chop it roughly.

Pour the reserved tangerine juice into a large pan. Add the sugar and chopped peel and bring to the boil. Simmer for 15–30 minutes, until the syrup thickens and forms a firm jelly when a drop is left on a cold plate. Let the jam cool slightly, then pour into clean jars and seal tightly.

Strawberry Preserve

2 pounds barely ripe strawberries,
  preferably wild ones
2 pounds sugar
Juice of ½ lemon

Hull the strawberries and wash them very briefly if necessary. Spread layers in a bowl with sugar in between, and leave them to macerate for 12 hours or overnight. The sugar will draw out their juices.

Transfer the strawberries and their juices to a large pan. Add the lemon juice and bring to the boil very slowly, stirring gently with a wooden spoon or shaking the pan lightly, and skimming off the white froth as it rises to the surface. Simmer for 5–10 minutes, depending on the ripeness of the fruit. Wild strawberries will require only 5 minutes, sometimes even less.

When the strawberries are soft, lift them out gently with a slotted spoon and pack them into clean glass jars. Let the syrup simmer for a little while longer, until it has thickened enough to coat the back of a spoon, or until it sets when tested on a cold plate. Pour over the strawberries and, when cool, close the jars tightly.

Date Preserve in Syrup

This exquisite delicacy makes a ready dessert. Accompany if you like with vanilla ice cream or mascarpone. It is made with fresh dates—the yellow or red varieties, which are hard and sour and totally different from the dried dates with which people in America are familiar. (They are called *zaghlouli* in Egypt.) It is usual to peel them, but that is an arduous task and, in my view, not all that much worth the effort. They are stuffed with blanched almonds, with which they make a lovely combination.

2 pounds fresh yellow or red dates
Juice of ½ lemon
½–¾ cup blanched almonds (optional)
4½ cups sugar
8 cloves

Wash the dates well, peel them if you wish, and put them in a pan with water to cover (about 4½ cups) and the lemon juice. Bring to the boil and simmer, covered, for 1 hour, or until they are soft, adding a little water, if necessary, to keep them covered.

Lift them out of their water with a slotted spoon, and when they are cool enough to handle, push the pits out with a skewer or knitting needle. You will get the knack of doing it without breaking the dates. It helps to press them tightly in your hand. If you like, replace each pit with a blanched almond through the same hole.

Add sugar and cloves to the date liquor and bring to the boil. Simmer for a few minutes, until the sugar is dissolved, then drop in the dates and cook for a further 20–30 minutes. Lift the dates out carefully with a slotted spoon and put them in a clean glass jar, burying the cloves among them.

Thicken the syrup by boiling until it coats

the back of a spoon or sets when tested on a cold plate. Pour over the dates, let cool, and close the jar tightly.

Variation

These dates are also delicious stuffed with pieces of candied orange peel; use about 1 cup.

Clementine Preserve

This must be done with the very tiny clementines. Wash them well and cover with cold water overnight to get rid of some of the bitterness of the skin.

Make a syrup by boiling $4\frac{1}{2}$ cups of water and 2 pounds of sugar.

Drain the fruit and prick each one all over with a needle. Drop them into the syrup and simmer for about an hour. Lift them out with a slotted spoon, and transfer to a clean glass jar.

Reduce the syrup very much, until it is thick enough to coat a spoon, and pour it over the fruit. Let it cool before closing the jar tightly.

Apricot Preserve

2 pounds fresh apricots
$3\frac{1}{2}$ cups sugar

Wash and pit the apricots. Layer them, with sugar in between the layers, in a large bowl, and leave them overnight to macerate and release their juices.

The following day, pour the contents of the bowl into a large pan. Bring to the boil very slowly, and simmer gently over medium heat for about 20 minutes, or until the apricots are soft and the juices reduced and thickened enough to set when tested on a cold plate. Stir occasionally, to prevent the fruit from sticking to the bottom of the pan and burning.

Let the jam cool in the pan, then pour into clean glass jars and close tightly.

Apricots in Syrup

Use the same proportions of apricots to sugar as in the preceding recipe for apricot preserve. Wash and pit the apricots. Bring the sugar to the boil with $2\frac{3}{4}$ cups water and the juice of $\frac{1}{2}$ lemon, and simmer for a few minutes. Drop in the apricots and cook gently for 15–20 minutes, until soft. Lift them out carefully with a slotted spoon and put them in clean glass jars.

Reduce and thicken the syrup by boiling it down until it falls in heavy drops from a spoon. Cool slightly, and pour over the fruit, covering it entirely. Let cool before closing the jar tightly.

Green Walnut Preserve

A delicacy which should be attempted whenever green walnuts are available.

- 1 pound fresh shelled green walnuts
- 2¼ cups sugar
- 2 cups water
- 1 tablespoon lemon juice
- 4 or 5 cloves

Shell the walnuts carefully, trying not to break them. Soak them in cold water for 5 or 6 days, changing the water twice a day to remove any bitterness.

Make a syrup by boiling the sugar and water with lemon juice until thickened enough to fall in heavy drops from a spoon. Let the syrup cool, then add the well-drained walnuts. Bring to the boil gently and simmer for ½ hour. Remove the pan from the heat and leave the walnuts submerged in the syrup overnight at room temperature.

The following day, add the cloves, bring to the boil again, and simmer for ½ hour. Pour the walnuts and syrup into a clean glass jar, allow to cool, and close tightly.

Pumpkin Slices in Syrup

This Kurdish preserve makes a ready sweet to serve with chopped walnuts or clotted cream.

- 2 pounds orange pumpkin (weight free of skin, fibers, and seeds)
- 4 cups sugar
- 2 cups water
- A squeeze of lemon juice

Cut the peel off the pumpkin and remove seeds and fibers, then cut the flesh into slices about ½ inch thick and 2½ inches long.

Bring the sugar and water with the lemon juice to a boil in a large pan. Drop the pumpkin pieces in and cook for 15–20 minutes, or until tender.

Lift out the pieces with a slotted spoon and drop them into glass jars. Reduce the syrup until it is thick enough to coat a spoon, and pour over the pumpkin pieces. Let it cool before closing the jars tightly.

Pumpkin Conserve

2 pounds orange pumpkin (weight free
   of skin, fibers, and seeds)
3½–4½ cups sugar
1 tablespoon lemon juice
¼ teaspoon mastic (see page 44)
½–¾ cup slivered almonds

Grate the pumpkin flesh into thick shreds and
arrange alternate layers of pumpkin and sugar
(the jam lasts longer with the larger amount of
sugar) in a large bowl. Leave overnight at room
temperature, covered, for the pumpkin juices
to be drawn out.

Put all the contents of the bowl and the
lemon juice into a large pan. Bring to the boil
slowly, stirring occasionally with a wooden
spoon to make sure that it does not stick at the
bottom. Cook, uncovered, over low heat for
10–20 minutes, until the pumpkin is soft and
translucent and the syrup has thickened. Drop
a little on a cold plate to see if it sets.

Pound or grind the mastic to a powder with
a pinch of sugar and mix thoroughly into the
jam. Cook 1 minute more, and stir in the slivered almonds.

Pour into clean, warm, dry glass jars. Let
cool before closing.

Store in a cool place.

Variation

As an alternative flavoring instead of mastic, stir
in 1 teaspoon cardamom seeds or ground cardamom at the start of the cooking.

Green Fig Preserve

You can serve this with thick cream or mascarpone, or with vanilla ice cream. For the preserve to last a long time, it needs the same
weight of sugar as of figs. If you will be eating
it within 2 weeks you can make it much less
sweet, but keep it in the refrigerator.

2 pounds young green figs
4 cups sugar
2½ cups water
Juice of ½ lemon
1 tablespoon orange-blossom water or a
   few drops of vanilla extract (optional)

Choose small, unblemished, slightly underripe
figs. Do not peel them, but trim their stems,
leaving only a little part, and wash them carefully.

In a large pan, boil the sugar and water with
the lemon juice for a few minutes, until slightly
thickened. Soak the figs in this syrup overnight. The following day, bring to the boil and
simmer for 15 minutes, or until the figs are soft.
Lift them out with a slotted spoon and put
them in clean glass jars.

Reduce the syrup by simmering for a few
minutes longer, until it is thick enough to coat
the back of a spoon. Add orange-blossom
water or vanilla extract, mix well, and cook for
a minute or so.

Let the syrup cool, and pour over the figs,
then close the jars tightly.

Dried Fig Jam with Mastic, Aniseed, and Walnuts

The flavors here are rich and exciting.

2 pounds dried figs

2½ cups sugar

2 cups water

Juice of ½ lemon

1 teaspoon ground aniseed

3 tablespoons pine nuts

1 cup walnuts, coarsely chopped

¼ teaspoon pulverized mastic (optional)

Chop the figs roughly.

Boil the sugar and water with the lemon juice for a few minutes, then add the figs, and simmer gently until they are soft and impregnated with the syrup, which should have thickened enough to coat the back of a spoon. Stir constantly to avoid burning.

Add the aniseed, pine nuts and walnuts, and the mastic if you like. (To be properly pulverized, the mastic must have been pounded or ground with a pinch of sugar.) Stir well, and cook a few minutes longer.

Pour into clean glass jars and let it cool, then close tightly.

Wishna

Sour Cherry Jam

This can be served as a sweet, with thick cream to accompany. Or plunge 1–2 tablespoons of it into a glass of iced water, then drink the syrupy water and eat the fruit left at the bottom. Use an olive pitter to pit the cherries.

2 pounds pitted sour or morello cherries

4 cups sugar

Juice of ½ lemon (optional)

Layer the pitted cherries and sugar in a large glass or earthenware bowl, and leave them to macerate and release their juices overnight.

The following day, pour the cherries and juice into a large pan and bring to the boil very slowly, stirring frequently to prevent them from burning. Let the cherries simmer in their own juice for about ½ hour, or until very soft, adding a little water only if necessary. If the syrup is still too thin at the end, remove the cherries carefully to glass jars with a perforated spoon and simmer for a few minutes longer, until it coats the back of a spoon. A little lemon juice is sometimes added during the cooking.

Pour into clean glass jars, let it cool, and close tightly.

Quince Preserve

We start getting large quinces from Cyprus at the beginning of October, and later in the year smaller ones arrive from Iran and Turkey. I buy them as soon as I see them, and they last a pretty long time without going bad. Their heavenly scent pervades the whole house. In America they are available in the fall in farmers' markets.

> 2 pounds quinces
> Juice of $\frac{1}{2}$ lemon
> 4 cups sugar

Wash the quinces and rub off the gray down that covers them. Cut them in half and cut away the black ends, but do not remove the cores and pips, because these produce the jelly. You will need a large, strong knife and plenty of force to cut them: They are very hard. Put them in a pan with water barely to cover them and the lemon juice. Bring to the boil and simmer for 20–45 minutes, or until they are just tender. The time varies. It depends on the size and degree of maturity of the fruit. Lift them out carefully with a slotted spoon, and when they are cold enough to handle, quarter them, peel them, core them, and cut them into small slices.

Add sugar to the water left in the pan. Bring to the boil, and simmer until the syrup is thick enough to coat the back of a spoon. Return the quince pieces to the pan and cook for 20–30 minutes, until they are soft. The syrup keeps them firm. Pour into clean glass jars, and let the jam cool before closing.

Variation

For quince cheese, mash the cooked quinces in the pan with a potato masher or a wooden spoon.

Rose Petal Jam

In Egypt, vendors sold crates of rose petals, in their season, for making rose water and rose jam. Certain varieties of rose, such as the wild eglantine of Turkey and Syria, are the best for jam-making. I have not been able to make a good one with the roses from my garden. The petals remained tough under the tooth.

> 1 pound fresh rose petals, preferably red
> Juice of $1\frac{1}{2}$ lemons, or more
> 2 cups sugar
> 2–3 tablespoons rose water (optional)

Pick fresh petals. (Make sure they have not been sprayed with insecticide.) Cut off their white ends with scissors, and wash and drain the petals. Cover with water in a large pan, add the juice of $\frac{1}{2}$ lemon, and simmer for 30 minutes. Then drain.

In the same pan, make a syrup by boiling $2\frac{1}{2}$ cups of water with the sugar and the remaining lemon juice for 10 minutes. Let it cool, put the petals in, and leave them to macerate for 24 hours.

Bring the syrup and petals to the boil and simmer for 20 minutes, or until the petals are tender. Add rose water, if you like, and boil a moment more. Pour into a glass jar and let cool before closing.

Variation

Make the same jam with the blossoms of bitter Seville-orange trees.

Sweet Eggplant Preserve

A famous North African specialty with an exciting bittersweet flavor.

 2 pounds small, thin, long eggplants
 2 pounds sugar
 1–2 teaspoons cloves
 $\frac{1}{2}$ teaspoon ground ginger (optional)
 Juice of $\frac{1}{2}$ lemon

Wash the eggplants. Trim the stem end, leaving a little piece. Cut one or two thin strips of peel, so that the vegetables keep their shape but their flesh is better exposed to absorb the syrup. Some people leave them in water (changed daily) for 3 days to remove excessive bitterness, but it is sufficient to poach them in lightly salted water for 10–15 minutes, until they soften (you will need to weigh them down with a smaller lid), and then to let them drain very well before cooking them in syrup.

In a large saucepan, make a syrup by boiling the sugar in about $3\frac{3}{4}$ cups water with the spices and lemon juice. Gently press the juice out of the eggplants and throw them in. Simmer for about an hour, until the eggplants are very tender and engorged with syrup. Let them cool before you put them in a jar, and cover them with the syrup, which should be thick enough to coat a spoon. If it is not, reduce it by boiling fast. If it is too thick or caramelized, add a little water. Let the preserve cool before closing the jar.

Drinks and Sherbets

One of my most exciting memories of Turkey is the inaugural evening, some years ago, to celebrate the formation of the Turkish wine-lovers' branch of the Chevaliers du Tastevin. I happened to be in Istanbul, and my friend the gastronome Tuğrul Şavkai invited me to the ceremony and dinner. The venue was the grand ballroom of a yet-to-be-opened grand hotel. An enormous banqueting table was set in the middle of the empty hall with Ottoman lavishness. Course upon course of "modern" Turkish delicacies were accompanied by a succession of local and foreign wines. (Notable local wines are the red Buzbag, the white Trakya, and the Diren.) There were many toasts, in an atmosphere of convivial jollity. The scene was enchantingly fairylike, with a cloak-and-dagger atmosphere. The event had been secretly arranged to foil Islamic fundamentalists—there were whispers of a possible bomb; and velvet cloaks, hats, gold chains, and a great sword had been promised by the Chevaliers branch of California, who were renovating their wardrobes. These arrived an hour late, which created some anxiety. When they did arrive, the women were seated in rows to watch their men be knighted by the sword. As each man knelt on a velvet cushion and classical music created an elevated feeling of ceremony, the women laughed helplessly.

Wine and alcoholic liquor are prohibited by Islam, but in many Muslim countries arak (or raki), an anise-flavored liquor, is very much a national drink that all but the very religious drink with mezze. Beer and wine are also produced. In the past they were produced by the Christian and Jewish communities. Today, even while governments in Turkey, and also in Algeria, Morocco, and Tunisia, try to encourage a quality wine trade, they are faced with the growing forces of Islamic fundamentalism.

The Lebanese Château Musar is the most famous and perhaps the best wine in the region. Although Greece is known mostly for its pine-resin-flavored retsina, it now produces quality wines, as does Israel, with wines such as Gamla and Yarden in the Golan Heights. The French colonizers in Algeria, Tunisia, and Morocco produced large quantities of wine—in the 1950s their wine exports accounted for a third of the total world wine trade—much of it to be mixed with the wines of Burgundy, the Languedoc, and the south of France. Since the French left North Africa and the colonist wine-makers moved to Corsica, production has shrunk immeasurably, but some of the better wines (quality is always variable) can be surprisingly good. The dry and fruity rosés of Algeria and Morocco, the Moroccan Gris, and the Tunisian muscat (it can be sweet or dry) are especially good with couscous and tagines and spicy salads.

Arak (or raki) is made from the distilled fermented juice of white grapes flavored with aniseed. In Iraq they make it with dates. Another liquor is *mahia,* a specialty of the Moroccan Jews, which is distilled from figs. Like arak, it is drunk as an apéritif or a digestive. You will find it in Jewish stores in Paris now, while in Morocco, since most of the Jews left, it has been sorely missed. In Morocco they secretly make *samet,* which is based on the fermented juice of various fruits such as grapes, apples, pears, and plums.

Because of the alcohol prohibition, people appreciate many other types of drinks, among them fresh fruit juices and sherbets, milk (it is the drink of welcome and hospitality offered with dates), and yogurt, and, most of all, water. People sometimes perfume water with rose petals or with a slice of lemon. Spring water is especially popular. In Turkey people pride themselves on recognizing where it is from. Of course, in the desert water has magical qualities. In Islamic culture water has symbolic importance. It is seen as a divine gift, a purifier, and saintly. Colorfully dressed water-carriers, strapped with large earthenware jars (their porous surface helps to keep the water cool by its constant evaporation) and clanging brass goblets, are a familiar tourist attraction, but in reality the water-vendor has a powerful position in Middle Eastern folklore.

A story is told of the vendor who, greedy for power, established himself by a desert road, displaying cool and curvy earthenware jars. As a thirsty traveler approached and asked for a drink, the vendor would take a very long time to reply, then he would point to a jar. When the traveler approached the jar, the vendor would snap: "Not that one! The one next to it!" Then, as the unfortunate man took this one up to his lips, he would be sworn at again: "Not that one, you fool! That one, I said!" This would go on until the poor traveler was on his knees, begging to be allowed to buy a drink. As a protection from this sort of experience, an Arab proverb advises: "The water of the well is better than the favor of the water-vendor." However, beggars are never refused water, which is considered the most blessed of alms.

Limonada

Lemonade

Serves 6

6 cups ice-cold water
Juice of 4 lemons
$^1/_4$–$^1/_2$ cup sugar, to taste
The grated zest of 1 lemon
1 tablespoon orange-blossom water

Mix all the ingredients and leave, covered, in the refrigerator until the sugar is dissolved.

Karkade

Iced Hibiscus Drink

Serves 4 or 5 • If you go to Egypt, one thing to bring back home is wine-red dried hibiscus petals.

1 cup hibiscus petals (*karkade*)
5 cups water
Sugar to taste

Put the petals in a pan with the water. Bring to the boil and simmer for 5 minutes. Let cool, then filter into a jug and chill, covered with plastic wrap. Serve chilled. The drink is quite tart. Let everyone add sugar to taste.

Note: The drink can also be served hot like tea.

Laban

Yogurt Drink

Makes 4–6 glasses • This deliciously refreshing drink, called *doug* by Persians, *ayran* in Turkey, and *laban* by others, is consumed extensively all over the Middle East and particularly in Lebanon, Turkey, and Iran. It is prepared in the home, served in cafés, and sold by street vendors. It is good served chilled or with ice cubes.

3 cups plain whole-milk yogurt
4 cups water or carbonated mineral
   water
Salt
1–2 tablespoons chopped fresh mint or
   crushed dried mint (optional)

Pour the yogurt into a large jug. Gradually add the water and beat vigorously until thoroughly blended. Season to taste with very little salt, if any, and add mint if you like.

Serve chilled, preferably with a lump of ice in each glass.

*Someone asked Goha what was
his favorite music and he replied,
"The clanging of pots and pans and
the tinkling of glasses."*

Sahlab—Salep

Serves 4 • This wonderful, heartwarming winter drink is hot milk thickened with the starchy ground bulb of an orchid called *Orchis mascula*. This was sold by street vendors from the large copper urn in which it was made. The stone-colored powder called *sahlab* (*salep* in Turkish and Greek) is expensive and not easy to find. I have often bought it in Middle Eastern markets only to discover that it was a fake or adulterated mix. Cornstarch is an alternative which gives a creamy texture but not the same special flavor.

1½ tablespoons pulverized *sahlab* or
    2 tablespoons cornstarch
4 cups milk
3 tablespoons sugar, or to taste
2 teaspoons rose or orange-blossom
    water (optional)
2 tablespoons finely chopped pistachios
Ground cinnamon

In a bowl mix the pulverized *sahlab* or cornstarch with a few tablespoons cold milk.

Bring the remaining milk to a boil. Pour in the *sahlab* or cornstarch mixture, stirring vigorously so as not to let lumps form. Cook over very low heat, stirring all the time, until the milk thickens (about 10 minutes). Then stir in the sugar and, if you like, rose or orange-blossom water.

Serve in cups (a ladle is useful), with finely chopped or ground pistachios sprinkled on top and a dusting of cinnamon.

Variation

In Egypt it is the custom to sprinkle grated coconut on top.

An excellent account of how coffee was made in Egypt in the last century is given by E. W. Lane in Manners and Customs of the Modern Egyptians:

In preparing the coffee the water is first made to boil; the coffee (freshly roasted and powdered) is then put in and stirred; after which the pot is again placed on the fire, once or twice, until the coffee begins to simmer, when it is taken off, and its contents are poured out into the cups while the surface is yet creamy. The Egyptians are excessively fond of pure and strong coffee thus prepared, and very seldom add sugar to it (though some do so when they are unwell) and never milk or cream; but a little cardamom seed is often added to it. It is a common custom, also, to fumigate the cup with the smoke of mastic; and the wealthy sometimes impregnate the coffee with the delicious fragrance of ambergris. The most general mode of doing this is to put about a carat weight of ambergris in a coffee-pot and melt it over a fire; then make the coffee in another pot, in the manner before described, and when it has settled a little, pour it into the pot which contains the ambergris. Some persons make use of the ambergris, for the same purpose in a different way—sticking a piece of it, of the weight of about two carats, in the bottom of the cup, and then pouring in the coffee: a piece of the weight above mentioned will serve for two or three weeks. This mode is often adopted by persons who always like to have the coffee which they themselves drink flavored with this perfume, and do not give all their visitors the same luxury.

Kahwa

Turkish Coffee

Serves 1 • In my family, it was the men—my father or brothers—who made the coffee. Here is their method. My parents had many pots of different sizes—for two, three, four, five people.

1 very heaping teaspoon pulverized coffee

1 heaping teaspoon sugar, or less, to taste

1 small coffee cup water

Although it is more common to boil the water with the sugar alone first and then add the coffee, it is customary in my family to put the coffee, sugar, and water in the *kanaka* or pot (a small saucepan could be used, though it is not as successful), and to bring them to the boil together. By a "very heaping teaspoon" of coffee I mean, in this case, so heaping that it is more than 2 teaspoons. A level teaspoon of sugar will make a "medium" coffee.

Bring to the boil. When the froth begins to rise, remove from the heat, stir, and return to the heat until the froth rises again. Pour immediately into little cups, allowing a little froth (*wesh*) for each cup. The froth is forced out by making your hand tremble as you serve. But if you are making a larger amount of coffee in a

---

Coffee first became popular in the Middle East in the Yemen and Saudi Arabia. It was transplanted there from Abyssinia, where it grows wild. According to legend, coffee was particularly favored by the Yemeni Sufis, who believed that its effects facilitated the performance of their religious ceremonies, hastening mystical raptures. Accordingly, it became endowed with a ceremonial character.

Today the serving and drinking of coffee is still surrounded by tradition and ceremony. Walking past cafés, one cannot help remarking on the almost mystical ecstasy with which coffee-drinking still affects people. Men spend hours during the long summer nights, and as much time as they can during the day, sitting in cafés, sipping coffees one after another, sometimes accompanied by a *lokum* or pastry, while they entertain each other, telling jokes and playing charades and *tric-trac* (backgammon, also called *shish-bish*).

Business and bargaining are never done without coffee. At home, it is served as soon as visitors arrive, always freshly brewed, usually with freshly roasted and pulverized coffee beans. It is prepared in small quantities as each visitor arrives, in small long-handled tin-lined copper or brass pots called *kanaka* or *cezve,* holding from one to five cups. Another type of coffeepot, called an *ibrik,* has a curved spout like a pelican's beak.

Coffee cups are very small, usually cylindrical. In some countries they have no handles; in others, china cups fit into small metal holders that match the serving tray made of copper, brass, or silver. The tray is usually beautifully ornamented. Traditional patterns and Arabic writing (often blessings and words in praise of God) are chiseled into the metal. Sometimes the carvings are inlaid with a thin silver thread which is beaten in.

People have their favorite blends of coffee

---

big *kanaka,* it is easier to distribute the froth equally between the cups with a spoon before pouring. Serve very hot. The grounds will settle at the bottom of the cup. Do not stir them up or drink them.

Variation

Try flavoring the coffee with cardamom seeds (*heil*), or a little cinnamon, or a pinch of ground cloves, added at the same time as the coffee. Or pour in a drop of orange-blossom or rose water before serving.

Note: It is common practice for people in some circles to turn their coffee cups upside down on their saucers when they have finished drinking. As the coffee grounds dribble down the sides of the cup, they form a pattern or image from which at least one member of the company can usually read the fortune of the drinker. A friend has a coffee cup which she brought from Egypt and has kept in a cupboard in England for many years now, carefully wrapped in fine tissue paper and rarely disturbed. She is convinced that it bears the protective image of Rab Moshe (Moses) traced out in coffee grounds at the bottom of the cup.

---

beans. Mocha beans from the Yemen are popular, as are Brazilian and Kenyan beans.

Rules of etiquette are observed in the serving of coffee. A person of high rank is served first, then a person of advanced age. Until a few years ago, men were always served before women, but today, in the more Europeanized towns, women take precedence.

Since sugar is boiled in with the coffee, guests are always asked their preference—whether they would like sweet (*helou* or *sukkar ziada*), medium (*mazbout*), or unsweetened (*murra*)—and they are served accordingly. In cafés, it is customary for waiters to take thirty orders for coffee at a time, all varying in sweetness, and supposedly never to make a mistake. There is a well-known joke about the waiter who takes an order for a large gathering of inevitably differing tastes, makes them all exactly the same, medium-sweet, brings them all together on a huge tray, and hands them round

with a show of concentration, saying: "*Helou, mazbout, helou, murra, murra, helou . . .*"

The occasion may determine the amount of sugar added to the coffee. At happy ones, such as weddings and birthdays, the coffee should always be sweet, while at a funeral it should be bitter, without any sugar at all, regardless of the tastes of the mourners. At deaths it was customary for some families in Cairo to erect huge tents, which stretched right across the narrow streets. The ground would be carpeted and filled with gilt chairs, and the tents were decorated with sumptuously colored appliqués. Relatives, friends, and passersby came to pay their respects. They sat on the gilt chairs, solemnly drinking black, unsweetened coffee to the wailing of the professional mourners.

Kahwa Beida

White Coffee

A hot drink of boiled scented water taken as an alternative to coffee at night is an old tradition in Syria and Lebanon.

Pour boiling water into a small coffee cup and add a few drops of orange-blossom water. Sweeten with sugar if you like. It is very soothing.

When I was a child in Egypt, we used to take to bed a glass of cold water with a few drops of rose water to make us sleep.

Chai

Tea

Tea is relatively new in the Middle East, where it was introduced in the nineteenth century. Though not as important as coffee, it has been widely adopted, especially in times when coffee has been expensive. In Egypt it was drunk strong and black. In other parts, spices are often added. Make tea in the usual way and put a stick of cinnamon with 3 slices of lemon in the pot. Alternatively, add 2 teaspoons aniseed and garnish each cup with finely chopped walnuts.

Moroccan Mint Tea

Makes 10 small glasses in a 5-cup teapot • In Morocco tea—a refreshing infusion of both green tea and mint—is the symbol of hospitality, prepared with art, served with ceremony, and drunk at all times of the day. Introduced in the nineteenth century by the English, tea became an indispensable drink. It is traditionally served in richly engraved English-style silver teapots (the grandest are from Manchester) on silver trays with tiny legs. It is poured from a great height into small, ornamented colored glasses. Spearmint is the type of mint used, and the infusion is sweetened in the teapot. In Morocco they like it very sweet, with many lumps of sugar, but you can suit your taste.

1½ tablespoons green tea
Handful of fresh whole mint leaves
Lump sugar, to taste

Bring a kettle of water to a rolling boil. Heat the teapot by swirling some boiling water in it, then pour out. Add the tea leaves and pour a little boiling water over them. Swirl around, and quickly pour the water out again, taking care not to lose the leaves. Add mint leaves and sugar to taste, and pour in about 5 cups boiling water. Allow to infuse for about 5 minutes, then skim off any mint that has risen to the surface. Taste a little of the tea in a small glass, and add more sugar if necessary. Serve in small glasses.

Zhourat

Infusions or Tisanes

Infusions of all kinds, both hot and cold, are extremely popular throughout the Middle East for their soothing and medicinal properties as well as for their fragrance. They are made from dried fruits (apples and apricots), roots (ginger and licorice), pods (carob and tamarind), seeds (anise and caraway), and dried flowers and leaves. The following are used: dried mint, verbena, sage, sweet basil, sweet marjoram, chamomile and lime blossom, jasmine and orange blossom, rose petals, and hibiscus.

Make the tisanes in a teapot the same way you make tea, warming the teapot and pouring on boiling water. Sweeten in the cup, if you like, with sugar or honey.

Chai Hamidh

Dried Lime Tea

A hot lime drink is made by breaking open dried limes (*noomi basra,* see page 44) and pouring boiling hot water over them. Strain, and sweeten to taste.

Ginger Tea

This is made with ground ginger, but I prefer to use the fresh root. Drop 3 or 4 thin slices of ginger in each cup of boiling water. Stir in 1–2 teaspoons honey and a squeeze of lemon.

Laban al Loz

Milk of Almonds

Serves 8 • This fragrant drink was a favorite in my home. Commercial varieties of a concentrated version (a syrup) have an unpleasant synthetic taste.

1¼ cups whole blanched almonds

9 cups water

1 cup sugar

3 or 4 drops of almond extract

2 teaspoons rose or orange-blossom water, or to taste

Grind the almonds as finely as possible in the food processor (do not buy them already ground). Add about 3 cups of the water and blend very thoroughly for several minutes. Pour into a saucepan, add the sugar, and bring to the boil. Simmer for a minute or two, then add the almond extract. Pour the rest of the water in, and leave to macerate overnight. Strain into a jug through a fine sieve or cheesecloth. Add rose or orange-blossom water and chill, covered, in the refrigerator.

Variations

- In Morocco, they stir in ¼ teaspoon pulverized mastic after boiling.
- In Iraq, they flavor with ½ teaspoon ground cardamom.

Sharbat

SHERBETS—FRUIT DRINKS AND SYRUPS

In *Manners and Customs of the Modern Egyptians,* Edward William Lane writes:

> The Egyptians have various kinds of sherbets or sweet drinks. The most common kind is merely sugar and water, but very sweet; lemonade is another; a third kind, the most esteemed, is prepared from a hard conserve of violets, made by pounding violet-flowers and then boiling them with sugar. This violet-sherbet is of a green color. A fourth kind is prepared from mulberries; a fifth from sorrel. There is also a kind of sherbet sold in the streets which is made with raisins, as its name implies; another kind, which is a strong infusion of liquorice-root, and called by the name of that root; a third kind, which is prepared from the fruit of the locust tree, and called in like manner by the name of the fruit.

I have long been haunted by the cries and songs of street vendors in Cairo in my childhood. Most often, it was drinks that they were selling, to quench the thirst of passersby or, as they sometimes chanted, to give them strength and health. As they went by, singing their irresistible calls of "*Arasous!*" and "*Tamarhendi!*" accompanied by the tinkling of little bells and the clanking of metal cups, people would rush down from their flats to drink several glasses. The vendors carried a selection of sherbets in gigantic glass flasks, two at a time, held together by wide straps and balanced on their shoulders. The flasks glowed with brilliantly seductive colors: pink for rose syrup; pale green for violet juice; tamarind was a dark warm, rich, brown; and mulberry was purple-black.

Sherbets or syrups were also served at home at all times of the day, and when guests had already had Turkish coffee and it was time to have something else. Sherbets are very sweet and are meant to be diluted with ice-cold water. A tablespoonful is usually enough for one small glass.

Lane goes on to describe how the sherbet is served:

> The sherbet is served in colored glass cups, generally called "kullehs," containing about three-quarters of a pint; some of which (the more common kind) are ornamented with gilt flowers, etc. The sherbet-cups are placed on a round tray, and covered with a round piece of embroidered silk, or cloth of gold. On the right arm of the person who presents the sherbet is hung a large oblong napkin with a wide embroidered border of gold and colored silks at each end. This is ostensibly offered for the purpose of wiping the lips after drinking the sherbet, but it is really not so much for use as for display. The lips are seldom or scarcely touched with it.

Although this description was written more than a hundred years ago, the same customs still went on, as I remember from my own childhood.

Sharbat Bortokal

Orange Syrup

This is very sweet, but it is a syrup and not to be compared to orange juice. We used the smallish, slightly acid oranges with thin skins for this, but now that we have bottled freshly squeezed orange juice, that is what we use. Dilute 2 tablespoons in a glass of iced water.

2 cups freshly squeezed orange juice

3 cups sugar

Juice of ½ lemon

Pour the orange juice into a pan. Add sugar and lemon juice, and bring slowly to the boil, stirring to dissolve the sugar. Remove from the heat as soon as it reaches the boiling point.

Cool, and pour into thoroughly washed bottles. Serve diluted with ice-cold water.

Note: If you wish to store the syrup for a long time, here is a traditional method for preserving it. Grate the rind of 1 or 2 oranges, then squeeze it through a piece of fine muslin. Float a teaspoon of this oily "zest" at the top of each bottle. It will act as a perfect protection. Before using the syrup, remove the oily crust with the point of a knife.

Sharbat Sekanjabin

Vinegar and Sugar Syrup

A refreshing sweet-and-sour Persian syrup to be diluted in ice-cold water.

3 cups water

5 cups sugar

1½ cups white-wine vinegar

6 sprigs of fresh mint, washed

Bring the water to the boil with the sugar, stirring constantly until the sugar has dissolved. Add the vinegar and simmer for 20 minutes longer. Remove from the heat and submerge the sprigs of mint in the syrup. The flavor of the mint will penetrate the syrup as it cools. Remove the mint, and pour into clean bottles.

To serve, stir 5 tablespoons syrup into each glass of iced water (or water and ice cubes).

Variation

Sometimes a little peeled and grated cucumber is added when serving, and a mint leaf is used to garnish.

RIDDLE:
What is sweeter than honey?

ANSWER:
Free vinegar.

About Early Culinary Manuals

As early as the eighth century, writings on food were abundant and popular. So much so that the scientist Salih Abd al-Quddus, who was to be executed as a heretic, complained bitterly: "We live among animals who roam in search of pastures without seeking to understand. If we write about fish and vegetables we are invested in their eyes with great merit, but truly scientific subjects are for them painful and boring."

Many early cookbooks are mentioned in various works, but they have unfortunately been lost to us. Al Nadim, the well-known bibliographer who lived in Baghdad in the tenth century, lists eleven "Books Composed About Cooked Food" dating from between the eighth and the tenth centuries and gives the names of their authors.

At the Bodleian Library in Oxford there is a handwritten manuscript of one of the earliest existing Arabic cookbooks, copies of which are at the University Library of Helsinki and Topkapi Saray in Istanbul. It is an anonymous work adorned with poems and gastronomic anecdotes about famous men, written in the tenth century and entitled *Kitab al-Tabikh wa-Islah al-Aghdhiya al-Makulat* (*Book of Cooking and Better Eating*). It quotes recipes from older books, such as those of Ibn al-Masawaih and Ibn al-Mawsili of the early ninth century. In Istanbul there are two manuscript copies of a book called *Kitab al-Atima al-Mu'tada* (*Book of Daily Food*), which was written in the thirteenth century. Other very important culinary manuscripts of the same period exist in Baghdad, Damascus, Morocco, and Spain.

In the first edition of this book I featured many recipes from two of the works from Baghdad and Damascus, but I have left them out of this edition to make room for all the new recipes, and because they are primarily of academic interest and scholars have made them available today in new translations. In the last few years European and American scholars have studied all the medieval culinary works which have come down to us, and their analyses, with added commentaries and translated recipes, are now available in English. Most important are Lucie Bolens's book *La Cuisine andalouse, un art de vivre, XIe–XIIIe siècle,* now also in an English translation; David Waines's *In a Caliph's Kitchen—Medieval Arabic Cooking for the Modern Gourmet;* and the forthcoming *Medieval Arab Cookery—Papers by Maxime Rodinson and Charles Perry.*

Ibn Sayyar al Warraq's *Kitab Tabikh* (*Cookbook*) from Baghdad

A compilation of recipes recorded by a certain Abu Muhammad al Muzzafar ibn Nasr Ibn Sayyar al Warraq in Baghdad in the tenth century, during the Abbasid Caliphate, is the earliest collection of recipes to have survived. It is very extensive, includes culinary poems, and draws on previous, ninth-century sources. It reflects the cosmopolitan court cuisine at the heart of the Islamic Empire, and touches on subjects such as utensils, kitchen practices, and table manners.

The work has been edited by Kaj Ohrnberg and Sahban Mroueh (Helsinki, 1987). David Waines features some of the recipes in his *In a Caliph's Kitchen—Medieval Arabic Cooking for the Modern Gourmet.*

Muhammad ibn al-Hassan al-Baghdadi's *Kitab al-Tabikh*

In 1934 the Iraqi scholar Dr. Daoud Chelebi discovered two manuscripts written in Baghdad in the year 1226 by a certain Muhammad ibn al-Hassan ibn Muhammad ibn al-Karim al Katib al-Baghdadi, who died in 1239 A.D. Dr. Chelebi published it in Mosul with the same title, *Kitab al-Tabikh* (*Cookbook*). The late Professor A. J. Arberry translated it into English and included it in his article entitled "A Baghdad Cookery Book" published in the periodical *Islamic Culture* 13 (1939). This is the work that I studied and cooked from extensively years ago. You will find it in a new translation by Charles Perry in the forthcoming *Medieval Arab Cookery—Papers by Maxime Rodinson and Charles Perry.* David Waines features many of the recipes in *In a Caliph's Kitchen—Medieval Arabic Cooking for the Modern Gourmet.*

In the preface, after the obligatory praises to God and some remarks on the importance of good wholesome eating, the author says he wrote the book for his own use and for those interested in "the Art of Cooking." He divides pleasure into six classes: food, drink, clothes, sex, scent, and sound. Of these, he says, the noblest and most consequential is food, and he subscribes to the doctrine of the pre-eminence of the pleasure of eating above all other pleasures. It was for that reason that he composed the book. Al-Baghdadi chose to include, from among the recipes popular at the time, only those he personally liked, and discarded what he describes as "strange and unfamiliar dishes, in the composition of which unwholesome and unsatisfying ingredients are used." There is general advice about the necessity of keeping nails trimmed and pots clean, or rubbing copper pans bright with brick dust, potash, saffron, and citron leaves, and on such things as the value of using fresh and strongly scented spices ground very fine.

One hundred and sixty recipes follow, divided into ten chapters, which include "sour dishes," some of which are sweetened with sugar, syrup, honey, or date juice; and milk dishes made with "Persian" milk, which is actually curdled milk or yogurt. The "plain dishes" are not at all plain. The "fried" or "dry" dishes do not have much broth or sauce. The "simple" and "sweet" dishes are not desserts but meat dishes. Those grouped under "harissa" are of meats cooked with grains. There are fresh and salted fish dishes, and recipes for fish caught in Lake Wan in Armenia. And there are recipes for sauces, relishes and savories, vegetable pickles and salads, desserts, pastries, and sweetmeats.

The recipes are remarkable in their variety and in the imaginative combinations of a wide range of ingredients, including apples, prunes, quinces, currants, almonds, and pistachios, with vegetables and meats. They bear Persian names, and most are in the Persian tradition. Their delicate flavoring is the result of the subtle blending of herbs and spices, roots, resins, and flower extracts. Their preparation requires skill and patience, and their presentation calls for taste and artfulness. They are all perfectly explained and precise, but although they often give quantities of spices and aromatics, they do not usually give measures when dealing with main ingredients. A certain knowledge and experience on the part of the cook are assumed, but they are easy to follow in a modern kitchen more than seven centuries after they were written, and they are delicious if interpreted with taste.

The *Kitab Wasf al-At'ima al-Mu'tada* (*The Description of Familiar Foods*)

Charles Perry is bringing out a translation of a thirteenth-century cookbook called *Kitab Wasf al-At'ima al-Mu'tada* (*The Description of Familiar Foods*) in his forthcoming *Medieval Arab Cookery—Papers by Maxime Rodinson and Charles Perry*. Recipes are from Syria, Iraq, and Egypt. There is a chapter on drinks and one on vegetarian dishes.

Two copies of the manuscript are at Topkapi Library in Istanbul.

A Syrian Cookbook—The *Kitab al Wusla il al Habib fi Wasfi t-Tayyibati wat-Tib* (*Book of the Bond with the Friend, or Description of Good Dishes and Perfumes*)

This book exists in at least ten handwritten copies, each with minor variations and additions. One manuscript is in the British Library (shelfmark Or. 6388). Others are in Aleppo, Damascus, Cairo, Bursa, Mosul, Paris, and Bankipore in India. Professor Maxime Rodinson describes and analyzes the manuscripts at length in his study "Recherches sur les documents arabes relatifs à la cuisine" in the *Revue des études islamiques* (1949). Unfortunately, circumstances prevented him from giving a full translation of the recipes. Charles Perry has been working in the United States on a full edition and translation.

The true origin, date, and authorship of the original manuscript are uncertain; but it is very likely that it dates from before 1261, in the Ayyubid period in Syria, and that it was written by someone close to the courts, because of the many references to the Sultan, his cooks, and the royal kitchens. It may have been a prince or a grandson of Safadin and great-nephew of Saladin, or the historian Kamal ad-din ibn al-Adim, or the poet and historian Ibn al-Jazzar.

It is in two parts, one of which is on table manners, while the other contains the recipes. A chapter is devoted to perfumes and incense, another to drinks and juices. There are seventy-four recipes for cooking chicken, and recipes for fried and roast meats as well as omelets and stews. Vegetables, rice, wheat, fruit, and yogurt dishes are featured; and there is a chapter on desserts and pastries.

My father's family originally came from Aleppo in Syria, and I was thrilled to trace the origins of several of our own dishes. You will find a full translation of Maxime Rodinson's study "Recherches sur les documents arabes relatifs à la cuisine" in the forthcoming *Medieval Arab Cookery—Papers by Maxime Rodinson and Charles Perry.*

Spanish Arabic Cookbooks

Another source of old Arabic cookbooks is Islamic Spain of the period when the Moors were there. Two manuscripts have been recently published, from the thirteenth and early fourteenth centuries. The *Kitab Fadalat al-Khiwan fi Tayyibat al-Ta'am wal-Alwan (Book of Delicacies of the Table with the Pleasures from All Types of Food)* was written by Ibn Razin al Tujibi, a native of Murcia in Spain. It was translated by Fernando de la Granja, and was published in Madrid in 1960 under the title *La Cocina Arabigoandaluza segun un Manuscrito Inedito.* Another translation, by Huici Miranda, published in Madrid in 1966, is the *Traduccion Espanola de un Manuscrito Anonimo del Siglo XIII sobre la Cocina Hispano-Magribi.*

In *La Cuisine Andalouse, un Art de Vivre, XIe–XIIIe Siècle,* Lucie Bolens translates three hundred medieval Andalusian recipes into French and explains the place of gastronomy in that exceptional society. The majority of the recipes are from an anonymous thirteenth-century Arabic cookery manual first edited and translated into Spanish by Ambrosio Huici Miranda entitled *Kitab al Tabikh fil Maghrib wal Andalus (Cookbook of the Maghreb and Andalusia).* The book has also been translated into English and richly annotated by Charles Perry in *A Collection of Medieval and Renaissance Cookbooks* (David Friedman and Betty Cook, volume 2, 5th edition [Chicago, 1992]).

An Early Egyptian Cookbook

An anonymous collection of about eight hundred recipes, entitled *Kanz al Fawa'id fi Tanwi al-Fawa'id* (*Treasury of the Benefits in Food Organization*), which contains recipes similar to those of the same period in Baghdad and Damascus and many that are different, is believed to have been compiled in Egypt around the thirteenth and fourteenth centuries during Mamluk rule. It has been edited by David Waines and Manuela Marin and published with an introduction in English.

Persian Cookbooks

The earliest Persian cookbook to be found was written in 1520, during Safavid rule by a cook in the service of a prince, a certain Mohammad Ali Ba'urchi Baghdadi. His recipes represent dishes from the period of Timur, in the fifteenth century.

Another Persian collection of recipes—by Ostad Nurollah, who was the head cook of Shah Abbas at the end of the sixteenth century—reveals a courtly cuisine similar to the grand style of cooking in Iran today, where rice dishes hold a prominent place.

Apart from the recipes, there are references to health and nutrition.

BIBLIOGRAPHY

Cookbooks

Abdennour, Samia. *Egyptian Cooking—A Practical Guide.* Cairo: American University in Cairo Press, 1984.

Alford, Jeffrey, and Naomi Duguid. *Flatbreads and Flavors.* New York: William Morrow, 1995.

Aoun, Fayez. *280 Recettes de cuisine familiale libanaise.* Paris: Jacques Grancher, 1980.

Baron, Rosemary. *Flavours of Greece.* London: Ebury Press, 1992.

Basan, Ghillie. *Classic Turkish Cookery.* London: Tauris Parke Books, 1997.

Batmanglij, Najmieh. *A Taste of Persia.* London: I. B. Tauris, 1999.

Beattie, May H., ed. *Recipes From Baghdad.* With contributions from more than a hundred ladies. Baghdad: Indian Red Cross, 1946.

Benkirane, Fettouma. *La Nouvelle Cuisine marocaine.* Paris: J. P. Taillandier, 1979.

Bennani-Smires, Latifa. *Moroccan Cooking.* Casablanca: Al Madariss, n.d.

Detroit Women's Chapter of the Armenian General Benevolent Union. *Treasured Armenian Recipes.* New York, 1963.

Doniguian, Mireille. H. *La Cuisine armenienne et orientale.* Paris: Doniguian Frères, 1989.

El-Kareh, Rudolph. *Le Mezze libanais.* France: Actes Sud, 1998.

Eren Neset. *The Delights of Turkish Cooking.* Istanbul: Redhouse Press, 1988.

Guineadeau-Franc, Zette. *Fès vu par sa cuisine.* Morocco, 1958.

———. *Les Secrets des cuisines en terre marocaine.* Paris: Jean Pierre Taillandier Vilo, 1958.

Hal, Fatema. *Les Saveurs & les gestes—Cuisines et traditions du Maroc.* Paris: Stock, 1996.

Halici, Nevin. *Nevin Halici's Turkish Cookbook.* London: Dorling Kindersley, 1989.

———. *Siniden Tepsiye—From "Sini" to the Tray: Classical Turkish Cuisine.* Istanbul: Basim, 1999.

Hamady, Mary Laird. *Lebanese Mountain Cookery.* Boston: Godine, 1987.

Helou, Anissa. *Lebanese Cuisine.* London: Grub Street, 1994.

Kaak, Zeinab. *La Sofra—cuisine tunisienne traditionnelle.* Tunis: Ceres Editions, 1995.

Kahayat, Marie Karam, and Margaret Clark Keatinge. *Food from the Arab World.* Beirut: Khayats, 1965.

Karaoglan, Aida. *A Gourmet's Delight.* Beirut: Dar An-Nahar, 1969.

Khalil, Nagwa E. *Egyptian Cuisine.* Washington, D.C.: Worldwide Graphics, 1980.

Khawam, René. *La Cuisine arabe.* Paris: Albin Michel, 1970.

Kouki, Mohamed. *La Cuisine tunisienne—d'Ommok Sannafa.* Tunis, 1974.

———. *Poissons Méditerranéens.* Tunis: L'Officiel National des Pêches, n.d.

Krmezi, Aglaia. *The Foods of Greece.* New York: Stewart, Tabori and Chang, 1993.

Laasri, Ahmed *240 Recettes de cuisine marocaine.* Paris: Jacques Graucher, 1976.

Mallos, Tess. *The Complete Middle East Cookbook.* Sydney: Weldon Publishing, 1990.

Mardam-Bey, Farouk. *La Cuisine de Ziryab.* Marseille: Actes Sud, 1998.

Mark, Theonie. *Greek Island Cooking.* London: Batsford Ltd., 1978

Mazda, Maideh. *In a Persian Kitchen.* Rutland, Vt.: Charles E. Tuttle, 1960.

Mouzannar, Ibrahim. *La Cuisine libanaise.* Beirut: Librairie du Liban, 1983.

Pekin, Ersu, and Ayse Sumer, eds. *Timeless Tastes—Turkish Culinary Culture.* Istanbul: Vehbi Koc Vakfi, 1996.

Ramazani, Nesta. *Persian Cooking—A Table of Exotic Delights.* Charlottesville: University Press of Virginia, 1974.

Rayess, George N. *Art of Lebanese Cooking.* Beirut: Librairie du Liban, 1966.

Salaman, Rena. *Greek Food.* London: Fontana Paperbacks, 1983.

Saleh, Nada. *Fragrance of the Earth—Lebanese Home Cooking.* London: Saqi Books, 1996.

Shaida, Margaret. *The Legendary Cuisine of Persia.* London: Lieuse Publications, 1992.

Smouha, Patricia. *Middle Eastern Cooking.* London: André Deutsch, 1955.

Waines, David. *In a Caliph's Kitchen—Medieval Arabic Cooking for the Modern Gourmet.* London: Riad el Rayyes Books, 1989.

Weiss-Armush, Anne Marie. *Arabian Cuisine.* Beirut: Dar an-Nafaes, 1984.

Wolfert, Paula. *The Cooking of the Eastern Mediterranean.* New York: HarperCollins, 1994.

———. *Couscous and Other Good Food from Morocco.* New York: Harper & Row, 1973.

Yegen, Ekrem Muhittin. *Inkilàp-Kitabeir (A Cookery Book).* Istanbul: Third Impression, 1951.

Zeitoun, Edmond. *250 Recettes classiques de cuisine tunisienne.* Paris: Jacques Graucher, 1977.

Other Books and Publications

Allen Donaldson, Bess. *The Wild Rue.* London: Luzac & Co., 1938.

Arberry, A. J. "A Baghdad Cookery-book," in *Islamic Culture,* no. 13, 1939.

Barnham, Henry D., trans. *Tales of Nasr-ed-Din Khoja,* C. M. G. Nisbet and Co., 1923.

Bolens, Lucie. *La Cuisine andalouse, un art de vivre, XIe–XIIIe siècle.* Paris: Albin Michel, 1990.

Christensen, Arthur. *Contes persans en langue populaire.* Copenhagen: Andr. Fred. Høst & Son, 1918.

Foat Tugay, Emine. *Three Centuries—Family Chronicles of Turkey and Egypt.* Oxford: Oxford University Press, 1963.

Frayha, Anis. *Modern Lebanese Proverbs.* Beirut: American University of Beirut, 1953.

Giacobetti, le R.P.A. des Pères Blancs. *Recueil d'énigmes arabes populaires.* Algiers: Adolphe Jourdan, 1916.

Lane, Edward William. *Manners and Customs of the Modern Egyptians.* London: John Murray, 1896.

Maspéro, Gaston. *Chansons populaires recueillies dans la Haute-Egypte, de 1900 à 1914.* Cairo: Imprimerie de l'Institut Français d'Archéologie Orientale, n.d.

Rodinson, Maxime. "Recherches sur les documents arabes relatifs à la cuisine," in *Revue des études islamiques,* nos. 17 and 18, 1949.

"Ghidha," in *Encyclopédie de l'Islam.* 2nd ed., Livraison 39, 1965. (This edition now in *Encyclopedia of Islam,* vol. 2, pp. 1057–1072.)

Shah, Idries. *The Exploits of the Incomparable Mulla Nasrudin.* London: Jonathan Cape, 1966.

Sidqi Effendi, Muhammad. *Malja-at-tabbahin.* Translated from the Turkish into Arabic. Cairo, 1886.

Walker, Barbara. *Watermelons, Walnuts and the Wisdom of Allah and Other Tales of the Hoca.* New York: Parents Magazine Press, 1967.

Walker, John, trans. *Folk Medicine in Modern Egypt, by "A Doctor."* 1934.

Westermarck. *The Wit and Wisdom of Morocco: A Study of Native Proverbs.* London, 1930.

Zubaida, Sami, and Richard Tapper. *Culinary Cultures of the Middle East.* London: I. B. Tauris, 1994.

Claudia Roden was born and raised in Cairo. She completed her formal education in Paris and then moved to London to study art. She travels extensively as a food writer. Her previous books include the James Beard Award–winning *The Book of Jewish Food,* as well as *Coffee: A Connoisseur's Companion, The Good Food of Italy—Region by Region, Everything Tastes Better Outdoors,* and *Mediterranean Cookery,* which was published in conjunction with her BBC television series on the Mediterranean. In 1989 she won the two most prestigious food prizes in Italy, the Premio Orio Vergani and the Premio Maria Luigia, Duchessa di Parma, for her London *Sunday Times Magazine* series *The Taste of Italy.* She has won six Glenfiddich prizes, including 1992 Food Writer of the Year for articles in the *Daily Telegraph* and *The Observer* magazine, and the Glenfiddich Trophy awarded "in celebration of a unique contribution to the food that we eat in Britain today." In 1999 she won a Versailles Award in France, and Prince Claus of the Netherlands presented her with the Prince Claus Award "in recognition of exceptional initiatives and achievements in the field of culture." She lives in London.

A NOTE ON THE TYPE

The text of this book was set in Bembo, a facsimile of a typeface cut by Francesco Griffo for Aldus Manutius, the celebrated Venetian printer, in 1495. The face was named for Pietro Cardinal Bembo, the author of the small treatise entitled *De Aetna* in which it first appeared. Through the research of Stanley Morison, it is now generally acknowledged that all old-style type designs up to the time of William Caslon can be traced to the Bembo cut.

The present-day version of Bembo was introduced by the Monotype Corporation of London in 1929. Sturdy, well balanced, and finely proportioned, Bembo is a face of rare beauty and great legibility in all of its sizes.

Composed by
North Market Street Graphics, Lancaster, Pennsylvania

Printed and bound by
R. R. Donnelley & Sons, Harrisonburg, Virginia

All photographs on color insert pages
copyright © 1999 by Gus Filgate